Principles and Standards for Benefit–Cost Analysis

Principles and Standards for Benefit–Cost Analysis

Edited by

Scott Farrow

University of Maryland, Baltimore County, USA

Richard O. Zerbe, Jr.

University of Washington, USA

Edward Elgar

Cheltenham, UK • Northampton, MA, USA

Published by
Edward Elgar Publishing Limited
The Lypiatts
15 Lansdown Road
Cheltenham
Glos GL50 2JA
UK

Edward Elgar Publishing, Inc.
William Pratt House
9 Dewey Court
Northampton
Massachusetts 01060
USA

A catalogue record for this book
is available from the British Library

Library of Congress Control Number: 2012948850

This book is available electronically in the ElgarOnline.com
Economics Subject Collection, E-ISBN 978 1 78254 906 2

FSC www.fsc.org MIX Paper from responsible sources FSC® C018575

ISBN 978 1 78195 343 3

Typeset by Servis Filmsetting Ltd, Stockport, Cheshire
Printed and bound by MPG PRINTGROUP, UK

Contents

List of contributors vii
Acknowledgments viii

Introduction: professionalizing benefit–cost analysis 1
Scott Farrow and Richard O. Zerbe, Jr.

1 An assessment of important issues concerning the application of benefit–cost analysis to social policy 25
Aidan R. Vining and David L. Weimer

2 Toward standardization of benefit–cost analysis of early childhood interventions 63
Lynn A. Karoly

3 Principles and standards for benefit–cost analysis of public health preparedness and pandemic mitigation programs 110
Joseph H. Cook

4 Principles and standards for the benefit–cost analysis of crime 153
John R. Lott, Jr.

5 Towards principles and standards for the benefit–cost analysis of safety 172
Scott Farrow and W. Kip Viscusi

6 Developing general equilibrium benefit analyses for social programs: an introduction and example 194
H. Allen Klaiber and V. Kerry Smith

7 Appropriate discounting for benefit–cost analysis 247
David F. Burgess and Richard O. Zerbe, Jr.

8 Ethical benefit–cost analysis as art and science: ten rules for benefit–cost analysis 264
Richard O. Zerbe, Jr.

9 Incorporating distributional issues into benefit–cost analysis: why, how, and two empirical examples using non-market valuation 294
John B. Loomis

10 Behavioral economics and the conduct of benefit–cost analysis: towards principles and standards 317
Lisa A. Robinson and James K. Hammitt

11 Conclusion: principles and standards for benefit–cost analysis 364
Richard O. Zerbe, Jr., Tyler Blake Davis, Nancy Garland, and Tyler Scott

Index 445

Contributors

David F. Burgess, University of Western Ontario, Canada

Joseph H. Cook, University of Washington, USA

Tyler Blake Davis, University of Washington, USA

Scott Farrow, University of Maryland, Baltimore County, USA

Nancy Garland, University of Washington, USA

James K. Hammitt, Harvard University, USA and Toulouse School of Economics, France

Lynn A. Karoly, RAND Corporation, USA

H. Allen Klaiber, The Ohio State University, USA

John B. Loomis, Colorado State University, USA

John R. Lott, Jr.

Lisa A. Robinson, Harvard University, USA

Tyler Scott, University of Washington, USA

V. Kerry Smith, Arizona State University, USA

Aidan R. Vining, Simon Fraser University, Canada

W. Kip Viscusi, Vanderbilt University, USA

David L. Weimer, University of Wisconsin, USA

Richard O. Zerbe, Jr., University of Washington, USA

Acknowledgments

The following articles were reprinted with permission from the publisher:

Chapter 1, "An assessment of important issues concerning the application of benefit–cost analysis to social policy," originally appeared in *Journal of Benefit–Cost Analysis*, Volume 1, Issue 1, 2010. Reprinted with permission from De Gruyter. Also available at www.degruyter.com, DOI: 10.2202/2152-2812.1013.

Chapter 2, "Toward standardization of benefit–cost analysis of early childhood interventions," originally appeared in *Journal of Benefit–Cost Analysis*, Volume 3, Issue 1, 2012. Reprinted with permission from De Gruyter. Also available at www.degruyter.com, DOI: 10.1515/2152-2812.1085.

Chapter 5, "Towards principles and standards for the benefit–cost analysis of safety," originally appeared in *Journal of Benefit–Cost Analysis*, Volume 2, Issue 3, 2011. Reprinted with permission from De Gruyter. Also available at www.degruyter.com, DOI: 10.2202/2152-2812.1033.

Chapter 6, "Developing general equilibrium benefit analyses for social programs: an introduction and example," originally appeared in *Journal of Benefit–Cost Analysis*, Volume 3, Issue 2, 2012. Reprinted with permission from De Gruyter. Also available at www.degruyter.com, DOI: 10.1515/2152-2812.1083.

Chapter 7, "Appropriate discounting for benefit–cost analysis," originally appeared in *Journal of Benefit–Cost Analysis*, Volume 2, Issue 2, 2011. Reprinted with permission from De Gruyter. Also available at www.degruyter.com, DOI: 10.2202/2152-2812.1065.

Chapter 8, "Ethical benefit–cost analysis as art and science: ten rules for benefit–cost analysis," originally appeared in *University of Pennsylvania Journal of Law and Social Change*, Volume 12, Number 1, 73–105, 2009. Reprinted with permission from the University of Pennsylvania.

Chapter 9, "Incorporating distributional issues into benefit–cost analysis: why, how, and two empirical examples using non-market valuation," originally appeared in *Journal of Benefit–Cost Analysis*, Volume 2, Issue 1,

2011. Reprinted with permission from De Gruyter. Also available at www.degruyter.com, DOI: 10.2202/2152-2812.1044.

Chapter 10, "Behavioral economics and the conduct of benefit–cost analysis: towards principles and standards," originally appeared in *Journal of Benefit–Cost Analysis*, Volume 2, Issue 2, 2011. Reprinted with permission from De Gruyter. Also available at www.degruyter.com, DOI: 10.2202/2152-2812.1059.

Figure 10.2, "Exponential, hyperbolic, and quasi-hyperbolic discounting functions," originally appeared in *Trends in Cognitive Sciences*, Volume 11, Issue 11, "Intertemporal choice – toward an integrative framework," p. 482, by Gregory S. Burns, David Laibson and George Loewenstein, 2007. Reprinted with permission from Elsevier.

Introduction: professionalizing benefit–cost analysis

Scott Farrow and Richard O. Zerbe, Jr.

1 PRINCIPLES, STANDARDS AND PROFESSIONS

Many policy and economic analysts are familiar with benefit–cost analysis whether learned through formal courses or on-the-job training. These analyses are routinely developed at the federal level while many more are customized efforts at the federal, state, or local levels or in think tanks and academia. Various government agencies and the Executive Office of the President have taken time from mission-oriented tasks to develop BCA guidelines. Generally implicit in these guideline efforts is the goal of improving the quality of analysis. Within economics, the eminent economist Arnold Harberger called for a professionalization of BCA standards in the 1970s (Harberger, 1971).

However, professionalization, as it may involve aspects of licensing, quality signaling, or restricting entry, is not an automatically desirable practice to economists. A large literature exists on the role of professional licensing as a means to capture rents by limiting entry. Equally large is the literature on asymmetric information in which there is a concern that bad quality products will drive good quality ones from the market, for which one recommendation is a certification of quality. Organizational theory also points to the sometime role of professional identity in creating outstanding organizations, although economists have long considered and to date rejected a broad-based professional oath.

Our interest in developing principles and standards for benefit–cost analysis rests on the role of replication in science and the difficulty in discerning the quality of benefit–cost analyses. In our view it would be desirable if different analysts produced similar analyses when confronted with a common analytical problem; or, if those analyses differed, that they could be distinguished by readily communicated key differences. While this can be viewed as good science, it can also be viewed as good management of policy analyses. Similarly, although there is a frontier of analysis where new approaches are being used and tested, we view it as desirable that analyses that fail to apply reasonably appropriate methods should be omitted from consideration. We believe that organizational efforts to identify principles and standards, even if they evolve over time, can assist in signaling quality in the contentious field of benefit–cost analysis. However, no professional organization has existed to develop and guide the evolution over time of principles and standards for benefit–cost analysis. Only time will tell if the recently created Society for Benefit–Cost Analysis will fill this gap, and if it achieves the membership and broad-based credibility of longer-standing professional organizations such as those for financial analysts or accountants. Consequently, beginning with a workshop at the US Government Accountability Office in the early 2000s and continuing through meetings at the University of Washington, the creation of the Society for Benefit–Cost Analysis and work coordinated through the Benefit–Cost Center at the Evans School for Public Policy at the University of Washington, these chapters are offered in the hopes of furthering principles and standards and the quality of decisions supported by benefit–cost analysis.

2 A SHORT HISTORY OF PRINCIPLES AND STANDARDS

Benefit–cost analysis (BCA) as currently practiced represents the culmination of more than a century of theoretical advances in economics as well as empirical improvements in the art of public policy decision-making. BCA is, at its core, an accounting framework used to evaluate the financial consequences of decisions. In this sense, it is similar to analyses that corporations conduct in order to evaluate investment decisions and calculations individuals make on a daily basis prior to engaging in an activity or making a purchase. However, BCA differs from these frameworks in two significant ways. First, the objective of BCA is to increase public welfare; this increases both the technical and political complexity of the exercise, because the definition of "public welfare" is elusive. Second, because BCA often encompasses non-market goods, such as the value of a recreational visit or wildlife viewing at a park, the required data are often not found in market transactions, and instead must be generated through resource-intensive surveys or other statistical analyses.

Formalized BCA was first employed in the USA for the analysis of US Army Corps of Engineers' (hereafter "the Corps") public works projects such as canals and dams. These projects required significant allocations of federal expenditures to selected states or regions; as such, there was a need to justify the choice of a particular project or site objectively.

Economic theorists also spurred the growth of BCA through exploration of the concepts of efficiency and social welfare in public sector economic policy. BCA has thus developed as a means for welfare economists, policy analysts, and engineers to evaluate the effect(s) of economic policy and decision-making upon social welfare in order to inform policy decisions. Advances largely coalesced to foster widespread governmental application of BCA in the mid-twentieth century. In recent years BCA has been applied to the evaluation of social programs.

2.1 The Engineers

BCA in the United States primarily arose not through academic research, but out of a need to facilitate mutual accommodation in a political climate rife with distrust and disagreement (Porter, 1995). During the nineteenth century, the French were at the forefront of formalized attempts to develop analyses of public investments. Though US Treasury Secretary Albert Gallatin had advocated for the comparison of water project benefits and costs in 1808 (Hanley and Spash, 1993), American efforts to analyze public investments were usually ad hoc until the Corps, borrowing from the French model, entered the picture in the early twentieth century (Porter, 1995).

The Corps' use of BCA was motivated by a Congressional desire to allay conflict and build consensus. Attempting to better govern its own massive earmark spending on contentious water projects, Congress recognized the Corps as a relatively neutral and respected arbiter in federal water project controversies, and thus sought to use the prestige of the Corps to promote procedural regularity and give public evidence of fairness in project selection (ibid.). The subsequent passage of the Rivers and Harbors Act of 1902 mandated that the Board of Engineers for Rivers and Harbors, also established by the Act, certify water projects as beneficial (Hammond, 1966), as Congress evidently found the ideal of efficiency sufficient to serve as a coordinating principle to facilitate tractable decision-making and curb rampant spending. A later amendment to the Act in 1920 further required Corps-recommended projects to promise benefits in excess of costs (ibid.). Porter (1995) notes that this project approval process was not a mere formality: the Corps rejected more than half of proposed projects, usually on the basis of economic unfeasibility (ibid.).

Depression-era public works spending and ongoing flood concerns further spurred the application of BCA through the Flood Control Act of 1936. This Act stated that the Corps was to evaluate water resource project benefits and costs "to whomsoever they accrue" (Hanley and Spash, 1993). The Act allowed Congressional authorization only for projects that had been approved by the Corps. However, Porter (ibid.)

notes that the Act's explicit requirement for Corps approval on a BCA basis was already standard Corps practice. Though project approval methodology still left ample room for political influence and special interest legislation, Congressional passage of inefficient large public works bills was significantly curtailed; the Corps' economic analyses limited debate such that the approval of truly egregious projects became rarer (ibid.)

Initially, economic figures put forward by the Corps were accepted without reservation. However, the Flood Control Act had neglected to specify appropriate metrics for benefits and costs, which resulted in each federal agency developing criteria biased towards its own initiatives (Quade, 1971). Accordingly, rival techniques and standards for BCA were introduced. After 1940, this led to controversy regarding Corps decisions, as powerful interests including major utilities, railroads, and rival federal agencies (especially the Bureau of Reclamation and the Department of Agriculture) called various technical figures into question and pushed for rigorous standardization (Porter, 1995).

In 1945, four federal agencies—the Army Corps of Engineers, Federal Power Commission, Bureau of Reclamation, and Department of Agriculture (USDA)—commissioned a "subcommittee on costs and benefits" (N.A., 1945) in an attempt to resolve these differences by relying on basic economic principles. However, while the subcommittee's report served to clarify points of difference, such as project life and the degree of side-effect inclusion, they could not officially resolve different principles and standards as the committee lacked formal bargaining power to develop unilateral customary procedures (Porter, 1995). Thus, the committee largely left the task following their descriptive efforts, but a small USDA working group tasked by the subcommittee to prepare "an objective analysis of the problem" persisted (ibid.). In 1949, this working group distributed a report titled *Objective Analysis* (ibid.). However, this report, known colloquially as the *Green Book*, failed to reconcile benefit–cost practices and, while influential, did not gain official standing (Quade, 1971).

2.2 The Economists

The modern economic basis for BCA builds on the early formalization (1844) of consumer surplus associated with Jules Dupuit, civil engineer and self-taught economist (Ekelund and Hébert, 1999), and Vilfredo Pareto's foundational study of the distribution of income and economic efficiency (1896). Theoretical advancement of Pareto's work in the 1930s rendered economists significant actors alongside engineers in the benefit–cost field. From Pareto's work comes the concept of a "Pareto improvement," which occurs when, as the result of an allocation change, at least one person is made better off and no person is made worse off. A second term, "Pareto efficiency," is a state that is attained when no further Pareto improvements are possible. There are two forms of Pareto efficiency. In its strong form, Pareto efficiency holds that state A is preferred to state B when state A is ranked higher than state B for one person and all other persons rank A at least as high as B. In its weaker form, the utility (well-being) of each individual must be higher in state A for state A to be preferred (Boadway and Bruce, 1984). In practice, the unanimity requirement of the Pareto efficiency criterion is paralyzing as an empirical decision-making tool as almost every policy decision engenders winners and losers. A more pragmatic substitute for the Pareto criterion, developed in light of this limitation, is the "Potential Pareto," or "Kaldor–Hicks," criterion.

The Kaldor–Hicks criterion arose during the late 1930s out of discussions among leading British economists about the adoption of the Corn Laws in 1815 and their repeal in 1846 (Harrod, 1938; Robbins, 1938; Hicks, 1939). Earlier economists had generally assumed that each individual had an "equal capacity for enjoyment," and that gains and losses among different individuals could be directly compared (Mishan, 1981; Hammond, 1985). For example, Harrod (1938) argued that the net social benefit from a policy could be established on the assumption that the individuals affected were equal in their capacity to enjoy income. By 1939, however, leading British economists began to question the validity of making interpersonal comparisons of utility as required for such policy prescriptions (Hicks, 1939). For instance, Hicks's contemporary Lionel Robbins wrote that interpersonal comparisons of utility could not rest on a scientific foundation since utility cannot be measured, and thus the justification for such comparisons is more ethical than scientific (1938). Nicholas Kaldor proffered a solution, acknowledging the inability of economists to establish a scientific basis for making interpersonal comparisons of utility, but suggesting that this difficulty could be rendered irrelevant (1939). Kaldor sought to avoid interpersonal utility comparisons by separating equity from efficiency, arguing that policies engendering an increase in aggregate real income are always desirable because given such a change the *potential* then exists to make everyone better off:

> [T]he economist's case for the policy is quite unaffected by the question of the comparability of individual satisfaction, since in all such cases it is possible to make everybody better off than before, or at any rate to make some people better off without making anybody worse off. (Kaldor, 1939, pp. 549–50)

According to Kaldor's revised criterion of economic efficiency, a hypothetical project is desirable if the money measure of gains exceeds the money measure of losses, since there is then the potential for a transfer between winners and losers that could satisfy the basic Pareto criterion. Using the change in aggregate gains as the measure of efficiency was thought to separate efficiency and distributional effects and thus avoid interpersonal utility comparisons (ibid.). Contemporary thinking held that only politicians (or at least non-economists) should make judgments and decisions about income distribution effects. Eager to separate considerations of efficiency from those of distribution so as to put economics on safe ground as an objective policy instrument, Kaldor noted that whether *actual* compensation should take place "is a political question on which the economist, qua economist, could hardly pronounce an opinion" (ibid.). He thus proposed that decision-makers address ethical values regarding equity outside the purview of BCA. Hicks, perhaps the most prominent economist of the time, accepted the Kaldor approach, which eventually became known as the Kaldor–Hicks (KH) criterion.

The KH criterion did not truly obviate concern about making interpersonal comparisons of utility, however. The KH assumption of equal marginal utility of income in fact embraces such comparisons in a very particular way, where all people are treated equally in terms of the value they place on changes in income. To address this, Kaldor endorsed the procedure adopted by Pigou (1920), which Kaldor describes as "dividing welfare effects into two parts: the first relating to production, and the second to distribution" (ibid.). Kaldor suggests, "the economist should not be concerned with prescriptions at all . . . For, it is quite impossible to decide on economic grounds what particular pattern of income-distribution maximizes social welfare" (ibid.). By taking this approach, BCA has been led to largely ignore the concept of moral sentiments as goods even though they may in fact fit the economic definition of goods, in that there is a willingness to pay for them.

In recent decades, BCA has continued to evolve in keeping with economic theory. Many of the current principles and standards identified in this project reflect this. For instance, growth in economic theory regarding the valuation of non-market goods and services has fostered increasingly comprehensive economic analyses. Valuation methods for non-market goods and services such as the travel-cost method (Hotelling, 1949), hedonic valuation (Rosen, 1974), and contingent valuation (CV) surveys (e.g., willingness to pay) (Mitchell and Carson, 1989) have increasingly gained acceptance as means by which to estimate values for non-market resources in the absence of observable market transactions. Current work regarding stated preference methods, both CV and conjoined analysis, is at the forefront of current BCA research and development. Other aspects of continued growth and discourse in BCA concern the use of appropriate discount rates to account explicitly for distributional issues, and the treatment of uncertainty in producing estimates. Such refinement in economic methodology has enabled broader application of BCA to analyses of all types of government expenditures and regulatory activities.

Although the KH criterion remains the standard for BCA today, in recent years, it is of diminishing use in its restrictions. Analysts have lent increasing attention to ethical issues of distribution and intergenerational equity to the extent that KH has in practice been, if not abandoned, seriously eroded. Various approaches have been proposed to account for equity in BCA, including:

- distributional weighting, where net benefits, expressed in dollars, are weighted by income or some other metric to express an equity viewpoint (Brent, 1984; Farrow, 2011);
- using unweighted net benefits, but applying the KH criterion separately within each income class as well as in society as a whole (Ng, 1984; Farrow, 1998; Graham, 2008);
- using well-being rather than money as the metric, and employing a social welfare function that captures equity viewpoints (Adler, 2008);
- using benefits and costs expressed in dollars and measure willingness to pay for ethical sentiments to capture equity (Loomis, Chapter 9 this volume; Zerbe, 2001, 2007, 2009, and Chapter 8 this volume);
- taking a portfolio approach, whereby it is assumed that if a KH test is applied in multiple rule-makings, and that winners and losers are considerably mixed, then in the long run *most* (but not all) people will better off (Graham, 2008; Zerbe and Scott, 2012).

What is most commonly advocated though is for BCA to analyze equity issues qualitatively and separately from efficiency, by presenting policymakers with the best distributional information possible and letting them weigh equity concerns implicitly (e.g., Jones-Lee, 1976). To date, this final approach is the most common practice throughout the world. Recent findings (e.g., Zerbe, 2007; Cai et al., 2010; Zerbe and Scott, 2012) call into question the validity of the long-assumed separation between equity and efficiency, however, so future principles and standards revisions are likely to revisit this issue.

2.3 Application to Broader Governance

The use of BCA in the USA at the federal level expanded beyond Army Corps applications in the 1960s, as former Defense Secretary Robert

McNamara instituted BCA within the Defense Department's Planning and Programming Budgeting System (PPBS) (Fuchs and Anderson, 1987). Though President Lyndon Johnson expanded the use of the PPBS throughout the executive branch in 1965, the program failed due to its complexity, difficulty in implementation, and lack of sustained presidential support. The program was officially terminated in 1971 (ibid.). Six years later, in an attempt to solidify executive branch control over federal regulatory agencies, President Richard Nixon included BCA in his "Quality of Life Review" process for agency regulations (ibid.). In a similar vein, numerous executive orders, regulatory commissions, and other executive actions pertaining to federal agency regulations undertaken by President Gerald Ford and President Jimmy Carter contain language referencing the weighing of benefits and costs to one degree or another (ibid.).

The use of BCA in federal decision-making was formalized beyond simply referencing benefits and costs in 1981, when President Reagan issued Executive Order (EO) 12291. Executive Order 12291 required that Regulatory Impact Analyses be conducted for major government initiatives (Reagan, 1981). As noted by Philip Shabecoff in a *New York Times* article on 7 November, 1981, "[President Reagan] transformed with a stroke of his pen what had been a useful economic tool into an imperative of federal decision making." Among other things, the executive order declared that: (1) regulatory action shall not be undertaken unless the potential benefits to society for the regulation outweigh the potential costs to society; (2) regulatory objectives shall be chosen to maximize the net benefits to society; (3) among alternative approaches to any given regulatory objective, the alternative involving the least net cost to society shall be chosen; and (4) agencies shall set regulatory priorities with the aim of maximizing the aggregate net benefits to society, taking into account the condition of the particular industries affected by regulations, the condition of the national economy, and other regulatory actions contemplated for the future (Reagan, 1981). As a result of this order, the Office of Information and Regulatory Affairs (OIRA) within the White House Office of Management and Budget (OMB) became the central clearinghouse for all substantive agency rule-making, at the time reviewing between 2000 and 3000 rules per year. President Reagan's subsequent EO 12498, issued in January 1985, furthered this commitment, requiring each federal agency to submit a regulatory plan to OMB discussing all significant current or proposed regulatory activity for yearly review (Reagan, 1985).

In 1993, President Clinton introduced EO 12866, at once revoking both EO 12291 and 12498 and establishing a new format for OIRA reviews. Order 12866, titled "Regulatory Planning and Review," sought to promote four broad objectives: (1) to enhance planning and coordination with respect to both new and existing regulations; (2) to reaffirm the primary role of federal agencies in the regulatory decision-making process; (3) to restore the integrity and legitimacy of regulatory review and oversight; and (4) to make the process more accessible and open to the public (Clinton, 1993).

President Clinton's order stated that when making regulatory decisions, both qualitative and quantitative costs and benefits should be incorporated into an assessment of all alternatives, including the status quo, and that the alternative that maximizes net benefits should be clearly identified. Of particular relevance to this Principles and Standards project, EO 12866 established 12 prescriptive principles for adherence to the new regulatory philosophy. The EO specified that performance objectives of a chosen regulatory policy must be specified and that stakeholders significantly affected by a regulation must be consulted. Other sections within the EO reorganized the regulatory review structure (Section II), developed a planning mechanism (IV), and centralized regulatory review within OIRA (VI). Section III prescribed the litmus test for determining what regulatory decisions must be subject to these review standards, stating that any regulation action that is likely to "[h]ave an annual effect on the economy of $100 million or more or adversely affect in a material way the economy, a sector of the economy, productivity, competition, jobs, the environment, public health or safety, or State, local, or tribal governments or communities" qualifies as "significant regulatory action" (Clinton, 1993).

In compliance with EO 12866, OIRA organized an interagency review committee with representatives from every major federal regulatory agency to examine the state of the art for the economic analysis of regulatory action. Three years later, in 1996, the group released a "Best Practices" document detailing the appropriate standards and methodology under which to conduct analysis of significant regulatory action as mandated by Clinton's executive order (US OMB, 1996).

In 2003, the OMB under President George W. Bush issued Circular A-4 (US OMB, 2003), which details methods for identifying benefits and costs as well as informs agencies what should be included in a BCA. The document replaced the 1996 "Best Practices" publication and a subsequent guidance form issued in 2000 (US OMB, 2000). In Circular A-4, OMB refers to the combination of BCA and other information as "regulatory analysis." The document gives details regarding required aspects of a regulatory analysis, including a statement of need for a rule-making, an identification of regulatory alternatives, and an identification of benefits and costs. According to Circular A-4, regulatory analysis must also establish a baseline for the comparison and must separately describe the "distributional effects" of each alternative (i.e., how both benefits and costs are distributed among sub-populations of particular concern) so that decision-makers can properly consider these distributional effects along with the effects on economic efficiency.

The George W. Bush administration also produced more formal guidelines for agencies conducting BCAs, focusing analysis on the calculation of net benefit. In 2002, EO 13258 installed "regulatory policy advisors" in place of the Vice President for duties related to regulatory oversight, OIRA, and regulatory conflict resolution (Bush, 2002). EO 13422, issued in January 2007, amended Clinton's EO 12866 in five major ways:

1. it required that agencies identify the specific market failure or issue prompting regulation in writing;
2. it ordered agencies to designate a presidentially appointed intra-agency "regulatory policy officer" to control upcoming agency rule-making;
3. it required yearly estimates summing the cumulative benefits and costs of agency rules expected to reach publication in the coming year;
4. it expanded executive influence by broadening OIRA review to include significant guidance documents, defined as "agency statement[s] of general applicability and future effect, other than . . . regulatory action[s], that set forth a policy on a statutory, regulatory, or technical issue or an interpretation of a statutory or regulatory issue";
5. it permitted agencies to use more formal rule-making procedures when warranted (Bush, 2007).

In January 2009, President Barack Obama issued EO 13497, which formally revoked EO 13258 and EO 12866 and installed an updated version of President Clinton's EO 12866 (Obama, 2009a). The Obama Administration's October 2009 Executive Order (13514), titled "Federal Leadership in Environmental, Energy, and Economic Performance" significantly addressed regulatory review and benefit–cost analysis. EO 13514 mandates retrospective BCA policy analysis through annual performance evaluation to enhance accountability and extend or expand projects that have net benefits and reassess or discontinue under-performing projects (Obama, 2009b).

In keeping with this emphasis, a December 2009 proposal submitted by the White House Council on Environmental Quality to the National Academy of Sciences (NAS) for review seeks to update federal principles and standards for water resources planning and decision-making. The document seeks to update and expand the established principles and guidelines in place for water resource projects, currently collected as the *Economic and Environmental Principles and Guidelines for Water and*

Related Land Resources Implementation Studies (US Water Resources Council, 1983). The proposed revisions aim to modernize national water resources development by increasing the role of science in decision-making, incorporating both monetary and non-monetary benefits in the calculation of net benefits, and ensuring the transparency of analyses and determinations. Further, the proposal seeks to expand the purview of the proposed revisions to encompass all federal agencies that undertake water resource projects, whereas current guidelines only pertain to the US Army Corps of Engineers, Bureau of Reclamation, Natural Resources Conservation Service, and the Tennessee Valley Authority. The National Research Council (2010) reviewed the proposal and identified a number of weaknesses in the revised guidelines while being supportive of the overall intent. This effort at honing trans-agency principles and standards for BCA represents a significant development in the effort to achieve standardization while also illustrating its many difficulties.

The President's Budget proposed for FY2011 (Obama, 2010) also affirmed a move to increasingly cohesive, sophisticated federal BCA.[1] While no specific principles and standards are outlined within the document, the Budget proposal informs the development of principles and standards by addressing the underlying goals and intent of future federal BCA. Within the "Analytical Perspectives: Performance and Management" section, the Budget proposal states that more sophisticated evaluation methods are required to answer fundamental questions about the social, economic, or environmental impact of programs and practices by isolating the effect of government action from other possible influencing factors (Obama, 2010). Agencies seeking funding are required to demonstrate that their 2011 funding priorities are based upon credible empirical evidence—or a plan to collect that evidence—and to identify impediments to rigorous program evaluation in their statutes or regulations so that these might be addressed going forward (ibid.). For instance, the document notes "The Administration . . . has made a concerted effort to increase investments in early childhood education and home-visiting programs that are backed by strong evidence—because rigorous evidence suggests that investments in those areas have especially high returns" and further calls for retrospective BCA analyses, noting: "Historically, evaluations have been an afterthought when programs are designed—and once programs have been in place for a while it can be hard to build a constituency for a rigorous evaluation" (ibid.).

While such comprehensive federal legislation requiring the broad use of a formal, standardized BCA framework has yet to be approved by Congress, the presence of BCA as standard practice in governmental decision-making is nonetheless apparent within various levels of government. Since the initial expansion of BCA beyond the Army Corps, intra-agency application and development of BCA practices has mirrored Congressional and Executive Branch actions described above. Though space does not allow for a detailed discussion of each, the US Environmental Protection Agency, Department of Transportation, Federal Aviation Administration, Department of Homeland Security, Department of Justice, Department of Housing and Urban Development, Department of Education, and Department of Health and Human Services (to name several significant actors) have all developed internal guidelines and BCA protocols in response to the aforementioned executive orders and OMB circulars. However, there currently is no overarching framework of inter-agency principles and standards beyond general guidance as provided by OMB and the Executive Branch.

Momentum is building towards increasing standardization, largely precipitated at the agency level and by the Executive Branch. In a February 2009 Memorandum for the Heads of Executive Departments and Agencies (74 FR 5977), President Obama directed the head of OMB to prepare a comprehensive set of recommendations pertaining to regulatory review at the federal level. This call for input sought to examine the role of benefit–cost analysis and related distributional concerns, disclosure and transparency, in preparation for the coming issuance of an executive order on Federal Regulatory Review. These documents reveal interest in and impetus for the development of a comprehensive, coherent standardization of BCA for decision analysis and implementation. Likewise, as the proposed President's FY2011 Budget document notes, far beyond the desire for consistency and efficiency, there exists a public right to governmental accountability and a justified expectation for prudent allocation of scarce fiscal resources that increases the need for consistent, standardized BCA in practice (Obama, 2010). Currently, the most comprehensive set of guidelines for conducting BCA on government projects and regulation remain OMB Circulars A-94, "Guidelines and Discount rates for Benefit–Cost Analysis of Social Programs" (US OMB, 1992) and A-4 "Regulatory Analysis" (US OMB, 2003).

Although this national summary has focused on the USA, some other national governments and international organizations have their own guidance such as the UK (HM Treasury, 2008), the European Union (2008), Canada (Treasury Board, 2007), and the World Bank (1994). While there is no comparable set of standards or history of use of BCA in more local or regional governments, there is growing momentum to that end. For example, the State of Washington, through the Washington State Institute for Public Policy (WSIPP),[2] now performs analyses of significant new social programs, and many states have adopted regulatory review policies (though of widely varying structure, scope, and impact). A report by the Institute for Policy Integrity[3] at the New York University Law School provides a detailed discussion of the regulatory review process on a state by state basis (Schwartz, 2010). In addition, there is growing interest in using BCA in non-governmental settings, such as non-profit human services agencies. It is our belief that these principles and standards should apply to these growing areas as well.

3 CRITICISMS OF BCA

Given the role of BCA in governmental decision-making and the significant implications of policy decisions informed by such analysis, it is hardly surprising that both the process and application have long come under scrutiny. As noted previously, criticism has often served as the impetus for the growth and honing of BCA as a discipline and tool. Present criticism might best be divided into two categories: (1) philosophical concerns, generally broad questions of ethics, morality, and BCA usage; and (2) economic/technical issues, usually more pointed critiques involving questions such as non-market valuation and discounting. However, a more significant division is without doubt the dichotomous perspectives of BCA that inform BCA critics and proponents; much criticism of BCA has little to do with BCA, but rather with ongoing questions regarding the usage of science and expertise in decision-making.

Much of the criticism directed towards the use of BCA tackles a strawman: BCA as a mechanistic decision-making criterion. Conversely, its best proponents present and defend a method by which to provide knowledge and inform possible outcomes. This dichotomy is by no means unique to the discipline of BCA; rather, it is one example of the debate surrounding science in many forms and across many disciplines. Sarewitz (2004) writes that scientific inquiry is inherently and unavoidably subject to politicization in a controversial decision-making environment, and thus that "political controversies with technical underpinnings are not resolved by technical means" (ibid., p. 1). Fundamentally, most criticism of BCA stems from the pervasive and problematic notion that "science is a source of facts and theories about reality that can and should settle disputes and guide political action" (ibid., p. 386). Science of any discipline, including BCA, will not furnish a decision without direction as to policy goals or social mores. Yet agreement can sometimes be reached about the means to reach a decision, even if not about the decision itself.

The decision to use BCA is itself an ethical decision. The way in which it is used, however, can rest in considerable part on science. Concerns of intergenerational equity, discounting, and distribution are in the end political or ethical questions with economic or scientific components. Certainly, the approach and rationale utilized for a BCA must be explicitly stated alongside the analysis. While decisions made by the analyst or policy-maker are open to critique, it is illogical to condemn BCA itself on such grounds. This point, consistently emphasized in current BCA publications and analysis (as reviewed in Zerbe, 2007), obviates much of the criticism levied at BCA; BCA is not a mechanistic decision-*maker*, and should not be viewed or presented as such. The proper use of BCA is to furnish information and predictions. Thus, in reality, much disagreement surrounding BCA reflects democratic deliberation regarding values and usage, and does not speak to the legitimacy of BCA in and of itself.

A second overarching criticism contends that BCA is not sufficiently inclusive, encompassing, or informed. As a blanket criticism, such contention is inappropriate given that BCA is fundamentally an application of deterministic modeling. BCA is applied to complex, interrelated social, political, economic, and ecological systems; complex systems theory holds such systems to be non-linear and intrinsically uncertain (von Bertalanffy, 1968; Costanza et al., 1993), inherently limiting the potential accuracy and holism of a BCA model relative to its real-world analog. This is, however, the case with any model. Thus, any particular BCA model represents a gross simplification of the real world, intended not to reflect reality in comprehensive detail, but rather to inform decision-making about the likely efficiency of alternative policies. The very premise of modeling, as famously quipped by Einstein, is "to be as simple as possible, but not too simple." As such, BCA processes of system bounding, aggregation, and reduction are not and should not be expected to be wholly definitive and complete. Sarewitz (2004) similarly notes that more information often decreases consensus, as increased information provides an ever-larger pool out of which interested actors can strike differing positions on the history leading to current circumstances, on what is presently occurring, on what needs to be done, and on what the outcome(s) will be.

Certainly, the assumptions and choices made to facilitate a particular BCA might well neglect a crucial process or fail to reflect a key value, and thus appropriately garner criticism as poorly suited for its intended purpose. Criticizing a BCA for inappropriately or insufficiently representing reality in this capacity serves a crucial place in honing BCA principles and standards and increasing the utility of future analyses. However, such criticism fails to resonate when levied as an indictment of BCA more broadly; it is axiomatic that BCA *modeling* does not fully capture the breadth and depth of complex social-economic systems.

This is not to say that all criticisms of BCA are poorly founded; in fact, discerning critics have and continue to drive constructive growth and development within the field. Zerbe (2007) provides a fuller, iterated treatment of specific points of contention regarding BCA. Perhaps the most trenchant criticisms are, first, recognition that the usage of KH and the potential compensation test (PCT) entails a value judgment in and of itself, even though the fundamental premise of practical welfare economists has been to avoid value judgments and interpersonal comparisons of utility in conducting analysis and making policy prescriptions (Chipman and Moore, 1978). Second, there is widespread criticism that BCA is missing important values. This criticism reflects the valuation structure and scheme of classic KH and PCT analysis, which does not fully reflect the values and goals we hold as individuals and a society, as it often neglects equity and other moral values (Zerbe, 2007).

Critics are correct in asserting that much past BCA work has failed to incorporate existing moral sentiment into the model and output (ibid.). Axiomatically, unless BCA includes values held for distributional effects and other "equity goods" (ibid.), then values will necessarily be missing. And it is missing values that lie at the heart of most legal and philosophical criticism of BCA as a technique. To address this, traditional KH criteria can be expanded to include all sentiments, the realization of which there is a willingness to pay (Zerbe, 2007, 2009; Scarborough and Bennett, 2012).

4 SUMMARY OF THE VOLUME

The material in this book grew from the Principles and Standards project at the University of Washington funded by the John D. and Catherine T. MacArthur Foundation. White papers were commissioned on various subjects from leading experts and promising younger scholars in specific fields of applied benefit–cost analysis.

Each of the commissioned authors' papers was subject to professional review by another scholar in the field, and comments were provided to the author. Following revisions, each commissioned paper was opened up to public comment through posting on the website of the Benefit–Cost Analysis Center. Through this site, readers could view and download these pieces of cutting-edge scholarship, and leave comments for the authors and the benefit–cost analysis community. Several of the papers have since appeared in the *Journal of Benefit–Cost Analysis* and are reprinted here, courtesy of DeGruyter, as they appeared in that journal. In addition to directly commissioned papers, two other papers were developed as part of the project. The first, by David Burgess, delved into the complexity of the discount rate. The second, by Richard Zerbe, focused on the ethical foundation for benefit–cost analysis. The contributions of each of these papers are briefly summarized here.

Aidan Vining and David Weimer in Chapter 1 investigate issues in the application of benefit–cost analysis to social policy. Social policy includes a range of substantive policy areas including early childhood development, education, physical and mental health, juvenile justice, crime and corrections, housing, income support, and employment.

Because it is always valuable and important to understand the efficiency consequences of government interventions, including social policy interventions, there is no normative reason why these fundamental principles of BCA (and more generally welfare economics) should not apply to social policy. Therefore, they argue that *the standard principles of BCA should apply to social policy*. However, the application of BCA to social policy does raise a number of issues that deserve special attention in any effort to develop standards for benefit–cost analysts. The specific charge for the paper was to "address general considerations in conducting a BCA of social programs, the need for principles and standards for social programs and addiction in particular and point out any special problems facing those doing BCA in the field of addiction."

How best to evaluate programs and policies that affect early childhood is Lynn Karoly's topic in Chapter 2. She notes that while the BCAs of early childhood programs serve to make such investments more compelling, there are limitations in the current state of the art. Most importantly, there are a number of methodological choices required when implementing a BCA—from discount rates to shadow prices—and analysts typically do not follow a standardized approach. Moreover, there are a number of other challenges in applying the BCA approach to early childhood programs that further introduce potential differences in methodology. These challenges include the economic values attached to observed program outcomes, many of which do not have readily available economic values, and valuing potential benefits beyond the last observed outcomes. At present, most BCAs of early childhood programs provide proof of the principle that the economic returns can be positive for a given program, but they do not support decision-makers who may want to use the results to choose between alternative approaches to early intervention or to assess the difference in the economic returns obtained from investing in early childhood versus investing later in childhood or versus investing in some other type of social program.

Joseph Cook in Chapter 3 focuses on policies and programs for public health preparedness and pandemic mitigation (PHP/PM). These policies include the stockpiling and distribution of vaccines or antiviral drugs, disease surveillance networks, social distancing measures such as school closures, and quarantines or border closures. The focus is primarily on pandemic influenza in the US context. Cost-effectiveness analysis is compared with the benefit–cost approach followed by specific issues that arise in the economic analysis of PHP/PM programs. These include: modeling the macroeconomic impacts of pandemic outbreaks; modeling the effects on households of school closure policies; uncertainty; discounting; disparate impacts and equity; valuing mortality risk; and health externalities. A supplementary appendix provides a literature review on economic analysis of policies and programs for PHP/PM.

John Lott in Chapter 4 investigates the trade-offs involved in analyzing crimes and criminal justice. These investigations follow questions such as: Are we spending enough on police? What are the levels of penalties for different crimes? Are there trade-offs between different types of penalties? For example, does greater reliance on criminal penalties reduce the reliance on reputational penalties? There are many possible alternative methods of deterring crime. Longer prison terms are just one option. There are also issues of increasing the probability of arrest or conviction for those who are arrested. There are also private actions that can deter crime, of which private reputations are one example. Others are putting locks on doors, car alarms, or people owning guns. Some of these actions involve possible externalities and Lott discusses how those externalities might be measured and evaluated. Though Lott views the range of possible estimates for many of these actions to be too large to definitively say whether the actions pass a benefit–cost test, that is not an unusual result. It is still useful to know what actions can be said to pay for themselves and which ones do not.

Scott Farrow and Kip Viscusi focus on public safety in Chapter 5. They seek to provide an initial compilation of proposed principles and standards for benefit–cost analysis of public safety policies. In their view, public safety issues cover a wide range of governmental activities in general categories such as security, physical safety, health, natural hazards, and consumption of goods. Fundamental to each component is the element of risk of a bad outcome, including risks arising from nature as well as those that are the result of actions of people. Typically, there are also decisions that affect one's exposure to the risk as well as possibilities to either alter the risk or its consequences, as through the purchase of insurance.

Farrow and Viscusi note that the different contexts for BCA are associated with different literatures, communities of practice, and outlets for publication. What is similar across the applications in public safety is that there is an element of risk involving a probability of some negative outcome. Attending to general concepts such as public danger and public risk provides an important clue to the principles and standards that may be common across areas of public safety. Consequently, their chapter focuses on principles and standards for applying BCA where the unifying theme is that public safety is directed at reducing risk to the public. They develop a very modular approach to focus on specific principles and standards, which seems to point the way toward a process to reach agreement, or not, on the recommendations.

The challenges of general equilibrium analysis are investigated by Allen Klaiber and Kerry Smith in Chapter 6. They describe a conceptual framework for incorporating general equilibrium effects into benefit–cost analyses of social programs. To make the description tangible, Klaiber and Smith selected a specific example, the evaluation of reductions in the resources available for public primary education. They use a policy change that has been common in local public education due to the economic downturn—reductions in the teaching staff. To highlight the general equilibrium effects of exogenous reductions in the resources used to produce education and its effect on common measures of the quality of education, they use a locational sorting model applied to school districts in Maricopa County, AZ. Several of these districts experienced teacher cuts in the 2009–10 school year and these cuts were used to illustrate how the model would work. Their approach provides an illustration of how the general equilibrium effects influence our understanding of both the severity and distribution of changes in household well-being arising as a result of changes to local social programs.

David Burgess and Richard Zerbe in Chapter 7 discuss the challenging problem of the appropriate rate of discounting for the typical case when projects extend over a period of time. They review areas of concern in the literature such as: the effects of risk, displacement of private capital, the rate of time preference including whether rates should be hyperbolic, ethical issues such as evolving wealth and whether or not certain goods such as lives and health are special and should not be discounted. The authors proceed from the premise that the purpose of discounting is to select that rate that will lead to selection of projects that maximize net present values. They conclude that this will occur when the present value of benefits compensates for the capital forgone and the consumption displaced and so recommend using the social opportunity cost approach to the discount rate.

Richard Zerbe in Chapter 8 focuses on the ethical foundation for benefit–cost analysis, which so often stirs concerns among those opposed to benefit–cost analysis. His view is that properly conducted, BCA is an art form embodying elements of law, morality, judgment, and science. It is a method of structuring conversation and organizing knowledge. It is not a maxim, nor can it be acceptably reduced to mechanical objectivity. To recognize BCA as partly reductionist is not to prove it is without value, or without the flexibility to adapt to change. As a method it is necessarily reductionist and reductionist sciences have proven to be very powerful. The test of a method is whether it is useful, and BCA undeniably has been useful, notwithstanding claims to the contrary. Zerbe briefly considers the benefit–cost principle, the considerations that lie behind it, and the criticisms that have been made of it in light of these considerations. In response to criticisms, and to establish what BCA is more clearly, he describes a version of BCA that he calls ethical benefit–cost analysis.

Distributional issues are an important implication of ethical considerations and John Loomis in Chapter 9 traces the methods of analyzing who gains and who loses. The distribution of benefits and costs is certainly important to politicians as well as economists, but of course for different reasons. Traditionally, few BCAs explicitly analyze or provide a detailed discussion of equity. Historically, when equity was discussed it was in the context of a policy-induced change in market prices, taxes or incomes, not changes in utility from publicly provided non-market goods like human health and environmental quality. Loomis addresses that gap in his chapter. After first reviewing the importance of including equity in BCA, and the metrics to quantify distributional concerns, two case studies illustrating how to empirically evaluate distributional effects of non-market goods are presented.

Lisa Robinson and James Hammitt in Chapter 10 investigate the paradigm-shaking impact of behavioral economics. As traditionally conducted, benefit–cost analysis is rooted in neoclassical welfare economics, which assumes that individuals act rationally and are primarily motivated by self-interest, making decisions that maximize their own well-being. Its conduct is now evolving to reflect recent work in behavioral economics, which integrates psychological aspects of decision-making. Robinson and Hammitt consider several implications for analyses of social programs. First, benefit–cost analysis often involves valuing non-market outcomes such as reductions in health and environmental risks. Behavioral research emphasizes the need to recognize that these values are affected by psychological as well as physical attributes. Second, benefit–cost analysis traditionally uses exponential discounting to reflect time preferences, while behavioral research suggests that individuals' discounting may be hyperbolic. However, steep near-term rates may largely reflect impulsive behavior and self-control problems. Third, behavioral research emphasizes the influence of social preferences on valuation. In addition to acting altruistically, individuals may act reciprocally to reward or punish others, or use the status of others as the baseline against which to assess their own well-being. Fourth, behavioral economics identifies factors that can help develop valuation studies that provide well-informed, thoughtful preferences. Finally, while behavioral research has led some to argue for a more paternalistic approach to policy analysis, an alternative is to continue to focus on describing the preferences of those affected by the policy options while working to ensure that these preferences are based on knowledge and careful reflection. Benefit–cost analysis can be best viewed as a pragmatic framework for collecting, organizing, and evaluating relevant information.

The concluding chapter, Chapter 11, by Richard Zerbe, Tyler Blake Davis, Nancy Garland, and Tyler Scott both synthesizes and extends the earlier chapters. Their chapter is intended as a starting synthesis of detailed principles and standards for benefit–cost analysis in government and non-profit decision-making, with a particular emphasis on social programs. Foundational principles and details of almost 50 principles and standards are presented in the six categories of benefit and cost estimation, market extent, discounting, risk and uncertainty, equity and distribution, and presentation. References are provided in each section and an appendix provides a glossary of terms and abbreviations. The authors recognize that some principles and standards are contentious and all may need to adapt to future developments and advances in economics and benefit–cost analysis scholarship. Thus, the chapter is viewed as the beginning of a continuing endeavor but an important synthesis to conclude this volume.

ACKNOWLEDGMENTS

We thank the John D. and Catherine T. MacArthur Foundation for its support, particularly Michael A. Stegman, Valerie Chang, and Steven Casey. Mary Kokoski of University of Maryland, Baltimore County (UMBC) and managing editor of the *Journal of Benefit–Cost Analysis* along with Kiana Scott at the University of Washington were instrumental in crystallizing the many tasks needed to get this book to publication including detailed coordination and manuscript preparation. Zerbe also thanks the Evans School of Public Affairs for institutional support, including the efforts of Dean Sandra Archibald, Professors Alison Cullen and Joe Cook, and the support staff of the Benefit–Cost Analysis Center at the University of Washington, Deborah Fishler, Katie Ward, Aubri Wall, Camille French, and Kay Sterner. Farrow benefited from institutional support from UMBC and the Woods Hole Oceanographic Institution.

Several of the chapters have also appeared in the electronic *Journal of Benefit–Cost Analysis* (http://www.degruyter.com/view/j/jbca). We thank

BEPress and DeGruyter publishers for their assistance and willingness to provide several permissions to reprint articles for this volume.

Finally we thank the supportive and energetic people at Edward Elgar who helped so much to make this book a reality.

NOTES

1. The proposals in the President's Budget are also discussed in OMB's 2010 *Report to Congress* on the benefits and costs of federal regulations. More generally, the OMB's annual *Reports to Congress* provide updated information on federal regulatory analyses and related concerns, including issues relevant to the conduct of BCA (see http://www.whitehouse.gov/omb/inforeg_regpol_reports_congress/; accessed 3 October 2012).
2. http://www.wsipp.wa.gov/.
3. http://policyintegrity.org/.

REFERENCES

Adler, Matthew (2008), "Risk equity: A new proposal," *The Harvard Environmental Law Review*, **32** (1), 1–47.

Boadway, Robin and Neil Bruce (1984), *Welfare Economics*, New York: Basil Blackwell.

Brent, Robert (1984), "Use of distributional weights in cost–benefit analysis: A survey of schools," *Public Finance Quarterly*, **12** (2), 213–30.

Bush, George W. [President] (2002), "Executive Order No. 13258," *Federal Register* 76: 9385 (28 February 2002).

Bush, George W. [President] (2007), "Executive Order No. 13422," *Federal Register* 72: 2763 (23 January 2007).

Cai, Beilei, Trudy Cameron, and Geoffrey Gerdes (2010), "Distributional preferences and the incidence of costs and benefits in climate change policy," *Environmental and Resource Economics*, **46** (4), 429–58.

Chipman, John and James Moore (1978), "The new welfare economics 1939–1974," *International Economic Review*, **19** (3), 547–84.

Clinton, William [President] (1993), "Executive Order No. 12866," Code of Federal Regulations 3: 638, reprinted as 5 United States Code § 601.

Costanza, Robert, Lisa Wainger, Carl Folke, and Karl-Goran Maler (1993), "Modeling complex ecological economic-systems—toward an evolutionary, dynamic understanding of people and nature," *Bioscience*, **43** (8), 545–55.

Ekelund, Robert and Robert Hébert (1999), *Secret Origins of Modern Microeconomics: Dupuit and the Engineers*, Chicago: University of Chicago Press.

European Union–Regional Policy (2008), *Guide to Cost–Benefit Analysis of Investment Projects*, accessed 8 August 2012 at http://ec.europa.eu/regional_policy/sources/docgener/guides/cost/guide2008_en.pdf.

Farrow, Scott (1998), "Environmental equity and sustainability: Rejecting the Kaldor–Hicks criteria," *Ecological Economics*, **27** (2), 183–8.

Farrow, Scott (2011), "Incorporating equity in regulatory and benefit–cost analysis using risk based preferences," *Risk Analysis*, **31** (6), 902–7.
Fuchs, Edward and James Anderson (1987), "The institutionalization of cost–benefit analysis," *Public Productivity Review*, **10** (4), 25–33.
Graham, John (2008), "Saving lives through administrative law and economics," *University of Pennsylvania Law Review*, **157** (2), 101–245.
Hammond, Robert (1966), "Convention and limitation in benefit–cost analysis," *Natural Resources Journal*, **6** (2), 195–222.
Hammond, Peter (1985), "Welfare economics," in George R. Feiwel (ed.), *Issues in Contemporary Microeconomics and Welfare*, New York: Macmillan, pp. 405–34.
Hanley, Nick and Clive Spash (1993), *Cost–Benefit Analysis and the Environment*, Aldershot, UK and Brookfield, VT: Edward Elgar.
Harberger, Arnold C. (1971), "Three basic postulates for applied welfare economics: An interpretive essay," *Journal of Economic Literature*, **9** (3), 785–97.
Harrod, Roy (1938), "Scope and method of economics," *Economic Journal*, **48** (191), 383–412.
Hicks, John (1939), "The foundations of welfare economics," *Economic Journal*, **49** (196), 696–712.
HM Treasury (2008), *The Green Book: Appraisal and Evaluation in Central Government*, accessed 7 August 2012 at http://www.hm-treasury.gov.uk/data_greenbook_index.htm.
Hotelling, Harold (1949), "Letter to the National Park Service (dated 1947)," in *An Economic Study of the Monetary Evaluation of Recreation in the National Parks*, Washington, DC: US Department of the Interior, National Park Service and Recreational Planning Division.
Jones-Lee, Michael (1976), *The Value of Life: An Economic Analysis*, Chicago: University of Chicago Press.
Kaldor, Nicholas (1939), "Welfare propositions of economics and interpersonal comparisons of utility," *Economic Journal*, **49** (195), 549–52.
Mishan, Edward (1981), *An Introduction to Normative Economics*, New York: Oxford University Press.
Mitchell, Robert and Richard Carson (1989), *Using Surveys to Value Public Goods: The Contingent Valuation Method*, Washington, DC: Resources for the Future.
N.A. (National Archives) (1945), Record Group 315.2.1, Records of Interagency Committees and Councils Coordinating Water Use Programs: General Records (Meetings 12 [25 January 1945], 23 [27 December 1945], 24 [31 January 1946], 27 [25 April 1946]).
National Research Council (2010), *A Review of the Proposed Revisions to the Federal Principles and Guidelines Water Resources Planning Document*, Washington, DC: Committee on Improving Principles and Guidelines for Federal Water Resources Project Planning.
Ng, Yew-Kwang (1984), "Quasi-Pareto social improvements," *American Economic Review*, **74** (5), 1033–50.
Obama, Barack [President] (2009a), "Executive Order No. 13497," *Federal Register* 74: 6113 (4 February 2009).
Obama, Barack [President] (2009b), "Executive Order No. 13514," *Federal Register* 74: 52117 (8 October 2009).
Obama, Barack [President] (2010), "Analytical perspectives," in *Budget of the United States Government, Fiscal Year 2011*, Washington, DC: White House Office of Management and Budget.

Pareto, Vilfredo (1896), *Cours déconomie politique professé à lUniversité de Lausanne*, Lausanne: F. Rouge.
Pigou, Arthur (1920), *The Economics of Welfare*, London: Macmillan and Co.
Porter, Theodore (1995), *Trust in Numbers: The Pursuit of Objectivity in Science and Public Life*, Princeton, NJ: Princeton University Press.
Quade, Edward (1971), "A history of cost-effectiveness," IFORS International Cost Effectiveness Conference, 12–15 April 1971, Washington, DC, accessed 26 July 2012 at www.rand.org/pubs/papers/2006/P4557.pdf.
Reagan, Ronald [President] (1981), "Executive Order 12291," *Federal Register* 46: 13 193 (19 February 1981).
Reagan, Ronald [President] (1985), "Executive Order 12498," *Federal Register* 50: 1036 (8 January 1985).
Robbins, Lionel (1938), "Interpersonal comparisons of utility: A comment," *Economic Journal*, **48** (192), 635–41.
Rosen, Sherwin (1974), "Hedonic prices and implicit markets: Product differentiation in pure competition," *The Journal of Political Economy*, **82** (1), 34–55.
Sarewitz, Daniel (2004), "How science makes environmental controversies worse," *Environmental Science and Policy*, **7** (5), 385–403.
Scarborough, Helen and John Bennett (2012), *Cost–Benefit Analysis and Distributional Preferences*, Cheltenham, UK and Northampton, MA, USA: Edward Elgar.
Schwartz, Jason (2010), "52 experiments with regulatory review: The political and economic inputs into state rule-makings," Report No. 6, 2010, Institute for Policy Integrity, New York: New York University Law School.
Shabecoff, P. (1981), "Reagan order on cost–benefit analysis stirs economic and political debate," *New York Times*, 7 November.
Treasury Board of Canada (2007), *Canadian Cost Benefit Analysis Guide*, accessed 8 August 2012 at http://www.tbs-sct.gc.ca/ri-qr/documents/gl-ld/analys/analys-eng.pdf.
US Office of Management and Budget (OMB) (1992), "Guidelines and discount rates for benefit–cost analysis of federal programs," OMB Circular A-94, Washington, DC.
US OMB (Office of Management and Budget) (1996), *Economic Analysis of Federal Regulations Under Executive Order 12866*, Washington, DC: US Government Printing Office.
US OMB (Office of Management and Budget) (2000), *Guidelines to Standardize Measures of Costs and Benefits and the Format of Accounting Statements*, Washington, DC: US Government Printing Office.
US OMB (Office of Management and Budget) (2003), *Informing Regulatory Decisions: 2003 Report to Congress on the Costs and Benefits of Federal Regulations and Unfunded Mandates on State, Local, and Tribal Entities*, Washington, DC: US Government Printing Office.
US Water Resources Council (1983), *Economic and Environmental Principles and Guidelines for Water and Related Land Resources Implementation Studies*, 10 March 1983, Washington, DC: US Government Printing Office.
von Bertalanffy, Ludwig (1968), *Organismic Psychology and Systems Theory (Heinz Werner Lectures)*, Worcester, MA: Clark University Press.
World Bank (1994), *Operating Policy 10.04: Economic Evaluation of Investment Operations*, accessed 7 August 2012 at http://web.worldbank.org/WBSITE/EXTERNAL/PROJECTS/EXTPOLICIES/EXTOPMANUAL/0,,content

MDK:20064625~menuPK:4564185~pagePK:64709096~piPK:64709108~theSitePK:502184,00.html.

Zerbe, Richard O. (2001), *Economic Efficiency in Law and Economics*, Cheltenham, UK and Northampton, MA, USA: Edward Elgar.

Zerbe, Jr., Richard O. (2007), "The legal foundation of cost–benefit analysis," *Charleston Law Review*, **2** (1), 93–184.

Zerbe, Jr., Richard O. (2009), "Ethical benefit–cost analysis as art and science: Ten rules for benefit–cost analysis," *University of Pennsylvania Journal of Law and Social Change*, **12** (1), 73–106.

Zerbe, Jr., Richard O. and Tyler Scott (2012), "[Almost] everybody wins: A true Pareto justification for practical welfare economics and benefit–cost analysis," working paper available from authors.

1. An assessment of important issues concerning the application of benefit–cost analysis to social policy

Aidan R. Vining and David L. Weimer

1 INTRODUCTION

Social policy can be defined as the laws, rules, directives, programs, and other instruments employed by government to increase investments in human capital, encourage behaviors with positive externalities, discourage behaviors with negative externalities, or reduce disparities in wealth, income, or consumption. Social policy includes a range of substantive policy areas that encompass early childhood development, education, physical and mental health, juvenile justice, crime and corrections, housing, income support, and employment.

How should society in general, and government agencies in particular, assess the value of the vast array of social policy interventions that are either proposed or operating? Benefit–cost analysis (BCA) provides a framework for comprehensively taking account of the full range of social benefits and costs. Indeed, BCA is the only normative framework that explicitly claims to assess these costs and benefits comprehensively. Although BCA has traditionally been applied primarily to infrastructure investments, economic regulation, and environmental policy, it is now increasingly being applied to social policy (for a comprehensive review, see Weimer and Vining, 2009). The application of BCA to potential social policies requires both prediction of the effects of investments of scarce resources by society and the valuation of these effects in a money-metric, normally present-value dollars. The purpose of BCA is to identify the most efficient policy. Efficiency simply means getting the most value from the resources available. It includes technical efficiency—producing things of value in ways that involve giving up the smallest amounts of other things of value. More generally, however, it concerns the allocation of resources to generate the largest aggregate value, as assessed by summing individual valuations across all members of society. A policy or policy alternative is efficient if no other policy can be identified that offers a larger excess of benefits over costs. Any alternative policy that would create greater costs than benefits relative to the status quo is clearly inefficient. For example, a policy that would inflict $400 million in costs but only $300 million in benefits would decrease, rather than increase, efficiency.

Because it is always valuable and important to understand the efficiency consequences of government interventions, there is no normative reason why these fundamental principles of BCA (and more generally welfare economics) should not apply to social policy interventions. Therefore, we argue that the standard principles of BCA should apply to social policy. However, the application of BCA to social policy raises a number of issues that deserve particular attention in any effort to develop standards for BCA. An earlier version of this chapter was commissioned by the Society for Benefit–Cost Analysis. This commission asked us to "address general considerations in conducting a BCA of social programs, the need for principles and standards for social programs and addiction in particular, and point out any special problems facing those doing BCA in the field of addiction. An ideal methodology will be suggested in so far as this is possible." This chapter updates our earlier response to this charge (Vining and Weimer, 2010).

2 THE MAJOR ISSUES FACING THE APPLICATION OF BCA TO SOCIAL POLICY

After a comprehensive review of both the academic and more applied policy literatures, we can identify four issues as especially important in applying BCA to social policy: (1) the need for a comprehensive approach to assessing social policies; (2) the need to recognize and explicitly address the great uncertainty in prediction and valuation involved in applying BCA in most social policy areas; (3) the need to consider those behaviors, which occur frequently in social policy, that do not satisfy the assumptions of neoclassical welfare economics; and (4) the application to policies that often have strong distributional goals and consequences. Before considering each of these issues in detail, we seek to justify their importance.

Every BCA should be comprehensive in terms of taking account of all valued effects in predicting net benefits. Achieving comprehensiveness poses a special challenge in applying BCA to social policies because many of their effects are difficult to predict and value. Social policies often have effects that spill over from one domain to another, such as education and health investments that affect human capital and work effort. They also often have effects that are likely to persist over long periods of time but are difficult to predict. For example, investments in early childhood (e.g., subsidies for enriched day care) may affect labor market productivity (e.g., earnings) decades after the investment, requiring predictions of a chain of effects leading from cognitive development through school achievement to employment. Social policies also often involve the reduction of negative externalities, such as crime, that require valuation. However, the appropriate metrics, or "shadow prices," for a number of these externalities are currently uncertain.

The ubiquity of uncertain predictions of effects and uncertain shadow prices for valuation make the explicit recognition of uncertainty especially important in the application of BCA to social policy. Comprehensiveness requires the valuation of all effects, including those that might not achieve conventional levels of statistical significance in particular studies. The challenge is particularly great when a single study provides a number of important estimates of effects and few of these effects have statistical significance under the rules of multiple comparisons. As the focus of BCA is the hypothesis that net benefits are positive, analysts appropriately incorporate predictions based on statistically insignificant coefficients if they take account of their standard errors in the creation of predicted distributions of net benefits through Monte Carlo simulations. Indeed, because of the many uncertainties in the application of BCA to social policy, we argue that an explicit consideration of uncertainty, through Monte Carlo simulation or equivalent methods, is essential.

Social policies quite often involve behaviors that do not necessarily conform to the principles of neoclassical economics that underpin welfare economics generally, and BCA specifically. For example, an estimation of the opportunity cost of volunteer time depends on whether volunteers treat time as a standard economic good or as a "conscience good" that they feel morally obligated to provide (Freeman, 1997). Another behavior of particular importance is addiction. Should consumption that satisfies addiction be treated the same way as consumption that contributes to utility under the assumption of positive marginal utility? The correct application of BCA to policies that affect substance abuse often requires an answer, or plausible range of answers, to this question.

In contrast to many other policy areas, concerns about equity legitimately motivate the adoption of many social policies. Standard BCA itself is based solely on the value of efficiency. However, with advances in stated preference techniques, it may be possible to elicit people's willingness to pay for various sorts of redistribution and therefore changes in the equality of outcomes. For example, it may be possible to estimate how much the population would be willing to pay to move a child or family above the poverty line. Equity effects valued in this way may be included in BCA through a broader definition of efficiency, such as the one used in the application of BCA to environmental policies, that includes not only people's willingness to pay for the consumption (use) of private goods, but also their willingness to pay for consumption (non-use) of public goods. This approach is not common in social policy, partly because there are not yet good shadow price estimates of these external effects (but see, for example, Blomquist et al., 2009). Consequently, BCA analysts may want to embed their standard analyses within a multi-goal framework that takes account of equity as a second value. The consideration of equity may involve a trade-off between these two values. However, there may be some fortuitous situations in which well-targeted social policies increase both efficiency and equity.

The primary general guidelines for the conduct of BCA, the Office of Management and Budget Circulars A-4 and A-94 in the USA and the UK Treasury's *Green Book: Appraisal and Evaluation in Central Government*, do not provide much guidance that is specific to social policy. The most substantively relevant, but limited, guidance we were able to identify is the *Cost Benefit Framework* developed by the Department for Work and Pensions in the UK (Greenberg and Knight, 2007). Consequently, more explicit guidance is needed to facilitate the appropriate application of BCA to social policy. In particular, research that explicitly considers the special attributes of social policy is needed to develop more confident guidelines that could eventually become standards.

3 THE NEED FOR A COMPREHENSIVE SOCIAL ACCOUNTING STANCE

Of course, all BCA should strive for comprehensiveness. Yet, in order to be comprehensive, analysts need theoretically and empirically grounded estimates of all significant impacts. In practice, the constraints of time and data availability prevent analysts from developing their own empirically supported estimates of shadow prices for valuing the multiple effects of most policies. They must almost always draw on estimates of shadow prices from other sources. This is, of course, impossible if nobody has developed these shadow prices! Comprehensiveness is especially important in many areas of social policy because of the likelihood that policy interventions will produce significant impacts beyond those often thought of as being "primary." For example, early childhood interventions may produce the primary intended impact of increased cognitive development as well as later gains in schooling and employment that reduce criminal behavior. Just valuing cognitive development would substantially distort the measurement of net benefits.

Inevitably, the admonition to be comprehensive in the inclusion of valued effects in BCA will remain an aspiration unless the community of researchers invests in the development of commonly required shadow prices. It is straightforward to summarize our overall conclusion that guidelines or standards for those applying BCA to social programs should be bolstered with research to increase confidence in existing shadow prices and develop estimates of a number of additional shadow prices that are currently unavailable. Yet, what specifically should be the priorities? In the discussion that follows, we consider a number of issues relating to the required shadow prices. First, some shadow prices are of such importance that continued efforts to improve their estimates are needed (crime, marginal excess tax burden). Second, we identify important shadow prices that require research efforts because they are largely missing (increments of cognitive development, schooling quantity and quality), and shadow prices that require conceptual clarifications to facilitate the development of estimates (volunteer time and addiction). Third, we note available shadow prices that should but are not routinely used (marginal excess tax burden).

3.1 The Social Benefits of Avoided Crime

Many social policy interventions affect the incidence of crime (Butts and Roman, 2009; Roman and Visher, 2009). Indeed, crime reduction is one of the primary impacts in policy areas such as juvenile justice and prisoner re-entry. Additionally, taking an appropriately long-term perspective, crime reduction may also be an important benefit category in early childhood development programs and substance abuse treatment. The incidence of crime may also be affected and (ideally) reduced to some small degree by interventions in almost all areas of social policy, such as mental health and primary and secondary education. Thus, it is useful to have accurate and current estimates of the cost of crime because avoided crimes are an important source of benefits. The development of appropriate shadow prices for crimes that take account of their full social costs are thus extremely important for promoting good social policy BCA. The costs of crime can be divided into three parts: tangible costs to victims, intangible costs to victims, and criminal justice system costs. Weimer and Vining (2009) argue that there is a clear need for improvement of all three parts—better shadow prices for both tangible and intangible victim costs and better and state-specific estimates of criminal justice system costs.

Currently, the primary source for estimates of the costs of crime that are used in BCAs is Miller, Cohen, and Wiersema (1996). Miller et al. (MCW) have estimated the costs of fatal crimes (rape, assault, arson, driving while intoxicated), child abuse (sexual, physical, emotional), non-fatal rape and sexual assault, assault or attempted assault (with and without injury), robbery or attempted robbery (with and without injury), drunk driving (with and without injury), arson (with and without injury), larceny or attempted larceny, burglary or attempted burglary, and motor vehicle or attempted motor vehicle theft. MCW's estimates of the private monetized costs of these crimes included property damage and loss, the costs of medical care and mental health care, the cost of police and fire services, the cost of victim services, and productivity losses. Their estimates of intangible costs were based on estimates of the average value of life revealed by people's willingness to bear mortality risks. Following Cohen (1988), estimates of the costs of pain, suffering, fear, and lost quality of life were based on jury awards. Despite the reliance on jury awards, which do not necessarily reflect people's willingness to pay to avoid such harms, MCW's effort is an important contribution to the promotion of comprehensiveness in social policy BCA. Miller and Cohen (1997) also provide useful estimates of the victim cost of intentional gunshots and stabs. However, alternative estimation methods, including contingent valuation (CV) surveys to estimate willingness to pay for crime reductions (Ludwig and Cook, 2001; Cohen et al., 2004) and estimates of the capitalization of crime risk into housing prices (Lynch and Rasmussen, 2001), suggest that the intangible costs may be much larger than suggested by the MCW approach. For example, Cohen and colleagues (2004) find intangible costs for assaults to be about twice as large and those for armed robbery to be between five and ten times as large as MCW. In view of the various validity threats to contingent valuation, replications of these studies would be valuable.

Recently, McCollister et al. (2010) have produced a new set of estimates of the total societal cost of specific crimes (in 2008 dollars) for use in policy and program evaluation. These cost estimates are comprehensive and include victim costs (both tangible and intangible), criminal justice system costs, and crime career costs. Their research provides social (average) cost estimates for 13 crimes: murder, rape/sexual assault, assault, robbery, arson, larceny/theft, motor vehicle theft, household burglary, embezzlement, fraud, stolen property, forgery/counterfeiting, and vandalism. Estimates for several of these crime categories are new and have not been previously available. The authors also provide sensitivity analysis around these estimates.

Despite these commendable efforts, more still needs to be done. In some cases these estimates of the victim costs of crime (and therefore the benefits of avoided crime) are not comprehensive and are best thought of as lower-bound estimates. Additionally, the current research does not cover all crimes, despite recent expansions of coverage. Comprehensive and current cost estimates are needed for both tangible and intangible victim costs of all types of crime. As avoided victim costs are often a benefit of social policy interventions, multiple methods and replications are desirable to bolster confidence in particular estimates.

The third crime cost category of importance is the marginal cost of criminal justice resources. For any given social policy intervention, these costs could either increase or decrease. Hereafter, our parlance assumes system cost reduction. This is commonly the case, but ultimately it is an empirical question. System cost is an important category because reductions in crime not only benefit those who would otherwise be victimized, but also society more broadly through the reduction of real resources devoted to the criminal justice system.

Ideally, we wish to estimate these benefits in terms of avoided marginal costs. However, the estimation of changes in marginal cost is complicated, especially for correctional resources. The most common approach to estimating the criminal justice system benefits of an avoided crime is to estimate the time savings to various criminal justice system employees, typically including police, public defenders, prosecutors, judges, court staff, and probation officers, and valuing these time savings at the employees' hourly wages and benefits. One problem with this approach is that criminal justice agencies are not necessarily equating marginal cost to marginal benefit in their application of labor and other resources. The expenditure of additional employee hours could produce marginal benefits in terms of crime reduction and justice that were either smaller or larger than the full wage rate. For example, adding the time of an additional police officer might very well reduce crime costs to victims by more than the wages and benefits of that officer. Further, an exclusive focus on employee costs may result in an underestimation of marginal cost because non-employees, victims, witnesses, jurors, and innocent defendants, also bear time costs in the operation of the criminal justice system.

Estimating the marginal cost of incarceration in jails, prisons, and other correctional facilities poses the most serious challenge to measuring criminal justice system marginal costs. These sorts of facilities often require large capital costs that, although sunk for any existing facility, would have to be expended if the inmate population grew sufficiently to require new construction. Average operating costs that include wages and benefits of security personnel, maintenance, and hotel services (food service and laundry), rehabilitation, and medical care almost certainly overestimate the marginal cost of adding an additional inmate to the facility in the absence of overcrowding. (The addition of another inmate to an already overcrowded facility could conceivably result in marginal costs larger than the average operating cost if it increases violence among prisoners or against prison personnel.) Urban Institute researchers John Roman and P. Mitchell Downey are preparing estimates of the marginal costs of criminal justice events (arrest, jail, prison, and probation) for each of the 50 states. These estimates should be available by the time this chapter is published (Henrichson, 2012).

Incarceration within existing arrangements may involve large externality costs. Approximately a quarter of the HIV population in the USA, and an even higher fraction with hepatitis C, pass through correctional facilities within any given year (Hammett et al., 2002). These inmates have the potential to spread these infections to other inmates, and to members of the community after release. Such external costs are potentially very large. Inmates may also impose external costs on their families, especially if it necessitates foster care of dependent children. The list of tangible and intangible externalities that could arise from incarceration is potentially long. These few sentences hardly do justice to them. Rather, they make clear that considerable analytical effort is required to assess the marginal costs of incarceration.

The issue of standing may also arise when assessing the marginal costs of jails or correctional services provided on a for-fee basis to local jurisdictions. Often these charges are based on budgetary expenditures and do not correspond to marginal costs. For example, the fees for correctional services provided to counties for juveniles may be based on the average costs of operation (Engle and Weimer, 2005). It is unclear whether these average costs approximate the long-run marginal costs.

Better estimates of the marginal costs of criminal justice system resources, especially the marginal costs of incarceration, including marginal external costs, would improve the comprehensiveness of BCAs in the many social policy areas that affect crime. Practical guidelines that analysts could apply in moving from available budgetary and average operating cost data in specific states or locales to appropriate shadow prices would also be useful.

3.2 Productivity Benefits

Most investments in human capital aim to increase the labor productivity of the target population in some way. This is a direct benefit. Additionally, this increased productivity may induce further indirect benefits, such as improvements in the health, self-esteem, and happiness of participants (i.e., their consumer surplus) and the welfare of participants' children. Even more indirectly, there might also be reduced administrative costs in those agencies that administer income transfer programs. These indirect effects are also real benefits or costs, albeit they are much more difficult to measure; indeed, they are rarely measured in practice (Greenberg and Knight, 2007). For suggestive studies on how some of these impacts might be measured and included in BCAs, see Morris (2001) and Grogger et al. (2002).

The usual procedure employed by labor economists for assessing direct productivity gains focuses on measuring the resulting increases in wages, rather than increases in hours worked. This follows the reasoning that, at the margin, the value of the lost leisure from additional hours of work equals the full wage rate: the gain to society from the added production is fully offset by the loss to the worker providing it. In other words, additional hours worked are a transfer from the worker to society; there is no net gain in social benefits. However, BCA analysts generally make the case that the equality is actually between the value of lost leisure and the after *tax* wage rate, and consequently they argue that the tax revenue resulting from additional hours worked should be counted as an external benefit—this portion of the additional production is gained by the rest of society and it is not offset by the worker's loss of leisure. There is, therefore, a net social gain.

A slightly more sophisticated argument suggests that workers most likely have upward sloping supply schedules that indicate their marginal opportunity costs at various levels of hours worked (Greenberg and Robbins, 2008). Programs that increase hours worked at the same wage rate may yield net productivity gains on the additional infra-marginal units if the worker could not work as many hours as they desired before the intervention.

The usual procedure for measuring productivity gains can be readily monetized: the productivity benefit accruing to the worker is the increase in income due to higher wages, and the external productivity benefit is the additional wage taxes paid. The more sophisticated treatment, however, requires an estimate of the worker's elasticity of supply of labor. Either procedure is implicitly based on the (strong) assumption that labor markets are perfectly competitive, such that all workers are able to smoothly adjust the hours they work in response to changes in wage rates. Many characteristics of real-world labor markets, such as involuntary unemployment or underemployment, removal from the labor market due to mortality, and work absences due to morbidity render this assumption unrealistic. This, in turn, raises questions about the proper approach for measuring productivity changes resulting from social policies.

The labor market access issue is likely to be particularly central to mental health and prisoner re-entry interventions. For example, people with mental illnesses may be unable to satisfy the requirements of normal labor market participation (Baron and Salzer, 2002). Interventions that allow those with significant mental illnesses to gain employment may provide benefits that exceed an estimate obtained from the difference between total after-tax wages and the total opportunity cost of supply as measured using a typical labor supply schedule. Indeed, Weisbrod (1981) reached this conclusion in his BCA of a comprehensive community treatment program. Consequently, Weisbrod estimated productivity benefits as equaling the total increases in earnings.

Researchers in health policy have extensively debated the appropriate treatment of lost labor due to morbidity or mortality (Olsen, 1994; Weinstein et al., 1997; Olsen and Richardson, 1999). The standard approach is to treat absences from work due to illness as costing society an amount equal to the missed hours times the full wage rate (even though this assumes that an individual receives no surplus from this time off work). Nicholson et al. (2006), however, find that, because of team production, absences may involve social costs that exceed the value of the lost labor of the absent worker. They provide estimates of these external costs for 35 job types, reporting a median multiplier of 1.28.

The direct productivity costs of mortality, or other involuntary labor market exit, have generally been treated as included in the value of quality-adjusted life years. Assuming the availability of replacement workers, the external costs of involuntary exit from the labor market have been assumed to equal the recruitment and training costs firms incur to replace the lost worker.

In view of the central importance of productivity as a benefit category in almost all areas of social policy, comprehensive and consistent standards for the measurement of the effects of interventions that increase human capital or affect the use of human capital would help improve BCA and contribute to comparability across BCAs. More empirical work to develop rules of thumb for productivity-related parameters such as non-wage benefits and tax rates, the externalities of network production in various categories of employment, the replacement costs of workers, and the decay rate for induced productivity gains would also be extremely useful.

3.3 Opportunity Cost of Public Expenditures: Marginal Excess Tax Burden

The use of public funds involves an opportunity cost greater than the amount of the funds. There are two reasons why raising one dollar of revenue from taxes typically costs society more than one dollar of resources. First, a tax creates inefficiency, or deadweight loss, that results from taxpayers' responses to the tax. For example, income taxes induce taxpayers to work less or take other actions to reduce their tax payments. These actions involve real social costs, whether in terms of forgone production or consumption. There are, of course, some well-defined exceptions to this rule, such as an excise tax on a good that produces a negative externality. Second, the collection of taxes requires the use of real resources that have an opportunity cost.

It is common practice in applied BCA not to include the opportunity cost of government expenditures. However, most social policy interventions do, and would, require net public expenditures, at least in the short run: one way or another, whether currently or in the future, these expenditures must be funded by taxation. The ratio of these additional costs of taxation to the amount of revenue collected is the marginal excess tax burden (METB) of the taxation. Each dollar of expenditure funded by tax revenue costs society (1 + METB) dollars in real resources. Some estimates, for example, suggest that the US METB appears to be on the order of 1.10 for excise taxes (on goods other than alcohol, tobacco, and gasoline) and about 1.30 for income taxes (Ballard et al., 1985). Boardman et al. (2011, p. 433) suggest that for most BCA purposes the appropriate income-tax-based METB is around 1.23 (see also Fujiwara, 2010). However, other scholars, including Feldstein (1997, 1999), have argued that these are lower-bound estimates of the METB for several reasons, including the fact that they do not include the effect of tax avoidance on labor supply. Saez et al. (2012, p. 4) go even further and emphasize that "taxes trigger a host of behavioral responses . . . all such responses are sources of inefficiency." For example, they point out that the METB of an excise tax on cigarettes should include the impact of the tax on smuggling and online internet purchases. Even so, they conclude that for almost all income earners the METB is around 1.20, slightly lower than the Boardman et al. (2011) estimate.

In spite of these lower estimates of the METB, the implication of not using the METB is that the conventionally described net benefits of interventions involving an excess of government expenditures over revenues will be too large, while those for interventions involving an excess of government revenue over expenditures will be too small.

The preponderance of positive net benefits found in published BCAs does suggest that quite a few proposed social policy interventions would still show positive net benefits if the appropriate opportunity cost of public funds were included. Yet, from a comprehensiveness perspective, this does not excuse the exclusion of these costs, especially as the pursuit of all apparently cost-beneficial interventions would require much larger budgets and the greater taxation required to fund them.

BCA practitioners commonly view redistribution as purely a transfer that nets out in the aggregation of the costs and benefits of individuals. Thus, they typically treat a dollar raised by a government tax and transferred to an individual as a one-dollar cost to government that is exactly offset by a one-dollar benefit to the recipient. The correct opportunity cost perspective, however, is that the transfer would result in a net cost of the METB times the number of dollars transferred. As we have emphasized, the METB is rarely included in actual BCAs. Indeed, Weimer and Vining (2009) found no examples of its use in the published BCAs in the social policy areas they reviewed, and only a few examples of its use in government-sponsored reports (e.g., Greenberg and Davis, 2007). Although we have been hesitant to go beyond a guideline level for most of our prescriptions, we think this can be elevated to a standard: an estimate of the marginal excess tax burden should be included in social policy BCAs. However, this elevation also requires that research efforts be directed at updating and improving this important shadow price.

3.4 Better Measures of the Benefits of Further Schooling

A variety of social policy interventions may affect the quantity and quality of schooling. Most obviously, education-based interventions are designed to increase the number of years of schooling and completion of degrees. So too do interventions in the areas of early childhood development, juvenile justice, mental and physical health, and substance abuse. For example, a pre-school program may increase the number of years a child voluntarily stays in school. Thus, increasing the number of years of schooling or the completion of degrees are important sources of benefits in several social policy areas. We have emphasized increments of school quantity because there is less prima facie evidence that increasing the "quality" of schooling (at least in developed countries) produces incremental benefits. The important caveat to this conclusion is that classroom, school, or school district quality is a multi-dimensional concept. It is possible that most empirical studies of quality have been looking for it in the wrong places (standard school inputs, such as teacher/student ratios, appear to be one of the clearly wrong places). The right places appear to be school attributes that raise cognitive skills (Hanushek and Woessmann, 2008). While it is certainly possible to treat any benefits arising from schooling increments as simply one form of productivity enhancement, there are sufficient differentiating characteristics to treat them separately.

Economists have provided estimates of the productivity gains from greater quantity (and, to some extent, quality) of schooling as measured in terms of the impact on higher earnings and non-wage labor market remuneration (Card, 2001). The contribution of increments of schooling to earnings appears to be highly robust (Harmon et al., 2003; Heckman et al., 2006; Oreopoulos, 2006), however, schooling may have other benefits. Some of these benefits, such as improved health, accrue directly to the schooled persons (Grossman, 2006). Their families may benefit from improved consumption efficiency and effectiveness in choosing the desired number of children. Children benefit in terms of cognitive development, health, and even longevity (van Kippersluis et al., 2011) and these benefits may carry over to some extent to successive generations. Communities enjoy some external benefits, such as reductions in crime.

Haveman and Wolfe (1984) have set out the standard framework for valuing many of these effects using a household utility function in which schooling is one of the inputs. Haveman and Wolfe were able to extract shadow prices for schooling in the production of outputs as a function of the marginal productivity of other inputs, such as family income. The total non-productivity benefit of schooling could then be estimated by summing across the various outputs other than productivity to which it contributes. Based on the then available studies, they estimated that the non-productivity benefits of schooling were comparable to the commonly measured productivity benefits. Thus, their estimates suggest that in BCA the appropriate shadow price for a year of schooling is roughly double the estimated productivity benefit.

Wolfe and Haveman (2001) updated their 1984 review with more recent empirical evidence concerning the non-productivity benefits of schooling, and they also expanded the categories of benefits. For example, studies indicate that parental education not only affects their fertility choices, but also affects the probability that their teenage daughters will give birth out of wedlock (Hayward et al., 1992; Lam and Duryea, 1999). Although they do not provide monetary estimates, they conclude that their earlier finding of approximately equal magnitudes for the labor and non-labor market benefits of schooling most likely still holds. Drawing on data from the US General Social Surveys, Oreopoulos and Salvanes (2011) quantify, but do not monetize, positive effects of schooling beyond productivity both within the labor market (job characteristics, satisfaction, and unemployment) and outside the labor market (health, marriage, parenting, encouragement of good behaviors, and consumption benefits).

Davies (2003) reviews the empirical macroeconomic literature and concludes that there are likely additional external benefits of education that go beyond those considered by Wolfe and Haveman. Dee (2004) finds that education contributes to voter participation and support for free speech, suggesting the possibility of eventually monetizing the "civic return" to education (see also Milligan et al., 2004 and Blomquist et al., 2009).

A consensus range of shadow prices for further schooling would be an extremely valuable contribution to improving BCA. As much of the non-labor market benefit arises through the increased earnings that result from schooling, a practical rule of thumb for scaling up productivity gains measured in markets to the full social benefits would also be valuable. Although such a rule of thumb would not necessarily incorporate all the benefits of schooling, it would not become obsolete as estimates of the benefits of productivity gains changed over time.

3.5 Better Measures of the Benefits from Cognitive Development

A number of social policy interventions, such as pre-natal, nutritional, and early education interventions, have the potential to improve the cognitive development of children. Indeed, preschool investments that improve the cognitive development of disadvantaged children may offer higher rates of return than any schooling improvements and job training programs provided later in their lives (Heckman, 2006). The cognitive benefits are most easily conceptualized, and measured, in terms of IQ improvements, although it can also be derived from measures of change on basic skills assessment tests, including those for math, science, and reading (Hanushek and Woessmann, 2008). Improvements in cognitive development or cognitive skills, in turn, contribute to other desirable, but more indirect, participant outcomes. The most obvious contributions are to educational inputs or outputs: increased school readiness, which reduces grade retention and the need for special education; higher achievement within school; more years of schooling completed; and higher graduation rates. It may raise the happiness and self-esteem of participants. It may also contribute to better social skills that reduce costs that are largely external to participants, such as delinquent and criminal behavior, teen pregnancy, and substance abuse. Other external benefits from improved cognitive development might include more civic-minded behavior. Obviously, some of the issues discussed in this section overlap with those discussed under the benefits of further schooling.

BCA of interventions that affect childhood development interventions would ideally take account of all of these possible impacts. The rare long-term longitudinal studies, such as those of Perry Preschool or the Carolina Abecedarian Project, measure many of the impacts that may result from improved IQ (Wolfe and Tefft, 2009). Although there may be a small residual effect of IQ gain that is not captured in these studies, it is likely to be relatively small, especially as IQ gains appear to be less likely to persist over time than scholastic success (Currie, 2001).

How might the shadow price of this benefit be refined? Weimer and Vining (2009) argue that a plausible starting point would be analyses of data from existing longitudinal studies to relate short-term IQ gains to longer-term outcomes. The shadow prices of schooling discussed in the previous section could be used to link the IQ gains to monetized outcomes through schooling. That is, IQ gains would be related to schooling gains, which in turn would be shadow priced to take account of their productivity and non-productivity benefits. There would also be potential gains in terms of fewer grade repeats and less need for special education that would not be captured in the shadow prices for schooling. Any additional impacts of IQ gain that can be identified should also be monetized and included in the IQ shadow price. The long chains of inference that are required might very well yield such a wide range of values for the shadow price that it would be of little value. Nonetheless, having at least some idea of the value of IQ gains would be useful in BCA if for no other reason than assessing whether such gains could potentially be large enough to affect the sign of net benefits.

3.6 Better Estimates of, and Consistent Use of, the Opportunity Cost of Volunteer Time

At first view, the appropriate treatment of the opportunity cost of volunteer time appears conceptually straightforward. The two leading sources of economic evaluation guidelines in health policy, for example, argue that this opportunity cost should be included in program cost (Gold et al., 1996; Drummond et al., 2005). That is, it is normally argued that volunteers' time has some positive opportunity cost, whether it is spent in leisure or labor. However, a recent review of reviews of health policy costing studies found that almost no studies actually included volunteer time as a program cost (Adam et al., 2003). Even when analysts are prepared to include this cost, they face the practical difficulty of choosing a shadow price based on the value of the services being provided or the value of the time of the donor. In practice, those analysts that have included this cost have skirted detailed consideration of this issue by simply shadow pricing as some fraction of the median wage in the local market, although some efforts have been made to value the important category of informal care using contingent valuation surveys (De Meijer et al., 2010)

Nonetheless, implementing a more refined shadow price requires addressing a fundamental question: Why would someone who has skills highly valued in the marketplace volunteer to do much lower-skilled labor? A guiding principle of welfare economics is that revealed preferences should be taken at their face value unless there is a good reason to do otherwise. The recognition of this principle suggests that volunteers realize utility from the activity at least as large as their opportunity costs of time, otherwise they would not be volunteering! From this perspective the shadow price of volunteer time may reasonably be treated as zero—the opportunity cost of the time is fully offset by the benefit realized by the volunteer. Indeed, if volunteers derive significant utility from volunteering, it would make sense to treat this value as a benefit of an intervention. In contrast, the treatment of volunteering as a conscience good, something that many donors feel morally obliged to provide when asked, casts doubt on the argument that the benefits of volunteering exceed the opportunity costs (Freeman, 1997). Because conscience goods are provided as a perceived duty rather than as a weighing of economic choices, donors might very well assess their own welfares as being worse for having provided the goods than if they had not been asked to do so.

Mukamel et al. (2001) explicitly incorporated the revealed preference argument for sensitivity analysis purposes and therefore shadow priced volunteer time at both the wage rate and zero. The shadow pricing of volunteer time can be substantively important. For example, a study of Big Brother/Big Sister programs by Aos et al. (2004) reported benefit–cost ratios of over three when volunteer time was shadow priced at zero, but very close to one when volunteer time was shadow priced at the wage rate.

However volunteer time itself is treated, it is clear that organizations making use of volunteer time bear the costs of recruiting, training, and monitoring volunteers. These costs should be included in the shadow price of volunteer time. Further, there may be externalities involved in these functions. An organization that provides poor experiences for volunteers may depress the total supply of volunteers in the community. Wasting volunteers' time or assigning volunteers tasks that members of the organization see as undesirable or low priority may encourage some volunteers to withdraw their contributions of time.

Having a greater consensus on the proper method for valuing volunteer time strikes us as important, especially when comparing faith-based and other privately delivered social services to those delivered by government agencies. More sophisticated guidelines that take account of the nature of the volunteering would be valuable to analysts. The minimum standard for the treatment of volunteer time would be sensitivity analysis that includes the boundary values of zero and the wage rate.

3.7 Plausible Estimates of the Social Costs of Substance Abuse

An important feature of the recent growth in BCA has been its wider application to substance abuse policy (e.g., Egerton et al., 1997; Cartwright, 1998, 2000; French et al., 2002). However, most evaluations of drug prevention or treatment interventions have short follow-up periods even though the participants involved in the interventions might well experience long-term behavioral changes. Therefore, the current evaluations often provide limited opportunity to observe directly socially relevant behaviors that relate to the social costs of drug consumption. This problem is particularly serious because intervention effects may be highly non-linear with time. Reductions in consumption might accelerate with time as a result of a "virtuous cycle" or decay increasingly quickly. Therefore, the application of BCA to these interventions through direct shadow pricing of all major effects is either impractical or highly speculative. Most evaluations can provide plausible estimates of reductions in drug consumption of effective interventions during the program participation period and the (typically short) follow-up period. Consequently, most economic analyses in what can be broadly defined as substance abuse policy are actually cost-effectiveness analyses that estimate cost per unit of reduction in substance consumption. So, at a minimum, robust shadow prices for reductions in the consumption of specific illicit drugs would make it more feasible to assess and compare programs using BCA, primarily by allowing researchers to monetize drug reduction effects in the numerous existing cost-effectiveness analyses.

To the extent that these shadow prices reflect streams of future costs and benefits, they would allow analysts to convert the short-run impacts measured in most program evaluations to more appropriate measures of social costs and benefits. Ideally, such shadow prices would be developed based on long-term experiments designed specifically to estimate future effects. In practice, rough estimates of these shadow prices may be developed from the body of evidence from observational studies linking changes in substance abuse to future labor market and other impacts. Zarkin et al. (2012) use a lifetime simulation model to estimate the present value of net benefits of prison-based substance abuse treatment programs.

A number of studies have estimated the social costs of drug use. For example, Harwood et al. (1999) provide estimates of the health, productivity, crime, and other social costs of alcohol and illicit drug abuse. Using these estimates, as well as other sources of information such as school-based treatment evaluations, drug use surveys, and various literatures, Caulkins et al. (2002) estimate the average social cost per unit of marijuana consumption and cocaine consumption. Moore (2007) estimates the social costs in terms of health and crime effects in Australia per gram for cannabis, cocaine, opiates, and amphetamines. He also estimates the annual social costs for dependent and non-dependent users of these substances. Caulkins (2009) argues that it is particularly important to develop further estimates of the social costs of stimulants (cocaine and crack) and amphetamines, as these probably generate approximately three-quarters of the social costs of illicit drug use in the USA.

In view of the magnitude of the social costs of drug consumption, much more research is needed to develop shadow prices for both legal and illicit drug consumption based on marginal social costs. To be practically useful, these estimates should be disaggregated by type of consumer, most critically by non-addicted versus addicted (see addiction below) but also by demographic groups such as age and sex.

Estimating the costs associated with consumer use, though, raises a major conceptual issue with respect to the social costs of price changes of addictive goods. In BCA, the standard approach to valuation assumes fully rational consumers. In such cases, increases (decreases) in the prices of these goods would result in social surplus losses (gains) for consumers of the good (Weimer et al., 2009). In many areas of drug policy, however, perhaps because of implicit unease with the standard BCA approach, the practice is to ignore social surplus changes to consumers (French et al., 2002; Ettner et al., 2006).

Relatively little attention has been given to the important questions surrounding this issue with the exception of the Australian Productivity Commission (1999) and Laux (2000). What should be the correct approach? How can the correct approach be implemented? Even more controversially, should any alterations to standard practice be extended to psychological or socio-psychological addiction? The Australian Productivity Commission (1999), for example, has argued that gambling can be addictive. The Commission argues that approximately 2 percent of Australian gamblers should be considered to be addicted. Although a small percentage, the Commission argues that the social costs arising from gambling by these problem gamblers could offset all the consumer surplus gains of recreational ("non-addicted") gamblers. Other recent studies suggest that the percentage of pathological gamblers in the gambling population is somewhat higher (Potenza et al., 2001; Narayanan and Manchanda, 2008). There also appear to be systematic interactions between gambling and, at least, nicotine addiction (Grant et al., 2009). Because of the importance of this question, we devote a subsequent section of this chapter to the BCA treatment of social surplus in social policy relating to addiction.

Is it important to distinguish between legal or illegal (i.e., illicit) drugs in assessing the social costs of drug abuse? There might be a case for doing so if one could reasonably conclude that legal status was based on some coherent assessment of social cost. However, the evidence suggests that this is not the case, perhaps because historically much drug policy was formulated before the pharmacological and genetic bases of addiction were clearly understood and appreciated. The nicotine in tobacco, a legal substance, is now recognized as one of the most addictive substances known to science (Hogg and Bertrand, 2004; Tapper et al., 2004). This suggests that legal status should be considered a policy choice (see MacCoun et al., 1996, for a fuller exposition of this argument). If this were not the case, then many alternatives that might pass the net benefits test would be eliminated from analysis.

4 DEALING WITH HEIGHTENED UNCERTAINTY IN SOCIAL POLICY ARENAS

The application of BCA to social policies typically involves producing predictions of net benefits based on imprecise predictions of numerous effects and their monetization with relatively uncertain shadow prices. Effectively, net benefits are the sums of products of random variables. Predicting net benefits using mean values for the random variables does not necessarily produce a good prediction of the mean of net benefits, the common metric for assessing efficiency. A much more appropriate approach is to treat the uncertainty in the predictions of effects and their shadow prices explicitly through Monte Carlo simulation. However, Monte Carlo simulation is thus far not standard practice in the application of BCA to social policy. In view of the multiple uncertain effects contributing to predictions of net benefits in most social policy applications, Monte Carlo simulation should be the standard basis for assessing net benefits in social policy.

The application of Monte Carlo simulation in BCA is conceptually straightforward. First, probability distributions for each parameter (predicted effect or shadow price) are specified. These distributions may involve covariance among parameters, for example when several coefficients and their variance–covariance matrix specify the multivariate t-distribution for several BCA parameters. Often the distributions themselves are highly uncertain and modeled as uniform distributions over some plausible range. Second, a trial is conducted in which a specific parameter value is drawn from each distribution and used to calculate a corresponding net benefit. Third, a large number, typically in the thousands, of trials are conducted to produce a distribution of net benefits, which can be displayed as a histogram. Fourth, summary statistics are computed for the distribution of net benefits. The "point prediction" of net benefits would typically be the mean net benefits across trials, which may differ from the net benefit predicted based on a calculation using the mean values of all parameters. (In applications where the mean may be overly influenced by a small number of trials with large net benefits, the analyst may choose the median of the distribution as the point prediction of net benefits.) The spread of the distribution, measured as a standard error, can also be readily calculated. For examples of well-developed Monte Carlo simulations in the BCA context, see Nicol (2001), Weimer and Sager (2009), and Zarkin et al. (2012).

BCA analysts usually do not explicitly frame BCA as testing the hypothesis that net benefits are positive. However, if the hypothesis of positive net benefits is viewed as the central concern of BCA, then the fraction of Monte Carlo trials with positive net benefits can be interpreted as a test of the null hypothesis of zero net benefits. If the fraction of trials with zero or negative net benefits is very small, then one can confidently reject the null hypothesis in favor of the alternative of positive net benefits.

Focusing on the hypothesis of positive net benefits differs from the statistical inference approach commonly employed in social science research. Particularly in the case of estimating parameters from a single study, whether experimental or observational, the common social science approach would be to treat parameter estimates that do not achieve conventional levels of statistical significance as "zero" to guard against Type I error. Nonetheless, under standard statistical assumptions, the estimated coefficient is the best estimate (in terms of mean square error) of the parameter even if it is not statistically significant at conventional levels. Returning to the importance of comprehensiveness in BCA of social policies, it is more appropriate to use the estimated but statistically insignificant coefficient, rather than zero, as the parameter value in calculating net benefits. However, incorporating the imprecision of the estimate in the predicted distribution of net benefits is all the more important. Hence, Monte Carlo simulation, or some other explicit accounting of uncertainty, is necessary.

Note that focusing on the hypothesis of positive net benefits avoids the necessity for addressing the issue of multiple comparisons. Analysts concerned about the statistical significance in the context of estimating many effects from the same experiment or observational study often make adjustments to statistical tests or p-values to take account of the fact that, while any particular test may limit the probability of falsely rejecting the null hypothesis to the stated p-value, the probability of having false rejections rises above the p-value in each individual test for the collection of tests—see, for example, Perneger (1998) and Anderson (2008). This adjustment process, while preserving the overall p-value for a false rejection to some level, typically results in some parameters being judged as statistically insignificantly different from zero despite their individual tests showing significance. From a BCA perspective, this aggravates the problem of treating statistically insignificant parameters as zero, making focusing on the hypothesis of positive net benefits even more important.

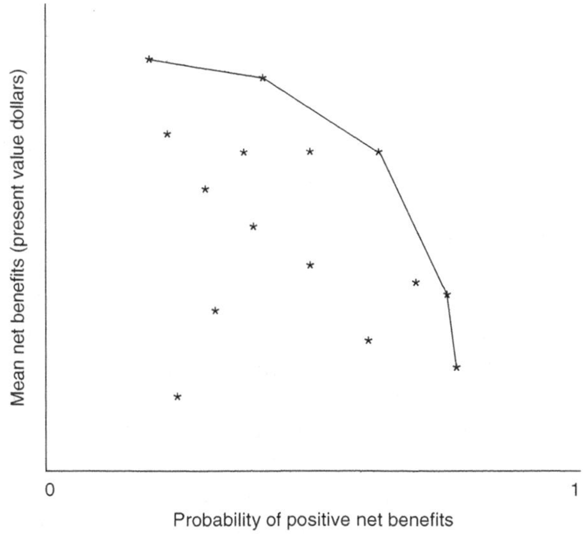

Figure 1.1 *Frontier of mean net benefits and probability of positive net benefits*

In terms of communicating the uncertainty of estimates to decision-makers, reporting the fraction of trials with positive net benefits along with the mean net benefits may be particularly effective. Specifically, the "probability of positive net benefits" as estimated from the fraction of trials with positive net benefits is likely to be more meaningful to a decision-maker than, say, "the standard error of the distribution of outcomes." The results from assessing multiple alternatives may be presented in a diagram like that shown in Figure 1.1. The points represent various combinations of mean net values and probabilities of positive results. The line segments show the alternatives that are not dominated by any other alternatives in the sense that none of the other alternatives offer increases in either dimension without decreases in the other. The line segments can thus be thought of as forming a production possibility frontier for trade-offs between mean net benefits and probability of positive net benefits. Although BCA under the assumption of risk neutrality provides no basis for choosing among policies with the same mean net benefits, decision-makers who are risk averse would certainly prefer less risky policies with the same mean net benefits. More generally, decision-makers who are risk averse would prefer policies somewhere on the frontier in Figure 1.1. Their particular choices would depend on how they trade off mean net benefits with probability of positive net benefits. If these preferences were represented in indifference curves, then they would each choose the policy that allowed them to reach their indifference curve giving them the highest utility. That is, the one furthest to the northeast.

The use of distributions based on empirical estimates of parameters should be viewed as the starting point for Monte Carlo simulations for two reasons: the danger of regression to the mean and optimism bias.

Statisticians recognize the implications of the difference between estimation and prediction (Copas, 1997). Social scientists most often focus on estimation, relying on the statistical properties of estimators. However, analysts conducting ex ante BCA are generally not concerned about the value of a parameter as estimated with respect to a particular set of data, but rather using the estimate as a basis for prediction of the parameter for assessing a policy that has not yet been adopted. Beginning with Stein's paradox (Effron and Morris, 1997), statisticians have recognized that regression to the mean implies that the best estimates are not the best predictions. Typically, estimates tend to be predictions that are too large in absolute value terms. Consequently, it is desirable that analysts adjust estimates downward in making predictions, especially when the estimates come from a single study—estimates from meta-analysis are less prone to the problem because it is less likely that multiple studies would all produce extreme estimates. Providing a systematic basis for making such adjustments should be a research priority for the BCA community.

Individuals may exhibit cognitive biases that make them overly optimistic about the potential for policies that they develop or advocate. The UK *Green Book* explicitly warns against the danger of optimism bias, especially in the context of large and complex projects (HM Treasury, 2009, p. 86). Drawing on research suggesting that programs closely controlled by developers or researchers systematically show better results than programs in "real world" administrative settings, analysts at the Washington State Institute for Public Policy routinely discount effects from studies not in "real world" settings by 50 percent in their meta-analyses (Drake et al., 2009, p. 178). Developing guidelines for guarding against optimism bias would contribute to more effective BCA of social programs. Although there have been some studies comparing ex ante BCA estimates with ex post assessments (see, for example, Boardman et al., 1994; Anguera, 2006), more such studies are needed to provide a better empirical basis for assessing the risks of optimism bias.

5 IMPORTANCE OF EQUITY IN SOCIAL POLICY

BCA is a protocol for assessing efficiency. Many social programs, however, also have equity goals. Indeed, some programs have the explicit goal of improving the conditions of disadvantaged segments of the population, perhaps by raising their incomes or consumption of specific goods, such as food or housing, closer to the population average. Recognition of declining marginal utility opens the door for incorporating equity into BCA. Further, to the extent that people in the general population have willingness to pay for improving the status of the lowest-income people, it is conceptually possible to employ stated preference methods to estimate this willingness to pay and incorporate it into BCA as an efficiency effect. When this approach is not feasible, policy analysts have no choice but to treat both equity and efficiency as distinct goals; that is, assessing efficiency through the prediction of net benefits and making explicit comparisons among alternative policies in terms of trade-offs between the two goals. Fortunately, well-targeted social policies often do not pose stark trade-offs.

5.1 Stretching Standard BCA: Recognizing the Declining Marginal Utility of Money

BCA takes the existing distribution of wealth as given and assesses the relative efficiency of alternative policies given that distribution. The rationale for a significant subset of social policies is that they seek to improve the conditions of disadvantaged groups in society, such as the poorly educated and unhealthy. Should BCA of these kinds of policy be adapted to take account of the social value of these improvements?

Some economists have proposed the use of BCA with distributional weights as a way to incorporate desirable distributional effects of policies (Boardman et al., 2011, Chapter 19). The normative rationale for distributional weighting is an application of the standard idea of declining marginal utility—in this case, the declining marginal utility of money. Given the differences in the level of wealth, an equal marginal increase in wealth increases the utility of poorer persons more than richer persons. An obvious problem with this approach is that, for a practical (and relatively consensual) use, ratios of marginal utilities at various levels of wealth are required. Researchers have postulated plausible proxies for relative marginal utilities based on tax rates (Eckstein, 1961; Haveman, 1965) or patterns of public expenditures (Weisbrod, 1968). Yet, in general, distributional weighting in BCA heretofore has been generally viewed by economists as a supplement to, rather than replacement for, standard BCA (Harberger, 1978). However, this solution sits somewhat less easily in social policy areas than in the traditional domains of BCA.

The severity of this problem is somewhat offset by the fact that some distributional weighting is indirectly introduced in BCA through the use of average shadow prices for normal goods. For example, economists generally use a single (average) shadow price for the value of a statistical life despite the empirical evidence that willingness to pay for reductions of mortality risk rise with income. They also tend to use some ratio of average wage rates in determining the value (cost) of changes in waiting time. We recommend research designed to establish a gradient giving guidance for adjusting these values depending on the characteristics of the population affected by the policy intervention.

5.2 Willingness to Pay for Redistribution

An alternative approach to measuring the social benefits of improvements to the circumstances of the least advantaged is based on the observation that many people derive utility from helping the disadvantaged. In other words, they are willing to pay something to help the most disadvantaged. The spontaneous outpouring of charitable giving after major disasters is one indication of such altruism. Experiments that attempt to put subjects behind a "veil of ignorance" in terms of the consequences of distributive policies for their own circumstances suggest general preferences for providing everyone with at least some minimum level of income (Frohlich et al., 1987). Experiments that use the so-called "dictator game" also provide some indirect evidence on this question. In the dictator game, "proposer" has a fixed sum of money that he or she allocates between self and "responder" (i.e., potential recipient). Although responders have no way to sanction proposers if they give nothing, the experimental evidence shows that they often offer between 20 and 30 percent of the total allocation (Camerer, 1997). To the extent that these preferences can be translated into standard willingness-to-pay measures, they can be incorporated into standard BCA. It would be valuable to have more work on this question. The starting point would be in terms of income or wealth disparities, but it is not clear that many people would not have greater preferences for redistribution if the "willingness-to-pay" question were framed in terms of other dimensions of disadvantage: for example mental or physical disability. (This could flow from a belief that these forms of disadvantage are less subject to moral hazard than, say, work effort.)

The conceptual starting point for valuing improvements in circumstances for the disadvantaged is a hypothetical (or contingent) comparison between the current situation and an alternative to it that differs only in terms of the number of people who are "disadvantaged." In terms of income or wealth disparity, for example, the alternative state of the world might be described as having one less family with an income below the poverty line. If a person were willing to pay to have the alternative over the current state of the world, then this amount would be interpreted as the person's willingness to pay to have one less family in poverty. This would provide a shadow price for valuing changes in the number of families in poverty resulting from alternative policy interventions.

CV (contingent valuation) surveys could provide data for estimating such shadow prices. Although critics remain, CV is now widely used and accepted; CV studies now number in the thousands (Carson, 2011). Its application is now widespread in health policy (Diener et al., 1998; De Bekker-Grob et al., 2012) and is beginning to emerge in other areas of social policy (e.g., Garbacz and Thayer, 1983; Ludwig and Cook, 2001; Van den Berg and Ferrer-i-Carbonell, 2007; De Meijer et al., 2010), although it is still not common. The potential application of CV to estimating willingness to pay for reduced poverty can be illustrated from its use in a somewhat related context: Dickie and Messman (2004) assessed parents' willingness to pay to relieve both their own acute illness and that of their children. They estimate that parents of 3-year-olds are willing to pay about twice as much to relieve their children's symptoms as they are to relieve their own symptoms. (Perhaps not surprisingly, they also find that this ratio falls to one-to-one as the children go through their teenage years!)

Using CV to develop shadow prices for the populations' altruistic value of improving the circumstances of the disadvantaged would make an important contribution to the application of CBA to social policy. As CV requires clear descriptions of the good being valued, a relatively narrow research focus on shadow prices for moving a child, an adult, or a family above the poverty line would be a good starting point. In view of the remaining controversy over CV in general as well as over-specific methods of willingness-to-pay elicitation, it would be unrealistic to think that convincing shadow prices could be developed from a single study, or even a small number of studies.

5.3 The "Efficiency–Equity Trade-off"

Efficiency and equity often involve a trade-off, but not always. In some situations involving market failures or the targeting of low-wealth groups with larger marginal benefits, efficient policies may involve desirable redistribution (Aghion et al., 1999; Rogers, 2003). Consider a good with a positive externality, such as vaccination against a communicable disease. Increasing consumption of the vaccine by lower-income families through a subsidy would both increase efficiency and provide greater income equality in preventive health care. Sometimes targeting disadvantaged groups may even lead to higher levels of efficiency than would be the case with a broadly targeted intervention because the intervention has a larger marginal effect on the disadvantaged than the general population. Such may be the case with class size reductions, which have larger marginal effects for lower-income than higher-income families; increased access to private schooling, which may produce larger educational gains for minority than majority children; and drug treatment programs, which may produce greater reductions in external costs for lower- rather than higher-income drug abusers. These situations produce what might be called a "double dividend" because they increase both efficiency and equity.

Social policy analysts cannot assess the potential for a double dividend, however, unless they disaggregate benefits and costs by potentially relevant social or economic groups. Currently, disaggregation is most often done (Boardman et al., 2011, pp. 310–13) or discussed (Krutilla, 2005) in terms of program participants as a group versus the rest of society or taxpayers. However, disaggregating among program participants may be possible when predictions of effects are based on experiments or quasi-experiments that allow sorting of participants by demographic characteristics.

6 THE SPECIAL PROBLEM OF ADDICTION

The standard assumption in applied BCA is that market demand schedules are marginal valuation schedules and therefore the appropriate basis for the measurement of benefits. However, addiction brings into question this correspondence. The addicted demand may not provide gains in utility in the same way as demand not driven by addiction. BCA that ignores the problem of addiction generally overestimates the costs of interventions that reduce consumption of the addicted good.

What is addiction? Clarke and Danilkina (2006, p. 1) provide the following working definition:

> a substance is addictive if, as the duration and intensity of consumption increases, (i) the agent becomes tolerant to the substance so they progressively want more of it; (ii) the agent finds it increasingly difficult to cease consumption; (iii) if they do quit, they suffer withdrawal disutility. Finally, (iv) if use is interrupted or ceases, the agent experiences unpleasant, and perhaps long-term, cravings for the substance.

With the modification that the agent may actually reach a plateau of demand for the substance, we accept this definition.

Figure 1.2 illustrates the addiction problem. The market demand schedule for a good is shown as D_A. It includes the demand for both addicted and non-addicted consumption. The schedule labeled D_R shows demand

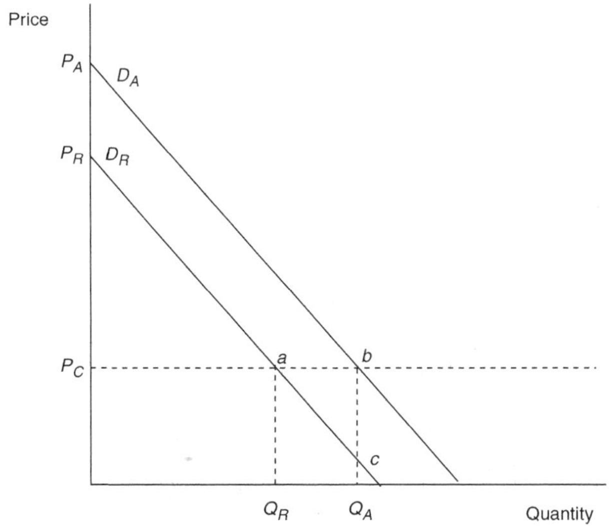

Source: Adapted from Australian Productivity Commission (1999, Appendix C, pp. 11–13).

Figure 1.2 Consumer surplus in the presence of addiction

in the absence of addiction. For example, if D_A is the total demand for cigarettes, then D_R is the demand for cigarettes if no one were addicted to cigarettes. Suppose a policy removed this good from the market. Standard BCA would count the area of triangle P_AbP_C as the consumer surplus loss and therefore a cost of the policy. However, if the non-addicted demand schedule is taken to be the marginal valuation schedule, then the consumer surplus would be $P_RaP_C - abc$, a much smaller cost than measured relative to the market demand schedule.

This illustration raises two questions. First, is the non-addicted demand schedule the proper basis for measuring changes in social surplus? Second, if it is the proper basis, how can it be estimated?

Becker and Murphy (1988) argue that if consumers fully take account of the future effects of their current consumption, then the market demand schedule would be the appropriate basis for measuring welfare changes absent any externalities. They describe this as rational addiction. It is beyond the scope of this analysis to assess fully whether the behavior they model can be described as rational as posited in standard welfare economics. We would argue that if so, it is a very strong and not particularly useful definition of rationality. Most particularly, their model employs constant exponential discounting, which in turn implies time-consistent decisions and allows for no "weakness of will" lapses or regret. Clarke and Danilkina (2006) note that Samuelson introduced constant exponential discounting into consumer choice models (Samuelson, 1937) and point out that Samuelson (ibid., p. 160) himself emphasized its mathematical arbitrariness and potential lack of generalizability:

> it is extremely doubtful whether we can learn much from considering such an economic man, whose tastes remain unchanged, who seeks to maximize some functional form of consumption alone, in a perfect world, where all things are certain and synchronized. For in any case such a functional [*sic*] would have to be dependent upon certain parameters which are socially determined . . . In general, there is strong reason to believe that changes in such parameters are not of an equilibrating nature.

Bernheim and Rangel (2004) propose an alternative model of individual choice to rational addiction in which addicts make mistakes and their experiences sensitize them to environmental cues that trigger mistaken usage.

The empirical case for rational addiction is also questionable. It is generally based on analysis of aggregate demand for the good over time. As noted by Auld and Grootendorst (2004) and others, the econometric methods employed find many goods addictive, not just the ones for which there is scientific evidence of physical addiction. This problem arises because it is empirically difficult, although not impossible (Farrell et al., 1999; Gruber and Koszegi, 2001; Guryan and Kearney, 2009), to distinguish between serial correlation in consumption arising from stable preferences and some fundamental causal relationship between present and future consumption.

If consumers are time inconsistent or are otherwise myopic in the sense of not fully anticipating the consequence of future consumption, then the market demand schedule is not the proper basis for measuring welfare change. Myopia refers not just to extreme impatience as would be modeled with very high discount rates, but any significant failure to take account of the future. With respect to goods that are generally physiologically addictive, there are a number of causal pathways through which consumers may misjudge their addictive properties. For example, most smokers begin smoking as juveniles who underestimate the addictive properties of nicotine (Taylor and Brown, 1988; Gruber 2002/2003). Similarly, those experimenting with recreational drug use are unlikely to be fully aware of the risks many of these drugs, especially the stimulants, pose for physical addiction. One increasingly recognized reason for individuals' inability to anticipate addiction risks may be lack of knowledge about their own genetic make-up that could predispose them to heightened risk of addiction. Current estimates are that genetic factors contribute between 40 and

60 percent to addiction vulnerability (Uhl, 2004; Goldman et al., 2005). For example, the A1 allele of the dopamine receptor gene DRD2 appears to be more common in those addicted to cocaine or alcohol (for a recent review, see Li et al., 2008).

With respect to goods that are psychologically or behaviorally addictive, consumers are unlikely to know prior to use whether or not they will be prone to addiction. While most people can gamble without escalating their gambling expenditures to destructive levels, a small fraction of people cannot restrain themselves. Prior to some experience with gambling, people are unlikely to know their type so that those who are prone to addiction inadvertently become addicted.

To determine how to take account of addiction in BCA an explicit utility model is required. Weimer et al. (2009) employ one such simple utility model:

$$U = x + \alpha c - \rho(c - S)^2$$

where c is consumption of the addictive good, x is the consumption of all other goods, S is the index of addiction, and α and ρ are non-zero parameters. Assuming a budget constraint of B_A and prices for x of p_x and of addictive good c of p_c, respectively, and solving the first order conditions for x and c and substituting them into the above, yields the following expression for the maximum utility, W^*:

$$W^* = \left[\frac{B_A - p_c S}{p_x}\right] - \left[\frac{\alpha p_c}{2\rho p_x}\right] + \left[\frac{p_c^2}{2\rho p_x^2}\right] + \rho\left[\frac{\alpha}{2\rho} - \frac{p_c}{2\rho p_x}\right]^2$$

In this simple case, if S were set to 0, that is, the person were no longer addicted, then decreasing B_A by an amount $p_c S$ would leave the utility unchanged. Therefore, $p_c S$ is the compensating variation for the elimination of the addiction. That is, the person would be willing to pay $p_c S$ in return for removal of the addiction.

Letting p_x = \$1, yields the following demand schedule for the additive good:

$$c = \frac{\alpha}{2\rho} + S - \frac{p_c}{2\rho}$$

where the slope is $-1/2\rho$. As S becomes larger (the good is more addictive), the amount demanded at every price increases. Also, as ρ becomes larger, demand becomes less elastic.

Weimer et al. (2009) employ contingent valuation to estimate smokers' willingness to pay for removal of addiction, and therefore to estimate p_cS. This enables them to remove addicted demand from the market demand schedule. Their procedure results in estimates of social cost of a price rise in the cost of cigarettes of only about 75 percent of the social surplus loss measured using the market demand schedule. It should be viewed as an upper bound, for two reasons. First, despite the overwhelming scientific evidence on the addictiveness of cigarettes, about 14 percent of cigarette smokers responding to the survey reported that they believed that they were not physically addicted. Second, the treatment removing addiction in the contingent valuation elicitation question was described as involving injection, which may have depressed positive responses to bid prices—one relevant study suggests that about 15 percent of respondents may have rejected bid prices solely because of aversion to injection (Steiner et al., 2002). Consequently, this one study is only suggestive. It also relates only to the demand for cigarettes. Therefore, more studies are needed to develop confident estimates of non-addicted demand for goods with addictive properties.

Absent confident estimates of the fraction of market demand resulting from addicted demand, how should changes in consumption of addicted demand be treated in BCA? As a first step, the analysts should assess the degree of addictiveness of the good. This requires analysts to address two questions. First, what is the evidence about the physical addictiveness of the good in question? Nicotine perhaps anchors that upper end of the scale, followed by stimulants, opiates, alcohol, and marijuana. Second, what is the evidence concerning psychological or behavioral addiction? Especially with this latter category, it is important to assess the extent to which people are susceptible to addiction. For example, most people are susceptible to nicotine addiction while evidence suggests that only about 2 percent of the population is susceptible to gambling addiction. Answering these questions provides at least some basis for assessing whether or not addictive demand is a large component of market demand. At a minimum, analysts applying BCA to policies affecting the consumption of addictive goods should be explicit about their assumptions concerning the proportion of addicted consumers and their estimate of the consumer surplus reduction. In view of the uncertainty surrounding the affects of addiction on market demand, these BCAs should incorporate a range of estimates for additive demand in their Monte Carlo and other sensitivity analyses.

7 CONCLUSION

BCA offers great potential for informing choices about desirable social policies. Realizing this potential, however, requires that the community of scholars with skills in BCA invest in developing evidence-based shadow prices required for monetizing the most common social policy impacts. In some cases, such as shadow prices for the costs of crime or marginal excess tax burden, estimates are available but require more research to narrow their ranges and verify their validities. In other cases, such as shadow prices for the social benefits of schooling, willingness to pay for redistribution, or the treatment of addictive demand, creativity is needed to develop estimates where none are now available. Analysts should also look for opportunities to develop appropriate shadow prices for short-run impacts of the sort most commonly estimated from program evaluations and experiments. Such efforts will most likely require the creative use of empirical evidence of all kinds to link short-run effects to outcomes for which we have or can develop shadow prices.

In view of the large number of uncertain effects and shadow prices involved in applying BCA to social policies, analysts must take special care in dealing with uncertainty. Rather than setting estimates of effects equal to zero when their estimates are statistically insignificant, a more appropriate approach is to take account of the uncertainty of these effects in Monte Carlo simulations.

REFERENCES

Adam, Taghreed, David B. Evans, and Marc A. Koopmanschap (2003), "Cost-effectiveness analysis: Can we reduce variability in costing methods?," *International Journal of Technology Assessment in Health Care*, **19** (2), 407–20.

Aghion, Philippe, Eve Caroli, and Cecilia Garcia-Penalosa (1999), "Inequality and economic growth: The perspective of the new growth theories," *Journal of Economic Literature*, **37** (4), 1615–60.

Anderson, Michael L. (2008), "Multiple inference and gender differences in the effects of early intervention: A reevaluation of the Abecedarian, Perry Preschool, and early training projects," *Journal of the American Statistical Association*, **103** (484), 1481–95.

Anguera, Ricard (2006), "The Channel Tunnel—an ex post economic evaluation," *Transportation Research Part A: Policy and Practice*, **40** (4), 291–315.

Aos, Steve, Roxanne Lieb, Jim Mayfield, Marna Miller, and Annie Pennucci (2004), *Benefits and Costs of Prevention and Early Intervention Programs*, Olympia, WA: Washington State Institute for Public Policy.

Auld, M. Christopher and Paul Grootendorst (2004), "An empirical analysis of milk addiction," *Journal of Health Economics*, **23** (6), 1117–33.

Australian Productivity Commission (1999), *Australia's Gambling Industries*, Inquiry Report No. 10, 26 November, accessed 12 July 2012 at http://www.pc.gov.au/projects/inquiry/gambling/docs/finalreport.

Ballard, Charles L., John B. Shoven, and John Whalley (1985), "General

equilibrium computations of the marginal welfare costs of taxes in the United States," *American Economic Review*, **75** (1), 128–38.
Baron, Richard C. and Mark S. Salzer (2002), "Accounting for unemployment among people with mental illness," *Behavioral Sciences and the Law*, **20** (6), 585–99.
Becker, Gary S. and Kevin M. Murphy (1988), "A theory of rational addiction," *Journal of Political Economy*, **96** (4), 675–700.
Bernheim, B. Douglas and Antonio Rangel (2004), "Addiction and cue-triggered decision processes," *American Economic Review*, **94** (5), 1558–90.
Blomquist, Glenn C., Paul A. Coomes, Christopher Jepsen, Brandon C. Koford, and Kenneth R. Troske (2009), "Estimating the social value of higher education: willingness to pay for community and technical colleges," IZA DP No. 4086, Bonn, Germany.
Boardman, Anthony E., Wendy L. Mallery, and Aidan R. Vining (1994), "Learning from ex ante/ex post cost–benefit comparisons: The Coquihalla Highway example," *Economic Planning Sciences*, **28** (2), 69–84.
Boardman, Anthony E., David H. Greenberg, Aidan R. Vining, and David L. Weimer (2011), *Cost–Benefit Analysis: Concepts and Practice*, 3rd edition, Upper Saddle River, NJ: Prentice Hall.
Butts, Jeffrey A. and John K. Roman (2009), "Juvenile crime interventions," in David L. Weimer and Aidan R. Vining, (eds), *Investing in the Disadvantaged: Assessing the Benefits and Costs of Social Policies*, Washington, DC: Georgetown University Press, pp. 103–26.
Camerer, Colin (1997), "Progress in behavioral game theory," *Journal of Economic Perspectives*, **11** (4), 167–88.
Card, David (2001), "Estimating the return to schooling: progress on some persistent econometric problems," *Econometrica*, **69** (5), 1127–60.
Carson, Richard T. (2011), *Contingent Valuation: A Comprehensive Bibliography and History*, Cheltenham, UK and Northampton, MA, USA: Edward Elgar.
Cartwright, William S. (1998), "Cost–benefit and cost-effectiveness analysis of drug abuse treatment services," *Evaluation Review*, **22** (5), 609–36.
Cartwright, William S. (2000), "Cost–benefit analysis of drug treatment services: Review of the literature," *Journal of Mental Health Policy and Economics*, **3** (1), 11–26.
Caulkins, Jonathan P. (2009), "Illicit substance abuse and addiction," in David L. Weimer and Aidan R. Vining (eds), *Investing in the Disadvantaged: Assessing the Benefits and Costs of Social Policies*, Washington, DC: Georgetown University Press, pp. 83–102.
Caulkins, Jonathan P., Rosalie Liccardo Pacula, Susan Paddock, and James Chiesa (2002), *School-based Drug Prevention: What Kind of Drug Use Does it Prevent?*, Santa Monica, CA: RAND.
Clarke, Harry and Svetlana Danilkina (2006), "Talking rationally about rational addiction," unpublished manuscript, LaTrobe University.
Cohen, Mark A. (1988), "Pain, suffering, and jury awards: A study of the cost of crime to victims," *Law and Society Review*, **22** (3), 537–56.
Cohen, Mark A., Roland T. Rust, Sara Steen, and Simon T. Tidd (2004), "Willingness-to-pay for crime control programs," *Criminology*, **42** (1), 89–109.
Copas, J.B. (1997), "Using regression models for prediction: Shrinkage and regression to the mean," *Statistical Methods in Medical Research*, **6** (2), 167–83.

Currie, Janet (2001), "Early childhood education programs," *Journal of Economic Perspectives*, **15** (2), 213–38.
Davies, Jim (2003), "Empirical evidence on human capital externalities," Economic Policy Institute Working Paper No. 2003–5, London, Ontario: University of Western Ontario.
De Bekker-Grob, Esther W., Mandy Ryan, and Karen Gerard (2012), "Discrete choice experiments in health economics: A review of the literature," *Health Economics*, **21** (2), 145–72.
Dee, Thomas S. (2004), "Are there civic returns to education?," *Journal of Public Economics*, **88** (9–10), 1607–720.
De Meijer, Claudine, Werner Brouwer, Marc Koopmanschap, Bernard van den Berg, and Job van Exel (2010), "The value of informal care—a further investigation of the feasibility of contingent valuation in informal caregivers," *Health Economics*, **19** (7), 755–71.
Dickie, Mark and Victoria L. Messman (2004), "Parental altruism and the value of avoiding acute illness: Are kids worth more than parents?," *Journal of Environmental Economics and Management*, **48** (3), 1146–74.
Diener, Alan, Bernie O'Brien and Amiram Gafni (1998), "Health care contingent valuation studies: A review and classification of the literature," *Health Economics*, **7** (4), 313–26.
Drake, Elizabeth K., Steve Aos, and Marna G. Miller (2009), "Evidence-based public policy options to reduce crime and criminal justice costs: Implications in Washington State," *Victims and Offenders*, **4** (2), 179–96.
Drummond, F. Michael, Mark J. Sculpher, George W. Torrance, Bernie J. O'Brien, and Greg L. Stoddart (2005), *Methods for the Evaluation of Health Care Programmes*, 3rd edition, New York: Oxford University Press.
Eckstein, Otto (1961), "A survey of the theory of public expenditure criteria," in James M. Buchanan (ed.), *Public Finances: Needs, Sources and Utilization*, Princeton, NJ: Princeton University Press, pp. 439–94.
Effron, Bradley and Carl Morris (1997), "Stein's paradox in statistics," *Scientific American*, **236** (5), 119–27.
Egerton, J., D. Fox, and A. Leshner (1997), *Cost–Benefit and Cost-effectiveness Analysis: Issues in the Evaluation of Illicit Drug Abuse*, Malden, UK: Blackwell.
Engle, Pär Jason and David L. Weimer (2005), "Enhancing criminal sentencing options in Wisconsin: The state and county correctional partnership," *La Follette Policy Report*, **15** (1), 15–18.
Ettner, Susan L., David Huang, Elizabeth Evans, Danielle Rose Ash, Mary Hardy, Michael Jourabchi, and Yih-Ing Hser (2006), "Benefit–cost in the California Treatment Outcome Project: Does substance abuse treatment 'pay for itself'," *Health Services Research*, **41** (1), 192–213.
Farrell, Lisa, Edgar Morgenroth, and Ian Walker (1999), "A time series analysis of U.K. lottery sales: Long and short run price elasticities," *Oxford Bulletin of Economics and Statistics*, **61** (4), 513–26.
Feldstein, Martin (1997), "How big should government be?," *National Tax Journal*, **50** (2), 197–213.
Feldstein, Martin (1999), "Tax avoidance and the deadweight loss of the income tax," *Review of Economics and Statistics*, **81** (4), 674–80.
Freeman, Richard B. (1997), "Working for nothing: The supply of volunteer labor," *Journal of Labor Economics*, **15** (1), S140–S166.
French, Michael T., Helena J. Salome, Jody L. Sindelar, and A. Thomas McLellan

(2002), "Benefit–cost analysis of addiction treatment: Methodological guidelines and empirical application using the DATCAP and ASI," *Health Services Research*, **37** (2), 433–55.

Frohlich, Norman, Joe A. Oppenheimer, and Cheryl L. Eavey (1987), "Choices of principles of distributive justice in experimental groups," *American Journal of Political Science*, **31** (3), 606–36.

Fujiwara, Daniel (2010), "The Department for Work and Pensions social cost–benefit analysis framework: Methodologies for estimating and incorporating the wider social and economic impacts of work in cost–benefit analysis of employment programmes," Working Paper No. 86, Department for Work and Pensions, UK, accessed 12 July 2012 at http://research.dwp.gov.uk/asd/asd5/WP86.pdf.

Garbacz, Christopher and Mark A. Thayer (1983), "An experiment in valuing senior companion program services," *Journal of Human Resources*, **18** (1), 147–53.

Gold, Marthe R., Joanna E. Siegel, Louise B. Russell, and Milton C. Weinstein (1996), *Cost-effectiveness in Health and Medicine*, New York: Oxford University Press.

Goldman, David, Gabor Oroszi, and Francesca Ducci (2005), "The genetics of addictions: Uncovering the genes," *Nature Reviews. Genetics*, **6** (7), 521–32.

Grant, Jon E., Desai Rani, and Marc Potenza (2009), "Relationship of nicotine dependence, subsyndromal and pathological gambling, and other psychiatric disorders: Data from the National Epidemiologic Survey on Alcohol and Related Conditions," *The Journal of Clinical Psychiatry*, **70** (3), 334–43.

Greenberg, David H. and Abigail Davis (2007), "Evaluation of the New Deal for disabled people: The cost and cost–benefit analyses," Research Report No. 431, Leeds, UK: Department for Work and Pensions.

Greenberg, David and Genevieve Knight (2007), *Review of the DWP Cost Benefit Framework and How It has Been Applied*, Leeds, UK: Department for Work and Pensions.

Greenberg, David H. and Philip Robbins (2008), "Incorporating nonmarket time into benefit–cost analyses of social programs: An application to the self-sufficiency project," *Journal of Public Economics*, **92** (3–4), 766–94.

Grogger, Jeffrey, Lynn A. Karoly, and Jacob Alex Klerman (2002), *Consequences of Welfare Reform: A Research Synthesis*, Santa Monica, CA: Rand.

Grossman, Michael (2006), "Education and nonmarket outcomes," in Erik Hanushek and F. Welch (eds), *Handbook of the Economics of Education, Volume 1*, Amsterdam: Elsevier/North-Holland.

Gruber, Jonathan (2002/2003), "Smoking's internalities," *Regulation*, **25** (4), 52–7.

Gruber, Jonathan and Botond Koszegi (2001), "Is addiction 'rational'? Theory and evidence," *Quarterly Journal of Economics*, **116** (4), 1261–303.

Guryan, Jonathan and Melissa Schettini Kearney (2009), "Is lottery gambling addictive?," NBER Working Paper Series, No. 14742.

Hammett, Theodore M., Mary Patricia Harmon, and William Rhodes (2002), "The burden of infectious disease among inmates of and releasees from US correctional facilities, 1997," *American Journal of Public Health*, **92** (11), 1789–94.

Hanushek, Erik A. and Ludger Woessmann (2008), "The role of cognitive skills in economic development," *Journal of Economic Literature*, **46** (3), 607–68.

Harberger, Arnold C. (1978), "On the use of distributional weights in social cost–benefit analysis," *Journal of Political Economy*, **86** (2), S87–S120.

Harmon, Colm, Hessel Oosterbeek, and Ian Walker (2003), "Returns to education: Microeconomics," *Journal of Economic Surveys*, **11** (1), 115–55.
Harwood, Henrick J., Douglas Fountain, and Gina Livermore (1999), "Economic cost of alcohol and drug abuse in 1992: a report," *Addiction*, **94** (5), 631–47.
Haveman, Robert (1965), *Water Resources Investment and the Public Interest*, Nashville, TN: Vanderbilt University Press.
Haveman, Robert and Barbara Wolfe (1984), "Schooling and economic well-being: The role of nonmarket effects," *Journal of Human Resources*, **19** (3), 377–407.
Hayward, Mark D., William Grady, and John O. Billy (1992), "The influence of socioeconomic status on adolescent pregnancy," *Social Science Quarterly*, **73** (4), 750–72.
Heckman, James J. (2006), "Skill formation and the economics of investing in disadvantaged children," *Science*, **312** (5782), 1900–902.
Heckman, James J., Lance J. Lochner, and Petra E. Todd (2006), "Earnings functions, rates of return and treatment effects: The Mincer equation and beyond," in Eric A. Hanushek and Finis Welch (eds), *Handbook of the Economics of Education, Volume 1*, Amsterdam: Elsevier/North-Holland.
Henrichson, Christian (2012), "April focus: Upcoming studies that are on our radar screen," *Cost–Benefit Knowledge Bank for Criminal Justice*, Vera Institute, accessed 25 June 2012 at cbkb.org/2012/04/.
Her Majesty's Treasury (2009), *Green Book: Appraisal and Evaluation in Central Government*, accessed 16 June 2009 at http://www.hm-treasury.gov.uk/data_greenbook_index.htm.
Hogg, R.C. and D. Bertrand (2004), "What genes tell us about nicotine addiction," *Science*, **306** (5698), 983–4.
Krutilla, Kerry (2005), "Using the Kaldor–Hicks tableau format for cost–benefit analysis and policy evaluation," *Journal of Policy Analysis and Management*, **24** (4), 864–75.
Lam, David and Suzanne Duryea (1999), "Effects of schooling on fertility, labor supply, and investments in children, with evidence from Brazil," *Journal of Human Resources*, **34** (1), 160–92.
Laux, Fritz L. (2000), "Addiction as a market failure: using rational addiction results to justify tobacco regulation," *Journal of Health Economics*, **19** (4), 421–37.
Li, Chuan-Yun, Xizeng Mao, and Liping Wei (2008), "Genes and (common) pathways underlying drug addiction," *PLoS Computational Biology*, **4** (1), e2.
Ludwig, Jens and Philip J. Cook (2001), "The benefits of reducing gun violence: Evidence from contingent-valuation survey data," *Journal of Risk and Uncertainty*, **22** (3), 207–26.
Lynch, Allen K. and David W. Rasmussen (2001), "Measuring the impact of crime on house prices," *Applied Economics*, **33** (15), 1981–9.
MacCoun, Robert, Peter Reuter, and Thomas Schelling (1996), "Assessing alternative drug control regimes," *Journal of Policy Analysis and Management*, **15** (3), 330–52.
McCollister, Kathryn E., Michael T. French, and Hai Fang (2010), "The cost of crime to society: New crime-specific estimates for policy and program evaluation," *Drug and Alcohol Dependence*, **108** (1), 98–109.
Miller, Ted R. and Mark Cohen (1997), "Costs of gunshot and cut/stab wounds

in the United States, with some Canadian comparisons," *Accident Analysis and Prevention*, **29** (3), 329–41.

Miller, Ted R., Mark A. Cohen, and Brian Wiersema (1996), *Victim Costs and Consequences: A New Look*, Washington, DC: National Institute of Justice.

Milligan, Kevin, Enrico Moretti, and Philip Oreopoulos (2004), "Does education improve citizenship? Evidence from the United States and the United Kingdom," *Journal of Public Economics*, **88** (9–10), 1667–95.

Moore, Tim (2007), "Working estimates of the social costs per gram and per user for cannabis, cocaine, opiates and amphetamines," Drug Policy Modelling Program Monograph Series, No. 14, Sydney: National Drug and Alcohol Research Centre.

Morris, Pamela (2001), *How Welfare and Work Policies Affect Children: A Synthesis of Research*, New York: MDRC.

Mukamel, Dana B., Heather Taffet Gold, and Nancy M. Bennett (2001), "Cost utility of public clinics to increase pneumococcal vaccines in the elderly," *American Journal of Preventive Medicine*, **21** (1), 29–34.

Narayanan, Sridhar and Puneet Manchanda (2008), "An empirical analysis of individual level casino gambling," Stanford Graduate School of Business, Research Paper No. 2003.

Nicholson, Sean, Mark V. Pauly, Daniel Polsky, Claire Sharda, Helena Szek, and Marc L. Berger (2006), "Measuring the effects of workloss on productivity with team production," *Health Economics*, **15** (2), 111–23.

Nicol, Kristin L. (2001), "Cost–benefit analysis of a strategy to vaccinate healthy working adults against influenza," *Archives of Internal Medicine*, **161** (5), 749–59.

Olsen, Jan Abel (1994), "Production gains: Should they count in health care evaluations?," *Scottish Journal of Political Economy*, **41** (1), 69–84.

Olsen, Jan Abel and Jeff Richardson (1999), "Production gains from health care: what should be included in cost-effectiveness analyses?," *Social Science and Medicine*, **49** (1), 17–26.

Oreopoulos, Philip (2006), "Estimating average and local average treatment effects of education when compulsory schooling laws really matter," *American Economic Review*, **96** (1), 152–75.

Oreopoulos, Philip and Kjell G. Salvanes (2011), "Priceless: The nonpecuniary benefits of schooling," *Journal of Economic Perspectives*, **25** (1), 159–84.

Perneger, Thomas V. (1998), "What's wrong with Bonferroni adjustments," *British Medical Journal*, **316** (7139), 1236–8.

Potenza, Marc T., Thomas R. Kosten, and Bruce J. Rounsaville (2001), "Pathological gambling," *Journal of the American Medical Association*, **286** (2), 141–4.

Rogers, Mark (2003), "A survey of economic growth," *Economic Record*, **79** (244), 112–35.

Roman, John K. and Christy Visher (2009), "Prisoner re-entry programming," in David L. Weimer and Aidan R. Vining (eds), *Investing in the Disadvantaged: Assessing the Benefits and Costs of Social Policies*, Washington, DC: Georgetown University Press, pp. 127–50.

Saez, Emmanuel, Joel Slemrod, and Seth H. Giertz (2012), "The elasticity of taxable income with respect to marginal tax rates: A critical review," *Journal of Economic Literature*, **50** (1), 3–50.

Samuelson, Paul A. (1937), "A note on measurement of utility," *Review of Economic Studies*, **4** (2), 155–61.

Steiner, MaryAnn, Lee C. Vermeulen, John Mullahy, and Mary S.S. Hayney (2002), "Factors influencing decisions regarding influenza vaccination and treatment: A survey of health care workers," *Infection Control and Hospital Epidemiology*, **23** (10), 625–7.

Tapper, Andrew, Sheri McKinney, Raad Nashmi, Johannes Schwarz, Purnima Deshpande, Cesar Labarca, Paul Whiteaker, Michael J. Marks, Allan C. Collins, and Henry A. Lester (2004), "Nicotine activation of a4* receptors: Sufficient for reward, tolerance, and sensitization," *Science*, **306** (5698), 1029–32.

Taylor, Shelley E. and Jonathon D. Brown (1988), "Illusion and well-being: A social psychological perspective on mental health," *Psychological Bulletin*, **103** (2), 193–210.

Uhl, G.R. (2004), "Molecular genetic underpinnings of human substance abuse vulnerability: Likely contributions to understanding addiction as a mnemonic process," *Neuropharmacology*, **47** (Supplement 1), 140–47.

Van den Berg, Bernard and Ada Ferrer-i-Carbonell (2007), "Monetary valuation of informal care: The well-being valuation method," *Health Economics*, **16** (11), 1227–44.

van Kippersluis, Hans, Owen O'Donnell, and Eddy van Doorslaer (2011), "Long-run returns to education: Does schooling lead to extended old age?," *Journal of Human Resources*, **46** (4), 695–721.

Vining, Aidan R. and David L. Weimer (2010), "An assessment of important issues concerning the application of benefit–cost analysis to social policy," *Journal of Benefit–Cost Analysis*, **1** (1), 1–38.

Weimer, David L. and Mark A. Sager (2009), "Early identification and treatment of Alzheimer's disease: Social and fiscal outcomes," *Alzheimer's and Dementia*, **5** (3), 215–26.

Weimer, David L. and Aidan R. Vining (2009), *Investing in the Disadvantaged: Assessing the Benefits and Costs of Social Programs*, Washington, DC: Georgetown University Press.

Weimer, David L., Aidan R. Vining, and Randall K. Thomas (2009), "Cost–benefit analysis involving addictive goods: Contingent valuation to estimate willingness-to-pay for smoking cessation," *Health Economics*, **18** (2), 181–202.

Weinstein, Milton C., Joanna E. Siegel, Alan M. Garber, Joseph Lipscomb, Bryan R. Luce, Willard G. Manning, Jr., and George Torrance (1997), "Productivity costs, time costs and health-related quality of life: A response to the Erasmus Group," *Health Economics*, **6** (5), 505–10.

Weisbrod, Burton A. (1968), "Income redistribution effects and cost–benefit analysis," in S.B. Chase (ed.), *Problems in Public Expenditure Analysis*, Washington, DC: The Brookings Institution, pp. 177–208.

Weisbrod, Burton A. (1981), "Benefit–cost analysis of a controlled experiment: Treating the mentally ill," *Journal of Human Resources*, **16** (4), 523–48.

Wolfe, Barbara and Robert Haveman (2001), "Accounting for the social and non-market benefits of education," in John F. Helliwell, (ed.), *The Contribution of Human and Social Capital to Sustained Economic Growth and Well Being*, Vancouver, BC: University of British Columbia Press, pp. 221–50.

Wolfe, Barbara and Nathan Tefft (2009), "Early childhood interventions," in David L. Weimer and Aidan R. Vining (eds), *Investing in the Disadvantaged: Assessing the Benefits and Costs of Social Policies*, Washington, DC: Georgetown University Press, pp. 17–29.

Zarkin, Gary A., Alexander J. Cowell, Katherine A. Hicks, Michael J. Mills, Steven Belenko, Laura J. Donlap, Kimberly Houser, and Vince Keyes (2012), "Benefits and costs of substance abuse treatment programs for state prison inmates: Results from a lifetime simulation model," *Health Economics*, **21** (6), 633–52.

2. Toward standardization of benefit–cost analysis of early childhood interventions

Lynn A. Karoly

1 INTRODUCTION

There is a growing body of evidence regarding the favorable effects of investing early in the lives of disadvantaged children through such programs as home visiting and early childhood education. Such programs have demonstrated short- and longer-term benefits for both participating children and their families through rigorous experimental and quasi-experimental evaluations (Karoly et al., 2005). Advocates who call for devoting more resources to such programs have drawn attention to the associated benefit–cost analyses (BCAs) that also show positive economic returns, whether to the participating families and children or to society more generally. As funders in the public and private sectors consider such investments, the evidence of favorable benefit–cost ratios, net benefits, or internal rates of return have further boosted enthusiasm for directing more resources to early childhood programs. Ultimately, the BCAs of early childhood programs fulfill the increased demand for results-based accountability when allocating public and private sector resources.

Although the BCAs of early childhood programs serve to make such investments more compelling, there are limitations in the current state of the art. Most importantly, there are a number of decisions about the methods to employ when implementing a BCA—from discount rates to shadow prices—and analysts typically do not follow a standardized approach.[1] Moreover, there are several other challenges in applying the BCA approach to early childhood programs that further introduce potential differences in methods. These challenges include the economic values to attach to observed program outcomes, many of which do not have readily available economic values, and valuing potential benefits beyond the last observed outcomes. At present, most BCAs of early childhood programs provide proof of principle that the economic returns can be positive for a given program, but they do not support decision-makers who may want to use the results to choose between alternative approaches to early intervention or to assess the difference in the economic returns obtained from investing in early childhood versus investing later in childhood or versus investing in some other type of social program.

In this context, the objective of this chapter is to delineate a set of standards for conducting BCAs of early childhood programs. Such standards can guide the choices that analysts need to make about the methods to use when performing BCAs for one or more early childhood programs and they can support greater transparency in the results the analysts provide. The standards can also support consumers of the BCA results in their need to understand the methods employed and the comparability across different studies. The standards outlined in this chapter are intended to address issues specific to the use of BCA for early childhood programs. As such, this chapter complements the related efforts to identify a set of principles and standards for the application of BCA to social programs more generally (see, for example, Vining and Weimer, 2010 and Chapter 1 this volume; Loomis, Chapter 9 this volume; Zerbe et al., Chapter 11 this volume), as well as recommendations for the use of BCA to assess social policy interventions in other areas such as crime (Lott, Chapter 4 this volume), public safety (Farrow and Viscusi, Chapter 5 this volume), and public health preparedness and pandemic mitigation (Cook, Chapter 3 this volume).

To set the stage for the discussion of standards in the early childhood context, this chapter proceeds in the next section by considering what early intervention is and the existing evidence of the economic returns from such programs. The discussion highlights the diversity of early intervention models and also calls attention to some of the challenges that arise in applying the BCA methodology to assess the economic returns to programs that serve children and families in the first five years of life. Despite this diversity, the available BCAs tend to show favorable economic returns, both modest and more sizeable, across effective programs.

In the third section, the chapter provides a more in-depth discussion of the challenges of applying the BCA methodology to early intervention programs, considering each stage of the BCA process, from program evaluation to valuing program outcomes to generating estimates of net economic benefits or benefit–cost ratios. The discussion continues with a consideration of how these challenges are addressed in practice by reviewing the specific methods employed in existing BCAs of early childhood programs. This review underscores the general lack of standardization across BCA methods to date, although there is more agreement on some elements than others.

Motivated by the current state of the art, the fourth section lays out a set of standards for applying the BCA methodology to early childhood programs. These recommendations are designed to encourage greater uniformity of methods and hence a higher degree of comparability across BCAs. For some components of the BCA methodology, the rationale for standardization is clear and standardization is feasible in practice. For others, even with clear principles, there are practical considerations that limit the possibility of fully standardized methods. However, even in such cases, sensitivity analyses can support comparative analyses that will highlight the importance of key methods and resolve possible differences in findings across BCAs. Finally, this chapter makes the case for greater transparency and uniformity in reporting BCA methods and results, even if the BCAs are not fully standardized across studies.

2 ECONOMIC RETURNS FROM INVESTING IN CHILDREN PRIOR TO SCHOOL ENTRY

Before delving into a discussion of BCA methodology for early intervention, I first provide an overview of the approaches to early intervention. The section continues with a brief review of the BCAs conducted to date for such programs.

2.1 Strategies for Intervention with At-risk Children

As detailed in Karoly et al. (2005), early childhood intervention programs incorporate a diverse array of strategies for improving the developmental trajectory of participating children, especially children facing various disadvantages such as low family income, low parental education, or early health risks (e.g., low birth weight), among other stressors. Table 2.1 illustrates some of this variation by delineating a series of program features and examples of how those features might be defined for any given early intervention program. For example, programs are designed to influence various outcomes for the participating child or the child's family (typically the mother), outcomes that might include some of those shown in Table 2.1 such as the child's own health or behavioral or cognitive development or outcomes for the child's mother such as her pregnancy outcomes (e.g., birth weight, gestation, or substance use), parenting skills, or education level. Programs vary in the extent to which they target the child, the parents, or both as the focus of the intervention. Most early intervention programs have some means of targeting services to those families that will benefit the most, although some take a universal approach and

Table 2.1 Approaches to early childhood intervention

Program Feature	Examples	
Outcome targeted	Child behavior Child cognition Child health	Pregnancy outcomes Parenting skills Parent education
Target person(s)	Child Parent	Child–parent dyad Family unit
Targeting mechanism	Family income Child health problems	Parental problems Universal
Services offered	Family supports Health/nutrition	Parenting Early education
Location of services	Home Center, school	Health provider Other provider
Age of focal child	Prenatal to age 5 years, for shorter or longer durations	
Intensity of intervention	Starting to ending age	Hours per week Weeks per year

Source: Based on Karoly et al. (2005, Table 2.1).

make the program available to all children or families regardless of their circumstances. Programs offer various combinations of services, depending on their objectives, and provide services in one or more settings that might include the child's home, a school or center, or a service provider's office such as a pediatric practice. Programs may begin their interventions as early as the prenatal period or wait to start until the child is closer to age five years when they would typically enter kindergarten. Depending on the nature of the services offered and the starting and ending ages, there is tremendous variation in the intensity of the services offered, ranging from full-day year-round services from birth to age 5 years to 15–20 hours of parent training classes at some point during the early childhood period.

The varied ways in which these program features are combined can be demonstrated with the following illustrative programs, drawn from 19 programs with rigorous research evaluations and demonstrated benefits reviewed by Karoly et al. (2005) and ordered by the age of the focal child at intervention:

- *Nurse–Family Partnership (NFP)*. Provides a sequence of approximately 32 home visits to low-income first-time young mothers by public health nurses starting in the prenatal period and continuing until the child reaches age two years, with a focus on improving pregnancy outcomes, the mother's self-efficacy, and parenting skills.

- *Infant Health and Development Program (IHDP).* Provides periodic home visits and full-day year-round developmentally appropriate center-based child care services and other family supports to low birth weight babies starting a few weeks after birth and continuing to age 3 years.
- *Carolina Abecedarian Project.* Provides periodic home visits and full-day year-round developmentally appropriate center-based child care and early education services, as well as other family supports, to very low-income children starting a few weeks after birth and continuing to kindergarten entry.
- *HIPPY (Home Instruction Program for Preschool Youngsters) USA.* Provides low-income low-education parents of children ages 3 to 5 years with a two-year structured curriculum and associated materials that is delivered daily by parents at home, augmented with biweekly home visits from a paraprofessional trainer and biweekly meetings with the trainers and other parents.
- *Chicago Child–Parent Centers (CPC).* Provides children in high-poverty neighborhoods with a one- or two-year part-day school-year center-based developmentally appropriate preschool program with a strong parent involvement component.
- *High/Scope Perry Preschool Project.* Provides children with low income and low IQ scores with a one- or two-year part-day school-year center-based developmentally appropriate preschool program that also includes periodic home visits.

These six programs also happen to have accompanying BCAs, as discussed further in the next subsection.

The variation in early intervention programs contributes to some of the challenges for using BCA as part of policy evaluation of these programs. First, there is a diversity of outcomes that may be affected by programs and that would need to be valued in economic terms. Many of these outcomes—child development, parenting skills, and so on—may be considered "soft," in other words, not readily valued in monetary terms. Depending on the nature of the intervention, changes in outcomes may occur for the child, the parents, or both. Moreover, the evaluations for early interventions may not all assess the same outcomes or for the same targets or using the same measurement tools. Second, many early intervention programs aim to improve outcomes while the program is under way but most also expect to improve outcomes into the future, well beyond the end of program services. This may require longer-term follow-up or some method of projecting longer-term benefits and not all program evaluations may have the same capacity for such longer-term assessments. Third, programs may intervene at different points in early childhood, from the prenatal period to a year or less before kindergarten entry. When comparing the economic returns to different intervention strategies, it will be important to account for this temporal difference when resources are spent and benefits accrue. The discussion returns to these challenges and others, along with the implications for the BCA methodology, in the next section.

2.2 Evidence of the Economic Return to Early Childhood Investments

BCAs have been conducted for the six early childhood interventions described in the previous subsection, either by the same team of researchers that conducted the program evaluation or through an independent analysis.[2] In some cases, more than one estimate has been made, either by different research teams or based on program evaluation results at different points in time. The estimated societal benefit–cost ratios for the BCAs of the six early childhood programs are reported in the top panel of Table 2.2. In addition, the bottom panel of Table 2.2 reports estimates that have been made for two early childhood program types—home visiting for at-risk mothers and children and early childhood education for low-income 3- and 4-year-olds—based on estimates of program effects from a meta-analysis of multiple interventions. The resulting benefit–cost ratios across both panels of Table 2.2 range from 0-to-1 to over 16-to-1.

As discussed further below, there are a number of differences in how the BCAs recorded in Table 2.2 were performed so that the resulting benefit–cost ratios are not strictly comparable across the interventions. However, these results offer "proof of principle" that early interventions can yield positive returns to society (Kilburn and Karoly, 2008). With one exception, the ratio of societal benefits to costs exceeds 1 for the array of early interventions. In the case of the IHDP, the program produced favorable child developmental benefits as of the last follow-up available at the time (age 8 years), but all benefits were in areas that could not be readily monetized (e.g., improved child IQ, home environment, and mother–child interactions). Hence, there were no dollar benefits to weigh against the program costs.[3]

For the other five intervention programs, the favorable economic returns are not only limited to smaller-scale demonstration projects such as Perry Preschool but they are also evident for larger-scale programs such as Chicago's CPC program that operated in the Chicago public school system. The positive benefit–cost ratios also apply to higher-cost more

Table 2.2 Reported benefit–cost ratios for early childhood interventions

Program/Program Type	Source	Benefit–Cost Ratio[e]
Estimates for specific programs		
NFP—full sample	Aos et al. (2004)	2.88[a]
NFP—higher-risk sample	Karoly et al. (1998)	5.06[b]
NFP—lower-risk sample	Karoly et al. (1998)	1.10[b]
IHDP	Aos et al. (2004)	0.00
Abecedarian	Masse and Barnett (2002); Barnett and Masse (2007)	2.49[c]
HIPPY USA	Aos et al. (2004)	1.80
Chicago CPC—Age 21 follow-up	Reynolds et al. (2002)	7.14
Chicago CPC—Age 26 follow-up	Reynolds et al. (2011)	10.83[a]
Perry Preschool—Age 19 follow-up	Berrueta-Clement et al. (1984)	3.56
Perry Preschool—Age 27 follow-up	Karoly et al. (1998)	4.11[b]
Perry Preschool—Age 27 follow-up	Barnett (1993, 1996), Schweinhart et al. (1993)	8.74[a]
Perry Preschool—Age 40 follow-up	Barnett et al. (2005); Nores et al. (2005); Belfield et al. (2006)	16.14[a]
Perry Preschool—Age 40 follow-up	Heckman et al. (2010)	7.1–12.2[a,d]
Estimates from meta-analysis of intervention types		
Home visiting for at-risk mothers and children	Aos et al. (2004)	2.27[a]
Early childhood education for low-income 3- and 4-year-olds	Aos et al. (2004)	2.36[a]

Notes:

a. Includes value of reduced intangible crime victim costs.
b. Discount rate is 4%.
c. From revised estimate in Barnett and Masse (2007).
d. Reported range of estimates under alternative assumptions regarding the economic cost of crime.
e. The benefit–cost ratios are the ratio of the present discounted value of total benefits to society as a whole (participants and the rest of society) divided by present discounted value of program costs. The discount rate is 3% unless otherwise noted. The value of reducing intangible crime victim costs are excluded unless otherwise noted.

Source: Based on the cited sources.

intensive programs such as Abecedarian (which provided full-day year-round center-based child care and early education services for the child's first five years) and to lower-cost less intensive programs such as HIPPY USA (a two-year parent-delivered in-home curriculum with periodic home visits and parent training). Furthermore, the favorable BCA results accrue to both types of early intervention: home visiting and center-based care and early education.

The results in Table 2.2 also illustrate the intuitive result that programs that target the population that the program is designed to serve can have higher benefit–cost ratios. In the case of NFP, the original trial of the program in Elmira, New York, so as not to stigmatize participants, served both the targeted higher-risk population of unmarried pregnant women with low socioeconomic status (SES) and a somewhat more advantaged group of pregnant women who were either married or had higher SES. As expected, compared with the lower-risk group, the program impacts were larger for the higher-risk group and hence estimated dollar benefits and the resulting benefit–cost ratio were also higher (a ratio just over 5-to-1 compared with a ratio just over 1).

Finally, the results for the BCAs of the Perry Preschool and Chicago CPC programs at each successive follow-up age demonstrate the advantage of being able to observe, rather than project, future benefits. For example, for the Perry Preschool program, based on observed outcomes as of age 19 years and with some projection of future benefits, the program was estimated by the High/Scope research team to produce a benefit–cost ratio of just under 4-to-1 (Berrueta-Clement et al., 1984). Using a similar set of methods, the ratio more than doubled based on data analyzed by the team through age 27 years (again with some projection of future benefits) (Barnett, 1993, 1996; Schweinhart et al., 1993) and then topped 16-to-1 when the study participants were observed again at age 40 years (Barnett et al., 2005; Nores et al., 2005; Belfield et al., 2006). In this case, the projections of future earnings gains after age 19 years or after age 27 years were too conservative, in part because those projections were based solely on the difference in educational attainment between participants and non-participants, whereas favorable effects of the program on other factors such as cognitive abilities, attitudes, and behavior also contributed to earnings gains (Karoly, 2008).[4] The BCAs for the Chicago CPC program as of age 21 years and then age 26 years show a similar pattern, with a 50 percent increase in the estimate benefit–cost ratio with additional follow-up data. Such a pattern of increasing economic returns with more follow-up data is not always assured. Program benefits may fade out over time, in which case projections beyond the age of the last follow-up may overstate future benefits.

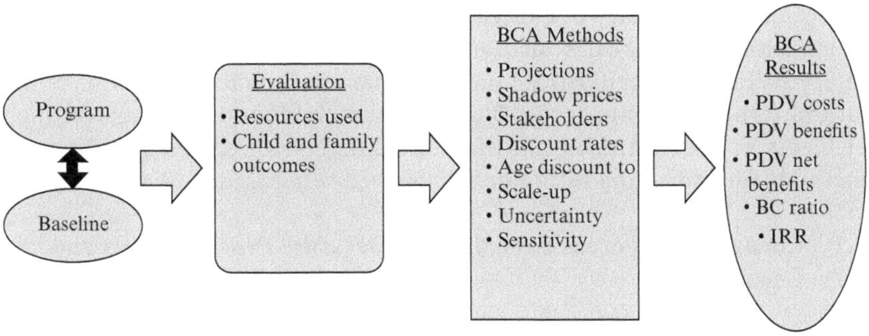

Source: Karoly (2009) and National Research Council (NRC) and Institute of Medicine (IOM) (2009, Figure 1.1).

Figure 2.1 Elements of benefit–cost analysis

3 CHALLENGES IN APPLYING BCA TO EARLY CHILDHOOD INVESTMENTS

The use of BCA for evaluating early childhood interventions requires a series of steps that define the BCA methodology, as illustrated in Figure 2.1 (Karoly, 2009; National Research Council [NRC] and Institute of Medicine [IOM], 2009). The starting point is a program of interest (the top left oval) that is compared with a baseline or alternative (the bottom left oval), typically a "no program" alternative but the comparison may also be made to another type of early childhood program or programs. Next, an evaluation is conducted that compares the program of interest with the baseline (the first rectangle), in terms of both program costs and outcomes for program participants. This may be done through an experimental evaluation where the participants in the experiment are randomly assigned to receive the treatment of interest or to be in the control group (which receives the baseline or alternative). When an experiment is not feasible or is too costly, quasi-experimental methods may be used to evaluate differences in costs and outcomes for the program group against a comparison group. The results of the evaluation then form the basis for implementing the BCA methodology (the second rectangle), which requires making decisions about such aspects as projecting outcomes into the future, valuing outcomes using shadow prices, applying discount rates, addressing uncertainty, and conducting sensitivity analyses. A given set of methods finally leads to the BCA results (the right-hand oval), which may be expressed in terms of present discounted value (PDV) costs, benefits, and net benefits, or in terms of benefit–cost ratios or internal rates of return (IRR).

Keeping this framework in mind, I now highlight the key challenges in implementing the BCA methodology in the context of early childhood interventions.[5] I then illustrate the consequences in practice in terms of the lack of standardization across BCAs of early childhood programs on such elements as discount rates, age discounted to, benefits that are monetized, methods for projecting future or unobserved benefits, and shadow prices.

3.1 Conducting Rigorous Evaluations to Measure Program Costs and Causal Effect

The field of early childhood intervention has been characterized by a long history of evaluation research, with a proliferation of evaluation studies beginning in the 1960s including those for Perry Preschool, the Early Training Project, and the Head Start Project (Karoly et al., 1998).[6] Although many early intervention programs do not include a well-implemented formal experimental or quasi-experimental evaluation, there are many that do. For example, Karoly et al.'s (2005) review identified 20 early intervention programs with rigorous evaluations that met specific criteria such as a published evaluation that had an adequate control or comparison group and a sufficient sample size. However, even well-designed experimental or quasi-experimental evaluations may have issues with missing data, sample attrition over the follow-up period, or other threats to validity (e.g., treatment-control crossovers). For example, Heckman et al. (2010) re-analyze the Perry Preschool evaluation data, accounting for several problems with the experimental evaluation including compromised randomization due to reassignment of treatment and control group members after randomization and missing data.

One issue in the use of BCA for early childhood interventions is that the evaluations do not always employ the same baseline or alternative to compare with the program of interest. Of the programs listed in Table 2.2, for example, the Perry Preschool program was evaluated in the 1960s when the alternative or status quo for most children was no formal early education. By contrast, in the recent national experimental Head Start evaluation, many children in the control group attended some other type of early education program, whereas some who were randomized into the treatment group did not attend Head Start (US Department of Health and Human Services, 2005; Ludwig and Phillips, 2007). In some cases, the control group children just attended a different Head Start than the one they had been randomized out of. As another example, IHDP and Abecedarian, also listed in Table 2.2, provided some health, developmental, or family services to the control group. For these two programs, the measures of program effects are relative to a baseline that includes some remedial services rather than a "no program" baseline.

In the case of the Head Start evaluation, Ludwig and Phillips (2007) convert the "intent-to-treat" (ITT) estimates reported in the Head Start evaluation into "treatment-on-treated" (TOT) estimates, an approach that is valid under certain assumptions.[7] When it is not possible to generate program impact estimates relative to no participation, differences in the baselines used in the evaluations of different interventions will in turn affect the validity of direct comparisons of the BCA results for these programs. We might expect the gains from more recent interventions to be lower compared with programs implemented several decades ago because of the change in the baseline or "no program" alternative. In the same way, an evaluation that provided some limited services to the control group might be expected to produce smaller benefits than would have been found if no services were offered to the controls. Thus, a head-to-head comparison between old and new generation programs or between programs with other differences in the baseline services would not be valid.

Another issue with evaluations of early childhood programs is that costs are not always measured with the same rigor as benefits. Ideally, the evaluation would capture the incremental costs associated with the program relative to the baseline or alternative. In cases where the alternative includes some services, this means collecting cost data for both the program group and the no program group. For both groups, the cost data should allow for estimation of the full economic costs associated with program delivery, including both resources that require cash outlays, as well as the opportunity costs associated with resources that may be provided in kind (e.g., space provided without charge or at a subsidized rate or volunteer labor). The most rigorous approach uses the resource cost method (RCM) outlined by Levin and McEwan (2000), an ingredients-based approach that collects detailed information on the actual quantities of labor and non-labor resources used and then attaches market prices or shadow prices to each resource employed. Instead of this ideal, it is not uncommon with early childhood evaluations to base estimates of program costs on budget or expenditure data, without fully accounting for in-kind resources utilized or the full economic costs associated with each resource. The opportunity costs of the time that participants spend in the program are also often overlooked.

3.2 Measuring Program Effects on Child or Family Outcomes in Shorter Term and Longer Term

Given the varied objectives of and approaches to early intervention, it is perhaps not surprising that evaluations have measured a diverse

Table 2.3 Outcomes with favorable impacts from early interventions

Domain	Outcomes for Participating Child	Outcomes for Participating Parent(s)
Behavioral/emotional and cognitive development	Behavior Social competence IQ Developmental milestones	Parent–child relationships Home environment
Education	School readiness Achievement tests Grade repetition Special education use Grades High school completion College attendance	Educational attainment
Health	Abuse and neglect Health care utilization Teen pregnancy	Reproductive health
Economic	Employment Earnings Use of social welfare programs	Employment Earnings Use of social welfare programs
Crime and substance abuse	Criminal activity Use of tobacco, alcohol, and drugs	Criminal activity Use of tobacco, alcohol, and drugs

Source: Based on Karoly et al. (1998, 2005).

array of outcomes and found favorable effects for many of these outcomes in both the shorter term and longer term, with benefits for both participating children and their parent(s). It is even possible that early interventions would have effects on the children of program participants or even their grandchildren (Masse and Barnett, 2002). Table 2.3 lists outcomes within five domains where early intervention programs have demonstrated statistically significant benefits, at least in the short term. For several evaluations where long-term follow-up has been possible, the outcomes in Table 2.3, such as higher rates of high school graduation, increased earnings, reduced welfare use, and lower rates of crime and delinquency, represent favorable effects for program participants long after the program has ended. Indeed, in the case of Perry Preschool, statistically significant favorable impacts were still evident when the participants were age 40 years, around 35 years after the program ended (Schweinhart et al., 2005).

The types of outcomes affected, how they are measured and for whom, and the timing of program effects create several challenges for the use of BCA to assess early childhood programs. First, given resource constraints, evaluations of early intervention programs are not able to measure and assess all possible outcomes that may be favorably affected. Typically, each evaluation focuses on a set of outcomes given the goals of that particular intervention. As a result, at any given point in time during or after an intervention, there may be outcomes affected by the program that are not measured as part of the evaluation and hence cannot be captured in the BCA. For example, most early childhood interventions focus on outcomes for the participating child and do not attempt to assess effects on their parent(s). For programs that provide center-based early care and education, it is possible that parents benefit in terms of their ability to work, which can raise their labor market experience and earnings, and thereby reduce welfare use or even criminality. In the case of home visiting programs, improved maternal outcome is often a central objective and thus evaluations have incorporated parental outcomes. Indeed, favorable effects on parent outcomes have been found in selective evaluations (e.g., Abecedarian, NFP), but most have not assessed parental outcomes and thus any benefits are unknown.

Second, for a number of the potential benefits of early interventions, the evaluation field has not converged on a common set of measures. Thus, for example, while one goal of the intervention may be to increase child IQ or to raise school readiness, researchers rely on different assessment tools to measure those constructs. In other cases, evaluators have to rely on measures that are feasible, thus it is not always possible to include the same outcomes measure as other evaluations. In the case of criminal activity in adolescence or adulthood, for example, researchers often rely on administrative data that may capture criminal activity only one way, such as by arrests, adjudications, convictions, or time in jail or prison.

Third, resource constraints can also affect the ability to conduct long-term follow-up of the interventions. This can be a real detriment as many of the benefits of early intervention may persist into the future, as has been found in those interventions with longer-term follow-up, as noted above. The longer-term favorable effects for such outcomes as high school completion, earnings, and criminality also happen to be the outcomes with some of the largest dollar benefits, even after discounting. In the absence of longer-term follow-up, potential future benefits remain unknown or researchers must rely on methods for projecting those outcomes into the future. For example, favorable effects on achievement tests may be used to project an effect on high school graduation rates. Effects on crime and delinquency in adolescence may be used to project criminality during adulthood. The use of projections, while typically based on other empirical research, introduces considerable uncertainty. This is especially true for longer-term benefits that have been theorized—such as effects on descendants—but not yet confirmed in any evaluations. The use of projections to value unmeasured future benefits is another source of variation in methods across BCAs.

With each study measuring a different set of outcomes, using different measures, for different participants, or over different time horizons, it is not possible for BCAs of different programs to value the same set of observed outcomes or to make projections for those outcomes over the same future horizon. This may mean that interventions measuring a smaller set of outcomes or with little or no longer-term follow-up will leave more potential benefits unmeasured compared with evaluations that measure a broader range of outcomes over a longer time horizon.

3.3 Generating Economic Values or "Shadow Prices" for Resources Used and Outcomes Affected

The range of domains and specific outcomes measures shown in Table 2.3 also presents a challenge for BCA of early intervention programs because many outcomes do not have an economic value that can be observed in the marketplace. In such cases, shadow prices are used in BCAs to capture the appropriate economic value in terms of willingness to pay: what consumers are willing to forgo to obtain a given benefit or avoid a given cost. Shadow prices may be used when markets exist but there is a need to correct for distortions in market prices (e.g., as a result of externalities, monopoly power, rent-seeking, underemployed labor or other resources, taxes or subsidies, or other market imperfections). Shadow prices may also be used to value outcomes for which there are no market prices or those for which there are both tangible and intangible benefits (Karoly, 2008).

Many of the outcomes listed in Table 2.3 do not have a market value to readily apply as a benefit or cost. What is the economic value of raising a child's IQ or their school readiness?[8] What dollar value should be placed on a reduction in child abuse and neglect?[9] Even outcomes such as increased earnings, which are valued in dollars, may need to be adjusted to account for effects on participant well-being (or utility) or externalities. For example, if an increase in employment and earnings for a program participant comes through displacing another worker in the labor market, the gain in individual earnings is not the same as the social benefit. In addition, if all or part of the earnings gain derives from an increase in hours, the value of reduced leisure time may also need to be taken into account (Karoly, 2008). As another example, BCAs for early childhood programs do not always account for the marginal excess tax burden when assigning a value to the increased taxes generated from higher participant earnings.[10] Often, such adjustments, which are consistent with economic theory, are not taken into account in practice either because of data limitations or current practice. Shadow prices may also vary across markets so that geographic differences come into play. In some cases, BCAs are conducted with a specific jurisdiction in mind (e.g., a given state or city), thus the shadow prices used for that jurisdiction may not be appropriate for another.

The economic valuation of the effects of early intervention also need to account for the benefits or costs to different stakeholders in society. Typically, the stakeholders are divided into the government sector (i.e., individuals as taxpayers), program participants (as private individuals), and the rest of society (i.e., program non-participants as private individuals).[11] Table 2.4 illustrates how some of the potential benefits from early interventions would accrue across different stakeholders. Even though all the outcomes are specific to a participating parent, child, or the child's descendants, the positive benefits (or in some cases the negative benefits) may accrue to one or more stakeholders. There are economic effects (benefits, positive and sometimes negative) for the public sector from all but one of the outcome changes listed in Table 2.4. These benefits come in the form of reduced (or increased) costs for publicly provided services (e.g., education, child welfare, criminal justice) or changes in taxes and transfers (e.g., from changes in earnings or welfare use). Participants are also listed as beneficiaries (or losers) in Table 2.4 for many of the same outcomes, and even when they are not listed there may be psychic or intangible positive benefits (or negative benefits) that are typically not taken into account. For example, in addition to the savings to the public education system from reducing special education use, there may be a psychic benefit to the child or parent from being in regular education classes, rather than in special education. Finally, the one outcome that most clearly can have private effects on non-participants is changes in crime, as non-participants are potential crime victims with associated tangible and intangible economic consequences.

The issue of which outcomes to value, the economic value to use for those that are measured, and the disaggregation of economic values by the stakeholder are especially challenging issues for BCAs of early interventions because so many outcomes are not observed in the market and many affect multiple stakeholders and have both tangible and intangible components. How these issues are addressed in the application of the BCA

Table 2.4 Potential benefits (positive or negative) of improved outcomes from early childhood intervention programs

Whose Outcome Changes			Outcome Affected	Positive Benefits (Negative Benefits)	Stakeholder		
Parent(s) of participant	Participating child	Descendant(s) of participant			Government	Participants	Rest of society
X			Increased child care	Value of subsidized child care for parents of participating children		X	
	X	X	Reduced child maltreatment	Lower costs to child welfare system and lower abuse victim costs	X	X	
	X	X	Reduced child accidents and injuries	Lower costs for emergency room visits and other public health care costs	X	X	
	X	X	Reduced incidence of teen childbearing	Lower costs for public health care system and social welfare programs	X		
	X	X	Reduced grade repetition	Fewer years spent in K-12 education	X		

	X	X	Reduced use of special education	Lower costs for special education	X		
X	X	X	Increased high school graduation rate	(More years spent in K-12 education when dropping out is avoided)	(X)		
X	X	X	Increased college attendance rate	(More years spent in post-secondary education)	(X)	(X)	
X	X	X	Increased labor force participation and earnings in adulthood	Increased lifetime earnings for participants (net of taxes) and increased tax revenue to government	X	X	
X	X	X	Reduced use of welfare and other means-tested programs	Reduced administrative costs for social welfare programs; reduced welfare program transfer payments	X	(X)	
X	X	X	Reduced crime and contact with criminal justice system	Lower costs for criminal justice systems and lower crime victim costs	X		X

Table 2.4 (continued)

Whose Outcome Changes			Outcome Affected	Positive Benefits (Negative Benefits)	Stakeholder		
Parent(s) of participant	Participating child	Descendant(s) of participant			Government	Participants	Rest of society
X	X	X	Reduced incidence of smoking and substance abuse	Lower costs for public health care system and from premature death	X	X	
X	X	X	Improved pregnancy outcomes	Lower medical costs due to low birth weight babies	X		

Note: Parentheses denote costs as opposed to benefits.

Source: Based on Karoly et al. (2005, Table 4.1).

methodology may have implications for whether a given program passes a benefit–cost test or shows a higher economic value compared with other early interventions or other policy options.

3.4 Standardizing Other BCA Methods to Support Comparability

If BCAs for early childhood interventions are to go beyond the "proof of principle" and be used for comparative purposes, there is a need to standardize other aspects of the BCA methodology listed in the second rectangle in Figure 2.1, beyond the methods for projecting outcomes, valuing outcomes, and disaggregating values by stakeholders as already discussed. These issues include the discount rate or rates to use, the age (or time point) to discount to, accounting for scale-up effects, addressing uncertainty, and performing sensitivity analyses.

The appropriate discount rate to use is not unique to BCAs of early childhood interventions. However, the time point that costs and benefits should be discounted is a more distinctive concern to the early childhood context. That is because early intervention programs may start at different ages of the child, from before birth up to age 5 years. If discounting is taking to the age when a program starts some BCAs will be discounting to birth (or earlier), whereas others will discount as late as age 4 years. When the discounting applies to different points in the lifecycle, the BCA measures of present value costs, benefits, and net benefits will not be comparable.[12] If the choice is between investing in a program at birth or waiting until age 4 years, all costs and benefits should be equated to a common age.

Of the other issues listed above, the concern about scale-up effects is particularly relevant for the early childhood field because many programs that have been evaluated were implemented as a demonstration project or on an otherwise limited scale. Yet, in many cases, the purpose of conducting a BCA is to inform policy-makers who are considering a larger-scale implementation of the program. Typically, the expectation is that a larger-scale program may have diminished effects relative to a small-scale program. This might hold if larger-scale implementation means a loss of fidelity to the proven model or a reduction in quality because sufficient funding is not available. Alternatively, larger-scale implementation of a program may amplify the effects found at a smaller scale if there are synergies when a program covers a larger share of the population. For example, if there are positive (or negative) externalities or spillovers of early intervention for the peers of program participants when they are in K-12 education, having larger-scale implementation of an early childhood program could lead to a realization of those benefits that otherwise might not appear when only a few children have access to the program.

The need to address uncertainty and perform sensitivity analyses are two other salient issues for the use of BCA for early childhood programs. One source of uncertainty is that program effects on various outcomes are based on estimates derived from study samples, which results in sampling variability. Statistical uncertainty may also arise from the use of other model-based parameters such as projecting future benefits based on observed outcomes. Sensitivity analysis is relevant for determining whether the myriad number of choices regarding methods is critical for obtaining the results under the preferred set of methods. Sensitivity analyses can account for the choice of outcomes to value, whether outcomes are projected, the values applied, the application of scale-up factors, and other basic BCA methods such as the discount rate to use.

3.5 Addressing Challenges in Practice

This discussion has served to highlight several challenges with the application of the BCA methodology to early childhood interventions. In practice, the field has yet to coalesce around a common set of methods to ensure as much comparability as possible across the various BCAs. To illustrate the lack of standardization, Tables 2.5 and 2.6 summarize key method choices made in the BCAs listed in Table 2.2. Table 2.5 features some of the general issues, whereas Table 2.6 puts a spotlight on the valuation of outcomes. Although a total of 14 BCAs for early intervention programs are listed in Tables 2.5 and 2.6 (some conducted for the same program by different research teams or with differing amounts of follow-up data), several of the BCAs were performed as part of the same study using a common set of methods. For example, Aos et al. (2004) use the same BCA methods for the five programs or program types listed in Tables 2.5 and 2.6. Likewise, Karoly et al. (1998) use a common approach for the BCA of NFP and Perry Preschool, and Reynolds et al. (2002, 2011) use similar, although not identical, methods for their BCA of Chicago CPC based on two rounds of follow-up data. Finally, three of the BCAs for Perry Preschool conducted by different configurations of authors associated with that program's evaluation team apply a very similar approach to the follow-up data collected at ages 19, 27, and 40 years (Heckman et al., 2010 is not included in this group). Thus, effectively there are six different approaches applied in the 14 BCAs.

A comparison of the key elements of the methods used can be summarized as follows:

Table 2.5 General methods in BCAs for early childhood interventions

BCA Study/ Program	Age at Intervention Start	Age at Last Follow-up	BCA Discount Rate(s) (%)	BCA Discounts to Age	BCA Dollar Year	BCA Has Stakeholder Disaggre-gation?	BCA Reports Standard Errors?	BCA Reports Sensitivity Analyses?
Aos et al. (2004)/NFP	Up to 30th week of gestation	15	3	0	2003	Yes	No	To outcomes valued
Aos et al. (2004)/IHDP	Birth	8	3	0	2003	Yes	No	To outcomes valued
Aos et al. (2004)/HIPPY USA	3 to 4 years	6	3	3	2003	Yes	No	To outcomes valued
Aos et al. (2004)/Home visiting (meta)	Varies (*in utero* min.)	Varies (age 15 max.)	3	0	2003	Yes	No	To outcomes valued
Aos et al. (2004)/Early childhood education (meta)	Varies (age 3 min.)	Varies (age 27 max.)	3	3	2003	Yes	No	To outcomes valued
Karoly et al. (1998)/NFP	Up to 30th week of gestation	15	4, 0–8	0	1996	Yes	For $ savings to government	To discount rate, outcomes valued

Table 2.5 (continued)

BCA Study/ Program	Age at Intervention Start	Age at Last Follow-up	BCA Discount Rate(s) (%)	BCA Discounts to Age	BCA Dollar Year	BCA Has Stakeholder Disaggre-gation?	BCA Reports Standard Errors?	BCA Reports Sensitivity Analyses?
Karoly et al. (1998)/Perry Preschool	3 to 4 years	27	4, 0–8	0	1996	Yes	For $ savings to government	To discount rate, outcomes valued
Masse and Barnett (2002); Barnett and Masse (2007)/ Abecedarian	6 weeks to 3 months	21	0, 3, 5, 7, 10	0	2002	No	No	To discount rate, outcomes valued
Reynolds et al. (2002)/Chicago CPC	3 to 4 years	21	3, 0–7	3	1998	Yes	No	To discount rate, outcomes valued, projection method
Reynolds et al. (2011)/Chicago CPC	3 to 4 years	26	3, 0–7	3	2007	Yes	Yes	To discount rate, outcomes valued, projection method

Berrueta-Clement et al. (1984)/Perry Preschool	3 to 4 years	19	3	3	1981	No[a]	For $ benefits by stakeholder	To outcomes valued
Barnett (1993, 1996); Schweinhart et al. (1993)/Perry Preschool	3 to 4 years	27	3, 5, 7, 9, 10, 11	3	1992	No[a]	No	To discount rate, outcomes valued, projection method
Barnett et al. (2005); Nores et al. (2005); Belfield et al. (2006)/Perry Preschool	3 to 4 years	40	0, 3, 7	3	2000	No[a]	No	To discount rate, outcomes valued, projection method
Heckman et al. (2010)/Perry Preschool	3 to 4 years	40	0, 3, 5, 7	3	2006	Yes	Yes	To discount rate, outcomes valued, cost of crime, projection method

Note: a. Benefits for taxpayers (i.e., the government) are not separated from private benefits to non-participants (e.g., crime victims).

Source: Based on Karoly et al. (2005, Tables 2.4 and 4.2), and the cited sources.

Table 2.6 Valuation of outcomes in BCAs for early childhood interventions

BCA Study/ Program	Outcomes Observed and Valued	Outcomes Observed But Not Valued	Outcomes Projected in Time	Outcomes Projected for Third Parties?	Value Parent Time?	Value Intangible Crime Benefits?
Aos et al. (2004)/ NFP	Child abuse and neglect Achievement tests Crime (mother and child)	Emergency room use Earnings (and taxes) Welfare use (mother) Total births and birth spacing (mother) Substance abuse (mother)	Child abuse and neglect Earnings (and taxes) Crime (mother and child)	No	No	Yes
Aos et al. (2004)/ IHDP	None	Achievement tests IQ scores Mother–child interactions Home environment	None	No	No	n.a.
Aos et al. (2004)/ HIPPY USA	Achievement tests	None	Earnings (and taxes)	No	No	Yes

Aos et al. (2004)/ Home visiting (meta)	Child abuse and neglect Achievement tests	Contraceptive use (mother)	Child abuse and neglect Achievement tests	No	No	Yes
Aos et al. (2004)/ Early childhood education (meta)	Child abuse and neglect Achievement tests K-12 net savings High school graduation Crime	None	Child abuse and neglect Earnings (and taxes) Crime	No	Value child care benefit for parents	Yes
Karoly et al. (1998)/NFP	Emergency room use Earnings (and taxes) (mother) Crime (mother and child) Welfare use (mother)	Child abuse and neglect Achievement tests Total births and birth spacing (mother) Substance abuse (mother)	Crime (child)	No	No	No
Karoly et al. (1998)/Perry Preschool	K-12, college and adult education net savings Earnings (and taxes) Crime Welfare use	Academic success Teen pregnancy	Earnings (and taxes) Crime Welfare use	No	Value child care benefit for parents	No

Table 2.6 (continued)

BCA Study/ Program	Outcomes Observed and Valued	Outcomes Observed But Not Valued	Outcomes Projected in Time	Outcomes Projected for Third Parties?	Value Parent Time?	Value Intangible Crime Benefits?
Masse and Barnett (2002), Barnett and Masse (2007)/ Abecedarian	K-12 net savings Educational attainment Smoking Welfare use Earnings (mother)	None	College costs Earnings (and taxes) Mortality Welfare use Earnings (mother)	Earnings of descendants (three generations)	Value child care benefit for parents	n.a.
Reynolds et al. (2002)/Chicago CPC	Child abuse and neglect K-12 net savings Crime	None	College costs Earnings (and taxes) Crime	No	Value (a) required parent time in centers; (b) child care benefit for parents	No

Reynolds et al. (2011)/Chicago CPC	Child abuse and neglect K-12 and college net savings Crime Depression Substance use Smoking	None	Child abuse and neglect (intangible victim costs) Earnings (and taxes) Crime Depression Substance use Smoking	No	Value (a) required parent time in centers; (b) child care benefit for parents	Yes
Berrueta-Clement et al. (1984)/Perry Preschool	K-12 net savings Earnings (and taxes) Crime Welfare use	Academic success Teen pregnancy	College costs Earnings (and taxes) Crime Welfare use	No	Value child care benefit for parents	Unclear
Heckman et al. (2010)/Perry Preschool	K-12, college and adult education net savings Earnings (and taxes) Crime Welfare use	Academic success Mortality (intrinsic value of loss of life)	Earnings (and taxes) Crime Welfare use	No	No	Yes

Note: All outcomes pertain to the participating child unless otherwise noted; n.a. = not applicable.

Source: Based on Karoly et al. (2005, Table 4.3), and the cited sources.

- *Discount rate*. With the exception of the Aos et al. (2004) study and the age-19 Perry Preschool BCA by Berrueta-Clement et al. (1984), a range of discount rates is employed, with 3 percent or 4 percent selected as the preferred rate (see Table 2.5). Aos et al. (2004) and Berrueta-Clement et al. (1984) both use 3 percent as the sole discount rate.
- *Age discount*. Karoly et al. (1998) is the only study to apply a common age to discount to (in this case the child's birth), regardless of the age of entry into the program (see Table 2.5). The other BCAs use the age at entry, which is either effectively birth or age 3 years.
- *Stakeholder disaggregation*. With the exception of the BCAs for Abecedarian and the three related BCAs for Perry Preschool, all the BCAs present results disaggregated for the public sector (government or taxpayers), participants, and the rest of society (see Table 2.5).
- *Accounting for uncertainty*. With four exceptions, the BCAs do not account for uncertainty in the BCA results by reporting standard errors (see Table 2.5). In two of the cases where standard errors are reported (Berrueta-Clement et al., 1984; Karoly et al., 1998), they only apply to a portion of the BCA results (the dollar savings to government in the former and the dollar benefits by the stakeholder in the latter). Reynolds et al. (2011) report standard errors for all cost and benefit dollar estimates and benefit–cost ratios for each stakeholder, whereas Heckman et al. (2010) provide standard errors estimated benefit–cost ratios and internal rates of return.[13]
- *Performing sensitivity analyses*. Sensitivity analyses are primarily limited to two types (see Table 2.5). All the methods report the disaggregated estimates of benefits by outcome valued, so that it is possible to determine which outcomes are relatively more or less important drivers of the estimated benefits. The use of alternative discount rates in all but two studies can also be viewed as a type of sensitivity analysis. Four of the study groups also examine the sensitivity of results to the method for projecting future benefits, primarily future earnings. Heckman et al. (2010) is the only study to also present sensitivity analyses associated with different values for the social cost of crime.
- *Outcomes valued*. For programs with follow-up only to the early elementary grades (i.e., HIPPY USA at age 6 years and IHDP at age 8 years), at most the effects on achievement tests are valued in dollar terms (see Table 2.6). For the IHDP program, Aos et al. (2004) discount the effect size to zero and thus no outcomes are valued.

The other BCAs have access to follow-up data through at least age 15 years and as late as age 40 years. The most common outcomes valued are child abuse and neglect, K-12 education savings, earnings, welfare use, and crime.

- *Outcomes not valued.* For several of the BCAs, the early intervention programs had statistically significant effects on outcomes that were not valued (see Table 2.6). Some of these outcomes such as achievement test scores, child abuse and neglect, and substance use were valued in other BCAs. For the Aos et al. (2004) approach, for example, program effects were adjusted to account for the scale of the intervention and other concerns, thus the adjustments often resulted in the outcome not being valued at all. Several outcomes were not valued in any of the studies, notably because they do not have ready shadow prices. These include IQ scores, mother–child interactions, the home environment, contraceptive use, total births and birth spacing, and teen pregnancy.
- *Outcomes projected.* For each of the studies that valued observed outcomes, at least one outcome was also projected beyond the last follow-up and valued in the BCA (see Table 2.6). The most common outcomes projected were college costs, earnings (sometimes based on test scores or educational attainment), welfare use, and crime. Based on observed child abuse and neglect, the Aos et al. (2004) approach also projected and valued future outcomes in terms of crime, high school graduation, K-12 grade repetition and test scores, alcohol use, and illicit drug use. The Abecedarian and age-26 Chicago CPC BCAs projected future mortality based on smoking rates observed at the last follow-up, and the long-term costs of depression were also projected in the same Chicago CPC BCA. The Abecedarian BCA was also the only analysis to project and value future earnings for descendants of program participants.
- *Valuing participant time.* For programs that included parent participation, only the BCA for Chicago CPC by Reynolds et al. (2002, 2011) valued the time costs for parents (see Table 2.6). In the other BCAs, the argument was made that parental time spent in home visits and other activities was usually voluntary, so that if parents chose to participate there must have been intrinsic benefits that outweighed the cost of their time. The BCAs for all but two of the center-based early childhood programs (the IHDP BCA and the Heckman et al., 2010 Perry BCA are the exceptions) also included the value of the child care benefits parents received.
- *Valuing intangible crime benefits.* Table 2.6 does not summarize differences in the shadow prices applied to the outcomes that were

valued. However, one potentially important choice is whether to account for the intangible benefits to potential victims of reductions in crime, as the dollar amounts from such benefits can be large. Table 2.6 shows that some BCAs opt to exclude these intangible benefits to generate more conservative estimates, whereas others include them.

This summary demonstrates that there is convergence on some elements of the BCA methodology used for early childhood programs, but other elements are a source of variation that limits the comparability of BCA results across studies. Usually with at most one exception, the studies use and report alternative discount rates, include stakeholder disaggregation, value child care benefits, and project a common set of outcomes. There is less standardization in the age to which costs and benefits are discounted, in accounting for uncertainty by reporting standard errors, in performing a range of sensitivity analyses, in valuing a common set of outcomes, and whether to incorporate the intangible costs of crime. Another source of variation that has not been discussed in detail here, but will be taken up in the next section, is the actual economic values or shadow prices attached to each outcome.

4 TOWARD STANDARDIZATION OF BCA FOR EARLY CHILDHOOD INTERVENTION

In the above section, the review of BCAs for early childhood interventions as practiced highlights the need for standards to bring more uniformity and comparability to BCAs in this field. As noted, there is greater comparability regarding the application of some elements of the BCA methodology to early childhood interventions, such as the discount rate to use and disaggregation of results by the stakeholder. These and some other elements are most readily standardized, thus I discuss them first. The greatest variation in practice concerns which outcomes, either observed or projected, to value and the values to attach. Although complete standardization may not be possible, I discuss the potential for movement in this direction. I then discuss sensitivity analyses as a principle for BCA of early intervention programs that also contributes to greater standardization in methods. Moreover, sensitivity analyses can help address the lack of standardization on other elements of the methodology. Finally, I suggest some standards for reporting BCA methods and results to ensure greater transparency. Table 2.7 provides a summary of the cumulative set of recommendations.

Table 2.7 Recommended standards for BCAs of early intervention programs

BCA Methodology Element	Recommendation
Discount rate	Use 3% as the standard real discount rate but report results using alternative discount rates as part of the sensitivity analyses (see below)
Age discount to	Discount costs and benefits to the focal child's birth but report results for at least age 5 years as part of the sensitivity analysis (see below) to support comparison with school-age programs
Stakeholder disaggregation	Disaggregate costs and benefits for key stakeholders, which at a minimum includes government, participants, and the rest of society
Accounting for uncertainty	Report standard errors accounting for sampling error; account for non-sampling error (e.g., model uncertainty associated with projections or other modeling) and other sources of uncertainty (e.g., program scale-up) through sensitivity analyses (see below)
Valuing program costs	Calculate the full economic costs of the incremental resources used for the program group versus the no program group, accounting for goods and services provided in kind Any induced costs (e.g., remaining in school longer) should be treated as negative benefits and not as additional program costs
Outcomes to value, shadow prices, and projections	Value all the outcomes available for all relevant parties, including participating children and their parents, siblings, and peers Use economic values that capture the willingness-to-pay concept Where intangible costs or benefits are involved, develop shadow prices to account separately for both tangible and intangible components and generate estimates of both types of dollar benefits (or costs) Account for the value of participant time spent in the program, especially if participation is mandatory and not voluntary

Table 2.7 (continued)

BCA Methodology Element	Recommendation
Performing sensitivity analyses	Conduct a range of sensitivity analyses that provide, at a minimum: • Results for alternative discount rates (e.g., 0%, 5%, 7%, and 10%) • Results for alternative ages to discount to (e.g., age 3 years, age 5 years) • Results for alternative shadow prices (e.g., with and without intangible crime costs) • Results for alternative approaches to future projection When relevant, also include: • Results for different assumptions about the effects of program scale-up • Results based on reduced information, such as data from later follow-ups or for specific outcomes, to mirror what is available for BCAs of other programs • Results based on alternative distributional assumptions
Reporting results	Be transparent in reporting key features of the evaluation and BCA methodology and results, including: • The baseline or status quo that the program is compared to • The evaluation method, the program impacts and their statistical significance, potential biases in estimates of causal effects, and any adjustments to estimated program impacts • Which outcomes measured in the evaluation are valued in the BCA and which are not valued • Which outcomes are observed versus projected, for whom they are projected, and the projection method • For the outcomes valued, the valuation used, its derivation, and the geographic or jurisdictional boundary the valuation applies to: • The method for estimating program costs and any omitted resources, including in-kind goods and services • The calendar year for all dollar amounts, discount rate, and age discounted to: • Aggregate results for present discounted value societal costs, benefits, and net benefits and the benefit–cost ratio; use appropriate adjustments if reporting the internal rate of return • The present discounted value benefits (or costs) of each outcome valued, with a disaggregation by outcomes observed versus projected and disaggregation, where possible and relevant, by tangible versus intangible benefits (e.g., for crime or child abuse and neglect)

Table 2.7 (continued)

BCA Methodology Element	Recommendation
	• Disaggregated present discounted value costs and benefits in total and by outcome valued for the key stakeholders defined above • The estimated standard errors, at least in aggregate, for present discount value costs (if relevant) and benefits • The results of any sensitivity analyses

4.1 Discount Rates and Discounting Age

In practice, there is no agreed upon discount rate to use in BCAs more generally or specifically for early intervention programs. Candidates for the social discount rate may be based on the social marginal rate of time preference, the marginal rate of return on private investments, the social opportunity costs of public sector investment, or the shadow price of capital (US Government Accountability Office, 1991; Boardman and Greenberg, 1998). The social discount rates may vary through time and may even be zero or negative when benefits occur far in the future or when society values the well-being of future generations more highly than the current generation (Boardman and Greenberg, 1998; Dasgupta et al., 2000). For convenience, however, discount rates are almost always assumed to be constant. Variation in the rate is provided for in US Government Accountability Office (GAO) guidelines, which recommends a base case that applies the real yield on US treasuries with maturity consistent with the time horizon of the project being evaluated, combined with sensitivity analysis to alternative rates (US Government Accountability Office, 1991). Constant real discount rates of 3 percent and 5 percent are recommended in medicine (Gold et al., 1996). Moore et al. (2004) suggest a 3.5 percent social discount rate for government projects that are intragenerational (i.e., do not last beyond 50 years) and there is no crowding out of private investment. The Office of Management and Budget (OMB) guidelines favor a real discount rate of 7 percent, "the approximate pre-tax rate of return on an average investment in the private sector in recent years" (Office of Management and Budget, 1992), whereas the Congressional Budget Office typically applies a 2 percent real discount rate, an approximation of the long-run average annual borrowing costs for the federal government (Hartman, 1990).

The most common preferred discount rate employed in the BCAs of early childhood programs listed in Table 2.5 was 3 percent, a rate that is within the range of the recommended rates cited above. Among the studies cited in Table 2.5, it was also routine to report results for a range of rates as part of a sensitivity analysis. This approach is reasonable and the practice should be adopted as the standard. Thus, a 3 percent real discount rate can be used for baseline results and then results can also be presented for alternative rates such as 0 percent, 5 percent, 7 percent, or 10 percent, where the rates at the low end are potentially appropriate given the long horizon over which the benefits from early intervention may accrue. Moreover, providing results for a range of discount rates can be used to see how high the discount rate can go before net benefits are zero (or how low it must go before net benefits are positive).

As noted earlier, although it may be standard to discount benefits and costs to the start of the program of interest, in the context of early interventions, this can mean that discounting is made to different ages during the first five years of life. Thus, to ensure greater comparability of BCA results—notably measures of present value costs, benefits, and net benefits—across early childhood programs, discounting should be made to one or more common ages. The birth of the focal child is a natural measurement point, as the decision-maker's problem is whether to start investing as early as birth or to defer an investment until later in the period before children enter school.[14] A dollar spent on a program that started at birth could be invested instead and used to pay for a more expensive program that began at age 2 or 3 years, for example. Thus, a fair benefit–cost comparison across programs with different investment profiles requires discounting to a common age. Of course, standardization could occur at any age and there are reasons to consider additional ages for purposes of reporting. Thus, for example, discounting to age 5 years would allow comparisons with programs that begin in kindergarten or other school-age programs if they are also discounted to the same age.

4.2 Stakeholder Disaggregation

Depending on the perspective of the decision-maker, there may be an interest in benefits and costs of early childhood interventions from the perspective of society as a whole or from the perspective of specific stakeholders, such as the public sector or private program participants. Thus, it is common in BCAs to report results disaggregated by the stakeholder, in addition to the societal perspective. At a minimum, the stakeholders in the disaggregation should include government, program participants, and the rest of society. The government sector could be further disaggregated by jurisdiction (e.g., federal, state, and local) and private benefits could be calculated for subcategories of participants (e.g., focal child, parents, siblings, descendants).

4.3 Accounting for Uncertainty

Although it is not typically done in the early childhood intervention application, BCAs should recognize the uncertainty associated with estimates of costs and benefits (see also Vining and Weimer, Chapter 1 this volume for a discussion of this issue and the application of Monte Carlo methods). First, there is the statistical uncertainty associated with sampling error because program impacts are estimated using a sample-based evaluation. An evaluation with a smaller sample size will produce estimates of program impacts with larger error bands, and that higher degree of uncertainty should be reflected in the standard errors associated with the estimates of present value costs and benefits. Reporting standard errors also addresses the concern as to whether outcomes for which there is a statistically non-significant program impact should be valued.

Of the BCAs reported in Tables 2.5 and 2.6, sometimes only outcomes with statistically significant impacts are valued in the BCA, whereas others also value outcomes with non-significant effects. The lack of statistical significance may result from small samples, which give low power for detecting program impacts with magnitudes that would produce meaningful dollar benefits or cost. Rather than assuming that effects and dollar benefits are zero based on the standard errors, the statistically non-significant evaluation impacts can be included in the calculation of benefits and costs, but the greater degree of statistical uncertainty will be reflected in the size of the standard errors (Vining and Weimer in Chapter 1). In addition, as recommended below as part of transparency in reporting, by presenting the statistical significance of all program impacts and the present discounted values disaggregated by the outcomes valued, it is possible to determine if the BCA results are sensitive to the inclusion or exclusion of outcomes that are not statistically significant. The Heckman et al. (2010) BCA of Perry Preschool and the Reynolds et al. (2011) BCA of Chicago CPC are exemplary in generating standard errors for the key BCA summary outcomes reported (e.g., costs, benefits, net benefits, benefit–cost ratios, or internal rates of return [IRRs]), as well as reporting the statistical significance of the program impacts and the present value estimates disaggregated by outcome.

Other sources of uncertainty, non-sampling error, can be associated with having to estimate the various parameters used to calculate costs and benefits, such as shadow prices or projected future benefits. Another source of uncertainty is whether the costs and program effects estimated for a smaller-scale or demonstration program will be replicated when the program is implemented at a larger scale. As noted earlier, such scale-up effects could lead to effects that are diminished or amplified, and there may be little basis for knowing the direction or magnitude of the scaling factor. The implications of these various sources of non-sampling error can be examined through the types of sensitivity analyses, discussed below, that can determine how robust results are to alternative modeling assumptions and parameter estimates.

4.4 Valuing Program Costs

The valuation of program costs relative to the baseline or alternative should be as rigorous as the valuation of the program benefits, with a full accounting of the economic costs associated with the delivery of the program. Ideally, this means collecting costs data prospectively, as the program is delivered, using the RCM approach to capture the quantities of resources used so the appropriate valuations can be applied. Any resources that are not accounted for or valued should be noted as part of the reporting of the BCA methodology and results, as discussed below.

4.5 Outcomes to Value, Shadow Prices, and Projections

Across the BCAs for early childhood interventions summarized in Tables 2.5 and 2.6 there is variation in the outcomes that are valued as well as the economic values attached to those outcomes that are included in the calculations. At the same time, given the nature of the potential for lasting effects of early interventions, all the BCAs reviewed above projected at least one outcome into the future, often based on a different observed outcome (e.g., achievement scores during the K-12 years are used to project future earnings).

In principle, all outcomes in both the short and long run affected by the program for all relevant parties should be valued in the BCA, whether those outcomes produce benefits or costs to the various stakeholders. The parties could include the focal child, the participating parent(s), the child's siblings, and even their peers. The application of this principle in practice for any given early childhood intervention is limited by the outcomes actually measured in the evaluation, who the outcomes are measured for, and the length of the follow-up period over which outcomes are observed. Moreover, comparability across the BCAs for different programs would require that all evaluations measure the same outcomes, using the same measures, for the same parties, and over the same time period. Although such standardization does not characterize the evaluations of early childhood interventions to date, it may be more feasible in the future if research teams coordinate their evaluation efforts to ensure greater comparability.

Given current limitations in the standardization of evaluation methods, greater standardization could be applied to the economic values or shadow prices attached to the available outcomes. Although it is not feasible in this chapter to make recommendations regarding specific shadow prices to employ for all possible outcomes affected by early intervention programs at a national level or for more disaggregated geographic locales, I do offer recommendations regarding several of the more generic issues that arise in valuing outcomes from early intervention.[15]

Given the nature of many of the outcomes affected by early intervention, one of those issues is whether both tangible and intangible benefits or costs should be incorporated into the shadow price. For example, as noted earlier, when crime is reduced, the potential victims of crime experience the tangible benefit of not having the property loss or medical costs from injuries, as well as the intangible benefits of reduced pain and suffering. Intangible benefits may also apply to program participants, such as the psychic benefit a child or parent would receive when the child performs better in school. Intangible benefits may also accrue to the rest of society beyond program participants, such as having improved educational outcomes for children, a reduction in welfare, or a more equal distribution of income.

In principle, such intangible benefits should be incorporated into the shadow price in the same way that tangible benefits are included. In practice, as shown in Table 2.6, BCAs for early childhood interventions have both included and excluded intangible crime benefits. The challenge in practice is that such intangible benefits are more difficult to quantify, hence there is often more controversy with the methods used to estimate intangible benefits and in the resulting estimates. For example, the available estimates of the intangible benefits from reductions in crime, especially some types of crime such as murder or other violent crimes, are typically several times larger than the tangible benefits (see, for example, Miller et al., 1996, 2001). Consequently, the intangible crime benefits can account for a substantial share of the estimated benefits for a given early intervention program (Barnett et al., 2005; Nores et al., 2005; Belfield et al., 2006). For this reason, I recommend separate reporting of the present value benefits for tangible and intangible components of a given outcome's value, so the contribution of each to total benefits is clear.

As many early intervention programs work directly with parents, another valuation issue is whether to account for the opportunity cost of parents' time. As noted earlier, the BCAs to date summarized in Tables 2.5 and 2.6 have made a distinction between parent participation that is voluntary (e.g., time spent with a home visitor or in a parenting workshop) versus parent participation that is mandatory (i.e., a requirement to spend time in the child's classroom). No value is placed on parent time in the first instance, as voluntary participation implies non-pecuniary benefits to the parent that at least equal the opportunity cost of their time. When participation is required, that assumption may no longer be valid.[16] In practice, the full opportunity cost of time has been used even though parents may still derive intrinsic benefits that may offset at least some of the value of their time. I recommend that this approach be continued, although the value of parent time should be reported separately so that a sensitivity analysis is possible.

Finally, because many of the benefits of early childhood interventions have the potential for long-lasting effects, BCAs for early childhood interventions typically project at least one outcome beyond the age of the last follow-up. Of the BCAs listed in Tables 2.5 and 2.6, there is variation in the projection method adopted for the common outcomes projected such as earnings, crime, and welfare use. Greater standardization could be applied to the methods used to project these and other outcomes, although one challenge to such standardization is that the age from which projections are made often vary across BCAs because of variation in the age at the last follow-up. Thus, it may be possible to standardize on the nature of the modeling assumptions made, even if the specific projections made vary with the starting age.

4.6 Performing Sensitivity Analyses

Sensitivity analyses can be used to examine the implications for BCA results of making alternative choices regarding various benefit–cost methods. In areas where there is no clear consensus about the methods or parameters to use (e.g., shadow prices), sensitivity analyses can illuminate the importance of the choices made in the preferred or baseline methods. At a minimum, I recommend sensitivity analyses to examine the effects of employing alternative discount rates, discounting to alternative ages, using different shadow price estimates, and adopting alternative methods for projecting future outcomes. When there are concerns about the effects of program scale-up on program costs and effects, sensitivity analyses can also be performed using different scaling factors.

Sensitivity analyses can also be used to estimate comparable benefit–cost results when programs have different follow-up periods or measure different outcomes. For example, if program A had a shorter follow-up period or measured fewer outcomes than program B, the BCA for program B can be recalculated to match that for program A, using only data through the same age as the last follow-up in program A and for the same outcome measures. In effect, to achieve comparability, this approach assumes that program B has less information available about longer-term effects or effects on a wider range of outcomes than in reality, so that the BCA for program B is based only on the information that is comparable to what is available for program A.

Finally, alternative distributional assumptions can be explored as part of the sensitivity analyses. Although the BCAs for early interventions reviewed earlier in the chapter have not applied alternative distributional weights (i.e., each dollar of benefits or costs are weighted equally regardless of individual characteristics such as income or wealth), such weights can be applied and the implications reported as part of the sensitivity analyses.

4.7 Transparency in Reporting

Standardization of methods in the application of BCA to early childhood interventions will provide a foundation for sound policy analysis, yet that foundation will be compromised if results are not reported in a way that the research and policy communities can understand and discern the methods choices applied and how they vary across studies. Thus, transparency in reporting is key to ensuring that the results of BCAs are used at all and used appropriately. In this final section, I highlight key aspects of the underlying program evaluation and the BCA methodology and results that should be incorporated into the reporting of BCAs for early childhood programs.

4.7.1 Program evaluation methods

Details of the evaluation of the early intervention program are often reported separately, so it is important to summarize key features that may affect the validity of the BCA or that provide relevant context. For example, the evaluation methods should be described and any potential biases should be identified, such as deviations from a well-implemented randomized experiment, issues in using a quasi-experimental approach, or attrition rates for studies with longitudinal data collection. Where possible, appropriate statistical methods should be used to remedy these problems, such as imputation for missing data and corrections for treatment–control crossovers.

The experience of control group members should be discussed, such as whether they received any services as part of the evaluation or if the status quo for control group members included services similar to those received by the treatment group. This serves to clarify what incremental services were received by the treatment group for which the causal effects were measured in the evaluation. Where possible, ITT ("intent-to-treat") estimates may be converted to TOT ("treatment-on-treated") estimates so that cross-program comparisons are more valid. The estimated program effects and their statistical significance should be reported, along with any adjustments to estimate program impacts to adjust for potential biases in estimation, to convert from ITT to TOT estimates, or to account for other factors such as program scale-up.

4.7.2 BCA methods

The description of the BCA methods employed should make clear which of the outcomes affected by the program were valued in the BCA and which were not. Outcomes that were projected, for whom they were projected (e.g., participating children or parents or other third parties such as descendants, siblings, or peers), and the projection method should also be described. Another key element for disclosure is the economic values applied to each outcome, whether they are intended to capture either tangible or intangible benefits or both, and the geographic or jurisdictional boundaries (e.g., specific markets or levels of government) used to derive the values. The discussion should also delineate the method for collecting program cost data. Any omission of resources used and their associated valuation, whether or not they required cash outlays, should be identified. Other elements discussed above such as the discount rate, age discounted to, estimation of standard errors, approach to sensitivity analysis, and so on should also be made explicit.

4.7.3 BCA results

In reporting BCA results, the year for dollar amounts should be stated. The reported BCA metrics should include the present discounted value societal costs, benefits, and net benefits (net present value), along with the benefit–cost ratio. Reliance on the IRR is problematic because of the well-known issues that the IRR may not be unique and will not necessarily rank projects in the same order as the net benefit metric will (Zerbe and Dively, 1994). A similar issue with respect to inconsistent rankings may also occur with the benefit–cost ratio when projects of a different size (i.e., cost) are compared. However, adjustments can be made to the benefit–cost ratio and IRR calculations, which will then produce consistent rankings.[17]

In addition to presenting aggregates, disaggregated results should show estimates for each outcome valued and for the key stakeholders. Ideally, the estimates by program outcomes would differentiate dollar benefits (or costs) based on observed outcomes versus projected outcomes and, where possible and relevant, based on tangible versus intangible benefits (or costs). Presenting disaggregated results facilitates identifying which outcomes make relatively large or relatively small contributions to estimates of net benefits, determining of the effect of including or excluding benefits for program effects that were not statistically significant, and identifying whether specific stakeholders, in addition to society as a whole, are net beneficiaries. Finally, the estimated standard errors, at least in aggregate for present discounted value costs (if relevant) and benefits, and the results from any sensitivity analyses should also be reported.

5 CONCLUSION

Decision-makers in the public and private sectors considering investments in early intervention programs have gravitated towards BCA results that demonstrate that effective programs can also generate favorable economic returns. The BCA estimates reviewed in this chapter, based on results published to date, suggest that early interventions can generate dollar benefits to society as a whole that exceed program costs. When there are effects on outcomes that can be valued, the BCAs show returns that range from approximately $2 to $16 for every dollar invested, results that are modest to sizeable compared with other social policy programs. However, the current practice with respect to BCA for early childhood programs does not ensure comparable results across different estimates. Thus, a program with a higher estimated net benefits or higher benefit–cost ratio does not necessarily have a higher return compared with a program that has a lower estimate of net benefits or the benefit–cost ratio. That is because some of the differences in BCA estimates arise from different implementation of the BCA methodology, rather than true differences in economic returns.

To support greater standardization of BCA methods applied to early childhood interventions and to encourage greater transparency in reporting of the methods used, this chapter has developed recommendations regarding standards that analysts can apply in practice. These recommendations concern issues such as the discount rate to use and the age to which costs and benefits should be discounted; stakeholder disaggregation; outcomes to value, the associated values, and projections of future outcomes; accounting for uncertainty; sensitivity analysis; and reporting of results. If these recommendations are embraced by those who conduct BCAs for early childhood programs, consumers of the BCAs will also benefit as they seek to make decisions regarding which programs to support and whether early intervention should receive greater investment relative to other uses of scarce resources.

However, even these recommendations will not ensure complete uniformity in the application of BCA to early childhood programs. The methods component where standardization is most problematic, given the current state of practice, is in the valuation of the outcomes affected by early intervention programs. As noted by Vining and Weimer (Chapter 1 this volume), the use of BCA for social policy more generally will benefit from the refinement of economic values for outcomes such as cognitive development, educational attainment, crime (specifically tangible and intangible victim crime costs, as well as the marginal cost of criminal justice system resources), and the opportunity cost of volunteer time.[18] For several of these outcomes, it is relevant to value observed outcomes and also to project benefits (or costs) into the future. Until researchers converge upon an agreed set of valuations for the key outcomes affected by early childhood programs, sensitivity analysis can be used to determine how robust BCA results are to the specific economic valuations and projection methods used. The use of sensitivity analysis, combined with the other recommendations offered in this chapter, will help to advance the appropriate use of BCA in support of decision-making regarding investments in early childhood programs.

NOTES

1. One exception is the report by the Washington State Institute of Public Policy (WSIPP), which applies a common set of methods to estimate benefit–cost ratios and net benefits for an array of different early childhood programs (Aos et al., 2004). However, the comparability of even these estimates is limited by the fact that the underlying evaluations of the early childhood programs do not measure a common set of outcomes nor do they have a common follow-up period.
2. Although the Federal Head Start program has been evaluated using experimental and quasi-experimental designs, the program has not been subject to a formal benefit–cost analysis comparable to those for the other programs reported in Table 2.2. Ludwig and Phillips (2007) provide an assessment of whether the magnitude of the estimated Head Start impacts would translate into sufficient dollar benefits to outweigh the program costs. They conclude that the program would probably pass a benefit–cost test, consistent with a "back-of-the-envelope" assessment provided earlier by Currie (2001).

3. A follow-up at age 18 years of the IHDP program participants and non-participants showed continued positive program impacts in areas such as academic achievement (McCormick et al., 2006), an outcome that could potentially be valued in terms of future projected earnings differentials.
4. The results from Heckman et al. (2010) indicate, however, that the estimated benefit–cost ratios from the series of High/Scope studies of Perry Preschool are sensitive to the use of alternative methods, as discussed later in the chapter.
5. Most of these issues apply more generally to BCAs of other types of social programs. See Karoly (2008) for additional discussion.
6. There are many comprehensive reviews of this literature, often with a particular focus on different types of intervention models (e.g., preschool or home visiting) or benefits for particular participants (e.g., children or parents). Earlier and more recent examples include Meisels and Shonkoff (1990), Benasich et al. (1992), Barnett (1995), Yoshikawa (1995), Karoly et al. (1998), Brooks-Gunn et al. (2000), Shonkoff and Phillips (2000), and Karoly et al. (2005).
7. See Ludwig and Phillips (2007) for further discussion of the Head Start case, along with Heckman et al. (1999) for a more general discussion of accounting for intent to treat and substitution bias.
8. The association between IQ and earnings has been used to assign an economic value to IQ gains. See, for example, the method employed by the US Environmental Protection Agency (EPA) in estimating the benefits from lead reduction (US Environmental Protection Agency, 2008).
9. Again, estimates are available of the economic costs of abuse and neglect.
10. The Heckman et al. (2010) BCA for Perry Preschool is one exception in incorporating alternative assumptions about the magnitude of the deadweight loss from taxation.
11. Further disaggregation with these general categories of stakeholders is possible, such as different agencies within the government or different generations within the group of program participants (e.g., children versus parents).
12. The benefit–cost ratio and internal rate of return (IRR) will be the same regardless of the age reference point for discounting, provided both costs and benefits are discounted to the same age.
13. The standard errors account for different sources of uncertainty and are estimated using different approaches. For example, among the two recent studies, Reynolds et al. (2011) account for the uncertainty in the estimated program impacts, both by monetizing the standard errors associated with each impact estimate and by Monte Carlo simulation assuming a normal distribution of program effect sizes. Heckman et al. (2010) use a combination of bootstrap resampling and Monte Carlo simulation to account for both errors in estimation and in prediction. Both studies assess the impact of other sources of uncertainty through sensitivity analyses.
14. A case could be made that conception is the appropriate reference point, as some early childhood interventions begin before birth. The choice of birth as the reference point is offered for expediency, expecting that results will not be that sensitive to accounting for the 40-week potential gestational period.
15. See Karoly (2008) for additional detail on the shadow prices used for BCAs of early intervention programs and other social programs. Vining and Weimer (Chapter 1 this volume) also discuss the need for better shadow prices to use in BCAs of social programs, many of which are relevant to the application of BCAs for early childhood programs.
16. See Vining and Weimer (Chapter 1 this volume) for additional discussion of this issue.
17. See, for example, Zerbe's (2010) proposed "reliable" IRR and the discussion in Zerbe and Dively (1994) regarding adjusting for projects with different costs.
18. See also National Research Council (NRC) and Institute of Medicine (IOM) (2009) for a discussion of approaches to valuing outcomes affected by early childhood interventions and projecting future outcomes based on observed results.

REFERENCES

Aos, Steve, Roxanne Lieb, Jim Mayfield, Marna Miller, and Annie Pennucci (2004), *Benefits and Costs of Prevention and Early Intervention Programs for Youth*, Olympia, WA: Washington State Institute for Public Policy, 17 September.

Barnett, W. Steven (1993), "Benefit–cost analysis of preschool education: Findings from a 25-year follow-up," *American Journal of Orthopsychiatry*, **63** (4), 500–508.

Barnett, W. Steven (1995), "Long-term effects of early childhood programs on cognitive and school outcomes," *The Future of Children*, **5** (3), 25–50.

Barnett, W. Steven (1996), *Lives in the Balance: Age-27 Benefit–Cost Analysis of the High/Scope Perry Preschool Program*, Monographs of the High/Scope Educational Research Foundation, No. 11, Ypsilanti, MI: High/Scope Press.

Barnett, W. Steven and Leonard N. Masse (2007), "Comparative benefit–cost analysis of the Abecedarian program and its policy implications," *Economics of Education Review*, **26** (1), 113–25.

Barnett, W. Steven, Clive R. Belfield, and Milgros Nores (2005), "Lifetime cost–benefit analysis," in Lawrence J. Schweinhart, Jeanne Montie, Zongping Xiang, W. Steven Barnett, Clive R. Belfield, and Milagros Nores, *Lifetime Effects: The High/Scope Perry Preschool Study Through Age 40*, Monographs of the High/Scope Educational Research Foundation, No. 14, Ypsilanti, MI: High/Scope Press, pp. 130–57.

Belfield, Clive R., Milagros Nores, W. Steven Barnett, and Lawrence Schweinhart (2006), "The High/Scope Perry Preschool Program: Cost–benefit analysis using data from the age-40 follow-up," *Journal of Human Resources*, **41** (1), Winter, 162–90.

Benasich, April A., Jeanne Brooks-Gunn, and Beatriz Chu Clewell (1992), "How do mothers benefit from early intervention programs?," *Journal of Applied Developmental Psychology*, **13** (3), 311–62.

Berrueta-Clement, John R., Lawrence J. Schweinhart, W. Steven Barnett, Ann S. Epstein, and David P. Weikart (1984), *Changed Lives: The Effects of the Perry Preschool Program on Youths Through Age 19*, Monographs of the High/Scope Educational Research Foundation, No. 8, Ypsilanti, MI: High/Scope Press.

Boardman, Anthony E. and David H. Greenberg (1998), "Discounting and the social discount rate," in Fred Thompson and Mark T. Green (eds), *Handbook of Public Finance*, New York: Marcel Dekker, Inc., pp. 269–318.

Brooks-Gunn, Jeanne, Lisa Berlin, and Allison Fuligni (2000), "Early childhood intervention programs: What about the family?," in Jack P. Shonkoff and Samuel J. Meisels (eds), *Handbook of Early Childhood Intervention*, 2nd edition, New York: Cambridge University Press.

Currie, Janet (2001), "Early childhood education programs," *Journal of Economic Perspectives*, **15** (2), 213–38.

Dasgupta, Partha, Karl-Göran Mäler and Scott Barrett (2000), "Intergenerational equity, social discount rates and global warming," unpublished manuscript (updated from a paper with the same title that appeared in Paul Portney and John Weyant (eds), *Discounting and Intergenerational Equity*, Washington, DC: Resources for the Future, 1999), Department of Economics, University of Cambridge.

Gold, Martha R., Joanna E. Seigel, Louise B. Russell, and Milton C. Weinstein (eds) (1996), *Cost-effectiveness in Health and Medicine*, New York: Oxford University Press.
Hartman, Robert W. (1990), "One thousand points of light seeking a number: A case study of CBO's search for a discount rate policy," *Journal of Environmental Economics and Management*, **18** (2), S3–S7.
Heckman, James J., Robert J. LaLonde, and Jeffrey A. Smith (1999), "The economics and econometrics of active labor market programs," in Orley Ashenfelter and David Card (eds), *Handbook of Labor Economics, Vol. III*, Amsterdam: North-Holland, pp. 1865–2097.
Heckman, James J., Seong Hyeok Moon, Rodrigo Pinto, Peter A. Savelyev, and Adam Yavitz (2010), "The rate of return to the High Scope Perry Preschool Program," *Journal of Public Economics*, **94** (1/2), February, 114–28.
Karoly, Lynn A. (2008), *Valuing Benefits in Benefit–Cost Studies of Social Programs*, TR-643, Santa Monica, CA: RAND Corporation.
Karoly, Lynn A. (2009), 'Overview of benefit–cost analysis for early childhood interventions', presentation at the Workshop on Strengthening Benefit–Cost Analysis Methodology for the Evaluation of Early Childhood Interventions, 4–5 March, National Academies, Washington, DC.
Karoly, Lynn, Rebecca Kilburn, and Jill Cannon (2005), *Early Childhood Interventions: Proven Results, Future Promise*, Santa Monica, CA: RAND Corporation, MG-341.
Karoly, Lynn A., Peter W. Greenwood, Susan S. Everingham, Jill Houbé, M. Rebecca Kilburn, C. Peter Rydell, Matthew Sanders, and James Chiesa (1998), *Investing in Our Children: What We Know and Don't Know about the Costs and Benefits of Early Childhood Interventions*, Santa Monica, CA: The RAND Corporation, MR-898.
Kilburn, M. Rebecca and Lynn A. Karoly (2008), *The Economics of Early Childhood Policy: What the Dismal Science Has to Say About Investing in Children*, OP-227, Santa Monica, CA: RAND Corporation.
Levin, Henry M. and Patrick J. McEwan (2000), *Cost-effectiveness Analysis: Methods and Applications*, 2nd edition, Thousand Oaks, CA: Sage Publications, Inc.
Ludwig, Jens and Deborah Phillips (2007), "The benefits and costs of Head Start," *Social Policy Report*, **XXI** (3), 3–18.
Masse, Leonard N. and W. Steven Barnett (2002), "A benefit–cost analysis of the Abecedarian Early Childhood Intervention," in Henry M. Levin and Patrick J. McEwan (eds), *Cost-effectiveness and Educational Policy*, Larchmont, NY: Eye on Education, Inc., pp. 157–73.
McCormick, Marie C., Jeanne Brooks-Gunn, Stephen L. Buka, Julie Goldman, Jennifer Yu, Mikhail Salganik, David T. Scott, Forrest C. Bennett, Libby L. Kay, Judy C. Bernbaum, Charles R. Bauer, Camilia Martin, Elizabeth R. Woods, Anne Martin, and Patrick H. Casey (2006), "Early intervention in low birth weight premature infants: Results at 18 years of age for the Infant Health and Development Program," *Pediatrics*, **117** (3), 771–80.
Meisels, Samuel J. and Jack P. Shonkoff (eds) (1990), *Handbook of Early Childhood Intervention*, New York: Cambridge University Press.
Miller, Ted R., Mark A. Cohen, and Brian Wiersema (1996), *Victim Costs and Consequences: A New Look*, Washington, DC: National Institute of Justice, January.

Miller, Ted R., Deborah A. Fisher, and Mark A. Cohen (2001), "Costs of juvenile violence: Policy implications," *Pediatrics*, **107** (1), 1–7.

Moore, Mark A., Anthony E. Boardman, Aidan R. Vining, David L. Weimer, and David H. Greenberg (2004), "'Just give me a number!' Practical values for the social discount rate," *Journal of Policy Analysis and Management*, **23** (4), 789–812.

National Research Council (NRC) and Institute of Medicine (IOM), Committee on Strengthening Benefit–Cost Analysis Methodology for the Evaluation of Early Childhood Interventions (2009), *Strengthening Benefit–Cost Analysis for Early Childhood Interventions: Workshop Summary*, Washington, DC: National Academies Press.

Nores, Milagros, Clive R. Belfield, W. Steven Barnett, and Lawrence Schweinhart (2005), "Updating the economic impacts of the High/Scope Perry Preschool Program," *Educational Evaluation and Policy Analysis*, **27** (3), Fall, 245–61.

Office of Management and Budget (OMB) (1992), "Guidelines and discount rates for benefit–cost analysis of federal programs (revised)," Circular No. A-94, Washington, DC: OMB, accessed 1 December 2012 at http://www.whitehouse.gov/omb/circulars/a094/a094.html.

Reynolds, Arthur J., Judy A. Temple, Dylan L. Robertson, and Emily A. Mann (2002), "Age 21 cost–benefit analysis of the Title I Chicago Child–Parent Centers," *Educational Evaluation and Policy Analysis*, **24** (4), Winter, 267–303.

Reynolds, Arthur J., Judy A. Temple, Barry A. White, Suh-Ruu Ou, and Dylan L. Robertson (2011), "Age-26 cost–benefit analysis of the Child–Parent Center Early Education Program," *Child Development*, **82** (1), 379–404.

Schweinhart, Lawrence J., Helen V. Barnes, and David P. Weikart (1993), *Significant Benefits: The High/Scope Perry Preschool Study Through Age 27*, Monographs of the High/Scope Educational Research Foundation, No. 10, Ypsilanti, MI: High/Scope Press.

Schweinhart, Lawrence J., Jeanne Montie, Zongping Xiang, W. Steven Barnett, Clive R. Belfield, and Milagros Nores (2005), *Lifetime Effects: The High/Scope Perry Preschool Study Through Age 40*, Monographs of the High/Scope Educational Research Foundation, No. 14, Ypsilanti, MI: High/Scope Press.

Shonkoff, Jack P. and Deborah A. Phillips (eds) (2000), *From Neurons to Neighborhoods: The Science of Early Child Development*, Washington, DC: National Academy Press.

US Department of Health and Human Services (2005), *Head Start Impact Study: First Year Findings*, Washington, DC: Administration for Children and Families, US Department of Health and Human Services, June, accessed 1 December 2012 at http://www.acf.hhs.gov/programs/opre/hs/impact_study/reports/first_yr_finds/first_yr_finds.pdf.

US Environmental Protection Agency (EPA) (2008), *Regulatory Impact Analysis of the Proposed Revisions to the National Ambient Air Quality Standards for Lead*, Research Triangle Park, NC: Office of Air Quality Planning and Standards, US EPA, accessed 1 December 2012 at http://www.epa.gov/ttnecas1/regdata/RIAs/finalpbria.pdf.

US Government Accountability Office (GAO) (1991), *Discount Rate Policy*, Washington, DC: Government Printing Office, May.

Vining, Aidan R. and David L. Weimer (2010), "An assessment of important issues concerning the application of benefit–cost analysis to social policy," *Journal of Benefit–Cost Analysis*, **1** (1), 1–38.

Yoshikawa, Hirokazu (1995), "Long-term effects of early childhood programs on social outcomes and delinquency," *The Future of Children*, **5** (3), 51–75.
Zerbe, Jr., Richard O. (2010), "A reliable internal rate of return," working paper, July.
Zerbe, Jr., Richard O. and Dwight D. Dively (1994), *Benefit–Cost Analysis in Theory and Practice*, New York: HarperColllins College Publishers.

3. Principles and standards for benefit–cost analysis of public health preparedness and pandemic mitigation programs

Joseph H. Cook

1 INTRODUCTION

In the spring of 2009, the world saw the outbreak of a new strain of influenza virus (H1N1). Although earlier interest had been focused on the possibility of strains of avian (H5N1) influenza coming from Asia, the H1N1 strain had jumped carriers from pigs to humans, and was first detected in Mexico. Known as H1N1 or "swine flu," it quickly spread around the world.

The World Health Organization (WHO) declared the outbreak a Phase 6 pandemic (the highest alert level) on 11 June 2009. As of late February 2010, H1N1 caused 16200 deaths in 213 countries.[1] The US Centers for Disease Control estimates that there were 41–84 million cases in the USA, 183000–378000 hospitalizations, and 8330–17160 deaths attributable to H1N1.[2] Nevertheless, the disease was milder than initially feared, and during much of 2009 attention among citizens and public officials was focused intensely on preparations for the pandemic.

There are a number of policies and programs that can be implemented in both the private and public sector at the local, state, and federal level to either contain the spread of epidemic or pandemic[3] influenza or mitigate its effects once it is already widespread. These containment and mitigation strategies have been studied extensively in the public health and epidemiology literature, often with state-of-the-art mathematical modeling approaches, to find "optimal" strategies. These analysts typically had a clear objective in mind when defining optimality: reduce the number of cases or deaths.

Many of these policies, however, imply large costs and benefits outside the health sector. For example, school closures are thought by many epidemiologists to be effective at slowing the spread of a pandemic or at least reducing peak caseloads, and are widely used. They may impose few costs on the health care system, but may involve large costs to families. Parents may need to miss work or arrange alternative child care. These effects may differ by socioeconomic status, such as whether a household has one or two adults or whether they have access to a paid leave policy. On the other hand, the benefits of containment and mitigation programs may have very large macroeconomic effects that have only recently begun to motivate careful research. These types of economic costs and benefits have not been widely incorporated into existing economic analyses.

In addition to identifying the proper mix of policies to contain a pandemic disease, an important economic and ethical question concerns the optimal level of public sector preparatory investment. How do we evaluate expensive investments in systems and stockpiles to prevent low-probability but extreme-outcome events?

Here is one illustration. The influenza pandemic of 1918 killed many young, healthy adults because of an over-reaction of the healthy immune system known as a "cytokine storm." Patients died of pneumonia when their lungs filled with fluid. Had these patients had access to ventilators, however, most would have survived. A ventilator is therefore arguably the best insurance policy against preventing influenza deaths. At an extreme, should hospitals therefore stock one ventilator for each American? Should they stockpile ventilators using the expected mortality rate? For example, if the overall mortality rate for the 1918 pandemic influenza was four per 1000, should they stock four ventilators per 1000 people? There were estimated to be approximately 105 000 ventilators in US hospitals in 2006, of which 100 000 are in use during a normal flu season. The Strategic National Stockpile stores an additional 4000–5000 ventilators, but the National Pandemic Plan calls for 742 500 in a worst case scenario (approximately 1 for every 410 Americans). A ventilator costs approximately $30 000, however, and neither hospitals nor local or federal governments are willing to buy and store excess ventilators. They would also need to ensure adequate staff capacity to operate them. "We only have a certain amount of money to spend on preparedness," said Thomas W. Skinner, a spokesman for the federal Centers for Disease Control and Prevention in Atlanta. "We can't invest strictly in respirators."[4]

Two economic frameworks that could be used for these types of questions are cost-effectiveness analysis (CEA) and benefit–cost analysis (BCA). The CEA approach is more widely used in the health field, although BCA may prove a more useful tool for some types of questions, as I discuss below. Like any methodology, however, a lack of standardization about common assumptions and techniques in both CEA and BCA may lead to different policy recommendations. The main goal of this chapter is, therefore, to begin a discussion of a set of principles and standards to be used in benefit–cost analyses of public health preparedness and pandemic mitigation policies. It is meant to be suggestive, not definitive. Neither is it meant to suggest that analysis should be *completely* standardized in parameter assumptions or in approach. Good analysis will always require good judgment, particularly in determining the appropriate scale of research given the scale of the question and the time and financial resources available for the study.

The audience for this chapter is assumed to be practitioners and economic analysts (benefit–cost and cost-effectiveness) at research institutions as well as various local, state and federal agencies charged either directly or indirectly with protecting health and minimizing the economic disruption of a major infectious disease outbreak. My focus is primarily on policies and strategies in the context of the USA.

In the remainder of this section, I define more comprehensively the types of problems and policies intended under the rubric "public health preparedness and pandemic mitigation" (which I abbreviate throughout as "PHP/PM") and briefly describe previous influenza pandemics. Section 2 provides a brief conceptual comparison between the CEA and BCA. (A review of existing economic evaluations of PHP/PM programs, both CEA and BCA, is provided in the appendix at the end of the chapter.) Section 3 discusses a specific set of empirical issues that may arise in conducting a BCA in this area. Section 4 concludes.

1.1 What Diseases and Interventions?

The types of infectious diseases that could become widespread in the USA and cause significant economic damage might include pandemic influenza, severe acute respiratory syndrome (SARS), multi-drug-resistant tuberculosis (MDR-TB), MRSA (methicillin-resistant staphylococcus aureus) or other antibiotic-resistant bacteria, smallpox, and hepatitis, as well as others. The types of preparedness and response policies and interventions will vary by disease; the disease focus in this chapter is primarily on pandemic influenza in order to maintain tractability for such a broad topic and because it has received the most attention among health analysts and modelers.

The chapter is limited to the economic analysis of public (rather than private) policies, programs, and investments to prevent the spread of an infectious disease and mitigate the disease's effects once it becomes widespread. Table 3.1 lists these interventions in three broad categories of preparation, containment, and mitigation. Although some of these

Table 3.1 Programs, interventions, and investments in PHP/PM

PREPARE (Before an outbreak)	CONTAIN (Prevent a disease from entering a geographical region)	MITIGATE (Slow the spread of the disease within a geographical region, reduce morbidity and mortality from the disease)
Stockpiling antiviral medicines (e.g., oseltamivir, zanamivir, amantadine, rimantadine) that can be used prophylactically or as treatment	Close borders to people	Production and distribution of targeted high-efficacy vaccines (lead times generally estimated to be six to nine months after first appearance of disease, though highly uncertain). Could be distributed to target groups (frontline responders, close contacts of existing cases), or to the entire population
Stockpiling low-efficacy vaccines (until vaccines more targeted to the specific agent can be manufactured)	Close borders to goods (trade restrictions)	Antiviral distribution. Could be used to treat all or a fraction of existing cases, or distributed prophylactically to target groups (frontline responders, close contacts of existing cases), or to the entire population
Disease surveillance networks (state or county health depts) and information technology systems to share information (nationally or internationally)	Ground airplane travel	Social distancing policies[b] such as: school closures, ban on public gatherings (sporting events, parades, etc.), mandatory closure of some types of private business (theaters, restaurants)
Emergency preparedness plan formation and drills[a]	Quarantine existing cases (requires adequate surveillance capacity)	General recommendations to avoid contact, stay home[c]
Programs targeted at changing prevention behavior (e.g., hand washing, improved infection control procedures in hospitals)		

Notes:
a. For detailed plans for state and local governments on measures see http://www.pandemicflu.gov/.
b. All of the policies listed occurred during the 1918 influenza pandemic in the United States; see Hatchett et al. (2007).
c. There is also some concern that a strong recommendation for social distancing measures may lead to a breakdown in social cohesion. When families and communities must rely on each other for care during outbreaks (especially if the health infrastructure is overwhelmed), government recommendations to avoid the sick could be problematic (Middaugh, 2008).

programs will have spillover benefits to other national security threats such as bioterrorism (e.g., contingency planning, emergency drills, etc.), I do not address bioterrorism specifically.[5]

What public sector agencies might be doing such analyses? The public health system in the USA is highly decentralized, with much of the funding, monitoring and surveillance, and policy responses such as school closures occurring at the local (i.e., county, city) and state levels. Nevertheless, federal agencies like the Centers for Disease Control (CDC) and Health and Human Services (HHS) play important roles in providing information, setting recommendations and guidelines for local public health agencies, and aggregating monitoring information. They also provide some funding to support monitoring. The Department of Homeland Security also has a limited role in a federal monitoring system called BioWatch, initiated in response to the anthrax attacks in the fall of 2001. The BioWatch program has deployed a series of outdoor air samplers in 30 major cities with the aim of rapid detection and characterization of aerosolized biological threats. All levels of government have the legal authority to enforce quarantines of patients, and the federal government theoretically has the power to close national borders and halt airline travel in the event of a pandemic.

1.2 Historic Pandemics

Because much of the existing economic analysis on PHP/PM deals with pandemic influenza planning, a brief introduction to the history of influenza pandemics may be helpful in understanding some of the key assumptions of these studies described later in the chapter.

There have been three large influenza pandemics in modern times. The worst, and most well known, is the 1918 influenza pandemic (Barry, 2004). A mild "heralding" wave was noted in the American Midwest in the spring of 1918, although it received little attention at the time (James and Sargent, 2006).[6] In the fall of 1918, the virus returned in a more lethal form, sickening approximately 20–25 percent of North Americans and spreading worldwide. The virus was unusual in that it disproportionately killed predominantly young, healthy adults from pneumonia (rather than the young, old, and infirm), and that it spread very rapidly. In any given location, approximately 80 percent of cases occurred within one month. Excess mortality was estimated to be 4.1 per 1000 (0.4 percent) in the USA, but between 8 and 55 per 1000 worldwide because of much higher mortality rates in poor countries like India (total mortality from the epidemic has been estimated at between 15 and 100 million deaths).

The two other pandemics occurred in 1957 and 1968–69. Both were much milder than the 1918 pandemic. Although the 1957 pandemic is believed to have sickened a higher percentage of people (35 percent vs 25 percent in 1918), excess mortality was an order of magnitude lower (0.4 per 1000 in the USA and 0.7 per 1000 globally). As with normal seasonal influenza, the deaths were concentrated in the very young and very old. The 1968–69 pandemic was milder still, with an excess mortality rate in the USA of 0.2 per 1000.

2 COMPARING BENEFIT–COST AND COST-EFFECTIVENESS

There are a number of texts devoted to the theoretical underpinnings and practical implementation of both benefit–cost analysis (Boardman et al., 2005; Zerbe, 2008) and cost-effectiveness/cost-utility analysis (Gold et al., 1996; Drummond et al., 1997; Haddix et al., 2003; IOM, 2006). What follows is an introduction for readers who may be less familiar with one or both methodologies.

2.1 Cost-effectiveness

Cost-effectiveness analysis (CEA) seeks to achieve a given health objective at lowest cost. This health objective may be narrowly defined. For example, a CEA analyst may evaluate the cost of three different blood pressure medications in relation to their clinical effectiveness at reducing blood pressure (the health objective). (When all three medications have equal clinic effectiveness, the analysis would become a cost-minimization exercise.) CEA is more useful, however, for comparing broader sets of health policies or interventions to inform health sector budget allocation decisions. For example, if the health objective is defined more broadly as preventing mortality, several different types of programs within the health sector (i.e., R&D into new cancer-fighting drugs, expanded vaccination, public health education programs to reduce smoking) can be compared by their cost per life saved. Though conceptually straightforward, accurately determining the direct health care costs of various policies or interventions is by no means simple (see Lipscomb et al., 2009 for a recent review). The analytical perspective for CEA is typically either from the health system perspective (only costs incurred or avoided by the health care provider are included) or the social perspective, which also includes costs borne by patients and society.

Because programs often have effects on both mortality (quantity of life) and morbidity (quality of life), CEA researchers developed measures in the

1970s that combine the two effects. The quality-adjusted life year (QALY) approach is the most common. To combine the effects of a program on morbidity and mortality, an analyst first calculates the incremental effect of the program compared to a status quo option in terms of extension of life and reduction in the amount of time spent in disability, pain, and so on. The analyst then weights time spent in the disabled condition with a QALY weight, which is equal to 1 for perfect health and 0 for death. This time can then be added to life years lost to premature death to calculate QALYs gained from the program.

QALY weights, the subject of hundreds of studies, are generally elicited from the general population (not experts) using a variety of techniques.[7] The most common and theoretically uncontroversial is the standard gamble approach. Respondents are described some condition or illness that involves pain or disability (i.e., a kidney disease that requires weekly dialysis). They are then asked to choose between two alternatives. In the first alternative, there is a treatment option for the kidney disease that will return the respondent to "perfect health" for their remaining t years of life with probability p, or will result in instant death with probability $(1 - p)$. In the second alternative, respondents will live with the kidney disease for the remaining t years of their lives. The probability is varied until a respondent is indifferent between these two alternatives, and the resulting probability is the QALY weight for that kidney disease. Again, weights near zero indicate that living with the condition is almost as bad as death, and indeed negative weights are possible for conditions considered worse than death. Because of the elicitation approach, QALY weights are based on von Neumann-Morgenstern expected utilities, so this approach has also been called cost-utility analysis. These utilities, however, are cardinal and not tied in any way to how respondents might trade *income* for health improvements or risk reductions. These should not be confused with the ordinal utilities (only ordering is possible, and is sufficient) used by welfare economists.

A second type of weight used to combine morbidity and mortality effects is the disability-adjusted life year (DALY). The DALY approach was initiated by the World Health Organization and is more commonly used in the context of developing countries. It is different from a QALY in several respects. First, DALY weights are coded on a scale of 0 as perfect health and 1 as death, exactly the opposite of the QALY scale. The effect of interest is therefore DALYs avoided, rather than QALYs gained. Second, DALY weights have been constructed from a process of expert elicitation rather than a survey-based approach from the general population. Third, DALYs as originally proposed weight effects by when the morbidity occurred in life. These age weights are lowest for the young and the old, and peak at middle age when people are most productive (Murray and Lopez, 1996). These age weights have proved controversial, however, and have not been commonly applied in recent CEA studies using the DALY approach (Jamison et al., 2006).

Health policy-makers are advised to invest more health resources in programs with lower cost-effectiveness ratios and less in programs with higher cost-effectiveness ratios. There are not, however, generally clear guidelines for when a program has such poor cost-effectiveness that it should not be undertaken at all. Is a health program with a cost-effectiveness of $5 000 000 per life saved worth undertaking? CEA can tell us to prefer a program with a ratio of $4 million per life saved, but if this program has the lowest cost-effectiveness ratio it cannot be used to justify whether that program is worth doing. There are reference values that are widely used in CEA, although they are not grounded in welfare theory. Using a definition first suggested in the World Bank's 1993 *Investing in Health* report, interventions are often considered "very cost effective" if the ratio of cost per DALY avoided is less than per capita GDP. An intervention is "cost effective" if the ratio is less than three times per capita GDP. In Britain, the National Health Service will generally not cover interventions that have cost-effectiveness ratios higher than £20 000–30 000 per QALY gained.[8] In this sense, CEA can be thought of as achieving *technical efficiency* in spending resources that have been budgeted to the health sector by higher-level decision-makers (Drummond et al., 1997). In this framework, these decision-makers (i.e., Congress, Parliament, etc.) make implicit decisions about sectoral allocations.

2.2 Benefit–Cost Analysis

Benefit–cost analysis, on the other hand, can be used to answer these types of questions of *allocative efficiency*. Unlike CEA, the BCA framework is firmly grounded in welfare economics (in addition to the BCA texts cited above, see also Just et al., 2004). As such, it relies on several basic tenets that are normative in nature. First, social welfare is derived from the welfare (utilities) of the individuals that make up that society. Second, those individuals are the best judges of their own welfare (i.e., consumer sovereignty). Finally, a "Pareto-improving" program that would make at least one person better off but make no one else worse off is welfare enhancing and should be implemented. In practice, because such improvements are nearly impossible to find, welfare economists rely on the potential Pareto test, also known as the Kaldor–Hicks criteria: if the winners from a policy could fully compensate the losers and still be better off, the policy is welfare enhancing. This framework focuses on increasing efficiency, and takes the existing income distribution as given. Like CEA, it does not explicitly consider equity effects, although this has been, and continues to be, the subject of debate among welfare economists and BCA analysts.

To assess potential Pareto improvements, a full BCA places shadow prices on all positive and negative impacts of a policy or program. In other words, a health BCA requires monetizing all health impacts by determining consumers' willingness to trade income (or wealth) for the health improvements or a reduction in mortality risk. Although these shadow prices are often unavailable and frequently controversial, they have the advantage of allowing economic comparisons with programs or policies outside the health sector. Willingness to pay is then summed over the affected population[9] to calculate total social benefits. The proper decision rule is to select projects with the highest net benefits: total social benefits less total social costs.[10] There will, of course, be categories of benefits or costs that are difficult or impossible to monetize. These should be presented alongside BCA results; BCA is intended to be a decision-making aide rather than the sole normative criterion for evaluating a policy or program.

Shadow values can be elicited using four types of approaches: a human capital approach, cost-of-illness, revealed preference, and stated preference. The human capital approach uses changes in the productive capacity of individuals with changes in health state as the measure of economic welfare. For example, if a 35-year-old is expected to earn $1.5 million over the remainder of his or her life, a program that would prevent his or her death at age 35 would increase economic welfare by $1.5 million. This approach, however, is not consistent with the underlying theory of BCA in that it does provide information on individuals' willingness to pay (WTP) for risk reductions or health improvements (Drummond et al., 1997; Freeman, 1999). Although commonly used in wrongful death suits in the court system, the human capital approach is uncommon in modern BCAs.

Cost-of-illness (COI) captures both the financial and economic costs of being ill. COI estimates are available for a number of illnesses in a number of populations, and provide an uncontroversial measure of the economic benefits of avoiding an illness. Public COI refers to the cost incurred by the public sector health system in treating an illness, such as staff salaries, publicly provided treatments, capital costs of facilities, and so on. Private COI measures financial and economic costs incurred by patients (i.e., lost work days, cost of medicines not covered by the public system, etc.). In a BCA framework, ex ante COI (COI weighted by the probability of falling ill) can be compared with the costs of reducing the illness. From a health care provider perspective, the analysis may focus only on public COI avoided. A social perspective would include private COI avoided as well.

Avoided COI is also sometimes netted out of the numerator of cost-effectiveness ratios, although this may double-count benefits by placing one element of the monetized value of reducing illness in the numerator as well as the non-monetized QALY or DALY measure in the denominator.[11] The main problem with COI estimates in the BCA framework is that they do not capture the value of reductions in mortality risk. Treatment costs for a fatal illness are likely to underestimate ex ante willingness to pay to reduce mortality risk.

The third approach—revealed preference—relies on observing consumer behavior in markets related to health improvements. The most important application of the revealed preference approach in health is valuing changes in mortality risk through labor markets. By observing wages and fatality risks in a large number of jobs in the labor market, economists can deduce the wage premium that workers in less risky occupations forgo to avoid the higher mortality risk (or the additional wages demanded by those who chose the riskier occupation). This willingness to pay for mortality risk reduction can then be used as the shadow price in a health BCA of a policy or program that would reduce the risk of death (see Viscusi and Aldy, 2003 for a comprehensive review). Because risk changes are often presented as the number of deaths prevented, analysts often need to value these aggregate risk changes. If among a large group of people average willingness to pay to avoid a 1 in 100 000 risk of dying from a particular cause is \$45, then the average willingness to pay to reduce one death among the group would be (\$45/0.00001), or \$4.5 million. This value has unfortunately been termed the "value of a statistical life" (VSL), a label that draws ire from the general public, obscures the economic relationship of interest (WTP for small risk changes), and belies the large heterogeneity in these preferences depending on both individuals and contexts. A related concept is the "value of a statistical life year" (VSLY), or a VSL estimate that reflects remaining life expectancy by dividing the VSL by the discounted expected number of life years remaining (Robinson, 2007). This approach assumes that VSLs are proportional to remaining life expectancy, an assumption not grounded in theory and that has not been borne out by empirical studies (Aldy and Viscusi, 2007; Krupnick, 2007; Viscusi, 2010).

The fourth approach to valuing health outcomes is stated preference (SP). Researchers use either contingent valuation or stated choice methodologies to present respondents with a hypothetical product that would reduce their risk of dying, treat a condition, or prevent an illness. Respondents are asked if they would be willing to purchase the product at a given price. Prices are randomly chosen from a range of prices that allow the analyst to construct a bid curve (the percentage of respondents purchasing the product by price). The area under this curve represents average willingness to pay for the health impact of interest. For mortality risk reductions, the WTP can be used to estimate the VSL.

Because of the hypothetical nature of the exercise, these SP techniques have been subject to two decades of close scrutiny and testing, much of it in the environmental and transport literatures. Although hypothetical biases in SP studies remain a threat and many poorly conceived and executed SP studies routinely appear, the technique has gained acceptance in federal government economic analysis and increasingly among economists. There are now a number of documents that provide guidance on how to conduct high-quality stated preference studies (Arrow et al., 1993; US Office of Management and Business [OMB], 2003; US Environmental Protection Agency [EPA], 2008). Analysts using shadow prices from SP studies should consult these references for criteria to evaluate the quality of the underlying research. Researchers experienced in SP methods know these recommendations and criteria well (i.e., scope tests, high-quality survey administration, extensive focus group and pre-testing, "cheap talk" scripts etc.). On the positive side, the hypothetical nature of SP provides a larger scope for valuing morbidity changes than revealed preference approaches. They may also capture categories of benefits in morbidity changes that are not captured in COI measures (e.g., fear, dread, suffering).[12]

2.3 Existing Principles and Standards

There are a number of well-known sources for principles and standards in both cost-effectiveness and benefit–cost analyses. In the USA, the federal government is required to assess the benefits and costs of all major federal regulations.[13] The Office of Management and Budget is responsible for reviewing these benefit–cost assessments, and its Circular A-4 "Regulatory Analysis" (most recently updated in 2003) serves as a source of both analytical requirements and more general preferred practices. Most of the federal regulations examined under the requirements of Exec. Order 12866 have been environmental rules (Robinson, 2010). As such, the Environmental Protection Agency, responsible for many of these rules, publishes its own guidance, *Guidelines for Preparing Economic Analyses*. First published in 2000, the US EPA is in the process of updating these guidelines, and circulated a draft revised document in 2008. There are to my knowledge no guidelines specifically related to BCA in health care or public health preparedness, though the discussion of analytical framework, methods for deriving shadow prices, discounting, and so on in Circular A-4 and US EPA (2008) would be an appropriate place to begin. I will reference these throughout the next section discussing individual analytical challenges for PHP/PM. Canada, the UK, and the European Union have also developed regulatory impact analyses in recent years similar in approach to those used in the USA (for more details see Robinson, 2010).

Cost-effectiveness analysis also has a well-developed set of principles and guidelines specifically in health-related applications because of its widespread use. The most commonly cited is Gold et al. (1996), a report from a US Public Health Service-appointed expert panel titled *Cost-Effectiveness and Health in Medicine*. Other sources include the World Health Organization's CHOICE framework,[14] the UK's National Institute for Clinical Excellence (NICE),[15] Weinstein et al. (2003), the guidelines for submissions to the *British Medical Journal* (Drummond and Jefferson, 1996), the Institute of Medicine's report on valuing health for regulatory CEA (2006), and the standards used in the compilation of cost-effectiveness studies in the recent Disease Control Priorities project (DCP2, outlined in Musgrove and Fox-Rushby, 2006). US OMB Circular A-4 also discusses CEA for major regulations, largely echoing recommendations from the Gold et al. expert panel and explicitly stating a preference for BCA where possible. Since my focus here is on BCA, a complete discussion of these guidelines for CEA is beyond the scope of this chapter.

3 SPECIFIC ISSUES

3.1 Modeling Macroeconomic Impacts

Perhaps the most important element missing from many existing economic evaluations of PHP/PM is the potential for effects outside the health sector, including large-scale macroeconomic effects. Beutels et al. (2008) argue that:

> traditional health economic analysis is ill-equipped to estimate the cost-effectiveness and cost–benefit of interventions that aim at controlling and/or preventing public health emergencies of international concern (such as pandemic influenza) . . . Since traditional economic forms of evaluation are being used to inform decisions about controlling and preparing for these emergencies, they do not appear to be fit for the purpose.

How might we adapt them to fit the purpose? I begin this section with a review of the existing literature on the macroeconomic impacts of pandemic influenza and the effects of school closure policies on households. I then offer some suggestions for how and when these types of effects should be included in BCAs.

3.2 Existing Literature

Several studies have attempted to document the macroeconomic consequences of infectious disease outbreaks, namely pandemic influenza. These studies do not attempt an economic evaluation of specific policies or programs, but seek to understand the various linkages between a pandemic and the wider economy using theory, models, and historical evidence. These linkages could include: a decline in the size of the labor force due to illness and death, a reduction in household income as a result of missed work, a reduction in consumer demand for products and services that require more social contact, and a re-evaluation of investment risk, particularly with regards to price inflation (McKibbin and Sidorenko, 2006). Several government reports and non-academic outlets have discussed these possible macroeconomic effects of influenza (US CBO, 2006; Langton, 2008),[16] or the effect of the SARS in 2002–03 (Conference Board of Canada, 2003). Langton (2008), from the US Congressional Research Service, analyzes possible trade disruptions due to an avian flu pandemic. Disruptions could include banning imported goods from infected regions, de facto bans or boycotts due to health concerns, or supply-side constraints from exporting countries. The study considers the potential impact of import restrictions from countries with confirmed avian flu cases from January 2004 to January 2008. Of those countries, imports from China, which account for 15 percent of total US imports, would have the largest potential impact on the US economy. Overall the effect on the macroeconomy would depend on the severity of the outbreak, the duration of the outbreak, and the number of countries affected.

Several studies have attempted to model these effects for a future pandemic (see Table 3.2). All of the studies take case attack rates and mortality rates from historical pandemics as various case scenarios, typically using the 1957 and 1968–69 pandemics as more moderate cases, and the 1918 pandemic as the worst case (McKibbin and Sidorenko, 2006 and US Congressional Budget Office [CBO], 2006 use mortality rates double that of 1918 as their worst case). With the exception of Bloom et al. (2005), the studies have predominantly been conducted by authors in developed countries with a focus on developed country economies, although several make predictions about effects in developing countries.

The studies use a variety of modeling approaches, although none uses a full computable general equilibrium (CGE) model. McKibben and Sidorenko (2006) use a multi-sector structural model called G-Cubed, Jonung and Roeger (2006) use a QUEST model, Keogh-Brown et al. (2009) use a structural model. James and Sargent (2006) estimate individual morbidity, mortality, and absenteeism impacts separately based on

Table 3.2 Studies of macroeconomic effects of pandemic influenza

Study	Primary Country	Key Scenario Characteristics	Total Pandemic Year GDP Effects	Decomposition of GDP Effects: Absenteeism from Mortality, Illness, and Workplace Avoidance	Remaining Indirect GDP Effect
James and Sargent (2006) (1)	Canada	1918 mortality (0.44%), base case	Canada: −0.4 to −0.9%; similar impacts in other advanced economies and in emerging economies	−0.6%	−0.4%
James and Sargent (2006) (2)	Canada	1918 mortality (0.44%), with workplace avoidance absenteeism	Canada: −0.4 to −1.1%; similar impacts in other advanced economies and in emerging economies	−0.7%	−0.4%
James and Sargent (2006) (3)	Canada	1957 mortality (0.04%)	Canada: −0.1 to −0.3%; similar impacts in other advanced economies and in emerging economies	−0.3%	−0.1%
US CBO (2006) (1)	USA	Mortality double that of 1918 (0.75%)	USA: −5%	−3.0%	−2.0%
US CBO (2006) (2)	USA	1957 mortality (0.03%)	USA: −1.5%	−1.0%	−0.5%
Kennedy et al. (2006)	Australia	Mortality half that of 1918 (0.2%)	Australia: −9.3%	−1.5%	−7.8%
McKibbin and Sidorenko (2006) (1)	Global	Mortality double that of 1918 in advanced economies	USA: −5.5%; Canada: −5.7%; Japan: −15.8%; Europe: −8.0%; Singapore: −21.7%; Philippines: −37.8%; LDCs: −12.2%	−0.6%	−0.1%

Table 3.2 (continued)

Study	Primary Country	Key Scenario Characteristics	Total Pandemic Year GDP Effects	Decomposition of GDP Effects: Absenteeism from Mortality, Illness, and Workplace Avoidance	Remaining Indirect GDP Effect
McKibbin and Sidorenko (2006) (2)	Global	1918 mortality	USA: −3.0%; Canada: −3.1%; Japan: −8.4%; Europe: −4.3%; Singapore: −11.2%; Philippines: −19.3%; LDCs: −6.3%	−0.7%	−0.8%
McKibbin and Sidorenko, 2006 (3)	Global	1957 mortality	USA: −1.4%; Canada: −1.5%; Japan: −3.3%; Europe: −1.9%; Singapore: −4.4%; Philippines: −7.3%; LDCs: −2.4%	−0.8%	−2.3%
McKibbin and Sidorenko (2006) (4)	Global	1968 mortality	USA: −0.6%; Canada −0.7%; Japan −1.0%; Europe −0.7%; Singapore −0.9%; Philippines −1.5%; LDCs −0.69%	−1.0%	−4.7%
Bloom et al. (2005)	Asia	Mortality double that of 1957 (0.1%)	Asia: −2.6% to −6.8%	−0.3%	−6.5%
Jonung and Roeger (2006)	EU	Same as CBO (1) (0.75%)	EU: −1.6%	−1.1%	−0.5%

Source: Adapted largely from James and Sargent (2006); LDCs = less developed countries.

historical data from 1918, 1957, and 1968–69. They also differ in several key assumptions about the level of absenteeism due to workplace avoidance policies or school closures, and the degree to which demand shocks "bounce back" after the pandemic ends. A full discussion of the macroeconomic modeling approaches taken is beyond the scope of this chapter.

For 1918-like scenarios, estimates for the drop in GDP during the pandemic year range widely. James and Sargent's estimates range from 0.4 to 0.9 percent in Canada specifically, though they believe the effects would be representative of other "advanced economies." McKibben and Sidorenko predict a drop of roughly 3 percent in the USA and Canada (and much higher in Asia and developing countries) for a 1918-like pandemic and mortality rate. Kennedy et al. (2006) predict the largest effects: for mortality rates half as high as 1918, they predict a fall in GDP of 9.3 percent for Australia. As points of reference, real GDP fell by roughly 30 percent from 1929 to 1933 in the United States.[17] In two more recent recessions, US GDP fell 1.9 percent from 1981 to 1982, and 0.2 percent from 1990 to 1991 (though these annual figures mask larger quarterly changes). The recession in 2008–09 is currently estimated to have shrunk US GDP by 6.3 percent in the fourth quarter of 2008 and 5.5 percent in the first quarter of 2009.

James and Sargent further break out the component of GDP effects caused by absenteeism due to avoidance behavior (e.g., school closures, workplace avoidance, home care for ill family members) and mortality. Mortality in these models is not valued using a VSL calculation, but rather through the macroeconomic effect of losing workers in the economy. On average, these comprise roughly half of the total GDP effects across the various countries and models studied.

As can be seen from Table 3.2, however, there is not a consensus on how large the impacts might be, depending largely on assumptions about how households' economic behavior (purchasing, travel, workplace avoidance) may change in reaction to a pandemic. Estimates of the costs of a 1918-like pandemic flu for the USA range from 0.4 percent to 5.5 percent of GDP (see Table 3.2). If current US GDP is approximately $14.1 trillion,[18] the range of costs implied is $56 billion to $775 billion (approximately the same size as the economic stimulus package passed in the USA in 2009). The results of a BCA that includes general equilibrium effects will clearly be extremely sensitive to the distribution chosen for this parameter.

However, most of the data on what types of behaviors the public would undertake is based on historical analyses with sparse data or assumptions with little empirical support. Using a survey-based approach, Sadique et al. (2007) asked residents in five European countries and two Asian countries what types of behavioral modifications they might make under one of two scenarios for a pandemic influenza outbreak. Nearly three-quarters of respondents said that they would avoid public transportation, avoid places of entertainment, and restrict their shopping to the essentials. Similarly, a survey by Balicer et al. (2006) found that approximately half of public health workers in the USA said they would avoid work in the wake of a pandemic.

3.3 School Closure

Similarly, relatively little is known about the economic and social impact of school closure or "class dismissal" policies. This is of particular relevance because school closures policies are thought by some to be an effective policy for slowing the spread of outbreaks for many infectious diseases, although this is still the subject of debate among epidemiologists (Cauchemez et al., 2009 provide an excellent introduction to this issue, including a discussion of the epidemiological evidence, the social/economic impacts, and practical issues of school closure policies). They were widely used in the H1N1 pandemic.

Sadique et al. (2008) use a large nationally representative survey data from the UK to estimate the percentage of working adults with dependent children who may need to stay home to care for children in the event of a school closure. They estimate that 16 percent of the UK workforce would be primary caregivers, although this may be lower if parents find other informal care arrangements with friends, neighbors, or extended family. The effect may also differ by sector, with workers in the health care and education sectors more likely to be a primary caregiver for a child than workers in other sectors. Because of this, school closure policies may have important effects on the capacity of the health care system to deal with large patient loads if health care workers are forced to miss work because of school closures. Using average sector-specific wage data, they estimate the cost of this absenteeism to be on the order of £0.2 to £1.2 billion per week, or 0.2 to 1 percent of British GDP for a closure lasting for the duration of a 12-week pandemic wave. They note (p. 6) that although these costs "might appear to be large, the benefits of the policy in terms of cases and deaths might be acceptable . . . only a fully economic analysis can shed light on whether such a policy should be adopted."

Similarly, Blendon et al. (2008) surveyed 1697 American adults about prospective behaviors during an influenza pandemic. Among the subset of respondents with at least one school-aged child and one employed adult in the household, 86 percent reported that they could arrange care so that one adult could continue to work. Interestingly, though, they found that among the low-income (<$25000 per year) subset of this group, 93 percent said they would have serious financial difficulties if they had to stay home because of a school closure lasting three months, compared to 64 percent of higher-income (>$75 000) respondents.

Effler et al. (2010) surveyed retrospectively 233 households affected by an H1N1-related closure of three schools in Perth, Australia in June 2009. Parents were advised to place their children under "home quarantine." Nearly half of parents (45 percent) of asymptomatic children reported taking at least one day off work to care for their child (range one to five days, median three days). Thirty-five percent said that they made special child care arrangements for at least one day as a result of the closure (median of two days). One-third of parents thought the closure was inappropriate, while half thought it appropriate. In addition, they found that 74 percent of students reported going outside the home for sporting events, shopping, or outdoor recreation during the school closure period, despite the recommendation to avoid public gatherings. Parents of children with more outside activities were more likely to think the school closure was inappropriate. The survey did not solicit information about wages or income, and did not attempt to identify whether the effect on households differed by socioeconomic status.

In contrast, Johnson et al. (2008) found relatively modest impacts on 220 families from a one-week school closure due to an influenza B outbreak in a rural county in North Carolina. Although one-quarter of adults reported missing work during that period, most were absent because of their own illness or to treat a sick child. The only respondents who missed work solely due to the school closure were school employees. Three-quarters of respondents said that someone was regularly available to provide child care, and although 10 percent said they needed to make special child care arrangements, only two respondents (1 percent) reported spending extra money. The closure was widely supported by parents, with 91 percent feeling the closure was appropriate. The authors note, however, that the rural county may not be representative as schools frequently close for large winter storms and parents may be more prepared with alternative arrangements. They also note that the county has a smaller share of single-parent households than the national average.

3.4 Existing Guidance and Principles and Standards

When should BCAs for PHP/PM incorporate larger-scale macroeconomic effects? There is little existing guidance on whether BCA models should use partial or general equilibrium frameworks. All existing CEA guidance assumes a partial equilibrium framework by definition, since only effects within the health sector are included. US OMB (2003) does not discuss when general equilibrium frameworks might be advisable, let alone required. US EPA's draft 2008 guidance suggests that a general equilibrium (GE) framework may be more appropriate when it is clear that an environmental rule will affect many markets, although it neither provides exact guidance on when a GE framework would be required, nor how a GE model should be constructed.

The structural models described above are time-consuming to build and run, and the expertise needed is likely beyond that available to many government agencies charged with economic analysis. In addition, the errors arising from such models are likely to swamp any of the uncertainty in other parts of the analysis. Clearly, analyses should be proportionate to the scale of their analytical goals and available resources. A state health department conducing a BCA of an antiviral stockpiling program will probably neither need, nor have the resources, to model the general equilibrium effects on the benefits side in their state, let alone nationwide. A full GE model may be a more appropriate investment for a federal analysis of a very expensive national-level program (such as stockpiling respirators, for example, or recommending nationwide school closure guidelines).

Incorporating macroeconomic effects may also be more important for BCAs of infectious disease outbreaks that appear suddenly and spread very quickly, producing a shock to the system. For diseases that spread more slowly, like MRSA or drug-resistant tuberculosis, it seems more likely that individuals and economies would adapt over time, although there are certainly large macroeconomic effects on countries with very high prevalence rates of disease such as malaria, HIV/AIDS, or tuberculosis.

For CEA, approaches like the one taken by Sander et al. (2009) are a useful first step towards consideration of non-health impacts. As described in the appendix, Sander et al. include as costs the estimate of work days lost as a result of child illness (for parents) and school closure policies (to teachers, staff, and parents). They also include travel and time costs of vaccination and antiviral treatment. Because the authors estimate a CEA model, they need not model the more difficult benefits side of the equation, but rather find the policies (or combination of policies) that have the lowest cost per QALY gained. Beutels et al. (2008) also suggest ways that constrained treatment capacity (which would lead to longer waits for care for patients) could be translated into QALYs in a cost-effectiveness approach.

For BCAs, it may be prudent at this point to include best estimates of macro-level impacts on the cost side in a partial equilibrium framework but stop short of full-scale GE models for the benefits side. Decision-makers can examine these results, which provide a more complete picture of the costs of PHP/PM programs, alongside the emerging estimates of the potential GDP effects from pandemics described above. An alternative would be to model the range of impacts in the literature in a probabilistic sensitivity analysis, though as noted before, the error in these estimates will almost surely drive the distribution of net benefits. Given the number of recent working papers in this area, as well as the attention brought by the H1N1 pandemic and the possibility of an H5N1 pandemic, this line of research may expand dramatically. If better estimates become available and GE models become easier to implement, these principles and standards would need to be adapted.

3.5 Uncertainty

The treatment of uncertainty will be central to any economic evaluation of PHP/PM programs because so many parameters[19] are not known with a high degree of certainty. First and foremost, the probability of a pandemic occurring[20] as well as its severity is highly uncertain.

Existing guidelines and texts in both BCA and CEA stress the importance of addressing uncertainty (Gold et al., 1996; Drummond et al., 1997; Boardman et al., 2005; US OMB, 2003). This may take the form of univariate sensitivity analysis, where key uncertain parameters are varied in the analysis ceteris paribus, often in an attempt to identify "break-even" values where net benefits are equal to zero or where C/E ratios are equal to "cost-effective" or "very cost-effective" levels.[21] All six PHP/PM studies reviewed included a univariate sensitivity analysis.

Probabilistic approaches like Monte Carlo analysis are increasingly common in many fields as the availability of software and computing power has made conducting them fairly simple (Caulkins, 2002; Weinstein et al., 2003; Krupnick et al., 2006). They are now required by US OMB (2003) for regulations expected to have an economic impact of $1 billion or more. Monte Carlo techniques allow the analyst to allow several uncertain parameters to vary simultaneously and construct a range of possible outputs (e.g., net benefit measures). Specifically, the analyst defines a distribution of plausible values for each uncertain parameter. Parameters can be correlated. These distributions can be elicited from experts using Delphi methods (see Morgan and Henrion, 1990), or can be estimated from existing literature. The Monte Carlo model then randomly draws from this distribution for each uncertain parameter and calculates the net benefits that would result from the "draw." It repeats this process many times (e.g., 10 000), each time generating a net benefit estimate. The result is a distribution of net benefits estimates, which can then be described probabilistically. US OMB recommends reporting both measures of central tendency from this distribution (median net benefits and expected value [mean]) as well as 95 percent confidence intervals. Results can also be presented as the probability of observing positive net benefits. Four of six PHP/PM papers reviewed used Monte Carlo simulation approaches.

For preparedness programs, the probability of an infectious outbreak is perhaps the most important uncertain parameter, and an obvious but critical standard in any economic evaluation of preparedness programs is to vary the probability of an outbreak occurring in a sensitivity analyses framework (as Balicer et al., 2005 do). For the sake of transparency, this should include a univariate sensitivity analysis (probability of pandemic alone) in addition to any multivariate Monte Carlo simulations. Although historical data will continue to provide the best guide to the probability of a new outbreak, globalization has dramatically changed the ease and speed with which new diseases can be spread throughout the world (as modeled by Colizza et al., 2007). Furthermore, for some diseases in some countries the impact of a changing climate may also be an important factor in the probability of attack. A useful form of sensitivity analysis here might be a break-even analysis.

For containment and mitigation programs like quarantines, border closures, and social distancing policies, however, the analyst is concerned with identifying the optimal policies given that the pandemic is occurring. Thus, the probability of a pandemic occurring is unimportant. Rather, the uncertain parameters that are likely to be of the most importance are the characteristics of the pandemic (transmissibility and attack rate, mortality rate), the characteristics of the intervention (e.g., how much will a school closure slow transmission[22]), and the macroeconomic consequences of containment and mitigation programs, especially social distancing measures. Because of the large number of uncertain parameters, these types of programs would probably be best suited for multivariate, probabilistic Monte Carlo analysis.

The challenge lies in communicating probabilistic results to policy-makers. One approach is to design models with accessible user interfaces so that policy-makers can personally run various scenarios with different assumptions. For a more in-depth discussion of approaches for presenting probabilistic information to policy-makers and to the public, see Morgan and Henrion (1990), Caulkins (2002), and Krupnick et al. (2006).

3.6 Discounting

The issue of discounting, or how to adjust the value of benefits or costs that occur in the future to be commensurate with benefits and costs in the current period, will be important in many types of BCAs for PHP/PM.

On the benefits side, for pandemics that have fairly short case durations and few long-term associated disabilities (like influenza), the choice of a discount rate will primarily affect the valuation of avoiding premature deaths. In other words, if most patients are sick for a few weeks and recover completely, there are few health effects occurring in future years to be discounted. On the other hand, some types of programs may involve costs in the current period but accrue potential benefits in future years. Preparedness training programs and the stockpiling of antiviral drugs or low-efficacy vaccines with relatively long shelf lives[23] are two examples. For many other types of programs, however, discount rates may have little impact on net benefits. For example, mitigation or containment programs (e.g., social distancing programs like school closures, travel cessations, high-efficacy vaccine research and deployment) would have most benefits and costs occurring within a small time frame.

Because of its key role, the choice of an appropriate social discount rate has long been the subject of considerable discussion in the literature (Portney and Weyant, 1999) and in benefit–cost texts (Zerbe and Dively, 1994; Brent, 1996; Boardman et al., 2005). An approach using the shadow price of capital (SPC) has the most theoretical appeal, but requires knowledge of how projects are financed in order to estimate the fraction of benefits and costs measured as increments to consumption versus private sector investment. It also requires assumptions about the shadow price of capital, and the more common assumptions about the marginal social rate of time preference and marginal rate of return on investments.

The predominant analytical approach remains constant exponential discounting.[24] One alternative to this approach is hyperbolic discounting, which tends to make benefits or costs in the near future somewhat less important and those in the distant future more important (they are discounted less heavily). There is behavioral evidence that hyperbolic discounting may capture time preferences more accurately. In addition, much of the debate over constant exponential versus hyperbolic discounting has centered around analyses of policies, programs or investments with intergenerational equity concerns, chief among them climate change (see Portney and Weyant, 1999). This may be less of a concern for PHP/PM programs, which have time frames where both costs and benefits occur within a generation.

The US OMB, in both Circular A-4 and A-94, provides clear guidance. In addition to undiscounted benefits and costs, results should be presented using two real discount rates. A rate of 7 percent represents the rate of return to private capital, while a 3 percent rate represents the consumption rate of interest.[25] Both US OMB (2003) and US EPA (2008) discuss discounting in the presence of intergenerational concerns. US

OMB recommends using a positive rate lower than 3 percent in sensitivity analysis when rules have "important intergenerational benefits and costs." US EPA (2008) recommends using a schedule of discount factors based on a stochastic "random walk" (Newell and Pizer, 2003) for programs with time horizons longer than 50 years. US OMB recommends lower rates (based on the marginal rate of return on investments) for cost-effectiveness analyses (these were 0.9 percent for a three-year time horizon to 2.7 percent for a 30-year time horizon[26] as of December 2008).

There is considerable agreement in the health evaluation field to use a real discount rate of 3 percent, and this rate has been codified in several cost-effectiveness guidelines (Gold et al., 1996; Musgrove and Fox-Rushby, 2006).[27] This rate is applied to both discounting of health states (i.e., comparing life years saved in one year versus those saved in ten years) as well as financial outlays in the current and future periods. (Many studies do not adjust specifically for inflation in future direct health care costs, implicitly assuming that health costs will rise in parallel with overall price inflation; an assumption that seems unwarranted in the USA.[28]) This consensus is largely reflected in the PHP/PM evaluations in the appendix below. Five of six studies (both CEA and BCA) use a base case discount rate of 3 percent (the sixth uses a base case of 3.5 percent). Only two studies varied the discount rate in a sensitivity analysis. Siddiqui and Edmunds (2008) use a discount rate of 6 percent as an upper bound, and Nichol (2001) uses 5 percent.

To maintain consistency with the bulk of the health economic literature and because it is also consistent with existing US OMB guidance, analysts should continue to present results using a real discount rate of 3 percent. All studies should also present results using a 7 percent rate, or whatever rate is currently recommended by US OMB. Where the choice of discount rate has a substantial impact on results, analysts should avoid presenting the 3 percent rate as the "base case" value but rather both sets of results as equally plausible. In all cases, however, the discount rate should be varied in a sensitivity analysis. Results should also be presented in undiscounted form, which may be especially useful to policy-makers given the uncertainty in the timing and magnitude of a pandemic.

3.7 Disparate Impacts and Equity

Pandemics may have disparate impacts within the US population. These disparities may occur because some groups could be more or less susceptible to infection (age, health status, prior infection, occupation) or to have more severe cases that end in death. There is a considerable amount of research on these types of impacts, and epidemiologists often focus their efforts on identifying and giving preferential treatment to these high-risk groups. Among groups that are similar in these characteristics, however, disparate disease impacts could also occur by socioeconomic status if (1) lower-income groups have more difficulty accessing the health care system, (2) low-income communities are targeted less by public health departments both in disease surveillance and in mitigation, and (3) low-income groups are less able to cope with school closures or other social distancing programs because they may hold hourly-wage jobs with less generous leave policies. Although plausible, there is little existing evidence of disparate health impacts of pandemic infectious disease outbreaks by socioeconomic status in the USA.[29] This type of research would be useful, and the H1N1 pandemic may have provided an opportunity to evaluate prevalence rates controlling for socioeconomic factors.

Just as evidence of disparate age or health impacts are important to tailoring epidemiological responses, disparate impacts by income might imply different approaches to a benefit–cost analysis. In other words, should we treat programs that reduce illness and death in an economically disadvantaged group differently? Even without disparate impacts, applying "distributional" or "equity" weights to groups by income may affect the results of a BCA. The use of distributional weights in economic analysis to accomplish equity goals has been widely discussed in standard benefit–cost texts (Sugden and Williams, 1978; Zerbe and Dively, 1994; Brent, 1996; Boardman et al., 2005), but has rarely been implemented in practice. Economists for several decades have generally agreed that analyses should focus on increasing economic efficiency and take the existing income distribution as given. According to Pearce (1997, p. 212), "the procedure for integrating efficiency and equity into project appraisal fell largely into disuse, partly because it was not always easy to see the scientific basis for the equity weights,[30] but partly because using projects to correct for fundamental inequities in income distribution is the wrong way to deal with inequality." Although US OMB (2003) recommends providing "a separate description of distributional effects (i.e., how both benefits and costs are distributed among sub-populations of particular concern)," it does not recommend explicitly applying equity weights. For more recent approaches to incorporating equity into economic analysis without using equity weights, interested readers should consult Adler (2008) and Graham (2008).

Similarly, cost-effectiveness analysis has generally avoided the use of distributional weights. Gold et al. (1996, p. 24) discuss distributional equity noting that the "assumption that all QALYs are valued equally may lead to some ethically unsettling distributional implications," though the guidelines do not recommend the use of distributional weights. As noted earlier, however, there has been some use of age weights in the calculation of DALYs (Murray et al., 2000), where health improvements or prevented deaths are weighted more heavily for working-age adults.

Of the economic evaluations of PHP/PM programs I reviewed, several used epidemiological models to separate populations by age, gender, and occupation (principally to identify high-risk occupations like frontline health workers). Unsurprisingly, none attempted to quantify impacts by socioeconomic status, and thus did not attempt to explicitly weight outcomes.

I will leave suggested principles and standards on this topic to another paper in this project examining methods for incorporating distributional equity (Loomis and Gonzalez-Caban, 2010). As noted earlier, however, research on whether pandemics impact socioeconomic groups within the USA differently would be helpful. If such impacts occurred, it would be important to separately report benefits and costs for various groups as US OMB (2003) suggests.

3.8 Valuing Mortality Risk

As described in section 2, a key distinction between CEA and BCA is the monetization of health impacts. For many health programs, how the analyst values changes in mortality risk will be a key decision. This will also be true for many or most pandemics like influenza or SARS that do not have long-lasting morbidity effects in many patients but do cause a number of premature deaths.

There has been an extensive discussion in both the economic and policy analysis literature on the proper approach for valuing mortality risk changes, largely in response to environmental regulations in the USA like the Clean Air Act. Readers who come from backgrounds where CEA predominates may be unfamiliar with this large literature, and with the fact that the concept of mortality risk valuation is now well established in regulatory BCAs. As described above, the two sources for establishing WTP for risk reduction that are theoretically consistent with the BCA framework are revealed preference (typically wage hedonic studies or safety product studies) and stated preference (contingent valuation or stated choice). The EPA convened a Science Advisory Board panel in 2009 to review the agency's 2010 White Paper *Valuing Mortality Risk Reductions for Environmental Policy*[31] and Robinson (2007) reviews estimates used in government regulation. There have also been two recent contingent valuation studies that examined WTP for mortality risk reduction in the context of pandemics. Gyrd-Hansen et al. (2008) examined WTP for a course of the antiviral drug Tamiflu in Norway, and Liu et al. (2005) examined WTP for a hypothetical vaccine against the SARS virus in Taiwan.

The most important continuing source of debate in the profession is whether to use "differentiated" VSLs for different population sub-groups (e.g., by age, income, health status, or voluntariness of risk) or for different rule-making settings (e.g., cancer vs pandemics).[32] This is an important debate in the context of pandemic planning and mitigation because of the differential impacts likely to be observed by age, health status, and risk. Although representative of preferences found in a number of revealed and stated preference studies, differentiation has proven controversial. An attempt by US EPA to use an age-adjusted VSL estimate in 2003 was characterized by the media as a "senior death discount," triggering a public backlash. The proposal was subsequently dropped by the US EPA. US OMB (2003) does not recommend using differentiated VSL estimates, and provides a range of VSL estimates from $1 million to $10 million while not endorsing a specific value. The US EPA (2008) continues to recommend using a central estimate of $7.3 million per life saved (in 2009 dollars), while recommending analysts note the limitations inherent in using a single estimate and presenting the distribution of impacts by age or risk category if possible. As noted above, the US EPA has also convened a Science Advisory Board panel that is expected to take up this topic further.

Of the four PHP/PM benefit–cost studies reviewed, three use the human capital approach to value mortality risk reductions, and one does not attempt a monetization at all.[33] None of the studies use estimates of individual WTP for risk reductions (e.g., a value of a statistical life [VSL] calculation).

In summary, there is a large amount of evidence suggesting that it is possible to derive a welfare-theoretic measure of individuals' WTP for mortality risk reductions and the practice of incorporating these values into BCAs is now well accepted in government practice in the USA and elsewhere. The question of what estimates to use, and whether there is sufficient evidence to justify the use of differentiated estimates, continues to evolve. Analysts should consult current guidance from the US OMB. Because much of the research and policy decisions on VSLs involve environmental rules, analysts should also be sure to consult the US EPA's most current estimates and recommended practices in this area. As the US EPA suggests, where analysts can quantify the impacts of a PHP/PM program by age, health status or risk, they should present this analysis in the BCA without necessarily applying differential values. When using a central estimate of WTP for mortality risk reduction, this parameter should clearly be included in a univariate sensitivity analysis (reporting a break-even VSL would be helpful) as well as any probabilistic Monte Carlo analysis.

3.9 Externalities

An externality occurs when a transaction imposes costs on (or provides benefits to) a party outside that transaction. These are sometimes called "spillover" effects, and represent a market failure. In public health, the presence of positive or negative externalities is one justification used for public provision of health services. There are several types of externalities that may be relevant to a BCA of PHP/PM and which should be included in the analysis where sufficient data exist and where appropriate to the scale of the analysis. These include the possibility of positive externalities from vaccination or antiviral treatment and negative externalities from increasing microbial resistance.

Vaccines against some types of diseases provide indirect protection.[34] As the vaccinated population increases, the remaining unvaccinated population enjoys a lower probability of infection (i.e., "herd immunity"). The policy response here is old and uncontroversial in theory (Pigou, 1920): vaccines will be underprovided in the private market, and a Pigouvian subsidy is needed to equate marginal costs with marginal social benefits. The extent of the externality *may* justify public provision with no user fees, although free provision runs the risk of vaccinating a higher fraction of the population than is socially optimal (i.e., the disease can be eradicated with less than 100 percent coverage precisely because of herd immunity).

Although vaccines are often cited as a textbook example of a positive externality, relatively few economic evaluations of health interventions have included an analysis of the effect of vaccination externalities (some exceptions include Beutels et al., 2002; Brisson and Edmunds, 2003; and Jeuland et al., 2009). There has been only one study to attempt to identify the socially optimal vaccine subsidy with field data (Cook et al., 2008). Widespread treatment with antiviral drugs like Tamiflu may also produce positive externalities if they reduce virus loads in infected patients and thus shedding of the virus to others (analogous to the effect of widespread use of anti-retrovirals on HIV/AIDS prevalence).

To the extent that epidemiological data are available on the magnitude of indirect protection from either targeted vaccination[35] or provision of antivirals, these should be incorporated into economic evaluations of such programs using either a static model (like Jeuland et al., 2009) or a stochastic, agent-based model (like the one used in Sander et al., 2009, although they did not model vaccination or treatment externalities).

A second externality is the potential for the infectious agent to involve resistance to antimicrobial treatment (Regoes and Bonhoeffer, 2006). Building on earlier work by Stilianakis et al. (1998), Alexander et al. (2007) use a mathematical modeling approach to show the connection between various antiviral treatment strategies and the potential for the resistance emerging (although the paper attempts no economic analysis). It may be possible, however, to incorporate these externalities into either a CEA framework as an indirect cost in the numerator or a BCA framework. The best economic work to date on this resistance externality is on resistance to antibiotics (Laxminarayan, 2002) and anti-malarial treatments (Laxminarayan et al., 2006). There is sufficient evidence for anti-microbial resistance for many diseases that analysts in most cases should make an attempt to incorporate this into their analysis, again either through a static model or stochastic agent-based models. These models should allow the effectiveness of a treatment to vary stochastically and negatively correlated with the level of use of the treatment.

Finally, economic evaluation of containment strategies across jurisdictional borders presents a similar problem, though not technically an externality. Areas with poor quality public health infrastructure may allow a nascent outbreak to spread to areas that have invested heavily in preparation and monitoring. Barring drastic and high-cost measures such as complete border closures, cessation of air travel, and trade restrictions, a more prepared region or country may be unable to contain the disease.[36]

At the international level, the principal policy of interest may be in investments to strengthen public health systems in poor countries that may be the source of the initial outbreak (e.g., SARS, avian influenza, multidrug-resistant tuberculosis).[37] A full social benefit–cost analysis of such an investment program, however, would be extremely difficult. There is little epidemiological research to provide support for the magnitude of the spillover effects, and finding appropriate shadow prices would be more analytically and ethically challenging still. For example, should different shadow prices for prevented deaths be used in different countries? Furthermore, strengthening public health systems in poor countries would potentially create large social benefits in the country, which donor countries may value for humanitarian reasons beyond pandemic containment. Although perhaps a useful exercise for large donors in the health sector or multilateral agencies (WHO, World Bank), a national agency like the US CDC would be unlikely to set its planning area for an analysis so wide.

Within the USA, should an analysis of public health preparedness spending in one county or state incorporate the spillover benefits to a neighboring county or state? Ideally, the scope of analysis would be large enough to encompass all relevant benefits and costs of a program. Still, I am unaware of completed evaluations of the economic value of surveillance or monitoring systems, even at the federal level.[38] The value of information for planning responses may also be quite high. As suggested in Handel et al. (2007), it is critical that, at an early stage of an outbreak, information on the transmission characteristics of the pathogen be determined and provided to disease modelers. This would allow them to evaluate the potential effectiveness of various control strategies. Again, though, the epidemiological data seem to be lacking, and I am unaware of research examining whether county-level public health spending is correlated with the number of reported cases during a pandemic (i.e., how effective is local preparedness in practice?).[39] Although crucial in identifying the optimal level of PHP spending at both the local and national levels, incorporating these effects would seem impractical at this stage.

4 CONCLUDING REMARKS

This chapter has illustrated a number of issues that might arise in conducting economic analyses of public health preparedness or pandemic mitigation programs. Some of the issues raised have been debated extensively elsewhere, such as the choice of a social discount rate, the importance of sensitivity analyses, and the use of distributional weights. Other issues such as incorporating externalities or macroeconomic effects have received less attention in the economic evaluation literature. The aim has been to begin a discussion of appropriate principles and standards on both types of issues.

When might benefit–cost analysis be preferred to cost-effectiveness analysis? The choice of methodologies can unfortunately be contentious, and may be driven by the academic training and peer groups of analysts more than underlying theoretical justifications. I humbly offer a few thoughts in conclusion.

As described above, many of the policies and programs for pandemic mitigation may have large economic costs outside the health sector. Proponents of CEA might argue that those additional indirect costs should simply be added to the numerator of the cost-effectiveness ratio; the objective would remain minimizing illness and death at lowest cost. This is the approach taken by Sander et al. (2009). Considerations such as constrained health capacity could also be incorporated into the CEA framework as well (Beutels et al., 2008). When examining policies to prevent the spread of a pandemic that is under way (i.e., containment or mitigation strategies), it may well make the most sense to continue to use CEA to improve the technical efficiency with which health funds that have already been allocated should be spent.

There is, of course, no guarantee that a strategy with the lowest cost-effectiveness ratio would pass a benefit–cost test. That would require an understanding of how individuals value a QALY saved or DALY avoided; most importantly, it involves understanding how individuals value reductions in mortality risk. However, given the likely magnitude of the macroeconomic costs of a pandemic, it would appear a priori that many containment and mitigation interventions would likely pass a benefit–cost test. The risk of a costly policy mistake would seem low, though this is an empirical question

Public health preparedness problems, however, may lend themselves more to BCA methods. Here the principal issue is not simply which policies or programs will "work" best, but what overall level of preparation society is willing to pay for. This can still be incorporated into a CEA framework, but the derivation of the QALY or DALY effect will depend very heavily on the assumed probability of a pandemic occurring. This probability will also drive the BCA analysis, but it may be more transparent to present these trade-offs in a BCA framework. Returning to the ventilator example mentioned in the introduction, how many ventilators should the US stockpile for pandemic influenza? Ventilators (and the health professionals trained to use them) will not slow the spread of a pandemic, but will greatly enhance the health system's ability to minimize deaths from influenza or other acute respiratory illnesses. They are, however, very costly. By using information on how individuals reveal or report trading income for reductions in mortality risk,[40] it might be straightforward to identify the socially optimal level of ventilator (and staff) investments that would equate marginal costs and marginal benefits. A similar argument could be made for the optimal size of stockpiles of poorly targeted vaccines or antivirals, though these calculations would be more complicated for several reasons,[41] including the externality of indirect protection.

In either approach, however, analysts should first and foremost bear in mind that their economic evaluations should serve as useful decision-making aids for policy-makers. They should also aim to make clear the trade-offs that policy-makers face in designing public policies and making investment decisions, especially when some of those trade-offs may not be immediately apparent. I would echo Weinstein et al. (2003) and Garrison (2003) that health economic analyses should first and foremost be transparent and reasonable.

NOTES

1. "Pandemic H1N1 2009, Update 89," accessed 6 October 2012 at http://www.who.int/csr/don/2010_02_26/en/index.html.
2. http://www.cdc.gov/h1n1flu/estimates_2009_h1n1.htm#Table, accessed 6 October 2012.
3. I will generally use the term "pandemic" throughout the chapter, although epidemic

and pandemic are not synonymous. A pandemic is an epidemic that "occurs over a very wide area (several countries or continents) and usually affects a large proportion of the population" (http://www.cdc.gov/reproductivehealth/epiglossary/glossary.htm, accessed 6 October 2012). An endemic infectious disease is one that is present on a regular basis in an area, such as seasonal influenza in the USA, or malaria in sub-Saharan Africa.

4. "Hospitals short on ventilators if bird flu hits," *New York Times*, 12 March 2006, accessed 6 October 2012 at http://www.nytimes.com/2006/03/12/national/12vent.html.
5. For more on the economics of terrorism and homeland security, see the CREATE program (create.usc.edu), or Richardson et al. (2007). In addition, the journal *Medical Decision-Making* recently published a special issue discussing bioterrorism; see Vol. 29, No. 4, July–August 2009. Finally, the Institute of Medicine commissioned an expert panel evaluating the costs and benefits of its BioWatch program, as well as "enhanced national surveillance through hospitals" (described in more detail below). See http://www8.nationalacademies.org/cp/ProjectView.aspx?key=HSPX-H-08-03-A, accessed 6 October 2012.
6. This section draws heavily from James and Sargent (2006, pp. 5–16).
7. Researchers interested in conducting or evaluating a study eliciting QALY weights should consult IOM (2006) for best practices in these survey techniques.
8. See http://www.nice.org.uk/newsroom/features/measuringeffectivenessandcosteffectivenesstheqaly.jsp, accessed 6 October 2012.
9. In other words, which groups have "standing" in the analysis. This will generally hinge on the purview of the agency conducting the analysis (i.e., state vs federal).
10. It is well known that benefit–cost *ratios* can be misleading because (1) the placement of categories of benefits in the numerator versus the denominator can change b/c ratios and (2) ratios can hide differences in the scale of projects, potentially favoring many smaller projects (each of which has a high b/c ratio but provides small net benefits in absolute terms) rather than larger projects with lower b/c ratios but higher net benefits in absolute terms. Internal rates of return, or the discount rate that equalizes benefits and costs, is also not a reliable decision criterion from the perspective of welfare economics.
11. As noted earlier, QALY and DALY measures already include morbidity. This will not be double-counting if respondents were carefully told to exclude these potential costs of illness during the elicitation process for QALY weights, as is recommended by Gold et al. (1996).
12. There are a number of forthcoming papers on valuation of both morbidity as well as mortality risks from a large, representative web panel of Americans. The research group was headed by Trudy Cameron and J.R. DeShazo; for more information, see http://pages.uoregon.edu/cameron/vita/, accessed 7 October 2012.
13. This requirement began with President Reagan's Executive Order 12291 (1981), and was updated under President Clinton in 1993 (Exec. Order 12866) and G.W. Bush in 2002 and 2007 (Exec. Orders 13258 and 13422). Exec. Order 12866 requires an assessment of benefits and costs of any regulation expected to "have an annual effect on the economy of $100 million or more or adversely affect in a material way the economy, a sector of the economy, productivity, competition, jobs, the environment, public health or safety, of State, local or tribal governments or communities."
14. See http://www.who.int/choice/en/, accessed 7 October 2012.
15. See http://www.nice.org.uk/. Cost-effectiveness analysis is used extensively to support decision-making in the UK's National Health Service.
16. See also *The Economist*, 2 May 2009, "Flu and the global economy: the butcher's bill."
17. Based in chained 2000 dollars, Bureau of Economic Analysis (http://www.bea.gov/national/index.htm#gdp, accessed June 2009).
18. First quarter of 2009, in current dollars. Accessed from Bureau of Economic Analysis, June 2009.

19. I address principally parameter uncertainty here, although it is important for analysts to also acknowledge and test for model uncertainty. Since most of this type of uncertainty comes in the approach for modeling epidemiological effects, I defer to the existing standards for CEA (Gold et al., 1996; Weinstein et al., 2003), as well as a recent paper specifically targeted at modeling disaster responses (Brandeau et al., 2003).
20. One interesting source for these probabilities may be "prediction markets"—see Philip Polgreen's presentation at the 7 October 2009 session on pandemics at Resources for the Future (http://www.rff.org/events/pages/the-economics-of-pandemics.aspx, accessed 7 October 2012).
21. As discussed above, these cutoffs are fairly arbitrary and not grounded in what consumers might or might not be willing to pay for the health effects of interest.
22. Annex 1 of the recent WHO guidance (WHO, 2009) provides the most up-to-date information on assumptions that analysts should make about these first two categories of uncertain parameters.
23. The shelf life for oseltamivir (Tamiflu) is five years (Siddiqui and Edmunds, 2008).
24. Constant exponential discounting applies a discount weight to benefits or costs occurring in time t of the form $w_t = 1/(1 + r)^t$, where r is the discount rate. Hyperbolic discount weights are of the form $w_t = (1 + \alpha t)^{-r/\alpha}$.
25. Circular A-94 does permit an analyst to use the SPC approach with "OMB concurrence."
26. http://www.whitehouse.gov/omb/circulars_a094_a94_appx-c/, accessed 7 October 2012.
27. It is interesting to note that Gold et al. (1996, p. 159) recommend that "costs and health effects should be discounted to present value at a rate consistent with the shadow price of capital (SPC) approach to evaluating public investments" and recommend a 3 percent real discount rate; in practice most studies seem to have adopted the latter recommendation but not the former.
28. The cost of health care has in fact increased considerably faster than overall price inflation in the USA (inflation-adjusted health spending has taken an increasingly larger share of GDP). See Chernew et al. (2003). It is certainly possible to use only the health care components of the CPI to correct for this.
29. Differences between rich and poor countries, however, are clearer (Bloom and Canning, 2006). In addition to vast differences in public health infrastructure and other private and public health investments, resource-poor countries may not have access to limited supplies of antivirals and vaccines in the event of an outbreak. This is an important ethical consideration raised in the WHO's recent guidance on pandemic influenza planning (WHO, 2009). In practice, it seems unlikely that a global-level economic analysis of mitigation programs like stockpiling would be carried out, as there is currently neither a centralized purchasing mechanism large enough to accomplish the task nor institutional rules about how limited supplies would be distributed.
30. Several authors have attempted to back-calculate the distributional weights implied by various government policies such as progressive income taxation or railroad closures in the UK (see Brent, 1996 and Boardman et al., 2005).
31. The most recent Science Advisory Board panel on VSL was convened in September 2009. See http://yosemite.epa.gov/sab/sabproduct.nsf/298E1F50F844BC23852578DC0059A616/$File/EPA-SAB-11-011-unsigned.pdf, accessed 14 October 2012.
32. For an introduction to this topic, see Viscusi (2010) and Robinson (2009). Aldy and Viscusi (2007) summarize the evidence for heterogeneous WTP for risk reductions from revealed preference studies, and Krupnick (2007) reviews the evidence from stated preference studies.
33. The study is framed as a "lower-bound" benefit–cost analysis, but given that estimates for WTP for mortality risk are widely available, omitting this category of benefits might lead one to question whether the study could be properly called a benefit–cost analysis.
34. This externality will tend to be larger for diseases that depend primarily on human hosts, and smaller (or zero) for diseases that also have non-human hosts or can survive for long periods of time in the environment.

35. There is, at least, evidence of indirect protection for annual influenza vaccination (Reichert et al., 2001).
36. Although several studies use stochastic models to evaluate the effectiveness of various containment strategies (Cooper et al., 2006; Colizza et al., 2007), I am unaware of any studies that have attempted a cost-effectiveness or benefit–cost analysis of these strategies.
37. Another analogous policy would be to improve *reporting* of disease outbreaks and information sharing, even if the public health systems themselves are not improved. China's delay in reporting early SARS is believed to have increased the scope of the SARS outbreak. See "Learning from SARS, China vows swift flu reporting," ABC News, 27 April 2009.
38. Congress directed the National Academies to "evaluate the effectiveness of BioWatch [described in Section 1]," including a comparison of benefits and costs as well as "the benefits and costs of an enhanced national surveillance system that relies on U.S. hospitals and the U.S. public health system." The expert committee issued their report in 2009, later published as National Research Council (2011). The committee described the challenges in modeling the costs of the surveillance systems (see Appendix C of NRC, 2011), but did not attempt to monetize the benefits, instead discussing the "merits" of the program.
39. Bloom and Canning (2006) discuss the correlation between income and epidemics at the national level. One problem with a county-level analysis that would arise is measurement error—areas with lower levels of public health infrastructure might be less likely to detect and report cases.
40. One issue that arises would be "benefits transfer," or the use of shadow prices derived in one application or setting to another. Many of the existing revealed preference studies of WTP for mortality risk reductions are from labor market studies where the mortality risks are of fatal on-the-job injuries. Many of the stated preference studies have been in the context of familiar conditions with long latency periods (i.e., cancer, diabetes, heart disease). Individuals may view reductions in the risk of dying from a sudden and widespread pandemic differently because of fear, dread, and so on.
41. Because the shelf life for oseltamivir (Tamiflu) is five years, optimal stockpiling policies are of particular economic interest (Siddiqui and Edmunds, 2008). Although several of the evaluations described in the appendix discuss stockpiling, only one uses them in an optimization framework. Rowthorn et al. (2009) combine an epidemiologic model with an economic optimization approach to find the optimal strategy for allocating a fixed stockpile of antiviral drugs when outbreaks occur in two locations. Using an objective of minimizing the discounted sum of total infection in the two regions, they find that the seemingly intuitive strategy of deploying the most resources to the area with the highest number of infected is in fact the worst possible strategy. They instead find that the optimal strategy is to treat the area with the highest number of susceptibles (and thus lowest number of infected) preferentially. The result is robust to several extensions and assumptions, although the authors note that further work combining economic optimization with epidemiological modeling is needed.

REFERENCES

Adler, Matthew D. (2008), "Risk equity: a new proposal," *Harvard Environmental Law Review*, **32**, 1–47.

Aldy, Joseph E. and W. Kip Viscusi (2007), "Age differences in the value of statistical life: Revealed preference evidence," *Review of Environment and Economic Policy*, **1** (2), 241–60.

Alexander, Murray E. and Christopher S. Bowman et al. (2007), "Emergence

of drug resistance: Implications for antiviral control of pandemic influenza," *Proceedings of the Royal Society B: Biological Sciences*, **274**, 1675–84.
Arrow, Kenneth and Robert Solow et al. (1993), "Report of the NOAA Panel on contingent valuation," *Federal Register*, **58** (10), 4601–14.
Balicer, Ran and Michael Huerta et al. (2005), "Cost–benefit of stockpiling drugs for influenza pandemic," *Emerging Infectious Diseases*, **11** (8), 1280–82.
Balicer, Ran D. and Saad B. Omer et al. (2006), "Local public health workers' perceptions toward responding to an influenza pandemic," *BMC Public Health*, **6** (99).
Barry, John M. (2004), *The Great Influenza: The Epic Story of the Deadliest Plague in History*, New York: Viking.
Beutels, Philippe and W. John Edmunds et al. (2002), "Economic evaluation of vaccination programmes: A consensus statement focusing on viral hepatitis," *Pharmacoeconomics*, **20** (1), 1–7.
Beutels, Philippe and W. John Edmunds et al. (2008), "Partially wrong? Partial equilibrium and the economic analysis of public health emergencies of international concern," *Health Economics*, **17** (11), 1317–22.
Blendon, Robert J. and Lisa M. Koonin et al. (2008), "Public response to community mitigation measures for pandemic influenza," *Emerging Infectious Diseases*, **14** (5), 778–86.
Bloom, David E. and David Canning (2006), "Epidemics and economics," *Program on Global Demography of Aging Working Paper*, Boston: Harvard Center for Population and Development Studies.
Bloom, Eric and Vincent de Wit et al. (2005), "Potential economic impact of an avian flu pandemic on Asia," *Economics and Research Department Policy Brief*, Manila: Asian Development Bank.
Boardman, Anthony and David H. Greenberg et al. (2005), *Cost–Benefit Analysis: Concepts and Practices*, Upper Saddle River, NJ: Prentice Hall.
Brandeau, Margaret L. and Greg S. Zaric et al. (2003), "Resource allocation for control of infectious diseases in multiple independent populations: Beyond cost-effectiveness analysis," *Journal of Health Economics*, **22** (4), 575–98.
Brent, Robert J. (1996), *Applied Cost–Benefit Analysis*, Cheltenham, UK and Brookfield, VT, USA: Edward Elgar.
Brisson, Marc and William J. Edmunds (2003), "Economic evaluations of vaccination programs: The impact of herd immunity," *Medical Decision Making*, **23** (1), 76–82.
Conference Board of Canada (2003), "The economic impact of SARS," accessed 7 October 2012 at http://www.conferenceboard.ca/e-Library/abstract.aspx?did=539.
Cauchemez, Simon and Neil M. Ferguson et al. (eds) (2009), "Closure of schools during an influenza pandemic," *The Lancet Infectious Diseases*, **9** (8), 473–81.
Caulkins, Jonathan P. (2002), "Using models that incorporate uncertainty," *Journal of Policy Analysis and Management*, **21** (3), 486–91.
Chernew, Michael E. and Richard A. Hirth et al. (2003), "Increased spending on health care: How much can the United States afford?, *Health Affairs*, **22** (4), 15–25.
Colizza, Vittoria and Alain Barrat et al. (2007), "Modeling the worldwide spread of pandemic influenza: Baseline case and containment interventions," *PLoS Medicine*, **4** (1), e13.
Cook, Joseph and Marc Jeuland et al. (2008), "Using private demand studies to

calculate socially optimal vaccine subsidies in developing countries," *Journal of Policy Analysis and Management*, **28** (1), 6–28.
Cooper, Ben S. and Richard J. Pitman et al. (2006), "Delaying the international spread of pandemic influenza," *PLoS Medicine*, **3** (6), 845–55.
Drummond, Michael F. and Tom Jefferson (1996), "Guidelines for authors and peer reviewers of economic submissions to the BMJ," *British Medical Journal*, **313** (7052), 275–83.
Drummond, Michael F. and Bernie O'Brien et al. (1997), *Methods for the Economic Evaluation of Health Care Programmes*, Oxford: Oxford University Press.
Effler, Paul V. and Dale Carcione et al. (2010), "Household responses to pandemic (H1N1) 2009-related school closures, Perth Australia," *Emerging Infectious Diseases*, **16** (2), 205–11.
Ferguson, Neil and Dale A.T. Cummings et al. (2006), "Strategies for mitigating an influenza pandemic," *Nature*, **442** (7101), 448–52.
Fowler, Robert A. and Gillian Sanders et al. (2005), "Cost-effectiveness of defending against bioterrorism: A comparison of vaccination and antibiotic prophylaxis against anthrax," *Annals of Internal Medicine*, **142** (8), 601–11.
Freeman, A. Myrick (1999), *The Measurement of Environmental and Resource Values: Theory and Methods*, Washington, DC: Resources for the Future.
Garrison, Lou P. (2003), "The ISPOR good practice modeling principles: A sensible approach: be transparent, be reasonable," *Value in Health*, **6** (1), 6–8.
Germann, Timothy C. and Kai Kadau et al. (2006), "Mitigation strategies for pandemic influenza in the United States," *PNAS*, **103** (15), 5935–40.
Gold, Marthe R. and Joanna E. Siegel et al. (eds) (1996), *Cost-effectiveness in Health and Medicine*, New York: Oxford University Press.
Graham, John D. (2008), "Saving lives through administrative law and economics," *University of Pennsylvania Law Review*, **157** (2), 101–244.
Gyrd-Hansen, Dorte and Peder A. Halvorsen et al. (2008), "Willingness to pay for a statistical life in the times of a pandemic," *Health Economics*, **17** (1), 55–66.
Haddix, Anne C. and Steven M. Teutsch et al. (eds) (2003), *Prevention Effectiveness: A Guide to Decision Analysis and Economic Valuation*, New York, Oxford University Press.
Handel, Andreas and Ira M. Longini Jr. et al. (2007), "What is the best control strategy for multiple infectious disease outbreaks?" *Proceedings of the Royal Society B: Biological Sciences*, **274**, 833–7.
Hatchett, Richard J. and Carter E. Mecher et al. (2007), "Public health interventions and epidemic intensity during the 1918 influenza pandemic," *PNAS*, **104** (18), 7582–7.
Institute of Medicine (IOM) (2006), *Valuing Health for Regulatory Cost-effectiveness Analysis*, Washington, DC: National Academies Press.
James, Steven and Tim Sargent (2006), "The economic impact of an influenza pandemic," *Canadian Department of Finance Working Paper*.
Jamison, Dean T. and Joel G. Breman et al. (eds) (2006), *Disease Control Priorities in Developing Countries*, Washington, DC: The World Bank and Oxford University Press.
Jeuland, Marc and John Clemens et al. (2009), "Incorporating herd protection into cost-effectiveness calculations of new-generation oral cholera vaccines: a multi-site analysis," *Value in Health*, **12** (6), 899–908.
Johnson, April J. and Zach S. Moore et al. (2008), "Household responses to school

closure resulting from outbreak of influenza B, North Carolina," *Emerging Infectious Diseases*, **14** (7), 1024–30.

Jonung, Lars and Werner Roeger (2006), "The macroeconomic effects of a pandemic in Europe—a model-based assessment," *Economics Papers*, European Commission Directorate-General for Economic and Financial Affairs.

Just, Richard E. and Darrell L. Hueth et al. (2004), *The Welfare Economics of Public Policy*, Cheltenham, UK and Northampton, MA, USA: Edward Elgar.

Kennedy, Steve and Jim Thomson et al. (2006), "A primer on the macroeconomic effects of an influenza pandemic," *US Treasury Working Paper*, Washington, DC.

Keogh-Brown, Marcus and Simon Wren-Lewis et al. (2009), "The possible macroeconomic impact on the UK of an influenza pandemic," University of Oxford Department of Economics Discussion Paper Series, Oxford, UK.

Krupnick, Alan (2007), "Mortality-risk valuation and age: stated preference evidence," *Review of Environmental Economics and Policy*, **1** (2), 261–82.

Krupnick, Alan and Richard Morgenstern et al. (2006), *Not a Sure Thing: Making Regulatory Choices under Uncertainty*, Washington, DC: Resources for the Future.

Langton, Danielle (2008), "Avian flu pandemic: Potential impacts of trade disruptions," Washington, DC: Congressional Research Service.

Laxminarayan, Ramanan (2002), *Battling Resistance to Antibiotics and Pesticides: An Economic Approach*, Washington, DC: Resources for the Future Press.

Laxminarayan, Ramanan and Mead Over et al. (2006), "Will a global subsidy of new antimalarials delay the emergence of resistance and save lives?," *Health Affairs*, **25** (2), 325–36.

Lipscomb, Joseph and K. Robin Yabroff et al. (2009), "Health care costing: Data, methods, current applications," *Medical Care*, **47** (7), S1–S6.

Liu, Jin-Tan and James K. Hammitt et al. (2005), "Valuation of the risk of SARS in Taiwan," *Health Economics*, **14** (1), 83–91.

Loomis, John and Armando Gonzalez-Caban (2010), "How two non-market valuation techniques can improve compliance with environmental justice requirements: Three case studies using hedonic property and contingent valuation methods to quantify the distribution of benefits by ethnicity and income," Benefit–Cost Analysis Center, University of Washington.

McKibbin, Warwick and Alexandra Sidorenko (2006), "Global macroeconomic consequences of pandemic influenza," Research Paper, Sydney, Australia: Lowy Institute for International Policy, Australian National University.

Meltzer, Martin and Nancy J. Cox et al. (1999), "The economic impact of pandemic influenza in the United States: Priorities for intervention," *Emerging Infectious Diseases*, **5** (5), 659–71.

Meltzer, Martin I. and Kathleen M. Neuzil et al. (2005), "An economic analysis of annual influenza vaccination of children," *Vaccine*, **23** (8), 1004–14.

Middaugh, John P. (2008), "Pandemic influenza preparedness and community resiliency," *Journal of the American Medical Association*, **299** (5), 566–8.

Morgan, M. Granger and Max Henrion (1990), *Uncertainty: A Guide to Dealing with Uncertainty in Quantitative Risk and Policy Analysis*, New York: Cambridge University Press.

Murray, Christopher and Alan D. Lopez (eds) (1996), *The Global Burden of Disease: A Comprehensive Assessment of Mortality and Disability from Diseases, Injuries and Risk Factors in 1990 and Projected to 2020*, Global Burden of Disease and Injury Series, Cambridge, MA: Harvard University Press.

Murray, Christopher J.L. and David B. Evans et al. (2000), "Development of WHO guidelines on generalized cost-effectiveness analysis," *Health Economics*, **9** (3), 235–51.

Musgrove, Philip and Julia Fox-Rushby (2006), "Cost-effectiveness analysis for priority setting," in Dean T. Jamison, Joel G. Breman and Anthony R. Measham et al. (eds), *Disease Control Priorities in Developing Countries*, Washington, DC: The World Bank.

National Research Council (2011), *BioWatch and Public Health Surveillance: Evaluating Systems for the Early Detection of Biological Threats: Abbreviated Version*, Washington, DC: The National Academies Press.

Newell, Richard G. and William A. Pizer (2003), "Discounting the distant future: How much do uncertain rates increase valuations?" *Journal of Environmental Economics and Management*, **46** (1), 52–71.

Nichol, Kristin (2001), "Cost–benefit analysis of a strategy to vaccinate healthy working adults against influenza," *Archives of Internal Medicine*, **161** (5), 749–59.

Nichol, K.L. (2003), "The efficacy, effectiveness and cost-effectiveness of inactivated influenza virus vaccines," *Vaccine*, **21**, 1769–75.

Pearce, David W. (1997), "Benefit–cost analysis, environment and health in the developed and developing world," *Environment and Development Economics*, **2** (2), 210–14.

Pigou, Arthur C. (1920), *The Economics of Welfare*, London: Macmillan.

Portney, Paul R. and John P. Weyant (eds) (1999), *Discounting and Intergenerational Equity*, Washington, DC: Resources for the Future Press.

Regoes, Roland R. and Sebastian Bonhoeffer (2006), "Emergence of drug-resistant influenza virus: Population dynamical considerations," *Science*, **312** (5772), 389–91.

Reichert, Thomas A. and Norio Sugaya et al. (2001), "The Japanese experience with vaccinating schoolchildren against influenza," *The New England Journal of Medicine*, **344** (12), 889–96.

Richardson, Harvey W. and Peter Gordon et al. (eds) (2007), *The Economic Costs and Consequences of Terrorism*, Cheltenham, UK and Northampton, MA, USA: Edward Elgar.

Robinson, Lisa A. (2007), "How US government agencies value mortality risk reductions," *Review of Environmental and Economic Policy*, **1** (2), 283–99.

Robinson, Lisa A. (2009), "Valuing lives, valuing risks and respecting preferences in regulatory analysis," *Regulation and Governance*, **3** (3), 298–305.

Robinson, Lisa A. (ed.) (2010), "Assessing regulatory costs and benefits," *Encyclopedia of Environmental Health*, Oxford: Elsevier.

Rowthorn, Robert and Ramanan Laxminarayan et al. (2009), "Optimal control of epidemics in metapopulations," *Journal of the Royal Society Interface*, **6** (41), 1135–44.

Sadique, M.Z. and Elisabeth J. Adams et al. (2008), "Estimating the costs of school closure for mitigating an influenza epidemic," *BMC Public Health*, **8** (1), 135.

Sadique, M.Z. and William J. Edmunds et al. (2007), "Precautionary behavior in response to perceived threat of pandemic influenza," *Emerging Infectious Diseases*, **13** (9), 1307–13.

Sander, Beate and Azhar Nizam et al. (2009), "Economic evaluation of influenza pandemic mitigation strategies in the USA using a stochastic microsimulation transmission model," *Value in Health*, **12** (2), 226–33.

Schmier, Jordana and Su Li et al. (2008), "Benefits and costs of immunizing children against influenza at school: An economic analysis based on a large-cluster controlled clinical trial," *Health Affairs*, **27** (2), w96.

Siddiqui, M. Ruby and W. John Edmunds (2008), "Cost-effectiveness of antiviral stockpiling and near-patient testing for potential influenza pandemic," *Emerging Infectious Diseases*, **14** (2), 267–74.

Stilianakis, Nikolaos and Alan S. Perelson et al. (1998), "Emergence of drug resistance during an influenza epidemic: Insights from a mathematical model," *Journal of Infectious Diseases*, **177** (4), 863–73.

Sugden, Robert and Alan Williams (1978), *The Principles of Practical Cost–Benefit Analysis*, New York: Oxford University Press.

US Congressional Budget Office (CBO) (2006), "A potential influenza pandemic: An update on possible macroeconomic effects and policy issues," Washington, DC: Congressional Budget Office.

US Environmental Protection Agency (EPA) (2008), *Guidelines for Preparing Economic Analysis: External Review Draft*, Washington, DC: Environmental Protection Agency.

US Office of Management and Budget (OMB) (2003), Circular A-4, "Regulatory analysis," Washington, DC: OMB.

Viscusi, W. Kip (2010), "The heterogeneity of the value of statistical life: Introduction and overview," *Journal of Risk and Uncertainty*, **40** (1), 1–13.

Viscusi, W. Kip and Joseph. E. Aldy (2003), "The value of a statistical life: a critical review of market estimates throughout the world," *Journal of Risk and Uncertainty*, **27** (1), 5–76.

Weinstein, Milton. C. and Bernie O'Brien et al. (2003), "Principles of good practice for decision analytic modeling in health-care evaluation: Report of the ISPOR Task Force on Good Research Practices¾Modeling Studies," *Value in Health*, **6** (1), 9–17.

WHO (2009), *Pandemic Influenza Preparedness and Response: A WHO Guidance Document*, Geneva: World Health Organization.

World Bank (1993), *Investing in Health*, accessed 7 October 2012 at http://files.dcp2.org/pdf/WorldDevelopmentReport1993.pdf.

Zerbe, Jr., Richard. O. (2008), *Benefit–Cost Analysis*, Cheltenham, UK and Northampton, MA, USA: Edward Elgar.

Zerbe, Jr., Richard O. and Dwight D. Dively (1994), *Benefit–Cost Analysis in Theory and Practice*, New York: Harper Collins College.

APPENDIX

A.1 Cost-effectiveness Studies of Public Health Preparedness

Sander et al. (2009) examine the cost-effectiveness (dollars per QALY gained) of several interventions for mitigating an influenza pandemic (see Table 3A.1 for a summary of this and other CEA studies on PHP/PM). They take a societal perspective of costs and benefits, and use a six-month time horizon (the time assumed to be needed to develop a more effective vaccine). Although several earlier papers explored pandemic mitigation or containment strategies with a stochastic agent-based model (Cooper et al., 2006; Ferguson et al., 2006; Germann et al., 2006; Colizza et al., 2007), Sander et al. are the first to use stochastic modeling in an *economic* evaluation. They compare 17 different combinations of: targeted antiviral prophylaxis (TAP), targeted either at the households of identified cases (they assume 60 percent of symptomatic cases can be identified), or at all contact groups of identified cases; school closures; and pre-pandemic immunization with low-efficacy vaccines. Costs of the status quo (no mitigation strategy) included physician visits, hospitalizations, and use of antibiotics and over-the-counter drugs. Households with children under 12 are assumed to lose 2.5 days of work per week if the child is sick or if schools are closed. School closure programs also cause teachers and other school professionals to lose five days of work per week. These workdays lost were valued using a human capital approach (average compensation plus fringe benefits for parents, average earnings for teachers separately). Travel and time costs were also included as costs. They also varied assumptions about the size of the stockpile of antiviral drugs (as a percentage of the population). They find that both fully targeted antiviral treatment and pre-pandemic vaccination are cost-saving from a social perspective (i.e., the reduction in health care expenditures from the base case are greater than costs of intervention). Also, the full TAP strategy reduced the 54 percent of cases at the lowest cost to society or $127 per capita.

Fowler et al. (2005) compare vaccination and antibiotic prophylaxis against a bioterrorist anthrax attack. They take a societal perspective, and examine three post-attack strategies (in addition to a baseline do-nothing strategy): vaccination alone, antibiotic prophylaxis alone, or a combination of the two. They include lost wages but not time or travel costs of vaccination or treatment. They find that, should an attack occur, a combination of vaccination and antibiotic prophylaxis is the most cost-effective strategy.

Siddiqui and Edmunds (2008) examined the cost-effectiveness of

Table 3A.1 Summary of cost-effectiveness/cost-utility studies of public health preparedness and pandemic influenza

	Country	Disease/ Problem	Interventions Evaluated	Epidemiological Approach	Macroeconomic Effects	Discount	Sensitivity Analysis
Sander et al. (2009)	USA	Pandemic flu mitigation	Cost-effectiveness of 17 strategies—targeted antiviral prophylaxis (TAP) alone and in combination with school closures and pre-vaccination	Stochastic agent-based microsimulation model	Lost work days for parents of sick children and teachers (school closure) using average wage rates	3% for life years saved	Univariate sensitivity analysis on attack rate, basic reproduction number (R_0), resource use, school closure, mortality rates
Fowler et al. (2005)	USA	Anthrax bioterrorism	Vaccination, antibiotic prophylaxis	Static, decision-analytic model	Lost work days	3%	Univariate sensitivity analysis.on probability of attack; multivariate Monte Carlo
Siddiqui and Edmunds (2008)	UK	Pandemic influenza	Stockpiling of antivirals (oseltamivir), enough to treat cases, or to treat cases and (tested) close contacts	Static, decision-analytic model	None (health care provider perspective)	3.5%, varied up to 6% in sensitivity analysis	Univariate sensitivity analysis (all params and charts for major params); multivariate Monte Carlo

stockpiling antiviral drugs in the UK. They use the baseline epidemiologic scenarios from the UK Department of Health's Pandemic Contingency plan, which assumed an attack rate of 25 percent over one wave lasting 15 weeks. They modeled a 1918 scenario with a case fatality rate of 2.3 percent and a 1957/1968–69 scenario with an overall case fatality rate of 0.3 percent. Using a static decision-analytic model, they find that stockpiling enough antivirals to treat the expected number of cases only would be cost-effective (by standards adopted for the UK's national health insurance system). A stockpiling program that also tested close contacts of index cases and treated those as well was much less cost-effective (and would not pass the threshold under any conditions if case fatality rates were as low as in 1957/1968–69).

A.2 Benefit–Cost Studies of PHP/PM

Table 3A.2 summarizes the existing BCA studies on PHP/PM. Meltzer et al. (1999) analyze the potential effects of a pandemic flu in the USA. They estimate the economic costs of an outbreak, and evaluate the costs, benefits, and policy implications of several possible vaccine-based interventions. Using a Monte Carlo simulation model the authors estimate 89 000 to 207 000 deaths; 314 000 to 734 000 hospitalizations; 18 to 42 million outpatient visits; and 20 to 47 million additional illnesses. The overall impact to the US economy is estimated between \$71.3 and \$166.5 billion, *not* including disruptions to commerce and society. Loss of life accounted for approximately 83 percent of all economic losses. If the vaccine could be provided for \$21, the authors found that a program to vaccinate the entire US population would pass a benefit–cost test. If vaccination proved more expensive (\$62 per vaccinated person), a program targeting only high-risk populations would pass a BCA, but a mass (untargeted) program would not.

Balicer et al. (2005) estimated the health-related impact of pandemic flu in Israel, calculated direct costs to the health system associated with those outcomes, and analyzed strategies for stockpiling antiviral drugs for a possible pandemic flu outbreak (including therapeutic use, long-term pre-exposure prophylaxis, and short-term post-exposure prophylaxis for close contacts of flu patients). Although the study took a social perspective and valued lost workdays (at US\$72 per day), it did not attempt to monetize the benefits of avoiding flu deaths. Even omitting this large category of economic benefits (the aim of the study was "to elicit minimum cost–benefit estimates"), the study found that current stockpiling of oseltamivir (Tamiflu) would pass a benefit–cost test if the probability of a pandemic occurring were greater than 1 in 80. Furthermore, stockpiling would be cost-saving to the health care sector (i.e., not counting work days lost) if the stockpile were only large enough to treat patients at high risk.

There have been a number of pharmacoeconomic studies on vaccination against seasonal, rather than pandemic, influenza. I will discuss one illustrative example only; interested readers can find more detail on studies of annual influenza vaccination of the elderly in Nichol (2003) and of schoolchildren in Meltzer et al. (2005) and Schmier et al. (2008). Nichol (2001) examined vaccination of healthy adults for seasonal influenza from a societal perspective. Costs of the intervention included the direct cost of vaccination (vaccine and administration), indirect costs from work absenteeism in order to be vaccinated, and direct and indirect costs from side-effects of the vaccine. Benefits (which Nichol frames as "costs averted due to vaccination") include reduced medical care, reduced work absenteeism, reduced loss of life (valued using a human capital approach), and increased "work effectiveness" (decreased work productivity was calculated by scaling down the average wages paid). Net benefits were presented in the paper per vaccinated person rather than for the program as a whole. Using a probabilistic Monte Carlo framework, Nichol estimated that net benefits averaged $13.66 per person vaccinated, though the 95 percent confidence interval included values implying a net cost of vaccination (−$2.18, $32.97). Reductions in indirect costs (lost work days and reduced productivity) accounted for 78 percent of benefits. Nearly all of the pharmacoeconomic studies reviewed in Nichol (2003) find that vaccinating the elderly against seasonal influenza would be cost-effective or even cost-saving, and Meltzer et al. (2005) and Schmier et al. (2008) find similar results for vaccinating high-risk school children.

Table 3A.2 Benefit–cost studies in public health preparedness

Author	Country	Disease/ Problem	Which Interventions	How are Lives Valued	Macroeconomic Effects	Discount	Sensitivity Analysis
Meltzer et al. (1999)	USA	Pandemic flu	Vaccination—targeted by age, risk, group	Human capital approach (~$1.0 million for those under age 65, $65 thousand for those over)	Lost work days only	3%	Multi-parameter sensitivity analysis and Monte Carlo simulation
Balicer et al. (2005)	Israel	Pandemic flu	Stockpiling antiviral drugs for (1) therapeutic use, (2) long-term pre-exposure prophlyaxis, (3) short-term post-exposure prophylaxis	Not included	Lost work days only; overall direct and indirect costs ~0.5% of Israeli GDP	3%	One-way sensitivity on the yearly probability of a pandemic
Nichol (2001)	USA	Seasonal influenza	Vaccination of healthy working adults	Human capital approach	Lost work days	3% base case, 5% "worst case scenario"	One-way sensitivity analysis on several parameters; Monte Carlo simulation

4. Principles and standards for the benefit–cost analysis of crime

John R. Lott, Jr.

1 OVERVIEW

Criminal justice involves many trade-offs. Are we spending enough on police? What are the levels of penalties for different crimes? Are there trade-offs between different types of penalties? For example, does greater reliance on criminal penalties reduce the reliance on reputational penalties?

One complicated example is the death penalty. There is still some debate over the deterrence effect of the death penalty. But even if one accepts that such deterrence exists, how large does that effect have to be to outweigh the costs? The legal process for the death penalty is costly. What are the costs of accidentally convicting innocent individuals? The death penalty might save imprisonment costs after a certain point, but executions are so delayed that the present value of those costs might be small. Numbers cannot easily be assigned to all these costs and benefits, but it is still possible to give examples of how large different values have to be for people to change their decisions on whether the death penalty passes a benefit–cost-type test.

Prison provides another interesting trade-off. Crime is overwhelmingly committed by young men. The incapacitation effect of prison is thus likely to decline with the prisoner's age. If criminals have a high discount rate (and there is considerable evidence that is true) (Block and Gerety, 1995), after a certain point lengthening prison sentences might not have much of an impact on deterring criminals. If society uses a different discount rate for the cost of imprisonment than criminals do for the penalty that they face, long prison terms might impose very little penalty on criminals despite imposing a very large financial burden on society.

There are many possible alternative methods of deterring crime. Longer prison terms are just one option. There are also issues of increasing the probability of arrest or conviction for those who are arrested. There are also private actions that can deter crime. Private reputations are one example. Others include putting locks on doors, car alarms, or people owning guns. Some of these actions involve possible externalities and we will discuss how those externalities might be measured and evaluated.

Though the range of possible estimates for many of these actions will be too large to definitively say whether the actions pass a benefit–costs test, that is not an unusual result. It is still useful to know what actions can be said to pay for themselves and which ones do not.

Cost–benefit analysis is a technique designed to determine the feasibility of a project or plan by quantifying its costs and benefits. Below is a brief rough outline of what is involved with measuring and calculating these costs and benefits.

2 FOUR TYPES OF PENALTIES

2.1 Prison, Fines, Reputations, and Collateral Penalties

There are generally four types of criminal penalties, all of which have significant costs and benefits: prison, fines, reputations, and so-called collateral penalties, the loss of the ability to hold different jobs or various rights. All these punishments deter crime, though with the exception of prison and fines there is no evidence of their different abilities to deter crime. The costs of these penalties vary dramatically. The two most costly are prison and collateral penalties. For prison, there is the obvious cost of running the prison, but there is another cost: anything beneficial that the criminal could have produced outside of prison. Many criminals might have continued spending most of their time committing crime, but others would have produced benefits that people pay for. Michael Milken might have been charged with stock parking crimes, a violation that would normally have been punished with a \$10 000 fine, but presumably there was some reason why companies were willing to pay Milken \$500 million per year to help them get financing. During the mid-1980s the average person convicted of insider trading was making \$365 000 per year in legal income prior to conviction.

Just as women's human capital depreciates when they leave the labor force to have children, putting people in prison also leads to depreciated human capital. It is possible that their human capital that facilitates their ability to commit crime increases, but there is a clear drop in earnings that occurs the longer the criminals are in prison.

In 2001 (Table 4.1), annual prison operating costs averaged \$22 600 per inmate, ranging from \$8128 in Alabama to \$44 379 in Maine (Stephan, 2004). Much of this range depends on factors beyond the control of correctional officials: differences in the cost of living, the mix

Table 4.1 Inmate prison expenditures by state in 2001

State	Annual Cost per Inmate (US$)	State	Annual Cost per Inmate (US$)	State	Annual Cost per Inmate (US$)
Alabama	8128	Kentucky	17818	North Dakota	22415
Alaska	36780	Louisiana	12951	Ohio	26295
Arizona	22476	Maine	44379	Oklahoma	16309
Arkansas	15619	Maryland	26398	Oregon	36060
California	25053	Massachusetts	37718	Pennsylvania	31900
Colorado	25408	Michigan	32525	Rhode Island	38503
Connecticut	26856	Minnesota	36836	South Carolina	16762
Delaware	22802	Mississippi	12795	South Dakota	13853
District of Columbia	26670	Missouri	12867	Tennessee	18206
		Montana	21898	Texas	13808
Florida	20190	Nebraska	25321	Utah	24574
Georgia	19860	Nevada	17572	Vermont	25178
Hawaii	21637	New Hampshire	25949	Virginia	22942
Idaho	16319			Washington	30168
Illinois	21844	New Jersey	27347	West Virginia	14817
Indiana	21841	New Mexico	28035	Wisconsin	28622
Iowa	22997	New York	36835	Wyoming	28845
Kansas	21381	North Carolina	26984		
Average by prisoner					22600
Average by state					24105

Source: Stephan (2004).

of high- and low-security prisoners, variation in prevailing wage rates, climate, building codes, as well as other factors (ibid.). For example, prisoners who are serving life sentences are very difficult to maintain. The only additional penalty that could restrain the behavior of these criminals is the threat of a death penalty. But there is no reduced prison time for good behavior.

Fines do not have many of the costs involving prison. Paying the fine does not interfere with the criminal's ability to continue working. There can be costs to collecting the fine, but those are similar to the costs of trying to put the criminal in prison. The question is whether it is easier to hide assets or the individual. However, while fines have many desirable attributes, they are not simply applicable for most criminals since the harm caused by the criminal vastly outweighs most criminals' assets.

Collateral penalties share aspects of both prison and fines. For collateral penalties, the loss of business and professional licenses, the inability to work for many unions or to work for the government, as well as the loss of the ability to own a gun, all have their own costs. A criminal conviction because of debarment is likely to result in lawyers losing their licenses, executives in the defense industry from being allowed to work in those businesses, and stockbrokers being banned from working in the securities industry (The National Advisory Commission on Criminal Justice Standards and Goals, 1973).[1] The penalties involving jobs are similar to those faced by people in prison. Even banning convicted felons being able to own guns can have its costs. The question is whether the felons will be more likely to use their guns for self-protection (many felons will presumably live in high crime areas) or whether they use the guns to commit yet more crimes. Presumably these risks vary by the type of crime the criminal was convicted of. White-collar criminals seem unlikely to be the people who are at risk of using a gun in a crime.

The debate over these collateral penalties goes back decades and the types of penalties are indeed very broad. Ex-convicts face many other forms of penalties such as being prevented from inheriting property, suffering partial or complete divestment of their assets, losing life and automobile insurance, and losing pension funds and facing the discontinuance of pension payments even if the individual is already retired (Grant et al., 1970). Since the loss of inheritance and pension funds and divestment of assets undoubtedly impose a larger absolute penalty on the well to do than it will on the poor, the estimates presented here will underestimate how much penalties increase as a function of pre-sentence income. Conviction also affects voting, parental rights, divorce, public employment, ability to serve as a juror, and holding public office. Several Presidential Task Forces have emphasized the importance of these collateral penalties and expressed concern over how ignoring collateral penalties will create inequities in criminal penalties (e.g., President's Commission, 1967, p. 88). Many of these collateral penalties, such as the loss of property or other assets, are the same as fines. Losing assets in a divorce is no different than losing assets in the form of a fine. The only difference is that these collateral penalties transfer assets to a spouse or someone else instead of as restitution to the crime victim or as a fine to the government.

Finally, reputational penalties have similarities to all the other penalties. As with prison and collateral penalties, reputational penalties can mean that employment is ended. Those who commit a crime may find that people are unwilling to hire the criminal because they no longer trust them. While the government imposes collateral penalties, reputations involve voluntary exchange, but there is another difference between prison and collateral penalties versus reputational penalties. As noted earlier, a cost of prison and collateral penalties could involve the loss of productive labor. Reputational penalties seem less likely to have the same problem since reputational penalties are only imposed voluntarily. Jobs where reputations are important in ensuring the worker's behavior will be foreclosed to those workers. Jobs where reputations are not important will not be foreclosed.

Reputations also have another similarity to fines and collateral penalties in that they apply most to the highest-income criminals. People who lose professional licenses tend to be relatively well to do. Reputations, where individuals are paid a premium, almost by definition mean that the criminal is earning a higher income.

2.2 Comparing the Penalties in Real Life

A criminal's income plays a major role in how they are penalized. Penalties thus end up being extremely progressive. If optimal penalties mean that two criminals who commit the exact same crime should face the same penalty, this penalty structure could mean that prison penalties right for low-income criminals are too high for high-income criminals. Similarly, penalties that are right for high-income criminals would be too low for low-income criminals. If the latter case is closer to the truth, it implies that we are able to get closer to the right penalty simply because fines and reputations, which are readily available for high-income criminals, are lower-cost ways of imposing penalties.

Take the case of a bank embezzler from California in the mid-1980s shown in Table 4.2 based on material in Lott (1992a, 1992b). The total criminal monetary penalty that a person bears from conviction consists of the reduction in legitimate income, the lost income while in prison, fines, legal costs, and the lost time resulting from the legal process leading up to conviction. Assuming the exact same crime in terms of the amount taken and the circumstances under which it was committed, an embezzler with an income 1 standard deviation above the mean faces a total monetary penalty that is 4.94 times greater than that for an average income embezzler. The analogous bank larcenist faces a 2.1-to-1 ratio over the one with the mean income. Therefore, if the low- and high-income criminals in both cases are to face the same expected penalties from conviction, the high-income embezzler must face a probability of conviction that is only 20.7 percent of that of the mean-income embezzler and the high-income

Table 4.2 Total monetary penalty from committing a crime (July 1984 US$)

Crime Category	Income Level	Income 12 Months Prior to Sentencing (US$)	Expected Monetary Reduction in Post-sentence Income (US$)	Expected Percentage Reduction in Post-sentence Income (%)	Expected Fine	Expected Imprisonment Times Pre-sentence Income (US$)	Expected Restitution (US$)	Total Monetary Penalty (US$)	Reduction in Post-sentence Income Divided by the Total Monetary Penalty (%)	Prob. of Convic. as a % of that for Mean*
Bank	½ mean	8406	1315	15.6	175	897	1133	3520	37.5	284
embezzle-	Mean	16813	6581	39.1	360	1769	1299	10010	65.7	100
ment	+1 std dev.	49362	40484	82.0	1052	4914	1929	48370	83.7	20.7
	+2 std dev.	81911	77232	94.3	1670	7699	2500	89130	86.7	11.2
Bank	½ mean	4127	597	14.5	315	673	1883	3468	17.2	200
larcenist	Mean	8255	3408	41.3	334	1302	1908	6952	49.0	100
	+1 std dev.	14986	10107	67.4	364	4914	1948	14654	69.0	47
	+2 std dev.	21717	17678	81.4	391	7699	1984	23117	76.5	30

Heroin/	½ mean	5580	5059	91	0	1077	5	6140	82	100
cocaine	Mean	11161	10620	95	0	2032	5	12657	84	49
distribu-	+1 std dev.	22613	22049	98	90	3893	6	26039	85	24
tion	+2 std dev.	34065	33.477	98	776	6100	7	40360	83	15
Heroin/	½ mean	6537	5778	88	24	788	3	6593	88	100
cocaine	Mean	13074	12285	94	0	1426	3	13713	90	48
possession	+1 std dev.	24792	23969	97	278	2528	4	26779	90	25
	+2 std dev.	36510	35654	98	1078	4108	4	40843	87	16
Narcotics	½ mean	3483	3276	94	162	112	1	3550	92	100
District of	Mean	6967	6751	97	78	166	1	6996	96	51
Columbia	+1 std dev.	7329	7113	97	71	169	1	7354	97	48
	+2 std dev.	7692	7475	97	66	171	1	7714	97	46

Note: * Inc. if Exp. Monetary Penalties are to be Equal (%).

larcenist a probability that is only 47 percent of that of mean income larcenist. When the corresponding values for 2 standard deviations above the mean are used, the relative probability of convictions fall to only 11 and 30 percent.

These numbers can underestimate the true differences across criminals. For example, if the real reduction in earnings persisted for five years beyond the last year of probation or parole and the real interest rate was 2 percent, the present value of lost earnings for an average bank embezzler is \$31 020 and for embezzlers with income 1 and 2 standard deviations above the mean the present values are \$190 818 and \$364 028.

2.3 Understanding the Trade-off between Government-imposed Penalties and Reputational Penalties

Government-imposed penalties are not simple substitutes for reputational penalties. Increasing government-imposed penalties will reduce the use of reputational penalties, but the trade-off is not one-to-one. Consider a simple case in which a single person is selling a product to consumers. Consumers value reducing the probability of being defrauded, but reducing that probability is costly. In the absence of government penalties, consumers can reduce the probability of fraud by having sellers face larger reputational losses or higher civil penalties for fraud.[2] Reputational penalties are costly because they arise from the quasi-rents established when consumers pay high prices for high quality-assurance.[3] Civil (and criminal) fines are also costly. In addition to administrative and enforcement costs, fines produce higher prices to customers of even legitimate sellers because higher fines increase legitimate sellers' returns from protecting themselves against false charges of fraud.

At some total penalty level, the cost to consumers of extra fraud deterrence exceeds the incremental expected cost of the fraud. When the cost of fraud is low or when customers have lower-cost alternative methods of insuring themselves against fraud, sellers will invest less in reputation and provide little quality-assurance. People who buy cars at flea markets are probably not making systematic mistakes—they simply value additional quality-assurance less than do people who buy from new car dealers. Flea market customers are more likely to be defrauded, but they also pay lower prices for their cars. They are also probably people who can better evaluate car quality.

This argument clarifies why the optimal amount of fraud is not zero: at some point the costs of reducing the probability of fraud exceed the expected benefits. Furthermore, and despite the presence of fraud, there is no externality in this case. Fraud deterrence is purchased until the marginal cost equals the marginal benefit.

A role for criminal penalties arises when a fraud imposes external costs on other parties. However, not all frauds that directly affect third parties represent negative externalities. Suppose a fraud committed by one seller causes the customers of other similar sellers to invest more resources to assure quality and detect fraud. These extra costs may represent external costs of the fraud. But they may not. The fraud may simply reveal that the net gain to fraud is higher than the customers previously realized, and that greater investments in quality-assurance and fraud detection are optimal. Such customers may demand greater investment in reputation to ensure quality. Learning that it paid for the seller to commit fraud represents an external benefit, not a cost, because the detection of the fraud has informed the customers that the probability of being defrauded was higher than they had realized. The external benefit is not produced by the fraud itself, but rather, by the information that at least one seller considered fraud to be profitable. In fact, the sooner the information about the fraud is communicated, the shorter the period of time that consumers will be making purchases with less quality-assurance than they would have purchased had they had the additional information.[4]

External costs arise when the seller committing the fraud has designed new methods that lower others' costs of committing frauds. The fraud may then motivate increased investment in quality-assurance because it increases the likelihood that other sellers will also engage in fraud. The external cost arises because one seller's fraud lowers other sellers' costs of committing fraud.

For consumer fraud, externalities, and thus a role for criminal penalties, arise when the fraud represents an innovation in fraud technology. Even in these cases, however, it is the innovation that imposes the external cost, not the fraud itself. External costs of the fraud itself arise when the fraud corresponds with an innovation in fraud technology that changes the costs of other frauds occurring. We do not know the fraction of frauds that also represent innovations in fraud technology. But these cases surely represent a subset of actual frauds. For all other consumer frauds, privately contracted penalties will optimally internalize the expected cost of the fraud.

2.4 Substitution of Criminal Fines for Private Quality-assurance

Since private quality-assurance mechanisms typically do not completely eliminate incentives to commit fraud, why not increase criminal penalties to deter fraud further? Can greater reliance on criminal penalties further reduce the incidence of fraud? The answer depends on the substitutability of criminal penalties and reputation in deterring fraud. If criminal penalties and reputation are perfect substitutes, an increase in penalties will have no effect on the incidence of fraud. Increases in criminal penalties will simply reduce customers' reliance on reputation as a guarantor of quality.

However, criminal penalties typically are not perfect substitutes for reputation. As a result, an increase in the criminal penalty will cause a smaller decrease in reputational investments, causing an overall increase in sellers' expected penalties. This will work to decrease fraud occurrences. But if there are no externalities for the criminal penalty to internalize, the penalty increase will also harm consumers and dissipate wealth.

One reason penalties and reputation are not perfect substitutes is that reputation relies on the threatened loss of supra-competitive prices and their associated (quasi-) rents, while reliance on penalties does not. As Klein and Leffler (1981) point out, sellers will compete to obtain those rents by providing additional goods and services (e.g., information, comfort, etc.). A dollar increase in fines will deter fraud as much as a dollar of lost reputation, but customers will prefer reputation because the sunk investments that guarantee quality via reputation also yield other services.[5] As long as customers attach a positive value to the services lost from a reduction in sunk investments, a dollar increase in fines must result in less than a dollar reduction in sunk investments if consumers are to remain indifferent. An increase in criminal penalties therefore will result in smaller than dollar-for-dollar reductions in reputational investments.

Another reason reputation and criminal fines are not perfect substitutes in guaranteeing quality is that some types of fraud are very costly for a third party such as a court to arbitrate, for example, the taste of a hamburger (see Klein and Leffler, 1981; Darby and Lott, 1989). Customers through the prospect of their repeat purchases can police such frauds more efficiently. Therefore, criminal penalties can protect consumers from only a subset of the frauds from which reputation protects them.

Furthermore, the net costs of criminal penalties increase at an increasing rate because the marginal substitutability of criminal penalties for reputation decreases with penalties. Fines and reputation are most similar in their ability to protect customers when the frauds can be demonstrated to third parties. At low fine levels, a relatively large portion of the reputational investment protects consumers from the types of fraud for which fines are also effective; higher fines therefore will cause a relatively large decrease in reputation. As the fine level gets larger, however, reputation and fines become progressively less close substitutes because reputation is increasingly relied on to prevent frauds that are costly to demonstrate to third parties. Further increases in fines therefore cause relatively small reductions in reputation and larger increases in the total penalty for fraud.

To illustrate, assume that expected criminal penalties increase to the point where the fines alone completely internalize those damages from frauds that can be demonstrated to third parties. At that point, further increases in fines are unlikely to reduce reputation to zero because only reputation and not fines would be useful in preventing frauds that cannot be readily proved to third parties. Still further increases in fines would result in little or no reduction in the use of reputation.

Even if reputation and fines were perfect substitutes over a broad range of criminal penalties, there would come a level of fines such that the optimal level of reputational bonding is zero. Further increases in fines will then unambiguously result in higher total penalties. In fact, we show that the more extreme estimates of the US Sentencing Commission's recent penalty increases imply that this increase completely offsets our estimated values of the minimum reputational penalties sellers suffer when they are accused of fraud.

Because reputation and criminal penalties are not perfect substitutes, an increase in penalties increases sellers' total expected penalty of fraud. This works to deter some frauds, but it also increases the expected costs of all sellers, as even innocent sellers may have to defend against fraud charges and will take extra measures to decrease the chance of being accused of fraud.[6] Some such measures will involve investing in production processes that provide a higher level of quality-assurance. That is, sellers will choose a higher level of quality-assurance than consumers would otherwise prefer.

An increase in criminal fines will also decrease sellers' abilities to meet demands for different levels of quality-assurance. Different sellers, or different product lines produced by the same seller, can meet the demands of different consumer clienteles by investing in different amounts of reputation. Criminal penalties that increase the total expected penalty, however, discourage sellers from providing low quality-assurance items. Flea markets may be hotbeds of fraud, but they satisfy a clientele of customers who attach a low value to buying additional quality-assurance. Such consumers undoubtedly value not being cheated, but they are relatively unwilling to pay for quality-assurance. For example, they may have alternative means to determine quality or may suffer relatively low costs from fraud. Large criminal penalties can eliminate the flea markets, but at a net cost to customers who prefer the low levels of quality-assurance.

Robert Crandall, the Chief Executive Officer of American Airlines, illustrates the effects on consumers of imposing high criminal penalties on sellers in the following comment (Castro, 1991):

> Suppose [regulators] said, "We don't want you guys to lose our bags anymore. And every time you lose a bag we're going to fine you a million dollars." Well,

> I can fix that tomorrow morning! We will never lose another bag. But it will be very inconvenient to travel. Today you come into Dallas-Fort Worth from all these different places, and in 45 minutes you make your connection and you go out. But in the world of the future, where bags are never lost, I'm going to keep you there for three hours, because I'm going to make sure I get every bag.

Increased penalties will reduce the number of bags lost, but at a cost most consumers would not pay voluntarily.

These arguments imply that higher criminal penalties can reduce the incidence of fraud, but at a cost. At the very least, higher criminal penalties force some consumers to pay for a higher level of quality-assurance than they would otherwise be willing to pay. It is also likely, however, that higher criminal penalties increase all consumers' costs, as all sellers' costs rise. This latter conclusion is supported by observation. Criminal penalties could conceivably be lower-cost guarantors of quality. But the fact that we observe very little private arbitration or other third-party enforcement of quality indicates that the additional cost of third-party penalties exceeds the benefit.[7]

These conclusions directly contradict the current conventional wisdom on the topic, as represented by the US Sentencing Commission's guidelines that substantially increase criminal penalties for fraud. To this point, our argument has been based on the premise that private contracting controls and penalizes sellers that commit fraud. In the following sections we present empirical evidence that supports this premise. The private wealth loss suffered by sellers alleged, indicted, or convicted of fraud is statistically significant and much larger than court-imposed penalties.

2.5 The Length of Prison Sentences

So how long should prison sentences be? Higher fines, greater reputational losses, larger collateral penalties, and longer prison sentences deter people from committing crimes. But when these penalties are imposed can have a big difference on their level of deterrence. Fines, reputation, and collateral penalties can be entirely imposed on the criminal on the day that they are convicted. By contrast, while prison sentences can start right away, the punishment takes place over a number of years. The reason why this is particularly important for criminals is that there is strong empirical evidence that criminals have much higher discount rates than the general population. Compared to other people, criminals are unwilling to wait to have their desires satisfied. Discount rates of 30 percent or more seem quite plausible for criminals.

If a law-abiding citizen had a real discount rate of 4 percent, they would be willing to pay about $0.68 for a dollar ten years from now. But a criminal with a discount rate of 30 percent would only be willing to pay $0.07 for that same dollar. The problem is that it means longer prison terms represent relatively little additional penalty for criminals. An additional year of prison 20 years from now is valued at less than 1 percent of the disutility of a year of prison today. What this says is that the discount rate used to evaluate the cost of prison for society is likely to be radically different from the discount rate used to estimate the increased deterrence from adding an additional year onto a criminal's sentence.

There are also two reasons for prison. The first is deterrence, and the high discount rate for criminals is relevant for that. The second is incapacitation, keeping criminals from committing more crimes. A relatively small percentage of the population commits most of the crimes. Whether it is that certain people are callous to the harm they impose on others or it is simply their high discount rates, certain people are much more prone to committing crime than others. However, crime is a young person's activity. Young males who are 18, 19, and 20 years old commit most murders. By the time a criminal is 45 he is likely to commit crime at about a sixth the rate that he would have done so at age 20 (Lott, 2007). Unfortunately this type of data is only available for murder. This reduced incapacitation effect also reduces the benefit from longer prison sentences.

3 THE IMPORTANCE OF DIFFERENT LAW ENFORCEMENT STRATEGIES

Arrest rates of criminals are usually the single most important factor in reducing every type of crime. Sensational topics like the death penalty may get the most media attention but it is everyday police work that really makes a neighborhood safer. Changes in the arrest rate account for around 16 to 18 percent of the drop in the murder rate (Mustard, 2003). Conviction rates explain another 12 percent. Arrest and conviction rates have an even larger effect on other types of violent crime, while their effect on property crimes is often two or three times larger than for violent crime overall.

While boosting arrest rates indisputably has deterrence, the evidence on longer prison sentences is much less clear. The reason is simple: methodologically, it's surprisingly difficult to measure how long criminals expect to be in prison. The length of a criminal's sentence is often much longer than the actual time served. Furthermore, the time that is served varies widely, even for a single type of crime, depending on a suspect's criminal history and the severity of the offense. Unfortunately, this kind of data is not readily available to researchers.

Arrest and conviction rates and expected prison sentence lengths all deal with deterrence—the cost to the criminal of committing a crime. But some people commit crimes despite those threats. Obviously, locking up the most crime-prone individuals will further decrease crime by keeping habitual criminals off the streets. Indeed, putting more people in prison explains another 10 to 12 percent of the drop in crime rates (Mustard, 2003; Lott, 2007, 2010). Other factors also matter. Overall, the rise in executions during the 1990s accounts for about 12 to 14 percent of the overall drop in murders. Right-to-carry laws explain around another 6 percent. Simply being arrested or convicted, even without a prison sentence, carries its own substantial penalties. Indeed, as noted earlier, these reputational penalties are the most meaningful penalties that many criminals face.

From a benefit–cost perspective, the ultimate question is: what did it cost for these different policies to produce their reductions in crime? Some rough calculations are possible. For police, a 1 percent increase in non-unionized police with arrest powers lowers the murder rate by less than 0.65 percent (Lott, 2010). With starting police salaries averaging just below \$40 000 per year (with benefits costing about \$55 000) and a 1 percent increase in police equaling about 7000 officers, that comes to about \$385 million (not including training costs). Assuming a value of life at \$4 million, the value of reduced murders is around \$423 million. Other estimates have been made of the cost of crime by looking at jury awards for injuries to victims (Miller et al., 1996). Looking at these different types of crime puts the value from additional police at closer to \$500 million.

While police are the single most important factor for reducing crime, concealed handgun laws might be the most cost-effective. Increasing the percentage of the adult population with concealed handgun permits by one percentage point reduces the murder rate by about 4 percent (Lott, 2010). Each additional law enforcement officer has a much bigger effect on the amount of crime than each additional citizen with a concealed handgun permit, but the cost of each additional law enforcement officer is also much bigger.

If permit-holding policy was a national one, increasing the number of permit holders by about 2.25 million would imply 650 fewer murders in 2008 and the saving from fewer lives lost would equal about \$2.6 billion. That comes to a benefit of about \$1156 per permit holder. The costs to states from issuing permits is essentially zero as most states actually make money on issuing concealed handgun permits. Given that someplace between 70 and 90 percent of permit holders already own a handgun, the primary cost of having new permit holders involves the cost of training (and about half the states do not require formal training, although individuals appear to train even when it is not required). An eight-hour training course can easily cost $200–300. In addition, there are the individual's time costs to go through training.

3.1 Externalities from Punishing Criminals

While penalties will deter some criminals from committing crime, penalties can also cause criminals to shift to other types of crimes or to move to other areas to commit them. Ignoring these complications can bias estimated benefits or costs of law enforcement activity.

Suppose the death penalty were imposed on a crime such as robbery. If a robber thought that they were going to get caught by the police, they might find it in their interest to kill all the witnesses to their crime. They can only be executed once and they already face execution for committing the robbery. In contrast, leaving the witnesses alive means that it might be easier for police to catch and convict them. The only factor that might work in the other direction is that police might spend more resources trying to catch a murderer than a robber and so murdering people could actually still increase the robber's expected penalty. On the other hand, the death penalty for murder might also work to reduce the rate that other crimes are committed. Because capital punishment can be imposed if a victim dies during the commission of a rape, robbery, or aggravated assault, statistics show the death penalty also acts as a deterrent to these crimes as well (Lott, 2010). This, however, does not mean that the death penalty should be applied directly to these crimes.

The point is that externalities mean that one has to think more broadly in evaluating the costs and benefits of criminal penalties. In this case, one cannot measure the benefits of the death penalty by simply looking at the impact that this penalty has on robberies. Similar concerns have been pointed out for other penalties, such as three-strike laws, where there is also evidence of small increase in murders when criminals face life sentences (Marvell and Moody, 2001).

These types of "spillover" effects can also be seen in private actions to stop crime. Take right-to-carry laws, which allow law-abiding citizens to carry concealed handguns. While violent crimes fall after these laws are adopted and after more people get permits, there is some evidence that property crime rises. Criminals appear to switch from violent crimes where criminals come into direct contact with victims, crimes that would be affected by the victims being able to defend themselves, and into property crimes where there is no contact between criminals and victims. So criminals may move from a crime such as robbery and into larceny.

But criminals might also move from one jurisdiction to another. Stephen Bronars and I found significant evidence that criminals move out of areas where concealed handguns are legalized (Bronars and Lott, 1998). Our study analyzed counties that border each other on opposite sides of a state line. In such cases, counties in states that adopt right-to-carry laws see a drop in violent crime that is about four times larger than the simultaneous increase in violent crimes in the adjacent counties without such laws. The spillover was greatest when you had two urban counties across the border from each other. These results imply that looking narrowly at the change in crime rates for states that adopt these right-to-carry laws will overestimate the benefit from the law.

3.2 Other Types of Externalities Regarding Crime

In 1982, James Q. Wilson and George L. Kelling articulated a persuasive new theory about crime. They argued that petty crime such as window breaking creates a vicious cycle whereby law-abiding citizens in a deteriorating neighborhood continually leave, to be replaced by criminals. If crime is rampant as evidenced by broken windows, criminals find it even easier to commit crimes with fewer law-abiding citizens around to witness them. So the key to fighting crime is to begin by cracking down on petty offenses. Some experts credit the huge drop in crime in New York City during the 1990s to a "broken windows" policy that strictly enforced laws against minor crimes like vandalism, public drunkenness, panhandling, and public urination.

3.3 How the Cost of Catching Criminals May Vary with the Size of the Crime

Prior to the US Sentencing Commission corporate penalty guidelines in the early 1990s, those who committed major environmental crimes—such as a massive oil spill from a tanker running aground—had to pay fines equivalent to the amount of the damages. In contrast, for minor environmental crimes—for example, dumping a barrelful of waste off the side of a ship—the fines were many times greater than the damage estimates. The commission reversed this relationship so that penalties for the more serious crimes became many times bigger than the damages. Understanding this pattern helps understand how the costs of catching criminals can sometimes vary with the harm done by the crime. While the new regulations seem logical, there was a sound reason for the earlier policy. A major oil spill is something that is nearly impossible to hide—we will know with near certainty that the crime occurred and which ship was responsible. But it is much more difficult to identify the culprit—or even to detect the crime—for a smaller transgression like dumping just a barrelful of waste off the side of a boat. That's why the Sentencing Commission's policy change was actually counterproductive; if we want to create disincentives to environmental crime, we need to ensure that small-time offenders face relatively harsher penalties that act to offset the high probability that they will get away with their crime.

4 CONCLUSION

Penalties, police, and private actions by individuals all impact crime rates. Prison is all too frequently the only focus of legally imposed penalties, though there are many other ways that criminals are punished. On the enforcement side, there are different choices there also. In law enforcement there are many areas where it will not be possible to quantify the benefits or costs of different policies, but hopefully those areas where numbers are available can reduce the uncertainty facing decision-makers in their final analyses. At the very least, the numbers that are available give decision-makers a rough idea of how large other considerations will have to be to offset those factors that can be measured.

NOTES

1. The National Advisory Commission on Criminal Justice Standards and Goals (1973, p. 592) notes that, "every State and the Federal government make it difficult for persons convicted of a felony to obtain licenses to practice occupations regulated by the government. In many instances conviction of a felony is automatic grounds for denial of a license. In others, it is in practice impossible for a former offender to obtain a license."
2. Common law prohibits privately negotiated penalty clauses in civil cases. But if existing efficiency prohibitions are valid, they would seem to apply to government-determined criminal penalties as well. That is, if frauds are not punished sufficiently because civil fines are restricted, the efficient reform is to change the common law prohibition, not to increase criminal penalties. We also distinguish between two issues: the mix of fines and reputation to police fraud, and whether private parties or government agents are better suited to determine the fine levels through civil or criminal procedures. To address the latter issue, one must examine whether the government has lower costs of determining the fine levels than do parties directly involved in the transactions. Block has argued that criminal fines involve a much more costly process than that involved with civilly imposed fines (Lott, 1988; Block, 1991).
3. In the Klein-Leffler model sellers either cheat or not with certainty. Lott extends this model by admitting the stochastic nature of the seller's decision to cheat. The size of the reputational bond is set so that the marginal value consumers obtain from a lower probability of fraud is equal to the marginal cost of increasing the bond (Darby and Karni, 1973; Klein and Leffler, 1981).
4. Consumers also value learning about potential frauds sooner if it is costly for sellers to quickly change their investments in reputation.
5. For simplicity, this discussion assumes that the probability of detection and punishment are the same for criminal fines and lost reputation.

6. The fact that many business people actively oppose increases in criminal penalties for corporate fraud, as indicated by the intense lobbying by the Business Roundtable on this issue, implies that these people expect their sellers to be guilty of fraud, or they expect their sellers' expected costs of defending against charges of fraud to increase with the criminal penalties even when the sellers are innocent. This latter possibility provides anecdotal evidence that Type II errors (accusing innocent sellers) are important for these sellers (see Epstein, 1990).
7. One third-party role we do not rule out is the role of a governing body to enforce agreements, as privately arbitrated decisions can be turned over to the public legal system to enforce. But it does not follow that governments have a comparative advantage in determining the penalty level upon conviction (see Karpoff and Lott, 1993, pp. 757–802). Individuals are likely to have better information than a government about how much they value higher levels of quality assurance.

REFERENCES

Block, Michael K. (1991), "Optimal penalties, criminal law, and the control of corporate behavior," *Boston University Law Review*, **71**, March, 395–419.

Block, Michael K. and Vernon E. Gerety (1995), "Some experimental evidence on differences between student and prisoner reactions to monetary penalties and risk," *Journal of Legal Studies*, **24** (1), 123–38.

Bronars, Stephen and John R. Lott, Jr. (1998), "Deterrence, right-to-carry concealed handgun laws, and the geographic displacement of crime," *American Economic Review*, May, 475–9.

Castro, Janice (1991), "The man who fired a dog to save a buck: Robert Crandall," *Time*, 28 October, p. 18.

Darby, Michael R. and Edi Karni (1973), "Free competition and the optimal amount of fraud," *Journal of Law and Economics*, **16** (1), April, 67–88.

Darby, Michael R. and John R. Lott, Jr. (1989), "Qualitative information, reputation, and monopolistic competition," *International Review of Law and Economics*, **9** (1), June, 87–103.

Epstein, Aaron (1990), "Companies resist having punishment fit big-ticket crimes," *Seattle Times* and *Seattle Post-Intelligencer*, 22 April, A3.

Grant, Walter M., John LeCornu, John A. Pickens, Dean H. Rivkin, and C. Roger Vinson (1970), "Special project—the collateral consequences of a criminal conviction," *Vanderbilt Law Review*, **23** (3), October, 929–1241.

Karpoff, Jon and John R. Lott, Jr. (1993), "The reputational penalty firms bear for committing criminal fraud," *Journal of Law and Economics*, **36** (2), 757–802.

Klein, Benjamin and Keith B. Leffler (1981), "The role of market forces in assuring contractual performance," *Journal of Political Economy*, **89** (4), 615–41.

Lott, Jr., John R. (1988), "The optimal level of criminal fines in the presence of reputation," United States Commission Working Paper, August.

Lott, John R. Jr. (1992a), "Do we punish high income criminals too heavily?," *Economic Inquiry*, **30** (4), October, 583–608.

Lott, Jr., John R. (1992b), "An attempt at measuring the total monetary penalty from drug convictions: The importance of an individual's reputation," *Journal of Legal Studies*, **21** (1), January, 159–87.

Lott, Jr., John R. (2007), *Freedomnomics*, Washington, DC: Regnery Publishers.

Lott, Jr., John R. (2010), *More Guns, Less Crime*, 3rd edition, Chicago: University of Chicago Press.

Marvell, Thomas and Carlisle Moody (2001), "The lethal effects of three-strikes laws," *Journal of Legal Studies*, **30** (1), 89–106.

Miller, Ted R., Mark A. Cohen, and Brian Wiersema (1996), *Victim Costs and Consequences: A New Look*, Washington, DC: National Institute of Justice.

Mustard, David B. (2003), "Re-examining criminal behavior: The importance of omitted variable bias," *Review of Economics and Statistics*, **85** (1), 205–11.

President's Commission on Law Enforcement and Administration of Justice (1967), *Task Force Report: Correction*, Washington, DC: US Government Printing Office.

Stephan, James J. (2004), "State-prison expenditures, 2001," Bureau of Justice Statistics, June, 2004.

US National Advisory Commission on Criminal Justice Standards and Goals (1973), Corrections, Washington, DC: Supt. of Docs., US Govt. Print. Off.

Wilson, James Q. and George L. Kelling (1982), "Broken windows," *The Atlantic Monthly*, 1 March.

5. Towards principles and standards for the benefit–cost analysis of safety

Scott Farrow and W. Kip Viscusi

1 INTRODUCTION

This chapter proposes principles and standards for benefit–cost analysis (BCA) that are of particular importance to public safety policies. Applied economists and policy analysts are often under pressure to deliver their analysis in a specified time frame subject to a particular budget (Committee to Evaluate Measures, 2006; DeMartino, 2011). In the US government and in some US states, analysts may be creating BCAs for which comparison of results across policies is desirable. Moreover, application of consistent standards for analysis facilitates public scrutiny of the economic basis for the policies. It is in such applied work where analytical principles and standards may facilitate producing analyses and encourage replicability, comparability, credibility, and usability. Our principles and standards provide a set of recommended best practices for the analysis of policies affecting public safety but do not necessarily reflect requirements that the analysis must meet.

Public safety issues arise with respect to both privately marketed goods that affect the public and government policies that have a strong public good component, such as highway safety. Public safety concerns arise in a wide range of activities in general categories such as security, physical safety, natural hazards, environmental risks, public health, product safety, and employment hazards. Each of these areas of potential risk exposure has specific component risks such as those posed by crime, terrorism, food products, floods, and transportation. Fundamental to each component is that there is a chance of a bad outcome including risks arising from nature as well as those arising from individual behavior. Typically, there are also personal choices that affect one's exposure to risk as well as possibilities to alter the risk or its consequences through adaptive actions, preventative activities, and the purchase of insurance.

Just as the range of public safety policies is quite broad, the applications of BCA to policy decisions involving public safety are also diverse. The different contexts in which BCA is utilized are associated with different literatures, communities of practice, and outlets for publication. Agencies implementing risk policies range from local police and health departments to state offices and national agencies such as the Federal Emergency Management Agency (FEMA), the US Coast Guard, the Transportation Security Administration (TSA), the US Environmental Protection Agency (EPA), the Consumer Product Safety Commission (CPSC), the Food and Drug Administration (FDA), the US Army Corps of Engineers, and the US Department of Transportation (DOT). Agencies at different levels of government use formal BCA with varying frequency in all these applications. In many instances, preparation of a formal BCA is required by law or by executive order. The role of BCA in the decision-making process ranges from being a minor component of the policy decision to being the key test that the policy must pass.

Consequently, this chapter focuses on principles and standards for applying BCA with respect to public safety actions directed at reducing risk to the public. How risks should be incorporated theoretically and empirically into BCA is the focus of our proposed principles and standards. One can view these guidelines as being embedded in a larger set of principles that may be generally applicable to BCA.

1.1 Context: Applied Welfare Economics and Risk

Economic behavior and markets play a fundamental role in determining the levels and consequences of risk. However, the effect of these economic contexts on risk levels is often less direct than for standard consumption goods as the risk may be bundled as one of many product attributes. It is often possible to buy, sell, and manage risk in various direct or indirect ways so as to change probabilities, reduce damages, and shift the cost associated with adverse outcomes.

In general, theoretical economic analysis of uncertain outcomes such as those involved with public safety has as its foundation expected utility theory (e.g., Luce and Raiffa, 1965; Raiffa, 1968; Hirshleifer and Riley, 1992; Pratt et al., 1995; Just et al., 2004; and Eeckhoudt et al., 2005). Although alternative models of choice under uncertainty have proliferated in recent decades, most of these have been developed to incorporate empirical anomalies and various forms of irrationality and inconsistencies in behavior. The expected utility model remains the standard reference point for normative decisions. The expected utility model is based on a series of assumptions that establish a rational basis for decision, such as the assumption that increasing the probability of an adverse outcome makes the risky "lottery" less attractive.

The expected utility model hypothesizes that individuals have a utility value for each of the possible outcomes and that they weight the utility values linearly using the probabilities associated with those outcomes as the weights. Such analyses focus on the probability and the utility of outcomes without a distinction regarding good or bad probabilistic outcomes. In other words, in the theoretical literature "risk" is not necessarily linked to a negative outcome, only a probabilistic outcome in which the dispersion of possible outcomes has implications that either increase or decrease utility. The chance that you will win the lottery, and its complement that you will lose and win nothing, is consequently a "risk." Abstracting from the cost associated with the lottery ticket, this risk has favorable implications unlike the adverse risks that tend to be the focus of public policy efforts.

What role expected utility theory should play in policy decisions involving risk depends on who is affected and to what extent. When asking how beneficiaries of flood control projects value the reduction in flood risks, there should be recognition of the preferences over uncertain outcomes of those who will be protected by the policy. Thus, individual risk preferences may be quite germane in constructing society's willingness to pay for the benefit, which is the fundamental benefits principle of BCA. However, some policy risks, such as the uncertain cost of the flood control project, can be spread across the entire population with little financial consequence for any particular individual. In this case, the individual stakes are sufficiently small that risk aversion is not a concern for a societal BCA. How risk enters the societal tally of benefits and costs depends on the distribution and magnitude of the outcomes. Most applied benefit–cost analyses, consistent with standard practice for analyzing expected value outcomes, undertake the analysis in a such a manner that it is possible to reduce expected utility to expected value. This approach is typical both for individuals and aggregates based either on reasoning that projects have a small impact on individual income either directly or through the availability of insurance, or that society effectively holds a portfolio of policy investments that insures against individual risk (Arrow and Lind, 1970; US OMB, 1992, 2003; Boardman et al., 2011, pp. 215–18). When large risks are borne by individuals, ex ante measures of the willingness to pay of individuals will incorporate recognition of individual risk aversion, such as an option price (Just et al., 2004; Boardman et al., 2011, pp. 203–14). People's willingness to pay to avoid personal catastrophic losses from natural disasters could, for example, enter the analysis, but even here the valuation of the risk can be converted to a certain monetary equivalent.

Where risks are more collective or systematic, perhaps because they involve large interrelated systems such as finance or broadly scaled public health concerns, then a stronger case might be made for departures from expected value (Boardman et al., 2011, pp. 215–18).

Perhaps more than many other areas of economic scholarship, the research relating to risk and uncertainty is rapidly evolving. How people actually make such decisions may be quite different than what expected utility theory predicts. For example, making decisions involving very small probabilities of catastrophic outcomes may be quite difficult. The creative tension brought by those working at the boundary of psychology and economics, which has developed into a field known as behavioral economics, is appropriately pushing the structure of theories with empirical observation and competing theories. Recent reviews include those by DellaVigna (2009) and Robinson and Hammitt (2011). Similarly, policy issues with large degrees of uncertainty, such as homeland security and long-term environmental policies, have pushed research on decision modeling towards greater robustness or adaptability (Dixit and Pindyck, 1994; Lempert and Collins, 2007; Hansen and Sargent, 2008).

However, for purposes of providing guidance with respect to how the government should make decisions involving public risks, the expected utility framework provides the current standard default framework for decisions in the economics literature. Although there are political pressures that often lead the government to institutionalize individual irrationalities, as discussed in Viscusi (1998), these tendencies should be resisted. Notwithstanding the substantial research that has demonstrated numerous inconsistencies and irrationalities in individual choice, we generally advocate a set of principles and standards that embody a consistent and rational approach to policy evaluations and governmental decisions.

Risk and uncertainty are used here synonymously. The probabilities associated with different possible outcomes or states of the world are often based on a subjective risk framework since there may be few classical risks that are known with precision (Raiffa, 1968; Hirshleifer and Riley, 1992, pp. 9–10). Probabilities such as the average motor vehicle fatality risk are well-understood risks because we have a great deal of information about the probabilities based on observing a large population and events with frequent occurrence. In contrast, hazards such as the dangers of climate change or the mortality risks posed by newly identified diseases such as swine flu are not as well understood and fall into the category of uncertainties. In situations in which a distinction between risk and uncertainty appears useful so as to emphasize the important role of unknown randomness in situations of uncertainty, then it will be used. However, for purposes of policy decisions, we will treat probabilities of an adverse outcome symmetrically whether they are precisely understood risks or dimly understood uncertainties. Perhaps the most important distinction is that in situations of uncertainty there is often the opportunity to learn more about the level of the probabilities, creating opportunities for information acquisition. Because elements of risk are important in areas outside of public safety, many of the same concerns surveyed here are also relevant in other application areas. A more extreme case than uncertainty is that of ignorance in which we do not know even the different possible states of the world to assign probabilities.

Even if the underlying policy context does not involve an element of risk, the empirical analysis of the policy choice may introduce aspects of uncertainty. Most obviously there can be measurement error of theoretically correct components of the BCA as well as variability across responses in the system and random error. Morgan and Henrion (1990, pp. 56–69) elaborate on the various sources of uncertainty in quantitative analysis and list the following categories:

- random error and statistical variation;
- systematic error and subjective judgment;
- linguistic imprecision;
- variability;
- inherent randomness and unpredictability;
- disagreement;
- approximations.

Debate has gone on for centuries about the distinctions embodied in these and other possible categories, in part because some uncertainties may be associated with more than one category. The purpose of this listing is not to establish a framework to compartmentalize the different sources of uncertainty but to point out that a variety of issues about risk and uncertainty occur at both theoretical and empirical levels of a policy analysis.

1.2 Principles and Standards: Sources and Scope

This chapter is not the result of a committee deliberation. Nor is it based on an explicit hierarchy of sources such as used in accounting (US GAO, 2005), as there are no existing standard-setting organizations for BCA. The result is that we place substantial reliance on textbooks, professional articles, and current government guidance as well as our views based on teaching, consulting, research, and government practice.

Common sources of standards for the benefit–cost analyst in government are guidance documents issued by the US Office of Management and Budget (US OMB, 1992, 2003) or similar institutions in some other countries. These documents and supplemental guidance issued by individual agencies describe expectations about BCA in the text, but generally do not break out individual standards. The guidance applies to government projects and regulation pertaining to safety, risk, and uncertainty. In addition, some prominent authors on BCA have published their consensus views on principles and standards (Arrow et al., 1996), and recent texts on benefit–cost analysis and applied welfare analysis include those by Stokey and Zeckhauser (1978); Gramlich (1990); Hanley and Spash (1993); Zerbe and Dively (1994); Brent (1998); Jones (2005) and Boardman et al. (2011), as well as collections of major articles such as those in Layard and Glaister (1994); Zerbe (2008) and Schmitz and Zerbe (2009).

Essentially all applications of ex ante BCA used to project policy outcomes involve aspects of risk and uncertainty, such as uncertainties about particular variables in the analysis. Evaluations of public safety policies often bring the issues to the core of the analysis since various aspects of risk are intrinsically involved. The areas of application that may be considered as pertaining to public safety and that are significantly driven by risk and uncertainty include but are not limited to the following:

- security: crime, terrorism, defense;
- safety: traffic, building codes;
- natural hazards: waterway control, fire, wind, flood, earthquake, tsunami;
- environment: water, hazardous waste, pollution, climate change;
- public health: disease, sanitation;
- products: food, motor vehicles, tobacco, drugs, and other consumer products;
- employment: occupational risks.

Our principles for analyzing such policies are intended to be general, few in number, and to provide a touchstone for more detailed standards. Standards are meant to provide specific guidance for modeling or empirical estimation in BCA, and in fact could be called guidance. We do not consider the "standards" as being necessary and sufficient for a good analysis, but we believe that analyses that are inconsistent with these standards could either be improved by following the standard or should depart from the standard only after a reasoned justification.

While the standards are not explicitly linked to principles in the presentation here, their development included that link. Theoretical and empirical issues related to risk and public safety issues addressed here may be usefully combined with principles and standards for other issues such as those related to general versus partial equilibrium, the cost of public funds, or other topics. The standards are separated into standards with respect to the theory of BCA and empirically oriented standards, where each of these has sections devoted to established and emerging standards. The modularized format for such principles and standards is somewhat unusual in that they are short, follow a specific template, and provide broad-based references; the proposed principles and standards are presented this way in order to focus discussion and to facilitate possible decisions regarding their use.

2 PROPOSED PRINCIPLES FOR THE BENEFIT–COST ANALYSIS OF PUBLIC SAFETY

1. *Provide realistic representation of the risks and the policy context.* The analysis should faithfully represent economic reality based on behavioral responses and uncertainty based on our current understanding. Where components of the analysis are not well understood, there should be an explanation of the lack of understanding due, for example, to resource limitations or inherent uncertainties that cannot be resolved.
2. *Applied welfare economics is the theoretical foundation for public safety and BCA generally.* The foundational principles defining what is to be measured are those that are generally accepted in professional economics literature. There is explicit recognition that such foundational elements are not unanimous and evolve, often through interaction with other disciplines.
3. *Do not become paralyzed by the impossibility of preparing an ideal analysis.* Analyses may be informative even if they do not adhere to all principles of welfare economics or other theoretical tools. It is often possible to adopt theoretical refinements in an analysis and to refine estimates of the risk but doing so may not alter the overall policy assessment or optimal policy choice.
4. *Provide unbiased risk analyses so as not to usurp the decision-makers.* Generate information that is valuable to decision-makers using a range of decision approaches involving uncertainty. However, do not embed in these analyses conservatism and similar adjustment factors that prevent the decision-maker from learning about the actual risk probabilities. Do not usurp the decision-maker's role unless the decision-maker has previously given approval or if abiding by the results of the BCA is a requirement imposed on the decision-maker.

5. *Strive to report monetized outcomes of risks so that risk outcomes can be compared to costs and other policy benefits.* Qualitative, quantified, and monetized measures are all useful, but the goal is a series of numerical analyses that allow a decision-maker to understand the impacts of a decision in a monetary or equivalent metric while also being able to view key quantities and values that lead up to the monetization. Establishing a single monetary metric for policy benefit and cost components facilitates comparisons. While some policy impacts by necessity may remain in qualitative terms, if there are too many such components the analysis tends to become unwieldy and with an accompanying danger that the policy choice will be made independent of the non-monetized components and the overall economic merits of the policy.
6. *Assume that there is statistical randomness in the components of the analysis.* If a numerical value is considered to be important and not analyzed as a random variable, one should explain why it is not. Discussing uncertainties is an essential component, but the existence of uncertainties with respect to parameters in a policy analysis should not be a barrier to identifying the policy that maximizes the difference between the appropriately risk-based level of net benefits.
7. *Avoid false accuracy that abstracts from underlying uncertainties.* The modeling assumptions and reporting of numerical values should convey information about the accuracy of the estimates.
8. *Consider proportionality of effort.* Analytical effort should be expended to the extent that it might change the policy decision as indicated by the value of information gleaned from such an effort. Many policy decisions hinge on a single key component. Identifying the critical parameters and ascertaining their value is a critical aspect of judgment required for effective policy analysis.
9. *Choose the appropriate scope of analysis.* Judgment is required in selecting the breadth and temporal dimension of the analysis that is pertinent for the risk policy decision, but the scope is often dictated by what factors are relevant for the BCA. For example, the time period for analyzing policy decisions may be different than the time period for assessing policy effects. Longer-term technology uncertainties may make it infeasible to analyze decisions with temporally remote effects, such as those affecting future generations. Nevertheless, the analysis should assess important longer-term consequences of the decisions and should not be truncated so as to coincide with the period over which policy decisions are being made. In some settings, this is similar to a life-cycle analysis.

10. *Acquire information economically.* Acquire information about key uncertainties when it is feasible and may affect the outcome of the analysis. The presence of hazards that are uncertain and do not entail precisely estimated risks creates a potential for acquiring information that will foster better understanding of the probabilities. Refining risk assessments is often desirable, but often the best that can be done is to utilize judgmental probabilities. Perfect information about risks is seldom available, and there is a cost to information acquisition. One of these costs is that failure to act often has important opportunity costs.
11. *Policy-makers should not usurp the policy analysts' role.* Political forces and agency biases should not dictate technical issues. Nor should policy investigations of feasible and potentially desirable alternatives be unduly limited.

3 PROPOSED STANDARDS

3.1 Proposed Established Standards (S): Theoretical and Empirical

3.1.1 Theory

S-THEORY-1
Issue: Does the potential exist to increase economic efficiency?
Standard: Identify some type of market failure or government failure.
Discussion: The focus of welfare economics and hence of BCA is determining whether an action increases economic efficiency. In the absence of theoretical or empirical evidence suggesting a market or government failure there is little expectation that there will be positive net benefits from action. For example, the existence of externalities from pollution and transaction costs that establishes barriers to Coasean bargains to externalities implies that private actions by consumers or firms will be inefficient. Consequently, it is possible for policies to increase efficiency compared to market outcomes. If the analysis claims that the policy will raise individuals' welfare or firms' profits, then a useful check on the analysis is to inquire what market failure currently prevents these gains from being realized. Analyses that claim that a policy that imposes costs on firms but nevertheless will boost firm profitability are often based on faulty assumptions and should include a compelling demonstration of a market failure that would generate such an outcome.
References: US OMB (1992); and most texts such as Zerbe and Dively (1994) and Boardman et al. (2011).

S-THEORY-2
Issue: What are the benefits of increased safety?
Standard: The standard benefit measure is the willingness to pay of those affected by the policy to reduce the risks of the bad outcomes that would have occurred compared to the base case. In some policy contexts, the benefit measure for policy may be specified as a willingness-to-accept measure. However, empirical anomalies in willingness-to-accept values make willingness-to-pay approaches preferable. Standard practice in assessing policy consequences remains the use of after-the-fact (ex post) consumer surplus although ex ante values are preferred (see Frontier Theory Standard 1 below) for prospective analyses and from the standpoint of unbiased benefit assessment.
Discussion: Public safety issues generally involve probabilities of outcomes perceived as socially "bad," for example, floods, crimes, and illness, which may or may not be at inefficient levels. As the primary outcome of concern is "bad," the policy achieves benefits by reducing the frequency or severity of the bad outcome. The problem can be framed as a trade-off between two types of costs: reduced value (cost) of harm and the implementation cost of avoiding the harm. Those benefiting from the forecasted reduction in harm are assumed to treat such reductions symmetrically with more standard benefits. Examples include reductions in pollution that reduce bad health outcomes and reductions in damage from natural disasters or terrorist attacks.
References: Freeman (2003, pp. 324–36) and Boardman et al. (2011, pp. 202–18).

S-THEORY-3
Issue: What welfare measure should be used?
Standard: Marshallian demand based on willingness to pay.
Discussion: Welfare measures based on consumer surplus typically use Marshallian (uncompensated) demand functions. Willig (1976) developed bounds on the error from the use of Marshallian consumer surplus instead of that based on a compensated (Hicksian) demand. The Willig article has been reprinted in a number of places including Zerbe and Dively (1994, pp. 111–13) and Jehle and Reny (2000, p. 170). The error in using the Marshallian demand can be large if only the deadweight loss is being measured (Hausman, 1981; Haveman et al., 1987).

Further, linear or constant coefficient approximations are frequently used when better information is lacking. Linear forms allow relatively easy closed form solutions and permit basic analytic geometry to be used to construct estimating equations. More advanced work often deals with more general functional forms such as constant elasticity or "exact"

surplus measures. See Frontier Theory Standard 2 below for exact measures of surplus.
References: Zerbe and Dively (1994); Freeman (2003, pp. 53–68); and Boardman et al. (2011).

3.1.2 Empirical

S-EMPIRICAL-1
Issue: What value should be used for point estimates?
Standard: Use the statistical expected value (mean) for point estimates or, lacking that, a measure of central tendency.
Discussion: There are two justifications. The first is statistical as the fundamental operations in BCA are addition and subtraction. The addition or subtraction of expected values is also the expected value. Other measures of a random variable are not generally additive in this fashion. Further, first-order approximations of functions of random variables such as products or division use expected values. The second justification is decision-analytic. A risk-neutral individual or social decision-maker makes decisions based on expected values (e.g., Arrow and Lind, 1970; Boardman et al., 2011). If the decision has a small effect on income or other major determinants of preferences, then the decision-maker may be risk-neutral. In situations of risk aversion, the expected willingness-to-pay values for benefits should recognize the influence of risk aversion so that from the standpoint of making the policy choice the expected benefits and costs should be the guide.
References: US OMB (1992); Arrow et al. (1996).

S-EMPIRICAL-2
Issue: When should some number be used instead of no number?
Standard: In contexts in which there are available data to assess the precision of a number, that number can be used when the mean is significantly different from zero, where statistical significance is often taken to be a 5 percent level of confidence in situations in which such bounds are computable. In some contexts, one must rely on judgmental probabilities as there are either no data or insufficient data to calculate these probabilities.
Discussion: Specifying these values and incorporating them in the analysis can promote sound analyses that systematically recognize the decision-maker's estimates of the likely effects. Often such judgmental probabilities can be provided as a sensitivity analysis; for example, how large must the probability of a terrorist attack be for a particular precaution to pass a benefit–cost test?

A different context for this question arises regarding the use of shadow prices estimated elsewhere, some of which may be generally accepted by analysts and others of more contention. Analysts are typically encouraged to consider whether the shadow price can be adapted for the specific population at hand. See Empirical Standard 3 below; Desvousges et al. (1998); and Boardman et al. (2011, pp. 406–36).

The role of significance tests depends on whether the information available for the analysis makes this a situation in which principles of classical statistical inference are pertinent, or whether by necessity judgmental probabilities and valuations must be used following Bayesian decision theory. Since numbers are assumed to be random variables, if the point estimate can be tested and a null hypothesis of zero is rejected then the number should be used in the classical statistics case. Perhaps the greatest danger is to abandon quantitative analyses altogether because of the imprecision of available data. Systematic thinking about policy effects is generally assisted by analyses in concrete numerical terms even when such numbers may be imprecise so that the best estimates of the distribution must be relied upon when undertaking the analysis.

Sensitivity analysis or other uncertainty methods may investigate the implications of the standard. For instance, although an estimate (coefficient) may be insignificantly different from zero, theory may indicate that the estimate is unbiased and the best available (e.g., minimum variance among linear unbiased estimates). The lack of significance may be viewed as an issue of needing more information or an inadequate sample size. Analysts may wish to investigate the robustness of their results using insignificant estimates. Further, classical measures may be unknown or poorly understood, as with terrorism risk, and so Bayesian methods for elements of a statistical distribution may be used.

References: Standard econometrics textbooks; Raiffa (1968); Pratt et al. (1995).

S-EMPIRICAL-3

Issue: When should the analyst use a point estimate developed in one location or context in a new analysis, which is a procedure often called benefit transfer or cost transfer?

Standard: To the extent possible, the point estimate should be adjusted for conditioning factors using a benefit transfer function. Whether such adjustments are made or not, the analyst should explain the reasons why the data and results obtained elsewhere are applicable to the new analysis.

Discussion: The underlying statistical population should be similar between the initial study site and the new analysis. For example, the use of recreational benefits in one area, such as a beachfront, may not be appropriate in another. There also may be differences in the population characteristics and utilization of the beachfront and these often can be recognized through the use of the pertinent elasticity of demand with respect to these characteristics, such as income. Also, the value of a statistical life based on workers may not be appropriate in other settings in which deaths occur, such as those due to terrorism, or to other populations, such as the elderly. The willingness to pay based on estimates for the average US population may not be reflective of the willingness to pay of those affected by the policy. Sensitivity analysis or other uncertainty methods may investigate the implications of a point estimate transferred by one location to another as from Empirical Standard 4 below.

References: Desvousges et al. (1998); Freeman (2003, pp. 453–6); Boardman et al. (2011, pp. 433–6); Viscusi (2011).

S-EMPIRICAL-4

Issue: How should the variability in outcomes due to parameter assumptions be assessed?

Standard: Investigate the sensitivity of the point estimate result at least with respect to key alternative values as might exist in the literature. In addition, consider a systematic adjustment of key variables in the analysis by changing their value by a common amount, such as 25 percent (stress testing).

Discussion: Sensitivity analysis as a "what if" investigation of empirical alternatives can investigate specific issues in the literature or policy debate; systematic variation in parameter values improves comparability of outcomes. More advanced approaches are discussed as Frontier Empirical Standard 1 below.

References: Boardman et al. (2011, pp. 177–87).

S-EMPIRICAL-5

Issue: What is the link, if any, between the discount rate and uncertainty?

Standard: Use the appropriate real or nominal discount rate as specified by the sponsoring agency. Do not add an uncertainty premium into the discount rate. Various justifications for different levels of the discount rate implicitly include some return for risk when private sector crowding out is assumed; and the risk-free rate has been supported based on risk pooling across governmental investments. Lower interest rates are often based on pure time preference rates.

Discussion: Consider a typical discounting calculation as involving a value, which is the numerator, and a discount rate term in the denominator. Some initial approaches in the literature suggested adjusting the discount rate using information on the price of dispersion (risk) and the quantity of risk associated with the project (Zerbe and Dively, 1994, pp. 332–3; see also Burgess and Zerbe, 2011). More recently, the focus has been on adjusting the numerator for risk and discounting at rates believed to be associated more directly with time. Thus, the role of risk can be incorporated in the expected benefits at any point in time rather than through the discount rate, which imposes a mathematical structure on the influence of uncertainty over time that may not be reflective of the temporal influence of uncertainty.

What are being discounted are the monetized values—the expected benefits and costs at different points in time—not physical units. If the unit dollar benefit value is constant over time, then discounting physical units is appropriate. But often there is a growth in these unit benefit values due, for example, to increases in income or greater scarcity of resources. If the unit benefit value is growing at a rate g and the discount rate is r, where $r > g$, then it is appropriate to discount the value of physical units over time or the benefit value based on current unit benefit amounts using a discount rate of $r - g$. See also Frontier Empirical Standard 2 below.
References: Lind (1982); US GAO (1991); Portney and Weyant (1999); Viscusi (2007); Summers and Zeckhauser (2008); Dasgupta (2008); Boardman et al. (2011, pp. 263–5).

S-EMPIRICAL-6
Issue: What characteristics of random variables should be reported?
Standard: The mean, median, and measures of dispersion such as the range, the interquartile range, and standard deviation of key outcomes such as benefits, costs, and net present value.
Discussion: In practice, the social welfare function is not known nor is that of the decision-maker. It is useful to provide to stakeholders and decision-makers information about the variability in the outcomes so that the decision-maker(s) can be informed about elements that may influence their choice. The range, meaning the minimum and maximum, leaves interpretation to the decision-maker of the probability within that range. To the extent possible additional information such as a 95 percent confidence level or full information about the distribution should be presented. Further, the visual display of quantitative information can be valuable. Probability density and cumulative distributions have been used with varying success to communicate uncertainty to decision-makers. There may of course be values at the extreme of a particular distribution that may imply quite different policy choices than derived from the mean values. This may provide a reason for further assessment of the key parameter values, but the potential influence of extreme values on the policy choice does not imply that the decision based on the means is incorrect.
References: Arrow et al. (1996); Krupnick et al. (2006).

3.2 Proposed Frontier Standards (FS): Theoretical and Empirical

3.2.1 Theory

FS-THEORY-1
Issue: How should the analyst value uncertain outcomes?
Frontier standard: Monetize individual values using an ex ante measure that explicitly accounts for uncertainty.
Discussion: Current thinking is that elements of uncertainty are appropriately captured in people's valuations of ex ante costs and benefits taking into consideration risk preferences such as risk aversion. The value of a statistical life is one such ex ante measure that reflects prior individual preferences with respect to reducing risks of death. Addressing the value of uncertain outcomes more generally, such as valuing the chance that one might be interested in using a natural resource at some future date, has turned out to be empirically difficult although substantial theory exists. Approaches include obtaining the option price that is the monetary metric linking the expected utility of the gamble with the utility of the certainty equivalent; adjusting expected damage (ex post measure) using theoretical adjustments; using the larger of expected surplus or option price if fair insurance is available; and using quasi-option or real option values if the decision-maker can adapt to new information and decisions are irreversible. For example, committing to irreversible capital investment today may give up the option value of investing tomorrow as new information arrives, which is a real option value. Alternatively, people may be willing to pay for a form of (approximately) state-independent payment consistent with option price, for example the purchase of sprinkler irrigation that incurs a certain cost but may stabilize income in either wet or dry years.
References: Viscusi (1992); Dixit and Pindyck (1994); Viscusi and Aldy (2003); Freeman (2003, pp. 209–52); Boardman et al. (2011, pp. 202–13).

FS-THEORY-2
Issue: What welfare measure should be used?
Frontier standard: Use "exact" consumer surplus based on compensated demand.
Discussion: Duality theory provides methods for exactly calculating compensating or equivalent variation measures of consumer surplus given estimated parameters. Methods are based either on integrating an estimated Marshallian demand curve back to underlying expenditure and indirect utility functions, or to assume a known utility function to derive appropriate Marshallian demands. If econometric methods are used to estimate

the parameters, the variance of the estimate can be computed given the known, but generally non-linear, structure of the exact consumer surplus measure. Under some conditions, non-market valuation linked to market observables can be carried out although failure of integrability, separability, or some non-market conditions may invalidate exact estimation.
References: Hausman (1981) and Freeman (2003, pp. 69–72, 101–22).

FS-THEORY-3
Issue: How should insurance be included in the BCA?
Frontier standard: Use to inform an ex ante evaluation based on premiums or an ex post measure of damages based on insurance claims paid.
Discussion: If insurance were actuarially fair, then by definition insurance premiums would equal the expected loss. Notwithstanding the practical difference between insurance premiums and losses, risk-averse people often purchase insurance and the premiums they pay would provide an estimate of the ex ante willingness to pay for the level of risk reduction. With insurance loading and multiple risks, the estimate is biased. Many people may forgo the purchase of insurance even though they are risk-averse if the premiums are too high so that their valuations will not be entirely captured by insurance premiums. When an insured event occurs, there is a transfer of funds based on a partial estimate of damages given the degree and extent of coverage. For example, voluntary risk premiums paid to avoid flooding may inform estimates of the value of structural improvements to reduce flooding.
References: Krutilla (1966); Schlesinger (2000); Freeman (2003, pp. 210–21); Boardman et al. (2011, pp. 211–13).

FS-THEORY-4
Issue: Does a budget constraint change the recommended decision rule?
Frontier standard: With constrained budgets the incremental net welfare measure, usually expected net present value, should equal or exceed a threshold value larger than zero.
Discussion: Equality-constrained optimization problems typically yield the result that the change in the objective function due to a choice variable (the first-order condition identifying the incremental impact) should equal the shadow price of the constraint, the Lagrangian multiplier. As all first-order conditions equal the same shadow price for a budget constraint, the standard follows. The implication is that some projects that may pass an unconstrained benefit–cost test (positive expected net present value) will fail the test based on limited resources. For example, the optimal allocation of homeland security expenditures across sites should equalize the marginal expected social costs avoided and the shadow price of the

constraint. A related standard based on benefit–cost ratios is discussed in the references for choosing among a set of projects with a fixed budget.
References: Stokey and Zeckhauser (1978); Bellinger (2007, p. 157); Farrow (2007).

3.2.2 Empirical

FS-EMPIRICAL-1
Issue: How does one estimate the statistical distribution of outcomes?
Frontier standard: Implement Monte Carlo simulation analysis using information on the statistical distribution of input assumptions and their interrelations in the model.
Discussion: Many software applications now allow Monte Carlo simulation when the user specifies input distributions and interrelations. The output of such simulation can be reported via tables, graphs, and interpretive data such as the correlation of inputs with outcomes, tornado diagrams, and similar diagnostics. For example, models such as BENMAP (US EPA, 2010) or FERET (Farrow et al., 2001) utilize different simulation tools to estimate the benefits or net benefits of pollution reduction based on distributions for concentration-response functions and for the value of various health outcomes. More unusually, the random error may be modeled (Farrow, 2012).
References: US OMB (2003); Boardman et al. (2011).

FS-EMPIRICAL-2
Issue: What is the appropriate discount rate with long-term risks?
Frontier standard: As indicated in Standard Empirical 5 above, the discount rate for near-term effects is generally specified by agency or OMB guidance. Discounting of remote risks, such as those faced by future generations, is more problematic and remains an active area for emerging economic research. We do not believe there is widespread acceptance of a common alternative approach other than investigating the sensitivity of the analysis to the assumed discount rate although many approaches are under consideration (see references).
Discussion: With exponential discounting, very long-term effects will play a very minor role in the analysis unless the valuation of the magnitudes being discounted also increases over time due to a positive income elasticity or increasing scarcity of the good being valued. Thus, if the discount rate is 3 percent and benefits are increasing in value by 2.5 percent, then the net discount rate of 0.5 percent has a much more modest effect on discounted long-term benefit values than would a 3 percent rate.

How effects for future generations should be discounted remains a

matter of continuing debate that we do not believe has resolved into a specific standard. Such long-term effects have been primarily of academic interest and are included in very few benefit assessments although climate change analyses have brought greater attention to the issue. The most fundamental task is to include longer-term consequences when they are potentially important to the policy assessment. Some economists have advocated preferential, lower discount rates for future generations based on intergenerational equity concerns. Suggestions that a zero discount rate be used have been widely rejected since a permanent $1 annual loss would have an infinite value and would swamp all other concerns in the analysis. Others have advocated discounting of future benefits in the same manner as effects for the current generation. A less future-oriented position is based on an assumption that future generations will be more affluent than the current generation so that there should be no preferential treatment of future generations if one ignores intergenerational income inequality. Should differential discount rates be used, such as a declining rate of discount over time, there is also a potential problem of time inconsistency. For example, will the discount rate sequence being applied to policies that have effects on future generation effects be in line with the preferences of that generation, which may have more present-oriented preferences for benefits and costs within their generation than suggested by a steadily declining discount rate over time?
References: Viscusi (2007); Dasgupta (2008); Summers and Zeckhauser (2008); Boardman et al. (2011); and Jamison and Jamison (2011).

FS-EMPIRICAL-3
Issue: How can distributional weights be incorporated?
Standard: The basic standard is that no adjustment (weighting) is made for those who receive the benefit or pay the cost. The frontier standard is that sensitivity analysis of this assumption be carried out based on guidance from policy decision-makers.
Discussion: The aggregation of individual benefits is problematic, both because individual marginal utility of incomes are not known and because there is no agreement on a social welfare function. The basic standard assumes a constant marginal utility of income across all people and no income inequality aversion as a society. These assumptions should be investigated if there are important distributional implications of the action (e.g., income, race, age, gender). For example, an analyst could adjust impacts by income categories of those affected using "Atkinson" values published by the Bureau of the Census that imply relative marginal utilities of income based on differing incomes. This adjustment is formally equivalent to a risk aversion to income inequality. In the absence of a

consensus on distributional weights, a more limited approach is to provide separate information on the distribution of benefits and costs among the various stakeholders of concern and to be able to provide breakdowns of interest to policy decision-makers.
References: Layard and Walters (1978); Boardman et al. (2011).

4 CONCLUSION

Benefit–cost analysis is frequently applied to decisions involving public safety that require analyzing risk and assessing options to manage risks. Developing principles and standards may assist analysts, decision-makers, and the public in developing and interpreting such BCAs. Principles and standards at best represent commonly held views among a community of practice. Such views are continually evolving with advances in the field. As a result, the proposed principles and standards are presented here as representing standard and frontier practice as of 2011. Over time, some frontier practices may become standard and new frontier standards may develop. The modularized format for the principles and standards may assist in focusing discussion and decisions about whether such proposals actually reflect principles and standards within the BCA community of practice.

REFERENCES

Arrow, Kenneth and Robert Lind (1970), "Uncertainty and the evaluation of public investment decisions," *American Economic Review*, **60** (3), 364–78.
Arrow, Kenneth, Maureen Cropper, George Eads, Robert Hahn, Lester Lave, Roger Knoll, Paul Portney, Milton Russell, Richard Schmalensee, V. Kerry Smith, and Robert Stavins (1996), "Is there a role for benefit–cost analysis in environmental, health, and safety regulation?," *Science*, **272** (April), 221–2.
Bellinger, William (2007), *The Economic Analysis of Public Policy*, New York: Routledge.
Boardman, Anthony, David Greenberg, Aidan Vining, and David Weimer (2011), *Cost–Benefit Analysis: Concepts and Practice*, Upper Saddle River, NJ: Pearson-Prentice Hall.
Brent, Robert (1998), *Cost–Benefit Analysis for Developing Countries*, Cheltenham, UK and Lyme, NH, USA: Edward Elgar.
Burgess, David and Richard Zerbe (2011), "Appropriate discounting for benefit–cost analysis," *Journal of Benefit–Cost Analysis*, **2** (2), Article 2.
Committee to Evaluate Measures of Health Benefits for Environmental, Health, and Safety Regulation (2006), Wilhelmine Miller, Lisa Robinson, and Robert Lawrence (eds), *Valuing Health for Regulatory Cost-Effectiveness Analysis*, Washington, DC: National Academies Press.

Dasgupta, Partha (2008), "Discounting climate change," *Journal of Risk and Uncertainty*, **27** (2/3), 141–69.
DellaVigna, Stefano (2009), "Psychology and economics: Evidence from the field," *Journal of Economic Literature*, **47** (2), 315–72.
DeMartino, George (2011), *The Economist's Oath*, Oxford: Oxford University Press.
Desvousges, William, Reed Johnson, and Spencer Banzhaf (1998), *Environmental Policy Analysis with Limited Information: Principles and Applications of the Transfer Method*, Cheltenham, UK and Lyme, NH, USA: Edward Elgar.
Dixit, Avinash and Robert Pindyck (1994), *Investment Under Uncertainty*, Princeton, NJ: Princeton University Press.
Eeckhoudt, Louis, Christian Gollier, and Harris Schlesinger (2005), *Economic and Financial Decisions Under Risk*, Princeton, NJ: Princeton University Press.
Farrow, Scott (2007), "The economics of homeland security expenditures: Foundational expected cost-effectiveness approaches," *Contemporary Economic Policy*, **25** (1), 14–26.
Farrow, Scott (2012), "A missing error term in benefit–cost analysis," *Environmental Science and Technology*, **46** (5), 2523–8.
Farrow, Scott, Rafael Ponce, Eva Wong, Elaine Faustman, and Richard Zerbe (2001), "Facilitating regulatory design and stakeholder participation: The FERET template with an application to the Clean Air Act," in Scott Farrow and Paul Fischbeck (eds), *Improving Regulation: Cases in Environment, Health and Safety*, Washington, DC: Resources for the Future Press.
Freeman, Myrick III (2003), *The Measurement of Environmental and Resource Values*, 2nd edition, Washington, DC: Resources for the Future Press.
Gramlich, Edward (1990), *A Guide to Benefit–Cost Analysis*, 2nd edition, Englewood Cliffs, NJ: Prentice Hall.
Hanley, Nick and Clive Spash (1993), *Cost–Benefit Analysis and the Environment*, Aldershot, UK and Brookfield, VT, USA: Edward Elgar.
Hansen, Lars and Thomas Sargent (2008), *Robustness*, Princeton, NJ: Princeton University Press.
Hausman, Jerry (1981), "Exact consumer surplus and deadweight loss," *American Economic Review*, **71** (4), 662–76.
Haveman, Robert, Mary Gabay, and James Andreoni (1987), "Exact consumer's surplus and deadweight loss: A correction," *American Economic Review*, **77** (3), 494–5.
Hirshleifer, Jack and John Riley (1992), *The Analytics of Uncertainty and Information*, Cambridge, MA: Cambridge University Press.
Jamison, Dean and Julian Jamison (2011), "Characterizing the amount and speed of discounting procedures," *Journal of Benefit–Cost Analysis*, **2** (2), Article 1.
Jehle, Geoffrey and Philip Reny (2000), *Advanced Microeconomic Theory*, 2nd edition, New York: Addison Wesley.
Jones, Chris (2005), *Applied Welfare Economics*, Oxford: Oxford University Press.
Just, Richard, Darrell Hueth, and Andrew Schmitz (2004), *The Welfare Economics of Public Policy*, Cheltenham, UK and Northampton, MA, USA: Edward Elgar.
Krupnick, Allen, Richard D. Morgenstern, Michael B. Batz, Per-Kristian C. Nelson, Dallas Burtraw, Jhih-Shyang Shih, and Michael R. Williams (2006), *Not a Sure Thing: Making Regulatory Choices Under Uncertainty*, Washington, DC: Resources for the Future Press.

Krutilla, John (1966), "An economic approach to coping with flood damage," *Water Resources Research*, **2** (1), 183–90.
Layard, Richard and Stephen Glaister (1994), *Cost–Benefit Analysis*, 2nd edition, Cambridge, UK: Cambridge University Press.
Layard, Richard and A. Walters (1978), "Income distribution," in Richard Layard and Stephen Glaister (eds), *Cost–Benefit Analysis*, 2nd edition, Cambridge, UK: Cambridge University Press.
Lempert, Robert and Myles Collins (2007), "Managing the risk of uncertain threshold responses: Comparison of robust, optimum, and precautionary approaches," *Risk Analysis*, **27** (4), 1009–26.
Lind, Robert (ed.) (1982), *Discounting for Time and Risk in Energy Policy*, Washington, DC: Resources for the Future Press.
Luce, Duncan R. and Howard Raiffa (1965) (original was 1957), *Games and Decisions: Introduction and Critical Survey*, 5th edition, New York: John Wiley and Sons, Inc.
Morgan, M. Granger and Max Henrion (1990), *Uncertainty: A Guide to Dealing with Uncertainty in Quantitative Risk and Policy Analysis*, Cambridge, UK: Cambridge University Press
Portney, Paul and John Weyant (eds) (1999), *Discounting and Intergenerational Equity*, Washington, DC: Resources for the Future Press.
Pratt, John, Howard Raiffa, and Robert Schlaifer (1995), *Introduction to Statistical Decision Theory*, Cambridge, MA: MIT Press.
Raiffa, Howard (1968), *Decision Analysis: Introductory Lectures on Choice under Uncertainty*, Reading, MA: Addison-Wesley.
Robinson, Lisa and James Hammitt (2011), "Behavioral economics and the conduct of benefit–cost analysis: Towards principles and standards," *Journal of Benefit–Cost Analysis*, **2** (2), Article 5.
Schlesinger, Harris (2000), "The theory of insurance demand," in George Dionne (ed.), *Handbook of Insurance*, Boston, MA: Kluwer Academic Publishers.
Schmitz, Andrew and Richard O. Zerbe (eds) (2009), *Applied Benefit–Cost Analysis*, Cheltenham, UK and Northampton, MA, USA: Edward Elgar.
Stokey, Edith and Richard Zeckhauser (1978), *A Primer for Policy Analysis*, New York: W.W. Norton.
Summers, Lawrence and Richard Zeckhauser (2008), "Policymaking for posterity," *Journal of Risk and Uncertainty*, **37** (2/3), 115–40.
US Environmental Protection Agency (2010), *Environmental Benefits Mapping and Analysis Program: 4.0*, accessed 4 April 2011 at http://www.epa.gov/air/benmap/basic.html.
US Governmental Accountability Office (GAO) (1991), "Discount rate policy," Office of the Chief Economist, Washington, DC, accessed 4 April 2011 at http://www.gao.gov/.
US Governmental Accountability Office (GAO) (2005), *Economic Performance: Highlights of a Workshop on Economic Performance Measures*, GAO-05-796SP, Washington, DC: GAO.
US Office of Management and Budget (OMB) (1992), "Guidelines and discount rates for benefit–cost analysis of federal programs," OMB Circular A-94, Washington, DC.
US Office of Management and Budget (OMB) (2003), "Regulatory analysis," OMB Circular A-4, Washington, DC.

Viscusi, W. Kip (1992), *Fatal Tradeoffs: Public and Private Responsibilities for Risk*, New York: Oxford University Press.
Viscusi, W. Kip (1998), *Rational Risk Policy*, Oxford: Oxford University Press.
Viscusi, W. Kip (2007), "Rational discounting for regulatory analysis," *University of Chicago Law Review*, **74** (1), 209–46.
Viscusi, W. Kip (2011), "Policy challenges of the heterogeneity of the value of statistical life," *Foundations and Trends in Microeconomics*, **6** (1), 99–172.
Viscusi, W. Kip and Joseph Aldy (2003), "The value of statistical life: A critical review of market estimates throughout the world," *Journal of Risk and Uncertainty*, **27** (1), 5–76.
Willig, Robert (1976), "Consumer surplus without apology," *American Economic Review*, **66** (4), 589–97.
Zerbe, Jr., Richard O. (ed.) (2008), *Benefit–Cost Analysis*, Cheltenham, UK and Northampton, MA, USA: Edward Elgar.
Zerbe, Jr., Richard O. and Dwight Dively (1994), *Benefit–Cost Analysis in Theory and Practice*, New York: Harper Collins.

6. Developing general equilibrium benefit analyses for social programs: an introduction and example

H. Allen Klaiber and V. Kerry Smith

1 INTRODUCTION

This chapter describes an approach for incorporating general equilibrium effects into benefit–cost analyses of social programs. To make our description tangible we selected a specific example: the evaluation of reductions in the resources available for public primary education. To highlight the general equilibrium effects of exogenous reductions in the resources used to produce education and its effect on measures of the quality of education, we use a locational sorting model applied to school districts in Maricopa County, AZ, USA. Several of these districts experienced teacher cuts in the 2009–10 school year. These cuts provide a tangible basis for illustrating how the model would work. General equilibrium effects allow non-market feedbacks to be aligned with the interrelationships between markets that are widely acknowledged in conventional multimarket analyses. In the context of sorting models, general equilibrium effects influence our understanding of *both* the severity and distribution of changes in household well-being arising as a result of changes to local social programs.

Most discussions of the distinctions between partial equilibrium (PE) and general equilibrium (GE) frameworks for benefit–cost analysis focus on policies that directly alter the prices of marketed goods and services. Many follow the seminal contributions described in Just et al. (2004). When these analyses consider policies altering the amounts, quality or conditions of access to non-market resources, there are added complexities. Nonetheless, the basic concepts defining PE and GE measures of net benefits are comparable.

After providing context for our analysis, section 3 defines benefit concepts and explains the difference between PE and GE welfare measures. Section 4 describes two approaches for developing models capable of measuring GE effects with non-market interactions that might arise from social or environmental policies. The first of these approaches uses the computable general equilibrium (CGE) logic originally developed by Scarf (1973) and made easily accessible through the MPSGE (mathematical programming system for general equilibrium) framework developed by Rutherford (1997).[1] The second modeling approach involves locational sorting models. The locational equilibrium approaches are different from the CGE logic. They do not represent GE welfare measures in the same way that the conventional CGE framework does.[2] We discuss locational equilibrium models because they are especially relevant to situations where social programs are provided by local governments. To extend the CGE framework to include market and non-market policies, the framework must describe how the services that result from these programs influence preferences and/or production activities. These specifications, in turn, influence how non-market feedbacks influence model outcomes. As a result, we include a discussion of how most CGE models have addressed these issues. Our review is somewhat critical of the most popular maintained assumption of separability between market and non-market influences. To help document our argument, we describe some of the existing analyses of PE versus GE measures associated with environmental policies.

Finally, our example of PE versus GE welfare measures for educational policy is developed in two sections. Section 5 describes how a vertical locational sorting model is estimated to characterize household preferences for the quality of local public education. Our application is based on housing sales data and the differences in performance of primary school students on standardized tests for 46 school districts in Maricopa County, AZ, USA. Our analysis allows school quality to be endogenous to equilibrium household sorting and solves the model as a Nash equilibrium. Each household is assumed to respond to housing prices and to recognize what other households will do in response to exogenous changes in resources for public schools. Households decide to relocate based on both housing prices and the implied effects of all household movements on the resulting school quality in each district, which is influenced by student/teacher ratios.

An outline of the conceptual features of this model and our example describing the PE and GE costs of eliminating different numbers of teachers in each of a subset of the school districts in Maricopa County are presented in section 6. The last section summarizes what is known about developing GE benefit–cost assessments for social programs and outlines a few areas where further research would be likely to yield significant payoffs.

2 BACKGROUND

2.1 Conventional Practice

Most of the economic analyses of the GE consequences of policies have been in the context of marketed goods and services. The focus has been on the effects of distortions in markets or the effects of new interventions. These can be pre-existing taxes, environmental regulations, or non-competitive markets. These effects are represented as creating wedges between what demanders pay and suppliers receive for the goods and services involved. There have been a number of interesting findings. For example, a pre-existing distortion can influence the measured effects of a new tax depending on whether a partial versus general perspective is adopted. The measured excess burden from introducing a new, relatively small tax can vary substantially due to GE effects (see Goulder and Williams, 2003). In another context, Goulder et al. (1999) demonstrate that similar GE "surprises" can arise in comparing the cost-effectiveness of environmental policy instruments with pre-existing distortions. These existing distortions raise the efficiency costs of all environmental policies relative to the costs in a first-best world.[3] In addition, they can alter the superiority of tradable permits over performance standards and mandated technologies from an efficiency perspective.

The evaluation of the differences of PE and GE effects cannot be distinguished from the assumptions made in defining the "size" of an intervention in relation to one or more markets. In most public economics applications involving taxes or regulations the evaluation typically focuses on the direct effects of the tax or regulation on prices. For these applications, size is interpreted in terms of a policy's effect on a PE or a GE measure of excess burden. The direct effect on excess burden is often proportional to the square of the size of the policy, and the policy is treated as a price wedge. For the case of taxes, size is based on the size of a change in tax rates. In practice, there has not been a specific definition of large or small changes. Early literature such as Shoven and Whalley (1972) or Whalley (1975) motivated their assessments using previous studies of tax distortions. For example, Shoven and Whalley used Harberger's estimates of the efficiency costs of differential tax treatment of capital in the USA. Whalley used a specific reform in UK capital tax rates. More recently, Goulder and Williams (2003) used a range of hypothetical new tax rates on commodities in different sectors to illustrate their arguments for the importance of a PE versus GE perspective in measuring excess burden. For these types of examples the GE effects are often approximately linear in this price wedge.

With environmental applications size can have a somewhat different meaning. It can arise from a spatial dimension, such as the amount of undeveloped land that is preserved in a protected status or the number of households affected who might be demanders (or suppliers) of specific goods and services. In either context, size does not correspond to a price wedge in a single market. In these settings, Palmquist's (1992) arguments for how to evaluate localized externalities are frequently used as an analogy to describe how "size" affects benefit measures in differentiated markets. The challenge arises because for environmental applications the change associated with a market response takes place within a specific geographic context. At least two steps are involved in translating it into an equivalent price change experienced by different households.

The first of these steps involves the representation of the spatial features associated with the impacted amenity as an attribute of a location. For example, is open space measured as the amount (acres) within a distance zone of each property, a measure of distance to the closest open space, or both? Depending on the way the non-market attribute is represented, the effects on the hypothesized trade-offs people would make to obtain (or avoid) it will be different. Equally important, the number of locations affected will be different. These distinctions are important because they imply the selection of a modeling strategy and a metric for measuring the non-market good will influence the "size" of effects assigned to each policy. With this outcome we also have a difference in the potential importance of PE and GE responses. Thus, the characterization of the market and the policy are jointly related in determining the equivalent of a price effect. In this case, it is the price change for one or a small number of locations.[4] Related to this point is the description of how a non-market good is made available to a consumer. Many economic models do not describe the geographic extent of the market. For some applications this is not important. However, it is important for non-market services. Non-market goods have virtual prices that cannot be defined without reference to the geography of the processes that influence their availability.

These issues arise in many forms. Here, attention is focused on the geography for considering the distinction between GE and PE welfare measures. The geographical extent of the market must be assumed for any benefit–cost analysis. The Clean Air Act introduces regulations that improve air quality in the USA and may also affect air quality in Canada or Mexico. Whittington and MacRae (1986) considered the issue of who should "count" in benefit–cost analysis as a question of who has "standing." For national policies and associated rules, we may be comfortable with using the political entity responsible for the rules to provide this definition. However, if we consider a local change for an important resource the question of the extent of the market may not be easily resolved in these terms. Removing dams on the Klamath River affects a river system. It is a federal decision with input from the states and stakeholders but the extent of the market for the changes in environmental services is not as clearly national.

Two important distinctions arise in these examples. First, what domain defines the affected individuals and do their responses influence markets that might signal trade-offs they would make to get (or to avoid) changes that are taking place due to an exogenous policy change. Second, are these services also influenced through a natural system that responds to what people do in response to an exogenous policy change? This system might be related to spatial markets but is separate and not market based. It leads to what we label here, non-market feedbacks, and need not have the same spatial definition as the market system used in describing a GE response.

2.2 Just et al.'s General Equilibrium Demand Functions

In a conventional summary of GE analysis in a static multi-market setting, such as Just et al. (2004), the analysis would begin by describing the features of GE demand functions.[5] When an exogenous distortion, such as a tax or a regulation, is introduced into an otherwise undistorted market equilibrium their analysis demonstrates how the PE and GE benefit measures can be compared in a single market. This explanation is based on the concept of a GE demand function. In the GE demand function the measure of how the quantity demanded of a good changes with a change in its price is defined so that this response measure is adjusted by the contributions that substitute or complementary markets make to equilibrium outcomes (observed in that good's market because its price has changed). When demand and supply functions describing all markets are linear the derivation is straightforward. The reduced form expressions for equilibrium prices in all other markets are used to eliminate their price effects in the demand for the commodity of interest. The term describing the price effect is the algebraic counterpart to assuming equilibrium adjustments in all markets have taken place when evaluating a price change in the one market of interest. It is consistent with GE welfare measures because there are no distortions in any other market. By assumption, each consumer's marginal willingness to pay is equal to the marginal cost for each good in these other markets. The action in the market of interest does not change that outcome. It may change the levels of consumption of these goods, and correspondingly the levels for their marginal willingness to pay and marginal cost in the new equilibrium. Only the market with the intervention has a wedge if the intervention is a tax or regulation that affects demanders and suppliers differently.

Harberger's (1964) strategy for measuring excess burden exploits a similar logic for the case of a single distortion. Recently, in arguing that the Harberger formula can be interpreted as a sufficient statistic, Chetty (2009) outlines two conditions. The first is that behavioral responses to price changes for other goods, induced by a new tax on a separate commodity (or service) are not first-order effects. In this context, he means that the majority of the effect will be captured in the market experiencing the change. He is making an analogy to a first-order (linear) approximation that would ignore "interaction" effects. The second is that in the absence of other distortions, the other price effects cancel between consumers and producers. Of course, this assessment does rely on our ability to measure the full effect of the new tax on the good being taxed.

When we consider the analog to a GE demand for non-market goods a parallel result could be suggested. That is, if a policy intervention affects multiple uses of an environmental resource we might not observe adjustment in response to a change in one context but would observe it in another. This would not mean "equality" of marginal willingness to pay and marginal cost (i.e., price and marginal cost in the context of multiple markets without imperfections). Here, it might mean considering the costs of adjustment along some margins such that the differences would not be large enough to motivate changes. The natural question that might arise concerns the mechanism that would lead to these types of outcomes.

One possibility would be through a hedonic model, but for the question to have meaning we would need to consider a non-market good that served multiple purposes for the same household. In this context, we could observe it affecting different types of choices. The reason is that one might be assumed to be capable of being adjusted by adapting behavior with relatively low cost and another might require larger adjustment costs. The example discussed in Phaneuf et al. (2008) is water quality in local lakes and its influence on housing prices and on local recreation trips. The changes in water quality could be small enough that they did not influence the hedonic equilibrium (e.g., the disparity between marginal willingness to pay and marginal price was not large enough, given the transaction costs of moving, to warrant relocation) but there could be a reason to measure the gains in terms of local recreation.[6] Recreationists would change the location and number of trips based on the change in water quality. Larger changes would be required to see the market feedback through housing markets. As a rule, however, the ways that are available to households to select different amounts of non-market goods are limited.

3 HOW SHOULD THE NET BENEFITS OF A PUBLIC INTERVENTION BE DEFINED?

The question posed in this heading is general. Our focus here will be targeted. We accept a conventional economic definition for what constitutes a benefit. It is either the amount a person would be willing to give up to realize some specific change from his or her baseline conditions (in the case of a willingness to pay for a desirable change) or it is the amount of compensation a person would require to be indifferent between having the change versus remaining with the baseline condition and receiving monetary compensation (the willingness-to-accept measure). A key element in the PE versus GE distinction is the characterization of "the change." In most standard discussions it would be described as a price, quantity, or quality change. However, when one considers policy evaluation, a key question is translating the change we associated with the specific policy, into a change in one or more of the exogenous factors that influence people's (and firms') decisions. This translation is directly connected to the differences we will classify into PE and GE measures of net benefits.

3.1 Some Definitions

A Hicksian consumer surplus assumes we can represent a person's choices within a constrained utility-maximizing framework. In the simplest static example, the constraint is a budget constraint relating income to the prices of the goods and services consumed. The outcome of these choices is represented with an indirect utility function, where realized well-being, V, is a function of income, prices, and any other exogenous factors contributing to well-being and outside a person's control.

We will adopt the convention that a superscript 0 defines the baseline condition and a 1 is the new or altered condition with the policy. Equation (6.1) defines the well-being that a person realizes in the baseline as a function of income, prices, public goods, and other exogenous factors contributing to well-being.[7]

$$V^0 = V(m^0, p^0, Z^0, q^0) \tag{6.1}$$

where m = income, p = a vector of prices of marketed goods, q = a vector of public goods (produced by local governments) and/or available natural assets such as air quality, and Z = a vector of quasi-fixed private commodities assumed outside an individual's direct control.

Willingness to pay is the income a person would give up to obtain some desirable change. Thus, if we assume one price (in our example the price for the first good) is lower in the new state (superscripted with 1) than in the baseline condition so the vector p^1 corresponds to $p^1 = [p_1^1 p_2^0 p_3^0 \ldots p_k^0]$ and $p^0 = [p_1^0 p_2^0 p_3^0 \ldots p_k^0]$, then the willingness to pay (WTP) for this improvement (from p_1^0 to p_1^1) is defined in equation (6.2a) and the willingness to accept (WTA) to forgo the same improvement is in equation (6.2b):[8]

$$V_1(m^0 - WTP, p^1, Z^0, q^0) = V(m^0, p^0, Z^0, q^0) \tag{6.2a}$$

$$V(m^0, p^1, Z^0, q^0) = V(m^0 + WTA, p^0, Z^0, q^0) \tag{6.2b}$$

To use equations (6.2a) and (6.2b) to describe the difference between PE and GE measures of WTP and WTA requires a specification for the source of the change in p_1. This source is often illustrated by supposing a tax is introduced. That is, we might suggest $p_1^1 = p_1^0 + t$ for the representative consumer. It is important to recognize this specification makes an implicit assumption about market conditions by maintaining that there is a perfectly elastic supply for the good being taxed. We can assume consumers are heterogeneous in the ways that they are affected by the tax. These need not be considered, as Chetty explains, because what matters for aggregate welfare change is the total change in behavior induced by the new tax. Assuming this can be measured at the aggregate level, compositional effects would not influence the overall assessment. They would be relevant for estimating distributional effects of a tax change.

Consider a more general case; assume there is a policy designated with the symbol θ. It could be a regulation, a tax, or new information about a product or service. The definition is not limited to situations where only one thing changes.[9] It could be a new rule that includes a way to finance the costs of the rule. Thus, there might be a tax change to pay for the enforcement activities required to assure the rule is implemented. In this case, θ represents a vector of actions.[10] A GE measure would consider the change in θ from θ^0 (the baseline conditions) to θ^1. Evaluating this change *requires a model of how the change influences the variables taken to be exogenous from the individual's perspective*. Thus, with direct effects of θ impacting several prices through some mechanism outside each individual's choice process, we would define the GE measure of WTP as:

$$V(m^0 - WTP^{GE}, p(\theta^1), Z^0, q^0) = V(m^0, p(\theta^0), Z^0, q^0) \tag{6.3}$$

We could assume Z^0 and q^0 also change but, in this case, the process that causes them to change would need to be specified. Income could also be assumed to change either through the revaluation of endowments, a change in the wage, or both.

The specific features of a GE benefit measure cannot be considered to be completely separate from the model used to estimate them. This conclusion follows from the logical structure of each model. That is, different models capture the elements of the policy delivery system that are outside market exchanges in different ways. In the environmental case, most policies are linked to a spatial delineation of people's choices. In the case of social policy, the process can be spatially delineated if the policy is delivered at a local level or is conditional on the local situation. Equally important, there is increasing recognition of the importance of the heterogeneity of consumer preferences to the full outcomes of policy. Often, people can respond outside of markets in ways that influence the policy outcomes. Suppose, for example, the policy involves the quality of local education at the primary level and that we hypothesize that the education outcomes for all students depend on peer group effects. That is, classes with the same minimum number of high-ability students experience better learning outcomes for all students than those classes with more homogeneous students, all with average ability. In these cases, the ways in which models incorporate preference heterogeneity and its effects on locational choices and schooling decisions will influence this dimension of their ability to represent GE effects.

To help develop this point in the remainder of this section we discuss PE benefit measures at the individual level. Partial equilibrium measures select a subset of the effects of a policy. One of the best examples of how this separation of effects can influence the way models are developed is to consider the organization of most benefit–cost staff conducting policy evaluation. As a rule, one group does costs and another group does benefits. This classification assumes each part can be done separately from the other. In a PE world, we might be willing to accept this assumption. In a GE world, as we explain below, we should not be satisfied with this division of labor.

To illustrate interplay between the definition of the GE measures for the net benefits of a policy and the model used to compute how GE effects arise, consider the argument developed more completely in Smith and Carbone (2007).[11] To begin it is helpful to define the consumer surplus measures in terms of expenditure functions. Thus, we invert the indirect utility function, equation (6.1), solving for the total expenditures needed to realize a given utility level. This function is the Hicksian expenditure function.[12] The definitions for WTP and WTA parallel to equations (6.2a) and (6.2b) using expenditure functions, designated here with the function, $e(.)$, are given in equations (6.4a) and (6.4b):

$$WTP = e(p^0, Z^0, q^0, u^0) - e(p^1, Z^0, q^0, u^0) \tag{6.4a}$$

$$WTA = e(p^0, Z^0, q^0, u^1) - e(p^1, Z^0, q^0, u^1) \tag{6.4b}$$

where u describes the utility level with the superscript of 0 corresponding to the baseline condition and 1 the new situation. Our definition follows the standard convention in applied welfare economics.[13]

In our example of a tax, we assumed $p_1^1 > p_1^0$, where the subscript 1 indicates this price is for the first good. We would expect it is necessary to spend more with the higher prices to realize the baseline utility. Similarly, the level of well-being with the higher prices would be lower in the new situation ($u^1 < u^0$) so that income would need to be reduced in the baseline condition to be equivalent.

A second issue of interpretation arises when we consider the connections between equations (6.2a) and (6.2b) with equations (6.4a) and (6.4b). The definitions acknowledge that income (or expenditures) are constant when evaluated at the baseline and at the new price and utility so:

$$m^0 = e(p^0, Z^0, q^0, u^0) = e(p^1, Z^0, q^0, u^1) \tag{6.5}$$

This relationship implies that the two measures could also be defined in alternative ways. They might be described as different ways of evaluating (monetizing) the change in well-being due to the policy (i.e., using the new prices—WTP—or using the old prices—WTA).[14]

Now turning to why the organization of policy analysts can be important. Suppose benefits and costs of policies are computed separately by distinct groups. Assume further that the tax policy in our example uses the tax revenues to improve q from q^0 to q^1. The WTP measure for an individual's benefits, ignoring effects of the change in p_1 and q on other prices, would be given in equation (6.6):

$$WTP^{PE} = e(p^0, Z^0, q^0, u^0) - e(p^1, Z^0, q^1, u^0) \tag{6.6}$$

Here the sign of WTP^{PE} is not clear. Indeed, this might be described as the individual level net benefits of introducing the new tax, t, to improve q from q^0 to q^1. Hazilla and Kopp (1990) used this logic to define the "social costs" of policy. Their example was environmental policy. They asked about the importance of a GE perspective for measuring these social costs. Before considering this point, we might ask what conditions are required for equation (6.6) to be consistent with separately measuring the costs and benefits of a policy. One answer, as Smith and Carbone (2007) note, follows from the definition of the expenditure function, provided it is separable in q, and can be written as:

$$e(p^0, Z^0, q^0, u^0) = \tilde{e}(p^0, Z^0, u^0) - h(q^0) \tag{6.7}$$

In this case, the net benefit measure can be separated into a cost and a benefit computation, as in equation (6.8):

$$WTP^{PE} = \underbrace{\tilde{e}(p^0, Z^0, u^0) - \tilde{e}(p^1, Z^0, u^0)}_{\text{Incremental cost}} + \underbrace{(h(q^1) - h(q^0))}_{\text{Incremental benefit}} \tag{6.8}$$

With this restriction, the distinction between GE and PE welfare measures depends on whether the analysis takes account of the full price effects of a policy change. That is, we assume there is a policy change from θ^0 to θ^1 and we ask how, given everything else is held constant, does this change influence the set of exogenous conditions that constrain each individual's ability to realize a given level of utility? The policy could be confined to one market, or a small number of markets. Alternatively, it could be assumed to influence conditions outside markets. The PE/GE distinction arises in how we convert the policy changes into changes in the prices and other exogenous conditions that influence people's choices. Thus, this is one of the ways there can be an interplay between the modeling assumptions used to describe how a policy influences market outcomes, the assumptions used to define preferences, and the resulting PE/GE distinctions.

In the context of education programs, Heckman (2006, 2008) has argued that efforts to improve preschool programs for children will improve the educational outcomes associated with these children. He notes this improvement is also associated with lower rates of teen pregnancy, drug addiction, crime, and other consequences of high dropout rates. It also limits the choice sets these children may experience in their future activities. These added choices can involve further education or jobs for some teenagers and young adults. Do we count all of these effects as a result of the policy improving preschool programs or as just a subset? This question illustrates the GE versus PE question. The issue of model interplay arises here because the decision of what is counted often depends on the reliability of the modeling frameworks used to describe the connections between the policies and each of these outcomes. Can the results leading to changes in education outcomes, teenage pregnancy, drug addiction, and so forth be attributed to the policy intervention in a convincing way that leads to reliable predictions? Equally important, can these outcomes be incorporated in an economic framework that describes the processes determining prices and incomes?

In a different context involving education, the side-effects do not have to be positive. Improvements in educational outcomes in one school district may well attract more families. This in-migration could lead to greater competition for homes in the neighborhoods that are assigned to the district experiencing the improvement. With a fixed supply of houses in the districts with better schools, we would expect that home prices would increase. Those households owning homes in the district would gain, whereas renters would lose as their rents increase. Indeed, poorer households could well lose because higher rents might force them to leave and accept a lower-quality school district in order to obtain affordable housing. These outcomes would not be intentional and might be missed with a framework that failed to allow for the full scope of GE adjustments. They are part of the distributional effects of a policy.

The importance of a GE/PE distinction depends on the size of the program being evaluated, the size of the markets, the social/economic context being described as relevant to the policy, and the assumed interconnections between the market and non-market influences to individual behavior. If a model focuses on the pure exchange of goods and services, the concept of size has a different meaning. Add a small amount of spatial context and ask how well an addition to the tax on gasoline in one county in the USA affects the world market price of gasoline and the answer is direct—not at all. However, if we recognize that even within a small region there is variation in the price of gasoline, the effect of such a tax on the prices of other fuels in *that* region may well depend on the volume of gasoline sold in the county relative to adjoining counties that might be part of the same metropolitan area.

Gauging the difference in a PE versus a GE assessment of the welfare effects of the tax depends on what we assume. As Goulder and Williams (2003) demonstrate, with pre-existing labor taxes (at 40 percent) small taxes on a product such as cigarettes can lead to *large percentage* errors in PE compared to GE measures of excess burden. Their analysis does not consider using the tax revenue for a non-market intervention. At a national scale this can make a large difference, as Carbone and Smith (2008) demonstrate using their model of energy taxes. A small tax (5 percent) with the same pre-existing labor tax and recognition of the non-market effects (on air pollution) of the tax can increase the differences in PE and GE by 100 percent when leisure and air pollution are complements as compared to *reducing* the discrepancy by approximately 50 percent when they are substitutes. Of course, the absolute size of the error in excess burden is also large in this case.

Now, if we return to the spatial dimension of the policy—a small regional clinic—then it is unlikely the feedback effects would be important enough to be considered at a national level. However, an analysis at a local level might need to consider another type of feedback. If the improvements in the clinic's quality of care were dramatic and capacity at the clinic remained limited, the net results for local patients might not be completely positive. There could well be congestion and delayed treatment for patients due to that congestion.

These examples suggest that market and non-market effects can both matter. Moreover, the spatial scale that we use in representing the non-market process and who is affected by a policy also matters. This is how the choice of models influences the characterization of PE and GE welfare measures. Some models will not be able to easily reflect the spatial dimensions of the social process or the heterogeneity in agents and their opportunities to adjust. Decisions to use simple, market-oriented, GE models to evaluate social processes then "build in" these potentially important conditioning assumptions.[15] Thus, the definitions of GE and PE are straightforward, but the real "action" arises in the definition of the models and their implementation.

With that background, PE measurement selects a subset of the possible effects of the change in θ and measures WTP for the change in θ recognizing only that subset of changes. One might suggest that GE includes everything, but this statement needs to be qualified. GE includes everything *that is in the model* used to assess the effect of the policy. Here again, we have an example of the interplay between the modeling choices and the interpretations of the PE/GE benefit measures. Examples using an abstract representation of the issues are in equations (6.9a) and (6.9b), with two prices assumed to be affected for the PE case and everything, p, q, and Z for the GE:

$$WTP^{PE} = e(p_1^0, Z^0, q^0, u^0) - e(p_1(\theta^1), p_2(\theta^1), \ldots p_k(\theta^0), Z^0, q^0, u^0) \tag{6.9a}$$

$$WTP^{GE} = e(p^0, Z^0, q^0, u^0) - e(p(\theta^1), Z(\theta^1), q(\theta^1), u^0) \tag{6.9b}$$

Another important issue that is implicit in these definitions and is also described in some of our examples arises from the differences in the WTP measures for different individuals. As previously discussed, when people are assumed to be heterogeneous the PE/GE distinction must be considered together with the distribution of effects across people. There are at least two aspects of this issue.

People may well experience the *same* price changes but react (due to preference heterogeneity) quite differently. Moreover, once we admit effects outside markets, there may not be complete mechanisms to adjust to differences. It is also possible that the adjustment could well have feedback effects on the policy intervention. Households in different circumstances may well be more or less prone to being impacted by these non-market effects as well.

3.2 Approximations

As a practical matter it is often difficult to measure the full GE willingness to pay. With revealed preference information we usually have the ability to estimate a subset of the demand functions or will specify a choice function that assumes each person has a limited range of decisions and other choices are not affected by the one being studied. Most policy applications of benefit–cost analysis rely on the existing literature to adapt a point estimate to evaluate the benefits from a policy.[16] Here, we will define two of many such approximations and describe one potential GE/PE distinction. These measures use what is sometimes labeled as the virtual price or marginal willingness to pay for a change in something available outside the market. The marginal willingness to pay for a change in one element in q (say q_1) would then be given in equation (6.10) using the indirect utility function in equation (6.1):[17]

$$MWTPq_1 = \frac{V_{q_1}}{V_m} \tag{6.10}$$

The distinction between PE and GE measures in this context might arise with whether the virtual price is evaluated at the baseline levels of prices (and other "parameters" entering the indirect utility function) or at the new level, after the policy change. Thus equation (6.11a) would be PE and equation (6.11b) GE with the superscript 0 designating the point of evaluation:

$$\Delta B^{PE} = \frac{V_{q_1}^0}{V_m^0} \cdot \Delta q_1 \tag{6.11a}$$

$$\Delta B^{GE} = \frac{V_{q_1}^1}{V_m^1} \cdot \Delta q_1 \tag{6.11b}$$

Smith and Carbone discuss these measures as adjustments to measures of excess burden of a tax to reduce pollution externalities. Using a small-scale computable GE model, they find that the differences due to PE versus GE evaluation points for the virtual price can be important. The size of the effect they illustrate depends on how the commodity that is taxed ultimately affects the non-market good of interest. Their results suggest that the role q plays in preferences is also important to the GE/PE effects on these approximations.[18]

3.3 General Equilibrium Market Demand

As we noted in situations with undistorted markets, the welfare costs (or gains) associated with a change can be evaluated using the affected market alone. They must be evaluated using the aggregates of compensated demand functions across individuals consuming the good involved and aggregate commodity supply functions. Both must be evaluated at the values of the general equilibrium prices after the change.

This ability to focus on one market relies on two key assumptions. First, it assumes all markets are in equilibrium before and after the intervention, and second all the GE effects arise exclusively through markets. As there is only the one market affected, the GE price effects of the intervention on other goods' prices will be the same for households and firms. Thus, the line integral (or equivalently the measure used for the contribution to economic surplus) will be exactly 0, given the equilibrium condition.[19] In the market experiencing the change in price, the size of the price change realized by consumers compared to what is experienced by suppliers will be different. It depends on the relative elasticities of the demand and supply functions. Thus, even though this market is also in equilibrium after the intervention, the sharing of the price change due to the new distortion is different. As a result, we have the consumer and producer contributions to economic surplus.[20]

In the context of non-market effects, the same result would hold in marginal willingness to pay for each non-market good equal to marginal social cost before and after a change. However, aside from specialized cases such as those discussed in our hedonic example there is usually no mechanism that assures that this condition will be satisfied. This typical set of conditions is what motivates the need for a structural model to describe GE responses. It allows analysts to compute the full GE effects and to consider the distribution of their impacts.

4 GENERAL EQUILIBRIUM MODELS WITH NON-MARKET INTERACTIONS

To this point the discussion has sought to persuade readers that the "action" in GE benefit–cost analysis is in the selection of the models used to describe how policies create GE effects. The theory concerning what should be measured is reasonably straightforward. This section considers two different, static approaches describing a composite of market and non-market GE outcomes. The first extends the logic of computable GE models to include non-market effects. The primary non-market effects that have been represented in these models to date have focused on environmental externalities. While other social programs could, in principle, be represented there are significant information gaps concerning just how they would be introduced into the models that would need to be addressed. The second modeling strategy is not a full GE framework. It relies on locational sorting models. They describe situations where price determination is limited to multiple land/housing markets. This set of prices can influence and be influenced by non-market outcomes, but the model does not provide a full description of other markets with effects on both prices and components of income, as has been done in the earlier CGE frameworks.

4.1 Non-market Effects in a CGE Framework

A CGE model is a consistent description of individual and firm behavior that recognizes the joint determination of product and factor market prices. In a static competitive setting, these models assure the conditions for budget constrained utility maximization by individuals and profit maximization of firms yield a price vector consistent with: equilibrium in all markets, budget exhaustion, and zero profits in all sectors. In the simplest cases, production functions are restricted to constant returns to scale and preferences are often assumed to be homogeneous of degree one. Both relationships are often described with constant elasticity of substitution (CES) functions.

CGE models are calibrated to match the observed baseline expenditures on final goods, payments to factors, taxes and government spending (if included in the model), as well as expenditures on any intermediate goods in a base year. Developing the calibrated version of such a model that realizes the consistency condition is greatly facilitated by using the homogeneous CES specification for preference and production functions. Rutherford (1997) has documented how the process of establishing a consistent link is straightforward for this case. In the case of marketed goods for the benchmark case, all prices are normalized to unity. As a result, quantities of the marketed goods can be measured by observed expenditures. Because the objective of the analysis is to evaluate how relative prices change, this normalization does not compromise the models' relevance (given the assumption of homogeneity of degree one for preference and production functions).[21] As a result, after selecting substitution elasticities, the benchmark data can be assembled into a consistent social accounting matrix and a limited number of parameters calibrated to match the labor/leisure conditions.[22]

4.1.1 Non-market calibration

When non-market resources are introduced into CGE models, they are either public goods or activities that reduce externalities. In the case of externalities, we might assume that one set of agents in the model produces them and the consumer receives them. However, the price "paid" for the amount received is usually not a per unit price. There may be no price. For the case of public goods, the costs may be covered through taxes on other goods.[23] The consumer may not have a mechanism to choose how much is received.

Considering the task of calibrating the model with these goods, three important issues concern how we measure: (1) the amounts of these goods, (2) the nature of the relationships between them and the private goods or (factor inputs) entering preferences (production functions), and (3) the information we have about the trade-offs people would make to change the amounts of the non-market goods. Non-separability, together with the fixed level of these non-market goods *from the perspective of the individual*, implies that the preference (production) functions with non-market goods are non-homothetic.[24] This change alters all of Rutherford's conditions for calibrating the GE to match baseline conditions. They no longer hold. Calibration must match another set of conditions that define the source for trade-off information while producing the social accounting matrix and equilibrium prices in the other goods and services in the model.

Calibration of these models exploits one or more envelope conditions to define a point where each non-homothetic function "appears" homothetic. Starting with a CES specification (with one or more arguments fixed), the same Rutherford calibration strategy used for the homogeneous case can be applied in the non-homothetic provided it is assumed to hold for the levels of consumption, input use, and values for the non-market good(s) consistent with satisfying the envelope condition(s) associated with the virtual prices for the non-market goods. This assumption means we are nesting a GE problem within the calibration.[25] In the case where non-market goods influence consumers, these conditions also require we define virtual income as a sum of expenditures on market goods plus virtual expenditures on non-market goods. The latter correspond to what is implied by the virtual prices derived from the envelope condition linking the levels of the fixed (non-market) goods to the other goods consumed for the benchmark solution. Parameters are set so that this amount of the non-market goods, given the externally observed marginal willingness to pay, would be selected to match the level observed in the benchmark case.

The calibration also needs to assure the benchmark reproduces the social accounting matrix for market goods, and any relationship defining how the amount of that non-market good is derived. These equations would be conditional to assumptions about substitution elasticities. Once this is solved then the model no longer treats the non-market good as a choice argument. It is treated as quasi-fixed—changing in response to other choices but not through any optimizing rule associated with households in the model. With non-separable preferences the level for the non-market good affects choices of market goods and the levels of these market goods can in turn affect the non-market good, but there is no direct choice of the non-market good. It is determined as a byproduct of other choices.

4.1.2 Examples

There is very little experience with introducing non-market goods within CGE models when they are treated as making non-separable contributions to preferences or production. Espinosa and Smith (1995) appear to offer the first treatment in a CGE framework. They resolved the calibration by assuming the non-market good had a private good serving as a perfect substitute. They also assumed a Stone Geary preference function. These two assumptions allowed them to adjust the translating (or subsistence) parameters so the level of each non-market good in the benchmark was consistent with its "production activities" and with external estimates for the marginal willingness to pay for each non-market good.

De Mooij (2000) used a log-linear GE model (following the Jones, 1965 format) to describe how non-separable externalities affect the impacts of an energy tax on employment, pollution, and income. He does not discuss how the non-market component is calibrated and does not consider the consistency conditions required to link market and non-market sectors. Although the welfare effects of taxes as measured with marginal excess burden are discussed for the separable case, they are not treated with non-separable effects.

Carbone and Smith (2008) appear to be the first to treat these issues in general terms. Their findings for a small CGE model lead to three direct conclusions:

- Even in cases where the non-market good has a small fraction of virtual income, the substitution or complementarity relationship between this good and a private good (leisure) has a large effect on the costs attributed to a new tax in an economy with pre-existing distortions.
- The nature of the production relationship linking activities with private goods to the level of a non-market good is important for the

measured effect of this good on measures of the welfare cost of a tax. A comparison of different response functions holding the share of the non-market resource in virtual income constant found large differences in the effects of the non-market sector on GE measures of excess burden.

- In a new analysis with several non-market goods, Carbone and Smith (2010) found that GE feedback effects may appear small based on substitution relationships to market goods. However, this criterion may be misleading. Feedback effects can have larger effects in the interactions among the non-market goods themselves. In this exercise, changes in the virtual price of one of the non-market goods was the best indicator of the importance of the changes in feedbacks arising from different substitution or complementarity relationships between *another* non-market good and labor.[26]

4.1.3 Using CGE for policy evaluation with non-market goods

Several tentative lessons emerge from the work with CGE models that are relevant to using this strategy for evaluating the GE effects of social policies. First, the structure of the interconnections between the non-market and market goods is important. Even for situations where the share of (virtual) national income attributed to the non-market sector is small, feedback effects can be very important to the difference between PE and GE welfare measures. Second, the strategy used to evaluate the nature of consumers' preferences for these goods also seems to be important. To date, the evidence has been largely through the interaction of estimates of consumers' preferences and the shape of the "production relationship" for the non-market good (i.e., in the case of air pollution it would be the dose-response function). Little has been done to systematically study the effect of alternative specifications for these relationships.

Third, most of these models use simple characterizations of the consumers and of the jurisdictions within which they select private goods. Carbone and Smith assumed a single aggregate consumer and abstracted from jurisdictions providing public goods. For many social programs there are multiple opportunities for people to adjust by changing locations.

Finally, benefit–cost analyses are increasingly being expected to include measures of the uncertainty in estimates. In the case of the CGE model, there has been limited work on how uncertainty in estimates used to calibrate these models would affect their results.[27] We should draw a distinction between treating the parameters used in GE policy analyses as random variables and sensitivity analysis. The former attempts to develop distributions for the computed GE effects—whether price changes or measures of willingness to pay. The latter recognizes a range of values for potential point estimates and considers the sensitivity of results to different values. It is not clear which strategy is most informative.

There are a number of complex issues in sorting through the arguments associated with estimation uncertainty and economic models. One line of argument might be the estimation uncertainty in our measures of parameters for any model. PE or GE is so large that the best an analyst can do is keep models simple until we can narrow the degree of uncertainty. Another argument would be to argue that one reason for the imprecision we observe is the GE nature of the world. Under this view, we need to do a better job of representing it at all stages—estimation and policy analysis. Another position might be to suggest that all policy evaluations rely on calibrated models so estimation uncertainty is only important if it affects the confidence of those using the models to inform policy judgments. Under this view, full-blown efforts to derive the probability distributions induced in PE or GE effects due to distribution for estimates are not likely to be useful.

Our view is that selecting one of these perspectives for all problems does not make sense. At this stage in our understanding of how to use models to inform policy we believe a strategy that relies exclusively on simple assessments is likely to be best. The choice of the type of modeling strategy to adopt should instead be guided by answering some progressively refined questions:

1. Is there agreement on the nature and empirical importance of the primary features and parameters of the models needed for an assessment, at least for first-order problems, in the literature? If yes, proceed to a detailed model of the system. If no—keep it simple!
2. Within a detailed model, can we agree on some stylized facts or parameters that we have confidence have credible estimates within a relatively narrow range? If no, then a large meta-like sensitivity analysis of modeling outcomes is required (see Banzhaf and Smith, 2007 as an example). If yes, then a target sensitivity analysis using the parameter(s) with largest variability in estimates is likely to be informative.[28]
3. Within a targeted analysis, are there thresholds that identify decision points such as positive net benefits that can be described and corresponding questions about the importance of what has been left out? If no, then the analysis may help to reference the policy choices. If yes, then the GE/PE distinction and structured sensitivity analysis may be especially important.[29]

4.2 Non-market Effects in a Locational Equilibrium Framework

Some of the services provided by local governments as well as environmental services available at different geographic locations have the characteristics of a local public good. The amounts available vary between the different locations. In the case of environmental goods these differences could be due to variations in natural conditions. For other goods they could be the result of decisions made by local communities. They are what led Tiebout (1956) to suggest that for local public goods, communities were the "supermarket" allowing households to select the best match, given their preferences and abilities to pay.

A number of authors, in public and urban economics, have attempted to evaluate the analytical properties of Tiebout models.[30] This literature offers two approaches for discussing PE versus GE benefit measures. The first uses calibrated models such as Fernandez and Rogerson (1998) and the second directly estimates a sorting model and is due to Epple and Sieg (1999). The Epple–Sieg paper demonstrates how a consistent description of a locational equilibrium could be used to estimate a model that: (1) recovered measures of heterogeneous households' preferences for housing and local public goods, and (2) offered the means to describe how that equilibrium would change with exogenous changes affecting the amounts of those public goods.[31]

The models can be grouped depending upon how they characterize the heterogeneity in household preferences. The first specification has been labeled a pure characteristics model and the second is labeled a random utility model. The Epple–Sieg version or pure characteristics model assumes each household (or each type of household) has a different taste parameter for the locationally differentiated good. However, the households all evaluate the locational attributes or services contributing to the amount of the local public good in the same way. The alternative random utility model allows the parameters of location-specific goods to vary more generally.[32] Our example uses the pure characteristics framework. As a result, we focus the remaining discussion on estimating, interpreting, and using these models for policy evaluation.

4.2.1 Structure and estimation of the pure characteristics model

A key assumption allowing these models to estimate the locational equilibrium in a way that facilitates estimation is the single crossing condition. To appreciate what this condition implies for preferences we need to develop its structure more specifically. Suppose we can define the price for a homogeneous unit of housing in each location and measure the amount of the non-market good a household acquires by locating in a specific community. The Epple–Sieg model maintains that two sources of household heterogeneity influence their sorting across communities. One is household income and the second is the household taste for public goods, represented by an unknown (to the analyst) parameter b. Income and the taste parameter are assumed jointly distributed to represent household heterogeneity. To characterize the equilibrium we must assume that both income and the taste parameter satisfy the single crossing condition.

The single crossing condition restricts how the price equivalent change in a good related to the non-market good changes with income and with the taste parameter. We describe it as restricting the price equivalent because the first step in understanding the condition is to characterize a price change in the related market good that is equivalent to a change in the non-market good (in terms of its effects on household utility). Once this price change is defined we ask how would it change with either income or household tastes. This relationship is formally described using the indirect utility function in equation (6.1). Assume p_1 is the annual rental price for a unit of homogeneous housing in community 1 and denote the amount of the non-market good in that community as q_1, then the single crossing condition in income can be defined in equation (6.12):

$$\frac{\partial}{\partial m}\left(\frac{Vq_1}{Vp_1}\right) = \frac{\partial}{\partial m}\left(\frac{dp_1}{dq_1}\right) > 0 \tag{6.12}$$

The variation in preferences stemming from the taste parameter (β) also must be consistent with the single crossing condition (i.e., $\frac{\partial}{\partial \beta}(\frac{Vq_1}{Vp_1}) > 0$) for all communities. Taken together these features assure that the sorting equilibrium satisfies three conditions. These three features are especially important to using the equilibrium for estimation and policy evaluation. They include the following:

- When communities are ranked by the public good index and by the equilibrium community-specific housing price and the two rankings are the same (this is called the ascending bundles condition).
- With a continuous array of different types of households, there is a set of households indifferent between communities with adjoining ranks based on price and the index of public goods (this is called the boundary indifference condition).
- When households are ordered among communities, given a level of income, the equilibrium ordering implies that households with the greatest preference for the locational public good locate in the community with the largest amount of that good. Thus, conditional on

income, households are stratified by their taste for the public good (this is called the stratification condition).

Using a CES specification to describe preferences, the three characteristics of the equilibrium allow the ordering of communities by price and the ordering of households by the unobservable taste parameter. This ordering is used to "predict" a distribution of income for each location. This feature provides the intuition for an estimator to recover preference parameters (see Epple and Sieg, 1999 for details).[33] An important feature of the model arises from the boundary indifference condition. This property of the equilibrium allows the definition of a relationship between the equilibrium prices for adjoining communities (in the ranking implied by the equilibrium) and the index for the levels of the community-specific public goods. That is, given estimates of the equilibrium price indexes it is used to define recursively an index for the quantity of the community-provided public goods. For policy analyses of how to introduce an exogenous change in one or more community's public goods, this relationship is reversed and used to define how prices "must" relate to the revised indexes of public goods across communities. These prices are used in a framework that derives housing demands, compares demand in each community to supply, and then updates prices and re-sorts households until housing demand equals supply in all communities and no households have an incentive to move given the quantities of public goods and the housing prices in each community.

4.2.2 Examples

There are two published examples of the vertical model that discuss welfare measurement. The first by Sieg et al. (2004) uses the model to describe sorting among school districts in Southern California for educational quality and air quality. They demonstrate how the sorting framework can be used to estimate preference parameters and to compute the benefits for improvements in air quality in a framework that allows a comparison of partial and GE WTP measures. These measures were defined for an exogenous improvement in air quality.[34] The simulated results permit an assessment of the role of preference heterogeneity for measures of the differences in welfare across communities and income groups. This approach also allows the differences in PE versus GE measures to be considered using these same categories.

In their application the difference between PE and GE results are defined by how the change in air quality is treated and whether the housing price effect is taken into account. That is, each simulated household "controls" the air quality it ultimately experiences by moving. To implement equations (6.2a) and (6.2b) we propose a thought experiment. For the partial equilibrium measure we consider how the "simulated" households assigned to a location (based on their income and taste for a public good) would evaluate an air quality improvement in that location, assuming housing prices don't change. The GE measure allows households to re-sort, with prices adjusting until the quantity of housing demanded in each community equals supply at the new set of prices and households have no incentive to move. This measure compares the baseline prices and public goods to the new prices and public goods at the locations each household selects under the new conditions. Both the realized air quality through adjustment and the price change contribute to the distinction between PE and GE measures in this case.

Several possible scenarios were considered in this study and the illustrative computations presented in the chapter suggest that even though air quality might improve everywhere, some households might experience losses because housing prices increase more than the improved air quality was worth to them. To some extent this result may be due to the simulation's inability to capture exit. The set of communities is a closed system in the simulation. Thus, a household must sort within the locations described by the model.

The second application by Walsh (2007) is similar in structure. The locational amenity in this case is open space and the sorting process is similar to what was used in the air quality application. There is, however, one important difference. Open space in Walsh's model is defined so that it is produced in part through the outcomes of household sorting. In the Sieg et al. (2004) paper, each household can select an air quality from a finite set so there is some endogeneity as part of the equilibrium amount realized by specific households. However, these choices do not feedback and alter the amounts of air quality available in each community. They affect the prices of homes. For the Walsh model, choices affect both prices and the amount of open space! Open space is assumed to be a composite of protected land and undeveloped land. As a result if policies to protect land attract households, it is possible for the equilibrium to lead to smaller amounts of open space by developing more of the unprotected land. In this situation, both the prices of housing and the amount of the local public goods in each community are equilibrium outcomes.

Walsh's research illustrates how a Nash equilibrium can be computed for endogenous determination of prices and open space. Our example in the following section builds on this work and allows the level of the location-specific good to be determined jointly with prices through the sorting process.

5 GENERAL EQUILIBRIUM BENEFIT MEASURES FOR SOCIAL POLICY: LOCAL EDUCATION

In this section, we outline a new application of the vertical sorting model to illustrate the decisions that need to be made in developing a GE analysis of the benefits of a social policy. We consider local education in Maricopa County, AZ, USA. This section and the following section describe how the model was estimated and how it can be used to evaluate the PE and GE benefits associated with changes in the number of teachers available in this county's school districts. In this section, we outline the model, describe the data, and show how the data are used to estimate the model's parameters. Section 6 describes a policy analysis with the model.

Before getting started with our example, it is important to emphasize that our objective is illustrative. The model builds on existing research but is not intended as an alternative model for evaluating the gains for policy changes that affect local education. This is an important perspective because there is a large body of literature confirming the importance of school quality on housing prices. The magnitude of the effect is often debated, as illustrated by the contrast between Black's (1999) estimate and the more recent work by Bayer et al. (2007). These authors' findings suggest homeowners have a marginal willingness to pay that, on average, was approximately a quarter what Black found.[35] While our estimates of the marginal willingness to pay are consistent with the Bayer et al. estimates, as we discuss below, we believe a full analysis would need to take account of the roles of additional locational distinctions for community selections.

Assume each household selects an amount of housing and a numeraire good. Homogeneous housing is available in each of a finite number of communities with different amounts of local public goods. For our application, public education is the primary public good considered by households and the communities correspond to school districts. To describe the logic of the model, suppose the household decision process takes place in two stages. First, a household evaluates what the consumption choices would be if each community was selected, conditional on the housing price and local public goods in each location. This decision includes the selection of an amount of homogeneous housing in each location. Then, in this conceptual description of the process, suppose now a household considers the level of well-being realized in each community with a fixed income and selects the community that provides the highest utility. The numeraire good in this simple description of the choice process is determined by default. The CES specification for the indirect utility function is given in equation (6.13):

$$V_j = \left[\beta q_j^{\rho} + \left[e^{\frac{m^{1-\eta}-1}{1-\eta}} e^{\frac{-aP_j^{\varepsilon+1}-1}{1+\varepsilon}} \right]^{\rho} \right]^{1/\rho} \tag{6.13}$$

The subscript j indexes school districts. The term, q_j corresponds to a measure of public school quality and P_j the price of a standardized unit of housing in community j. η and ε correspond to the income (m) and price (P) elasticities, respectively. ρ is a parameter that measures the substitution between the constant quality housing bundle and local public goods conveyed by each community. We have omitted a subscript for households. As with Sieg et al., the model is estimated using moments based on the percentiles for the income and housing expenditure distributions predicted by the model in comparison to what is observed for each school district given information about prices and the public goods (q_j values).

Seven moment conditions are used in estimation—three income quantiles (25th, 50th, and 75th), three housing quantiles (25th, 50th, and 75th), and one expression to describe a measure for the public good index. The ascending bundle condition together with estimates for the housing prices can be used to derive the shares of all households in each community. The expressions for these equilibrium shares can be inverted (numerically) to derive estimates for the public good index that are a function of the model's other parameters. We stack the seven moment conditions and use the ranks of the prices as instruments for the endogenous price and public good measures. We follow Kuminoff (2009) and use Chebyshev polynomials in ranks as instruments.[36]

5.1 Data Construction, Education Quality, and Housing Price

The study area is Maricopa County, AZ, USA and includes the Phoenix MSA (Metropolitan Statistical Area). Our analysis considers the 46 school districts in this county containing a full set of school quality records and Census data. These districts are highlighted in Figure 6.1 and comprise most of the Phoenix MSA excluding Indian Reservations and uninhabited mountain and desert preserves. At the time of the 2000 Census, the Phoenix MSA had a population of over 3.2 million and was growing rapidly. The population in 2008 was nearly 4.3 million people. Our study considers the period from 2003 to 2006 (largely before the collapse of the housing market in the area). Our data include all of the single family housing transactions for the years 2003 through 2006 as well as school quality data derived from annual school report cards for each school year between 2003 and 2006. Information on income and the population in each school district were developed using the block group SF3 file from the Census 2000 public data.

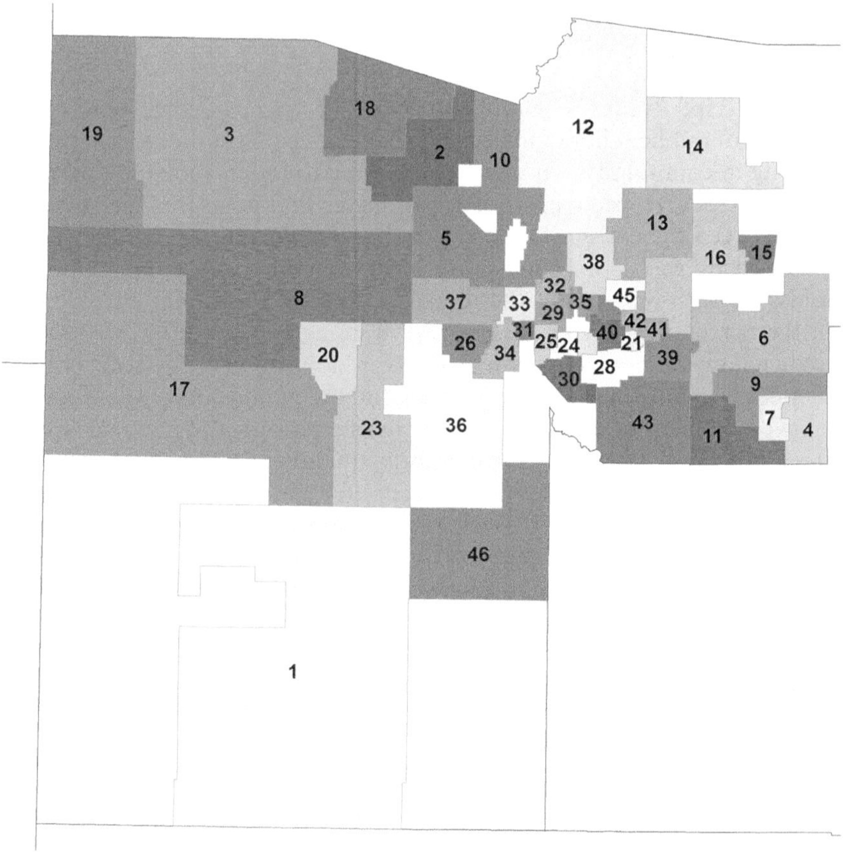

Figure 6.1 School districts in Maricopa County, AZ, USA

School quality is measured using the Arizona Department of Education School Report Cards. These reports are published for each school and are mandated by the No Child Left Behind Act. Test scores are available from Arizona's Instrument to Measure Standards (AIMS) test administered to students each spring. These reports contain test scores as well as the number of students in each school, the number of teachers, and teacher-aides. The summary of the scores differentiate English versus non-English-speaking students and are reported for grades 2 through 12 separately for categories of mathematics, language, and reading for 2003 through 2006. Our analysis considered the test results for grades 2 through 8 and was restricted to the scores for English-speaking students.

We developed measures for the average number of students, teachers,

Table 6.1 School quality regression model

Variable	Estimate	Std Err.	t-stat.
Student/Teacher	−0.2493	0.1074	−2.32
Student/Teacher-aide	0.0598	0.0061	9.81
Grade 3	−0.6073	0.8297	−0.73
Grade 4	0.3291	0.8293	0.40
Grade 5	0.1127	0.8285	0.14
Grade 6	1.1122	0.8293	1.34
Grade 7	2.7064	0.8317	3.25
Grade 8	2.1403	0.8333	2.57
Math	5.0642	0.5442	9.31
Reading	1.2624	0.5444	2.32
Year 2004	−0.3870	0.6327	−0.61
Year 2005	−1.5289	0.6308	−2.42
Year 2006	−2.6884	0.6290	−4.27
Constant	48.4230	2.0401	23.74
$R^2 = 0.0594$			
N = 3711			

and aides for each grade/district/year combination as well as a measure of the average math, reading, and language score for each grade/school/year combination. The individual school-level data were aggregated based on the school's district, the test type, the grade, and the year. Using these averages, we constructed measures for average student/teacher ratio as well as average student/teacher-aide ratio. Considering only the cases with complete records our sample consists of 3711 unique combinations of grade, district, year, and test score.

The measure of school quality used in the estimation of the sorting model is based on predictions from a model of these test scores. It is an index of performance that is associated with observable factors contributing to test scores. We hypothesize that test scores are related to the type of test, the grade level, the year, and the average number of teachers and aides present in each school. The specific measures used in the model are the averages for the student/teacher and student/teacher-aide ratios.

Table 6.1 provides the results for the model used to construct our school quality index. The estimates are consistent with the literature and our prior hypotheses about the importance of small class sizes. Higher student teacher ratios are associated with lower performance after controlling for the grade, test subject, and year.[37] Increases in the ratio of students to teacher-aides increases test performance. Although this finding may seem counterintuitive, there are a number of potential explanations. One would suggest that this result simply reflects the importance of teachers over aides. That is, the primary factor giving rise to improved test performance is the amount of teacher time devoted to students. If we assume there is a minimum number of staff required for class management and this threshold is met in all cases, then a *lower* number of aides for a given number of teachers would be consistent with an increase in scores because it implies that the class management threshold is more likely to be met with increased amounts of teacher time over that of aides. This outcome would imply that increasing the number of aides at the cost of teachers would not enhance school quality. These specific features are important to policies that are associated with teacher-aides. Our example involves reductions in teachers and relies on the effect of these reductions on teaching outcomes and assessments of education quality. Thus, what is important for our purpose is the ability to capture their effects on test performance. While the R^2 score is low the model does capture effects of teachers, recognizes differences for math and reading tests, and thus seems a credible basis for describing how test scores would respond to reductions in teachers at the school level. As a result, we adopt the predicted test score for the language test during the 2003 school year for grade 2 as our index of school quality for each district.

The price index for the homogeneous unit of housing is developed following the framework outlined in Sieg et al. (2002) using a transaction database for residential housing sales in Maricopa County. A log-linear price function is used to estimate district housing price indexes controlling for the attributes of each house sold and the year sold. The price indexes are derived from a set of fixed effect terms, one for each school district. For the period we considered, before the dramatic shift in the housing market, we felt that following Poterba (1992) and annualizing housing prices at a rate of 11 percent was consistent if not conservative as a description of buyer and seller expectations. The sample of housing sales includes 406 556 transactions between 2003 and 2006. It has all the transaction records for single family homes falling in the 46 school districts. Table 6.2 reports the estimated price equation. All of the school district fixed effects are significant. The estimated coefficients for the district fixed effects are used to construct price indexes. Their rank, generally, is in agreement with the rank of the districts based on the index of school quality. This consistency is what would be expected based on the ascending bundles condition. It offers confirmation for both the joint decisions in selecting the school districts as a reasonable characterization for the community and for our simple model relating test scores to students per teacher and using it as a gauge of school quality at the primary school level.

Table 6.2 Fixed effect hedonic property model for Maricopa County school districts, 2003–06

Variable	Estimate	Std Err.	t-stat.	Variable	Estimate	Std Err.	t-stat.
Lot acres	0.3020	0.0030	100.66	District 18	8.9333	0.0053	1676.05
Square feet (100s)	0.0569	0.0003	182.24	District 19	8.7462	0.0078	1114.49
Stories	−0.1452	0.0013	−109.92	District 20	9.1150	0.0055	1665.36
Bathrooms	0.0670	0.0012	57.27	District 21	8.7727	0.0055	1585.03
Age	−0.0083	0.0001	−71.06	District 22	8.8561	0.0065	1372.61
Lot acres sq	−0.0234	0.0006	−39.19	District 23	8.8902	0.0053	1677.99
Square feet (100s)	−0.0005	0.0000	−90.50	District 24	8.8079	0.0056	1585.03
Age sq	0.0001	0.0000	31.56	District 25	9.3861	0.0074	1267.62
Garage	0.0411	0.0020	20.41	District 26	8.9157	0.0049	1804.82
Pool	0.0758	0.0011	67.55	District 27	9.6041	0.0604	159.01
Year 2004	0.1116	0.0019	59.03	District 28	8.2523	0.0282	292.52
Year 2005	0.3936	0.0019	209.71	District 29	8.5662	0.0136	630.22
Year 2006	0.5521	0.0020	281.73	District 30	8.3126	0.0116	717.23
District 1	8.2976	0.0353	235.27	District 31	9.1222	0.0086	1066.71
District 2	8.8099	0.0067	1322.38	District 32	8.2997	0.0226	367.28
District 3	7.9440	0.0279	285.09	District 33	9.1620	0.0051	1789.31
District 4	8.7445	0.0057	1534.37	District 34	8.8030	0.0056	1574.50
District 5	9.0810	0.0114	798.06	District 35	8.9441	0.0050	1801.12
District 6	8.6239	0.0055	1556.11	District 36	9.0546	0.0076	1196.21
District 7	8.7563	0.0057	1545.80	District 37	8.7389	0.0065	1343.83
District 8	9.2811	0.0058	1606.96	District 38	8.7416	0.0098	889.23
District 9	8.9473	0.0049	1826.41	District 39	8.7555	0.0052	1683.18
District 10	9.1132	0.0072	1258.24	District 40	8.9351	0.0121	737.79

Table 6.2 (continued)

Variable	Estimate	Std Err.	t-stat.	Variable	Estimate	Std Err.	t-stat.
District 11	8.9726	0.0049	1833.24	District 41	9.4296	0.0054	1741.63
District 12	8.8057	0.0047	1866.59	District 42	9.0172	0.0061	1467.58
District 13	9.3064	0.0074	1264.40	District 43	8.7829	0.0079	1112.95
District 14	8.7443	0.0065	1339.52	District 44	8.9009	0.0055	1633.04
District 15	7.9725	0.0290	274.85	District 45	8.6870	0.0110	791.37
District 16	8.9419	0.0050	1781.48	District 46	8.3221	0.0305	273.00
District 17	8.7980	0.0058	1504.79				
$R^2 = 0.999$							
N = 406 556							

The final components of our data are the measures for population in each school district and the income quantities for each school district. These are developed using the block group 100 percent sample from Census 2000 data reported in the SF3 series of tables. The primary variables are total population counts within each district and the income classified into one of 16 distinct categories with the lowest ranging from \$0 to \$10 000 and the top category unbounded above \$200 000. To construct a spatially consistent measure by school district, the population counts for each block group are weighted based on the area falling within each school district. For example, a block group with half of the area falling in one school district and half the area falling in a second school district would be divided so that the population of people is split between the two districts. By using the total population in each district we construct the share of total population across all districts. This was also the approach used to allocate the count of households in each income bin.

A map of the block groups overlaid on our school districts is shown in Figure 6.2. Interval censored regression was used to estimate the mean and variance of a log-normal distribution based on the Census income categories. Using the results from the estimated distribution, the estimates for the 25th, 50th, and 75th income quantiles for each school district are recovered. Summary statistics for the school quality, housing price, housing expenditure, household income, and demographic measures for the population are provided in Table 6.3.

Table 6.4 presents the generalized method of moments (GMM) estimates for the preference parameters. The estimates for both the price and income elasticities for housing demand are consistent with the literature. The estimate for the rho (ρ) parameter is consistent with satisfying the single crossing property. The school quality measure is also a significant determinant of households' decisions about community location. Thus, the base model offers a plausible description of the link between community choice and local school quality and can serve to illustrate the PE/GE distinction.

It is also possible to develop some intuition about the model by comparing how our estimates for the marginal willingness to pay for a unit change in school quality align with the literature. Our results imply a range of annual values from \$40 to \$83 a year (in 2003 dollars). Bayer et al. (2007) compare hedonic property value estimates and results for a horizontal sorting model applied to the 1990 PUMA data for the six counties in the San Francisco Bay Area (including Alameda, Contra Costa, Maria, San Mateo, San Francisco, and Santa Clara counties). Two sets of estimates are reported in their study. The first of these estimates the effect of a 1 standard deviation change in average test scores using a hedonic price

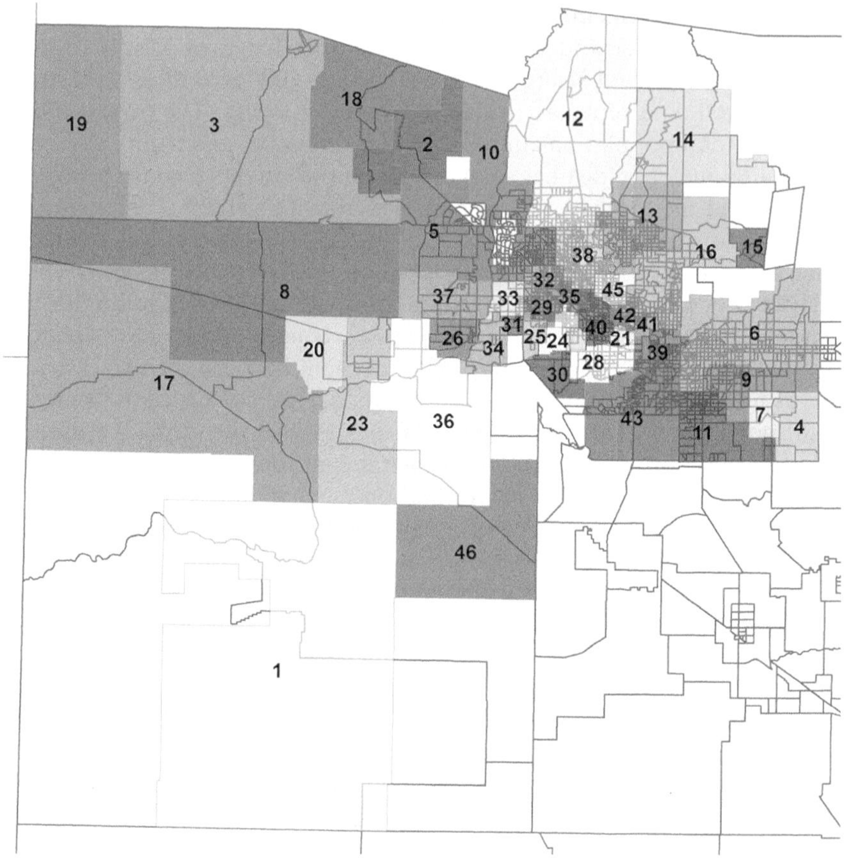

Figure 6.2 Census block groups overlaid with Maricopa school districts

function using their boundary fixed effects to control for neighborhood effects (i.e., the demographic attributes of the neighbors such as education and race). Their estimates are approximately a quarter the magnitude estimated by Black (1999) and range between \$14 and \$44 per month, with the variation based on the definition of the boundary and whether neighborhood socioeconomic characteristics are included in the model. Their preferred estimate was \$17 per month.

To compare this estimate with our results we need to adjust for price changes in residential housing, convert our measure to one in standard deviation units, and compute the monthly equivalent value.[38] After developing these adjustments, the range of estimates for the marginal willingness to pay implied by the parameter estimates of our model is \$5.24 to

Table 6.3 Summary statistics for characteristics of Maricopa County school districts used in sorting model

Variable	Mean	Std Dev.	Min.	Max.
Price index rank	23.5	13.4	1.0	46.0
Population share	0.0217	0.029	0.0003	0.1437
Test score	48.43	2.25	43.21	56.26
Price index rank	8.83	0.35	7.94	9.60
Income 25th pct	23 307	8 133	11 526	44 099
Income 50th pct	39 307	12 882	21 056	77 497
Income 75th pct	66 501	21 190	36 960	136 189
House price 25th pct	18 772	9 221	4 950	58 300
House price 50th pct	25 169	11 019	7 810	59 400
House price 75th pct	34 428	16 003	9 900	85 250
Household size	3.12	0.89	2.06	6.90
Students	12 562	13 972	21	59 701
Teachers	678	749	3	3 051
Teacher-aides	212	363	1	2 174
Number of schools	14	16	1	77
Number of districts = 46				

*Table 6.4 GMM estimation results for household preferences**

Variable	Estimate	Std Err.	t-stat.
Std dev. for ln(inc)	0.4332	0.0029	148.82
Mean for ln(inc)	10.5296	0.3154	
Mean for taste parameter	0.9092	0.0764	11.91
Std dev. for taste parameter	0.1806	0.0079	22.86
Lambda	−0.2758	0.0025	−112.47
Income elasticity	0.9214	0.0015	630.63
Price elasticity	−0.4781	0.0370	−12.93
Beta	1.3215	0.0254	52.10
Rho	−0.0438	0.0005	−88.66
q_initial	46.4400	0.1412	328.86

Note: * Standard errors are generated from bootstraps using five iterations, standard deviation for mean income based on census data. N = 1 000 000 for simulation.

$10.86. These estimates are in monthly 1990 dollars for a one standard deviation change in test scores. Given the differences in household incomes between the two areas, they are remarkably close to the Bayer et al. estimates. Based on this criterion, our model provides estimates for both the conventional parameters used to describe housing demand

and the relative importance of school quality to households' selections of homes that are consistent with the literature.

6 A POLICY SIMULATION TO ILLUSTRATE PE AND GE BENEFIT MEASURES

For our policy simulation we use a trivariate distribution with income, the taste parameter for schooling, and an assumed number of children per household. We allow for the fact that changes in resources can cause more children to be located in districts with greater resources and yet the ultimate educational outcomes may be inferior. That is, as households with children move to the districts with more resources the students per teacher increase and the school quality declines. To illustrate how recognition of these types of feedbacks can influence outcomes we compare a Nash equilibrium, where households move recognizing what others will do, with the case where households only consider the initial disruption to school quality and the effects it has on prices as households sort. In the Nash equilibrium, both school quality and housing prices are jointly determined in equilibrium. For the second case, only the prices change as a result of the equilibrium sorting. School quality is also a byproduct of movement but only the prices are recognized by households as they move.

To illustrate the effects of market and non-market feedbacks for PE versus GE measures of changes in resources for social programs, we selected a real policy change that involved reductions in state support for local education in Maricopa County. Based on reports distributed through the Arizona Education Association in April 2009, over 1600 teachers were fired in the county. These effects were unevenly distributed throughout the county's school districts.

Two simulations were developed. The first considers market and non-market feedback effects. It introduces the reductions in the teachers for each district. Using our estimated school quality function given in Table 6.1 we estimate, with existing students, the reduction in test scores. Recall that increased student/teacher ratios reduce test scores. With no moving costs any reduction in school quality creates incentives for some households to move. These changes, in turn, alter housing prices and create more incentives for households to re-sort until housing price adjustments imply there are no further gains to movement.

Three aspects of the development of our policy scenarios should be noted before turning to our results. The first concerns replicating the benchmark equilibrium. Our index of educational quality relies on the estimates for test scores as reported in Table 6.1. To assure they are consistent with the benchmark equilibrium and with our estimates for equilibrium housing prices, we begin our analysis by simulating the benchmark case and adjusting the intercept of the education function so we exactly match the population shares in each school district. The second issue concerns the assumed family size. Here we rely on Census estimates for the mean and variance of family sizes.[39] Finally, our analysis generated 1 million values for income, the taste parameter for education, and family size using a trivariate normal distribution based on the estimates for these parameters. The initial benchmark solution used to establish the corrections to the intercepts for the school quality equation assigns each household to a school district.

The first simulation considers the Nash equilibrium where households recognize the effects of sorting on both price *and* school quality through the children assigned to each simulated household. When households move the student/teacher ratio changes and school quality adjusts accordingly. In our analysis, the only exogenous change is the reduction in the number of teachers in each district based on the policies for Maricopa County with proposed cuts in teachers by district. Table 6.5 presents a selection of results for a few school districts for this simulation. The full details for all districts are in the Appendix (see Table 6A.1 for the first scenario with non-market feedbacks). The first column in Table 6.5 provides the school district name. The second column is the percentage reduction in teachers as part of the budget reduction. Out of 46 districts, 12 lost teachers with cuts ranging from 3 percent to 27 percent of the teaching staff. Columns 3 and 4 report the proportionate change in the equilibrium price and the index of public goods. We selected seven districts with varying effects of the policy to illustrate the results. The results for willingness to pay are grouped into GE and PE with the GE marginal willingness to pay (MWTP) corresponding to the marginal willingness to pay (i.e., V_q/V_m) for school quality evaluated at the new GE prices and quality. The PE corresponds to the same concept evaluated at the initial values. These are reported as a gauge of the effects of the point of evaluation for these marginal values.

Our analysis follows the Smith et al. (2004) convention and treats households as renters, so the capitalization effects due to price changes from the initial housing assignment accrue to absentee land owners. Consider first the proportionate change in school quality and housing prices created by comparing the benchmark solution to the new equilibrium. Several important results emerge from this comparison. First, averaging across households in a school district, it appears that everyone loses from cuts in teachers even though the cuts are restricted to approximately a quarter of the districts. Because there are no costs to moving, the model assumes households will adapt to attempt to find districts with better test scores

*Table 6.5 General and partial equilibrium measures for willingness to pay: Nash equilibrium**

School District	Loss of Teachers	Change in Housing Price	Change in Public Good Index	GE		PE	
				WTP	MWTP	WTP	MWTP
Palo Verde Elementary District	0	0.0069	0.0002	−490.16	40.59	6.30	40.64
Queen Creek District	27	0.0006	−0.0109	−501.36	41.34	−455.45	40.80
Litchfield Elementary District	18	−0.0024	−0.0134	−518.47	50.90	−786.98	50.07
Higley Unified District	21	−0.0023	−0.0137	−612.95	55.39	−1108.71	54.22
Roosevelt Elementary District	0	0.0070	0.0001	−514.48	45.29	4.25	45.35
Paradise Valley District	9	0.0008	−0.0093	−698.20	63.32	−553.28	62.81
Cave Creek District	18	−0.0088	−0.0191	−719.21	65.39	−1344.35	64.03

Note: * See Appendix Table 6A.1 for full details.

after the cuts. However, these actions result in a spreading of the "pain" through price increases in those districts where school quality increases slightly. When quality declines housing prices may decline.

We find that equilibrium schooling quality declines in most places. The quality changes because of two considerations. The policy reduces teachers and household sorting leads to a non-market feedback. Students move into districts with more teachers, raising the student/teacher ratio and reducing test scores. This effect also serves to spread the losses from the selective reduction in teachers throughout the county. For the seven districts we profiled, there is little difference between the marginal willingness to pay measures based on the point of evaluation. The primary impact of the GE and PE perspective can be seen through the difference in the WTP measures from a GE versus a PE perspective (averaged across households based on their original school district in the baseline solution of the model before the policy is implemented).

The PE results consider only the change in school quality. They include districts that would appear to have small annual gains and others with large losses, amounting to over $160 per month. These gains can be traced to situations where school quality increased slightly and the housing price increases are ignored. Palo Verde and Roosevelt experience small gains from the PE perspective because we allow for sorting after the change in teachers but do not change housing prices in the computation of the willingness to pay. In all other cases in Table 6.5, the school quality declines and the distinction between PE and GE arises in whether the housing price change is recognized. As the details of the computations suggest, we could also define other benefit measures, assuming, for example, no sorting and using the school quality based on the initial number of students with whatever number of teachers was implied by the policy change. This possible alternative highlights how the distinction between the definition of the policy to be evaluated and how it is represented in the model can matter for the interpretation of the results from PE and GE benefit measures.

It would be difficult without the structural model to anticipate some of these results. For example, Paradise Valley (a very expensive area north of Phoenix) experiences a cut in teachers, reduction in school quality but an *increase* in housing prices so the GE loss is larger than the PE, a contrast with most of the other findings where housing price reductions serve to reduce the net impact of the decline in school quality. These types of responses are most evident in the Higley Unified and Cave Creek districts shown in Table 6.5. Overall, the GE losses range from $41 to $91 per month.

Table 6.6 selects the same school districts (results for all are in Table 6A.2 in the Appendix) and compares the GE and PE estimates for a solution based on sorting on price alone with school quality exogenous.

Table 6.6 Comparison of GE and PE Nash equilibrium versus price only solution

School District	Loss of Teachers	Price Only				Nash			
		Change in Price	Change in Public Good	GE WTP	PE WTP	Change in Price	Change in Public Good	GE WTP	PE WTP
Palo Verde Elementary District	0	0.0068	–	−494	–	−0.0069	0.0002	−490	6
Queen Creek District	27	0.0009	−0.0106	−504	−441	−0.0006	−0.0109	−501	−455
Litchfield Elementary District	18	−0.0025	−0.0136	−523	−766	−0.0024	−0.0134	−518	−787
Higley Unified District	21	−0.0015	−0.0127	−618	−1132	−0.0023	−0.0137	−613	−1109
Roosevelt Elementary District	0	0.0069	–	−517	–	0.0070	0.0001	−514	4
Paradise Valley District	9	0.0003	−0.0100	−705	−561	0.0008	−0.0093	−698	−553
Cave Creek District	18	−0.0086	−0.0190	−726	−1338	−0.0088	−0.0191	−719	−1344

These are given in the four columns after restating the school district name and percentage cut in teachers. In this case, teacher cuts result in school quality declines using the initial distribution of students and reduced number of teachers as the assumed base for welfare computation. Households re-sort and this sorting process affects housing prices but school quality is assumed to be determined by the initial distribution of students.

In columns 7 through 10 of Table 6.6, we round the estimates of WTP to whole dollars from the Nash solutions (in Table 6.5) and include them for comparison. The Nash adjustment in school quality increases the estimates for GE losses (in absolute magnitude). The PE losses are smaller (in absolute magnitude) for the Nash than the solution that does not consider endogeneity in the non-market outcomes caused by sorting. GE losses are smaller, as might be expected when households are assumed to anticipate how their own and others' behavior will affect school quality. Consider, for example, Palo Verde school district or Roosevelt Elementary. The PE measures derived from the Nash equilibrium are positive, whereas they are negative when adjustment is based on price. In these cases, the assumed Nash adjustment leads to an increase in school quality, whereas sorting based on price alone implies a very small decline in school quality in one case and no change in another.

Overall, our sorting example illustrates three features of the comparison of GE and PE measures of the willingness to pay to avoid declines in school quality. First, it is possible to exploit revealed preference logic to develop models capable of reflecting multi-market adjustment in response to policies affecting social programs. Second, when the programs exist in different jurisdictions both market and non-market adjustments are possible. The non-market feedbacks are likely to be *more important* to discrepancies between PE and GE measures than price effects alone. Finally, measures of marginal willingness to pay were not as sensitive to the point of evaluation as comparisons of PE versus GE willingness to pay might lead an analyst to speculate would be the case.

7 SUMMARY AND RESEARCH AHEAD

This chapter has summarized definitions for PE and GE welfare measures when policy is assumed to affect only market goods. We generalized these definitions to consider market and non-market goods and outlined two modeling strategies for measuring the importance of GE effects. Finally, we illustrated how one of these frameworks, a locational equilibrium model, could be used to estimate PE and GE welfare measures for local public education policies as an example of a social policy. While our estimates closely match the literature relevant to the application, they are intended here simply as an example. A more complete analysis would need to consider air quality, crime, and a variety of other spatially delineated factors that influence neighborhood choices.

Several research issues are "buried" in the details of model implementation that should be considered in future research. We highlight three here: measures for the "amounts" of social programs; revealed preference and the non-use values for changes in social programs; and the extent of the market for social programs. We close with a short discussion of each issue.

7.1 Quantity Measures for Social Program Outputs

Our example of education policies as a social program focused on one measure of the output—school quality measured by test scores. If the objective of public education is to assure an informed electorate so that a democracy provides "better" decisions, then the relationship between test scores at the primary school level and an "informed electorate" is certainly not clear. If we believe education helps to avoid other social problems or enhances the likelihood for good social outcomes on a number of dimensions (i.e., crime, teenage pregnancy, childhood poverty, etc.) as Heckman has argued, then it seems reasonable to assume these effects are unlikely to be captured by the gains realized by individual households who seek to enhance the private skills of their children. How these individual choices "add up" to transform the collective outcome is certainly omitted from the types of models we discuss here. Of course, to deal with them we need a framework that links observable outcomes to the sequence of steps the improvements in the quality of local education will facilitate.

The task becomes more complex for social programs with limited direct private benefits. These issues must be addressed to quantitatively "scale" the output in a CGE setting. Measures of non-use value or the benefits from purely public outcomes of social programs cannot be recovered from revealed preference models. We need to consider integrating results from stated preference analyses with revealed preference measures of the trade-offs people would make for the private benefits associated with each specific program.[40]

7.2 Non-use Values for Social Programs

Environmental economists have been concerned about people who care about environmental resources that they may never want to "use." These preferences need not stem from an altruistic motive directed at the current or some future generation. It is certainly possible to consider preferences for a society that sustains social programs. It may be the case that individuals would make decisions (if they were available) to give up resources for these outcomes. We simply do not observe them. Once again this raises issues about how we measure trade-offs to calibrate preferences. In most CGE models for market goods, we assume these marginal trade-offs are revealed through ideal markets. In these cases we simply do not observe them.

7.3 Extent of the Market

At an aggregate level, judging the importance of GE effects will depend on these trade-off measures *and* the extent of the market. That is, how many people have them? Such questions do not come up for market transactions because expenditure flows allow the analyst to scale-up consumption levels and create the representative consumer. A comparable process can be used for user values for non-market goods on the revealed preference logic. Neither is available for social programs that largely resemble the concepts classified as non-use services. Both the characterization of the trade-offs with market goods and "the extent of the market" (or the aggregate resources that would be made available by people who would make these trade-offs) determine the importance of the GE effects of policies influencing these non-market goods.

These issues can be addressed. Some progress has been made for policies that are intended to change environmental resources. However, the record is much more limited with social programs. A prudent starting point would be to begin with social policies that can be addressed with some variant of the revealed preference logic, such as illustrated here with our sorting model for education and progressively extend the analysis to other situations with large benefits hypothesized to be associated with public good effects as we gain experience with the narrower set of problems where the revealed preference logic can be exploited.

NOTES

1. Shoven and Whalley (1992) provide an introduction and early review of this literature.
2. As we discuss in the next section, the use of the term general equilibrium can have a number of interpretations from considering effects through more than one market to a situation where the model describes a policy's effects on prices, incomes, and non-market services affected by market decisions. This is the definition we use when we refer to general equilibrium analyses. The definition of these measures in each modeling

strategy is conditional on the assumed structure of the choices made by economic agents and the rules governing their interactions.

3. Cost in this discussion is defined as the efficiency cost of a tax. This includes the costs due to abatement, output substitution, and input substitution. When pre-existing distortions are allowed and with them a second-best setting is considered there are marginal revenue recycling effects because new taxes can be used to reduce existing tax rates (while maintaining a consistent revenue) and there are interaction effects on measures of the marginal excess burden. See Goulder et al. (1999, pp. 336–7 and pp. 344–6).
4. Nonetheless, as Kuminoff and Pope (2010) demonstrate this argument is best interpreted as an approximation.
5. See Just et al. (2004, Chapter 9, pp. 311–50). Appendix 9B provides a detailed summary of general equilibrium welfare measurement for changes in a market economy.
6. We are grateful to a referee for suggesting the link to hedonic equilibria.
7. Our definitions for consumer surplus do not require that we measure utility or well-being. This characterization is an analytical abstraction. It allows formal definitions for the concept being measured (provided we make a set of assumptions about the functional forms for relationships linking variables describing choices and constraints).
8. For some specifications of $V(.)$ we could have a situation where WTP = WTA. This is not the case for a general specification of preferences. A great deal of effort has been devoted to explaining the size of the difference between the two measures. For example, Willig (1976) described the conditions required for the difference between these two measures of consumer surplus to be small *for price changes*. His conditions are based on the size of the income elasticity and the size of the Marshallian consumer surplus relative to the person's income. Hanemann (1991) demonstrated this intuition does not readily apply to situations involving quantity (or quality) changes where the commodity may not be available at a unit price. In this case, the price flexibility of income contributes to the definition of the Willig bounds and does not have a simple relationship to the income elasticity of demand. This distinction is important because we usually have some intuition about income elasticity of demand, considering necessities versus luxuries. The same intuition is not readily available for the price flexibility, which describes how the marginal willingness to pay changes with income. The simplest summary would suggest that the relationship depends on the structure of preferences, especially the availability of substitutes for the commodity affected by a policy and how its contribution to individual well-being changes with income.
9. Chetty's arguments, cited earlier, relate to cases where the first step in the process, the link between the policy and an impact on something that affects consumers' choices such as the tax and price increase, can be identified. In this example, a structural model is required to make this link.
10. See Hoehn and Randall (1989) for a discussion of piecemeal policy evaluation as compared to a strategy that defines policy composites. They suggest that without composite strategies for defining policies the potential biases in using benefit–cost analyses for individual projects can lead to movements away from efficiency when a sequence of individual choices is compared to the composite of the policies treated as an integrated whole. Their argument can be interpreted as reflecting factors that also contribute to the distinction between partial and general equilibrium benefit–cost analyses.
11. Their analysis was developed to explain the conditions required for Hazilla and Kopp's (1990) analysis of the social costs of environmental regulations to be valid.
12. See Diamond and McFadden (1974) for discussion of the duality features of the function and its role in early public economics.
13. See Freeman (2003, pp. 53–63) for further discussion.
14. This characterization—monetizing utility changes—has caused considerable confusion in the literature, as summarized by Freeman (2003).
15. These are part of what Chetty assumed were second-order effects for a national-level analysis. Our discussion does not overturn his judgment for the case of taxes. It does highlight that the situation can be much more nuanced for other policies.

16. This practice is called benefits transfer. See Boyle et al. (2010) for a current review and appraisal of these practices.
17. For small changes this would equal $\partial e/\partial q$; the definition in equation (6.10) holds income constant and in terms of the expenditure function, well-being or utility is assumed held constant. If the change is small they are usually assumed equal. At best, we usually have point estimates for marginal willingness to pay. The distinction between Marshallian measures as defined in equation (6.10) and Hicksian (based on the expenditure function) arise when we use these estimates to recover the marginal willingness to pay function. We do not consider these issues here—see Freeman (2003), or Bockstael and McConnell (2007) for discussion of the challenges involved with each.
18. In that example, one good had a pre-existing tax and the presence of it influenced the size of the excess burden for a new tax. The relationship of q to the good with the pre-existing tax was especially important.
19. This is what Chetty refers to as implication of the envelope condition.
20. See Just et al. (2004, pp. 360–61), especially equation (9.49) and the discussion.
21. Rutherford (2002) has demonstrated simple calibration strategies for the share parameters in CES functions.
22. One of the few stumbling blocks in these models is the calibration of leisure and work time because time allocations that are not associated with hours worked are incompletely measured (see Fullerton et al., 1984 for a description of the practice using Hicksian and Marshallian labor supply elasticities to resolve this issue).
23. Epple et al. (2001) discuss the prospects of developing models where voting determines the level of public goods and a budget balance condition, together with a specified production function for the public goods assures budget balance. This type of structure has also been included in models by Nechyba (1999, 2000) and Ferreyra (2007, 2009).
24. See Carbone (2005, 2007) for further discussion and Carbone and Smith (2008) for implementation of a model with these features.
25. Perroni's (1992) demonstration that a homothetic function can be used to represent non-homothetic responses provides the underlying logic for the calibration. This logic is used together with a more general insight developed by Carbone (2005) that is used in several applications. The insight is associated with combining conditions for GE calibration in the Carbone-Smith case or solving hybrid models. For example, in Carbone et al. (2009), a game theoretic model describing a sub-game perfect Nash equilibrium in the permit market for CO_2 permits is combined with a competitive CGE model to describe trade in marketed goods. The logic relies on describing GE as a mixed complementarity problem (see Böhringer and Rutherford, 2008, as one example) and combining it with equations that recognize the strategic decisions or permits are functions of local derivatives that are defined numerically. This allows the GE solution for the vector of equilibrium prices and quantities and the adjacent perturbed solutions for these variables to be solved simultaneously with the permit allocations treated as endogenous variables that result from the definition for the Nash equilibrium. A comparable process allows the definitions for the non-market valuation measures whether virtual prices (marginal willingness to pay) or willingness to pay to be solved simultaneously with the GE and calibrate a non-homothetic model for a baseline that uses properties of homothetic functions. (See online documentation for Carbone et al., 2009 for further discussion.)
26. In their example, changes in marginal willingness to pay for habitat provided a better indicator of how the substitution relationship between recreational fishing and leisure influenced the net of benefits of pollution policies intended to improve both. This measure was superior to using a simple comparison of PE versus GE measures of the net benefits of the pollution policy.
27. A notable exception is Harrison and Vinod (1992) who evaluate the sensitivity of CGE results to parameter values used in calibration in a statistical framework.
28. Farrow (1999) provides another illustration of an effort to evaluate how elasticities derived from an analytical GE model varied with estimation uncertainty. Using an

analytical model developed by Fullerton and Metcalf (1997), he assumed triangular distributions to characterize parameter uncertainty for the marginal labor tax rate, the aggregate income elasticity and the elasticity of substitution. Other variables were represented with uniform distribution and the analytical expressions derived in Fullerton and Metcalf were used to simulate the joint impact of uncertainty in all the parameters on the implied welfare effects of taxes.

29. See, for example, Goulder et al. (1999); Parry et al. (1999); and West and Williams (2004).
30. A review of these studies is beyond the scope here. See Epple and Platt (1998); Epple et al. (2009); Kuminoff et al. (2010); and Klaiber and Smith (2011).
31. Several of the calibrated models have considered educational policy but the focus was primarily on accounting for the effects of GE adjustment or outcome measures rather than benefit measures. See Kuminoff et al. (2010) for further discussion.
32. See Klaiber and Phaneuf (2010) for an example of a horizontal model that develops GE and PE welfare measures. Bayer et al. (2007) also estimate a horizontal model but do not compute welfare measures or consider the PE/GE distinction.
33. Klaiber and Smith (2011) provide more discussion of the intermediate steps in the logic in comparison to the horizontal or RUM formulation for the model.
34. The actual simulation of the equilibrium is numerical. It draws two random variables to characterize each household (i.e., income and the taste parameter for the index of public goods in each community) and selects a large number of these pairs of random variables. Each is assumed to represent a "household."
35. More recently, Kuminoff and Pope (2010) have extended the literature further, considering micro-housing sales data and replicating the Black methodology with the Bayer et al. instrument strategy for ten markets. They evaluate the federal No Child Left Behind program and find hedonic measures of the average value for the marginal WTP for improved school quality are four times larger than property value capitalization measures.
36. Thanks are due to Nicolai Kuminoff, who developed the Matlab Code for the Sieg et al. estimator.
37. The fixed effects for 2003, grade 2, and language test were omitted in these specifications so the effects that are measured are relative to these reference points for each variable.
38. The housing component of the CPI was 128.5 in 1990 and 184.0 in 2003. As Table 6.3 suggests, the standard in test scores for our sample was 2.25. This scaling the endpoints of our range by 2.25 × (128.5/184.0) × (1/12) will provide comparable measures.
39. The mean for family size was 3.116. We subtracted 2 to reflect parents and restricted the children to be a positive value or 0. The variance was 0.0326. Family size was assumed to be negatively correlated with income and independent of taste for education.
40. See Carbone and Smith (2010) for further discussion of the first point.

REFERENCES

Banzhaf, H. Spencer and V. Kerry Smith (2007), "Meta-analysis in model implementation: Choice sets and the valuation of air quality improvements," *Journal of Applied Econometrics*, **22** (6), 1013–31.

Bayer, Patrick, Fernando Ferreira, and Robert McMillan (2007), "A unified framework for measuring preferences for schools and neighborhoods," *Journal of Political Economy*, **115** (4) August, 588–638.

Black, Sandra E. (1999), "Do better schools matter? Parental valuation of elementary education," *Quarterly Journal of Economics*, **114** (2) May, 577–99.

Bockstael, Nancy E. and Kenneth E. McConnell (2007), *Environmental and Resource Valuation with Revealed Preferences*, Dordrecht: Springer.

Böhringer, Christopher and Thomas F. Rutherford (2008), "Combining bottom-up and top-down," *Energy Economics*, **30** (2), 574–96.

Boyle, Kevin J., Nicolai V. Kuminoff, Christopher F. Parameter, and Jaren C. Pope (2010), "The benefit transfer challenges," *Annual Review of Resource Economics*, **2**, 161–82.

Carbone, Jared C. (2005), "Calibrating non-separable general equilibrium models," unpublished working paper, CEnREP: North Carolina State University, March.

Carbone, Jared C. (2007), "The properties of non-price equilibria," unpublished working paper, Department of Economics, Williams College, 27 August.

Carbone, Jared C. and V. Kerry Smith (2008), "Evaluating policy interventions with general equilibrium externalities," *Journal of Public Economics*, **92** (5/6) June, 1254–74.

Carbone, Jared C. and V. Kerry Smith (2010), "Valuing ecosystem services in general equilibrium," March, *NBER Working Paper* No. 15844.

Carbone, Jared C., Carsten Helm, and Thomas F. Rutherford (2009), "The case for international emission trade in the absence of cooperative climate policy," *Journal of Environmental Economics and Management*, **58** (3), 266–80.

Chetty, Raj (2009), "Sufficient statistics for welfare analysis: A bridge between structural and reduced-form models," *Annual Review of Economics*, **1** (1), 451–88.

De Mooij, Ruud A. (2000), *Environmental Taxation and the Double Dividend*, Amsterdam: North Holland.

Diamond, Peter A. and Daniel L. McFadden (1974), "Some uses of the expenditure function in public finance," *Journal of Public Economics*, **3** (1), February, 3–21.

Epple, Dennis and Glenn J. Platt (1998), "Equilibrium and local redistribution in an urban economy when households differ in both preferences and incomes," *Journal of Urban Economics*, **43** (1), January, 23–51.

Epple, Dennis and Holger Sieg (1999), "Estimating equilibrium models of local jurisdiction," *Journal of Political Economy*, **107** (4), August, 645–81.

Epple, Dennis, Brett Gordon, and Holger Sieg (2009), "Drs. Mirth and Mills meet Dr. Tiebout: Integrating location specific amenities into multi-community equilibrium models," unpublished paper prepared for 50th Anniversary Conference of *Journal of Regional Science*, March.

Epple, Dennis, T. Romer, and Holger Sieg (2001), "Interjurisdictional sorting and majority rule: An empirical analysis," *Econometrica*, **69** (6), November, 1437–65.

Espinosa, J. Andrés and V. Kerry Smith (1995), "Measuring the environmental consequences of trade policy: A nonmarket CGE analysis," *American Journal of Agricultural Economics*, **77** (3), 772–7.

Farrow, Scott (1999), "The duality of taxes and tradable permits: A survey with applications in Central and Eastern Europe," *Environmental and Development Economics*, **4** (4), 519–35.

Fernandez, Raquel and Richard Rogerson (1998), "Public education and income distribution: A dynamic quantitative evaluation of education-finance reform," *The American Economic Review*, **88** (4), 813–33.

Ferreyra, Maria Marta (2007), "Estimating the effects of private school vouchers in multidistrict economies," *American Economic Review*, **97** (3), June, 789–817.

Ferreyra, Maria Marta (2009), "An empirical framework for large scale policy analysis with an application to school finance reform in Michigan," *American Economic Journal, Economic Policy*, **1** (1), February, 147–80.

Freeman, A. Myrick III (2003), *The Measurement of Environmental and Resource Values: Theory and Methods*, 2nd edition, Washington, DC: Resources for the Future.

Fullerton, Don and Gilbert Metcalf (1997), "Environmental controls, scarcity rents and pre-existing distortions," *NBER Working Paper* No. 6091.

Fullerton, Don, Yolanda K. Henderson, and John B. Shoven (1984), "A comparison of equilibrium models of taxation," in H.E. Scarf and J.B. Shoven (eds), *Applied General Equilibrium Analysis*, New York: Cambridge University Press.

Goulder, Lawrence H. and Roberton C. Williams III (2003), "The substantial bias from ignoring general equilibrium effects in estimating excess burden, and a practical solution," *Journal of Political Economy*, **111** (4), August, 898–927.

Goulder, Lawrence H., Ian W.H. Parry, Roberton C. Williams III, and Dallas Burtraw (1999), "The cost-cffectiveness of alternative instruments for environmental protection in a second-best setting," *Journal of Public Economics*, **72** (3), June, 329–60.

Hanemann, W. Michael (1991), "Willingness to pay and willingness to accept: How much can they differ?," *American Economic Review*, **81** (3), June, 635–47.

Harberger, Arnold C. (1964), "The measurement of waste," *American Economic Review*, **54** (1), 58–76.

Harrison, Glenn W. and H.D. Vinod (1992), "The sensitivity of analysis of applied general equilibrium models: Completely randomized factorial designs," *Review of Economics and Statistics*, **74** (2), 357–62.

Hazilla, Michael and Raymond J. Kopp (1990), "The social cost of environmental quality regulation: A general equilibrium analysis," *Journal of Political Economy*, **98** (4), August, 853–73.

Heckman, James J. (2006), "Skill formation and the economics of investing in disadvantaged children," *Science*, **312** (5782), 1900–902.

Heckman, James J. (2008), "Schools, skills and synapses," *Economic Inquiry*, **46** (3), 289–324.

Hoehn, John and Alan Randall (1989), "Too many proposals pass the benefit cost test," *American Economic Review*, **79** (3), 544–51.

Jones, Ronald W. (1965), "The structure of simple general equilibrium models," *Journal of Political Economy*, **73** (6), December, 557–72.

Just, Richard E., Darrell L. Hueth, and Andrew Schmitz (2004), *The Welfare Economics of Public Policy: A Practical Approach to Project and Policy Evaluation*, Cheltenham, UK and Northampton, MA, USA: Edward Elgar.

Klaiber, H. Allen and Daniel J. Phaneuf (2010), "Valuing open space in a residential sorting model of the twin cities," *Journal of Environmental Economics and Management*, **60** (2), 57–77.

Klaiber, H. Allen and V. Kerry Smith (2011), "Preference heterogeneity and non-market benefits: The roles of structural hedonic and sorting models," in Jeff Bennett (ed.), *The International Yearbook of Non-market Valuation*, Cheltenham, UK and Northampton, MA, USA: Edward Elgar, pp. 222–53.

Kuminoff, Nicolai V. (2009), "Decomposing the structural identification of non-market values," *Journal of Environmental Economics and Management*, **57** (2), 123–39.

Kuminoff, Nicolai V. and Jaren C. Pope (2010), "Hedonic equilibria, land value capitalization, and the willingness to pay for public goods," May, working paper, Arizona State University.

Kuminoff, Nicolai V., V. Kerry Smith, and Christopher Timmins (2010), "The new economics of equilibrium sorting and its transformational role for policy evaluation," *NBER Working Paper* No. 16349, September.

Nechyba, Thomas, J. (1999), "School finance induced migration and stratification patterns: The impact of private school vouchers," *Journal of Public Economic Theory*, **1** (1), 5–50.

Nechyba, Thomas, J. (2000), "Mobility, targeting, and private-school vouchers," *American Economic Review*, **90** (1), March, 130–46.

Palmquist, Raymond B. (1992), "Valuing localized externalities," *Journal of Urban Economics*, **31** (1), January, 59–68.

Parry, Ian, Roberton Williams, and Lawrence Goulder (1999), "When can carbon abatement policies increase welfare? The fundamental role of distorted factor markets," *Journal of Environmental Economics and Management*, **37** (1), 52–84.

Perroni, Carlo (1992), "Homothetic representations of regular non-homothetic preferences," *Economics Letters*, **40** (1), 19–22.

Phaneuf, Daniel J., V. Kerry Smith, Raymond B. Palmquist, and Jaren C. Pope (2008), "Integrating property value and local recreation models to value ecosystem services in urban watersheds," *Land Economics*, **84** (3), 361–81.

Poterba, James M. (1992), "Taxation and housing: Old questions, new answers," *American Economic Review*, **82** (2), 237–42.

Rutherford, Thomas F. (1997), "Applied general equilibrium modeling with MPSGE as a GAMS subsystem: An overview of the modeling framework and syntax," unpublished paper, University of Colorado, Boulder, CO, March.

Rutherford, Thomas F. (2002), "Lecture notes on constant elasticity forms," unpublished paper, University of Colorado, Boulder, CO, November.

Scarf, Herbert (1973), *The Computation of Economic Equilibrium*, New Haven, CT: Yale University Press.

Shoven, John B. and John Whalley (1972), "A general equilibrium calculation of the effects of differential taxation of income from capital in the United States," *Journal of Public Economics*, **1** (3/4), 281–322.

Shoven, John and John Whalley (1992), *Applying General Equilibrium*, New York: Cambridge University Press.

Sieg, Holger, V. Kerry Smith, H. Spencer Banzhaf, and Randy Walsh (2002), "Interjurisdictional housing prices in location equilibrium," *Journal of Urban Economics*, **52** (1), July, 131–53.

Sieg, Holger, V. Kerry Smith, H. Spencer Banzhaf, and Randy Walsh (2004), "Estimating the general equilibrium benefits of large changes in spatially delineated public goods," *International Economic Review*, **45** (4), 1047–77.

Smith, V. Kerry and Jared C. Carbone (2007), "Should benefit cost analyses take account of general equilibrium effects?," in Richard O. Zerbe Jr. (ed.), *Research in Law and Economics: A Journal of Policy*, **23**, 247–72.

Smith, V. Kerry, Holger Sieg, H. Spencer Banzhaf, and Randy Walsh (2004), "General equilibrium benefits for environmental improvements: Projected ozone reductions under EPA's prospective analysis for the Los Angeles Air Basin," *Journal of Environmental Economics and Management*, **47** (3), 559–84.

Tiebout, Charles M. (1956), "A pure theory of local expenditures," *Journal of Political Economy*, **64** (5), 416–24.

Walsh, Randall L. (2007), "Endogenous open space amenities in a locational equilibrium," *Journal of Urban Economics*, **61** (2), 319–44.
West, Sarah and Roberton Williams (2004), "Estimates from a consumer demand system: Implications for the incidence of environmental taxes," *Journal of Environmental Economics and Management*, **47** (3), 535–58.
Whalley, John (1975), "How reliable is partial equilibrium analysis?" *The Review of Economics and Statistics*, **57** (3), 299–310.
Whittington, Dale and Duncan MacRae Jr. (1986), "The issue of standing in cost–benefit analysis," *Journal of Policy Analysis and Management*, **5** (4), 665–82.
Willig, Robert (1976), "Consumer's surplus without apology," *American Economic Review*, **66** (4), September, 589–97.

APPENDIX

Table 6A.1 General and partial equilibrium measures of willingness to pay for all school districts: Nash equilibrium

School ID	District	Loss	GE WTP	PE WTP	MWTP Old	MWP New	dq	dp
1	ARLINGTON ELEMENTARY DISTRICT	0	−490.39	−13.53	40.26	40.23	−0.0004	0.0068
2	GILA BEND DISTRICT	0	−504.77	−7.51	44.44	44.39	−0.0001	0.0069
3	MORRISTOWN ELEM. DISTRICT	0	−491.40	−22.80	40.81	40.79	−0.0003	0.0066
4	AGUILA ELEM. DISTRICT	0	−510.08	−69.74	43.46	43.49	−0.0015	0.0060
5	PALO VERDE ELEMENTARY DISTRICT	0	−490.16	6.50	40.64	40.59	0.0002	0.0069
6	NADABURG DISTRICT	0	−490.90	−21.19	41.69	41.67	−0.0005	0.0065
7	WILSON ELEMENTARY DISTRICT	0	−502.50	−5.43	43.83	43.79	−0.0001	0.0067
8	MURPHY ELEMENTARY DISTRICT	0	−500.88	−102.44	42.39	42.46	−0.0061	0.0034
9	BUCKEYE ELEMENTARY DISTRICT	0	−498.99	−410.17	41.89	42.32	−0.0119	0.0001
10	WICKENBURG DISTRICT	0	−508.88	−538.05	42.22	43.22	−0.0131	−0.0006
11	QUEEN CREEK DISTRICT	27	−501.36	−466.45	41.34	41.34	−0.0109	0.0006
12	RIVERSIDE ELEMENTARY DISTRICT	0	−495.75	−265.47	40.21	40.21	−0.0060	0.0034
13	FOWLER ELEMENTARY DISTRICT	0	−515.36	−281.66	42.89	42.89	−0.0004	0.0067
14	AVONDALE ELEMENTARY DISTRICT	5	−517.91	−104.60	44.35	43.35	0.0002	0.0070
15	ISAAC ELEMENTARY DISTRICT	0	−517.63	−0.51	44.24	44.24	0.0000	0.0069
16	ROOSEVELT ELEMENTARY DISTRICT	0	−514.48	4.25	45.29	45.29	0.0001	0.0070
17	CARTWRIGHT ELEMENTARY DISTRICT	0	−511.40	−0.95	46.54	46.54	0.0000	0.0069
18	LAVEEN ELEMENTARY DISTRICT	0	−507.40	−78.41	46.86	46.86	−0.0015	0.0059
19	TOLLESON ELEMENTARY DISTRICT	0	−512.15	−168.53	47.61	47.61	−0.0019	0.0057
20	GLENDALE ELEMENTARY DISTRICT	0	−511.37	−58.75	47.65	47.65	−0.0026	0.0052
21	PENDERGAST ELEMENTARY DISTRICT	0	−512.96	−48.29	48.69	48.67	−0.0010	0.0062
22	DYSART DISTRICT	0	−514.62	−68.43	49.55	49.55	−0.0013	0.0060
23	LITTLETON ELEMENTARY DISTRICT	0	−513.22	−85.57	49.81	49.81	−0.0013	0.0060
24	ALHAMBRA ELEMENTARY DISTRICT	0	−512.76	−103.13	49.85	49.85	−0.0008	0.0064

Table 6A.1 (continued)

School ID	District	Loss	GE WTP	PE WTP	MWTP Old	MWP New	dq	dp
25	LIBERTY ELEMENTARY DISTRICT	0	−512.04	−491.55	49.92	49.92	−0.0083	0.0012
26	LITCHFIELD ELEMENTARY DISTRICT	18	−518.47	−786.98	50.90	50.91	−0.0134	−0.0024
27	WASHINGTON ELEMENTARY DISTRICT	0	−534.87	−841.57	51.49	51.49	−0.0146	−0.0032
28	MESA UNIFIED DISTRICT	7	−582.19	−975.10	53.91	53.91	−0.0166	−0.0046
29	HIGLEY UNIFIED DISTRICT	21	−612.96	−1108.71	55.99	53.99	−0.0137	−0.0023
30	SADDLE MOUNTAIN UNIFIED DISTRICT	0	−607.47	−1112.54	54.43	54.43	−0.0115	−0.0006
31	GILBERT DISTRICT	18	−622.49	−802.51	55.47	55.47	−0.0111	−0.0003
32	PEORIA DISTRICT	15	−631.55	−356.86	56.14	56.14	−0.0061	0.0037
33	CHANDLER DISTRICT	0	−636.70	−163.52	56.98	56.98	−0.0022	0.0069
34	DEER VALLEY DISTRICT	4	−643.30	−248.70	58.33	58.33	−0.0046	0.0049
35	TEMPE ELEMENTARY DISTRICT	0	−643.33	−206.41	58.50	58.50	−0.0093	0.0009
36	PHOENIX ELEMENTARY DISTRICT	0	−642.99	−308.77	58.92	58.92	−0.0128	−0.0022
37	BALSZ ELEMENTARY DISTRICT	0	−649.44	−503.58	59.92	59.92	−0.0083	0.0016
38	CREIGHTON ELEMENTARY DISTRICT	3	−654.93	−773.52	60.33	60.33	−0.0119	−0.0016
39	KYRENE ELEMENTARY DISTRICT	0	−670.03	−742.27	61.33	61.33	−0.0074	0.0025
40	OSBORN ELEMENTARY DISTRICT	0	−680.55	−550.47	61.97	61.97	−0.0079	0.0020
41	PARADISE VALLEY DISTRICT	9	−698.20	−553.28	63.32	63.32	−0.0093	0.0008
42	CAVE CREEK DISTRICT	18	−719.21	−1544.35	65.39	65.39	−0.0191	−0.0088
43	FOUNTAIN HILLS DISTRICT	19	−721.75	−1519.47	64.61	64.61	−0.0210	−0.0106
44	MADISON ELEMENTARY DISTRICT	0	−749.75	−1909.10	65.76	65.76	−0.0257	−0.0151
45	SCOTTSDALE DISTRICT	13	−919.32	−1925.90	70.97	70.97	−0.0071	0.0059
46	MOBILE ELEM. DISTRICT	0	−1093.20	6.67	83.31	83.31	0.0001	0.0155

Table 6A.2 General and partial equilibrium measures of willingness to pay: equilibrium for teacher cuts based on prices only

School ID	District	LOSS	GE WTP	PE WTP	dq	dp
1	ARLINGTON ELEMENTARY DISTRICT	0	−494.98	0.00	3.06E−16	7.01E−03
2	GILA BEND DISTRICT	0	−508.76	−1.77	−1.52E−16	0.0070
3	MORRISTOWN ELEM. DISTRICT	0	−495.02	−11.86	1.42E−16	0.0068
4	AGUILA ELEM. DISTRICT	0	−513.45	−12.16	0.0000	0.0068
5	PALO VERDE ELEMENTARY DISTRICT	0	−493.36	−0.24	0.0000	0.0068
6	NADABURG DISTRICT	0	−493.89	−1.07	−1.40E−16	0.0068
7	WILSON ELEMENTARY DISTRICT	0	−505.35	−0.87	−4.19E−16	0.0068
8	MURPHY ELEMENTARY DISTRICT	0	−503.77	−107.65	−0.0062	0.0034
9	BUCKEYE ELEMENTARY DISTRICT	0	−502.00	−414.89	−0.0121	1.19E−05
10	WICKENBURG DISTRICT	0	−511.91	−535.53	−0.0130	−0.0005
11	QUEEN CREEK DISTRICT	27	−504.23	−441.43	−0.0106	0.0008
12	RIVERSIDE ELEMENTARY DISTRICT	0	−498.50	−255.71	−0.0058	0.0036
13	FOWLER ELEMENTARY DISTRICT	0	−518.14	−271.87	−0.0006	0.0066
14	AVONDALE ELEMENTARY DISTRICT	5	−520.62	−107.14	−2.82E−05	0.0069
15	ISAAC ELEMENTARY DISTRICT	0	−520.40	−0.07	1.53E−15	0.0069
16	ROOSEVELT ELEMENTARY DISTRICT	0	−517.32	−0.42	−1.27E−16	0.0069
17	CARTWRIGHT ELEMENTARY DISTRICT	0	−514.28	−0.04	3.81E−15	0.0069
18	LAVEEN ELEMENTARY DISTRICT	0	−510.11	−28.64	−0.0003	0.0067
19	TOLLESON ELEMENTARY DISTRICT	0	−514.72	−102.33	−0.0018	0.0058
20	GLENDALE ELEMENTARY DISTRICT	0	−514.19	−90.19	−0.0026	0.0052
21	PENDERGAST ELEMENTARY DISTRICT	0	−516.64	−97.89	−0.0020	0.0056
22	DYSART DISTRICT	0	−518.98	−117.60	−0.0013	0.0061
23	LITTLETON ELEMENTARY DISTRICT	0	−517.83	−84.17	−0.0013	0.0061
24	ALHAMBRA ELEMENTARY DISTRICT	0	−517.33	−98.86	−0.0011	0.0062
25	LIBERTY ELEMENTARY DISTRICT	0	−516.50	−471.28	−0.0082	0.0013

Table 6A.2 (continued)

School ID	District	LOSS	GE WTP	PE WTP	dq	dp
26	LITCHFIELD ELEMENTARY DISTRICT	18	−522.90	−766.35	−0.0136	−0.0025
27	WASHINGTON ELEMENTARY DISTRICT	0	−539.33	−846.09	−0.0151	−0.0035
28	MESA UNIFIED DISTRICT	7	−587.16	−988.05	−0.0170	−0.0049
29	HIGLEY UNIFIED DISTRICT	21	−618.38	−1132.43	−0.0127	−0.0015
30	SADDLE MOUNTAIN UNIFIED DISTRICT	0	−612.85	−1136.05	−0.0123	−0.0012
31	GILBERT DISTRICT	18	−628.02	−810.72	−0.0101	0.0006
32	PEORIA DISTRICT	15	−637.38	−376.51	−0.0064	0.0035
33	CHANDLER DISTRICT	0	−642.98	−185.24	−0.0025	0.0067
34	DEER VALLEY DISTRICT	4	−649.95	−256.48	−0.0052	0.0045
35	TEMPE ELEMENTARY DISTRICT	0	−649.85	−198.31	−0.0093	0.0009
36	PHOENIX ELEMENTARY DISTRICT	0	−649.34	−302.57	−0.0126	−0.0019
37	BALSZ ELEMENTARY DISTRICT	0	−655.83	−507.62	−0.0082	0.0018
38	CREIGHTON ELEMENTARY DISTRICT	3	−661.34	−777.61	−0.0120	−0.0016
39	KYRENE ELEMENTARY DISTRICT	0	−676.53	−748.35	−0.0077	0.0024
40	OSBORN ELEMENTARY DISTRICT	0	−687.23	−567.67	−0.0083	0.0018
41	PARADISE VALLEY DISTRICT	9	−705.34	−560.93	−0.0100	0.0003
42	CAVE CREEK DISTRICT	18	−726.24	−1337.88	−0.0190	−0.0086
43	FOUNTAIN HILLS DISTRICT	19	−728.64	−1514.00	−0.0210	−0.0105
44	MADISON ELEMENTARY DISTRICT	0	−756.74	−1916.12	−0.0258	−0.0151
45	SCOTTSDALE DISTRICT	13	−923.52	−1878.00	−0.0047	0.0087
46	MOBILE ELEM. DISTRICT	0	−1055.41	0.00	0.0000	0.0149

7. Appropriate discounting for benefit–cost analysis

David F. Burgess and Richard O. Zerbe, Jr.

1 INTRODUCTION

Perhaps no methodological question within benefit–cost analysis (BCA) has been so widely discussed as the discounting of future benefits and costs. The body of literature regarding this subject is vast. However, it is also unresolved. Little consensus can be found on issues such as what should be discounted, or on the choice of a discount rate. Sources of discrepancy include: (1) the effects of risk; (2) displacement of private capital; (3) rate of time preference; (4) whether rates should be hyperbolic with respect to the time period in which effects are felt (an issue related to the use of time preferences); (5) ethical issues such as whether the changing wealth of future generations should allow for rates that reflect preferences for income (a marginal utility of money that is different from those at the time the project is initiated) (Weitzman, 2001; Moore et al., 2004; Dasgupta, 2008) and (6) whether or not certain goods such as lives and health are special and should not be discounted. Part of the problem lies in the fact that proponents of different approaches to discounting are frequently unclear about what they are maximizing, or what function the discount rate is supposed to perform. In this chapter we take the position that the basic principles that underlie benefit–cost analysis should be carried forward with respect to discount rates. The case for discounting arises from the concepts of time preference, uncertainty, and the opportunity cost of capital, all of which coalesce to underlie the simple premise that a dollar in hand today is held to be worth more than receiving that same dollar at any future point (US OMB, 1992, 2003).

This chapter assumes that the purpose of discounting is to select that rate that will lead to selection of the best projects in terms of maximizing net present values. We assume that projects should be chosen that meet the potential Pareto test: the gainers should be able to compensate the losers so that everyone is better off, though compensation need not be made.[1] This will occur when the present value of benefits compensates for the capital forgone and the consumption displaced. We find that the social opportunity cost approach to the discount rate is the most likely to meet this objective, and a major purpose of this chapter is to develop a rate, or a range of rates, that can serve as a standard for best practice in the context of the US economy.

1.1 Main Approaches

There are three main approaches to determining discounting rates:

1. The social opportunity cost of capital (SOC) approach, which proposes that the discount rate reflects the social (economic) opportunity cost of capital, a weighted average of the pre-tax and after-tax rates of return, and, in an open economy, the marginal cost of foreign funding, where the weights reflect the proportions of funding that are obtained from displaced investment, postponed consumption, and incremental funding from abroad when the government borrows to finance the project (Sandmo and Drèze, 1971; Harberger, 1972, 1985; Sjaastad and Wisecarver, 1977; Burgess, 2010a, 2012).
2. The social time preference (STP) approach (Marglin, 1963; Feldstein, 1972; Bradford, 1975; Lind, 1982), which discounts benefits and costs at the after-tax rate of return (or a politically determined social rate of time preference) but converts all investment displaced in financing (or induced by the project) into its consumption equivalent by multiplying by the shadow price of capital.
3. The marginal cost of funds criterion (MCF) (Liu, 2003; Liu et al., 2004), which discounts within-generation benefits at the after-tax rate, between-generation benefits at the pre-tax rate, and costs (including indirect revenue effects) at the pre-tax rate, but multiplies all costs and indirect revenue effects by a parameter reflecting the marginal cost of funds.[2] The MCF approach emphasizes the need for project evaluation to take into account the marginal social cost of raising the revenue necessary to cover any budgetary deficit that arises on account of the project.

Apparent differences between the SOC and MCF criteria arise from different interpretations of a project's indirect revenue effect. For the MCF criterion, the indirect revenue effect is the uncompensated effect of the project on tax revenue (holding income fixed) whereas for the SOC criterion it is the compensated effect (holding utility fixed). Apparent differences between the SOC and STP criteria arise from different assumptions about the private sector's knowledge of the project's benefits and costs.

Burgess (2012) shows that these approaches can be reconciled. He does not indicate discount rate estimates for the SOC and this is our primary purpose here.

All approaches recognize that the displacement of private capital must be taken into account, but they differ in terms of whether it should be incorporated into the discount rate or reflected by a shadow price. Liu (2003) and Liu et al.'s (2004) MCF criterion depends upon an exogenous rate of return to capital, but Burgess (2012) shows that the MCF approach can be extended to situations where the rate of return to capital is endogenous. In this more general setting the MCF criterion requires that (within-generation) benefits be discounted at the after-tax rate of return (consumption rate of interest) but costs and indirect revenue effects must be discounted at the weighted average rate that is appropriate for the SOC criterion. Costs and indirect revenue effects must be multiplied by the MCF parameter that measures the marginal cost of raising a dollar of revenue using the particular tax instrument that is relevant. In this more general setting the fundamental equivalence between the MCF and SOC criteria continues to hold. The key insight is that the MCF criterion is evaluating the impact of a project on private surplus (present value of consumption discounted at the consumption rate of interest) by converting the budgetary cost of the project (present value of project expenditures minus indirect revenue effects discounted at the SOC rate) into its consumption equivalent cost using the MCF parameter, whereas the SOC criterion is measuring the impact of the project on government revenue holding private surplus fixed at its pre-project level. While the standard SOC criterion assumes that the marginal tax instrument is a lump sum tax, the SOC criterion can be adapted to situations when a distortionary tax is used instead. The weighted average discount rate is appropriate for the SOC criterion whether or not the marginal tax instrument is a lump sum tax.

The SOC approach is justified by the straightforward principles of applied welfare economics—demand price measures marginal benefit, competitive supply price measures marginal cost, and adding up (i.e., dollars of benefits and costs are valued independently of to whom they accrue) (Harberger, 1971). The basic exercise is the extraction of resources from the economy, which displaces investment and stimulates saving and in an open economy attracts additional foreign funding. The discount rate should be consistent with choosing a project that is more productive over another that is less productive. The rate then must cover the productivity that is forgone as a consequence of displaced investment and the net-of-tax supply price of the newly induced savings and the marginal cost of incremental foreign funding. Any lower rate than the weighted average represented by the SOC will fail this test. Though one can find a number of ways to motivate lower rates, one cannot escape the penalty of ignoring the correspondingly higher social productivity of investment funds. Any higher rate will forgo desirable projects.

The STP approach plays a prominent role in the academic literature on the social discount rate. Because our ultimate position is in support of the SOC approach, we will focus on comparing how the STP and SOC criteria perform in simple situations.

In the case of two period projects, where costs are incurred in period 1 and benefits accrue in period 2, the SOC and STP criteria give equivalent results if benefits are just like income, as is the case of most commercial projects. Thus, for a project with costs $C1$ and benefits $B2$ it is a matter of indifference whether one converts costs and benefits into "consumption equivalents" and discounts at the STP rate, or discounts unconverted benefits and costs at the SOC rate. Assuming that the capital market is the marginal source of funds for all projects and (for simplicity) that the pre-tax rate of return p is exogenous, the SOC rate will equal the pre-tax rate of return and the STP rate will equal the after-tax rate of return r.[3] The wedge between the two rates is explained by the capital income tax so $r = p(1 - \tau)$. If the private sector consumes the annuity value of wealth the consumption equivalent of a dollar of investment displaced will be equal to the ratio of the pre-tax rate of return to the after-tax rate. In other words, the shadow price of a dollar of private investment displaced is p/r.

A project that costs $C1$ and provides benefits of $B2$ is worthwhile according to the SOC criterion if $-C1 + B2/(1 + p) > 0$. Using the STP criterion, the project's cost is converted into its consumption equivalent by multiplying by the shadow price of investment (because the costs displace private investment dollar for dollar), and the benefit $B2$ is separated into an income component, $B2 - C1$, which is available for consumption, and a "replacement of capital" component $C1$, which is reinvested. The project is worthwhile according to the STP criterion if $-C1\ (p/r) + [B2 - C1 + C1\ (p/r)]/(1 + r) > 0$. But this is equivalent to the SOC criterion.[4]

If the benefits are fully consumed (i.e., separable from private consumption) the project has no effect on private sector behavior, so ultimately it must be financed by raising taxes to balance the government's budget. If lump sum taxes are used, the project's cost has a consumption equivalent of $C1\ [p(1 + r)/r(1 + p)]$ and the project is worthwhile according to the STP criterion if $-C1\ [p(1 + r)/r(1 + p)] + B1/(1 + r) > 0$.[5] However, in this case the SOC criterion requires that an "indirect revenue effect" be included along with the conventional benefit and cost estimates, but the appropriate discount rate is still the SOC rate. The benchmark for the SOC criterion is a project whose benefits are "just like income." In other words, providing the project and increasing lump sum taxes by an amount equal to the private sector's willingness to pay for the project leaves capital income tax revenue unchanged. Any project whose benefits are not equivalent to income will have an indirect revenue effect. For a project whose benefit $B2$ is fully consumed (which may characterize certain non-pecuniary benefits), the indirect revenue effect is the effect on capital income tax revenue of a lump sum tax increase of $B2$ in period 2. Assuming that the private sector consumes the annuity value of wealth, capital income tax revenue will increase in period 2 by $\tau prB2/(1 + r)^2$, and decrease in periods 3 and thereafter by $\tau pB2/(1 + r)^2$. The present value of the project's indirect revenue effect (discounted at the SOC rate) is therefore $\tau B2(p.r - 1)/(1 + r)^2 (1 + p)$. Including the indirect revenue effect along with the conventional benefit and cost estimates, the SOC criterion becomes $-C1 + B2/(1 + p) + \tau B2(p.r - 1)/(1 + r)^2 (1 + p) > 0$. It is easy to verify that the SOC criterion with the indirect revenue effect taken into account is equivalent to the STP criterion specified above.

Bradford (1975) argued that for projects whose costs displace investment in the same proportion as the benefits induce investment, the appropriate discount rate is the STP rate with no need to shadow price benefits or costs. However, his result depends upon two critical assumptions: first, that the private sector behaves myopically so its saving is not governed by optimizing behavior but rather by a simple rule of thumb whereby a constant proportion of (disposable) income is saved independent of the rate of return; and second, that investments in the private sector are not feasible options for the government, because otherwise scarce resources should be invested in such projects rather than in any project that can pass muster only at the STP rate. Even if private sector investments are off limits for the government, whenever there is public debt outstanding, debt reduction is always an option and the rate of return on debt reduction is the SOC rate.

1.2 Estimating the SOC Rate for the United States

The SOC rate is a weighted average rate that takes into account both the displacement of capital and forgone consumption, and in an open economy the use of foreign funds. The general expression for the SOC rate in a multi-sector economy with different effective rates of tax on capital in each sector, and with different rates of personal income tax on different groups of savers, is:

$$SDR = \sum \beta_i r_i + \sum \theta_j p_j + \alpha f \quad (7.1)$$

Where:

$$\sum \beta_i + \sum \theta_j + \alpha = 1 \qquad (7.2)$$

Given that:
β_i = proportion of funds from increased savings of group i;
r_i = marginal rate of time preference, typically after-tax real rate of return, as perceived by group i;
θ_j = proportion of funds from displaced investment in sector j;
p_j = marginal rate of capital productivity in sector j in home country;
α = proportion of funds from incremental foreign funding;
f = marginal cost of incremental foreign funding.

While the SOC is conceptually straightforward, it is empirically challenging to arrive at a reliable estimate; not only must rates of return on alternative sources of funds be estimated, so must the proportions of funding drawn from each source.

A reasonable estimate of the opportunity cost of displaced investment is the pre-tax rate of return on capital in place.[6] National Accounts data can be used to estimate annual rates of return on reproducible capital (consisting of residential and non-residential structures, machinery and equipment, and inventories) as the ratio of the total income accruing to capital divided by the stock of capital. Rates of return estimated this way tend to exhibit low volatility, unlike financial rates of return, primarily because capital is measured at replacement cost rather than market prices (see Jenkins and Kuo, 2010). A major advantage of using national accounts data is that the estimated rate of return encompasses all sectors of the economy and all forms of reproducible capital and is thus likely to provide the best estimate of the rate of return that the economy as a whole will forgo when private investment is displaced.[7]

There are several challenges involved in estimating such a rate of return, however. They include: how to separate the return to capital from the return to labor in unincorporated businesses; how to reliably separate payments to unimproved land from the return to capital; how to determine appropriate rates of economic depreciation for the various capital types; and how to determine what proportion of the measured return to capital (GNP minus labor compensation) reflects monopoly profits that should not be fully attributable to capital. In this chapter we will have to rely on a less than fully comprehensive estimate of the rate of return to capital. Poterba (1999) estimated an average pre-tax rate of return in the US non-financial corporate sector of 8.5 percent over the period 1959–96. His estimates are based upon an improved methodology for determining the replacement cost of corporate capital. We will use this estimate as our baseline measure of the opportunity cost of displaced investment.

The consumer rate of interest is usually calculated as a group's after-tax rate of return, but for some groups (e.g., negative savers) it may be better approximated by the real interest rate on credit cards and other debt. Since the aggregate household sector is a net saver, a reasonable estimate of the marginal cost of forgone consumption is the pre-tax rate of return to capital net of all taxes on income from capital. Applying the corporate, property, and personal tax rates to Poterba's 8.5 percent estimate of the pre-tax rate of return gives an after-tax rate of return of approximately 3.5 percent. We will use this as our baseline estimate of the opportunity cost of postponed consumption.

Under certain conditions the average cost of foreign funding can be approximated as the rate of return that foreign investors earn on the capital invested in the country net of all taxes paid to the host government. If the supply price of foreign funding is upward sloping, the average cost will understate the marginal cost. If the withholding tax corrects the divergence between average and marginal cost, the marginal cost of foreign funding will be the rate of return to capital net of corporate and property taxes but gross of withholding taxes. Assuming a pre-tax rate of return of 8.5 percent and a combined corporate and property tax rate of 35 percent, the implied marginal cost of foreign funding is approximately 5.5 percent.

According to the SOC approach the marginal source of funding for all projects is the capital market, thus keeping the issue of tax reform separate from project evaluation. If a particular tax is being proposed to finance a particular project, the revenue from the tax could be used to pay down the debt instead of funding the project, so an alternative use of funds for any project is to pay down the debt.[8] Comparing the benefits from a proposed project to the benefits of debt reduction using the same funds (a comparison that is equivalent to the SOC criterion) ensures a level playing field for all projects, and avoids situations where a project is judged to be worthwhile solely on the merits of the efficiency of the tax intended to fund the project (Burgess, 2012). Thus, the capital market should appropriately be evaluated as the marginal source of funding for all projects, even if a project is funded by a tax.

The weights that enter the SOC formula reflect the proportions of an incremental dollar of funding that is obtained from each source when funding is drawn from a well-functioning, but distorted, capital market. Harberger (1969) and Sandmo and Drèze (1971) show that these weights can be expressed in terms of the rate of return elasticities of supply and demand for each source and the proportions of existing funding drawn from each source. Estimates of the elasticity of demand for investment spending on fixed capital with respect to the cost of capital typically range from −1.0 to −0.7 (Gilchrist et al., 2007; Department of Finance Canada, 2008), while estimates of the compensated elasticity of supply of indigenous saving with respect to the after-tax rate of return are in the range of 0.1 to 0.2.[9]

The elasticity of supply of foreign funding with respect to the rate of return is more problematic. Some would argue that this elasticity is close to infinite given the high degree of capital market integration, but it is crucial to recognize that what is relevant is the responsiveness of the net supply of real capital from abroad with respect to the real rate of return offered to attract this capital. If incremental funding for a project drives up the rate of interest it will crowd out some foreign direct investment as well as attract additional foreign portfolio investment. The net supply of real capital from abroad is the sum of these two competing effects. Burgess (2010b) shows that the SOC formula can be re-written in a way that does not depend (directly) upon an estimate of the elasticity of supply of external funding but instead upon an estimate of the "saving retention coefficient." Given an exogenous shock to indigenous saving, the saving retention coefficient is a ratio of the proportion of the indigenous savings increase that is invested within the country to the proportion of the savings increase that is invested abroad. Beginning with the widely cited paper by Feldstein and Horioka (1980), saving retention coefficients have been estimated by numerous researchers. The saving retention coefficient for OECD countries has been estimated by Helliwell (1998) to range from 0.5 to 0.7. Since the USA is the largest OECD country, and larger countries have more market power, they will tend to have larger saving retention coefficients. At the same time, national saving and investment rates have become increasingly decoupled in recent years due to globalization. In light of these considerations a reasonable estimate of the saving retention coefficient for the US is 0.6, with an upper bound of 0.67 and a lower bound of 0.5.

Burgess (2010b) shows that the SOC rate can be written as the following function of the relevant rates of return (opportunity cost of displaced private investment p, opportunity cost of postponed consumption r, and marginal cost of incremental foreign funding r^*), the (compensated) elasticity of supply of indigenous saving e, the elasticity of demand for investment n, the proportion of investment that is financed by indigenous saving S/I, and the saving retention coefficient SRC:

$$SOC = \{p - (e/n)(S/I)r + ((1/SRC) - 1)f\}/D \tag{7.3}$$

Where:

$$D = -(e/n)(S/I) + 1/SRC \tag{7.4}$$

Table 7.1 SOC rate for the United States

SRC	$e = 0.1, n = -1.0$	$e = 0.2, n = -1.0$	$e = 0.2, n = -0.7$
0.5	6.9%	6.7%	6.6%
0.6	7.1%	7.0%	6.7%
0.67	7.3%	7.1%	6.9%

Using the estimates for the rates of return p, r, and f identified above, the elasticity values $e = 0.2$ and $n = -1.0$, an assumed ratio of indigenous saving to investment S/I equal to 0.9 (which implies that 10 percent of private investment is financed from abroad), and a saving retention coefficient SRC equal to 0.6, the implied estimate of the SOC rate is 7.0 percent (which matches one of the two base-case rates recommended by the Office of Management and Budget for regulatory analysis, the other being 3 percent; see US OMB, 1992, 2003). The implied proportions of an incremental dollar of funding that is obtained from displaced investment, postponed consumption, and incremental foreign funding are 0.54, 0.10, and 0.36 respectively.

It is possible that the benchmark estimates of the rates of return are biased upward or downward.[10] The weights indicate the extent to which the SOC rate will change in response to a change of one percentage point in the respective rate of return. For example, if the opportunity cost of displaced investment is underestimated by one percentage point the SOC rate will be underestimated by 0.54 percentage points, whereas if the opportunity cost of postponed consumption is underestimated by one percentage point the SOC rate will be underestimated by 0.1 percentage points.[11]

Table 7.1 shows the sensitivity of the SOC rate to alternative values of the saving retention coefficient and alternative values of the elasticity parameters e and n. If plausible ranges for e are 0.1 to 0.2 and plausible ranges for n are -0.7 to -1.0 it is conceivable that the ratio could be as low as 0.1 and as high as 0.28. It is also possible that the saving retention coefficient could be as high as 0.67 or as low as 0.5. The results indicate that the implied SOC rate is in the range of 6.6 percent to 7.3 percent. Finally, the ratio of S/I could be as low as 0.8 but the implied SOC rate is only mildly affected by this change. It seems reasonable to conclude that an appropriate range of values for the SOC rate for the US economy is a lower bound of 6 percent and an upper bound of 8 percent.

Some have argued that the SOC rate obtained from national accounts data will be biased upward because it contains a risk premium that represents necessary compensation for bearing risk (Boardman et al., 2010). A dollar of forgone investment constitutes a well-diversified portfolio of assets in all sectors of the economy. This rate of return will be well approximated by the average rate of return on this broad mix of capital over a sufficiently long time period to encompass business cycle swings, and it may contain a premium to compensate risk-averse investors for bearing any non-diversifiable risk. If so, the "risk free" SOC rate will be somewhat lower. However, unless the project adds less risk to the aggregate portfolio than what is forgone on the private investment displaced the appropriate discount rate should include the risk premium that is embedded in the SOC rate.[12]

A frequent point of criticism regarding rates that arise from the SOC and related approaches is that they will materially reduce effects felt very far in the future. However, there is nothing inherently wrong with this. Nor will this mean that really large effects that occur in the future will necessarily be ignored. Suppose that unless corrective mitigation is taken now the world's GDP will suddenly fall to zero in 100 years. The current world GDP is about $62 trillion. This will grow to $1192 trillion (constant dollars) in 100 years at a 3 percent annual real rate. Assume that with the mitigation, GDP will continue to grow forever at 3 percent. The present value of the lost future GDP at year 100 will be $30 quadrillion, assuming infinite life for the world. When this is discounted at 7 percent, its present value today is $34 trillion. This is not a trivial sum to consider to place on the side of mitigating the future harm.

2 TIME PREFERENCE AND ETHICAL RATES

2.1 Time Preference Rates

There is recent interest in time preference and ethical discount rates. Time preference refers to a demonstrated behavioral economic preference for immediate or near-term benefits over future accruement, which skews economic decision-making towards near-term benefits. There is evidence that time preference rates do not correspond with the SOC rates. Evidence about the divergence of rates also suggests that the use of individuals' rates make choices practically difficult. Frederick et al. (2002) suggest that people have different discount rates for different activities and contexts. Thus, rates individuals might feel to be most appropriate for application to government social policy analyses might differ significantly from the rates they use in their own investment or consumption decisions. In addition, surveys of rates of time preference are so varied that no single rate seems possible (ibid.). More importantly there is no compelling rationale or motivation for using such rates even if available, since their use would result in a loss of efficiency and no clear gain in equity.

Recent work by Weitzman (1998, 2001) uses the opinions of economists about rates to form a set of discount factors:

$$1/(1/r)^t \tag{7.5}$$

Weitzman (2001) argues that it would be sensible to assume that each expert has an equal chance of knowing the "correct" social discount rate and thus we should compute the present value of a public project using each individual expert's discount rate, and then compute an average of these present values. One can then back out the implied social discount rate.[13] Weitzman fits a gamma distribution to the distribution of rates implied by the discount factors as suggested by the sample of economists. These rates are necessarily hyperbolic due to the divergence of rates. However, the gamma distribution over-weights the lower rates in his sample, significantly overestimating the frequency density of those with rates between 0 percent and 2 percent (see Weitzman, 2001, Figure 1); this leads to rates that are too low, especially for longer time periods. When Weitzman's data is used to calculate actual discount factors and a rate extracted that represents the average rate the result is rates for every time period higher than calculated by Weitzman (Long et al., 2011).

There are several other objections to using Weitzman's results. First, economists as a general class are unlikely to be experts on the discount rate. Weitzman assumes an equal probability of each economist being correct (a uniform distribution); however, there is no reason to assume this sample of experts consists of the most knowledgeable people, or that their opinions should have equal weight. Further, in using a sample of discount factors (the present value calculation for different people) one will necessarily find social rates to be hyperbolic and find very low rates for projects in the far future as the rates will asymptotically approach the lowest rate in the sample.[14] Third, the spread of rates is disconcertingly wide. Even when Weitzman restricts his sample to only 50 eminent economists, their opinions as to an appropriate discount rate for global warming mitigation policies (with all benefits and costs converted into consumption equivalent real dollars for each year) still range from 0 percent to 15 percent. Frederick et al. (2002) have found even greater spreads. Finally, there is little underlying rationale rooted in economic theory for using these rates.

2.2 Ethical Rates

The manner in which BCA addresses inter-temporal comparison is highly significant to project outcomes, as well as highly controversial philosophically. Some argue for a zero discount rate (i.e., no discounting of future benefits and costs) on philosophical and/or economic grounds (Schultze et al., 1981; Pearce and Turner, 1989; Parfit, 1992, 1994; Plater et al., 1998) (see Goodin, 1982 for an even-handed discussion of the limitations of discounting in policy analysis). Though it is commonly accepted that *money* should be discounted, both due to time preference and the investment value of money, the discounting of life and health (as is done in many social policy BCAs) is disputed (Sunstein, 2007). Philosophers and legal scholars often question such discounting on ethical or legal grounds (e.g., Cowen and Parfit, 1992; Revesz, 1999; Ackerman and Heinzerling, 2002, 2004; Shapiro and Glicksman, 2003). This concern is addressed by the principle of intergenerational neutrality (Sunstein, 2007), which holds that members of any particular generation should not be favored over members of any other. This principle is in fact a core tenet of benefit–cost analysis (Zerbe et al., 2010), and does not repudiate discounting life and health values.

A significant amount of disagreement about rates arises from those who wish to impose special conditions on particular projects. The most common candidates are health and life. The arguments center around considerations that lives or pain or other human health-related goods have equal value regardless of when they are incurred. This in a sense is true of virtually all goods. The capital penalty for avoiding the more productive investment is not avoided by this consideration and there is no sound reason to adjust discount rates for health and lives. The standard SOC criterion assumes that benefits are "just like income." If the benefits are not just like income there will be indirect revenue effects to include along with the "willingness-to-pay" (WTP) estimates of benefits, and they will be positive or negative depending upon the project. The appropriate discount rate remains the SOC rate. One might appropriately consider rates below the SOC rate for projects whose benefits are likely to induce private investment to an unusual extent, and conversely consider rates higher than the SOC for projects whose benefits are purely consumptive. However, these sorts of effects will be expensive to determine in many cases and could result in a ménage of various rates.

3 CONCLUSION

The SOC approach suggests discount rates in the range of 6–8 percent given the current state of knowledge and data. The SOC approach is consistent with the main alternative approaches to determining discount rates but it is generally easier to implement because (unlike the shadow price algorithm) it requires no shadow pricing of investment and (unlike the

MCF criterion) it applies a single discount rate to all benefits and costs. While the SOC approach may require the inclusion of indirect revenue effects along with conventional benefit and cost estimates (if project benefits are not pecuniary in nature), for the bulk of projects (i.e., those with commercial benefits) these effects will be zero (unlike the MCF criterion or the shadow price algorithm). Rates that are time varying are not consistent with the SOC unless the parameters that determine the SOC change. Adjusting rates for future benefits to account for a decline in the marginal utility of income is also inconsistent with the SOC. If the current generation wishes to subsidize or penalize future generations these sentiments can be expressed directly through the values given to future costs or benefits. The use of very low rates, such as found by Weitzman's experts and independently assumed by Stern (2007), seems to be a way to account for the present generation's perception of the risk of extreme damage to distant future generations. This sort of adjustment should be reflected in the values of benefits and costs and not through an adjustment of the discount rate. That is, where the current generation has moral values that apply to future generations these should be counted in terms of the current generation's WTP for such a moral value. An example is presented in Zerbe (2004). To use a lower discount rate than the SOC rate for long-term projects is to either transfer wealth from the present generation to the future at greater cost to the present generation than necessary, or to leave future generations worse off than they would be without the project.

Sunstein (2007) takes the correct stance when he recommends treating all generations the same.

NOTES

1. Elsewhere Zerbe and Scott (2012) argue for replacing the potential Pareto test with a Pareto relevance test, but for our purposes here this makes no difference.
2. A fourth approach to discounting comes from the literature on optimal growth. Gramlich (1981), for example, proposes that under certain conditions the growth rate of the economy be used to determine a government discount rate. The idea is to accumulate that quantity of capital that maximizes steady state consumption per effective worker. Thus capital formation is justified whenever the rate of return net of depreciation exceeds the growth rate. However, it does not follow that any project whose internal rate of return exceeds the growth rate is worthwhile because there is no assurance that undertaking the project will divert resources solely from consumption rather than from other projects.
3. The STP rate is interpreted by some as a "politically determined" rate that may lie below the after-tax rate of return, but we set aside this issue in this section.
4. Sjaastad and Wisecarver (1977) were the first to make this point. The SOC criterion and STP criterion yield different results for projects with long gestation lags, but the STP criterion fails to take into account the interim costs of financing such projects. See Burgess (2010a).

5. A lump sum tax increase of one dollar will reduce the present value of consumption by one dollar, but increase the present value of government revenue by just $r(1 + p)/p(1 + r)$ dollars. This is because the private sector discounts consumption at rate r but government revenue is discounted at rate p. If the government needs to raise $C1$ dollars to finance the project, the cost in terms of current consumption is $C1$ multiplied by $p(1 + r)/r(1 + p)$.
6. Under competitive conditions and constant returns to scale the rate of return to capital in place will equal the marginal productivity of an increment to capital.
7. Some have argued that the rate of return on real return bonds (TIPS) would provide a market-based measure of the risk-free rate of return, which could then be grossed up by adding the various taxes that apply to capital. If TIPS yield 3 percent and capital income is taxed at 35 percent, the implied pre-tax rate of return on "risk-free" capital would be in the order of 4.6 percent. Quite apart from whether this provides a reasonable estimate of the risk-free economic opportunity cost of private investment displaced, it would not be appropriate for the government to use a risk-free rate as the discount rate unless all project-specific risk could be eliminated by pooling and spreading. Bond rates of course are a part of rates that make up our opportunity cost of capital.
8. With the assumed benefit of debt reduction being a tax cut in the following period. For a more detailed discussion, see Burgess (2010a).
9. The compensated elasticity of supply of saving with respect to the after-tax rate of return is the product of the elasticity of inter-temporal substitution and the proportion of wealth that is consumed. The elasticity of inter-temporal substitution must be non-negative but Hall (1988) could not reject the hypothesis that it was zero. Attanasio and Weber (2010) review the literature and report estimates from reputable studies of 0.67 and higher. They perform simulations with an elasticity of inter-temporal substitution in the range from 0.25 to 0.5. The implied range of values for the compensated elasticity of supply of saving is less than this.
10. For example, Harberger (2010) makes the case that the pre-tax rate of return on investment is at least 10 percent. On the other hand, it could be argued that Poterba's estimate of 8.5 percent is biased upward because it pertains to the corporate sector only and ignores residential capital, which is more lightly taxed.
11. McGrattan and Prescott (2003) estimate that the real after-tax rate of return on US reproducible capital averaged approximately 4 percent over the period 1880–2002.
12. The analyst ideally should adjust for risk where the risk level is apt to be quite different from the average as is, for example, done for the capital asset pricing model. Unfortunately there are few if any relevant betas calculated for public projects.
13. Weitzman (2001) notes: "What is the expected value today of an extra expected dollar at time t? It should be the expected present discounted value of a dollar at time t, weighted by the 'probability of correctness' or the 'probability of actuality' of the rate at which it is being discounted" (p. 264). Weitzman infers that the probability that an individual expert is "correct" is given by the distribution of responses to a survey he conducted of 2160 PhD-level economists.
14. The US OMB (1992) recommends against time-varying discount rates on the grounds that it results in time inconsistency and that it is not ethically attractive. However, time inconsistency and hyperbolic rates for individuals appear to arise from uncertainty and risk (Farmer and Geanakoplos, 2009). Once risk is accounted for, no time inconsistency exists and individual rates are constant, that is, exponential.

REFERENCES

Ackerman, Frank and Lisa Heinzerling (2002), "Pricing the priceless: Cost–benefit analysis of environmental protection," *University of Pennsylvania Law Review*, **150** (5), 1553–84.

Ackerman, Frank and Lisa Heinzerling (2004), *Priceless: On Knowing the Price of Everything and the Value of Nothing*, New York: New Press.
Attanasio, Orazio P. and Guglielmo Weber (2010), "Consumption and saving: Models of inter-temporal allocation and their implications for public policy," *Journal of Economic Literature*, **48** (3), 693–751.
Boardman, Anthony E., M.A. Moore and Aidan R. Vining (2010), "The social discount rate for Canada based on future growth in consumption," *Canadian Public Policy*, **36** (3), 325–43.
Bradford, David F. (1975), "Constraints on government investment opportunities and the choice of discount rate," *American Economic Review*, **65** (5), 887–99.
Burgess, David F. (2010a), "Toward a reconciliation of alternative views on the social discount rate," in David Burgess and Glenn Jenkins (eds), *Discount Rates for the Evaluation of Public Private Partnership*, Montreal and Kingston: McGill-Queen's University Press, pp. 131–56.
Burgess, David F. (2010b), "Comment on 'The economic opportunity cost of capital for Canada: An empirical update,' by Glenn P. Jenkins and Chun-Yan Quo," in David Burgess and Glenn Jenkins (eds), *Discount Rates for the Evaluation of Public Private Partnerships*, Montreal and Kingston: McGill-Queen's University Press, pp. 289–97.
Burgess, David F. (2012), "Reconciling alternative views about the appropriate social discount rate," *Journal of Public Economics*, forthcoming.
Cowen, Tyler and Derek Parfit (1992), "Against the social discount rate," in Peter Laslett and James Fishkin (eds), *Justice Between Age Groups and Generations*, New Haven, CT: Yale University Press.
Dasgupta, Partha (2008), "Discounting climate change," *Journal of Risk and Uncertainty*, **37** (2), 141–69.
Department of Finance Canada (2008), "Considerations in setting Canada's corporate income tax rate," *Tax Expenditures and Evaluations*, accessed 11 October 2012 at http://www.fin.gc.ca/taxexp-depfisc/2008/taxexp08_4-eng.asp.
Farmer, J. Doyne and John Geanakoplos (2009), "Hyperbolic discounting is rational valuing the far future with uncertain discount rates," Cowles Foundation Discussion Paper No. 1719, New Haven, CT: Yale University, Cowles Foundation for Research in Economics.
Feldstein, Martin (1972), "The inadequacy of weighted discount rates," in Robert Layard (ed.), *Cost–Benefit Analysis*, Harmondsworth, UK: Penguin.
Feldstein, Martin and Charles Horioka (1980), "Domestic saving and international capital flows," *Economic Journal*, **90** (2), 314–29.
Frederick, Shane, George Loewenstein, and Ted O'Donoghue (2002), "Time discounting and time preference: A critical review," *Journal of Economic Literature*, **40** (2), 351–401.
Gilchrist, Simon, Fabio M. Natalucci, and Egon Zakrajsek (2007), "Investment and the cost of capital: New evidence from the corporate bond market," *NBER Working Paper* No. 13174, June.
Goodin, Robert E. (1982), "Discounting discounting," *Journal of Public Policy*, **2** (1), 53–71.
Gramlich, Edward M. (1981), *Benefit–Cost Analysis of Government Programs*, Englewood Cliffs, NJ: Prentice Hall.
Hall, Robert E. (1988), "Inter-temporal substitution in consumption," *Journal of Political Economy*, **96** (2), 339–57.
Harberger, Arnold C. (1969), "On measuring the social opportunity cost of public

funds," in *Proceedings of the Committee on Water Resources and Economic Development of the West: The Discount Rate in Public Investment Evaluation*, Denver, CO: Western Agricultural Economic Research Council.

Harberger, Arnold C. (1971), "Three basic postulates for applied welfare analysis: An interpretive essay," *Journal of Economic Literature*, **9** (3), 785–97.

Harberger, Arnold C. (1972), *Project Evaluation, Collected Papers of A.C. Harberger*, Chapter 4, Chicago: University of Chicago Press.

Harberger, Arnold C. (1985), "Reflections on social project evaluation," in Gerald M. Meier (ed.), *Pioneers in Development*, Oxford: Oxford University Press and the World Bank.

Harberger, Arnold C. (2010), "On growth, investment, capital and the rate of return," in David F. Burgess and Glenn P. Jenkins (eds), *Discount Rates for the Evaluation of Public Private Partnerships*, Montreal and Kingston: McGill-Queen's University Press, pp. 205–28.

Helliwell, John F. (1998), *How Much Do National Borders Matter?*, Washington, DC: Brookings Institution.

Jenkins, Glenn P. and Chan-Yun Kuo (2010), "The economic opportunity cost of capital for Canada: An empirical update," in David F. Burgess and Glenn P. Jenkins (eds), *Discount Rates for the Evaluation of Public Private Partnership*, John Deutsch Institute, Queen's University, Kingston, Ontario: McGill-Queen's University Press.

Lind, Robert C. (1982), "A primer on the major issues relating to the discount rate for evaluating national energy options," in Robert C. Lind (ed.), *Discounting for Time and Risk in Energy Policy*, Washington, DC: Resources for the Future.

Liu, Liqun (2003), "A marginal cost of funds approach to multi-period project evaluation: Implications for the social discount rate," *Journal of Public Economics*, **87** (7–8), 1707–18.

Liu, Liqun, Andrew Rettenmaier, and Thomas Saving (2004), "A generalized approach to multigenerational project evaluation," *Southern Economic Journal*, **71** (2), 377–96.

Long, Mark, Richard Zerbe, and Tyler Davis, (2011), "The discount rate for public projects: Incorporating heterogeneity in citizen preferences," working paper, Evans School of Public Affairs, University of Washington.

Marglin, Stephen A. (1963), "The opportunity cost of public investment," *Quarterly Journal of Economics*, **77** (2), 274–89.

McGrattan, Ellen R. and Edward C. Prescott (2003), *Average Debt and Equity Returns: Puzzling?*, Federal Reserve Bank of Minneapolis, Research Department, Staff Report No. 313.

Moore, Mark A., Anthony E. Boardman, Aidan R. Vining, David L. Weimer, and David H. Greenberg (2004), "Just give me a number! Practical values for the social discount rate," *Journal of Policy Analysis and Management*, **23** (4), 789–812.

Parfit, Derek (1992), "An attack on the social discount rate," in Claudia Mills (ed.), *Values and Public Policy*, Fort Worth, TX: Harcourt Brace Jovanovich.

Parfit, Derek (1994), "The social discount rate," in R.E. Goodwin (ed.), *Politics and the Environment*, Aldershot, UK and Brookfield, VT, USA: Edward Elgar.

Pearce, David A. and R. Kerry Turner (1989), *Economics of Natural Resources and the Environment*, Baltimore, MD: Johns Hopkins Press.

Plater, Zygmunt J.B., Robert H. Abrams, William Goldfarb, and Robert L.

Graham (1998), *Environmental Law and Policy: Nature, Law and Society*, St. Paul, MN: West Publishing.
Poterba, James M. (1999), "The rate of return to corporate capital and factor shares: New estimates using revised national income accounts and capital stock data," *NBER Working Paper* No. 6263.
Revesz, Richard L. (1999), "Environmental regulation, cost–benefit analysis, and the discounting of human lives," *Columbia Law Review*, **99** (4), 941–1017.
Sandmo, Agnar and Jacques H. Drèze (1971), "Discount rates for public investment in closed and open economies," *Economica*, **38** (152), 395–412.
Schultze, W., David S. Brookshire, and Todd Sandler (1981), "The social rate of discount for nuclear waste storage: Economics of ethics," *Natural Resources Journal*, **21** (4), 431–529.
Shapiro, Stuart A. and Robert L. Glicksman (2003), *Risk Regulation at Risk: Restoring a Pragmatic Approach*, Stanford, CA: Stanford University Press.
Sjaastad, Larry A. and Daniel L. Wisecarver (1977), "The social cost of public finance," *Journal of Political Economy*, **85** (3), 513–47.
Stern, Nicholas H. (and Great Britain Treasury) (2007), *The Economics of Climate Change: The Stern Review*, Cambridge, UK: Cambridge University Press.
Sunstein, Cass R. (2007), *Worst-case Scenario*, Cambridge, MA: Harvard University Press.
US OMB (US Office of Management and Budget) (1992), "Guidelines and discount rates for benefit–cost analysis of Federal programs," OMB Circular A-94, Washington, DC: US Government Printing Office.
US OMB (US Office of Management and Budget) (2003), "Regulatory analysis," Circular A–4, Washington, DC: US Government Printing Office.
Weitzman, Martin L. (1998), "Why the far-distant future should be discounted at its lowest possible rate," *Journal of Environmental Economics and Management*, **36** (3), 201.
Weitzman, Martin L. (2001), "Gamma discounting," *American Economic Review*, **91** (1), 260–71.
Zerbe, Jr., Richard O. (2004), "Should moral sentiments be incorporated into benefit–cost analysis? An example of long-term discounting," *Policy Sciences*, **37** (3/4), 305–18.
Zerbe, Jr., Richard O. and Tyler Scott (2012), "(Almost) everybody wins", working paper, University of Washington.
Zerbe, Jr., Richard O., Tyler Blake Davis, Nancy S. Garland, and Tyler Scott (2010), *Towards Principles and Standards in the Use of Benefit–Cost Analysis: A Summary of Work, and a Starting Place*, MacArthur Foundation Power of Measuring Social Benefits Initiative, Seattle, WA: Benefit–Cost Analysis Center, University of Washington.

8. Ethical benefit–cost analysis as art and science: ten rules for benefit–cost analysis

Richard O. Zerbe, Jr.*

1 INTRODUCTION

Benefit–cost analysis (BCA) is commonly viewed either as a mechanical tool for making decisions or as a failed technique of decision-making that avoids moral, interactive, and ethical components. Properly situated, it is neither. Benefit–cost analysis is an art form that can produce useful information with the potential to improve decision-making. To understand this we must consider current criticisms and come to another way of looking at BCA.

Benefit–cost analysis is widely seen as a rule by which preferences and emotions are valued, yet how can a maxim encompass these? It is hardly surprising then, that BCA is the object of longstanding and expansive contumely and even repugnance. Yet it is widely esteemed by practical people, "mere men of business," one might say. To put it crudely, BCA is generally approved, but is apt to be disparaged by those of a philosophic mind who see it as "a lust" for "mechanical objectivity."

Properly conducted, BCA is an art form embodying elements of law, morality, judgment, and science. It is a method of structuring conversation and organizing knowledge. It is not a maxim, nor can it be acceptably reduced to mechanical objectivity. To recognize BCA as partly reductionist is not to prove it is without value, nor without the flexibility to adapt to change. As a method it is necessarily reductionist and reductionist sciences have proven to be very powerful.[1] The test of a method is whether it is useful, and BCA undeniably has been useful (Porter, 1996), notwithstanding claims to the contrary such as those by Ackerman and Heinzerling (2002).

This chapter contributes to the process of attaining greater uniformity of principles and standards within BCA. Practitioners and critics alike are sometimes unclear about precisely what they mean when they speak of BCA, as there is no one uniform method or concept. Toward this end, I will briefly consider the benefit–cost principle, the considerations that lie behind it, and the criticisms that have been made of it in light of these considerations. In response to these criticisms, and to establish what BCA is more clearly, I then describe a version of BCA that I call ethical benefit–cost analysis (EBCA). I outline EBCA through establishing a set of rules—a meta-set of principles and standards to guide the practice of BCA. Finally, I show that in principle, this conception of BCA offers both a superior version of efficiency and a more accurate reflection of our moral compass.

2 THE BENEFIT–COST PRINCIPLE

Modern benefit–cost analysis arose out of discussions among prominent British economists during the late 1930s such as Lionel Robbins, John Richard Hicks, Nicholas Kaldor, and Roy Forbes Harrod, all writing in the *Economic Journal.* Before that time, it was generally assumed that each individual had an "equal capacity for enjoyment," and that gains and losses among different individuals could be directly compared (Mishan, 1981; Hammond, 1985). Robbins (1938) challenged this view by arguing that interpersonal comparisons of utility were unscientific so that no such direct comparison could be made. Kaldor (1939) acknowledged Robbins's point about the inability to make interpersonal utility comparisons on any scientific basis, but suggested it could be made irrelevant. He suggested that when a policy led to an increase in aggregate real income the economist's case for the policy is quite unaffected by the question of the comparability of individual satisfactions; since in all such cases it is *possible* to make everybody better off than before, or at any rate to make some people better off without making anybody worse off.

Kaldor went on to note that whether compensation should take place "is a political question on which the economist, *qua* economist, could hardly pronounce an opinion" (1939, p. 549). Hicks accepted this approach, which came to be called the Kaldor–Hicks test (KH), or, more often, the potential compensation test (PCT) as described in Zerbe and Bellas (2006). The PCT has been the standard for benefit–cost analysis for some 60 years. Its original justification was to separate economic efficiency from equity so as to avoid interpersonal comparisons. As Chipman and Moore (1978) and Zerbe (1991) have noted, this goal has not been achieved, nor should it be, nor can it be, nor need it be.

In BCA, preferences for gains in the form of projects or goods are measured by the willingness to pay for them (WTP). For example, if we are considering reducing noise levels at an airport by requiring new mufflers on airplanes, we would, inter alia, ask residents near the airport how much they would be willing to pay to achieve a certain reduction in noise and compare this amount to the costs to the airline of installing the mufflers. The preference to avoid losses (the cost) is measured by the willingness to accept payment to bear the loss (WTA). In the above example, airlines' WTA to avoid the cost is represented by the costs to the airlines of installing the mufflers. When the overall preference for obtaining a good is greater than the overall preference to avoid losing the good, the project passes the KH as discussed in Zerbe and Dively (1994). This is generally regarded as a reasonable maxim and as a reasonable way of ordering preferences for a single individual. These preferences are aggregated over several individuals and issues arise about the morality of aggregation (Zerbe, 2007). The original moral foundation for such aggregation was the concept of potential compensation as discussed by Brent (1997).

The concept of potential compensation justified KH on the grounds that when KH was passed the winners from the project *could* potentially compensate the losers. Thus the project could potentially be without losers, thereby satisfying the Pareto test, the precursor to the KH test, holding that the new state of the world is preferable to the status quo when someone gains from the new state of the world and no one loses. This would take judgments about the distribution of benefits and losses out of the hands of economists and put them into the political process. From the perspective of economists writing in the 1930s, this would make BCA more "scientific."

The WTP and WTA reflect time preferences—for example, the difference between how much right now I value \$50 you give me today weighed against how much I value \$50 you will give me a year from now—through the use of a discount rate. BCA is thus reduced to the simple formula of comparing the discounted value of the gains and losses as follows:

$$NPV = \sum_{t}^{T} \sum_{j}^{J} \frac{(Bjt - Cjt)}{(1 + r)^{t}} \tag{8.1}$$

where *NPV* is the net present value—the value of the benefits and costs of a project discounted to today's dollars, *Bjt* are benefits for person *j* measured in time *t* as measured by the willingness to pay, *Cjt* are costs to person *j* in time *t* measured by the willingness to accept payment, *r* is the discount rate, *J* is goods, and *T* is the time period of the project's effects.

This simple formulaic statement disguises deep considerations that lie behind the WTP, WTA, and the discount rate. These considerations include the role that rights and the law play in determining whether WTP or WTA is the appropriate measure of value, whose and what sort of preferences should be given economic standing, those persons, groups or values that are counted in an economic analysis, and how ethical considerations are to be used in BCA (Whittington and MacRae, 1990). The simple formulaic understanding of BCA, along with misunderstanding about the nature of goods, is nevertheless what drives the criticisms of BCA.

3 CRITICISMS OF THE BENEFIT–COST PRINCIPLE

The criticisms of BCA are wide-ranging, frequent, and repetitious. They are embodied mainly in academic legal-philosophical literature and appear motivated by the increasing use of BCA in decision-making, by the encroachment of economic thinking into law, and are related to the absence of clearly defined foundational values for BCA. Critiques include those by Fried (1978), who argues rights are more than mere entities determined to attain efficiency, Kelman (1981), who critiques benefit–cost analysis as applied to environmental, safety, and health regulation, Dworkin (1980), who rejects the economic analysis of law theory, while Richardson (2000) discusses flaws in the underlying standards of BCA and argues for "intelligent public deliberation."

Most of the critical literature is not aimed at improving the practice of BCA, or at identifying deficiencies of particular analyses. Rather, the literature critiques the foundational deficiencies of BCA, that is, it criticizes the use of BCA itself.

The leading criticism emphasizes the reductionist nature of BCA as a mechanical algorithm that is used to answer questions about what people want—the result of what Porter (1996. p. 187) describes as a "lust[ing] after . . . mechanical objectivity." Other criticisms of BCA include that it is missing values; that it pays too little attention to "good" values such as integrity and perhaps too much attention to "bad" values such as envy (Nussbaum, 2000); that it is rooted in a narrow utilitarianism (Dworkin, 1980), that it uses private values where public values are relevant (Anderson, 1993); that it favors the preferences of the rich and does not consider issues of income distribution or fairness; that it ignores transaction costs (Coase, 1988); and that it provides an answer that is without meaning as a result of attempting to combine incommensurables in a single metric. Some critics have also correctly noted that BCA's derivation by deductive logic is flawed.

A separate rationalist criticism is that BCA is rendered useless by the Scitovsky reversal paradox (Coleman, 1988). Scitovsky showed that using

Table 8.1 Reversal possibilities

	Status Quo		Proposed Project	
	X	Y	X	Y
Mr. A	2	0	1	0
Ms. B	0	1	0	2

Table 8.2 Reversals and Pareto superiority

	(1) Status Quo		(2) Proposed Project		(3) Pareto Superior Project to Status Quo		(4) Pareto Superior Project to Status Quo	
	Wheat	Cotton	Wheat	Cotton	Wheat	Cotton	Wheat	Cotton
Mr. A	2	0	1	0	1	1	1	0
Ms. B	0	1	0	2	0	1	1	1

KH one could move from state of the world A to B and then, having arrived at B, use KH to move back to A, thus continually cycling. The example used by Coleman is shown in Table 8.1.

The proposed project passes the KH test as, in the new state of the world, B could give one unit of Y to Mr. A, leaving him better off and Ms. B no worse off. However, in the status quo situation, Mr. A could give one unit of X to Ms. B leaving her better off than the proposed project and Mr. A no worse off than the proposed project. Thus there is a reversal using the PCT. On this basis Coleman argues that benefit–cost analysis is not a useful basis for decision-making.

One among other problems is that the example necessarily concerns second-best situations (Schmitz and Zerbe, 2009). This means there will be states of the world that are Pareto superior to the status quo and to the proposed project. The full array of possibilities is shown in Table 8.2 where we assume the two goods are wheat and cotton and retain Coleman's assumptions of one-to-one transformation ratio so that one acre produces one unit of either wheat or cotton and that the two parties value cotton and wheat equally.

It will be observed that situation 3 is Pareto superior to position 1, the status quo position and situation 4 is Pareto superior to position 2. Thus the relevant comparison is between positions 3 and 4 and here no reversal is possible. Elsewhere I have shown that reversals are not possible for normal goods (Zerbe, 2007).

As noted above, this technical problem generated by economists has been advanced by some as a reason to dismiss BCA entirely. In a recent book, Markovits (2008, p. 53) writes, "This Scitovsky Paradox invalidates the Kaldor–Hicks test because it implies that, if the test were accurate and a Scitovsky paradox arose, both the policy and its reversal would be economically efficient and, hence, the policy would simultaneously be economically efficient and economically inefficient."

Economists and practitioners using BCA generally ignore these criticisms for three good reasons. First, the critics fail to offer viable substitutes, except for vague references to political discussion (Sagoff, 1988; Hildred and Beauvais, 1995; Richardson, 2000; Wolcher, 2007). The critics do not compare the results of BCA with those of potential alternative approaches, and are therefore unable to answer whether BCA is better than its alternatives.

Second, such critics generally fail to address whether BCA is useful and, if it is, how it might be improved. Without determining empirically whether or not BCA is useful, how is it possible to argue persuasively against its use? Without being provided with suggestions for improvement, why should practitioners pay attention? This shortcoming is as true of recent criticisms, such as those by Ackerman and Heinzerling, critiquing the morality of benefit–cost analysis, as it is of the huge volume of past criticisms. Until recently, defects found by critics were generally unsupported by examination of actual projects using BCA (Hildred and Beauvais, 1995; Calandrillo, 2001), so it was uncertain whether, as a matter of fact, these defects existed. Though recent critics such as Ackerman and Heinzerling (2002) attempt to examine actual studies and uses of BCA, these criticisms contain important errors (Carlin, 2005) and are thus unconvincing.

Third, the invocation of the Scitovsky paradox is misplaced and incorrect. The conditions under which a Scitovsky reversal would occur are so rare and unlikely they can be ignored (Schmitz and Zerbe, 2009).

These criticisms are based on an outdated view of BCA that assumed moral sentiments, ethical considerations, and distributional consequences were not considered and saw BCA as a mechanical exercise (Ackerman and Heinzerling, 2002). The current view of BCA includes moral sentiments and ethical considerations, and considers BCA's role as an information-providing tool, rather than a method of giving a mechanical answer to the decision-making process. Therefore, because our view of BCA can be expanded to include moral sentiments as preferences that represent economic goods, BCA is put in proper context, and these criticisms are obviated.

The issues that garner criticism for BCA also contribute to my conception of BCA as an art form. In the sections below, I describe BCA as an art form, and clarify rules for its ethical and practical use.

4 ETHICAL BENEFIT–COST ANALYSIS: THE ART FORM

The term "art form" is meant to describe a procedure that relies on nuanced judgment. The basis for ethical BCA is an expansion of KH that I call in Zerbe et al. (2006) the Kaldor–Hicks–Moral (KHM). KHM adds to KH in five important ways. First, KHM adds the requirement that all ethical values for which there is a WTP or WTA be included in the analysis, including those concerning distributional and ethical considerations more generally. Second, KHM eliminates the PCT test and replaces it with the simple requirement that the net present value of a project be positive, *where the definition of benefits and losses are grounded in law*. Third, KHM incorporates the understanding that the proper use of ethical BCA is to furnish information and predictions, and not to furnish decisions. Fourth, KHM holds that transactions cost economics rather than market failure is the basis for a benefit–cost justification that government intervention might be useful. Finally, KHM provides a moral basis for BCA.

Ethical BCA requires an understanding and illumination of how benefits and costs are related to legal rights (Cohen and Knetsch, 1992). It insists on addressing the question of whether "bad" utility (in such forms as envy, malice, sadism, or gains from theft) is to be counted as part of BCA. It considers where the line should be drawn in determining standing to have values counted. It addresses the questions of whether the value of moral sentiments and considerations of equity are to be counted as part of BCA, and whether the role of BCA is to inform the decision-making process or to provide the answer to it. Answers to these questions bear both on the moral stature of BCA and its acceptability. The foundations of ethical BCA rest in law, as gains and losses are defined based on legal rights. Since rights are sometimes unclear, however, judgment may be required. In addition, subtle questions often arise about preferences. Whose preferences should count? Do "bad preferences" such as envy, malice, jealousy, and hatred count? Do the preferences count of those who are initially without knowledge of a project and who only care once they are informed? Do ethical sentiments count? How are preferences to be treated when preferences of the public differ from expert opinion?

When we consider BCA as an exercise that takes into account its foundations, the process shifts from what has been perceived as a mechanical exercise to the practice of a balanced science and art form. The science component of ethical BCA follows from its derivation from deductive reasoning and its striving for uniform and reproducible measurement. The following rules for BCA follow from ethical BCA and a consideration of foundational questions.

5 ARTISTIC RULES FOR ETHICAL BCA

Rule 1: Benefit–cost preferences rest on existing rights

The role of BCA is to suggest marginal improvements *given the existing pattern of rights* (Heyne, 1988). The definition of WTP and WTA rests on law. The WTA payment presupposes a right to some status quo position from which losses are to be counted.

This choice between WTP and WTA is properly based on psychological expectations and its connections to legal ownership. From a legal perspective, the use of WTA to measure losses and WTP to measure gains rests on a normative decision to recognize ownership. Gains and losses are to be measured from a psychological reference point that stems from one's beliefs about ownership. Legal rights largely determine one's beliefs about ownership. The WTP measure assumes that one does not have psychological or legal ownership of the good or the right and asks how much one would pay to obtain it. The WTA measure assumes that one owns the good or right and asks how much one would accept to sell it (Levy and Friedman, 1994).

The earlier example of the WTP and WTA to reduce airplane noise assumed the legal starting point was a society in which the residents had no right to quiet. If, however, we decide the residents at the airport have a legal right to quiet, then instead of asking them what they would pay (WTP) for quiet, we ask them what they would be willing to accept (WTA) to bear the noise.[2] This would then be considered the benefit of noise reduction, and would be compared with the airlines' WTP to avoid the loss.

Ownership establishes a reference point from which losses are to be calculated by WTA and gains by WTP. The law has long recognized that it is more serious to stop an owner from conducting an ongoing activity than to prohibit the owner from undertaking the same activity if he or she has not yet begun it. The currently fashionable expression of this view may be found in Justice Brennan's phrase in *Pennsylvania Central Transit Company* v. *City of New York* (1978), that a restriction is more likely to result in a taking if it destroys "investment backed expectations."

The law will determine whether WTP or WTA will be used. The law will be the major determinant of psychological reference points. Even if the economic standard is psychological ownership, the psychological point of view and the law will correspond to each other and to the sociological point of view (Rubin, 1977; Zerbe, 2006). The assumption is that a choice based on assigned legal entitlements is correct because of the correspondence between the legal and psychological states; it is not correct or incorrect as a matter of economic principle. Economic efficiency in the KHM form would recognize the psychological status quo as primary and change ownership to conform to it. As a matter of practice, the relevant psychological reference point cannot be just that of the individual but rather must be that of society generally. Insofar as the law embodies the general understanding, the law should govern. The underlying basis is the general psychological reference point. Where this reference point differs from the law, it furnishes a guide for further development of the law, as indeed it has done with the development of common law.[3]

Ethical BCA builds on the same WTP and WTA measures as BCA. As economists such as Knetsch (1995) have now shown, the WTP and WTA need to be embedded in legal rights. The nexus between legal rights and economic measurement has become apparent and is discussed in relevant literature. Many have argued for the inclusion of equity effects, including those on income distribution, and have suggested various schemes to accomplish this outcome.[4] Some such as Zerbe and Knott (2004) have applied these suggestions to actual policy issues. Recently, economists such as Andreoni (1995) have found it important to understand the role of social and cultural factors like altruism. Kaplow and Shavell's (2002) views of efficiency are in accord with KHM and note (pp. 18–19) that "[t]he only limit on what is included in well-being is to be found in the minds of the individuals themselves." Similarly, for environmental economists the importance of existence values, which are a type of ethical value, has forced their consideration. Although some economists would like to achieve the separation of the altruistic component from existence values, as some have claimed to have done, this is probably not possible, as Dana (2003) and others note, and moreover it is not desirable.[5] The evidence suggests that recognition of the importance of non-use values is intrinsically bound up with issues of ethical consideration. Respondents to surveys and experiments show a willingness to pay in regard to ethical considerations for the existence of environmental amenities that will be used by people other than themselves.[6]

George Stigler (Stigler, 1982; Gayer and Hahn, 2005), the Nobel Prize-winning economist, neatly summarizes this difference between ethical BCA and BCA in a statement to the effect that people don't always want efficiency. This can only be the case, however, when efficiency is defined incorrectly. The purpose of ethical BCA is to reflect actual preferences.

Error aside, if there is indeed a discrepancy between calculated efficiency and what people will pay for, it must arise from ethical values not included in the efficiency calculation. In principle, there should not be a discrepancy between what people want and the results of BCA. The discovery that people may be willing to pay for goods they never expect to use, such as existence values, has created enormous controversy about the validity of their inclusion in BCA. These values would be included in an ethical BCA. Though no consensus as to their proper place exists, the weight of practice is shifting towards the inclusion of ethical considerations.

The interesting questions are whose preferences count, which preferences count, how should they be weighted, and what are the relevant limitations?

Rule 2: Not everyone's preferences need to be measured in practice, but all should be considered

The traditional economic view as expressed by Trumbull (1990) is that everyone's preferences count and is consistent with a democratic point of view and the ethos of benefit–cost analysis. Economic welfare theory, however, typically assumes preferences have no transaction costs.

A preferable approach is to recognize that everyone's preferences count in the sense that they need to be considered but they do not always need to be measured. No BCA will measure all affected preferences; it is too expensive and inefficient. What is required is to reasonably measure significant preferences, to acknowledge preferences not measured, and to consider whether or not unmeasured preferences are likely to contradict the formulaic BCA test. These considerations should be included in reasonable principles and standards for BCA.

An ancillary rule suggests that in considering everyone's preferences greater efficiency in project development is achieved. Take for example Easterling's (1992) work, "Fair Rules for Siting a High-level Nuclear Waste Repository," in which he argues that the perceived fairness of a siting process influences the level of support for a facility among the potential host community. His survey of Nevada residents indicated that they would have been more supportive of the nuclear waste repository at Yucca Mountain if they had believed that the underground repository chosen by the federal government was the best option for high-level waste and that Yucca Mountain was the safest place for such a repository. If residents believed that these things were true, then they would be more likely to be altruistic regarding the site; they would accept "an increase in personal cost (i.e., risk) for the sake of improving the welfare of everyone else" (ibid., p. 449).

Based on his evaluation of the Yucca Mountain siting process and the results of the 1987 survey, Easterling recommended that four steps be followed in order to construct an ideal siting process. First, the process must consider all the possible options for dealing with the problem, with opportunities for a wide range of stakeholders to give their opinions. Second, there must be clear rules established for how the "best" option is chosen. For example, the criteria could be monetary cost, cultural impacts, biological impacts, or economic impacts on the surrounding area. Third, the alternatives should be compared using the predetermined criteria. Fourth, the results of the comparisons would be inputted to obtain a "suitability score." This score would then be used to select which course of action to follow and show the public that the best alternative was chosen.

In practice, political jurisdictions tend to confine their analyses in time or locations of their own interests. For many years, the conventional academic standard in the United States was that for US projects, preferences were confined to the United States. As a practical matter BCAs performed by a political jurisdiction do not usually consider the effects outside their jurisdiction. A municipal government will not normally consider the effects of its projects on another municipality. A state, unless required by law, will not usually consider effects on another state, and so forth. In fact, government BCAs often do not even fully consider, and sometimes do not consider at all, their own constituents' preferences in a project. Where significant preferences are ignored, or not considered, BCAs must be considered as politically constrained, and as not conforming to the highest principles and standards for BCA. Of course, this does not mean such analyses are not useful.

Rule 3: Better informed individual preferences are preferred to less informed. There will be a preference for expert opinion when it is recognized as superior

Preferences may differ over time, by knowledge and by contemplation. The following example is given by Frank (1997, p. 245):

> Cornell University has two sets of faculty tennis courts, one outdoor, the other indoor. Membership in the outdoor is available for a fixed fee per season. There is no additional charge . . . The indoor facility, by contrast has not only a seasonal fee, but also a $15 per hour charge for court time. The indoor facility opens in early October, a time when the Ithaca weather can be anything from bright sunshine and mild temperatures to blowing sleet and snow. The outdoor courts remain open . . . until early November. There is a similar 1-month overlap in the . . . spring . . . Having [paid for the indoor court] they must pay for the hour whether or not they use it. During good weather, almost everyone prefers to play on the outdoor courts . . .

> Here is the problem: You are committed to an indoor court at 3 p.m. on Saturday, October 20, the only hour you are free to play that day. It is a warm, sunny autumn afternoon. Where should you play, indoors or outdoors?
> I find that surprising many of my noneconomist [*sic*] partners balk when I say that playing on the outdoor courts is the only sensible thing to do. 'But we've already paid for the indoor,' they invariably complain. I ask, 'If both courts cost the same, which would you choose?' They immediately respond, 'Outdoors.' I then explain that both courts *do* cost the same—because our fee for the hour is going to be $15 no matter which place we play—indeed, no matter whether we play at all. The $15 is a sunk cost and should have no effect on our decision. Yet, even at this point, many people seem to feel uncomfortable about wasting the indoor court we have paid for. The alternative, however, is to waste an opportunity to play outdoors, which we all agree is something even more valuable! . . .
> Eventually, most people come around to the notion that it is more sensible to abandon the indoor court.

From this, one would conclude that the correct choice in a BCA context is to play outdoors and that the additional preference over playing outdoors rather than indoors is a measure of this preference. Because "most," but not all were persuaded by this argument, for some the avoidance of a feeling of waste, engendered by playing outdoors, is of sufficient value that they should play indoors. For these people, the additional value of playing outdoors only applies when one has not already paid for playing indoors.

Informed preferences are not at all the same as expertise. Expertise is clearly not the aim of requirements that adults be informed, as when, for example, they consent to medical procedures. Expertise is often hard won, for example, requiring about 10 000 hours of relevant experience in chess, violin or tennis, according to Ericsson and Lehmann (1996). Informed preferences are created when the respondent has a reasonable understanding of probable consequences of alternative actions. This is a higher standard than often imposed in product liability, community right-to-know, and medical practices where the standard is closer to information about the largest or most severe possible consequences of a choice but not always information about their probability of occurrence (Mertz, 1991). Preferences may be created or influenced by experts. In addition, preferences change with knowledge (Bostrom, 1997). Therefore a reasonable assumption is that people would prefer to use their preferences when they are knowledgeable. Their previous preferences are still available, but are no longer preferred.

Scholars in the field of psychology such as Payne et al. (1992) argue that, without good information, individuals and groups often make bad decisions when faced with complex issues involving uncertainties and value trade-offs. McDaniels et al. (1999), prominent scholars in the field of public affairs, show that public involvement in decisions that involve risk trade-offs is more successful when the participants are well informed about the technicalities of the decision. They also discuss experiments that show that, in situations where laypersons are not likely to fully understand all of the details of the risk related to the decision, a group participation process should be designed. They suggest the participation process should allow for the decision-makers to be educated about the risks involved in the decision through informational sessions. However, participants' consensus should be based on their own established hierarchy of values. These insights provided by scholars in psychology and public policy lead to the conclusion that the results of public participation in decisions involving risk assessment can be ameliorated by including well-conducted BCAs in the citizen participation process.

Rule 4: Expert opinion is better than uninformed preference[7]

It follows reasonably from Rule 3 that uninformed people will prefer the preferences of experts when they can assume that the preferences of experts lie closer to their own informed preferences than to their uninformed preferences. There is considerable literature on the differences between expert and lay opinion such as that by Chi et al. (1981), Flynn et al. (1993), Bostrom (1997), and Ericsson and Ward (2007). Bostrom (1997, pp. 105–6) notes that:

> Despite the numerous value judgments and biases that can influence expert risk assessments, such assessments are nevertheless based, ideally, on specialized information the average lay person is unlikely to know or have the resources to acquire. Knowledge about relative frequencies, causal mechanisms, and information sources often enables experts to make predictions about risky processes that are much more reliable than uninformed judgments. Most of us would rather not try to do for ourselves the jobs we usually delegate to experts, such as nuclear engineers, doctors, auto mechanics—or even lawyers.

In a charming note, Paul Portney (1992) presents a fantasy in which expert opinion and citizen opinion are in disagreement and then he asks what should be done. His example presents the situation of Happyville, a city afflicted with a disease residents believe is connected to contamination of the water supply. If experts find no risk attached to a particular substance in the water, yet citizens of Happyville are willing to each pay $1000 to get rid of it, should it be eliminated? If the residents themselves pay for the treatment, surely the argument for treatment is stronger. Yet the experts would presumably predict citizens would be happier in the short run but quite unhappy in the long run, when the treatment did not work. How should this be analyzed and decided?

If the residents refuse to believe the experts, should the residents' full WTP be included? This repeats the original conflict and question: now the experts' estimate of the future WTP of the residents differs from their own estimate. An approach is suggested in which greater weight is given to consumers' sentiments when the belief is so widespread and common that, for example, property values are or are likely to be materially affected. This approach appears to be one reasonably consistent with an economic analysis in that beliefs that are so widely and strongly held are less likely to change quickly so that material harm is done even if this harm is only psychological.

But, what if it isn't just the town contemplating paying for it, but the whole county? Suppose the citizens outside Happyville believe the experts. They will especially resent paying for a program they believe is worthless. Should their resentment be counted as part of a BCA analysis? Clearly it should. Such resentment is not barred by considerations of legal standing, and counting this resentment is required by ethical BCA, which recognizes all sentiments.

There is a conflict between scientific views of risk assessment and views that emphasize cultural and personal aspects. For example, the Environmental Protection Agency's generic guidelines—which apply to all substances—are an attempt to reduce the individual discretion and influence of experts and others (Pollak, 1996). These constitute a set of standards such as the following: no thresholds in dose response functions, linearity in dose response functions at low doses, cumulative lifetime exposure as measure of dose, and so forth. Pollak notes, however, that science does not resolve the underlying issues that generic guidelines are set to resolve. Justice Breyer (Breyer, 1993; Pollak, 1996) has suggested a bureaucratic structure to rationalize risk regulation across fields. But, Pollak notes, rationality in the form of "scientifically determined" guidelines is not attainable. Rationalizing procedures and standards leads to procedures that are less subjective. More importantly, it is possible to achieve "procedural objectivity" by reducing discretion. In the long run, standards can lead to better decisions as they create pressure to improve the standards. Similarly, this approach can be a means to think about ways to bring credible reassurance to the public.

Continuing the theme, Graham and Wiener (1995) ask how risk tradeoff decisions can be made more intelligently. They suggest the answer lies in how decisions are structured. First, many risk failures are intervention failures according to the authors. Why do decision-makers act without accounting for the full consequences of their decisions? Another major failure lies in the presence of "omitted voices." The basic solution suggested is more inclusive decision-making (National Research Council, 2000).

The use of expert opinion in civil and criminal trials illustrates how expert opinion is valued over uninformed lay opinion. Expert testimony is allowed according to Rule 702 of the Federal Rules of Evidence, where "scientific, technical, or other specialized knowledge will assist the trier of fact to understand the evidence or to determine a fact in issue." If it is a matter a layperson can understand without the help of an expert witness, an expert witness will not be allowed. Through the use of expert witnesses at trial, the legal system supports the notion that informed expert opinion is valued over uninformed lay opinion.

Rule 5: Where expert opinion differs from informed public sentiment, it is public sentiment that is relevant

It is well established that lay preferences, even if informed, will differ from expert preferences. In fact, informed public preferences often seem more nuanced and less narrow according to Flynn et al. (1993).

In BCA, public preferences are desired over the preferences of experts. What people perceive as an undesirable effect depends on their values and preferences. When a formal definition of risk is used people may disagree with it because the numerical combinations of magnitude and probabilities tend to assume equal weight for both values and preferences. However, there is evidence that lay definitions of risk depend on more than just the severity of the event and the uncertainty associated with that event.

Interactions between human activities and their consequences are more complex and unique than the interactions accounted for by the average probabilities used in technical risk analyses (see for example, Fischhoff et al., 1978 and Slovic et al., 1985). Researchers such as Bostrom (1997) conclude that risk perceptions are supported by sets of consistent beliefs, not just irrational fears and unbridled emotions.

In the tennis example offered by Frank above, there are informed people who nevertheless prefer to play tennis indoors—presumably to avoid the sentiment of waste. The fact is that people often appear not to treat sunk costs as irrelevant—the expert recommendation—due to the desire to avoid the sensation of waste. In such cases where the respondent is informed, preferences should be taken as they lie.

The use of expert witnesses at trial is also illustrative of this rule that informed lay opinion will be valued over expert opinion. Ultimately, in any jury trial, it is the jury's decision to decide whether and how much to value an expert's testimony.[8] The same is true for the judge in a bench trial. Many trials feature opposing expert witnesses, ensuring that the now-informed lay people's opinion has precedence over at least that of one expert.

Rule 6: It will be efficient and consistent with BCA to ignore socially disdained preferences as determined by law and custom (the use of the WTP and WTA are determined by law, norms, and customs)

Such sentiments as envy, hatred, jealousy, malice, sadism, or the rewards of thievery or murder need not count in a BCA by the requirements of efficiency itself. Where there is law forbidding behavior this may be taken as an indication that social sentiments are strongly against giving weight to that behavior. These anti-sentiments count as well. In the absence of law, sufficient social custom may in turn be taken to provide the same result. Thus, a balancing of sentiments in these cases suggests that, where law and custom dictate, those sentiments that reflect social opprobrium are outweighed and should be ignored.

As an illustration, consider this example as reworked from Dworkin (1980): Amartya, a rich man, steals a book from Derek, a poor man. Derek, who loves his book, sues for its return and costs. Derek would be willing to pay $10 for the book, but would sell it to Amartya for $15. Amartya, who cares very little for the book, would pay $20 for it, but would sell it for $22.50. At trial, a benefit–cost analyst hired by Amartya testifies that the book has more value to Amartya, because his willingness to pay exceeds Derek's. BCA would seem to suggest that giving the book to Amartya is wealth-maximizing. The Court, however, finds that because the book was stolen, it should be returned to Derek, regardless of the BCA analysis. Essentially, here, where there is a law against stealing, Amartya's WTP is outweighed by social sentiment, and therefore loses. Rule 6 then recommends, for example, that *the value of the stolen goods to the thief do not count.*

Rule 7: Where law and custom offer no guide then all preferences are to be counted

Rule 7 is ancillary to Rule 6. That is, where discussions concern whether or not theft *should* be illegal then thieves would have standing, assuming there is no prior understanding of a right to protection against thievery. Where the issue is the relative weight of the sentiment itself in order to decide whether or not theft should be illegal, then thieves' sentiments should be counted.

In situations where rights are undetermined the correct measure for BCA is the WTP, the payment to gain a right since there is not ownership of the right. That is, unowned goods should be sold at auction. Where rights are partial and in dispute, the correct measure of efficiency is determined by a combination of WTP and WTA of the various parties (Zerbe, 1991).

Navigating this balancing and enumeration of preferences can be seen in the Supreme Court's right to choose jurisprudence. Highly controversial subject matter aside, the court's decisions provide several examples of balancing parties' willingness to pay to secure certain rights.[9] *Roe* v. *Wade* (1973) balances, among other things, a woman's compelling interest in her body with the state's interest in the potentiality of life. More recently, the Court in *Planned Parenthood* v. *Casey* (1992) described sentiments in terms of an "undue burden" test, determining that if a pre-termination requirement (e.g., informing a spouse or a mandatory waiting period) did not unduly burden a woman's right to terminate pregnancy it was permissible under the Constitution. This decision affirmed a woman's right to terminate pregnancy established by *Roe* but applied a comparison test for the extent to which that right had to remain completely unburdened. Under the undue burden test, an undue burden can be conceptualized as a change in relative rights that is large enough that a woman who would pay to avoid the change could not afford to pay. This test was reiterated in *Gonzales* v. *Carhart* (2007), the Supreme Court's most recent major right to choose decision. The visceral majority and fiery dissent in this opinion serve as further illustration of the importance in balancing of all sentiments in an area where rights are still being negotiated. Regardless of one's feeling regarding the outcome of these cases, each is an example of undetermined rights or rights in dispute, and the balancing includes all sentiments that accompanied the firmer establishment or clarification of those rights. Such balancing is the essence of judicial decision-making and is illustrated further in other cases, such as *Mathews* v. *Eldridge* (1976) and *New York Times Co.* v. *Sullivan* (1964) and as discussed by Armitage (1985).

Rule 8: Moral sentiments are to be counted as preferences in ethical BCA

There is no reason to ignore ethical considerations in determining values. Ethical BCA logically includes values represented by ethical considerations. Economists as viewed by Carson et al. (2001) and Dana (2003) have improved the ability to measure moral values. For example, Andreoni (1995) found charitable values by examining the market for charity. Efficiency and the ethical values underlying it can often be found in experience—the sociological point of view. As stated in Zerbe (2006, p. 81), "Empirical evidence shows, and theory suggests, that the common law tends towards economic efficiency." Zerbe argues that the correlation between changes in the common law and efficiency is stronger when a measure of efficiency is used that includes moral sentiments. Thus, common law tendencies are explained using ethical BCA and enhanced by attention to issues of distribution and other ethical considerations. Schorr (2005) found that considerations of distributive justice have played an important role in the evolution of property rights. Zerbe and Anderson (2001) found that fairness played an important role in the creation of rights in the California gold fields after 1848. Goulder (2007) recently suggested an approach that incorporates important elements of the KHM framework. Ethical BCA using KHM codifies what has to a considerable extent been occurring in practice. For example, the heightened environmental movement starting in the 1970s led to common law approaches focused on fairness as well as efficiency. In the famous *Boomer* (1970) case, the New York Court of Appeals applied principles of equity and found that the Atlantic Cement Company's operation constituted a private nuisance to nearby residents, but allowed injunctive relief to be vacated upon the company's payment of permanent damages. The court's decision was based on the fact that the company employed over 300 people, had already made significant investments in the plant, and that techniques to address the annoying byproducts of cement production were unlikely to be developed in the near future.

These examples illustrate the importance of the process of determining benefits and costs. Lesbirel (2003) empirically shows that an offer of monetary compensation has a positive influence on an individual's support for a site, but that higher levels of compensation do not produce an additional increase in support. In other words, the level of compensation is not as important as compensation in principle.

Rule 9: Ethical sentiments are to be counted directly and not included in the discount rate

There has been very considerable criticism on moral or ethical grounds of BCA's discounting of future benefits and costs. Many critics would use discount rates of zero. To combine ethical preferences with the discount rate combines two disparate things, ethical preferences and the social opportunity cost of resources.

As soon as you use a discount rate that is lower than the actual time preference of those affected, you distort the choice between projects with shorter and longer time periods. This distortion will result in smaller benefits or larger costs so that net benefits are lower. Using the time preference discount rate and directly incorporating ethical preferences avoids this distortion.

In his article about risk–benefit trade-offs in hazardous facilities sitings as discussed above, Easterling (1992) argues that an individual's perception

Table 8.3 A comparison of KH and KHM involving future generations

Benefits and Costs	No Compensation or Mitigation Occurs (PV billions)	Compensation Occurs (PV billions)	Mitigation Occurs Compensation is Not Feasible (PV billions)
Ordinary benefits	100	100	100
Ordinary costs	60	60	60
Harm to future generations	0.017	0.017	[0.017]
Administrative costs of actual compensation	[10]	10	Infinite
Mitigation costs	[7.5]	[7.5]	7.5
Moral harm to present generation	50	[50]	[50]
KH NPV	39.983	39.983	39.983
KHM NPV	−10.017	29.981	32.5
Conclusion	Neither compensation nor mitigation appears worthwhile under KH as moral harm is ignored. The project is not worthwhile under KHM	Compensation eliminates moral harm	Mitigation eliminates moral harm

Note: A real discount rate of 3% is used to discount all figures. The 0.017 figure is the discounted value of future damage expressed in billions. Figures in brackets are costs not incurred in the given scenario. Note that not all figures are relevant to KH and that mitigation and compensation are substitutes so that one or the other but not both are included in the KHM calculation.

of seriousness of risk to future generations caused by a potentially hazardous site significantly impacts an individual's support for a site. Moral sentiments, in the form of concern for future generations, can be important in decisions about risk–benefit trade-offs.

Ethical preferences can be incorporated directly as part of WTP or WTA values. Under ethical BCA (KHM) we can give standing to ethical considerations of the present generation about future generations. This provides a solution to the ethical dilemma of the discount rate problem by acknowledging the validity of ethical concerns, while also acknowledging the values that commend use of a discount rate. Consider Table 8.3.

For purposes of this example, mitigation and compensation measures are assumed to completely eliminate future harm. However, mitigation does not enter the KH calculus, as the mitigation costs are less than the present value of the future harm. That is, mitigation does not occur under KH, as its costs are $7.5 billion and it eliminates only $0.018 billion in harm. This occurs because KH ignores the elimination of moral harm. Similarly, KH does not consider compensation, as it ignores distributional effects and costs of compensation.[10] Thus, the NPV under KH is the same under all scenarios.[11] KH misses values and information by ignoring moral harm and the cost of actual, as opposed to hypothetical, compensation.

The analysis of the nuclear waste example is quite different under ethical BCA using KHM. The NPV for a scenario without mitigation or compensation is negative, a negative $10 billion under KHM, instead of the positive nearly $30 billion under KH. This is because ethical considerations are included as required by KHM, but not included under KH. When compensation or mitigation occurs, the moral harm is eliminated and the missing values are now included under KHM. Some economists object, saying that moral harm cannot exceed the present value of the future loss. For example, some have asked, "If the current generation can compensate future generations for $0.017 billion, then wouldn't this represent the maximum willingness to pay?" The answer is no, for two reasons. First, the costs of compensating are clearly not $0.017 billion. The administrative costs of providing compensation so far into the future must be included, and these costs may well be enormous, perhaps infinite. The ability of government to provide the required long-lived institutions that would carry out compensation has been found in a study by Leschine and McCurdy (2001) to be improbable.

In addition, Zerbe and Knott (2004) conducted a survey of firms in charge of providing compensation for those found defrauded in Federal Trade Commission and certain former employees of the FTC. The survey showed administrative costs of compensation by firms or government in these actions is generally high and sometimes exceeds the amount to be compensated.

Second, the parties deciding on compensation may not be the same parties that suffer moral harm. For goods supplied by the public, there is a distinction between those who would purchase ethical satisfaction and those who make the decision to purchase it. The transactions costs of actually persuading decision-makers to compensate may be prohibitive, especially since any attempt at agreement may suffer from a free rider problem, a moral hazard issue in which one rides free on the coat-tails of those doing the work. As discussed in Gruber (2007) the possibility of free riding makes agreement more difficult as agreement would limit the possibility of getting a free ride. If no purchase of ethical satisfaction occurs, one must conclude that the transactions cost of purchase is at least as great as the moral harm to the present generations.

The highest NPV under KHM is $32.5 billion, which occurs with mitigation. The inclusion of the value of ethical considerations to reduce harm to future generations provides a justification for mitigation as long as its costs are less than the moral harm.

Under KHM, rough estimates of moral harm might suffice for the correct decision. The KHM approach is superior, as it gives a truer and fuller accounting. In this example mitigation gives a KHM net present value of about $32 billion. The use of ethical BCA-KHM accounts for all relevant values and results in a valuable project, whereas KH results in a project with a $10 billion loss.

Under KHM, analyses can give economic standing to ethical considerations about future generations. KHM allows us to correctly compare compensation, mitigation, and non-action. It avoids projects that appear worthwhile but impose moral harm greater than their value. It provides a solution to the ethical dilemma of the discount rate problem that recognizes ethical concerns as valid and seeks an ethical solution, while at the same time acknowledging the values that commend use of a discount rate. The economic efficiency of the project will then depend on the ethical values of the present generation. For example, the present generation may feel future generations should be free of problems caused by the current generation. Evidence from Kunreuther and Easterling (1990) and from Svenson and Karlsson (1989) suggests that, at least with regard to nuclear waste disposal, individuals tend to place a high emphasis on future consequences. On the one hand, the present generation may find that compensation for environmental harm is unwarranted, given their belief that future generations will be wealthier than the present one.[12] Alternatively, the present generation may feel that future generations should be free of problems caused by the current generation.[13]

Rule 10: The purpose of BCA is to furnish information to the decision process and not to make the decision

BCA should not to be separated from political discourse. When removed from public discourse, the most cogent criticism of BCA is that in attempting to portray preferences, BCA makes static what is fluid.[14] Preferences are formed out of human interaction and are not pre-existing values to be plucked from the brains of respondents. Decisions, however, are made in such interaction and BCA would be only one element in it. Moreover, sophisticated generators of questionnaire studies recognize that values are created and discovered in the course of administrating questionnaires. The proponents of BCA and benefit/risk analysis maintain that data from BCA can be used to enhance the relevant discussion. For example, Cook et al. (2007) examine the effect of giving respondents time to think about their stated choices in a survey of cholera and typhoid vaccine preferences in Hue, Vietnam. Because neither vaccine is widely available in Vietnam, they use a stated preference technique and gave half of their respondents overnight to think about their choices to make the hypothetical valuation scenario as similar to a real-life choice situation as possible. Respondents who were given extra time made fewer choices that violated internal validity tests of utility theory, and had lower average WTP, confirming a result found in similar studies in the contingent valuation literature.

My experience is that there is a tendency for hard numbers to drive out soft. Thus, political discourse is more important the greater the extent to which qualitative methodologies are not or cannot be well considered in a BCA. By paying more attention to qualitative methodologies as a part of BCA, the bias toward hard numbers can be mitigated or obviated.

6 CONCLUSION

Modern benefit–cost analysis has been mischaracterized by a wide spectrum of non-practitioner, mainly legal critics. Economists and users or producers of BCA in the past have chosen to ignore the need to make the foundation of benefit–cost analysis clear. Yet economists have come to realize that a more inclusive view of BCA allows a wider scope for evaluations, and a more solid framework for its use. Many of these realizations have come to the fore via economists' work in addressing issues of charity, environmental evaluation, and situations where moral sentiments and contingent valuation play a role. As part of the process of making the basis for BCA clearer and more useful, this chapter begins to develop rules and standards of practice. In doing this, it shows that BCA is not a mechanical exercise but rather an art form involving nuanced judgment about what information is most useful for public policy.

In introducing ethical BCA as an art form, most criticisms of BCA are obviated. Table 8.4 shows briefly the criticism and the response of ethical BCA. These responses are then shown to be governed by one or more of the rules for ethical BCA introduced here.

Table 8.4 Ethical BCA answers to BCA criticisms

Criticism and Basis for Criticism	Ethical BCA Responses	Governed By
1 BCA results reflect the existing pattern of wealth, thus the results will be unfair	The results are unfair only if the pattern of wealth is unfair. The solution is to change the pattern of wealth, not to throw out BCA	Rule 1
2 No weight is given to income distribution concerns and moral sentiments such as charity. Thus, BCA is morally deficient and suspect	This is not true for ethical BCA as defined here	Rule 8
3 Private values are used when community values are appropriate. The choices an individual makes as a public citizen may differ from those he or she makes as a private person. Thus, proper community values are missing in BCA	The correct measure is public preferences in the context of a public project, so criticism is not true of BCA	Rules 4, 10
4 BCA ignores moral considerations, e.g., by using discount rates to value future lives	Not the case with ethical BCA. No legitimate moral claims are ignored with ethical BCA. And discount rates are still used	Rule 9
5 BCA cannot recognize moral values without recognizing immoral ones, including "bad" utility. Thus, either immoral values are wrongly included, or moral values are omitted. BCA therefore fails to condemn rape or slavery in all cases	This is not the case if society gains from ignoring immoral values	Rule 6

6	BCA compares the incomparable and prices the priceless. It rests on market values. Values are aggregated improperly, and valuing moral sentiments degrades them	Ethical BCA provides information about preferences, including ethical or morally based ones	Rule 8
7	Absence of any "scientific" method of aggregating preferences, e.g., since one cannot measure utility, one cannot in general say if total happiness has increased if a project increases the wealth of some more than it decreases the wealth of others	This is a fact of nature, not of ethical BCA. The question is whether or not ethical BCA results in a useful metric	Rule 10
8	BCA favors the status quo and is therefore biased against change. It assumes the existing pattern of rights so that when there is sufficient disagreement, it would choose position A if starting from A; or B, if starting from B	This result is based on the importance of extant law and ethical BCA's relationship to it. Far from a failing, this is an ethical BCA strength	Rule 1
9	Ethical BCA may result in neglecting non-quantitative values, and as a result, it may miss important values	This is true and can be overcome with vigilance in presentation and discussion	Not discussed here. Consists of giving proper weight to quantitative and qualitative data

NOTES

* The author thanks Nancy Garland for valuable editorial assistance, including the addition of two paragraphs to this chapter, Ann Bostrom for very valuable information and suggestions concerning risk behavior and informed preferences, and William Stoebuck for a useful legal cite.

1. See Kauffman (2008) for an explanation of the central concepts of reductionism and delineating current and past scientists who adhere to the philosophy.
2. For normal goods where the WTA > WTP see Zerbe and Dively (1994).
3. This approach makes clear the irrelevancy of the objection in critical legal studies to BCA, as Heyne (1988) has shown. In brief (see Zerbe, 1991) the argument in such critical legal studies is that we cannot use the concept of efficiency without endorsing some concept of property rights. It is seen to follow from this argument that the concept of efficiency cannot be used to resolve disputes over property rights without begging the question. Just as the law does, BCA takes the existing structure of rights as extant. But there are disputes that reflect uncertainty about some small portions of these rights. BCA merely furnishes information relevant to the legal decision about the allocation of such a right. Take a simple case: a change in technology makes valuable rights to the radio wave spectrum that has hitherto been unowned. No party has a superior claim. The assignment of the right to a particular party will be a gain. Gains in economic analyses are to be measured by WTP, which will be partly determined by the existing pattern of wealth, which rests on the existing system of rights. Economic analysis suggests auctioning off the right. The right in general should go to that party who would pay the most for it if transactions costs were zero. Cases in which conflicting prior claims exist raise more difficult questions, but these are answerable with the logic of ethical BCA.
4. Harberger (1978) presents three suggestions on how to address the complications that distributional weights place on the cost-based analysis of commodity taxes, a topic also taken up by Feldstein (1972).
5. Dana (2003, p. 343) states "As an empirical matter, it is far from certain that one could accurately isolate the percentage of existence value valuations that is attributable to moral and spiritual values." McConnell (1997) suggests that to include existence value may result in double counting but Zerbe et al. (2006) shows that inclusion of existence value does not result in double counting.
6. An extensive flowering of the market failure concept has occurred in the field of law. The number of law review articles and court decisions using the concept runs into the thousands, with 239 references turned up by a search of law review articles for the 12 months between June 1995 and June 1996 alone. Similarly, court decisions referring to market failure and to externalities are made with great frequency. The bankruptcy of this approach is shown in Zerbe and McCurdy (1999) indicating that the raison d'être for government intervention has been shifting from market failure and externalities to transactions costs.
7. See generally Bostrom (1997), who analyzes the discrepancies between expert assessments and lay perceptions of risk. For an expression of what we are missing in our knowledge of expert and lay estimates of risk, see Rowe and Wright (2001), who evaluate nine empirical studies on expert versus lay estimates of risk.
8. See for example, Federal Civil Jury Instructions of the Seventh Circuit 1.21 Expert Witnesses (2005) at http://www.ca7.uscourts.gov/7thcivinstruc2005.pdf (accessed 15 October 2012), "You have heard [a witness] [witnesses] give opinions about matters requiring special knowledge or skill. You should judge this testimony in the same way that you judge the testimony of any other witness. The fact that such person has given an opinion does not mean that you are required to accept it. Give the testimony whatever weight you think it deserves," and *Amaru* v. *Stratton* (1985), which notes the jury can disregard expert testimony even absent contrary evidence.
9. Though poorer women seeking to terminate a pregnancy may not be able to pay as

much as wealthier women (and thus have a lower WTP, since WTP is finite and based on actual ability to pay), the Court's balancing aggregate WTP and WTA in these situations includes the moral sentiments of others and society. In essence, society's WTP to ensure access and equality to a right once established compensates for an individual's ability to pay.

10. Under KH, compensation costs are hypothetical and are merely the present value of the costs of future harm, or $0.017 billion.
11. The relevant amount of compensation here is not the amount actually required for those injured to be fully compensated, rather, it is the amount of compensation the current generation thinks is correct. This information is likely obtainable through a contingent valuation survey to determine, at least in principle, the WTP or WTA of "others" who have ethical considerations about the project.
12. The assumption that the marginal utility of income will decline as income increases, applies not simply to long-term discount rates, but short-term rates and distributional effects in general. If there is a declining marginal utility of income, then the benefits accruing to the wealthy should receive less weight. One can better take through valuations of benefits and costs rather than by changes in the discount rate. Current users can account both for their own sentiments for future generations as well as a probable increase in wealth of those generations. Attempting to use the discount rate to account for either of these can result in the wrong project choice (Zerbe and Lesser, 1994; Zerbe, 2004).
13. Again, it is not the amount of compensation actually required for those injured that is directly relevant here. Rather, it is the amount of compensation the current generation thinks is correct. This information could be determined, at least in principle, by a contingent valuation survey measuring the WTP or WTA of those who have ethical considerations about the project.
14. Wolcher (2007) delivers a particularly trenchant and clear criticism along these lines.

REFERENCES

Ackerman, Frank and Lisa Heinzerling (2002), "Pricing the priceless: Cost–benefit analysis of environmental protection," *University of Pennsylvania Law Review*, **150** (5), 1553–84.

Amaru v. *Stratton* 506 A.2D 1225 (Sup. Ct. NJ, 1985 (1985).

Anderson, Elizabeth (1993), *Values in Ethics and Economics*, Cambridge, MA: Harvard University Press.

Andreoni, James (1995), "Cooperation in public-goods experiments: Kindness or confusion?," *American Economic Review*, **85** (4), 891–904.

Armitage, Thomas C. (1985), "Efficiency as a legal norm," *Research in Law and Economics*, **7**, 1–27.

Boomer v. *Atlantic Cement Co.* (1970), 257 NE 2d 870 (NY).

Bostrom, Ann (1997), "Risk perceptions: 'experts' vs. 'lay people'," *Duke Environmental Law and Policy Forum*, **8**, 101–13.

Brent, Robert J. (1997), *Applied Benefit–Cost Analysis*, Cheltenham, UK and Lyme, NH, USA: Edward Elgar.

Breyer, Stephen (1993), *Breaking the Vicious Cycle: Toward Effective Risk Regulation*, Cambridge, MA: Harvard University Press.

Calandrillo, Steve P. (2001), "Responsible regulation: A sensible cost–benefit, risk versus risk approach to federal health and safety regulation," *Boston University Law Review*, **81**, 957–1032.

Carlin, Alan (2005), "The new challenge to cost–benefit analysis," *Regulation*, **28** (3), 18–23.

Carson, Richard T., Nicholas E. Flores, and Norman F. Meade (2001), "Contingent valuation: Controversies and evidence," *Environmental and Resource Economics*, **19** (2), 173–210.

Chi, Michelene T.H., Paul J. Feltovich, and Robert Glaser (1981), "Categorization and representation of physics problems by experts and novices," *Cognitive Science*, **5** (2), 121–52.

Chipman, John and James C. Moore (1978), "The new welfare economics 1939–1974," *International Economic Review*, **19** (3), 547–8.

Coase, Ronald (1988), *The Firm, the Market, and the Law*, Chicago: University of Chicago Press.

Cohen, David and Jack L. Knetsch (1992), "Judicial choice and disparities between measures of economic values," *Osgoode Hall Law Journal*, **30** (3), 737–70.

Coleman, Jules L. (1988), "Efficiency, utility and wealth maximization," in Jules L. Coleman, *Markets, Morals, and the Law*, New York: Cambridge University Press.

Cook, Joseph et al. (2007), "Reliability of stated preferences for cholera and typhoid vaccines with time to think in Hue, Vietnam," *Economic Inquiry*, **45** (1), 100–114.

Dana, David A. (2003), "Existence value and federal preservation regulation," *Harvard International Law Review*, **28**, 343–99.

Dworkin, Ronald M. (1980), "Is wealth a value?," *Journal of Legal Studies*, **9** (2), 191–226.

Easterling, Douglas (1992), "Fair rules for siting a high-level nuclear waste repository," *Journal of Policy Analysis and Management*, **11** (3), 442–75.

Ericsson, K.A. and A.C. Lehmann (1996), 'Expert and exceptional performance: Evidence on maximal adaptations on task constraints', *Annual Review of Psychology*, **47**, 273–305.

Ericsson, K. Anders and Paul Ward (2007), "Capturing the naturally occurring superior performance of experts in the laboratory: Toward a science of expert and exceptional performance," *Current Directions in Psychological Science*, **16** (6), 346–50.

Federal Rules of Evidence (2011), Rule 702.

Feldstein, Martin (1972), "Distributional equity and the optimal structure of public prices," *American Economic Review*, **32** (1), 32–36.

Fischhoff, Baruch et al. (1978), "How safe is safe enough? A psychometric study of attitudes towards technological risks and benefits," *Policy Sciences*, **9**, 127–52.

Flynn, James, Paul Slovic and C.K. Mertz (1993), "Decidedly different: expert and public view of risks from a radioactive waste repository," *Risk Analysis*, **13** (6), 643–8.

Frank, Robert H. (1997), *Microeconomics and Behavior*, New York: McGraw Hill Education.

Fried, Charles (1978), *Right and Wrong*, Cambridge, MA: Harvard University Press.

Gayer, Ted and Robert Hahn (2005), 'The political economy of mercury regulation', **28** (2), 26–33.

Gonzales v. *Carhart* (2007), 550 US 124.

Goulder, Lawrence H. (2007), "Benefit–cost analysis, individual differences, and third parties," *Research in Law and Economics*, **23**, 67–86.

Graham, John D. and Jonathan Baert Wiener (eds) (1995), *Risk vs. Risk: Trade-offs in Protecting Health and the Environment*, Cambridge, MA: Harvard University Press.

Gruber, Jonathan (2007), *Public Finance and Public Policy*, New York: Worth Publishers.

Hammond, Peter (1985), "Welfare economics," in George R. Feiwel (ed.), *Issues in Contemporary Microeconomics and Welfare*, Albany, NY: State University of New York Press.

Harberger, Arnold (1978), "On the use of distributional weights in social cost–benefit analysis," *Journal of Policy and Economics*, **86** (2), 87–120.

Heyne, Paul (1988), "The foundations of law and economics," *Research in Law and Economics*, **11**, 53–71.

Hildred, William and Fred Beauvais (1995), "An instrumentalist critique of cost-utility analysis," *Journal of Economic Issues*, **29** (4), 1083–96.

Kaldor, Nicholas (1939), "Welfare propositions of economics and interpersonal comparisons of utility," *Economic Journal*, **49** (195), 549–50.

Kaplow, Louis and Steven Shavell (2002), *Fairness versus Welfare*, Cambridge, MA: Harvard University Press.

Kauffman, Stuart (2008), *Reinventing the Sacred: A New View of Science, Reasons, and Religion*, New York: Basic Books.

Kelman, Steven (1981), "Cost–benefit analysis: An ethical critique," *AEI Journal on Government and Society Regulation*, **5**, 33–40.

Knetsch, Jack L. (1995), "Assumptions, behavior findings, and policy analysis," *Journal of Policy Analysis and Management*, **14** (1), 68–78.

Kunreuther, Howard and Douglas Easterling (1990), "Are risk–benefit trade-offs possible in siting hazardous facilities," *American Economic Review*, **80** (2), 252–6.

Lesbirel, S. Hayden (2003), "Markets, transaction costs and institutions: Compensating for nuclear risk in Japan," *Australian Journal of Policy and Science*, **38** (1), 5–23.

Leschine, Thomas and Howard McCurdy (2001), "The institutional challenge of sustaining high levels of reliability over extended periods of time" (submitted to the Consortium for Risk Evaluation with Stakeholder Participation) July, 2001.

Levy, Daniel and D. Friedman (1994), "The revenge of the redwoods? Reconsidering property rights and the economic allocation of natural resources," *University of Chicago Law Review*, **61** (2), 493–526.

Markovits, Richard S. (2008), *Truth or Economics: On the Definition, Prediction, and Relevance of Economic Efficiency*, New Haven, CT: Yale University Press.

Matthews v. *Eldridge* (1976), 424 US 319.

McConnell, Kenneth E. (1997), "Does altruism undermine existence value?," *Journal of Environmental Economy and Management*, **32** (1), 22–37.

McDaniels, Timothy L., Robin S. Gregory, and Daryl Fields (1999), "Democratizing risk management: Successful public involvement in local water management decisions," *Risk Analysis*, **19** (3), 497–510.

Mertz, Jon F. (1991), "An empirical analysis of the medical informed consent doctrine: Search for a 'standard' of disclosure," *Risk*, **27** (2).

Mishan, Ezra J. (1981), *An Introduction to Normative Economics*, Oxford: Oxford University Press.

National Research Council (2000), *Environment and Resources, Risk Analysis and*

Uncertainty in Flood Damage Reduction Studies, Washington, DC: National Academy Press.
Nussbaum, Martha (2000), "The costs of tragedy: Some moral limits of cost–benefit analysis," *Journal of Legal Studies*, **29** (2), 1005–36.
N. Y. Times Co. v. *Sullivan* (1964), 376 US 254.
Payne, John W., James Bettman, and Eric Johnson (1992), "Behavioral decision research: A constructive processing perspective," *Annual Review of Psychology*, **43** (1), 87–131.
Penn. Central Trans. Co. v. *City of New York* (1978), 438 US 104, 127.
Planned Parenthood v. *Casey* (1992), 505 US 833.
Pollak, Robert A. (1996), "Government risk regulation," *Annals of American Academy of Political and Social Science*, **545** (1), 25–34.
Porter, Theodore (1996), *Trust in Numbers: The Pursuit of Objectivity in Science and Public Life*, Princeton, NJ: Princeton University Press.
Portney, Paul (1992), "Trouble in Happyville," *Journal of Policy Analysis and Management*, **11** (1), 131–2.
Richardson, Henry S. (2000), "The stupidity of the cost–benefit standard," *Journal of Legal Studies*, **2** (29), 971–1003.
Robbins, Lionel (1938), "Interpersonal comparisons of utility: A comment", *Economic Journal*, **48**, 635–41.
Roe v. *Wade* (1973), 410 US 113.
Rowe, Gene and George Wright (2001), "Differences in expert and lay judgments of risk: Myth or reality?," *Risk Analysis*, **21** (2), 341–56.
Rubin, Paul (1977), "Why is the common law efficient," *Journal of Legal Studies*, **51** (6), 51–63.
Sagoff, Mark (1988), *The Economy of the Earth: Philosophy, Law, and the Environment*, New York: Cambridge University Press.
Schmitz, Andrew and Richard O. Zerbe, Jr. (2009), "The relevance of the Scitovsky principle for benefit–cost analysis," *Journal of Agriculture and Food Industrial Organizations*, **6** (2), Article 3.
Schorr, David B. (2005), "Appropriation as agrarianism: Distributive justice in the creation of property rights," *Ecology Law Quarterly*, **3** (32), 3–71.
Slovic Paul et al. (1985), "Characterizing perceived risks," in Robert Kates et al. (eds), *Perilous Progress: Managing the Hazards of Technology*, Boulder, CO: Westview Press.
Stigler, George (1982), "Economists and public policy," *Regulation*, **13** (1), 13–17.
Svenson, Ola and G. Karlsson (1989), "Decision-making, time horizons, and risk in the very long term perspective," *Risk Analysis*, **9** (3), 385–99.
Trumbull, W.N. (1990), "Who has standing in cost–benefit analysis?," *Journal of Policy Analysis and Management*, **9** (2), 201–18.
Whittington, Dale and Duncan MacRae, Jr. (1990), "Judgments about who has standing in cost–benefit analysis: A comment," *Journal of Policy Analysis and Management*, **9** (4), 536–47.
Wolcher, Louis E. (2007), "Senseless kindness: The politics of cost–benefit analysis," *Law and Inequality*, **147** (25), 147–205.
Zerbe, Jr., Richard O. (1991), *Economic Efficiency in Law and Economics*, Aldershot, UK and Brookfield, VT, USA: Edward Elgar.
Zerbe, Jr., Richard O. (2004), "Should moral sentiments be incorporated into benefit–cost analysis? An example of long-term discounting," *Policy Science*, **37** (3–4), 305–18.

Zerbe, Jr., Richard O. (2006), "Justice and the evolution of the common law," *Journal of Law and Economic Policy*, **3** (81).

Zerbe, Jr., Richard O. (2007), "The legal foundation of cost–benefit analysis," *Charleston Law Review*, **2** (94), 112–50.

Zerbe Jr., Richard O. and Leigh Anderson (2001), "Culture and fairness in the development of institutions in the California gold fields," *Journal of Economic History*, **61** (1), 141–3.

Zerbe, Richard O. and Allen S. Bellas (2006), *A Primer for Benefit–Cost Analysis*, Cheltenham, UK and Northampton, MA, USA: Edward Elgar.

Zerbe, Jr., Richard O. and Dwight Dively (1994), *Benefit–Cost Analysis in Theory and Practice*, Glenview, IL: Harper Collins College Division.

Zerbe, Jr., Richard O. and Sunny Knott (2004), "An economic justification for a price standard in merger policy: The merger of superior propane and ICG propane," *Resource Law and Economics*, **21**.

Zerbe, Jr., Richard O. and Jonathan Lesser (1994), "Discounting procedures for environmental (and other) projects: A comment on Kolb and Scheraga," *Journal of Policy Analysis and Management*, **13** (1), 140–56.

Zerbe Jr., Richard O. and H. McCurdy (1999), "The failure of market failure," *Journal of Policy Analysis and Management*, **18** (4), 558–78.

Zerbe, Jr., Richard O. et al. (2006), "An aggregate measure for benefit–cost analysis," *Ecological Economics*, **58** (3), 449–61.

9. Incorporating distributional issues into benefit–cost analysis: why, how, and two empirical examples using non-market valuation

John B. Loomis

1 WHY DISTRIBUTIONAL ISSUES ARE IMPORTANT IN THEORY AND PRACTICE

The origin of benefit–cost analysis (BCA), in both theory and practice, has its historical roots in the pursuit of economic efficiency, with less attention paid to distributional concerns. In the last decade there has been growing interest among federal and state agencies in displaying elements traditionally omitted from BCA, such as how the benefits and costs are distributed geographically, by income groups, and by ethnicity. In the case of applying BCA to evaluate social policies from preschool education to prison reform, distributional goals are often an explicit part of the policy design (Long et al., 1981; Vining and Weimer, 2010). The thrust of this chapter, and recent papers by others (Zerbe, 2007; Schmitz and Schmitz, 2010; Vining and Weimer, 2010), is that the information provided by BCA should be broadened to explicitly include discussion and display of the distributional effects of the project.

For the purposes of this chapter, distribution is an extension of positive economic analysis to quantify who gains (and by how much) and who loses (and by how much). Equity deals with the more normative issue of whether the distribution of these benefits and costs is "fair" or not using criteria such as ability to pay. While this discussion will address both distribution and equity, the empirical examples will focus on how to monetize the distribution of benefits from non-market goods and resources. For the purposes of this chapter, distributional consequences or effects primarily refer to how the benefits and costs are distributed by some classification of interest to the decision-makers such as income levels, ethnicity, age, and so on. Benefits are typically defined as net willingness to pay. Costs include real resource costs incurred by society. In some cases the analyst is also interested in how the burden of financing (e.g., taxes or fees paid) those real resource costs are distributed relative to the benefits. That is, how the real resource costs are paid for may moderate or exacerbate the distributional consequences of net benefits. When the term distributional consequences is used in the chapter, the context of the discussion will usually make apparent whether financing issues are being included or not.

The requirements to perform a distributional analysis as part of a BCA are now reflected in federal policies. Agencies are statutorily required to consider impacts on different groups: small businesses (Regulatory Flexibility Act of 1980, amended 1996); children (Food Quality Protection Act, EO 13045); vulnerable populations (Clean Air Act), and impact on state, local or tribal governments (Unfunded Mandates Reform Act of 1995).

To set the stage for this chapter's case study, we will examine the federal requirement to assess environmental effects on minorities and low-income populations. This requirement came about as a result of concerns raised by the NAACP (National Association for the Advancement of Colored People) regarding environmental racism in the siting of power plants, landfills, and petro-chemical facilities (especially in Louisiana). In 1994 President Clinton signed Executive Order (EO) 12898. Section 1-101 of the EO requires that "each Federal agency shall develop an agency-wide environmental justice strategy . . . that identifies and addresses disproportionately high and adverse human health or environmental effects of its programs, policies, and activities on minority populations and low-income populations."

Agencies such as the US Environmental Protection Agency (EPA) in its *Guidelines for Preparing Economic Analysis* (US EPA, 2000), provide a chapter on distributional issues. Within that chapter there is specific attention paid to the determination of whether environmental effects of changes in the natural or physical environment are adverse and disproportionately high to minority and low-income populations (ibid., p. 166). The disproportionate standard is relative to effects on the general population. This discussion appears geared toward determining health risks of environmental effects in a quantitative sense (e.g., parts per million concentration of a pollutant or acres mined near low-income or minority residents versus higher-income areas) but not in a monetary sense.

But how to monetize the distribution of health and environmental effects not priced in the market can be challenging. Little has been written on this topic. The purpose of this chapter is to show how to adapt two non-market valuation techniques in order to monetize the non-market benefits to different income and ethnic groups in order to address distributional issues that agencies are required to display in their analysis. The chapter proceeds as follows. First, we briefly set the stage for why distributional issues are important from a theoretical perspective. Next we highlight the general issue of partial equilibrium and general equilibrium approaches to calculating and displaying distributional effects. This is followed by a discussion of alternative approaches to incorporating distributional concerns and equity into BCA. The penultimate section discusses and provides empirical examples of how two non-market valuation methods can be used to calculate distributional effects. The chapter concludes with a summary of the findings of this chapter.

1.1 Distribution Matters in Economic Theory

For economists, social well-being is composed of two factors, economic efficiency and equity. By efficiency, economists mean selecting policies that maximize consumer well-being from use of a given amount of market and non-market scarce resources. Economists talk about economic efficiency as a positive or objective analysis, and it takes the distribution of income and resulting prices as given unless there are market failures such as monopoly or pollution (then shadow prices are used to correct for these distortions in the BCA). How project benefits and costs are distributed among different income or ethnicities is also a positive analysis.

The second factor is equity or fairness of the distribution of these goods and services. Using information on how benefits and costs are distributed to assess equity or fairness is a normative analysis as it requires society or its representatives (usually an elected official) to compare the well-being of a dollar's worth of benefit to one person versus another. While the choice of how to weight or trade-off benefits to people of different incomes is a societal choice, many people in society (but not all) would agree that publicly financed projects or policies should not seriously worsen the distribution of income. For an economist, nirvana would exist when an "optimum optimorum" (Boadway, 1979, p. 23) is achieved. Such an optimum requires attaining both efficient production and consumption (the first optimum), and a social welfare-maximizing distribution of those consumption goods and income (the second optimum). To obtain the second optimum regarding equity requires a social welfare function that reflects the relative contribution of each person's utility to social welfare. Of course such a function is generally considered a theoretical (not empirical) construct, and one that would be normative if empirical construction was possible. However, the concept of a social welfare function brings to the forefront the fact that economic theory is not just concerned with economic efficiency, but that it includes attention to equity as well. In fact, some economic policies are specifically designed to lessen the unequal distribution of income arising from the market economy, even if there is a cost in reduced economic efficiency. An example of one such policy is a progressive income tax along with income transfers to low-income households.

In a first-best world with perfectly competitive (price-taking) firms, and the ability of the government to offset any negative distributional effects through lump sum (non-distortionary) taxes and transfers (at little or no transactions costs), economic efficiency and equity can be separated. In this case BCA should focus on identifying economically efficient projects (Tresch, 1981). However, in many instances where a benefit–cost analysis is to be performed, the relevant industry structure is not perfectly competitive. Neither is the government able to engage in non-distortionary taxation of the high-income project beneficiaries in order to transfer these tax revenues to low-income households adversely affected by the project. In this more realistic, but what economists call "second-best world," attainment of social well-being requires ranking projects by both their levels of economic efficiency and equity (ibid.). Thus, we focus the remainder of the chapter on investigation of different means to conduct a distributional analysis that lays the foundation for an evaluation of the equity of a particular project or program.

1.2 Addressing Distribution in BCA in Partial and General Equilibrium Analyses

If the majority of the effects of a policy or project are limited in economic scope (i.e., primarily affecting one sector) or one relatively small geographic area, then a BCA limited to that sector or area is sufficient. That is, a partial equilibrium analysis may be sufficient to capture the vast majority of the effects. To incorporate distributional effects in a partial equilibrium analysis one approach is to adopt the "stakeholder accounting approach" (Jenkins, 1999; Krutilla, 2005). In this approach, the benefits and costs to each group of interest (i.e., stakeholders) are displayed in a table format. This approach lends itself to allowing decision-makers to decide how much weight to give each group.

However, oftentimes policies have widespread effects with backward linkages affecting suppliers of inputs to the project and forward linkages to end users of the project. For example, construction of a large hydroelectric dam could reduce the cost of electricity used by multiple industries. Or a national policy to reduce air pollutants from petroleum refining could affect prices of diesel fuel for airline and trucking industries and gasoline prices for consumers. In these examples a multi-market analysis is needed of the distributional effects to the relevant parties, as there will be multiple industries affected. In addition, there may be pecuniary spillover effects from these industries to those producing complement and substitute goods. Essentially, the interconnection of the airline and trucking industry on other industries must be explicitly accounted for when performing a distributional analysis. Economists have developed models to allow for multi-market BCA (Just et al., 1982; Berck and Hoffmann, 2002). Large policy changes (e.g., a cap and trade on carbon emissions) that have major economy-wide effects justify use of non-linear computable general equilibrium (CGE) simulation models. A properly constructed CGE simulation model allows an analyst to trace the effects of new policies on prices and quantities, labor, taxes, and so on throughout the entire economy (Berck and Hoffmann, 2002). This allows for a comprehensive analysis of both the economic efficiency and distributional consequences of pervasive policy change. In both the multi-market and CGE analysis, there may be several industry- and consumer-good-specific equity measures calculated, as well as one "net effect" measure. For example, new fuel economy standards will raise new car prices, but save consumers gasoline purchases over the life of the car. Further, the increase in new car prices may stimulate demand for used cars, boosting their price. Since the poor tend to buy used cars, this could have an unintended adverse equity effect, even though a single market analysis might show little effect since the poor usually do not purchase new cars. Fullerton (2009) provides a series of papers that illustrate the application of multiple market and general equilibrium analyses to analyze the distributional effects of energy and environmental policy. In sum, it is important to keep in mind when a multiple market or CGE analysis is warranted and perform such an analysis when appropriate. If a short-cut analysis using only the most directly affected market is performed, then these limitations discussed above should be discussed qualitatively based on the concepts of backward and forward linkages as well as substitute and complement goods. We now turn to the practical matter of possible ways distribution and equity concerns might be incorporated into a benefit–cost analysis.

2 APPROACHES TO INCORPORATING DISTRIBUTION AND EQUITY INTO BCA

There are several approaches to weighting benefits and costs based on income, ethnicity, or any other criteria. The more explicit the weights are, the more there is room for disagreement regarding the value judgments that underlie these weights. Nonetheless, differential weighting of benefits and costs may occur at some point in the policy process, and it behooves us as economists to help steer decision-makers away from obvious pitfalls that can arise with the use of weights. Some weighting schemes by being very explicit may be more controversial than others (some may recall the flap over the "senior discount" to the value of statistical life). As Harberger (1984) points out, there is an implicit efficiency cost associated with using differential weights for different groups. That is, the greater the range of weights between groups (e.g., a factor of four as in his example), the more possible it is for projects that provide significant benefits to a higher-weighted group to pass a benefit–cost test even if overall economic efficiency is inadequate (e.g., BCR < 1). We now review these different weighting schemes.

2.1 Implicit Weighting by Decision-makers

One of the easiest ways to account for distributional issues in a BCA is simply to display the benefits and costs disaggregated by income classes, rural versus urban, ethnicity, or whatever groups are relevant for this analysis (Zerbe and Dively, 1994; Jenkins, 1999; Krutilla, 2005). This "stakeholder" approach is also the easiest for decision-makers to understand. Most importantly, the decision-makers can then apply their own weighting regarding the relative emphasis to put on each grouping.

Like many elements in a BCA, such an approach is simple in concept, but can be difficult in practice. How does the analyst know how much of the benefits received or the costs paid/incurred are associated with different income classes or ethnicities? On the cost side, some of this may be known from the project financing. If the project is to be financed by user fees, then surveys of users may reveal the incomes, ethnicities, and so on of frequent versus infrequent users. From this the analyst could calculate the percentage of the project cost to be borne by each group of interest. If the project is to be financed by income taxes, sales taxes or property taxes, there is an extensive literature in public finance and tax journals on how these taxes are distributed by income.

On the benefit side, surveys can be used to estimate how the benefits vary with groups of interest (e.g., stakeholders) in the distributional analysis. As illustrated below, most surveys contain, or can be designed to contain, an extensive list of demographic characteristics such as age, education, gender, ethnicity, income, or whatever group the analyst thinks is relevant for distributional analysis of this project or policy (e.g., handicap status, single parent households, etc.). Benefits estimated by usage, willingness to pay, or other indicators can then be cross-tabbed with any of the demographic characteristics used in the survey. The analyst can even calculate and display multiple within-group, and between-group categories, for example, single parent households by ethnicity, senior citizens by race, and so on. In this way, the analyst can display multiple distributional measures that may be of political interest to elected officials. Combining these per capita effects based on the survey data with the number of households in each of the categories allows for a population-level incidence analysis. Once information on how benefits and costs are distributed has been assembled, a useful summary statistic is how the difference between benefits and costs, that is, net benefits, are distributed by each distributional strata of interest to the policy-makers (Graham, 2008; Hammitt, 2009). Net benefits involves combining information on the amount (if any) of project benefits to a typical individual in the group of interest (e.g., income class, ethnic group) along with the costs (e.g., higher prices, taxes, etc.) borne by a typical individual in those same groupings. Krutilla (2005) provides a tableau format that illustrates this approach for disaggregating project benefits, costs and net benefits for groups that are classified into residents, consumers, producers, taxpayers, and state government.

A second way to determine if the benefits do vary with key demographic characteristics is to include demographic variables in the statistical analysis used to estimate benefits. Many BCAs calculate benefits from demand or supply functions. If the analyst is using data to estimate these demand or supply functions, he or she can include variables such as income, age, gender, and so on in the demand or supply equations to statistically test (e.g., t-test) whether the usage, and hence the benefits, vary with these characteristics. If a demographic factor is significant, then the differential benefits received by each group can be calculated by setting that variable at the different levels of interest for that group. For example, if it is a dummy variable for gender, then the consumer or producer surplus could be calculated twice, once for males and once for females. The same approach would work for income quintiles. If a particular demographic factor is not statistically significant, then the fact that benefits do not vary with that demographic characteristic should be conveyed to the decision-maker. Knowing what distributional factors are not important can be valuable information to a decision-maker. We illustrate this approach below using the hedonic property method for determination of the changes in residential house prices in response to nearby forest fires. A parallel type of statistical analysis can be conducted in estimating the effects on suppliers, for example, including whether the firm is a small business, minority-owned business, and so on.

Even if the analyst does not estimate his or her own demand and supply functions, oftentimes the analyst is using someone else's demand or supply function to calculate benefits. Inspecting that function for significance of demographic factors will aid in determining if a particular demographic characteristic influences the benefits of the project. Even if an analyst uses elasticities or consumer surplus and/or producer surplus per unit of output, these are often derived from an underlying statistical function that can be inspected to determine if benefits vary by demographic variables of interest. If so, the benefits can be calculated for each relevant group by setting that variable at the levels of interest (e.g., income quintiles). The resulting distribution of benefits then can be displayed in a table for the decision-maker to review and implicitly weighted by the decision-maker in any way they want (including no differential weights at all).

2.2 Explicit Weighting of Net Benefits

One method to empirically incorporate equity or distributional concerns in the calculation of net benefits (i.e., benefits–cost) is to apply different weights to the net benefits of each group. Using an ad hoc pragmatic definition of groups, they could be any stakeholders of interest to the policy-maker. For example, the groups could be income classes (e.g., quintiles), ethnicities, gender, or rural versus urban consumers. Some groups have natural divisions such as gender or ethnicities, while for others it becomes the choice of the analyst. However, in the case where the grouping is chosen by the analyst, sensitivity analysis can be performed to determine if the segmentation of groups matter to the ranking of project or policy alternatives. Applying the weighting to net benefits has the advantage of incorporating the same weights on benefits and costs together in one number. However, displaying the original benefits and costs is often useful as well, as these essentially have a weight of 1 given to all income categories. This allows the decision-maker to see how the benefits and costs change from the baseline case of equal weights when alternative weights are applied. Weighted and unweighted net benefits need not be mutually exclusive, and together they may provide a more complete picture of the economic efficiency and equity dimensions of a project or policy.

However, ad hoc weights can undermine the utility theoretic foundation of benefits and costs as a measure of welfare or well-being. Prior to weighting, the theoretical measures of benefits and costs have a strong link to individual utility and well-being. Good practitioners strive to maintain the link between theory and empirical measurement of benefits and costs through estimation of demand functions consistent with utility maximization, for example. In order to link monetary net benefits to the social welfare function, the empirical distributional weights should reflect the marginal utility each distinct group receives from their net benefits. Drawing upon Starrett (1988), one way to do this is to weight the monetary net benefits received by each group by their marginal utility of income. If per capita incomes of each group are unequal, and there is diminishing marginal utility of income, then different income groups' monetary net benefits will be weighted differently in the social welfare function (ibid.).

But how strong is the case for diminishing marginal utility of income? Certainly it has some intuitive appeal in terms of the differences in utility of another $100 of income to a rich person versus a homeless person. Empirical observations of risk aversion when people make choices between uncertain outcomes is consistent with diminishing marginal utility of income. While Starrett lays out other rationales for diminishing marginal utility of income, in the end this is ultimately a value judgment. But of all the possible ways to weight benefits and costs, income-related weights have the tightest link to the underlying economic theory of welfare measurement. Thus, with income-based weights, the resulting net benefit measure is an attempt to provide a weighted sum of utilities to society. Alder (2008) suggests that benefit–cost analysts look to the optimal tax literature for a range of plausible social welfare functions. Along these lines Alder proposes risk-equity analysis of health and safety regulations that is "grounded" in the concept of the social welfare function.

2.3 A Revealed Preference Option for Calculating the Weights

Where might an analyst find empirical measures of these distributional weights? Herein lies the rub. One source of weights would be past government decisions involving equity trade-offs between groups. The differential tax rates in the US progressive income tax system might serve as a possible source of relative income weights (Gramlich, 1981). Thus, in the 2009 income tax year, a household with adjusted gross income of $10 000 pays a tax rate of 10 percent, with this tax rate increasing to 12 percent when income doubles to $20 000. A household earning $100 000 has a marginal tax rate of 28 percent on the earnings over $100 000 but less than $170 000. Households with earnings over $170 000 pay a marginal tax rate of 33 percent on this excess, up to $373 000. Earnings in excess of this amount are subject to a 35 percent marginal tax rate. There are of course numerous loopholes, including preferential treatment of capital gains, and clever accounting tricks to make the effective rate somewhat less for high-income households. Nonetheless, for the purposes of determining an explicit weighting of net benefits to each group, these tax rate percentages did reflect a consensus by a majority in Congress, with concurrence from the President of the United States, of a relative comparison of marginal utilities of income to different income groups. To use the tax rates as weights in a BCA, one would need to calculate the relative weights as the ratio of tax rates (Gramlich, 1981). For example, if we normalize on a 16 percent tax rate facing a middle class household ($50 000), then each dollar of benefit to the lowest-income household ($10 000) would be weighted by 1.6. Likewise, a dollar's worth of benefits to an upper-income household ($100 000) would be weighted by 0.57, and just 0.46 to richest households earning more than $373 000.

An advantage of relying upon a single nation-wide weighting standard is that it provides consistency in the weighting system used across projects and allows for greater comparability of the resulting benefit–cost ratios (BCRs). This avoids a concern about individual project by project weights chosen by decision-makers (a local agency official or locally elected representative with a stake in the outcome) that would not be comparable across projects.

2.4 A Relativist Approach to Calculating Weights

Brent (1996) discusses an approach by Thompson et al. (1984) to deal with equity in quantifying the net public benefits of reducing a health problem (i.e., different forms of arthritis) to patients. Thompson et al. used a stated preference type contingent valuation method survey to measure benefits in terms of willingness to pay (WTP). However, these authors were concerned that absolute dollar magnitude of WTP might be strongly influenced by income or ability to pay.[1]

If a strong positive link between WTP and income is believed to be the case, then Thompson et al. showed two ways to minimize this effect on benefit estimates. One is upfront in the survey itself, where in addition to eliciting the usual dollar amount of WTP, they also asked for WTP as a percentage of income. This willingness to pay a percentage of income would not be constrained by the absolute level of income. Arraying these percentages by income class would provide a relative comparison of the benefits to each income class. Second, the authors extended this first approach by multiplying the sample average percentage WTP by the *total* sample income to calculate the overall sample average dollar amount of WTP.

Brent suggests this approach by Thompson et al. is similar to calculating a weight for each group based on a comparison of the group income to the overall average income. Thus a low-income group with $20 000 per household income relative to the population average of say $40 000 would have its net benefits weighted by 2 ($W_i = (Avg\ Income/Income_i)$). Alternatively, net benefits to a high-income group with an income of $80 000 would get a weight 0.5.[2]

One advantage of this method is that the weights sum to 1, so that total net benefits are not overstated as would be the case if the weights summed to more than 1, or understated if the weights summed to less than 1. Another possible advantage is that since the weights are calculated as the ratio of household income of each group to the population's average income, the same weights could be applied across all project or policy BCAs. This provides consistency in the weighting system used across projects and allows for greater comparability of the resulting benefit–cost ratios.

Any of these approaches to weighting are not without their limitations. As such, regardless of the exact form of weights chosen, it is important to perform a sensitivity analysis using different weights to evaluate whether the ranking of projects by net present values (or benefit–cost ratios) is overly sensitive to a reasonable range of weights. One of those weights can be one for all groups, and hence would reflect the original benefits and costs. This can allow the decision-maker to see how the original benefits and costs change from the baseline case of equal weights when alternative weights are applied. If the BCRs or NPVs are not overly sensitive to the different weighting schemes chosen, then the analyst and decision-maker can have some confidence that the ranking of policy or project alternatives is not overly sensitive to how distribution concerns are treated. However, if the ranking of alternative projects is sensitive to the choice of weights, this too is important information for the decision-maker to know, as it focuses his or her attention on equity. Thus such a finding of sensitivity suggests the decision-maker devote some serious thought to what specific weights should be assigned to each group.

2.5 Lorenz Curve-based Approaches to Measure Distributional Effects

The inquiry regarding distributional concerns in economics is far broader than just BCA. As such, some measures of inequality that are commonly used to measure how equal or unequal the distribution of income is, can be useful for BCA. The Lorenz curve plots the cumulative percentage of income against the cumulative percentage of the population. If income was equally distributed, the relationship would be a straight line with a slope of 1. Of course it is not a straight line, as the first 20 percent of the population receives only about 4 percent of the income, and the upper 20 percent receives about 50 percent of the income. Farrow (2011) suggests this current relationship between income and population could be compared to a similar relationship for the project. In the case of the project, presumably the plot would be the cumulative percentage of the income versus cumulative percentage of project beneficiaries. If there is equal distribution of project benefits across the beneficiaries then the Lorenz curve would be a straight line with a slope of 1. The more the actual Lorenz curve bows or dips below this straight line, the more unequal the distribution of project benefits is. A further refinement of this procedure for policies that would have substantial effects on societal income would be to calculate what the Lorenz curve looks like before the new policy (i.e., the current situation), and then what the Lorenz curve would look like if the policy were implemented. This might provide a more complete and easily interpreted picture of the income distributional effects of such a major policy change.

One often overlooked aspect of BCA is that the results can provide feedback to project planners or policy analysts to modify the project or policy to make it more efficient or equitable. One way to apply the Lorenz curve to evaluate the distributional aspects of a project would be to display the distribution of net benefits of a project by income class. The resulting project Lorenz curve would be compared to the societal Lorenz curve of how income is distributed in the population to determine if the distribution of net benefits of a project would worsen the distribution of income. Such a calculation also illustrates how information on the distribution of benefits and costs of a project can be used to re-design elements of a project or its financing to change the distributional effects. If the project or policy has undesirable equity effects, then it may be possible to change the financing of the project to one emphasizing income taxes, rather than say sales taxes (as often used to finance open space, sports stadiums) or user fees (often used to finance mass transit). Alternatively, the beneficial projects such as light rail lines could have additional stops in poor neighborhoods so that poor households without cars could walk to stations. Of course the flip side would be that projects with undesirable distributional effects (e.g., new refineries) could be located further from poor neighborhoods.

A summary statistic that is derived from the Lorenz curve is called the Gini coefficient. This coefficient is defined as the ratio of two areas under the Lorenz curve. The numerator of the ratio is the area of the gap between the empirical Lorenz curve and the straight line. The denominator of the Lorenz curve is the total area under the straight line. The higher the Gini coefficient, the greater the inequality in the distribution. In the spirit of Farrow's above suggestion, the Gini coefficients could be compared between the project and the current income-based Gini coefficient to determine whether the project contributes to worsening or improving the distribution of income.

The Suits Index (Suits, 1977) is another measure of progressivity that can be applied to broad policies or changes in broad-based taxes, or to specific taxes (Loomis and Revier, 1988). As such, it has potential to provide an index of how project benefits vary with income and how specific taxes used to finance the project would vary with income. This information could provide feedback on modifying features of a project or policy, as well as the financing to improve equity.

Generating the type of data needed to calculate Lorenz curve measures can be accomplished using numerous techniques. As discussed in the previous sections, there can be single market or multiple market analyses, or economy-wide simulation models such as CGE. There is an extensive literature on empirically evaluating the distribution of market benefits and market costs on everything from the energy sector (i.e., natural gas—see Loury, 1983; gasoline—see Hughes, 1987) to minimum wages (Gramlich, 1990) to agricultural programs (Leuthold, 1969). However, for evaluating policies whose major benefits and costs are non-market in nature such as health or non-game wildlife and so on, these market-based models may be limited. While there has been recent research attempting to incorporate non-market values into CGE models (Espinosa and Smith, 1995), below we suggest adaptation of commonly used non-market valuation methods such as contingent valuation surveys and hedonic property models.

3 EMPIRICAL EXAMPLES OF INCORPORATING NON-MARKET DISTRIBUTIONAL CONCERNS INTO BCA

3.1 Using Survey Demographics to Display How Non-market Benefits Vary by Income

To illustrate the reliance upon surveys to display and evaluate whether there is any pattern of environmental benefits by income class, an example is developed in this section. Contingent valuation method (CVM) surveys are frequently used to quantify WTP for environmental quality (e.g., air quality, water quality, health, recreation) and can be framed to explicitly incorporate WTP for providing public goods to other low-income families (Loomis, et al., 2009) or for improving distributional consequences of a program (Vining and Weimer, 2010). In our case study the survey asked respondents for their WTP for river-based recreation and total economic value (use and passive or non-use value). Respondent WTP was then partitioned by income groups using survey respondent demographics. Of course CVM estimates of WTP are subject to significant controversy over their validity (Diamond and Hausman, 1994; Hanemann, 1994; Portney, 1994), but for our purposes,

Table 9.1 *Distribution of households' total economic value and visitors' recreation value by income*

Income ($)	Total Economic Value (Annual) ($)	Recreation Value per Trip ($)
7500	235	3
15000	174	11
25000	85	6
35000	93	6
45000	73	13
55000	81	17
68000	125	9
88000	167	23
125000	144	10
175000	95	10
250000	90	6
350000	500	0

Source: Loomis (2008).

it is the relative distribution of benefits across income groups that may be informative to decision-makers as there is no reason to believe that the hypothetical bias varies with income.

As an illustration of this approach, consider the results from a mail survey of Fort Collins, Colorado residents. The survey had a relatively high response rate of 65 percent of deliverable surveys. Of course a further check of the representativeness of the demographics contained in this sample could be conducted by comparing the sample demographics to the Census Bureau estimates of these same demographics, and weighting the sample demographics to reflect the population estimates.

In the CVM survey, residents were asked the maximum amount they would pay annually to avoid a 50 percent reduction in peak summer river flows. Visitors were also asked the maximum they would pay for a visit to the river as it flows through town. Table 9.1 illustrates the distribution of total economic value (use plus passive use) and recreation benefits of maintaining peak May–July instream flows in the Poudre River through the City of Fort Collins, Colorado by income level. Respondents were told the current May–July flows would protect riparian vegetation, as well as fish and bird populations. In addition, a paved bike path that thousands of residents use follows the river. During the high flow periods, the river provides locals with water-based recreation opportunities such as tubing and fishing.

As illustrated in Table 9.1, there is no real pattern of total economic values or recreation use values by income. This suggests that there would be no concerns on the distribution of benefits for either visitors or households of a policy that would maintain the current levels of instream flows.

However, on the cost side, the distributional burden may depend on how maintaining instream flows is to be financed. To address the cost side, the field of public finance can provide some insights. If maintaining instream flows was financed by increasing the sales tax rate or water bills, then it may be considered a regressive tax in that the tax would be a higher percentage of poor households' income than that of affluent households. If the instream flow program was financed by increasing property taxes, since housing expenditures rise with income (although the income elasticity is less than one; see Zabel, 2004 for a review), property taxes rise with income. However, given the income elasticity, financing by property taxes could still be regressive.

3.2 How the Hedonic Property Method Can Aid in Quantifying Distributional Impacts of Environmental Effects

As noted previously one way to determine if there are distributional differences in benefits or costs when using a statistical method such as multiple regression is to test whether the coefficient on different demographics is statistically different from zero. For example, is the coefficient on income or gender statistically significant? If not, then one could interpret this as no significant difference in response to price or consumer surplus calculated from the demand curve by income levels. To illustrate this procedure we use the hedonic property method or HPM. This method utilizes data from real estate transactions to infer how house prices change with changes in dozens of attributes surrounding a neighborhood. Using multiple regression of differences in house prices across different neighborhoods, HPM can estimate the absolute and percentage change in house prices related to, for example, reduction in air pollution, improvements in public transit, reduction in crime, improvement in school quality, and so on. Comparing the percentage change in house prices in low-income neighborhoods to other neighborhoods that arise due to a government permitting a new landfill would allow for identification of distributional effects on low-income residents relative to the general population.

More specifically, the HPM uses multiple regression to quantify how house prices fall with proximity to a waste site, source of pollution or adverse land use (e.g., landfill, oil refinery). A variable for distance to the pollution source is one way to measure the effect of pollution on house prices. If minority or low-income households are located closer to these pollution sources, the relative adverse effect of the pollution source on house prices would be substantially greater on these nearby houses than would be the effect on houses located further away. For example, if prices of similar size homes in a minority neighborhood located a half a mile from the pollution source are 20 percent lower than house prices in a non-minority neighborhood located two miles away from the pollution source, then one might conclude the environmental costs of this pollution source are disproportionately borne by nearby minority residents. However, on the flip side, a government clean-up program or order to the owner of the pollution source to reduce emissions would provide a disproportionate benefit to minority households, a desirable distributional effect, since minority-owned houses would rise in value by 20 percent.

Like many modeling analyses, this one would require certain assumptions be met for the results to be accurate. First, that most minority households are owners rather than renters, a condition that may not be met. If minorities are renters then any change in residence price accrues to the landowner. However, even in this case, the change in monthly rental rate may provide some indication of the gain from a government clean-up program to the renters. Second, to rely upon the marginal implicit prices that are estimated from the simple first stage regression requires that policy being evaluated is not so major that it changes the structure of the housing market. For large non-marginal changes in the housing market, the marginal implicit prices will overstate the value of gains, and understate the value of losses. In addition, there may very well be changes in relative mean incomes in the area (Banzhaf and Walsh, 2008) due to a shifting composition of households as a result of the public or environmental changes in the area brought about by the policy.

The strength of HPM is its utilization of actual market data on house prices to infer WTP for improving neighborhood attributes like air quality, public transit, public safety, and so on. In order to determine how much of the house price is related to pollution or crime versus the features of the house (e.g., number of bedrooms, bathrooms, lot size) and locational attributes (e.g., distance to work centers, recreation, and schools), a multivariate relationship is specified of the form:

$$P = \text{func}\,(E, S, N) \tag{9.1}$$

Where P is the house price, E are the location-specific attributes such as distance to amenities like public transit stations or disamenities such as landfills, or refineries or localized pollution concentrations in the area. S are the house characteristics such as the number of bedrooms and bathrooms. N are neighborhood social and demographic variables such as percentage non-white, income, and education levels. These are typically tied to zip code or Census Tract.

As shown in equation (9.2) below, it is by interacting the minority variable or income variable with the policy variable of interest (e.g., pollution, public transit) that allows an analyst to determine if there is a differential effect of the policy variable on house prices of low-income or minority households. Equation (9.2) provides an example of such a specification:

$$\begin{aligned}\text{Log (Real Sale Amount)} &= \beta_0 + \beta_1 * \text{(Distance to Refinery)} + \\ &\beta_2 * \text{(Square Feet of House)} + \beta_3 * \text{(Median Household Income)} + \\ &\beta_4 * \text{(Distance to Refinery * Median Household Income)} \\ &+ \beta_5 * \text{(\% Non-white)} + \\ &\beta_6 * \text{(\% Non-white * Distance to Refinery)} + \ldots \end{aligned} \tag{9.2}$$

From this model, the coefficient β_1 indicates how house prices increase as the distance the house is located from the refinery increases (since pollution would decrease). Whether that house price increase is different for houses located in low-income neighborhoods would be tested by whether the interaction term on β_4 is significantly different from zero. The same test on β_6 would indicate whether there is a differential effect on house price increase for minority neighborhoods.

Using the coefficients (the βs) in equation (9.2) an analyst can calculate the dollar change in house prices related to changes in environmental quality. This dollar change can be standardized into the percentage change in house prices making a relative comparison that adjusts for different house price values of minority or low-income residents relative to the general population.

Thus, HPM provides an economic model that monetizes the distribution of pollution costs or clean-up benefits to minority or low-income populations in urban areas. While the HPM is typically estimated on residential housing (e.g., single family homes), it has been applied to monthly rental rates paid at rental properties such as apartments.

3.3 Example of Hedonic Property Value Analysis of the Effect of Nearby Forest Fires on Hispanic and Low-income Residents' Home Prices

House price sales data were collected in the foothills region of Los Angeles including high-income areas such as Pasadena and lower-income areas such as San Fernando. Both of these areas were near two different, but equivalent size fires. House sale amount is hypothesized to be related to:

- distance the house is from the forest fire (which is treated as our hazard);
- square footage of the house;
- percentage of the Census block that is Hispanic;
- interaction of percentage of Hispanic with distance to the fire (to test for a differential effect of distance of forest fire on neighborhoods that have a higher percentage of Hispanics);
- median household income of the Census block;
- interaction of median household income with distance to the fire (to test for differential effect of distance to forest fire by income).

Three environmental control variables are included:

- distance to US Forest Service land (i.e., National Forest);
- distance to City of Los Angeles (the major employment center);
- elevation above sea level.

Equation (9.3) provides the multiple regression that is used to estimate the βs:

$$\begin{aligned} &\text{Ln (House Sale Amount)} = \beta_0 + \beta_1{*}\text{ (Distance to Fire)} + \\ &\beta_2 * \text{(House Square Footage)} - \beta_3 * \text{(\% Hispanic)} + \\ &\beta_4 * \text{(\% Hispanic * Distance to Fire)} + \beta_5 * \text{(Median Household Income)} \\ &+ \beta_6 * \text{(Median Household Income * Distance to Fire)} + \\ &\beta_7 * \text{(Distance to US FS Land)} + \beta_8 * \text{(Distance to Los Angeles)} \\ &+ \beta_9 * \text{(Elevation)} \end{aligned} \tag{9.3}$$

The slope coefficient β_1 is the baseline increase in house price as distance from the forest fire area increases. Statistical differences from the baseline effect of a forest fire on house prices between white and Hispanic neighborhoods are tested by whether β_4 is significantly different from zero using a t-test. The same t-test is employed on β_6 to determine if the effect of a forest fire varies with income.

The R-squared reported in Table 9.2 indicates the estimated model explains 50 percent of the variation in house prices in this area of Southern California. The house square footage is statistically significant and of the expected sign (e.g., as house square footage increases, house prices increase). The Hispanic–Distance to Fire interaction term is statistically significant and negative. This suggests that houses prices in neighborhoods with a higher percentage of Hispanic populations have a significantly ($p < 1\%$) different magnitude of response than white neighborhoods to nearby forest fires. The same pattern is evident with respect to low-income

Table 9.2 Relationship between house prices and distance to forest fires, Hispanics and income

Dependent Variable: Log House Sale Price, N = 7664				
Variable	Coefficient	Std Error	t-statistic	Probability
Constant	11.50900	0.2183	52.702	0.0000
Log(Distance to Fire)	0.087687	0.0272	3.2165	0.0013
Elevation	−0.00023	1.38E−05	−17.117	0.0000
House Sq. Feet	0.00032	5.84E−06	56.057	0.0000
% Hispanics	−0.00347	0.0005	−6.1571	0.0000
% Hisp* Distance to Fire	−5.59E−07	1.97E−07	−2.8404	0.0045
Household Income	4.00E−06	4.22E−07	9.4696	0.0000
Income*Distance to Fire	−5.77E−10	1.31E−10	−4.4156	0.0000
Distance to US FS Land	−1.19E−05	3.73E−06	−3.1979	0.0014
Distance to Los Angeles	−1.63E−06	4.82E−07	−3.3760	0.0007
R-squared	0.508	Mean dependent var.		12.38563
Adjusted R-squared	0.507	S.D. dependent var.		0.48238
F-statistic	879.500	Prob(F-statistic)		0.00000

neighborhoods. That is, the house price response to a nearby forest fire in low-income neighborhoods is statistically different ($p < 1\%$) than house price response in higher-income neighborhoods. To test the sensitivity of this analysis to one of the assumptions listed above with respect to owner versus renter occupied homes, the regression was re-run with percentage of renter occupied as one of the variables. This variable was statistically insignificant ($p = 0.1483$). Only about 24 percent of the residences in the study area were occupied by renters, so most of the benefits and costs of fire management is borne by owners of the properties who live there.

However, statistically significant differences between income groups or races are only part of the story. Whether those statistically significant differences are economically significant is equally important. We can convert the coefficients to an absolute change in house price by multiplying the coefficient times mean house price ($239 338 in 1993 prices). Houses in white neighborhoods adjacent to an area that has experienced a forest fire are worth $7884 less than houses a mile away, holding all other factors constant. This is due to homebuyers' perceived higher risk of being close to an area with forest fires. However, for predominantly Hispanic neighborhoods adjacent to an area that has experienced a forest fire, the reduction in house price is smaller, at $4539 less than houses a mile away. Thus forest fires have about half the effect on house prices in a predominantly Hispanic neighborhood as that of white neighborhoods. Considering house prices in predominantly Hispanic neighborhoods sell for less ($218 533, as our coefficient on percentage Hispanic suggests), the percentage drop in house price next to the fire represents a 2 percent loss in house price for Hispanic neighborhoods versus 3.3 percent for white neighborhoods. Expressing this percentage reduction in house price as a percentage of income, the loss in house price represents about 9 percent of income for Hispanic households and about 11 percent for white households. Similar calculations of the effect on house prices for lower-income neighborhoods show that low-income neighborhoods (those with incomes $20 000 less than our median) would lose $5212 by being adjacent to a fire versus a mile away. This too is smaller than the drop in house prices of median income neighborhoods.

These hedonic property analysis results can be utilized in two different ways. First, the impact of a federal government "let it burn" policy that has been applied to naturally started forest fires (e.g., lightning), especially those in Wilderness areas (some of which are adjacent to Wildland Urban Interface areas) would not have serious distributional concerns. Specifically, the absolute and percentage loss in house prices from being adjacent to a forest fire, is about half for minority and low-income neighborhoods compared with white and median-income neighborhoods. On the flip side, government agency expenditures on forest fire prevention projects that would reduce forest fires adjacent to white and Hispanic neighborhoods would yield larger absolute and percentage gains in value in white neighborhoods than in Hispanic neighborhoods. This might raise distributional concerns depending on how the government forest fire prevention programs were financed. Nonetheless, this example illustrates how the hedonic property method can be used to evaluate the absolute and relative effects of forest fire management decisions on minority and low-income households.

4 CONCLUSIONS

Government agencies are increasingly required to address distribution and equity in their economic analysis of projects, policies, and regulations. This discussion has presented a wide range of approaches to provide information on the distribution of benefits and costs by displaying the differential effects by income classes, age groups or ethnicity or any other stakeholder group of interest. Quantitative comparisons of the distributional consequences can also be made using a Gini coefficient, so as to formalize comparisons of distributional effects across BCA alternatives. In addition, specific weighting of net benefits can be performed to reflect judgments about relative importance of a dollar's worth of benefits to different income class, ethnicities or any other relevant stakeholder group characteristic. To judge the effects of major policies that affect market goods in multiple markets throughout an economy, simulation models of the economy such as computable general equilibrium models may be necessary. For the case of non-market goods, econometric methods and surveys provide a means to statistically test if non-market benefits such as health or environmental benefits vary by income, gender, age, ethnicity, and so on. Contingent valuation surveys that collect demographic data on respondents are a natural way to quantify how benefits and costs vary for each group of interest. This chapter illustrated the application of contingent valuation to measure the benefits to different income households by way of an empirical example of the benefits of protecting instream flows in an urban area. The chapter also illustrated how a hedonic property model can statistically test for and quantify differential effects of public policies or programs on house prices of minority or low-income owners. In the end, BCAs are likely to contribute more relevant information to decision-makers, and carry more weight in the ultimate decisions if we extend our BCAs to reflect distributional concerns associated with a project or policy.

NOTES

1. Not all health or even environmental CVM studies find a strong link with income, suggesting that substitution rather than income effects are often driving stated choices—see Loomis et al. (2009), and Loomis and duVair (1993), and a meta-analysis by Costa-Font et al. (2009).
2. A further refinement of this method would be to include an exponent on the W_i so that it is not just a linear function of the group's relative income.

REFERENCES

Alder, Matthew (2008), "Risk equity: A new proposal," *Harvard Environmental Law Review*, **32**, 1–47.

Banzhaf, Spencer and Randall Walsh (2008), "Do people vote with their feet? An empirical test of Tiebout's mechanism," *American Economic Review*, **98** (3), 843–63.

Berck, Peter and Sandra Hoffmann (2002), "Assessing the employment impacts of environmental and natural resource policy," *Environmental and Resource Economics*, **22** (1), 133–56.

Boadway, Robin (1979), *Public Sector Economics*, Cambridge, MA: Winthrop Publishers Inc.

Brent, Robert (1996), *Applied Cost–Benefit Analysis*, Aldershot, UK and Brookfield, VT, USA: Edward Elgar.

Costa-Font, Joan, Alistair McGuire, and Thomas Stanley (2009), "Health care

as a luxury: Winner's curse and publication selection bias," unpublished manuscript, London: London School of Economics and Political Science.
Diamond, Peter and Jerry Hausman (1994), "Contingent valuation: Is some number better than no number?," *Journal of Economic Perspectives*, **8** (4), 45–64.
Espinosa, Andrés and V. Kerry Smith (1995), "Measuring the environmental consequences of trade policy: A nonmarket CGE analysis," *American Journal of Agricultural Economics*, **77** (3), 772–7.
Farrow, Scott (2011), "Incorporating equity in regulatory and benefit–cost analysis using risk based preferences," *Risk Analysis*, **31** (6), 902–7.
Fullerton, Donald (2009), *Distributional Effects of Environmental and Energy Policy*, Farnham, UK: Ashgate Publishers.
Graham, James (2008), "Saving lives through administrative law and economics," *University of Pennsylvania Law Review*, **157**, 395–538.
Gramlich, E. (1981), *Benefit–Cost Analysis of Government Programs*, Englewood Cliffs, NJ: Prentice Hall.
Gramlich, Edward (1990), *A Guide to Benefit–Cost Analysis*, Englewood Cliffs, NJ: Prentice Hall.
Hammitt, James (2009), "Response—saving lives: Benefit–cost analysis and distribution," *University of Pennsylvania Law Review*, **157**, 395–538.
Hanemann, Michael (1994), "Valuing the environment through contingent valuation," *Journal of Economic Perspectives*, **8** (4), 19–43.
Harberger, Arnold (1984), "Basic needs versus distributional weights in social benefit cost analysis," *Economic Development and Cultural Change*, **32** (3), 455–74.
Hughes, Gordon (1987), "The incidence of fuel taxes: A comparative study of three countries," in D. Newbery and N. Stern (eds), *The Theory of Taxation for Development*, New York: Oxford University Press.
Jenkins, G. (1999), "Evaluation of stakeholder impacts in cost–benefit analysis," *Impact Assessment and Project Appraisal*, **17**, 87–96.
Just, Richard, Darrell Hueth, and Andrew Schmitz (1982), *Applied Welfare Economics and Public Policy*, Englewood Cliffs, NJ: Prentice Hall.
Krutilla, Kerry (2005), "Using the Kaldor–Hicks tableau format for cost benefit analysis and policy evaluation," *Journal of Policy Analysis and Management*, **24** (4), 864–5.
Leuthold, Raymond (1969), "Government payments and the distribution of income in agriculture," *American Journal of Agricultural Economics*, **51** (5), 1520–23.
Long, David, Charles Mallar, and Craig Thornton (1981), "Evaluating the benefits and costs of the job corps," *Journal of Policy Analysis and Management*, **1** (1), 55–76.
Loomis, John (2008), 'Estimating the economic benefits of maintaining peak instream flows in the Poudre River through Fort Collins, Colorado', Dept. of Agricultural and Resource Economics, Colorado State University, Fort Collins, Colorado.
Loomis, John and Pierre duVair (1993), "Evaluating the effect of alternative risk communication devices on willingness to pay: Results from a dichotomous choice contingent valuation experiment," *Land Economics*, **69** (3), 287–98.
Loomis, John and Charles Revier (1988), "Measuring regressivity of excise taxes: A buyers index," *Public Finance Quarterly*, **16** (3), 301–14.
Loomis, John, Paul Bell, Helen Zita-Cooney, and Cheryl Asmus (2009), "A

comparison of actual and hypothetical willingness to pay of parents and non-parents for protecting infant health: The case of nitrates in drinking water," *Journal of Agricultural and Applied Economics*, **41** (3), 697–712.
Loury, Gordon (1983), "Efficiency and equity impacts of natural gas regulation," in R. Haveman and J. Margolis (eds), *Public Expenditure and Policy Analysis*, 3rd edition, Boston, MA: Houghton Mifflin.
Portney, Paul (1994), "The contingent valuation debate: why economists should care," *Journal of Economic Perspectives*, **8** (4), 3–17.
Schmitz, Andrew and Troy Schmitz (2010), "Benefit–cost analysis: Distributional considerations under production quota buyouts," *Journal of Benefit–Cost Analysis*, **1** (1) Article 2.
Starrett, David (1988), *Foundations of Public Economics*, New York: Cambridge University Press.
Suits, Daniel (1977), "Measurement of tax progressivity," *American Economic Review*, **67**, 747–52.
Thompson, Michael, John Read, and M. Liang (1984), "Feasibility of willingness to pay measurement in chronic arthritis," *Medical Decision Making*, **4** (2), 195–215.
Tresch, Robert (1981), *Public Finance: A Normative Theory*, Texas: Business Publications.
US Environmental Protection Agency (2000), *Guidelines for Preparing Economic Analyses*, EPA 240-R-00-003, Washington, DC.
Vining, Aidan and David Weimer (2010), "An assessment of important issues concerning the application of benefit cost analysis to social policy," *Journal of Benefit–Cost Analysis*, **1** (1), Article 6.
Zabel, Jeffrey (2004), "The demand for housing services," *Journal of Housing Economics*, **13** (4), 16–35.
Zerbe, Jr., Richard O. (2007), "Ethical benefit–cost analysis," Berkeley Electronic Press (BEP), accessed 17 October 2012 at http://works.bepress.com/richard_zerbe/3.
Zerbe, Richard and Dwight Dively (1994), *Benefit–Cost Analysis in Theory and Practice*, New York: Harper Collins.

10. Behavioral economics and the conduct of benefit–cost analysis: towards principles and standards

Lisa A. Robinson and James K. Hammitt

1 INTRODUCTION

Policy-makers face difficult choices in determining how to best allocate scarce resources across social programs and other desirable goods and services. Benefit–cost analysis provides useful information for these decisions, by indicating the extent to which the values that individuals place on program outcomes are likely to exceed program costs. Determining these values has always been challenging, however. Most social programs lead at least in part to outcomes for which no market value exists, such as improved health and longevity or environmental quality. Instead, these values must be estimated from market behavior for related goods or by asking individuals about their willingness to pay. Recent research in behavioral economics adds to the complexity of this task, documenting ways in which individuals at times appear to act irrationally or contrary to their own interests.[1]

This chapter supports the development of principles and standards for conducting benefit–cost analyses of social programs, focusing on the implications of behavioral economics for how outcomes are valued in monetary terms. We review traditional practices, discuss findings from behavioral research, and recommend ways in which these findings might be integrated into benefit–cost analyses. We take the perspective of an analyst who has been asked to evaluate a given set of policy options and is curious about how behavioral economics might influence the assessment. We concentrate largely on empirical research results and their practical application, while recognizing that theory provides a useful, albeit simplified, model of reality that can help promote rigorous thinking about these issues.

Behavioral economics is a large and rapidly growing field, and has not yet evolved into a unified theory that provides a cohesive alternative or supplement to the standard economic model. Its status has several implications for our discussion. First, the dividing line between behavioral economics and conventional neoclassical economics is often murky. Both address behavior, and many findings identified as behavioral economics can be accommodated within the standard model. Second, while researchers have found an increasing number of behavioral deviations from neoclassical economic assumptions, it is not yet clear how significant many of these deviations are in terms of magnitude or pervasiveness. Much of the research involves small-scale laboratory experiments and needs to be supplemented by additional fieldwork to explore the real-world importance of the findings. Third, these deviations are often dependent on the context, and more work is needed to determine whether the deviations found in the contexts frequently studied (e.g., financial decisions) are equally important in the context of the policy decisions we consider. Finally, the rapid growth in related research means that it is not possible to be comprehensive. We select key topics for detailed consideration rather than attempting to review the entire literature. Because we are drafting this chapter as behavioral economics evolves in significant ways, we often raise questions or pose alternatives without attempting to resolve the underlying issues, describing concerns that researchers and analysts may wish to consider.

Below, we briefly summarize the distinction between behavioral and neoclassical economics, then introduce the features of the benefit–cost analysis framework that are the focus of this chapter. The remaining sections then discuss each topic in turn.

1.1 Behavioral vs Neoclassical Economics

"Behavioral" economics is somewhat of a misnomer, because all economics is concerned with how people behave in economic contexts. Behavioral economists often distinguish their work by noting that, in its simplest form, the standard economic model assumes that people behave self-interestedly and rationally (as "econs" or "homo economicus"), while they consider how human behavior may deviate from this model. However, this framing oversimplifies the neoclassical model and ignores other distinguishing features.

Behavioral economics has grown largely from the increased integration of psychological research into the models used to explain or predict economic behavior. In this respect, the distinction between neoclassical and behavioral economics may be largely a matter of emphasis. In addition, as discussed below, neoclassical economics often relies on expected utility theory as initially formulated by von Neumann and Morgenstern in the mid-1940s, while behavioral economics reflects challenges to that model, beginning most notably with work by Kahneman and Tversky and by Thaler in the late 1970s and early 1980s.

Thaler and Mullainathan (2008) provide an example of how behavioral economists distinguish their work. They argue that the standard economic model assumes three unrealistic traits: unbounded rationality, unbounded willpower, and unbounded selfishness. Bounded rationality recognizes that humans have limited capacity to process information, so often do not solve problems optimally. Instead, we may come to conclusions based on heuristics or simple decision rules. Bounded willpower reflects humans' incomplete self-control. We may engage in unhealthy behavior (such as eating or drinking too much, saving too little, or smoking) while at the same time recognizing that such behavior is damaging. Bounded selfishness refers to the fact that we may act selflessly. The neoclassical model is more complex than recognized in this description and can accommodate many behavioral findings, as discussed in more detail below. For example, other-regarding preferences (such as altruism and existence values) have long been recognized within the standard model.

An important element of behavioral economics is the rejection of expected utility theory as a model of decision-making under uncertainty. Expected utility theory assumes individuals assign utilities to consequences and prefer the choice that maximizes the expected value of this utility. In contrast, prospect theory (Kahneman and Tversky, 1979) and related models suggest that preferences depend on the reference point from which they are measured (with losses valued more than gains and diminishing sensitivity with increasing distance from the reference point) and that probabilities are evaluated non-linearly (with changes in probabilities near 0 and 1 more important than changes in intermediate probabilities). While some characterize the assumptions of expected utility theory as "rational" and alternatives to that theory as "irrational," both models are simplifications. For the purpose of benefit–cost analysis, our goal is to understand individual preferences over the outcomes of concern. If these preferences are reasonably well informed and stable, then they are useful for understanding the relative merits of different policies regardless of whether they are consistent with standard theory or an alternative model.

In this chapter, we are primarily concerned with the use of behavioral data to determine preferences for, or the value of, the outcomes of social programs. Bernheim and Rangel (2007, p. 7) note that:

> [p]ublic economics has positive and normative objectives; it aims both to describe the effects of public policies and to evaluate them. This agenda requires us to formulate models of human decision-making with two components—one describing choices, and the other describing well-being. Using the first component, we can forecast the effects of policy reforms on individuals' actions, as

well as on prices and allocations. Using the second component, we can determine whether these changes benefit consumers or harm them.

This distinction between behavior and welfare is not necessary under the traditional economic model. That model assumes that individuals choose what they want, that is, that their preferences are revealed through their behavior.

While there is no consensus on how to evaluate welfare given this distinction, Bernheim and Rangel (2007) describe two options.[2] One is to continue to rely on revealed preferences, expanding how we think about preferences to include deviations from the standard model. The second is to modify or reject revealed preferences, using preferences to measure welfare only in those cases where they appear consistent with the individual's self-interest. While proposed to protect against decision-making errors, this more paternalistic approach may be abused if individual preferences can be overridden without adequate, evidence-based justification. This tension between unquestioning acceptance of individual choices and acceptance of only those that are judged to be rational and welfare-enhancing is at the heart of many of the implications of behavioral economics for how we conduct benefit–cost analysis.

1.2 Behavior and Benefit–Cost Analysis

Implementing benefit–cost analysis involves several iterative and intertwined steps to characterize the affected universe, with and without the policy intervention, and assess the incremental social costs and benefits. We provide a simplified overview of this process in Figure 10.1.[3]

There is no principled distinction between costs and benefits: costs can be defined as negative benefits and vice versa. Typically, however, costs are defined as the opportunity costs of the real resources expended to develop, implement, and operate a program or to comply with government or other requirements, including any market impacts. Benefits typically include the monetary value of the outcomes that are the goal of the policy: improved education, increased safety, greater employment, enhanced housing, and so forth. Ideally, any significant side-effects (cost savings or ancillary benefits) are included, and the implications of non-quantified effects and uncertainty are carefully assessed. While these analyses provide important and useful information, policy decisions are rarely, if ever, based solely on their results. Decision-makers often seek additional information that cannot be easily captured in economic analysis.

Behavior, and the implications of behavioral economics research, permeate each step of a benefit–cost analysis. They also influence how

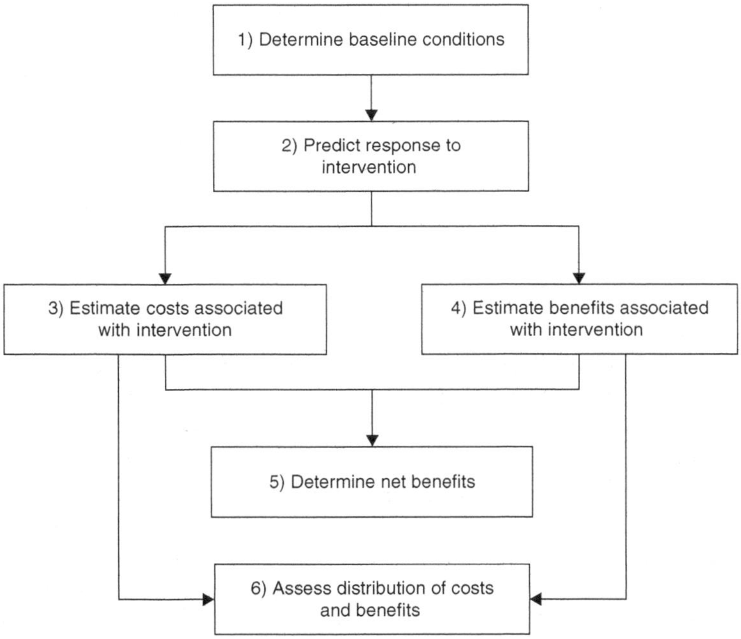

Figure 10.1 Simplified overview of benefit–cost analysis

policy decisions are made and how the public perceives the impacts. Some analytic steps involve predicting future behavior, while others use behavior more indirectly to value non-market outcomes. We focus largely on the latter issues, because they raise more difficult issues for the analyst.

We do not discuss the implications of behavioral economics in two areas that are also important in this context. First, we do not consider its implications for predicting how individuals or organizations will behave; neither for determining current and potential future baseline conditions in the absence of intervention, nor for estimating responses to different policies. For example, behavioral economics is helpful in forecasting how individuals are likely to respond to information provision (e.g., on the caloric content of food or on the energy efficiency of appliances or cars), including information on the trade-off between short-term costs and longer-term savings.[4] A well-conducted analysis attempts to be as realistic as possible; it seems self-evident that analysts should use whatever information appears likely to improve their predictions, regardless of whether the behavior appears rational or welfare-enhancing. The implications of behavioral economics for these types of predictions are diverse, vary significantly across different contexts, and are addressed in a large and rapidly growing literature.[5]

Second, we do not discuss the role of behavioral economics in estimating social costs. The focus on real resource expenditures means that market data are often used to estimate monetary values, and such data already reflect behavioral influences. In the case of a small program (such as a local addiction treatment center), the analyst is likely to be concerned primarily with direct expenditures on wages and benefits, space rental, equipment, supplies, and so forth, which can be directly estimated from market prices. Implementation of the program is not likely to significantly change these prices.

When a program is large enough to noticeably affect market conditions, price changes are more likely. In these cases, analysts again may be able to rely on market data that already reflect any associated behavioral anomalies (e.g., observed supply or demand elasticities). In other cases, analysts may need to predict impacts outside the range of the available data. In this case, consideration of behavioral factors becomes more important because resource costs may differ from those that would be estimated if the markets functioned in accordance with the standard model. As an example, if consumers undervalue future cost savings from adopting compact fluorescent light bulbs or more fuel-efficient motor vehicles (because of hyperbolic discounting, as discussed in section 3), the demand for these products will be lower than might otherwise be predicted. As a result, market prices and the estimated costs of requiring these more efficient products will be higher than if consumers evaluated future cost savings using exponential discounting.[6]

These considerations are closely linked. Predicting baseline and post-intervention conditions is intertwined with understanding how individuals and organizations react to costs and prices. For example, individual decisions (and any associated behavioral anomalies) may determine program size (e.g., the number of addicts served by a new center and the efficacy of the treatment), in turn affecting those costs that vary with participation rates.[7]

Once we begin to consider the monetary valuation of non-market outcomes, the potential distinction between choices and welfare increases in importance for two reasons. First, the value of these outcomes must be inferred; we generally cannot predict it directly from market prices. Second, if individuals' behavior suggests preferences that appear irrational, unstable, or contrary to their self-interest, choosing a policy to satisfy those preferences may not improve social well-being. In this case, we face difficult decisions. We could use the resulting values (or a range of values) in our analysis, we could explore the effects of providing more education or experience, or we could substitute expert judgment. Each of these options raises thorny practical and philosophical issues.

In this chapter, we take the perspective that benefit–cost analysis should attempt to describe, rather than prescribe, individual preferences. In other words, analysts should avoid making judgments about whether values are "rational" or "irrational," but instead attempt to ensure that studies are designed to elicit well-informed, thoughtful preferences. "Mistakes" or "errors" may occur when choices diverge from how an individual would define his or her own preferences given adequate reflection and self-control, absent the biases that may result from cognitive or emotional challenges. While perfection in decision-making may be impossible, our hope is to at least attempt to avoid paternalistic views of what individuals "should" prefer, deferring to the preferences that individuals express when provided opportunities for contemplation and learning. In other words, we maintain the traditional reliance on individuals' own definition of their welfare, while recognizing that education and experience may be needed to aid them in developing a reliable understanding of how particular choices might support their well-being.[8]

Data limitations play an important role in benefit–cost analyses, particularly in valuing non-market effects. The research base rarely includes studies that address an outcome that is identical in all respects to the outcome of a particular social policy. Time and resource constraints mean that analysts are generally unable to conduct new primary valuation research. Instead, they follow the benefit transfer framework, which involves taking values developed in one context (a primary research study or group of studies) and applying them in a somewhat dissimilar context (the policy analysis) based on careful review of the literature. While values may be adjusted to reflect differences in the characteristics of the outcomes or the affected population, the available research is often insufficient to support quantitative adjustment. These differences are frequently addressed in more qualitative terms. Analysts can explore the resulting uncertainty using sensitivity or probabilistic analysis, or by examining breakeven values, that is, the values at which the benefits of a policy no longer exceed its costs, or at which the ranking of the policy options changes. Because using multiple values and/or discussing these issues qualitatively can complicate presentation of the results, analysts need to carefully summarize the implications for busy decision-makers.

In the sections that follow, we begin by discussing several issues related to the implications of behavioral research for defining what it is that we are trying to measure, regardless of whether we are conducting primary research or reviewing studies for benefit transfer. In section 2, we focus specifically on benefits, considering how behavioral research might affect the attributes included in non-market valuation studies. In section 3, we turn to the discounting of costs and benefits to reflect their timing. Section 4 discusses the distinction between private and social preferences. In section 5, we turn to issues related to the quality of valuation studies, considering how behavioral research might affect their design and implementation.

Section 6 concludes by looking at the more general implications of behavioral economics. Although the goal of benefit–cost analysis is normative, that is, to identify the preferred policy from the perspective of economic efficiency, practitioners often advocate it because of its positive, descriptive components: it investigates what individuals would prefer (given the current distribution of income and other baseline conditions) and summarizes the results, rather than relying solely on the (perhaps unarticulated) preferences of decision-makers.[9] Substituting expert judgment for observed choices is a slippery slope: there is often no clear dividing line between irrational and rational decisions or stable and unstable preferences. Behavior that appears irrational or unstable on the surface may in fact reflect an underlying rationality; the problem may be that the investigator simply has not discovered or does not understand the rationale.[10] As Smith (2007) notes, experts make mistakes too, and there is no consensus on whose expert judgment should prevail. Thus, as discussed in section 6, we advocate a pragmatic view of these analyses as attempting to reflect the thoughtful, well-informed preferences of those affected to the greatest extent possible.

2 VALUING PSYCHOLOGICAL ATTRIBUTES

The value of the benefits of social programs—such as those targeted on reducing crime, increasing education, improving housing, or decreasing environmental, health, or safety risks—frequently cannot be fully captured by directly referencing market behavior. Instead, these values are estimated through revealed and stated preference research. Revealed preference studies use data from market transactions or observed behavior to estimate the value of related non-market goods, while stated preference studies involve asking respondents how they would behave in a hypothetical market. Regardless of whether they are conducting new primary research or transferring values from existing studies, analysts need to start with a clear definition of the key attributes of the outcome of interest. In this section, we discuss how behavioral research might affect the attributes that analysts consider important.

As noted earlier, behavioral economics highlights ways in which psychological responses may lead to values that appear irrational or inconsistent with the standard economic model. For example, prospect theory (Kahneman and Tversky, 1979) suggests that preferences vary depending on the reference point from which they are measured and whether the change is a loss or a gain.

The importance of psychological concerns has long been recognized in traditional research. For example, numerous studies have explored how risk perception affects the valuation of mortality risks, leading individuals to value risks of the same outcome and magnitude differently depending on their cause. Much of this work builds on research summarized in Slovic (1987), which suggests that individuals are more likely to want to see a risk reduced if it is more dreaded (i.e., perceived as more uncontrollable, catastrophic, likely to be fatal, inequitable, risky to future generations, difficult to reduce, risk increasing [rather than decreasing], and/or involuntary). Individuals also have a greater desire for addressing risks that are unknown or unfamiliar (i.e., that are unobservable, unknown to those exposed, new, unknown to science, or have delayed effects).

The effects of psychological responses on valuation, and the types of non-market outcomes associated with social programs, are too diverse for comprehensive review here.[11] Instead, we begin by addressing the distinction between willingness to pay (WTP) and willingness to accept (WTA) compensation. This distinction is fundamental to valuation in almost every context and has been identified by several scholars as an area where behavioral economics has significant implications. We then consider the valuation of mortality risk reductions in light of behavioral findings related to psychological attributes and the interpretation of probabilities. We use mortality risk reductions as an example both because they are an important outcome of many social programs and because their value has been relatively well studied.

2.1 Willingness to Pay versus Willingness to Accept Compensation

WTP and WTA can be used to value beneficial or harmful changes. For a beneficial outcome, WTP represents the maximum amount of money an individual would be willing to give up in exchange for the amenity, while WTA represents the minimum amount he or she would need to be paid to forgo the amenity. For a harmful outcome, WTP is the maximum an individual would pay to avoid the harm and WTA is the minimum he or she would require to accept the harm. Under conventional assumptions, Willig (1976) demonstrates that these values should be similar as long as income effects are negligible, that is, if purchases of the good represent a small proportion of income and if changes in income do not lead to large changes in demand. Willig's analysis pertains to private goods, where the individual chooses the quantity to purchase. For public goods, where the individual cannot choose the quantity, Hanemann (1991) finds that WTP and WTA may diverge significantly when there are no private goods that are good substitutes for the public good.

A number of empirical studies have found substantial differences between WTP and WTA (see, for example, Horowitz and McConnell, 2002).[12] Behavioral economists argue that these differences cannot be fully explained by income and substitution effects. Kahneman et al. (1991) and several subsequent studies highlight the implications of prospect theory for this divergence, identifying it as a major concern for benefit–cost analysis.

In particular, Knetsch (2005, 2010) notes that behavioral studies indicate that WTP and WTA differ due to the combined effects of two factors. First, values depend on whether individuals view the reference state as their present status or as their status after the change. Second, individuals value the change more highly if it is viewed as a loss from this reference state rather than as a gain. This implies that WTP for a gain will be smaller than WTA compensation to forgo the gain if the respondent takes his or her present status as the reference state for the WTP question and the status after the change as the reference state for the WTA question.

This divergence raises the question of which measure is most appropriate for policy analysis. Freeman (2003) argues that the choice should be based on property rights.[13] If the property right is associated with the status quo, then WTP to obtain an improvement is the correct measure. If the property right is instead associated with the change, then WTA to forgo the improvement is the correct measure. However, particularly for non-market goods, these property rights are often not well defined. In addition, the legal definitions of rights may not correspond with how individuals identify the starting point when assessing changes in their own welfare. In particular, they may view the status quo as the more intuitive basis for valuing the changes associated with implementation of new social programs.

Once a reference state is established, differing values could be applied depending on whether a policy results in a gain or a loss from that state. However, as discussed in Guria et al. (2005) and elsewhere, this approach could lead to recommendations that vary depending on the perspective: an ex ante evaluation of a proposed program could support a differing conclusion than an ex post evaluation of an existing program; a proposal to introduce a program could be evaluated differently than a proposal to abolish that program.[14] When the individuals who benefit from a policy change are the ones to bear the costs, it seems illogical for the evaluation of the policy to depend on the reference point. In addition, if a program involves both losses and gains, the use of different values could lead to counterintuitive results. The extent to which these sorts of problems arise will depend on the extent to which the values vary when viewed from these differing perspectives; for many outcomes these differences have not yet been well studied.

Much of the work identifying the behavioral anomalies that may underlie the divergence between WTP and WTA measures has been conducted in a laboratory setting with students as subjects, so often lacks the types of feedback mechanisms associated with real world exchanges. In addition, laboratory experiments usually involve exchanges of relatively simple goods (money, coffee mugs) that lack the multiple attributes associated with the outcomes of social programs. For more complex (and less familiar) non-market goods, differences between WTP and WTA measures may be driven at least in part by attributes of the outcomes themselves for which sufficient controls are not included in the data analysis and by challenges related to how the values are elicited or measured, as well as by loss aversion and other behavioral anomalies. Thus more study is needed (building on the work of Horowitz and McConnell, 2002), to better understand why WTP and WTA estimates diverge for particular types of outcomes and to estimate the size of the difference.

Policy analysts often focus on WTP estimates for more practical reasons, including skepticism about WTA estimates that appear implausibly large.[15] The extent to which these differences stem from problems with the data and methods used for non-market valuation, rather than from the sorts of concerns noted above, remains unclear. One particular methodological challenge arises from the relationship of these measures to income or wealth. Because WTP cannot exceed an individual's ability to pay, stated preference researchers can remind respondents to consider their budget constraints and can identify values that appear unrealistic given reported income levels. In contrast, WTA amounts are unconstrained, and may lead respondents to overstate what they would in fact accept when hypothetical surveys are used to elicit values. Large values also may be reported as protest bids when respondents do not accept the scenario presented by the researchers. Estimates of WTA that are consistent with an underlying utility function can be obtained instead using a preference-calibration approach using theoretically valid structural models and multiple data sources (Smith et al., 2006).

Thus more research is needed to examine the extent to which WTP and WTA estimates are likely to diverge for the particular outcomes of concern in benefit–cost analyses of social programs. In the interim, analysts can test the sensitivity of their findings to variation in these values. For example, if the benefits analysis relies on WTP estimates but consideration of the reference state and loss aversion suggests that WTA may be more appropriate, then the analyst may wish to test the impact of larger values on the results.

2.2 Psychological Responses to Risk

Behavioral research has other potentially significant implications for the attributes considered in non-market valuation, including how risks are perceived and valued. Some of these issues relate to the cognitive processing of risk information, including the misinterpretation of probabilities and the tendency to rely on simple heuristics or decision rules. In this section, we focus more directly on underlying preferences, while recognizing that it can be very difficult to distinguish "real" from "mistaken" choices or values. We illustrate these issues using research on the value of small mortality risk reductions.

Typically, the value of mortality risks is expressed as the value per statistical life (VSL). VSL represents the value of small risk changes (e.g., of one in 10 000) in a defined time period, expressed as a "statistical" life for convenience—it is not the value of saving an individual's life with certainty.[16] The VSL has been estimated in over 60 revealed preference studies (Viscusi and Aldy, 2003) and over 70 stated preference studies (Lindhjem et al., 2010); the implications of these studies have been assessed in numerous literature reviews and meta-analyses as well as in guidance for regulatory analyses.[17]

This research suggests that both personal characteristics and risk characteristics affect VSL; its variation is not limited to possible differences between WTP and WTA. The influence of income, age, and other personal characteristics can be described at least in part by standard economic theory. For example, the lifecycle consumption model takes into account the relationship between the probability of survival and the utility associated with consumption in each time period (see, for example, Shepard and Zeckhauser, 1984; Rosen, 1988; Hammitt, 2007; Hammitt and Robinson, 2011). This model suggests that expected lifetime utility is equal to the sum of the utility gained from the consumption associated with living in each future year, multiplied by the probability of surviving through that year.

Risk characteristics include both physical attributes (such as whether the risk is latent or involves significant morbidity prior to death) and psychological attributes (such as whether the risk is perceived as voluntarily incurred or under an individual's control). Research on the effects of these perceptions suggests that individuals may value risks of the same expected magnitude (e.g., one in 10 000) and same outcome (e.g., immediate death) differently if they stem from causes that are viewed differently. More work is needed to better understand how these perceptions affect valuation; however, the available empirical evidence suggests that risks viewed as less controllable, voluntary, or familiar, or as more feared or ambiguous, may be valued up to twice as much as other risks (Robinson et al., 2010).

Under the standard economic model, changes in attributes are expected to lead to changes in value. However, some stated preference research findings illustrate the influence of the types of anomalies emphasized by behavioral economists. First, when faced with uncertain risk information, individuals tend to respond differently than when faced with a point estimate equivalent to the expected value of the range, reflecting ambiguity aversion.[18] For example, work by Viscusi et al. (1991), Shogren (2005), and Riddel and Shaw (2006) indicates that WTP for fatal or non-fatal risk reductions increases as risk ambiguity increases. Second, some research shows that individuals tend to overweight small risks (particularly when they are viewed as fearsome), consistent with prospect theory (see, for example, the review in Johansson-Stenman, 2008). Third, individuals are often insensitive to small changes in risks, reporting the same or similar values for risk changes that differ in magnitude (Hammitt and Graham, 1999; Corso et al., 2001).

Some of these anomalies do not necessarily create problems for the analyst. Ideally, the values used in benefit–cost analysis would reflect all of the attributes of the risk, including the ambiguity and fear associated specifically with that risk (see, for example, Robinson et al., 2010). However, this may mean that the analyst needs to test a wide range of values either because of deficiencies in the research base or because of uncertainty regarding the applicability of the results.

Insensitivity to risk changes is troubling, however. Economic theory suggests that WTP should increase almost proportionately to the size of the risk change, as long as the change is small, which means that VSL would be nearly constant. Most studies find that WTP varies much less than proportionately to the risk change. For example, a recent review (US EPA, 2010a) found that when the sensitivity of WTP to the magnitude of the risk change could be tested, about 85 percent of studies found that the change was much smaller than proportional. While it is possible that individuals are indifferent between risk changes of these magnitudes, this explanation is contradicted by some studies. As discussed in Corso et al. (2001), individuals may be misinterpreting the probabilities; this misunderstanding can be reduced by using visual aids that more effectively communicate the size of the change. While many studies that use these aids find increased sensitivity to risk magnitude, some continue to find a degree of insensitivity (e.g., Alberini et al., 2004). Other work (e.g., Morris and Hammitt, 2001; Desaigues et al., 2007) suggests that expressing risk reductions as changes in life expectancy may lead to better comprehension of the effects of the small probabilities involved, although careful presentation is needed to ensure that the change in life expectancy is not misinterpreted as adding longevity only "at the end of one's life span."

It may be preferable to use the sensitivity of WTP to risk change as a criterion for evaluating the quality of the studies for benefit transfer, rather than assuming that it reflects indifference between risk changes of these magnitudes. More generally, differences between the risks studied and the risks associated with various social policies will lead to uncertainty in the estimates, the implications of which will need to be addressed in the analysis.

Our focus on mortality risks skirts some difficult questions, which we believe cannot be answered definitively. For example, there is substantial evidence that individuals' evaluations differ before, during, and after an experience (e.g., Kahneman, 2000a, 2000b). This means that, for example, the values for reducing the risk of a particular injury or illness may depend on whether the individual has experienced that health effect. One could argue it is the prospective, ex ante perspective of the inexperienced, healthy individual that matters in policy analysis, assuming that the goal of the policy is to help the currently healthy person avoid transitioning into the less healthy state.[19]Alternatively, one could argue that the experienced, ill individual is better informed and hence his or her values should be used. A third choice could involve somehow integrating values across inexperienced and experienced health states over time. These sorts of debates again argue for using a range of values in benefit–cost analysis, to determine how the differences affect the results.

2.3 Conclusions and Implications

The first step in valuing any outcome involves defining it, including both its physical and psychological characteristics. Behavioral economics suggests a number of attributes that may be worth investigating when valuing the non-market benefits of social programs. Assuming that our goal is to provide information on the amount of money that affected individuals would be willing to trade for the outcome of concern, it seems appropriate to examine the effects of these attributes regardless of whether the results appear consistent with the standard economic model; the findings may provide important insights. While inconsistencies in policy recommendations could potentially arise when such context-dependent values are used in benefit–cost analysis, it is difficult to determine the importance of these inconsistencies without more information on the extent to which values might vary. In addition, the effects of such uncertainties are useful information for decision-making; distinguishing cases where the evidence clearly supports a particular choice from those where the evidence is less clear is an important function of policy analysis.

As we discuss in more detail later, addressing these issues requires ensuring that valuation studies are well designed, to help separate values that reflect misinformation or misunderstanding from values that reflect more stable and carefully considered preferences. However, we also need more research that tests the effects of these attributes on valuation, so that we are better able to sort out what is and is not important in different contexts, as well as to determine the extent to which they are outweighed or counterbalanced by other considerations. For example, it is unclear whether differences between WTP and WTA are more or less important than whether a mortality risk is particularly feared or ambiguous. Regardless of whether we view these issues from a traditional or behavioral perspective, our understanding of how non-market values vary in different contexts is incomplete.

Two types of research would be helpful. First, because the effects of different attributes may be interrelated, studies are needed that consider them jointly—holistically assessing the specific outcome of concern. Second, studies that consider the effects of varying attributes one by one are also useful, because they provide insights that can be used to make adjustments (or to calibrate results) when benefit transfers are conducted. These studies should investigate the extent of heterogeneity in the population as well, to determine whether changes in attributes are perceived and valued similarly by different individuals.

Such studies can take years to complete, and funding for non-market valuation work is very limited. In the absence of reasonably consistent or conclusive research evidence, analysts will need to carefully describe the potential implications of differences between the study and policy outcome when interpreting benefit–cost analysis results, including both factors that are, and are not, consistent with the standard economic model. We expect that analysts will continue to use the benefit transfer framework to explore the effects of context differences both quantitatively and qualitatively; using sensitivity, breakeven, or probabilistic analysis where appropriate to test the implications of related uncertainties.

In conclusion, we recommend that analysts avoid making a priori judgments about whether values appear "rational" or "stable," and instead consider the following:

- Studies should be designed to test the effects of the psychologically salient attributes found in behavioral research on benefit values, as well as the effects of other physical and psychological attributes.

- Such studies should consider both the holistic effect of the full range of attributes relevant to a particular context and the effects of varying the attributes one by one to develop adjustments for transferring values to other contexts.
- Values should not be rejected unless the study does not meet basic criteria for quality or adhere to generally accepted principles for best practices. Rejected values, and the basis for rejecting them, should be clearly documented.
- When values are uncertain, sensitivity, probabilistic, or breakeven analysis should be used to test the effects of this uncertainty on the results.
- Where quantitative estimates are not available, the potential effects of both psychologically salient and physical attributes should be discussed qualitatively.

3 ESTIMATING TIME PREFERENCES

Evaluating the benefits and costs of social programs often involves comparing impacts that occur at different dates, using discounting to reflect time preferences. Two questions arise in this context: (1) what is the appropriate form of the discounting function, that is, should it be exponential or hyperbolic and (2) what is the appropriate basis for the discount rate, that is, should it be based on individual or market rates?

Traditionally, exponential discounting is used in benefit–cost analysis, while behavioral research suggests that hyperbolic functions may be appropriate. This distinction reflects simplifying assumptions more than theoretical differences. Exponential discounting can be traced to Samuelson's (1937) work on discounted utility, which was intended to highlight certain theoretical relationships. Samuelson himself recognized that his assumptions were a simplification, neither necessarily predictive of actual behavior nor associated with a normative view of welfare. More recent work (Weitzman, 2001) suggests that hyperbolic discounting is appropriate under the standard economic model when the discount rate is uncertain.[20] Gollier and Zeckhauser (2005) also discuss theoretical reasons why aggregating individual discount rates will lead to a rate that decreases over time. Thus the distinction that we explore in this section relates more to practical application than to theory. Figure 10.2 provides an example of exponential, hyperbolic, and quasi-hyperbolic functions.

To answer the questions about both functional form and the appropriate discount rate requires clearly defining what it is that we are trying to measure. In benefit–cost analysis, we are interested in estimating

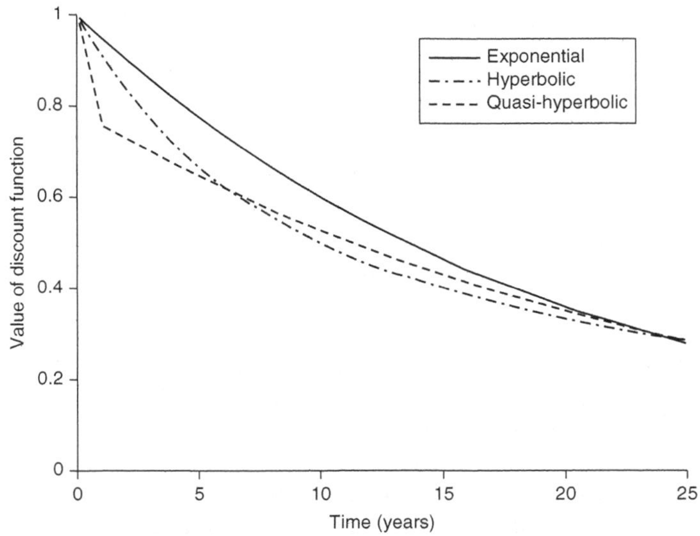

Source: Based on Berns et al. (2007, Figure 1).

Figure 10.2 Exponential, hyperbolic, and quasi-hyperbolic discounting functions

opportunity costs, that is, the value of the best alternative use of the resources to be devoted to the policy or program. In this case, discounting is intended to reflect real resource expenditures, and relying on market rates seems appropriate. Market rates result from the intersection of supply and demand conditions and reflect technological progress as well as individual tastes and preferences. Behavioral economics provides insight into how discounting affects individual choices, which in turn affect market rates.

One problem that arises in this context is the difficulty of disentangling the effect of timing from the effects of other characteristics of an outcome. Frederick et al. (2002, p. 362) note that, for a given time delay, the empirical evidence suggests that rates vary depending on the context:

> (1) gains are discounted more than losses; (2) small amounts are discounted more than large amounts; (3) greater discounting is shown to avoid delay of a good than to expedite its receipt; (4) in choices over sequences of outcomes, improving sequences are often preferred to declining sequences though positive time preference dictates the opposite; and (5) in choices over sequences, violations of independence are pervasive, and people seem to prefer spreading consumption over time in a way that diminishing marginal utility alone cannot explain.

As they note, these problems relate more to how the utility function is specified than to the discount rate. To avoid redundancy, below we focus on the effects of timing alone, while recognizing that the dividing line between pure time preferences and other types of preferences is somewhat murky.

In this discussion, we address discounting of the monetary value of costs and benefits, not the underlying physical impacts. To the extent that timing affects the value of these physical outcomes, its impact is best represented by using their time-specific monetary value rather than by adjusting the discount rate. For example, if latent health effects are valued differently than effects experienced immediately, this difference should be reflected in the unit values applied to the health effects at the time they manifest, which then can be discounted at the same rate as other monetary amounts included in the analysis.

The time period over which an analysis is conducted has important implications for discounting. We concentrate here on discounting annual quantities over an intra-generational time period, consistent with the likely timeframe of interest for analyses of social programs. We do not discuss the additional complications that arise when assessing programs (such as climate change or nuclear waste storage) where intergenerational impacts are of major importance. Below, we first briefly review the traditional exponential approach, then discuss the evidence from behavioral economics and describe the implications.

3.1 Exponential Discounting

Time can influence the value of costs and benefits in a variety of different ways. Outcomes further in the future may be more uncertain or risky; new opportunities, information, or technologies may arise while current options may disappear; and an individual's preferences may change as he or she ages. In theory, discounting as traditionally implemented should not reflect any of these factors (which may be addressed separately elsewhere in the analysis); it should simply reflect the "pure" effect of timing.

Typically, benefit–cost analysis is conducted with constant discount rates (using the same rate for both costs and benefits), although rates that change over time have been used in some cases for longer-term impacts.[21] Exponential (i.e., constant rate) discounting assumes that time preferences are constant over different periods.[22]

For government analyses of social programs, rates are established by US Office of Management and Budget (OMB) in Circular A-94 (1992) and Circular A-4 (2003); the former focuses more on government programs while the latter focuses on economically significant regulations.[23]

Both suggest the use of exponential discounting, using a 7 percent real annual rate to approximate the average marginal pretax rate of return on private investments.[24] Circular A-4 requires that analysts also report the results using a 3 percent rate to reflect consumption time preferences (or the "social rate of time preference").[25] US OMB derives the 3 percent rate from the pretax rate of return on long-term government debt to approximate the interest paid on savings, assuming that the savings rate represents the average by which consumers discount future consumption.

The use of two alternative rates reflects uncertainty about whether these programs primarily affect the allocation of capital or private consumption. In theory, the rates would not diverge in perfectly competitive markets, but in actuality economic distortions such as taxes lead to differences. Given this and other sources of uncertainty, US OMB also requires that agencies provide a schedule that shows how the undiscounted costs and benefits are likely to be distributed over time and discusses the use of alternative rates in sensitivity analysis. Thus the traditional approach for intra-generational discounting relies on a number of simplifying assumptions, and includes recommendations for testing these assumptions by considering the impact of alternative discount rates.

3.2 Hyperbolic Discounting

Time preferences have been one of the most active and well-developed components of behavioral economics research. As summarized in Chabris et al. (2008), numerous studies conducted over many years have found higher discount rates in the near term than over the longer term. As a result, behavioral economists have explored hyperbolic functions with discounted values that drop steeply in the immediate future and more gently over the longer run.[26] These functions are often described as "present-biased."

The exponential function is often described as the only discounting approach that yields dynamically consistent decisions.[27] Under hyperbolic and other functions, the preferred choice between policies having only future consequences can change solely because time passes. In other words, a project that appears desirable (e.g., the present value of its net benefits is positive) in time period 1 may appear undesirable (e.g., may have a negative net present value) in time period 2. As noted by Laibson (1997) "from today's perspective, the discount rate between two far-off periods, t and $t + 1$, is the long-term low discount rate. However, from the time t perspective, the discount rate between t and $t + 1$ is the short-term high discount rate" (pp. 445–6). This inconsistency is often referred to as a "preference reversal," although it can perhaps be better characterized as a sort of tug-of-war between these two perspectives or "as a game between a sequence of short-run impulsive selves and a long-run patient self" (Fudenberg and Levine, 2006, p. 1449).

Many of the studies that find declining rates were conducted in laboratory settings. In these experiments, a small number of subjects (often students) are offered choices between receiving differing amounts of money (or another reward, often small) sooner or later. Declining rates have also been found in some field studies that address real-world behavior. Frederick et al. (2002) list 42 studies conducted between 1978 and 2002, including 34 laboratory experiments and eight field studies. The number of studies is increasing rapidly. Laibson (2010) lists almost 20 additional studies completed since 2002, including several conducted under field rather than laboratory conditions.

The results are diverse. The studies reviewed by Frederick et al. imply annual discount rates ranging from 0 to thousands of percent, based on data collected for timeframes as short as one day to as long as 25 years. Frederick et al. note that this lack of agreement reflects at least in part the difficulties inherent in isolating pure time preferences from other (theoretically distinct) considerations.

While many studies demonstrate hyperbolic discounting, this pattern appears to apply primarily to relatively short near-term time periods. Frederick et al. report that if they exclude studies with time horizons less than one year, discount rates no longer decline over time, clustering around an average annual discount factor of 0.8. This factor implies an annual discount rate of 25 percent, however, well above market rates. Frederick et al. note that the high rates may be due to the effects of several confounding factors that tend to bias the results of these studies upwards.

Laibson et al. (2007) explore time preferences over the lifecycle more systematically, using a structural model with data on age-specific income, credit card borrowing, marginal propensity to consume, retirement wealth accumulations, household characteristics, mortality rates, and other factors. If they restrict their model to a single (exponential) function, they find an annual discount rate of about 16.7 percent. However, their analysis rejects this single rate hypothesis. Allowing a quasi-hyperbolic function, they find a short-term annualized discount rate of 39.5 percent and a long-term annualized rate of 4.3 percent.

Behavioral economists have explored a number of motivations behind these patterns. The high near-term rates are often described as resulting from imperfect self-control, which leads individuals to seek immediate gratification even if it diverges from their own longer-term preferences.[28] Examples of this behavior, such as eating dessert despite wanting to lose weight, are abundant. Individuals vary in the extent to which they correctly predict these types of problems. Behavioral researchers identify "sophisticated" consumers as those who are more fully aware of the potential for future self-control issues, while "naive" consumers are more likely to incorrectly predict their future behavior. Sophisticated consumers may implement self-control measures or use commitment devices (such as avoiding temptation or establishing penalties) to reinforce their self-control.

3.3 Conclusions and Implications

Although most economists agree that discounting is needed, there is some disagreement on the appropriate rate for social programs even within the traditional approach to benefit–cost analysis. Conceptually, under this framework, the rate should reflect the opportunity cost of investing in the intervention of concern, that is, the best alternative use of the resources. However, it is often unclear what types of investment or consumption are affected when particular social programs are implemented, leading to the widespread use of generic defaults for discount rates, usually accompanied by sensitivity analysis.

Traditionally, benefit–cost analysis involves discounting the monetary values of future impacts at a constant exponential rate, based on market data, with real rates often in the range of 3 percent to 7 percent annually. Behavioral economics suggests that individuals instead discount in a hyperbolic pattern, with varying rates.

In the context of social programs, rates reflecting a longer-term view appear more appropriate than the steep near-term rates found in behavioral research (regardless of whether they are exponential or hyperbolic) for two reasons. First, these programs are generally intended to operate over a several-year period, which means that the planning horizon is consistent with longer-term rates. Second, these programs are focused on providing lasting (rather than temporary) improvements in welfare. To the extent that short-term rates reflect impulsive behavior and self-control problems (rather than more patient and thoughtful consideration), they are inconsistent with this goal. To reflect true improvements in social welfare, it appears desirable to focus on the time preferences that result from more careful assessment of long-range well-being.

In addition, in benefit–cost analysis we are interested in market rates, which reflect both technological progress and individual preferences (including any behavioral anomalies), while most behavioral research focuses solely on individual decisions. Market rates indicate real resource costs, that is, the opportunity costs of investing in social policies or programs.

Behavioral research may be very useful, however, in predicting individual decisions, for example to participate in an addiction treatment or smoking cessation program, or to purchase an energy-efficient car. While the reviews cited earlier compile the results of numerous studies, they do not evaluate these studies against criteria for quality or for applicability to social programs. Systematic review is needed both to determine the extent to which individual discount rates might decrease over time (and whether they may be close to constant over the long run as suggested by Frederick et al.) and the extent to which they might differ from the 3 percent to 7 percent range now often used to represent market rates.

Given these considerations, we advise our prototypical policy analyst as follows:

- Discounting in benefit–cost analysis should reflect market rates, that is, the investment or consumption forgone when resources are diverted to social programs or policies. The appropriate functional form and discount rate are uncertain, however.
- Analysts should provide a schedule of undiscounted costs, benefits, and net benefits, in the form of bar charts (or other graphics) or a table, so that the decision-maker can inspect this pattern. Simply summarizing costs and benefits as a net present value does not provide adequate information.
- In choosing a discount rate or set of rates, as well as a functional form (exponential or hyperbolic) analysts must be clear about what, conceptually, they intend to represent for review by decision-makers. The quality of the underlying data and related assumptions should also be described.
- Analysts should consider the impact of alternative rates on their results, emphasizing the discount rates at which benefits do, and do not, exceed costs, and/or at which the relative ranking of different policy options change.[29] Comparing these switch points to rates reported in the empirical literature will provide insights into the implications of related uncertainties for decision-making.

4 SEPARATING PRIVATE FROM SOCIAL PREFERENCES

While the outcomes of social programs vary in the extent to which they meet the economic definition of a public good (i.e., are non-rival and non-excludable), these programs differ from markets for private goods and services along several dimensions, that interact with individuals' preferences regarding program effects on others. In its simplest form, the standard economic model assumes that individuals are primarily self-interested, yet other-regarding preferences have been long recognized within the traditional framework. As examples, we briefly discuss the treatment of altruistic motives and note issues related to valuing a social program rather than a private good and to assessing equity along with economic efficiency.

Behavioral studies reinforce the importance of these types of considerations, suggesting that individuals often act selflessly. They also identify other types of interpersonal considerations that may affect preferences, including vengeful as well as welfare-enhancing motives. Behavioral research on these issues is less well developed than research in the areas discussed previously, but provides potentially useful insights.

4.1 Social Preferences within the Traditional Framework

While self-interested preferences are a standard assumption of the most simplified version of the traditional economic model, scholars have long recognized that individuals also care about others' welfare. For example, existence values for natural environments (Krutilla, 1967) are well recognized within the standard model. Incorporating other-regarding preferences into benefit–cost analysis can be difficult due to data limitations as well as conceptual challenges; however, related issues have been explored extensively within the traditional framework.

In particular, the appropriate treatment of altruism has received substantial attention. Economic theory distinguishes between two forms. Pure, or non-paternalistic, altruism means that I respect the preferences of others: I weight the benefits they receive and the costs they incur exactly the same as they do. In contrast, paternalistic altruism involves ignoring others' preferences to some extent. If those affected by the costs and benefits of a policy are pure altruists, counting both their altruistic and private values in benefit–cost analysis simply scales the costs and benefits upwards without affecting the overall analytic conclusions, so that ignoring or including altruistic values leads to identical results (Jones-Lee, 1991; Bergstrom, 2006). If their altruism instead varies depending on the outcome (e.g., is greater for health than for other aspects of well-being) or depending on the individuals affected (e.g., is greater for poor individuals than for the wealthy), then it can affect the sign of net benefits.[30] In particular, there is some evidence that health and longevity are viewed more paternalistically than most other goods (e.g., Jacobsson et al., 2007).

Paternalistic motives also appear more plausible when inequalities exist: I may wish to help those in impaired health by funding a program that exceeds their willingness to pay for it (and decreasing my own consumption).[31, 32] Alternatively, selective paternalistic altruism could involve caring about the costs incurred by others rather than the risks they incur. For example, I may be willing to pay $75 for my own risk reductions plus $50 to offset the costs to poorer individuals, allowing them to use their funds for other purposes. In this case, the subsidy is a means to redistribute the costs of the program without changing its total costs nor the value of the benefits that accrue. With such a subsidy, the value may not be truly altruistic (i.e., reflect how I value these particular costs or benefits for others); it may instead reflect how I value the distribution of impacts. This means that analysts will need to carefully distinguish general preferences for redistribution from preferences related to the outcome of concern.

In more complex, real-world situations, determining whether and how the values of various outcomes are differentially affected by paternalistic altruism is a difficult task. For example, Viscusi et al. (1988) demonstrate that individuals are willing to pay additional amounts to reduce the risks of insecticide poisoning to others. However, they note that extrapolating their results to other contexts is not appropriate because the analysis was exploratory, the contributions were hypothetical, and the values are likely to vary across contexts. Due to these sorts of challenges, altruistic values are typically not quantified when valuing non-market goods.[33]

Another issue that is receiving increased attention is the difference between individual WTP for a "unit" of a particular good or service for private use versus WTP for a program that benefits the entire community of which the individual is a part. With purely self-regarding preferences, these values would be equal, if the outcomes are otherwise identical. However, while several stated preference studies consider public programs rather than, or in addition to, private goods, they have not yet been reviewed systematically to provide insights into the extent to which the values vary. Because it is difficult to design a believable scenario that is identical in all respects other than whether the good is provided privately or to a community, determining the extent to which such values diverge is challenging. For example, to be otherwise comparable, a risk-reducing program would need to deliver the same expected risk reduction as the private option, and to be described in a way that avoids strategic bias (e.g., free-riding).[34]

Finally, as traditionally practiced, benefit–cost analysis focuses on economic efficiency, supplemented at times by separate assessment of distributional equity. Advocates of this separation between equity and efficiency suggest that programs designed primarily to achieve outcomes other than income redistribution should focus on maximizing net social welfare; taxes and similar strategies can be used to more effectively achieve distributional goals.[35] However, if WTP for a particular outcome in part reflects altruistic motives (intentionally or inadvertently) that result from concerns about disparities, and this WTP is used in the analysis of efficiency, the results of the benefit–cost analysis will, at least in part, also reflect equity concerns.

Social programs can exacerbate or ameliorate current inequalities both directly (depending on who receives the benefits and who bears the costs) and indirectly (e.g., because improved health can lead to greater productivity and income). Proposals to weight costs and benefits to reflect equity concerns have generally not been accepted in the USA due to the lack of agreement on the appropriate weights as well as concerns about transparency.[36] However, several scholars have proposed approaches for more rigorously assessing equity (e.g., Sunstein, 2007; Adler, 2008; Graham, 2008; Zerbe, 2009; Johansson-Stenman and Konow, 2010; Farrow, 2011; Loomis, 2011). The feasibility and usefulness of these approaches have not yet been carefully tested. However, they suggest that equity effects could be addressed in more detail within the traditional framework, in part by taking advantage of the existing research on social welfare functions, optimal taxation, the marginal utility of income, and related topics.

4.2 Behavioral Research on Social Preferences

The strong interest in altruism, in valuing public programs as distinct from private goods, and in developing proposals to better incorporate equity into benefit–cost analysis, are consistent to a large extent with the emerging behavioral research on social preferences. Both laboratory and field studies suggest that individuals frequently consider others' welfare in decision-making. While this behavior is often altruistic, it may also involve acting reciprocally to reward or punish others.[37] In addition, individuals may use others' status as the baseline against which to assess their own well-being.

Charness and Rabin (2002, pp. 817–18) discuss three types of models that could explain behaviors found in laboratory settings:

> "[d]ifference aversion models" assume that players are motivated to reduce differences between theirs and others' payoffs; "social-welfare models" assume that people like to increase social surplus, caring especially about helping those (themselves or others) with low payoffs; reciprocity models assume that the desire to raise or lower others' payoffs depends on how fairly those others are behaving.

They conclude that their experimental results are consistent with the social welfare and reciprocity models, but suggest that difference aversion is less important, and indicate the need for further research.

The evidence from experimental research may be limited, however, in the extent to which it predicts behavior in more complex situations. As summarized in DellaVigna (2009), the role of social preferences has been studied in some field settings, particularly charitable giving and employer–employee relationships. The results suggest varied motives and do not necessarily match the experimental findings. DellaVigna notes that it can be difficult to separate social preferences from strategic decisions such as responses to social pressures, or from the "warm glow" associated with giving rather than with a particular outcome (see, for example, Kahneman and Knetsch, 1992; Andreoni et al., 2008). Thus while behavioral research provides support for the presence of altruistic (as well as malevolent) preferences, it does not provide values that can be directly used in benefit–cost analysis.

Finally, research also suggests that preferences are formed in part by interpersonal comparisons, indicating that private WTP will depend not only on one's current endowment of income, health, and so forth, but also on how this endowment compares to that of others (see, for example, Luttmer, 2005; Frank, 2005; and Solnick and Hemenway, 2005).[38] This research suggests that positional concerns are stronger in some areas and can lead to a sort of "arms race" involving cyclical increases as each individual responds to positional changes made by others, ultimately leading to an oversupply of positional goods relative to other goods.

Substantially more research is needed to determine how these positional concerns affect the valuation of outcomes from social programs. The results of the few studies to date are inconsistent. For example, Frank and Sunstein (2001) argue that ignoring the effects of relative income leads to benefit measures that are far too low, and suggest that the VSL estimates used in regulatory analysis may be significantly understated. However, Kniesner and Viscusi's (2005) analysis of wage-risk trade-offs suggests that the opposite is true: relative position appears to have little effect on compensating wage differentials for mortality risks and may decrease VSL. In addition, much of the behavioral research focuses on private goods; the effects of social preferences may have significantly different consequences in the case of public goods.

4.3 Conclusions and Implications

As indicated by the above discussion, practitioners have long struggled with how to represent social preferences (such as paternalistic altruism) in benefit–cost analysis, due to both research challenges and theoretical considerations. Behavioral research suggests additional ways in which concerns for others might affect valuation, such as reciprocating "good" and "bad" behavior or improving one's relative position.

The research on social preferences reinforces the discussion in section 2 on the potential importance of psychological attributes in valuation. For example, reciprocity may affect how individuals value mortality risks from crime (or from dangerous working conditions or polluting industries) in comparison to risks viewed as more accidental or naturally occurring; concerns about relative position may affect programs providing income transfers differently than programs promoting improved health. This research also foreshadows some of the issues in study design discussed in section 5, emphasizing the need to be clear about whether values reflect only an individual's private consumption or also reflect benefits to the household or community. To the extent that studies (intentionally or inadvertently) include other-regarding preferences related to disparities, the values used in the analysis of efficiency may incorporate some equity concerns, potentially blurring the distinction between the two types of analysis.

Behavioral research on social preferences is not as well developed as the research discussed in the prior sections, in part because of the complex interactions between social preferences and social pressures as well as the difficulty of extrapolating from experimental results to more complex real-world behaviors. Thus it is hard to offer much concrete advice to policy analysts that can be implemented immediately. However, this research suggests that these issues should be considered both when valuing particular non-market outcomes and when considering the distributional and other consequences of social programs.

This discussion leads to two recommendations for our prototypical policy analyst:

- In addition to other psychological attributes, studies should be designed to test the effects of social preferences on benefit values, focusing on outcomes associated with social programs rather than private goods or services.
- When reviewing studies for benefit transfer, analysts should consider whether the results are likely to reflect other-regarding as well as private preferences and discuss the implications for both the analysis of economic efficiency and its relationship to equity concerns.

5 IMPROVING VALUATION STUDIES

Thoughtful and well-informed preferences are desirable when valuing outcomes in policy analysis for several reasons. First, decisions to divert limited resources to achieving particular social goals warrant careful consideration. Given that there is no market to test the match between choices, preferences, and values for many of the outcomes associated with social programs, it seems that decisions to expend resources on these types of public goods should be justified with particular care. Interactions in real markets can provide various types of feedback and learning that may be lacking in non-market valuation studies, hence the studies may not capture market dynamics that could lead to more well-informed choices. However, in real markets firms face incentives to cater to consumer biases. They may also conceal information or provide misleading information to protect their market share or increase profits. Thus analysts need to recognize that review of market decisions could also lead to erroneous understanding of underlying consumer preferences.

Second, these programs and policies are generally focused on achieving long-term improvements in welfare, suggesting that we want to value the outcomes based on individuals' thoughtful assessment of how they might benefit over the long run. Third, and perhaps most relevant for the purposes of this chapter, behavioral research suggests that individuals may at times make "mistakes" or "errors" in expressing preferences or values, following simple decision rules or making choices that do not fully coincide with their assessment of their own welfare (see DellaVigna, 2009 for a recent review). However, evidence that suggests that values are stable or robust across studies and across contexts provides useful information for policy decisions, regardless of whether these preferences are consistent with the standard model.[39] While researchers have developed a number of strategies to address these issues, studies must be carefully designed so that the results do not ultimately reflect the values held by the researcher rather than the individuals studied.

5.1 Stated Preference Research

Stated preference researchers have a long tradition of considering psychological factors in designing their studies and behavioral concerns are well integrated into related guidance. Early work by Mitchell and Carson (1989) on best practices discusses approaches for encouraging honest and meaningful responses and controlling biases that may result from strategic behavior. In 1993, a National Oceanic and Atmospheric Administration (NOAA) expert panel (chaired by Kenneth Arrow and Robert Solow) issued guidelines for these studies in the context of natural resource damage assessment cases, particularly to assess non-use (or existence) values. They discuss several behavioral considerations, such as pretesting surveys to ensure that the responses are not biased by the desire to please an interviewer and using a referendum format (rather than an open-ended valuation question or payment card) to alleviate problems related to framing. Since that time, substantial additional research has been conducted that provides insights into how to best conduct these studies.

For example, in 2005 and again in 2010, the journal *Environmental and Resource Economics* published special issues that address these concerns. The 2005 issue includes seven articles on anomalies and stated preference research (Braga and Starmer, 2005; Guria et al., 2005; Hanley and Shogren, 2005; Kahneman and Sugden, 2005; Knetsch, 2005; List, 2005; Sugden, 2005a, 2005b). For example, List finds that experienced market participants behave in ways that appear consistent with the traditional economic model, while those with less experience exhibit some of the anomalies found in laboratory studies. Hanley and Shogren describe many options for improving stated preference research, such as using workshops to better inform respondents, allowing "maybe" responses to recognize that individuals may only know their preferences over a limited range, and including "cheap talk" that discourages free-riding. Researchers are increasingly using choice experiments that ask respondents to value varying combinations of attributes rather than a single outcome, to mimic market choices and avoid overly narrow framing of decisions.

The 2010 issue deals specifically with behavioral economics, and includes several articles that provide insights for stated preference research (particularly Carlsson, 2010; Hepburn et al., 2010; Johansson-Stenman and Konow, 2010; Knetsch, 2010; Smith and Moore, 2010; and Shogren et al., 2010). For instance, Carlsson notes that while stated preference researchers have much to learn from behavioral economics, behavioral economists can also learn from stated preference research. He discusses four topics: revealed versus normative preferences (see section 5.2), learning and constructed preferences, context dependence, and hypothetical bias. He indicates, for example, the importance of providing opportunities for learning, including practice and repetition. He also notes that while comparing results from studies with real and hypothetical payouts can be useful, there are several reasons for exercising caution in these comparisons.

The proliferation of these types of articles suggests that the intersection between behavioral research and the conduct of stated preference studies is fertile ground, with abundant lessons for researchers. However, it also means that there is a need to integrate the results of the numerous new studies to provide updated guidelines for best practices, including guidance on how to best tailor stated preference studies to different contexts and outcomes.

5.2 Revealed Preference Research

The issues raised by behavioral research also affect revealed preference studies. In particular, Beshears et al. (2008) distinguish between revealed (or positive) preferences (the choices people actually make) and normative preferences (the choices people think they should make). They note that actual choices result from combining normative preferences with the sorts of decision-making biases and anomalies found in behavioral research.

While Beshears et al. focus largely on how revealed and normative preferences diverge in savings and investment decisions, their findings have implications for many other contexts. They identify five factors that increase the likelihood of a disparity: (1) passive choice (acceptance of defaults); (2) complexity (delayed choice, avoidance of complicated options, or misunderstanding of options due to cognitive difficulties); (3) limited personal experience (lack of learning through feedback); (4) third-party marketing (manipulating preferences); and (5) intertemporal choice (inconsistent time preferences, discussed in section 3).

Beshears et al. then describe six approaches that can, in combination, help identify normative preferences:

> [*S*]*tructural estimation* specifies a positive model with a precise set of economic and psychological motives (perhaps including non-Bayesian thinking and other decision-making errors). This model is then estimated using data, and the resulting positive preferences are mapped into normative preferences using normative axioms.
>
> *Active decisions* eliminate some biases generated by default regimes. Under an active decision regime, individuals are required to *explicitly state their preference* without being influenced by (or being able to rely on) a default option. In some circumstances, this preference elicitation will be more reliable and more socially efficient than allowing consumers to express their preferences by opting into or out of a pre-chosen default.
>
> In most stationary economic environments, initial choices are likely to be further from normative optimality than choices made after many periods of experience. One should therefore give more weight to *asymptotic choices* when attempting to infer normative preferences.
>
> When homogeneous individuals make noisy, error-prone decisions, their individual decisions do not reflect normative preferences, but their aggregate behavior can. Hence, normative preferences can sometimes be inferred from the central tendencies of *aggregated preferences*.
>
> *Self-reported preferences* reveal something about an agent's goals and values. Normative economics should allow self-reports to have some standing. This is particularly true when self-reports can be used to distinguish confident consumer decisions from decisions that were made in a state of confusion.
>
> Informed opinions come in two forms. External observers may offer expert advice, and decision-makers may themselves gain more expertise when they receive training or education. When trained/educated decision-makers make a

> choice, we call this an *informed preference*. Economists measuring normative preferences should give disproportionate weight to the actors who are most likely to know what they are doing. (Beshears et al., 2008, p. 1793; italics in original)

When revealed preference studies are used to value non-market outcomes, researchers first identify a market good that includes the non-market outcome as one of its attributes. They then apply statistical methods to distinguish the value of the non-market outcome from the value of other attributes. For example, they may look at the trade-off between wages and job-related risks to value mortality risk reductions, or at residential decisions, recreational choices, or purchases of consumer goods to value various non-market attributes (see Freeman, 2003 for more detailed examples). It seems sensible to consider whether both the market outcome and preferences toward the non-market attribute of concern may be significantly affected by the factors identified by Beshears et al.

Although the data and methods used in revealed preference studies of non-market outcomes have been scrutinized (see, for example, Dockins et al., 2004), to the best of our knowledge these reviews have not systematically addressed the full range of behavioral issues listed above. More work is needed to determine the extent to which revealed preference studies reflect normative preferences, rather than decision-making biases, when used to value the diverse outcomes associated with social programs. Thus while there is substantial synergy between the findings of behavioral economics and the evolving conduct of stated preference research, more consideration of the implications of behavioral anomalies for revealed preference research may also be desirable.

5.3 Conclusions and Implications

Under the standard economic model, the goal of non-market valuation is to mimic a market: to estimate the amount of money that individuals would be willing to exchange for these outcomes if they could be directly bought and sold. Under standard assumptions, these choices would be consistent with individual welfare. However, implementing this approach presents challenges given the findings of behavioral research. If individuals make mistakes, and their choices do not correspond with their welfare (as self-defined), relying on choices for valuation may not lead to the identification of the policy option that best enhances social welfare. Improving related studies so that they result in well-informed, thoughtful preferences is thus an important goal for researchers and policy analysts.

These issues have received substantial attention over the years in stated preference research, although the proliferation of new studies suggests that more review and integration is now needed. They have received relatively little attention when revealed preference methods are used, although similar issues may arise in market contexts.

This discussion has implications for both researchers and policy analysts:

- Researchers should continue to incorporate the results of behavioral research into the design of valuation studies where useful and relevant, with the goal of identifying well-informed, thoughtful preferences, regardless of whether stated or revealed preference methods are used.
- When evaluating study quality for benefit transfer, analysts should consider possible decision-making bias along with other uncertainties, including any evidence that the study population did not fully understand the context or made other cognitive errors.

6 DETERMINING THE ROLE OF BENEFIT–COST ANALYSIS

Many reviews of the implications of behavioral economics compare and contrast a simplified version of the standard economic model with the findings of behavioral research. However, the standard model incorporates more complex considerations than suggested by these reviews. Some of these complexities reflect elaboration of the model, for example, to incorporate lifecycle consumption, household production, or social welfare functions. Others integrate behavioral findings, such as the effects of psychological factors on the valuation of non-market outcomes. Overall, the conduct of benefit–cost analysis reflects a number of pragmatic concerns, using economic theory as a starting point, incorporating behavioral considerations, and focusing on information that is useful for decision-making. In practice, the gap between the traditional and behavioral models is narrower than it might appear, and there is substantial synergy between non-market valuation and behavioral research.

The discussion in the prior sections of this chapter suggests additional avenues to explore. Below, we first summarize the recommendations from the previous sections. We then discuss the more general implications for the conduct and interpretation of benefit–cost analysis, focusing on its practical implementation.

6.1 Summary of Conclusions and Recommendations

In this chapter, we discuss the implications of behavioral economics for analyzing the benefits and costs of social policies and programs. While recognizing that behavioral research can aid in predicting program participation rates and effectiveness, as well as in predicting real resource costs conditional on these responses, we focus on the valuation of program benefits and costs. We take the role of the analyst who is asked to assess an exogenously determined program or policy and seeks advice on incorporating the results of behavioral research into the assessment given available data. We consider four areas: context-dependent valuation of non-market benefits (section 2); present bias and exponential versus hyperbolic discounting (section 3); social preferences such as altruism and equity (section 4); and the conduct of non-market valuation studies (section 5).

Because behavioral economics is a large and rapidly growing field, the significance or pervasiveness of many of its findings are not yet clear and these findings have not been combined into a widely accepted model that supplements or supplants the standard economic framework. As a result, we often raise questions for further research or note options for the analyst rather than trying to resolve the underlying issues. Throughout, we attempt to maintain the traditional perspective of benefit–cost analysis as describing the preferences of affected individuals (contingent on baseline conditions, including the distribution of income and other resources). While we recognize that individual choices may include errors, that is, diverge from what the individuals might choose given better information and more experience or reflection, we urge caution in substituting the judgment of the analyst for the information collected from representative members of the population.

In Box 10.1 we summarize our key recommendations.

As the summary in Box 10.1 indicates, behavioral research is not yet sufficient to support specific recommendations for adapting the practice of benefit–cost analysis in many areas. Our recommendations are thus similar to current best practice recommendations, which take into account uncertainty in the underlying data and analyses. In some cases (such as time preferences and the design of stated preference studies), the behavioral research base is relatively large and additional criteria-driven review may be helpful. In other areas (such as social preferences), the behavioral research is limited and does not necessarily address outcomes relevant to the evaluation of social programs. In the near term, the implications of behavioral research can be explored by testing the sensitivity of the results to different values, using probabilistic or breakeven analysis, or discussing impacts qualitatively. In the longer term, more significant changes may be warranted as new research becomes available that provides more robust and stable estimates of the effects of these factors.

BOX 10.1 SUMMARY OF MAJOR RECOMMENDATIONS

Valuing psychological attributes

1. Studies should be designed to test the effects of the psychologically salient attributes found in behavioral research on benefit values, as well as the effects of other physical and psychological attributes.
2. Such studies should consider both the holistic effect of the full range of attributes relevant to a particular context and the effects of varying the attributes one by one to develop adjustments for transferring values to other contexts.
3. Values should not be rejected unless the study does not meet basic criteria for quality or adhere to generally accepted principles for best practices. Rejected values, and the basis for rejecting them, should be clearly documented.
4. When values are uncertain, sensitivity, probabilistic, or breakeven analysis should be used to test the effects of this uncertainty on the results.
5. Where quantitative estimates are not available, the potential effects of both psychologically salient and physical attributes should be discussed qualitatively.

Estimating time preferences

1. Discounting in benefit–cost analysis should reflect market rates, that is, the investment or consumption forgone when resources are diverted to social programs or policies. The appropriate functional form and discount rate are uncertain, however.
2. Analysts should provide a schedule of undiscounted costs, benefits, and net benefits, in the form of a bar chart (or other graphic) or a table, so that the decision-maker can inspect this pattern. Simply summarizing costs and benefits as a net present value does not provide adequate information.
3. In choosing a discount rate or set of rates, as well as a functional form (exponential or hyperbolic) analysts must

be clear about what, conceptually, they intend to represent for review by decision-makers. The quality of the underlying data and related assumptions should also be described.

4. Analysts should consider the impact of alternative rates on their results, emphasizing the discount rates at which benefits do, and do not, exceed costs, and/or at which the relative ranking of different policy options change. Comparing these switch points to rates reported in the empirical literature will provide insights into the implications of related uncertainties for decision-making.

Separating private from social preferences

1. In addition to other psychological attributes, studies should be designed to test the effects of social preferences on benefit values, focusing on outcomes associated with social programs rather than private goods or services.
2. When reviewing studies for benefit transfer, analysts should consider whether the results are likely to reflect other-regarding as well as private preferences and discuss the implications for both the analysis of economic efficiency and its relationship to equity concerns.

Improving valuation studies

1. Researchers should continue to incorporate the results of behavioral research into the design of valuation studies where useful and relevant, with the goal of identifying well-informed, thoughtful preferences, regardless of whether stated or revealed preference methods are used.
2. When evaluating study quality for benefit transfer, analysts should consider possible decision-making bias along with other uncertainties, including any evidence that the study population did not fully understand the context or made other cognitive errors.

6.2 Benefit–Cost Analysis as Applied Pragmatism

Conducting benefit–cost analysis is challenging, regardless of whether framed by the traditional or behavioral economic model. However, denoting values in monetary terms has the advantage of providing information on the intensity as well as the direction of preferences. It also mimics the effects of policy decisions, which often require trading money for the outcomes of concern.[40] Thus we believe that valuation research provides useful information, despite its limitations—as long as the analyst is clear about the implications of these limitations for the conclusions of the analysis.

Although benefit–cost analysis has normative goals, those conducting such analysis may be most comfortable describing it as a positive, descriptive exercise, which provides decision-makers with factual information on the preferences of those potentially affected by the policy. Behavioral economics questions aspects of this model, suggesting that individuals do not always act rationally, are motivated in part by social preferences, and make choices that do not necessarily coincide with their own long-term welfare even as self-defined.

One possible response to these findings is to substitute a paternalistic approach for the positive or descriptive model, placing the analyst and/or policy-maker in the position of deciding which preferences are rational and welfare-enhancing and which are not. This is a task worthy of Solomon, because the dividing line will often be vague and preferences that appear nonsensical on the surface may become more sensible as one digs deeper. The alternative is to continue to work on developing information on the preferences that emerge when individuals are well informed and have the opportunity for reflection. But this task may require the endurance of Hercules. While we can clearly improve our understanding of these preferences, the complex attributes of social programs as well as the complexities of human judgment mean that our understanding of these preferences will always be somewhat imperfect.

Fortunately, the approaches currently used in benefit–cost analysis provide several practical tools for dealing with these uncertainties. These tools include quantitative sensitivity, probabilistic, and breakeven analysis, qualitative discussion of the implications of concerns that cannot be easily quantified, and explicit recognition that benefit–cost analysis should be only one of several inputs into policy decisions.

These concerns suggest a more pragmatic role for benefit–cost analysis than indicated by either the simplified version of the standard economic model or by behavioral economics.[41] Imagine again our prototypical policy analyst, asked to provide information that supports a recommendation about whether or not to proceed with an exogenously determined policy option. If well conducted, following the benefit–cost analysis framework provides the analyst with several advantages. While some of these advantages are not exclusive to benefit–cost analysis, in combination they help develop useful information for decisions:

- Benefit–cost analysis offers a well-established and tested approach for identifying and assessing the physical impacts of different policy options in addition to estimating their economic value, supported by substantial research and guidance documents that address best practices as well as by numerous examples of previously completed studies.
- Benefit–cost analysis's focus on monetization provides information on the intensity of preferences as well as on individuals' willingness to make the types of trade-offs implicit in many social policy decisions (which often involve exchanging money for social outcomes rather than for other goods and services) while not precluding the consideration of non-quantifiable effects and uncertainty.
- Benefit–cost analysis promotes a broad perspective, by incorporating the preferences of individuals affected by the costs and/or benefits of the policy options rather than being limited to the preferences of those most directly involved in the decision.
- Benefit–cost analysis encompasses several tools for incorporating uncertain outcomes and values, including sensitivity, probabilistic, and breakeven analysis as well as qualitative discussion.
- Benefit–cost analysis aids in focusing data collection and research and provides rough "stopping rules" for these efforts. These include the principle of proportionate analysis (matching the level of analytic effort to the stakes of the decision) and value of information considerations (focusing on research that is likely to affect the decision), essentially applying a benefit–cost test to the analysis itself.
- Benefit–cost analysis provides a transparent record of the data, assumptions, and analyses considered in the decision, if well documented.
- Benefit–cost analysis helps decision-makers and stakeholders to clarify areas of agreement and disagreement, separating data from assumptions and allowing those who disagree to test the effects of alternative analytic approaches.

Under this formulation, benefit–cost analysis becomes one of many sources of information for decision-making rather than providing *the* answer to a policy question. It is instead a method for collecting, organizing, and evaluating information relevant to the decision.

In summary, when taken to the extreme, traditional economic theory can be interpreted as suggesting that decisions are always rational and welfare enhancing, while behavioral economics could be interpreted as suggesting that individual choices are so unstable or inconsistent with well-being as to render the results of benefit–cost analysis meaningless. Both extremes substantially overstate the implications of related research. Analysts recognize that benefit–cost analysis as traditionally conducted is one of many sources of information, and must be supplemented by consideration of other concerns including non-quantified effects and equity. Behavioral researchers acknowledge that behavioral anomalies may be limited in occurrence and/or in significance, and that these anomalies can be counterbalanced to varying degrees by education and experience.

The introduction to this chapter suggests that the core issue raised by behavioral economics is whether choices in fact reflect welfare-enhancing preferences. The answer to this question appears to be "it depends." In some cases, behavioral research has identified attributes that individuals may truly value, that are not explicitly incorporated into the standard economic model. In other cases, decisions may reflect simplifying heuristics or emotional responses that drive a wedge between choices and underlying, normative preferences. We are far from fully understanding these distinctions, but the questions raised by behavioral economics provide useful insights for how we might further explore these issues. While benefit–cost analysis is useful for many reasons, it will inevitably have limitations. Clear discussion of its implications and uncertainties will always be required.

NOTES

1. Examples of seminal work and comprehensive reviews include Thaler (1992), Rabin (1998), Kahneman and Tversky (2000), Camerer et al. (2004), Fudenberg (2006), and DellaVigna (2009).
2. Other examples of alternative framing include: Sugden (2004, 2005a, 2009), Bernheim and Rangel (2009), Green and Hojman (2009), and Smith and Moore (2010).
3. See Robinson (2004, 2011) for more information on current practices for regulatory analysis; practices will vary in other policy contexts.
4. In its simplest form, neoclassical theory assumes perfect information. However, an entire field has developed within the standard model around the economics of information, including topics such as decision-making under uncertainty, insurance, the optimal acquisition of costly information, and the effects of information asymmetries (e.g., adverse selection and moral hazard).
5. See, for example, Diamond and Vartiainen (2007), Thaler and Sunstein (2008), and Congdon et al. (2011).
6. See, for example, Allcott and Mullainathan (2010) for discussion of the implications of behavioral research for energy policy.
7. See, for example, Bernheim and Rangel (2007) for discussion of the implications of behavioral research for addiction programs.

8. Manski (2011) goes further and proposes that economists should evaluate behavior in the context of the actual choice situation without imposing conditions about consistency with choices in other contexts. He notes (p. 1) that an individual "only wants to make a reasonable choice from the choice set that he actually faces. Hence, I reason that prescriptions for decision making should *respect actuality*. That is, they should promote welfare maximization in the choice problem the agent actually faces" (italics in original)
9. For more discussion of benefit–cost analysis as a normative or positive exercise, see, for example: Just et al. (2004), Adler and Posner (2006), and Hammitt (2009).
10. Smith and Moore (2010) note that: "[d]ecisions that appear incoherent or contradictory may simply reflect the analysts' failure to fully specify the constraints to choice" (p. 226). These constraints include factors such cognitive capacity, the energy available for decision-making, and physical dexterity, as well as budget constraints.
11. We do not discuss research on happiness (or life satisfaction) in detail. Several scholars have suggested that these approaches should replace the use of willingness to pay (WTP) or willingness to accept (WTA) measures in benefit–cost analysis (see, for example, Kahneman and Sugden, 2005 and Layard, 2010 as well as the August 2008 special issue of the *Journal of Public Economics*). However, more work is needed to improve related research methods, collect empirical data, and assess the implications for policy analysis. For a thoughtful critique of related issues, see Smith (2008).
12. This issue arises primarily in stated preference studies. As discussed in Smith and Moore (2010), hedonic models (such as those examining wage-risk trade-offs to estimate the value of mortality risks) result in point estimates of marginal WTP based on equilibrium conditions. Information on discrete changes is needed to detect disparities between WTP and WTA.
13. More precisely, these measures are based on the concepts of compensating and equivalent variation (or compensating and equivalent surplus for public goods). The two measures differ in their starting points: for a beneficial outcome, compensating variation references the level of utility without the improvement, while equivalent variation references the level with the improvement.
14. Even under conventional welfare economics, intransitivities can arise (e.g., the Scitovskzy reversal paradox) and the valuation of an intervention can depend on how its benefits and costs are distributed. For example, policies that prevent the same number of expected fatalities can be valued differently depending on how the risk reductions are concentrated or diffused in the population (Pratt and Zeckhauser, 1996; Hammitt and Treich, 2007).
15. This preference for WTP estimates due to perceived WTA measurement problems is reflected in current guidelines, such as US OMB (2003).
16. In other words, VSL is equal to individual WTP for a small risk change in a defined time period, divided by the risk change; it is the local slope of an indifference curve between risk and wealth (see Hammitt, 2000).
17. See, for example, the meta-analyses in Viscusi and Aldy (2003) and Lindhjem et al. (2010), the reviews in Robinson (2008), Robinson and Hammitt (2009), and US EPA (2010a), and the guidance in US OMB (2003) and US EPA (2010b).
18. The distinction between uncertain and ambiguous risks is not always clear. In principle, an uncertain probability may have a (subjective) expected value but an ambiguous one cannot. In his seminal work on this topic, Ellsberg (1961) notes that ambiguity depends on the amount, type, reliability, and unanimity of information on probabilities and the resulting degree of confidence one has in the data.
19. When assessing the cost-effectiveness of health policies and medical interventions, recommendations for best practices suggest that, while descriptions of health states should be based on information from patients or others familiar with the condition, preferences for different health states should be based on the community or societal perspective. One way of describing the desirability of this perspective "is to imagine that we are looking at the world before we are born, or at least before we encounter any serious health problems, and to ask what kind of world we would like it to be. In that

'ex ante' position we would not yet know what health problems we were destined to develop—only that there was some chance that we might develop any of them" (Gold et al., 1996, p. 7). Similar recommendations have been developed for cost-effectiveness analysis of environmental, health, and safety regulations (Institute of Medicine, 2006).

20. This results because the discount factor $[1/(1 + r)^t]$ is a nonlinear function of the discount rate r over time t, so the expected value of the discount factor corresponds to smaller values of r as t increases.
21. For example, the United Kingdom's guidance for evaluation of public programs (HM Treasury, 2003) suggests that declining discount rates be used for analyses that cover periods greater than 30 years. Wietzman (2001) also suggests declining rates for assessing climate change policies.
22. This means that the present value (PV) of a benefit or cost (S) at time (t) using a discount rate (r) is calculated as $PV = S_t/(1 + r)^t$.
23. Both Circulars note that the shadow price approach would be preferable but is not recommended due to difficulties in its implementation. In addition to discussing social programs, Circular A-94 also discusses rates to be used in analyses that reflect trade-offs within the federal budget, which are based on Treasury borrowing rates and updated annually.
24. All discount rates are reported as real rates, net of inflation.
25. Three percent is also recommended as the base rate for cost-effectiveness analysis of health and medical interventions, with an alternative of 5 percent (for comparability with older studies) and a range of 0 to 7 percent in sensitivity analysis (Gold et al., 1996).
26. Alternatives to the hyperbolic discounting model have been proposed by some to explain these research results, including subadditive discounting (Read, 2001) and similarity relations (Rubinstein, 2003).
27. If preferences are characterized by date rather than distance from the present, hyperbolic discounting can be dynamically consistent (Harvey, 1994).
28. As discussed in Berns et al. (2007) and Chabris et al. (2008), behavioral economists are also exploring the potential neurological basis of the tendency to discount hyperbolically.
29. In some cases, there may be more than one switch point (i.e., internal rate of return), depending on the distribution of costs and benefits over time.
30. We follow the usual assumption that the values to be counted in the benefit–cost analyses are those held by the individuals who bear its costs and/or receive its benefits. Decision-makers may, of course, have altruistic motives or other interests that differ from those of the affected individuals.
31. We default to the usual convention of referring to WTP rather than both WTP and WTA for ease of presentation. See section 2 for discussion of these measures.
32. It is worth considering, in this case, whether those receiving the excess health benefits (e.g., poorer members of the population) would benefit more if the altruists were willing to provide an additional $50 in cash rather than spending it on risk reduction.
33. One area where paternalistic values have been increasingly recognized is in valuing health risks to children; see, for example, Dockins et al. (2002).
34. A related issue is whether adult WTP reflects only personal values or also incorporates values associated with the well-being of other household members regardless of their age. See Munro (2009) for discussion of related issues in the context of stated preference studies. Similar issues may arise in revealed preference studies. For example, researchers generally assume that VSL estimates from wage-risk studies represent individual values, but decisions to trade income for risk changes may represent a household decision and include consideration of others' well-being.
35. In reality, such redistribution may be difficult to achieve due to administrative costs, political constraints, and other factors.
36. Other countries appear more willing to use distributional weights; for example, the United Kingdom suggests weighting to reflect the marginal utility of income in policy analyses (HM Treasury, 2003).

37. For example, Fehr and Schmidt (1999) explore inequity aversion, and find that the interaction between self-interested and inequity-averse individuals will affect each others' willingness to contribute to public goods.
38. Solnick and Hemenway (2005) trace this concern with relative position to work by Thorstein Veblen in 1899 and cite several theoretical treatments published since that time.
39. One underlying issue in this research is the effect of "constructed" preferences. Particularly when faced with unfamiliar goods, individuals are not likely to have pre-existing preferences. Rather, their preferences will be formed when related decisions are required. This raises the question of whether these preferences will then be stable over time and across different contexts, and of how education and experience relate to creating this stability.
40. In addition, given the Kaldor–Hicks potential compensation criteria, Hammitt (2009) notes, "[t]he justification for using a monetary metric is that money can be transferred among affected individuals at low or modest cost (e.g., through changes in the tax code and income-support programs), but other possible metrics are more difficult or costly to transfer" (p. 194).
41. There is a large literature on the rationale for conducting benefit–cost analysis that is too extensive to summarize here, including more philosophical discussions (e.g., Adler and Posner, 2006) as well as more detailed practical recommendations (e.g., Harrington et al., 2009). In particular, Sunstein (2000) argues that benefit–cost analysis "is most plausibly justified on cognitive grounds—as a way of counteracting predictable problems in individual and social cognition" (p. 1059), describing how such analysis can be used to counterbalance related errors.

REFERENCES

Adler, Matthew D. (2008), "Risk equity; a new proposal," *Harvard Environmental Law Review*, **32**, 1–47.

Adler, Matthew D. and Eric A. Posner (2006), *New Foundations for Benefit–Cost Analysis*, Cambridge, MA: Harvard University Press.

Alberini, Anna, Maureen Cropper, Alan Krupnick, and Nathalie Simon (2004), "Does the value of a statistical life vary with age and health status? Evidence from the U.S. and Canada," *Journal of Environmental Economics and Management*, **48** (1), 769–92.

Allcott, Hunt and Sendhil Mullainathan (2010), "Behavior and energy policy," *Science*, **327** (5970), 1204–5.

Andreoni, James, William T. Harbaugh, and Lise Vesterlund (2008), "Altruism in experiments," in Steven N. Durlauf and Lawrence E. Blume (eds), *The New Palgrave Dictionary of Economics*, 2nd edition, New York: Palgrave Macmillan.

Bergstrom, Ted C. (2006), "Benefit–cost in a benevolent society," *American Economic Review*, **96** (1), 339–51.

Bernheim, B. Douglas and Antonio Rangel (2007), "Behavioral public economics: Welfare and policy analysis with non-standard decision-makers," in Peter Diamond and Hannu Vartiainen (eds), *Economic Institutions and Behavioral Economics*, Princeton, NJ: Princeton University Press.

Bernheim, B. Douglas and Antonio Rangel (2009), "Beyond revealed preference: Choice-theoretic foundations for behavioral welfare economics," *Quarterly Journal of Economics*, **124** (1), 51–104.

Berns, Gregory S., David Laibson, and George Loewenstein (2007), "Intertemporal

choice—toward an integrative framework," *Trends in Cognitive Sciences*, **11** (11), 482–8.
Beshears, John, James J. Choi, David Laibson, and Brigitte C. Madrian (2008), "How are preferences revealed?," *Journal of Public Economics*, **92** (8/9), 1787–94.
Braga, Jacinto and Chris Starmer (2005), "Preference anomalies, preference elicitation, and the discovered preference hypothesis," *Environmental and Resource Economics*, **32** (1), 55–89.
Camerer, Colin F., George Loewenstein, and Matthew Rabin (eds) (2004), *Advances in Behavioral Economics*, Princeton, NJ: Princeton University Press.
Carlsson, Fredrik (2010), "Design of stated preference surveys: Is there more to learn from behavioral economics?," *Environment and Resource Economics*, **46** (2), 167–77.
Chabris, Christopher F., David I. Laibson, and Jonathan P. Schuldt (2008), "Intertemporal choice," in Steven N. Durlauf and Lawrence E. Blume (eds), *The New Palgrave Dictionary of Economics*, 2nd edition, New York: Palgrave Macmillan.
Charness, Gary and Matthew Rabin (2002), "Understanding preferences with simple tests," *Quarterly Journal of Economics*, **117** (3), 817–69.
Congdon, William J., Jeffrey R. Kling, and Sendhil Mullainathan (2011), *Policy and Choice: Public Finance through the Lens of Behavioral Economics*, Washington, DC: Brookings Institution Press.
Corso, Phaedra S., James K. Hammitt, and John D. Graham (2001), "Valuing mortality-risk reduction: Using visual aids to improve the validity of contingent valuation," *Journal of Risk and Uncertainty*, **23** (2), 165–84.
DellaVigna, Stefano (2009), "Psychology and economics: Evidence from the field," *Journal of Economic Literature*, **47** (2), 315–72.
Desaigues, Bridgette, Ari Rabl, Dominique Ami, Boun My Kene, Serge Masson, Marie-Anne Salomon, and Laure Santoni (2007), "Monetary value of a life expectancy gain due to reduced air pollution: Lessons from a contingent valuation," *Revue d'Economie Politique*, **117** (5), 675–98.
Diamond, Peter and Hannu Vartiainen (eds) (2007), *Behavioral Economics and its Applications*, Princeton, NJ, and Oxford: Princeton University Press.
Dockins, Chris, Robin R. Jenkins, Nicole Owens, Nathalie B. Simon, and Lanelle Bembenek Wiggins (2002), "Valuation of childhood risk reduction: The importance of age, risk preferences and perspective," *Risk Analysis*, **22** (2), 335–46.
Dockins, Chris, Kelly Maguire, Nathalie Simon, and Melonie Sullivan (2004), *Value of Statistical Life Analysis and Environmental Policy: A White Paper*, prepared by the National Center for Environmental Economics, US Environmental Protection Agency, for presentation to the Environmental Economics Advisory Committee of the Science Advisory Board.
Ellsberg, Daniel (1961), "Risk, ambiguity, and the savage axioms," *The Quarterly Journal of Economics*, **75** (4), 643–69.
Farrow, Scott (2011), "Incorporating equity in regulatory and benefit–cost analysis using risk-based preferences," *Risk Analysis*, **31** (6), 902–7.
Fehr, Ernst and Klaus M. Schmidt (1999), "A theory of fairness, competition, and cooperation," *The Quarterly Journal of Economics*, **114** (3), 817–68.
Frank, Robert H. (2005), "Positional externalities cause large and preventable welfare losses," *American Economic Review*, **95** (2), 137–41.
Frank, Robert H. and Cass R. Sunstein (2001), "Cost–benefit analysis and relative position," *University of Chicago Law Review*, **68** (2), 323–74.

Frederick, Shane, George Loewenstein, and Ted O'Donoghue (2002), "Time discounting and time preference: A critical review," *Journal of Economic Literature*, **40** (2), 351–401.
Freeman, A. Myrick III (2003), *The Measurement of Environmental and Resource Values: Theory and Methods*, 2nd edition, Washington, DC: Resources for the Future.
Fudenberg, Drew (2006), "Advancing beyond *Advances in Behavioral Economics*," *Journal of Economic Literature*, **44** (3), 694–711.
Fudenberg, Drew and David K. Levine (2006), "A dual-self model of impulse control," *American Economic Review*, **96**(5), 1449–76.
Gold, Marthe R., Joanna E. Siegel, Louise B. Russell, and Milton C. Weinstein (eds) (1996), *Cost-effectiveness in Health and Medicine*, New York and Oxford: Oxford University Press.
Gollier, Christian and Richard Zeckhauser (2005), "Aggregation of heterogeneous time preferences," *Journal of Political Economy*, **113** (4), 878–96.
Graham, John D. (2008), "Saving lives through administrative law and economics," *University of Pennsylvania Law Review*, **157**, 431–48.
Green, Jerry R. and Daniel A. Hojman (2009), "Choice, rationality, and welfare measurement," unpublished manuscript.
Guria, Jagadish, Joanne Leung, Michael Jones-Lee, and Graham Loomes (2005), "The willingness to accept value of statistical life relative to the willingness to pay value: Evidence and policy implications," *Environmental & Resource Economics*, **32** (1), 113–27.
Hammitt, James K. (2000), "Valuing mortality risk: Theory and practice," *Environmental Science and Technology*, **34** (8), 1396–400.
Hammitt, James K. (2007), "Valuing changes in mortality risk: Lives saved versus life years saved," *Review of Environmental Economics and Policy*, **1** (2), 228–40.
Hammitt, James K. (2009), "Response: Saving lives: Benefit–cost analysis and distribution," *PENNumbra—University of Pennsylvania Law Review*, **157**, 189–99.
Hammitt, James K. and John D. Graham (1999), "Willingness to pay for health protection: Inadequate sensitivity to probability?," *Journal of Risk and Uncertainty*, **18** (1), 33–62.
Hammitt, James K. and Lisa A. Robinson (2011), "The income elasticity of the value per statistical life: Transferring estimates between high and low income populations," *Journal of Benefit–Cost Analysis*, **2** (1), Article 1.
Hammitt, James K. and Nicolas Treich (2007), "Statistical vs identified lives in benefit–cost analysis," *Journal of Risk and Uncertainty*, **35** (1), 45–66.
Hanemann, W. Michael (1991), "Willingness to pay and willingness to accept: How much can they differ?" *American Economic Review*, **81** (3), 635–47.
Hanley, Nick and Jason F. Shogren (2005), "Is benefit–cost analysis anomaly-proof?," *Environmental and Resource Economics*, **32** (1), 13–34.
Harrington, Winston, Lisa Heinzerling, and Richard D. Morgenstern (2009), *Reforming Regulatory Impact Analysis*, Washington, DC: Resources for the Future.
Harvey, Charles M. (1994), "The reasonableness of non-constant discounting," *Journal of Public Economics*, **53** (1), 31–51.
Hepburn, Cameron, Stephen Duncan, and Antonis Papachristodoulou (2010), "Behavioural economics, hyperbolic discounting, and environmental policy," *Environment and Resource Economics*, **46** (2), 189–206.

HM Treasury (2003), *The Green Book: Appraisal and Evaluation in Central Government*, London: TSO.

Horowitz, John K. and Kenneth E. McConnell (2002), "A review of WTA/WTP studies," *Journal of Environmental Economics and Management*, **44** (3), 426–47.

Institute of Medicine (2006), *Valuing Health for Regulatory Cost-Effectiveness Analysis*, Wilhelmine Miller, Lisa A. Robinson, and Robert S. Lawrence (eds), Washington, DC: The National Academies Press.

Jacobsson, Frederic, Magnus Johannesson, and Lars Borgquist (2007), "Is altruism paternalistic?," *The Economic Journal*, **117** (520), 761–81.

Johansson-Stenman, Olof (2008), "Mad cows, terrorism and junk food: Should public policy reflect perceived or objective risks?," *Journal of Health Economics*, **27** (2), 234–48.

Johansson-Stenman, Olof and James Konow (2010), "Fair air: Distributive justice and environmental economics," *Environmental and Resource Economics*, **46** (2), 147–66.

Jones-Lee, Michael W. (1991), "Altruism and the value of other people's safety," *Journal of Risk and Uncertainty*, **4** (2), 213–19.

Just, Richard E., Darrell L. Hueth, and Andrew Schmitz (2004), *The Welfare Economics of Public Policy*, Cheltenham, UK and Northampton, MA, USA: Edward Elgar.

Kahneman, Daniel (2000a), "Experienced utility and objective happiness: A moment-based approach," in Daniel Kahneman and Amos Tversky (eds), *Choices, Values, and Frames*, Cambridge, UK: Cambridge University Press.

Kahneman, Daniel (2000b), "Evaluation by moments: Past and future," in Daniel Kahneman and Amos Tversky (eds), *Choices, Values, and Frames*, Cambridge, UK: Cambridge University Press.

Kahneman Daniel and Jack L. Knetsch (1992), "Valuing public goods: The purchase of moral satisfaction," *Journal of Environmental Economics and Management*, **22** (1), 57–70.

Kahneman, Daniel and Robert Sugden (2005), "Experienced utility as a standard of policy evaluation," *Environmental and Resource Economics*, **32** (1), 161–81.

Kahneman, Daniel and Amos Tversky (1979), "Prospect theory: An analysis of decision under risk," *Econometrica*, **47** (2), 263–91.

Kahneman, Daniel and Amos Tversky (eds) (2000), *Choices, Values, and Frames*, Cambridge, UK: Cambridge University Press.

Kahneman Daniel, Jack L. Knetsch, and Richard H. Thaler (1991), "Anomalies: The endowment effect, loss aversion, and status quo bias," *Journal of Economic Perspectives*, **5** (1), 192–206.

Knetsch, Jack L. (2005), "Gains, losses, and the US-EPA *Economic Analysis Guidelines*: A hazardous product?," *Environmental and Resource Economics*, **32** (1), 91–112.

Knetsch, Jack L. (2010), "Values of gains and losses: Reference states and choices of measure," *Environment and Resource Economics*, **46** (2), 179–88.

Kniesner, Thomas J. and W. Kip Viscusi (2005), "Value of a statistical life: Relative position vs. relative age," *American Economic Review*, **95** (2), 142–6.

Krutilla, John (1967), "Conservation reconsidered," *American Economic Review*, **57** (4), 777–86.

Laibson, David I. (1997), "Golden eggs and hyperbolic discounting," *Quarterly Journal of Economics*, **112** (2), 443–78.

Laibson, David I. (2010), "Behavioral economics," presented at American Economic Association Annual Meeting, Continuing Education Program.
Laibson, David I., Andrea Repetto, and Jeremy Tobacman (2007), *Estimating Discount Functions with Consumption Choices over the Lifecycle*, unpublished manuscript.
Layard, Richard (2010), "Measuring subjective well-being," *Science*, **327** (5965), 534–5.
Lindhjem, Henrik, Ståle Navrud, and Nils Axel Braathen (2010), "Valuing lives saved from environmental, transport, and health policies: A meta-analysis of stated preference studies," paper prepared for the Organisation for Economic Co-operation and Development.
List, John A. (2005), "Scientific numerology, preference anomalies, and environmental policymaking," *Environmental and Resource Economics*, **32** (1), 35–53.
Loomis, John B. (2011), "Incorporating distributional issues into benefit cost analysis: Why, how, and two empirical examples using non-market valuation," *Journal of Benefit–Cost Analysis*, **2** (1), Article 5.
Luttmer, Erzo F.P. (2005), "Neighbors as negatives: Relative earnings and well-being," *Quarterly Journal of Economics*, **120** (3), 963–1002.
Manski, Charles F. (2011), "Actualist rationality," *Theory and Decision*, **71** (2), 195–210.
Mitchell, Robert Cameron and Richard T. Carson (1989), *Using Surveys to Value Public Goods: The Contingent Valuation Method*, Washington, DC: Resources for the Future.
Morris, Jill and James K. Hammitt (2001), "Using life expectancy to communicate benefits of health care programs in contingent valuation studies," *Medical Decision-making*, **21** (6), 468–78.
Munro, Alistair (2009), "Introduction to the special issue: Things we do and don't understand about the household and the environment," *Environmental and Resource Economics*, **43** (1), 1–10.
National Oceanic and Atmospheric Administration (1993), "Natural resource damage assessments under the Oil Pollution Act of 1990," *Federal Register*, **58** (10), 4601–14.
Pratt, John W. and Richard J. Zeckhauser (1996), "Willingness to pay and the distribution of risk and wealth," *Journal of Political Economy*, **104** (4), 747–63.
Rabin, Matthew (1998), "Psychology and economics," *Journal of Economic Literature*, **36** (1), 11–46.
Read, Daniel (2001), "Is time-discounting hyperbolic or subadditive?," *Journal of Risk and Uncertainty*, **23** (1), 5–32.
Riddel, Mary and W. Douglass Shaw (2006), "A theoretically-consistent empirical model of non-expected utility: An application to nuclear-waste transport," *Journal of Risk and Uncertainty*, **32** (2), 131–50.
Robinson, Lisa A. (2004), *Current Federal Agency Practices for Valuing the Impact of Regulations on Human Health and Safety*, prepared for the Committee to Evaluate Measures of Health Benefits for Environmental, Health, and Safety Regulation, Institute of Medicine.
Robinson, Lisa A. (2008), *Valuing Mortality Risk Reductions in Homeland Security Regulatory Analyses*, prepared for US Customs and Border Protection, Department of Homeland Security, under subcontract to Industrial Economics, Incorporated.
Robinson, Lisa A. (2011), "Assessing regulatory costs and benefits," in J. Nriagu

(ed.), *Encyclopedia of Environmental Health*, Volume 5, Oxford: Elsevier Ltd., pp. 221–9.
Robinson, Lisa A. and James K. Hammitt (2009), *The Value of Reducing Air Pollution Risks in Sub-Saharan Africa*, prepared for the World Bank under subcontract to ICF International.
Robinson, Lisa A., James K. Hammitt, Joseph E. Aldy, Alan Krupnick, and Jennifer Baxter (2010), "Valuing the risk of death from terrorist attacks," *Journal of Homeland Security and Emergency Management*, **7** (1), Article 14.
Rosen, Sherwin (1988), "The value of changes in life expectancy," *Journal of Risk and Uncertainty*, **1** (1), 285–304.
Rubinstein, Ariel (2003), "'Economics and psychology'? The case of hyperbolic discounting," *International Economic Review*, **44** (4), 1027–216.
Samuelson, Paul A. (1937), "A note on the measurement of utility," *Review of Economic Studies*, **4** (2), 155–61.
Shepard, Donald S. and Richard J. Zeckhauser (1984),"Survival versus consumption," *Management Science*, **30** (4), 423–39.
Shogren, Jason F. (2005), "Economics of diet and health: Research challenges," *Acta Agriculturae Scand Section C*, **2** (3/4), 117–27.
Shogren, Jason F., Gregory M. Parkhurst, and Presenjit Banerjee (2010), "Two cheers and a qualm for behavioral environmental economics," *Environment and Resource Economics*, **46** (2), 235–47.
Slovic, Paul (1987), "Perception of risk," *Science*, **236** (4799), 280–85.
Smith, V. Kerry (2007), "Reflections on the literature," *Review of Environmental Economics and Policy*, **1** (1), 152–65.
Smith, V. Kerry (2008), "Reflections on the literature," *Review of Environmental Economics and Policy*, **2** (2), 292–308.
Smith, V. Kerry and Eric M. Moore (2010), "Behavioral economics and benefit cost analysis," *Environment and Resource Economics*, **46** (2), 217–34.
Smith, V. Kerry, Subhrendu K. Pattanayak, and George L. Van Houtven (2006), "Structural benefit transfer: An application using VSL estimates," *Ecological Economics*, **60** (2), 361–71.
Solnick, Sara J. and David Hemenway (2005), "Are positional concerns stronger in some domains than in others?" *American Economic Review*, **95** (2), 147–51.
Sugden, Robert (2004), "The opportunity criterion: Consumer sovereignty without the assumption of coherent preferences," *American Economic Review*, **94** (4), 1014–33.
Sugden, Robert (2005a), "Coping with preference anomalies in benefit–cost analysis: A market simulation approach," *Environmental and Resource Economics*, **32** (1), 129–60.
Sugden, Robert (2005b), "Anomalies and stated preference techniques: A framework for discussion of coping strategies," *Environmental and Resource Economics*, **32** (1), 1–12.
Sugden, Robert (2009), "Market simulation and the provision of public goods: A non-paternalistic response to anomalies in environmental evaluation," *Journal of Environmental Economics and Management*, **57** (1), 87–103.
Sunstein, Cass R. (2000), "Cognition and benefit–cost analysis," *Journal of Legal Studies*, **29** (2), 1059–103.
Sunstein, Cass R. (2007), "Willingness to pay vs. welfare," *Harvard Law and Policy Review*, **1**, 303–30.

Thaler, Richard H. (1992), *The Winner's Curse*, Princeton, NJ: Princeton University Press.
Thaler, Richard H. and Sendhil Mullainathan (2008), "How behavioral economics differs from traditional economics," in David R. Henderson (ed.), *The Concise Encyclopedia of Economics*, Indianapolis, IN: The Liberty Fund, Incorporated.
Thaler, Richard H. and Cass R. Sunstein (2008), *Nudge: Improving Decisions about Health, Wealth, and Happiness*, New Haven, CT: Yale University Press.
US Environmental Protection Agency (2010a), *Valuing Mortality Risk Reductions for Environmental Policy: A White Paper (Review Draft)*, prepared by the National Center for Environmental Economics for consultation with the Science Advisory Board–Environmental Economics Advisory Committee.
US Environmental Protection Agency (EPA) (2010b), *Guidelines for Preparing Economic Analysis*, EPA 240-R-10-001.
US Office of Management and Budget (OMB) (1992), Circular A-94: "Guidelines and discount rates for benefit–cost analysis of federal programs," Washington, DC: US Office of Management and Budget.
US Office of Management and Budget (OMB) (2003), Circular A-4: "Regulatory analysis," Washington, DC: US Office of Management and Budget.
Viscusi, W. Kip and Joseph E. Aldy (2003), "The value of a statistical life: A critical review of market estimates throughout the world," *Journal of Risk and Uncertainty*, **27** (1), 5–76.
Viscusi, W. Kip, Wesley A. Magat, and Anne Forrest (1988), "Altruistic and private valuations of risk reduction," *Journal of Policy Analysis and Management*, **7** (2), 227–45.
Viscusi, W. Kip, Wesley A. Magat, and Joel Huber (1991), "Communication of ambiguous risk information," *Theory and Decision*, **31** (2/3), 159–73.
Weitzman, Martin L. (2001), "Gamma discounting," *The American Economic Review*, **91** (1), 260–71.
Willig, Robert D. (1976), "Consumer's surplus without apology," *The American Economic Review*, **66** (4), 589–97.
Zerbe, Richard (2009), "Ethical benefit cost analysis as art and science: Ten rules for benefit–cost analysis," *University of Pennsylvania Journal of Law and Social Change*, **12** (1), 73–105.

11. Conclusion: principles and standards for benefit–cost analysis

Richard O. Zerbe, Jr., Tyler Blake Davis, Nancy Garland, and Tyler Scott

1 INTRODUCTION

This chapter is taken from a report for the MacArthur Foundation by the Center for Benefit–Cost Analysis entitled "Towards Principles and Standards in the Use of Benefit–Cost Analysis" (2010). The current chapter differs from the earlier one in the omission of certain historical material, some of which appears in the introduction of this volume, and the addition of small refinements. This chapter draws years of scholarship and work on benefit–cost analysis into a single document intended as a starting point to establish principles and standards for benefit–cost analysis in government and non-profit decision-making, with a particular emphasis on social programs. The responsibility for this chapter, including errors, mistakes, and choice of standards lies with the senior author and not with the student research assistants, authors of white papers, or the scientific committee members who helped with this chapter.

The Principles and Standards project commissioned white papers on various subjects from leading experts and promising younger scholars in specific fields of applied benefit–cost analysis. Each of these scholars was commissioned because of his or her experience and work in the field. The topics and commissions of these papers are as shown in Table 11.1.

Each of the commissioned authors' papers was subject to professional review by another scholar in the field, and comments were provided to the author. Following revisions, each commissioned paper was opened up to public comment through posting on the website of the Benefit–Cost Analysis Center. Through this site, readers could view and download these pieces of cutting-edge scholarship, and leave comments for the authors and the benefit–cost analysis community. Authors of papers responded to comments as appropriate, and the final papers have again been made available to the public.

Table 11.1 Commissioned papers, authors and reviewers

Topic	Author	Reviewer
General equilibrium analysis and social programs	H. Allen Klaiber and V. Kerry Smith	Roberton C. Williams III
Distributional issues	John Loomis	James K. Hammitt
Behavioral economics	Lisa A. Robinson and James K. Hammitt	Brigitte Madrian
Social policy	Aidan R. Vining and David L. Weimer	Robert Haveman
Early childhood interventions	Lynn Karoly	Clive R. Belfield
Crime	John R. Lott, Jr.	Bruce H. Kobayashi
Public safety	R. Scott Farrow and W. Kip Viscusi	Richard O. Zerbe
Public health	Joseph H. Cook	Lisa A. Robinson

The Benefit–Cost Analysis Center thanks the John D. and Catherine T. MacArthur Foundation for their support, particularly Michael A. Stegman, Valerie Chang, and Steven Casey. The Center also thanks the Evans School of Public Affairs for institutional support, including the efforts of Dean Sandra Archibald and Professors Alison Cullen and Joe Cook. The Center would also like to recognize its support staff, Deborah Fishler, Katie Ward, Aubri Wall, Camille French, and Kay Sterner. The Evans Communication Team, including Molly McCarthy and Joe Eastham, deserve thanks for creating the interactive sections of the Center's website to enable public comment on this project. Finally, the authors thank Nevena Lalic and Kiana Scott for their assistance reading and editing drafts.

1.1 The Scientific Committee

The authors are greatly indebted to the members of the Society for Benefit–Cost Analysis who served as a scientific review committee (Table 11.2). Their reviews and input served to significantly improve the chapter; any remaining faults, however, are the responsibility of the chapter authors alone.

In addition, Glenn Jenkins and David Burgess made very helpful suggestions. There are more citations to the principal author's work than he is comfortable with, and which in some cases could be replaced by better citations. Time constraints made this convenient but this author asks forbearance by other colleagues.

Table 11.2 Reviewers on scientific committee

Reviewer	Affiliation
Anton, Paul	Anton Economics
Aos, Steve	Washington State Institute for Public Policy
Cameron, Trudy	University of Oregon
Cole, Dan	Indiana University School of Law
Graham, John	University of Indiana
Hammitt, James K.	Harvard University
Harberger, Arnold C.	University of California, Los Angeles
Harrison, Glenn	Georgia State University
Kobayashi, Bruce H.	George Mason University
Krutilla, Kerry	Indiana University
Loomis, John	Colorado State University
Lott, John R., Jr.	University of Maryland
Robinson, Lisa A.	Independent Consultant
Schmitz, Andrew	University of Florida
Vining, Aidan	Simon Fraser University
Viscusi, W. Kip	Vanderbilt University Law School
Weimer, David	University of Wisconsin
Williams, Roberton C., III	University of Maryland

1.2 The Purpose and Goals of this Chapter

This chapter aims to establish principles and standards for the use of benefit–cost analysis for analyzing social programs. Most of these will apply also to benefit–cost analysis more generally. The chapter recognizes that these principles and standards necessarily will need to adapt to future developments and advances in economics and benefit–cost analysis scholarship; thus, we view our chapter as the beginning of a continuing endeavor. We hope that this ongoing project will be a collaboration of members of the field, including scholars, practitioners, policy-makers, and theorists. This chapter is a starting place for this effort.

Finally, there are several notable omissions from this chapter, which we were not able to fully address due to time and resource limitations. Among these, items to be addressed in future iterations include:

- a portfolio approach justification for BCA;
- standardized stated preference methodology;
- the validity of separating equity and efficiency given new research findings and theoretical advances;

- the role of behavioral models in valuation and prediction;
- the relation between benefit–cost and happiness research;
- a compilation of unit value for work in social program evaluation.

Although we touch on many of these issues within our principles and standards, a fuller review of the current literature is beyond the scope of this project. We envision that future editions of the Principles and Standards project will be able to provide more expansive and documented guidelines.

1.3 Organization

This section begins with a summary of all Foundational Principles, Theoretical Standards, and Technical Standards for benefit–cost analysis (BCA) found in the project. This is to provide a quick reference point for individual items; for further discussion, the reader should refer to the discussion of each item found starting in section 5. Following this, more-specific theoretical and technical standards for BCA are organized under subheadings of Benefit and Cost Estimation, Market Extent, Discounting, Risk and Uncertainty, Equity and Distribution, and Presentation. References and notes are provided in each section and an Appendix provides a glossary of terms and abbreviations.

2 SUMMARY OF COLLECTED PRINCIPLES AND STANDARDS

A fuller discussion of the structure and vision for our General Principles, Theoretical Standards, and Technical Standards is provided in section 3; however, principles are intended to be broad-based, fundamental concepts that define BCA. Theoretical and technical standards then apply these principles, providing more specific direction as to current best practices involving various aspects of BCA. The elements of this section provide a quick reference of collected principles and standards; each item is explained in detail later in the chapter.

We have not attempted here to separate well-established standards from newer concepts and recent research advances. Given that BCA is a continually evolving discipline, we thought it most advantageous to discuss commonly practiced and state-of-the-art standards in tandem. For any particular analysis component, where there exists a well-established standard practice as well as a different, newer approach gaining traction, we include both in the standard. In some instances, the new approach or finding is currently under development or poorly codified, and thus we provide the commonly practiced standard and provide the new concept as something the analyst must consider when using the older approach. Where both a newer and older approach are in use, a standard describes both approaches, and provides the analyst with guidance as to selecting the most appropriate methodology for an analysis given resources and context. Our reasoning is that this structure will allow for standards to evolve in keeping with empirical and theoretical developments as frontier practices become better established and less resource intensive, and subsequently supplant older methods.

Thus, our standards in part represent the state of the art, in part represent commonly accepted practices, and in part represent what we think should be the state of the art based upon the expert literature, comments, and reviews generated through this project.

2.1 Foundational Principles for Benefit–Cost Analysis (Details in Section 6)

- *Foundational Principle 1:* BCA is a financial evaluation tool that seeks to calculate values for all project inputs and outputs to determine the net benefit of a given project, policy, or intervention. It seeks to provide an objective framework for discussion, amendment, and decision-making by providing an accurate representation of policy outcomes.
- *Foundational Principle 2:* BCA is an aid to public policy decision-making; it is not, and should not, be regarded as a substitute for democratic, legislative, and administrative decision-making. Likewise, political influence should not intrude into technical analysis decisions and the analysis process.
- *Foundational Principle 3:* Transparency enhances the value of BCA for decision-making by facilitating a more comprehensive understanding of the analysis, and properly focuses the policy discussion upon political issues rather than technical aspects of BCA. Thus, both the analysis process and results should be made as transparent as possible.
- *Foundational Principle 4:* Pursuit of the "perfect" analysis should not prevent completion of a useful analysis. A BCA that meets basic acceptability requirements regarding objectivity and appropriate methodology can still be released even if it does not conform to all best practices or is data deficient.
- *Foundational Principle 5:* BCA should be conducted in accordance with the "principle of proportionality." This principle states that

the allocation analytical effort should be in direct proportion to the expected value of increased information, defined in this case as the extent to which it might affect a policy decision.

2.2 Standards for the Estimation of Benefits and Costs (Details in Section 7)

- *Benefits and Costs Theoretical Standard 1:* The standard theoretical measures of benefits and costs are the willingness to pay (WTP) for gains and the willingness to accept (WTA) losses. However, analyses should account for divergence between the two metrics stemming from the relative accuracy of qualifying effects as a gain or a loss.
- *Benefits and Costs Theoretical Standard 2:* Benefits and costs are defined relative to their appropriate counterfactual baseline (i.e., existing policy or currently expected outcomes).
- *Benefits and Costs Theoretical Standard 3:* As much as possible, analysts should use a consistent BCA approach across multiple public policy outcomes.
- *Benefits and Costs Theoretical Standard 4:* The fundamental summary metric of BCA is net present benefits. Though other summary statistics remain prevalent in the language of policy discussion, they provide accurate values only after appropriate adjustments. If the policy-maker desires a different metric (such as the benefit–cost ratio), this should be provided along with net benefits and adjusted to provide an accurate value.
- *Benefits and Costs Technical Standard 1:* The comprehensiveness of the analysis framework should be determined by the principle of proportionate analysis. BCA should consider general equilibrium (GE) effects where the effort required is justified by the expected importance of these effects in altering a policy decision.
- *Benefits and Costs Technical Standard 2:* Where possible WTP measures should be used for gains and WTA measures for losses. Where this is not done, the analysis should include a clear discussion of the bias from this omission and the rationale for the choice between WTP and WTA.
- *Benefits and Costs Technical Standard 3:* Values and estimates culled from secondary sources should be modified for relevancy using a benefit transfer function (also see section 9, Risk and Uncertainty below).
- *Benefits and Costs Technical Standard 4:* Non-market benefits and costs should be estimated using the current methodology appropriate for the given context.

- *Benefits and Costs Technical Standard 5:* Outcomes should be monetized to the degree necessary to facilitate faithful comparisons of economic merit. If an outcome category is monetized for one alternative, it should be monetized for all other alternatives.

2.3 Standards for Determining Market Extent/Economic Standing (Details in Section 8)

- *Market Extent Theoretical Standard 1:* As a theoretical stance, BCA should value all policy effects for all parties.
- *Market Extent Technical Standard 1:* Count all values and persons affected by the policy to the extent likely to affect results. Appropriate market extent should be based upon significance to model results and the need for proportionate analysis.
- *Market Extent Technical Standard 2:* The analyst should discuss the implications of excluded effects and present them alongside the focal results.
- *Market Extent Technical Standard 3:* The law and the policy question under consideration can furnish a guide as to values that are offset by opposing values. This provides an objective justification for the exclusion (or inclusion) of illegally derived benefits.
- *Market Extent Technical Standard 4:* Where legal rights are substantially controversial, they cannot be used to determine economic standing or reference points.

2.4 Standards for Addressing Risk and Uncertainty (Details in Section 9)

- *Risk and Uncertainty Theoretical Standard 1:* The treatment of risk and uncertainty when conducting BCA is itself subject to at least an informal BCA test.
- *Risk and Uncertainty Theoretical Standard 2:* Analyses should account for multiple sources of risk and uncertainty.
- *Risk and Uncertainty Theoretical Standard 3:* Assumptions of rationality may need to be modified in the face of risk or uncertainty.
- *Risk and Uncertainty Theoretical Standard 4:* BCA should not impose a particular form of risk-treating behavior, but should rely on empirical analysis.
- *Risk and Uncertainty Theoretical Standard 5:* The analyst should carefully account for the difference between predictions and estimates when transferring estimates and modeling outcomes.
- *Risk and Uncertainty Theoretical Standard 6:* Statistical significance levels for program and policy effect size are not relevant to BCA.

Regardless of the associated level of significance, all estimated effects should be included in the BCA model with the appropriate standard error.

- *Risk and Uncertainty Technical Standard 1:* Clearly delineate the accuracy and precision of numerical values and identify sources of uncertainty.
- *Risk and Uncertainty Technical Standard 2:* Explicitly define the concept of risk used in the analysis.
- *Risk and Uncertainty Technical Standard 3:* Use sensitivity analyses to evaluate implications of estimates and modeling assumptions.
- *Risk and Uncertainty Technical Standard 4:* Utilize probabilistic techniques to calculate net benefits so as to account for multiple uncertainties.
- *Risk and Uncertainty Technical Standard 5:* Analyze every value as a random variable, unless given evidence to the contrary.
- *Risk and Uncertainty Technical Standard 6:* Account for the legislatively mandated or desired stance towards risk at different agencies and levels of government.
- *Risk and Uncertainty Technical Standard 7:* Address potential for regression to mean, publication bias, and optimism bias when necessary by adjusting estimates.
- *Risk and Uncertainty Technical Standard 8:* Low-probability, high-consequence (i.e., catastrophic) risks should be treated with special attention according to contemporary protocol.

2.5 Standards for Selecting and Implementing Appropriate Discounting Procedures (Details in Section 10)

- *Discounting Theoretical Standard 1:* All benefits and costs expected to accrue in the future should be discounted.
- *Discounting Theoretical Standard 2:* A single, numerical discount rate should be applied consistently throughout the analysis. Where the current generation has moral values that apply to future generations these should be counted in terms of WTP at present and not incorporated into the discount rate.
- *Discounting Theoretical Standard 3:* No single rate will reflect the marginal preferences of all users.
- *Discounting Technical Standard 1:* The discount rate should be based on the social opportunity cost (SOC). The SOC will take into account both the displacement of private capital and forgone consumption, and the use of foreign funds. Its use is simpler than other similarly derived rates.

- *Discounting Technical Standard 2:* The discount rate period should match the period of the cash flow stream being analyzed.
- *Discounting Technical Standard 3:* Use real rates of discount with real benefits and costs.
- *Discounting Technical Standard 4:* Health and mortality risks should be discounted.
- *Discounting Technical Standard 5:* Adjustments for risk and uncertainty about the benefits and costs themselves should be applied to estimates of benefits and costs, and should not be factored into the discount rate. The sort of risk for which a risk premium should be attached to the discount rate is risk associated with covariance with other projects.
- *Discounting Technical Standard 6:* As an initial basis for developing a range of discount rates for social policy BCA, consult relevant published literature and standard government recommendations (such as that from the White House Office of Management and Budget [OMB]).

2.6 Standards for Addressing Equity and Distributional Issues (Details in Section 11)

- *Equity and Distribution Theoretical Standard 1:* Explicitly include the distribution of net benefits in the discussion and presentation of BCA results.
- *Equity and Distribution Theoretical Standard 2:* Present differentiated policy effects either implicitly or explicitly, but do not explicitly weight disaggregated benefits and costs (if effects are weighted, the analyst should take extreme care so that weighting does not distort estimates such that it fosters sub-optimal policy decisions).
- *Equity and Distribution Theoretical Standard 3:* Beyond displaying the distributed effects of a policy, BCA should aim to provide decision-makers with information as to how the current distribution of net benefits could be altered if so desired.
- *Equity and Distribution Technical Standard 1:* Disaggregate benefits and costs according to policy relevance and data availability.
- *Equity and Distribution Technical Standard 2:* When comparing projects, use congruent benefit and cost disaggregations.
- *Equity and Distribution Technical Standard 3:* Address potential relationship between distributional effects and policy valuation.

2.7 Standards for Analysis Presentation (Details in Section 12)

- *Presentation Theoretical Standard 1:* Presentations of benefit–cost analyses must be understandable and meaningful to the audience.
- *Presentation Theoretical Standard 2:* Analysis presentation should not overly emphasize the final estimate of net benefits. Each component of the analysis, from data gathering to modeling processes, potentially generates highly relevant policy information that deserves equal footing alongside model results in presentation.
- *Presentation Technical Standard 1:* Provide a brief (~ten page) summary for decision-makers describing analysis process, results, and implications.
- *Presentation Technical Standard 2:* Design models to allow replication and future revision. If possible, create models with accessible user interfaces so policy-makers can explore scenarios interactively.

3 THE CURRENT STATE OF BENEFIT–COST ANALYSIS AND ITS APPLICATION IN THE UNITED STATES

Momentum is building towards increasing standardization, largely precipitated at the agency level and by the Executive Branch. In a February 2009 Memorandum to the Heads of Executive Departments and Agencies (74 FR 5977), President Obama directed the head of OMB to prepare a comprehensive set of recommendations pertaining to regulatory review at the federal level. This call for input sought to examine the role of benefit–cost analysis and related distributional concerns, disclosure, and transparency, in preparation for the coming issuance of an Executive Order on Federal Regulatory Review. These documents reveal interest in and impetus for the development of a comprehensive, coherent standardization of BCA for decision analysis and implementation. Likewise, as the proposed Presidential FY2011 Budget document notes, far beyond the desire for consistency and efficiency, there exists a public right to governmental accountability and a justified expectation for prudent allocation of scarce fiscal resources that increases the need for consistent, standardized BCA in practice (Obama, 2010). Currently, the most comprehensive set of guidelines for conducting BCA on government projects and regulation remain OMB Circulars A-94, "Guidelines and Discount rates for Benefit–Cost Analysis of Social Programs" (US OMB, 1992) and A-4 "Regulatory Analysis" (US OMB, 2003).

While there is no comparable set of standards or history of use of BCA in state and local governments, there is growing momentum to that end. For example, the State of Washington, through the Washington State Institute for Public Policy (WSIPP),[1] now performs analyses of significant new social programs, and many states have adopted regulatory review policies (though of widely varying structure, scope, and impact) (Schwartz, 2010). A report by the Institute for Policy Integrity[2] at the New York University Law School provides a detailed discussion of the regulatory review process on a state by state basis (ibid.). In addition, there is growing interest in using BCA in non-governmental settings, such as non-profit human services agencies. It is our belief that these principles and standards should apply to these growing areas as well.

Notes

1. http://www.wsipp.wa.gov/.
2. http://policyintegrity.org/.

References

Obama, Barack [President] (2010), "Analytical perspectives," in *Budget of the United States Government, Fiscal Year 2011*, Washington, DC: White House Office of Management and Budget.
Schwartz, Joel A. (2010), *52 Experiments with Regulatory Review: The Political and Economic Inputs into State Rulemakings*, Institute for Policy Integrity, New York: New York University Law School, Chapter 6.
US Office of Management and Budget (OMB) (1992), Circular No. A-94, "Guidelines and discount rates for benefit–cost analysis of federal programs (revised)," Washington, DC: OMB.
US Office of Management and Budget (OMB) (2003), Circular A-4, "Regulatory analysis," Washington, DC: OMB.

4 CRITICISMS OF BCA

Without doubt, assigning WTP/WTA values to non-market goods and preferences is inexact; given the intangible, ethereal, nature of concepts such as happiness, how could it be otherwise? BCA does not claim to definitively assign value to such goods, but rather to better recognize the values held for spiritual, ethical, and moral preferences. Moreover, it bears reminder that no policy analysis tool purports to fully include such values; they are by definition inexact.

The facilitating role of BCA cannot be overstated on this point, as in the end democratic deliberation must determine value prescriptions and decide the suitable weight lent to any BCA analysis. There remains much room for improvement in economic assessment and valuation, particularly of non-market goods, and debate over such methods and frameworks serves a crucial, constructive role in improving BCA. In the classic words of statistician George Box, "All models are wrong, but some are useful." The task is to continue to hone and improve BCA as a *useful* policy tool; the application of the Kaldor–Hicks–Moral (KHM; see Chapter 8 this volume) and this Principles and Standards project represent such an endeavor. As a basis for rejecting BCA outright, however, arguments about the limitations of benefit–cost analysis as a justification for its abandonment are without foundation. One would not throw away a good hammer because it failed to tighten a screw, or even because it was used to build a poorly constructed house. Similarly, BCA should not be tossed aside for failing to accomplish what it is not intended, does not purport, nor cannot logically be expected to achieve.

In this vein, we note several technical criticisms that have been levied at either BCA or more particularly at the inclusion of moral sentiments or equity concerns in BCA. Much of this technical debate is discussed further within the following principles and standards, as these issues have driven refinement in BCA practices and methodology. One technical criticism concerning BCA at large lies in the existence of the Scitovsky reversal paradox (Scitovsky, 1941). Just et al. (2012) have shown that the paradox is unlikely to arise in most cases. The technical criticisms of including moral sentiments are primarily twofold; first the possibility that including moral sentiments could result in a positive net present value but not pass what is known as the potential compensation test (Milgrom, 1993), and second that their inclusion could lead to double counting (McConnell, 1997). Zerbe et al. (2006) have shown that even if the potential compensation test were to be retained (and we recommend it be dropped), the inclusion of moral sentiments only results in the problematic effects discussed by Milgrom in trivial cases. Further, Zerbe et al. also show that double counting will not result from the inclusion of moral sentiments, even in the case of non-paternalistic altruism.

References

Just, Richard E., Andrew Schmitz, and Richard O. Zerbe, Jr. (2012), "Scitovsky reversals and practical benefit–cost analysis," *Journal of Benefit–Cost Analysis*, **3** (2).

McConnell, Kenneth (1997), "Does altruism undermine existence value?," *Journal of Environmental Economics and Management*, **32** (1), 22–37.

Milgrom, Paul (1993), "Is sympathy an economic value? Philosophy, economics, and the contingent valuation method," in Jerry A. Hausman (ed.), *Contingent Valuation. A Critical Assessment*, Amsterdam/New York: North-Holland.

Scitovsky, Tibor D. (1941), "A note on welfare propositions in economics," *The Review of Economic Studies*, **9** (1), 77–88.
Zerbe, Jr., Richard O., Y. Bauman, and A. Finkle (2006), "An aggregate measure for benefit–cost analysis," *Ecological Economics: The Journal of the International Society for Ecological Economics*, **58** (3), 449–61.

5 DETAILED DESCRIPTION OF PRINCIPLES AND STANDARDS

The remainder of the chapter sets out cohesive guidelines for performing benefit–cost analyses of social programs, to foster maximally relevant, accurate, and comprehensive implementation of BCA in social policy decision-making. The remaining sections first delineate general, fundamental principles that form the underlying philosophical tenets of BCA, and then provide standards for conducting BCA that apply across all social policy sectors. The general principles might be considered the "non-negotiables" that underpin all BCA. The standards present more-specific guidance regarding currently held best theory and practices for different components of BCA. Standards are further divided into theoretical standards, broadly conceived concepts to guide analyses, and technical standards, appropriate methodological techniques for practitioners.

Many aspects of BCA remain fluid and will continue to evolve in keeping with research findings and theoretical advancements; where convention is unestablished or no general consensus exists, we have attempted to describe state-of-the-art practices and current research findings that indicate a way forward. These areas especially will demand revision and update in future principles and standards volumes. Rather than divide current and developing practices in BCA, we have attempted to combine the two as relevant; where an approach reflects a longstanding professional consensus, but recent research and theoretical advances advocate for a new methodology, we describe both and discuss what implications the new findings have for the old methodology. Many frontier findings and practices for BCA lack firmly established protocol, demand more research, or are currently cost prohibitive, and thus cannot be codified as explicit standards. However, such issues are hugely important to BCA, and presenting them as related to the relevant established standard allows the analyst room to chart a course that both leverages the best available research findings and is in keeping with resource demands and the scope of analysis.

The principles and standards that follow strive to further hone the way that BCA organizes knowledge and structures debate. We believe that implementation of the principles and standards presented, as gathered from a commissioned group of experts who practice and study BCA in their various disciplines, will help facilitate more compatible cross-sector policy comparisons, engender greater transparency so as to make policy debates more tractable, and improve the relevance and comprehensiveness of benefit–cost analyses. In turn, this should foster more equitable, efficient, and beneficial social policy decision-making.

Finally, we acknowledge past publications providing principles and standards for BCA (Arrow et al., 1996), texts on BCA and applied welfare analysis (Stokey and Zeckhauser, 1978; Gramlich, 1990; Hanley and Spash, 1993; Brent, 1998; Jones, 2005; Boardman et al., 2006) and major article collections (Layard and Glaister, 1994; Schmitz and Zerbe, 2009) that provide the foundation upon which these principles and standards are based. Where this chapter and the appended white papers fail to sufficiently address or describe a concept or practice, we point the reader to these sources. Further, US Office of Management and Budget Circulars A-94 and A-4 provide similar guidance in regards to government projects and regulation (US OMB, 1992, 2003); these documents also serve as common resources for BCA standards and practices.

References

Arrow, Kenneth, Maureen Cropper, George Eads, Robert Hahn, Lester Lave, Roger Knoll, Paul Portney, Milton Russell, Richard Schmalensee, V. Kerry Smith, and Robert Stavins (1996), "Is there a role for benefit–cost analysis in environmental, health, and safety regulation?," *Science*, **272** (5259), 221–2.

Boardman, Anthony E., David H. Greenberg, Aidan R. Vining, and David L. Weimer (2006), *Cost–Benefit Analysis: Concepts and Practice*, 3rd edition, Upper Saddle River, NJ: Prentice Hall.

Brent, Robert (1998), *Cost–Benefit Analysis for Developing Countries*, Cheltenham, UK and Lyme, NH, USA: Edward Elgar.

Gramlich, Edward (1990), *A Guide to Benefit–Cost Analysis*, 2nd edition, Englewood Cliffs, NJ: Prentice Hall.

Hanley, Nick and Clive Spash (1993), *Cost–Benefit Analysis and the Environment*, Aldershot, UK and Brookfield, VT, USA: Edward Elgar.

Jones, Chris (2005), *Applied Welfare Economics*, Oxford: Oxford University Press.

Layard, Richard and Stephen Glaister (1994), *Cost–Benefit Analysis*, 2nd edition, Cambridge, UK: Cambridge University Press.

Schmitz, Andrew and Richard O. Zerbe Jr. (eds) (2009), *Applied Benefit–Cost Analysis*, Cheltenham, UK and Northampton, MA, USA: Edward Elgar.

Stokey, Edith and Richard Zeckhauser (1978), *A Primer for Policy Analysis*, New York: W.W. Norton.

6 FOUNDATIONAL PRINCIPLES FOR BENEFIT–COST ANALYSIS

The fundamental role of BCA is to provide information that serves to improve decision-making and facilitate better policy outcomes. Graham (2008) makes a strong empirical case that despite various sources of criticism, BCA has proved efficacious in this regard. By monetizing policy outcomes, BCA produces comprehensive assessments of policy interventions that can be compared both within and between sectors. Rather than focusing on sector-specific metrics such as health outcomes, educational attainment, or crime statistics as policy end goals, BCA takes a broader approach to improving social welfare. This allows policy-makers to weigh investment decisions more holistically and pursue alternative solutions that increase efficiency and better outcomes. This is especially true for social policy decision-making, where significant effects typically accrue outside of the primary policy focus (Vining and Weimer, Chapter 1 this volume). For instance, by rendering all outcomes in a consistent format, BCA can reveal whether increasing funding for addiction treatments or drug enforcement will likely result in greater net benefits, or alternatively, where a reduction in specific aspects of educational funding is likely to result in the smallest reduction of net benefits. The comprehensiveness and comparability of BCA fosters more efficient governance and increased social welfare.

However, these same demands of comprehensiveness and consistency make BCA a highly demanding and complex endeavor. Given resource limitations and empirical realities, achieving uniformity of analyses is extremely difficult. Models are limited by the accuracy and availability of data, as well as by time and funding constraints. A sizeable proportion of social policy outcomes are experienced as non-market benefits, forcing analysts to develop means to quantify these impacts. Future outcomes are of course uncertain, and thus the analyst must predict expected policy effects. Different policy realms demand specific, nuanced approaches that can in turn make cross-sector comparisons difficult.

BCA is as much an art as it a science, since addressing these difficulties requires creativity, expertise, and careful objectivity on the part of the analyst. Moreover, these aspects drive a great deal of the controversy surrounding BCAs, both in terms of the mechanics of performing an analysis and how the analysis is utilized in decision-making. Debate can take on an ethical component, for instance regarding the issue of intergenerational equity and discounting. Some BCA decisions are inherently "judgment calls," and unfortunately, the decisions and assumptions an analyst must make when conducting BCA can become a source of controversy that obscures the true policy debate when BCA is not presented and utilized properly.

The desire to develop a consistent basis for the large number of decisions an analyst must make motivates this project's effort to establish a common framework for BCA. Developing standardized protocols and best practice guidelines, reflecting a consensus of expert practitioners and peer-reviewed literature, will make BCA a more effective and less controversial policy tool, which we believe will in turn affect social welfare decisions to good effect. The five foundation principles that follow form the basis for the more specific guidelines elaborated upon in the remainder of the chapter. These foundational principles provide the underlying philosophical framework for BCA work generally, and are not restricted to social policy analyses.

Foundational Principle 1: BCA is a financial evaluation tool that seeks to calculate values for all project inputs and outputs to determine the net benefit of a given project, policy, or intervention. It seeks to provide an objective framework for discussion, amendment, and decision-making by providing an accurate representation of policy outcomes.

BCA is distinguished from other types of financial evaluations by the fact that it seeks to value inputs and outputs of all forms to derive a comprehensive summary of the net benefits associated with a policy decision (Boardman et al., 2006). Its purpose is to identify the most efficient policy option (Vining and Weimer, Chapter 1 this volume). For social policy, BCA reflects the extent to which the values that individuals place on program outcomes likely exceed program costs (Robinson and Hammitt, Chapter 10 this volume). Though a private firm might focus on financial benefits and costs to the firm, BCAs for social policy incorporate all quantifiable outcomes, private and social, direct and indirect, and tangible and intangible (Brent, 1996), which are then monetized to facilitate holistic comparison of policy alternatives (Boardman et al., 2006). Valid BCA in this context comprehensively accounts for the full range of social benefits and costs (Vining and Weimer in Chapter 1); analyses that do not include significant indirect or spillover effects upon non-targeted populations or effects outside of the given policy spectrum (e.g., crime reduction engendered by improved education policy) do not meet the standard of BCA. While not all effects can be measured or estimated, any unmeasured or poorly understood effects thought significant must be addressed qualitatively or quantitatively within the analysis. BCA can either be ex ante, when considering an intervention or choosing amongst policy options, or ex post, to gauge project efficacy in order to guide future policy decisions (Boardman et al., 2006).

Though the two terms "benefit–cost analysis" (BCA) and "cost–benefit analysis" (CBA) are often used interchangeably, BCA is more closely associated with work of economists, while CBA has a stronger association with engineering disciplines and mechanistic analyses. Though the term CBA is more widely used, CBA can have a pejorative connotation, as it is frequently utilized by critics in referring to the archetype of a deterministic, value-free calculator of human livelihood. The type of analysis in practice today and codified in this chapter (BCA) has little (if anything) in common with the CBA straw man. Language plays a significant role in framing any policy discussion, and thus it is important to emphasize this distinction to increase the acceptability of BCA to policy-makers and the public. Practically, the use of "benefit–cost" instead of "cost–benefit" helps emphasize that net benefits are the appropriate welfare measure and speaks directly to the true role of BCA.

Finally, we note that before conducting a BCA one must first determine if BCA is the most appropriate tool to use (Zerbe and Dively, 1994). For instance, in some cases benefits or costs are prohibitively difficult to determine. In other situations, the policy choice has already been made and what remains is to decide how to meet the policy objective. For example, a policy-maker may decide that the quarantine and treatment of a deadly disease must be undertaken, but the method of achieving the policy goal has not been chosen. If the goal is already determined, cost-effectiveness analysis is an acceptable alternative to BCA, because it analyzes the least-cost option to achieve a predetermined goal. Again though, such financial analyses are not fully developed BCAs, and should be carefully distinguished from BCA in language and application. Moreover, in such situations, expanding the policy discussion to allow for BCA instead of a more limited analysis can identify alternative solutions, reveal indirect or unintended effects, and foster better policy.

Foundational Principle 2: BCA is an aid to public policy decision-making; it is not, and should not, be regarded as a substitute for democratic, legislative, and administrative decision-making. Likewise, political influence should not intrude into technical analysis decisions and the analysis process.

Properly used, BCA is not a mechanized decision-making tool, but rather a means of analysis that provides useful information to decision-makers (Zerbe and Dively, 1994). BCAs organize data and information in such a way that decision-makers can readily observe the trade-offs of various decisions (Gramlich, 1990; Zerbe and Dively, 1994). BCA should present clear information and use transparent methodology such that it structures constructive debate. Likewise, just as BCA should allow for policy-makers to make policy decisions, political actors should not unduly influence technical analysis components or limit the range of alternatives considered (Farrow and Viscusi, Chapter 5 this volume).

Although BCA is primarily used to provide information, at times the most appropriate action is to rely on the results of the BCA to make a decision. For example, in some situations wasteful, poor decisions are likely to be made in the absence of BCA due to the contentious or political nature of the issue. In other situations, agreement on BCA as a methodology—and on abiding by its results—may render a decision process tractable when an agreement is otherwise unlikely to be reached. In these situations, the role of discourse is confined to the decision to cement the use of BCA—or to require that any policy or project demonstrate net benefits in order to be approved.

Foundational Principle 3: Transparency enhances the value of BCA for decision-making by facilitating a more comprehensive understanding of the analysis, and properly focuses the policy discussion upon political issues rather than technical aspects of BCA. Thus, both the analysis process and results should be made as transparent as possible.

Given the complexity of most BCAs, and the large number of decisions that analysts must make when conducting an analysis, it is vital that both the analysis process and results be made as transparent as possible. This ensures that there is accountability for analyst decisions. More importantly, eliminating the "black box" makes BCAs more useful; allowing policy-makers to see where the data come from, what assumptions underlie the model, and what decisions were made regarding what values are included greatly enhances the value of a BCA by facilitating a more comprehensive understanding as to the meanings, implications, and uncertainty associated with final estimates. Thus, transparency is emphasized throughout our theoretical and technical standards, as relevant to that particular component of the analysis.

Foundational Principle 4: Pursuit of the "perfect" analysis should not prevent completion of a useful analysis. A BCA that meets basic acceptability requirements regarding objectivity and appropriate methodology can still be released even if it does not conform to all best practices or is data deficient.

Different situations may call for different styles or depths of analysis. A "quick and dirty" analysis may be appropriate to determine whether different policy alternatives should be fleshed out, or to point towards a decision for an organization with limited resources. Other situations may require intricate, comprehensive analysis in order to fully reflect the details and complexities of the proposed program or policy. In these situations, the elusive "perfect" or completely comprehensive analysis should not prevent a good analysis from going forward (Farrow and Viscusi, Chapter 5 this volume).

Farrow and Viscusi identify an axiomatic practical limit to BCA, in that BCA may only provide an analysis of identified benefits and costs. In most cases these known benefits and costs will not be exhaustive, whether because of resource or limitations to quantification. For instance, there are numerous instances where we know that non-market goods and ethical considerations have value, but are unsure of what those values are; any BCA is likely to encounter such instances where effects cannot readily be enumerated or valued, and thus the analysis becomes highly conjectural (Gramlich, 1990). Social policy analysis can prove particularly complicated, as it involves many effects that are highly difficult to predict and value (Vining and Weimer, Chapter 1 this volume). In these situations, BCA can contextualize existing information and present the known implications of policy options to decision-makers, while acknowledging and discussing the implications of unquantified and unknown effects. Incomplete knowledge and data-deficient aspects should not prevent an otherwise complete benefit–cost analysis from going forward, as long as appropriate measures for addressing and presenting uncertainty in BCA are taken.

Foundational Principle 5: BCA should be conducted in accordance with the "principle of proportionality." This principle states that the allocation analytical effort should be in direct proportion to the expected value of increased information, defined in this case as the extent to which it might affect a policy decision.

Essentially, an analysis should itself be subject to its own internal BCA. Additional time and resources expended towards gathering data, building more complex models, or disaggregating effects increase analysis costs. Thus, the cost of acquiring such information should at least be equaled by the expected decision-making benefit provided by the informational gain. Any expenditure should reflect the value of the information garnered, in terms of the extent to which it might change the policy decision (Farrow and Viscusi, Chapter 5 this volume). Aspects that should influence the allocation of analysis resources include: (1) the magnitude of the program; (2) the significance of particular effects to overall model outcomes; and (3) the context and relevance of affected markets. This principle applies equally to the various nested levels of analysis, including the number and types of policy options considered, types of benefits and costs, distributional impacts included, and the extent to which such impacts should be assessed (Wiener et al., 2009).

References

Boardman, Anthony E., David H. Greenberg, Aiden R. Vining, and David L. Weimer (2006), *Cost–Benefit Analysis: Concepts and Practice*, 3rd edition, Upper Saddle River, NJ: Prentice Hall.

Brent, Robert J. (1996), *Applied Benefit Cost Analysis*, Cheltenham, UK and Brookfield, VT, USA: Edward Elgar Publishing p. 4

Graham, John (2008), "Saving lives through administrative law and economics," *University of Pennsylvania Law Review*, **157** (2), 101–245.

Gramlich, Edward (1990), *A Guide to Benefit–Cost Analysis*, 2nd edition, Englewood Cliffs, NJ: Prentice Hall.

Wiener, Jonathan B., Chris G. Whipple, Paul Slovic, Elizabeth I. Anderson, Richard C. Schwing, D. Warner North, Robert G. Tardiff, M. Elizabeth Paté-Cornell, Rae Zimmerman, Yakov Y. Haimes, Gail Charnley, Roger Kasperson, John Ahearne, Robin Cantor, Bernie Goldstein, Baruch Fischhoff, H. Chris Frey, and Alison C. Cullen (2009), SRA (Society for Risk Analysis) (2009), Committee of Past Presidents, *Recommendations to OMB on Regulatory Review*, 16 March, 2009.

Zerbe, Jr., Richard O. and Dwight Dively (1994), *Benefit–Cost Analysis in Theory and Practice*, The HarperCollins Series in Economics, New York: HarperCollins College Publishers.

7 STANDARDS FOR THE ESTIMATION OF BENEFITS AND COSTS

The aim of BCA is to aggregate benefits and costs resulting from policy choices to evaluate their relative efficacy and equity. This seemingly mechanistic prescription actually entails a complex task on the part of the analyst. One challenge is that very few policy outcomes involve only goods and services traded directly on the open market where price is readily observable. Many other goods and services are not traded on the open market, yet these non-market values must be included to provide holistic economic comparisons for decision-makers.

Prices for some goods and services are available through existing research on non-market valuation. Some non-market economic values are found in published literature and established studies (for instance the marginal excess tax burden). For other goods and services, value estimates have not been sufficiently researched, are poorly understood, require further clarification, or are as yet undeveloped, thus there is no commonly accepted figure (Vining and Weimer, Chapter 1 this volume). For instance, the value of IQ gains and the treatment of volunteer time are not yet adequately quantified (ibid.). Given the need for a comprehensive accounting stance, a primary focus of BCA research is the development of better non-market value estimates.

The art of BCA is to leverage available resources so as to provide a useful analysis that reasonably addresses the base question for a given policy decision. Certainly, no BCA contains *all* benefits and costs; rather, the extent of relevant markets, available data and resources, and policy emphases serve to dictate the scope and breadth of values included in the analysis. The emphasis of this section is upon proper estimation of benefits and costs, in terms of building an accurate model and best portraying economic reality. Within this context, the rationale for governing what should be included or excluded from valuation and analysis is based solely upon relevance and significance to overall model outcomes. In a later section on market extent in BCA (section 8), we discuss legal and ethical aspects that might constrain economic standing and thus exclude some such benefits and costs; this section, however, discusses only guidelines for data gathering, estimation, and modeling. Below are principles and standards detailing current best practices for determining project benefits and costs.

7.1 Theoretical Standards for the Calculation of Benefits and Costs

Benefits and Costs Theoretical Standard 1: The standard theoretical measures of benefits and costs are the willingness to pay (WTP) for gains and the willingness to accept (WTA) losses. However, analyses should account for divergence between the two metrics stemming from the relative accuracy of qualifying effects as a gain or a loss.

The standard theoretical measure of benefits and costs in BCA remains WTP, defined as the maximum amount of money an individual would be willing to give up in exchange for a good (or pay to avoid a harm), and WTA, defined as the minimum amount an individual would require to forgo a good (or accept a harm) (Robinson and Hammitt, Chapter 10 this volume). This has long been thought to correspond to the concept of compensating variation (CV) and equivalent variation (EV) introduced into economic theory by Hicks (1939).

However, research has noted an empirical divergence between WTP and WTA, a discrepancy beyond that which is expected from the income effects encompassed by the CV–EV difference. This poses a longstanding problem for estimating effects in BCA. Classical consumer theory explains divergence between WTP and WTA as a product of income effects, and Willig (1976) proved that WTP and WTA metrics should produce close-to-equivalent values where income effects are negligible, as he argued they often were. This has encouraged analysts to use the WTP, occasionally with Willig adjustments, to calculate both benefits and costs, especially as the WTA is thought to be more difficult to calculate. However, the income effect has been found to be an inadequate explanation for the size of the divergence. Thus the Hicksian relationship between CV and EV, which relies on income effects, no longer holds (Zhao and Kling, 2004). Horowitz and McConnell (2003) empirically demonstrate substantial WTP and WTA divergence.

Kahneman and Tversky (1979) introduced the concept of "prospect theory" as a means to further explicate the WTA–WTP divergence. Several behavioral factors explain the greater than expected discrepancy. Divergence arises from: (1) income effects (McBride, 2001); (2) substitution effects (Hanemann, 1991); (3) loss aversion (Kahneman et al., 1991; Morrison, 1998); (4) endowment effects (Knetsch and Wong, 2009); (5) behavior in the face of uncertainty (Viscusi et al., 1987; Zhao and Kling, 2004); (6) the magnitude of change (whereby individuals demonstrate decreasing sensitivity as the change increment becomes larger) (Kahneman and Tversky, 1979); and (7) the existence of moral sentiments about the good in question (Anderson and Zerbe, 2010).

Benefits and Costs Theoretical Standard 2: Benefits and costs are defined relative to their appropriate counterfactual baseline (i.e., existing policy or currently expected outcomes).

The calculation of net benefits is a relative comparison, relative to a reference point, usually the status quo. The question of causality, whether a given expenditure actually engenders an increase (or decrease) in net benefits or if it in fact has little bearing on the outcome, is central to BCA (Drake et al., 2009). By carefully evaluating the counterfactual baseline, BCA helps identify causal effects and factors that might be unobserved otherwise.

In developing an appropriate comparison, the analyst must predict future conditions, estimate likely responses to a given policy, and determine the likely extent of non-compliance or non-participation. The source of comparison plays a very significant role in determining how BCA regards a policy. Thus, analysts must clearly identify the counterfactual being employed and discuss how this relates to comparisons used in similar analyses (Karoly, Chapter 2 this volume). This ensures that a BCA accounts for the true benefits and costs of inaction, and more importantly evaluates the degree to which the comparative outcome accurately represents the current decision point.

Benefits and Costs Theoretical Standard 3: As much as possible, analysts should use a consistent BCA approach across multiple public policy outcomes.

Analysts should use a consistent BCA methodology for all projects, since applying the same model to different projects best facilitates accurate comparisons. Even though the input assumptions of that particular BCA model might be biased, utilizing the same model and consistent analysis procedures at least ensures that mean values are biased in the same direction.

Similarly, the analyst should use a common source for basing shadow price estimates. For instance, when monetizing labor market outcomes, the analyst should use a common source, such as the US Department of Labor's Common Population Survey data, whether analyzing a public health project or an education program. This is not inconsistent with the need to adjust figures for the analysis's context. Rather, for an estimate such as that of labor market earnings, which is required in analyses of many different policy sectors, figures should stem from a common source and be adjusted for context using the same methodology utilizing a common method of conducting the benefit transfer. If multiple sources of shadow price information are combined, the analyst must take care to avoid the inconsistency of conflating study estimates derived using different discount rates and currency values.

Benefits and Costs Theoretical Standard 4: The fundamental summary metric of BCA is the net present value of benefits. Though other summary statistics remain prevalent in the language of policy discussion, they provide accurate values only after appropriate adjustments. If the policy-maker desires a different metric (such as the benefit–cost ratio), this should be provided along with net benefits and adjusted to provide an accurate value.

The five most widely used financial indicators are: (1) net present value (NPV); (2) the benefit–cost ratio (BCR), calculated as benefits/costs, or more rarely (benefits – costs)/costs; (3) the internal rate of return (IRR), which is the interest rate at which the NPV of investment benefits and costs are equal; (4) the modified internal rate of return, which adjusts for deficiencies in the IRR; and (5) the payback period, which is simply the time required to fully recover investment costs (Zerbe and Dively, 1994).

The fundamental summary metric of policy BCA is net social benefits, also termed net present value or simply net benefits. NPV reflects the present value of benefits minus the present value of costs, with all future benefits and costs discounted to a present value. This is the most appropriate metric as it most accurately presents the results of an analysis. One significant advantage of NPV is that it makes no difference whether the benefits are counted as benefits or as negative costs, or whether costs are counted as costs or negative benefits. This is important, because a cost to one individual might represent a benefit to someone else, and thus the concept of benefit and cost categories proves particularly useful (Boardman et al., 2006).

While other summary metrics are popular among non-economists, they are inappropriate for use in BCA unless carefully modified. For instance, policy-makers often look to a benefit–cost ratio, where benefits are divided by costs. Though using such a ratio can identify whether a project has positive net benefits, it does not facilitate comparison amongst projects that all demonstrate positive net benefits, as the ratios do not necessarily reflect an ordering of projects based upon net present benefits. Given that metrics such as benefit–cost ratio remain significant in the language of policy discussion, it might be appropriate to provide such a metric if desired by policy-makers. However, net benefits should always be the fundamental metric of BCA, and any other figures should be provided alongside net benefits and carefully adjusted to ensure their accuracy. Zerbe and Dively (1994) provide means by which to adjust other summary metrics to provide accurate figures.

7.2 Technical Standards for the Calculation of Benefits and Costs

Benefits and Costs Technical Standard 1: The comprehensiveness of the analysis framework should be determined by the principle of proportionate analysis. BCA should consider general equilibrium (GE) effects where the effort required is justified by the expected importance of these effects in altering a policy decision.

How resultant policy changes are characterized is a key distinction between partial and general equilibrium analyses (Klaiber and Smith, Chapter 6 this volume). Partial equilibrium (PE) measures select a subset of policy effects. General equilibrium (GE) analysis, on the other hand, aims to take into account most or all effects of a policy. In practice, the framework employed by most analyses falls on a spectrum between a strict PE framework that analyzes only the targeted market and a fully computable general equilibrium (CGE) model. Resource, data, and computational limitations often serve to determine the method used. Klaiber and

Smith note that the term "general equilibrium" in practice can represent several different types of analysis. A GE analysis might consider effects through more than one market, or describe a policy's effects on prices, incomes, and non-market services affected by market decisions (ibid.).

Most social policy analyses employ a modified PE framework that incorporates impacts in multiple (assumed-to-be) independent markets or takes account of interdependencies in several select markets, striking a compromise between practical limitations and the need for comprehensiveness. This model is much less resource intensive than CGE models, and can provide a suitable basis for sound decision-making. Moreover, in many instances, the stakes are simply not high enough to justify building a full CGE model. Direct cost analysis might even prove more appropriate than a simple PE model for smaller social policy programs (US EPA, 2008). Small interventions based on quasi-experiments or field research, community-based programs, and similarly small-scale policies can be modeled efficiently and with reasonable accuracy without the complexity of even a PE framework.

The inclusion of GE effects can significantly affect the results of BCA when there are significant distorted markets (Goulder and Williams, 2003; Fullerton and Heutel, 2010; Klaiber and Smith, Chapter 6 this volume). A policy that proves either beneficial or inefficient when analyzed for its effect within a specific market might prove otherwise when the same policy choice is evaluated across all relevant sectors. For instance, an educational policy that fails to provide full return on investment in terms of increased graduation rate or better classroom performance might prove warranted given expected benefits accruing from decreased crime, lessened social welfare expenditures, or increased public health (Heckman et al., 2006; Heckman, 2008).

A full GE analysis is a theoretical construct; it is impossible to measure the effect of a policy on every market in the economy. The intent of a GE framework should instead be to evaluate a sufficient number of markets alongside the targeted market so as to provide a reasonable approximation of the results of a theoretically complete GE analysis. Though it is somewhat counter-intuitive, Goulder and Williams (2003) demonstrate that the relative importance of including general equilibrium effects is largely independent of the size of the *targeted* market. Rather, it is crucial to include effects related to *affected* markets that exhibit some combination of: (1) a large difference between social marginal benefit and social marginal cost of the good (highly distorted); (2) size of affected market; and (3) tight linkage to the targeted market (significant cross-elasticity). Thus, the degree to which an analysis employs a partial or general framework should be a function of: (1) data and resource availability; and

(2) the presence of affected markets that are highly distorted, large scale, or tightly linked to the targeted market, and thus are highly relevant to the analysis (ibid.).

Benefits and Costs Technical Standard 2: Where possible, WTP measures should be used for gains and WTA measures for losses. Where this is not done, the analysis should include a clear discussion of the bias from this omission and the rationale for the choice between WTP and WTA.

The analyst often has to select between using WTP and WTA measures of policy effects. Though, typically, property rights can inform the appropriate choice, in many cases, such as that of non-market goods, property rights are poorly defined and legal definitions often prove incongruent with individuals' reference points (Robinson and Hammitt, Chapter 10 this volume). Thus, the analyst should carefully describe and examine the implications of choices made regarding the use of WTP and WTA variables.

In practice, BCA frequently utilizes unadulterated WTP estimates, even where WTA figures would be theoretically more appropriate. One constraint may be data limitations or the principle of proportionate analysis (see section 9, Risk and Uncertainty). However, the rationale behind using such an estimate should be discussed. Where WTP and WTA figures are likely to differ significantly for BCA analysis, attention should be paid to the effect this divergence might have on the results.

The analyst can use sensitivity analysis to examine impacts of potential variability (Robinson and Hammitt, in Chapter 10). For example, where the concepts of the reference state and loss aversion indicate that WTA values might be most appropriate, but the BCA utilizes WTP estimates, the analyst would likely need to examine model sensitivity to possible WTA values (ibid.).

Generally, in addressing WTP/WTA discrepancy, the analyst should avoid making a priori decisions as to whether values are rational or stable, and consider psychologically salient attributes of behavioral research on benefit values and the effects of other physical and psychological characteristics using the best available quantitative and qualitative methodology (ibid.).

Benefits and Costs Technical Standard 3: Values and estimates culled from secondary sources should be modified for relevancy using a benefit transfer function (see also section 9, Risk and Uncertainty).

Rather than being a specific, universally applied equation, a benefit transfer function is a correction developed specifically for the current analysis that reflects the focal statistical population. Given finite resources and time constraints, BCA usually entails applying estimates of effects, non-market benefits, and other figures derived elsewhere in a different study or decision context (Boardman et al., 2006). The point estimate might have been developed under assumptions inappropriate for the current analysis, or else the figure might simply pertain to a project of different magnitude, temporal context, or regional physical and socioeconomic characteristics (ibid.). For instance, differing population incomes might need to be accounted for using relevant demand elasticities (Farrow and Viscusi, Chapter 5 this volume). Similarly, commonly used values might require adjustment for the current situation; the value of a statistical life developed in a workplace context might be different for deaths due to other occurrences (e.g., terrorism) or other demographics (e.g., the elderly), and the recreational benefits of a beachfront park would lack relevancy to a landlocked town (ibid.).

A benefit transfer function thus adjusts the estimate for these conditioning factors (ibid.). Robinson and Hammitt (2009) provide five steps that comprise the benefit transfer process:

1. *Describe the study scenario*. Determine the characteristics of the risks and populations to be addressed by the target study, that is, in the case of the refinery study, the types of risks associated with air pollution and the characteristics of the affected Sub-Saharan African population.
2. *Identify potentially relevant existing valuation research*. Search the valuation literature for primary research studies that address similar populations and types of effects.
3. *Review existing studies for quality and applicability*. Assess the quality of the primary research studies by determining whether they follow generally accepted best practices in terms of the data and methods used. Assess applicability in terms of: (a) the similarity of the health effects; (b) the similarity of the populations experiencing the effects; and (c) the ability to adjust for differences between the scenarios in the primary research study and in the target study.
4. *Transfer the estimates*. Conduct the transfer, making any necessary adjustments to the primary research estimates and applying them to the target scenario. This transfer may be based on the results of a single study or several studies.
5. *Address uncertainty*. Address uncertainties in the estimates both qualitatively and quantitatively, for example, by conducting sensitivity or probabilistic analysis as appropriate and discussing the implications for decision-making.

Given that there are often numerous (and incongruent) estimates in use, the appropriateness of using a particular figure and of making subsequent adjustments should be discussed. Transferred values should be explicitly identified and the analyst should provide rationale for the use of each one. As stated in Step 5 of the benefit transfer function above, such "borrowed" estimates should be included in sensitivity analyses and Monte Carlo simulations to evaluate the significance of the figure overall within the BCA.

Finally, it is not always possible to develop a benefit transfer function. In such cases, the issue of transferability must be addressed using sensitivity analysis or qualitative methods. Hammitt and Robinson (Chapter 10 this volume) and Robinson et al. (2010) provide examples of how this can be accomplished.

Benefits and Costs Technical Standard 4: Non-market benefits and costs should be estimated using the current methodology appropriate for the given context.

Non-market values, defined as values for outcomes not directly traded in markets, can often comprise a large portion of total project outcomes for social policy evaluations. Thus, non-market valuation techniques are of vast importance. Non-market outcomes are valued using either revealed or stated preference methods.

In revealed preference valuation, the analyst utilizes data from market transactions or observable behavior to estimate the values of non-market goods associated with the observable transaction. One example of revealed preference valuation is hedonic regression. Hedonic regression uses revealed preferences to develop proxy values that reflect the value of various component characteristics not directly monetized as stand-alone values. Essentially, the overall value of a heterogeneous commodity that can be characterized as a bundle of distinct characteristics (e.g., the market price of a house) can be regressed on the quantities of each of these characteristics to impute a marginal price for each characteristic (such as the price per unit of local air quality) (Champ et al., 2003; Boardman et al., 2006).

For instance, values related to public safety interventions might be established hedonically through real estate prices. Variation in housing prices due to heterogeneously bundled risk components such as proximity to or possibility of exposure to environmental toxicity, natural disasters, crime, and other risk factors can reflect the values related to particular factors (Loomis, Chapter 9 this volume). Hedonic regression reduces concern regarding omitted variables and self-selection bias in the calculation of such values where the analysis lacks a true null analog (the textbook example being in real estate, where no two houses represent the exact same bundle of characteristics).

Stated preference valuation methodologies use answers generated in a hypothetical choice scenario to estimate the value of non-market goods (Champ et al., 2003). Individuals are asked how they would behave in a hypothetical market, and these responses are analyzed to produce valuation estimates. One commonly used stated preference method is contingent valuation (CV), where survey participants are presented with a policy scenario, and asked to give a WTP value for a gain or a WTA value for a loss regarding a good or service that is not directly or indirectly reflected in an expenditure or assess (ibid.). This technique primarily arose in environmental project analyses as a means to quantify use and non-use values such as an improvement in air quality or the continued existence of a species. CV is typically appropriate where a project has impacts that are not directly felt or experienced by people with standing in the analysis (Zerbe and Bellas, 2006).

A second stated preference method is conjoint analysis. Rather than asking participants to give a WTP or WTA value for a single good, conjoint analysis presents individuals with a bundle of component attributes; the participant is then asked to choose their most preferred bundle. The results of the survey can then be analyzed via multiple regression to estimate component values, or increasingly, hierarchical Bayesian analysis, which can then build models of individual decision-making behavior (Champ et al., 2003).

Non-market valuation is a complex exercise, with a vast body of both supporting and critical literature. It is beyond the scope of this project to recommend specific non-market valuation procedures, excepting that any methodology employed be in keeping with the principles and standards stated throughout this chapter. Statistical and behavioral findings continue to drive growth and development in the field, and each component of non-market valuation (e.g., survey techniques) has its own associated body of literature. Non-market valuation techniques continue to evolve and improve as the ongoing subject of extensive research. For instance, recent findings demonstrate that WTP and WTA values are greatly subject to the stated (or unstated but perceived) distributional consequences of a policy, which has significant implications for designing CV and conjoint analysis surveys going forward (Cook et al., 2007; Cai et al., 2010). Recent research also demonstrates the importance of informed preferences, showing large changes in WTP and WTA values when people are re-surveyed after having had time to process the information (e.g., Harsman and Quigley, 2010). These findings are just two examples of how non-market valuation continues to swiftly evolve. Furthermore, given our resource and time constraints for this project we are unable to meet the considerable task of codifying the current state of the art. Thus, the best practice standard for this chapter is to ensure that whatever non-market technique is employed be in keeping with the most up-to-date literature and expert-determined protocols. Champ et al. (2003) provides a definitive resource for practitioners conducting non-market valuation, and Boardman et al. (2006) serves as a valuable reference text. In future principles and standards updates, we hope to better codify non-market valuation and update it with new findings.

Benefits and Costs Technical Standard 5: Outcomes should be monetized to the degree necessary to facilitate faithful comparisons of economic merit. If an outcome category is monetized for one alternative, it should be monetized for all alternatives.

The utility of BCA is that it provides a comprehensive and explicit manner by which to evaluate decision alternatives on the criterion of economic efficiency (Vining and Weimer, Chapter 1 this volume). In order to furnish a truly comprehensive analysis, analysts must estimate all reasonable impacts, both tangible and intangible, market and non-market values. Values are aggregated into a single monetary metric and presented alongside key quantities and values that inform the monetized estimates to furnish the decision-maker(s) with an objective summation of the economic merit of a given policy option (Farrow and Viscusi, Chapter 5 this volume). Given that BCA is frequently utilized in social and environmental policy applications, many (if not most) policy outcomes lack an explicit, observable marketplace value (e.g., value of better dietary nutrition or of urban green space). Non-market outcomes are to be monetized through shadow prices derived using hedonic methods, WTP/WTA stated preference, or otherwise estimated. This method should correct for distortions (e.g., subsidies, externalities), non-existent market values, and intangible benefits (Karoly, 2008). Further, the development of shadow prices allows for comparison of outcomes across sectors, demonstrating the relative economic merits of allocation amongst various policy sectors (Cook, Chapter 3 this volume).

References

Anderson, Leigh and Richard O. Zerbe Jr. (2010), "Reference states, valuation disparities, and psychological entitlement in real property among Native Americans," working paper presented at Lincoln Institute Conference on Property Rights and Natural Resources, Cambridge MA, 20–21 September 2010.

Boardman, Anthony E., David H. Greenberg, Aiden R. Vining, and David L. Weimer (2006), *Cost–Benefit Analysis: Concepts and Practice*, 3rd edition, Upper Saddle River, NJ: Prentice Hall.

Cai, Beilei, Trudy Cameron, and Geoffrey Gerdes (2010), "Distributional preferences and the incidence of costs and benefits in climate change policy," *Environmental and Resource Economics*, **46** (4), 429–58.

Champ, Patricia A., Kevin J. Boyle, and Thomas C. Brown (2003), *Primer on Nonmarket Valuation*, The Economics of Non-Market Goods and Resources Series, New York: Springer.

Cook, Joseph, Dale Whittington, Do G. Canh, F. Reed Johnson, and Andrew Nyamete (2007), "Reliability of stated preferences for cholera and typhoid vaccines with time to think in Hue, Vietnam," *Economic Inquiry*, **45** (1), 100–114.

Drake, Elizabeth, Steve Aos, and Marna Miller (2009), "Evidence-based public policy options to reduce crime and criminal justice costs: Implications in Washington State," *Victims and Offenders*, **4** (2), 170–96.

Fullerton, Don and Garth Heutel (2010), "Analytical general equilibrium effects of energy policy on output and factor prices," NBER Working Paper No. 15788, Cambridge, MA: NBER.

Goulder, Lawrence and Roberton Williams (2003), "The substantial bias from ignoring general equilibrium effects in estimating excess burden, and a practical solution," *Journal of Political Economy*, **111** (4), 898–927.

Hanemann, W. Michael (1991), "Willingness to pay and willingness to accept: How much can they differ?," *American Economic Review*, **81** (3), 635–47.

Harsman, Bjorn and John M. Quigley (2010), "Political and public acceptability of congestion pricing: Ideology and self-interest," *Journal of Policy Analysis and Management*, **29** (4), 854–74.

Heckman, James J. (2008), "Schools, skills, and synapses," *Economic Inquiry*, **46** (3), 289–324.

Heckman, James J., Jora Stixrud, and Sergio Urzua (2006), "The effects of cognitive and noncognitive abilities on labor market outcomes and social behavior," *Journal of Labor Economics*, **24** (3), 411–82.

Hicks, John R. (1939), "The foundations of welfare economics," *Economic Journal*, **49** (196), 696–712.

Horowitz, J. and K.E. McConnell (2003), "Willingness to pay, willingness to accept and the income effect," *Journal of Economic Behavior and Organization*, **51**, 537–45.

Kahneman, Daniel and Amos Tversky (1979), "Prospect theory: An analysis of decision under risk," *Econometrica*, **47** (2), 263-91.

Kahneman, Daniel, Jack L. Knetsch, and Richard Thaler (1991), "Anomalies: The endowment effect, loss aversion, and status quo bias," *Journal of Economic Perspectives*, **5** (1), 193–206.

Karoly, Lynn A. (2008), "Valuing benefits in benefit–cost studies of social programs," Technical Chapter 643, Santa Monica, CA: RAND Corporation.

Knetsch, Jack L. and Wei-Kang Wong (2009), "The endowment effect and the reference state: Evidence and manipulations," *Journal of Economic Behavior and Organization*, **71** (2), 407–13.

McBride, Michael (2001), "Relative-income effects on subjective well-being in the cross-section," *Journal of Economic Behavior and Organization*, **45** (3), 251–78.

Morrison, Edward R. (1998), "Judicial review of discount rates used in regulatory cost–benefit analysis," *The University of Chicago Law Review*, **65**, 1333–63.

Robinson, Lisa A. and James K. Hammitt (2009), "The value of reducing air pollution risks in Sub-Saharan Africa," prepared for the World Bank under subcontract to ICF International.
Robinson, Lisa A., James K. Hammitt, Joseph E. Aldy, Alan Krupnick, and Jennifer Baxter (2010), "Valuing the risk of death from terrorist attacks," *Journal of Homeland Security and Emergency Management*, **7** (1), Article 14.
US EPA (US Environmental Protection Agency) (2008), *Guidelines for Preparing Economic Analysis* (external review draft), Washington, DC: EPA.
Viscusi, W. Kip, Wesley Magat, and Joel Huber (1987), "An investigation of the rationality of consumer valuations of multiple health risks," *RAND Journal of Economics*, **18** (4), 465–79.
Willig, Robert (1976), "Consumer's surplus without apology," *American Economic Review*, **66** (4), 589–97.
Zerbe, Jr., Richard O. and Allen Bellas (2006), *A Primer for Benefit–Cost Analysis*, Cheltenham, UK and Northampton, MA, USA: Edward Elgar, pp. 182–92.
Zerbe, Jr., Richard O. and Dwight Dively (1994), *Benefit–Cost Analysis in Theory and Practice*, The HarperCollins Series in Economics, New York: HarperCollins College Publishers.
Zhao, Jinhua and Catherine Kling (2004), "Willingness to pay, compensating variation, and the cost of commitment," *Economic Inquiry*, **42** (3), 503–17.

8 STANDARDS FOR DETERMINING MARKET EXTENT (ECONOMIC STANDING)

The traditional assumption in BCA is that all values should count (Trumbull, 1990; Cook, Chapter 3 this volume). No BCA, however, attempts to include or can include *all* values. Instead, the analyst is called to make decisions regarding the "extent of the market" (Smith, 1993) or "economic standing" (Whittington and MacRae, 1990). The extent of the market considers whether or not a person's or group's benefits and costs are counted, or, what subset of their values are counted.

The objective basis for determining market extent is in terms of the likely significance of effects with the principle of proportionate analysis. All principles and standards regarding those particular aspects of market extent can be found in section 2.2 above, Estimation of Benefits and Costs. This present section takes the exclusion of effects based upon insignificance or proportionality as a given, and is best viewed as a guide to addressing more subjective constraints often placed upon the inclusion of significant, feasibly estimated effects. Valid BCA requires an objective accounting stance and an analysis that is explicit about values imposed on the analysis and missing from it. Analyses that narrowly define economic standing, such as a public health project evaluation that defines program success in terms of a single unit of measure (e.g., quality-adjusted life years [QALYs]), do not represent a BCA, though they might represent part of one.

An aim to include all significant effects raises both practical obstacles, such as resource limitations, and theoretical problems, such as the issue of "bad" values. More commonly referred to as bad utility, the issue of bad values has frequently been illustrated using Nozick's (1974) concept of utility monsters (e.g., Posner, 1979). An example of such a monster is provided by Sen (1982), who poses a hypothetical situation in which, as the number of racist thugs wishing to beat up Ali increases, a point will be reached when their combined utility from the beating will exceed Ali's disutility, thereby justifying the beating on grounds of economic efficiency.[1] Scholars have raised numerous thought experiments demonstrating this conflict between efficiency and morality, such as a hypothetical action, motivated by utility theory, to hang an innocent man as a way to stop the murder of many other innocent people. These issues were brought to application in BCA especially by Whittington and Macrae's (1986) article on economic standing in BCA and the subsequent discussion (Trumbull, 1990; Zerbe, 1992).

This section provides an overarching theoretical principle for market extent in BCA, followed by standards that discuss how to address: (1) practical limitations to this theoretical principle; and (2) exogenous constraints that often enter into the analysis. Here we suggest an approach to these issues that is consistent with counting all values and moral considerations in so far as they are held by society.

8.1 Theoretical Standard for Determining Market Extent

Market Extent Theoretical Standard 1: As a theoretical stance, BCA should value all policy effects for all parties.

In theory, BCA should include all economic outcomes (Trumbull, 1990; Cook, Chapter 3 this volume). For objective analysis, all individuals should be counted and their values count equally. This is the appropriate theoretical stance, as it reflects the need for comprehensive BCA that portrays economic reality. In practice, however, the relevance of effects, constraints placed upon economic standing, resource limitations, and the inability to credibly estimate certain values all serve to limit the inclusion of policy benefits and costs. The remaining standards in this section provide guidance as to bounding BCA market extent in a pragmatic, appropriate manner.

8.2 Technical Standards for Determining Market Extent

Market Extent Technical Standard 1: Count all values and persons affected by the policy to the extent likely to affect results. Appropriate market extent should be based upon significance to model results and the need for proportionate analysis.

Many effects are minor and their inclusion proves inconsequential to analysis results. Other effects prove impossible or prohibitively difficult to quantify. In keeping with the principle of proportionate analysis discussed in section 2.2 above, the relationship between overall model significance and estimation costs appropriately constrains the inclusion of effects in BCA.

Any geographic, political, logistical, or legal constraints placed upon market extent that exclude certain values even though they are both quantifiable and significant may render BCA invalid. No constraint is an appropriate justification for omitting significant obtainable effects; no BCA accounting stance should simply exclude or ignore other effects.

Market Extent Technical Standard 2: The analyst should discuss the implications of excluded effects and present them alongside the focal results.

Just as a logistical inability to include a certain category of benefits or costs does not mean that those effects should simply be ignored, a BCA taking a particular accounting stance should still inform decision-makers as to the implications and importance of policy effects to non-targeted populations.

Often, the analyst will be asked by the client to focus on net benefits to a particular subset of the population. Such a geographic or political accounting stance can reflect a logical approach to policy decision-making. Stakeholders or representative agents of these principals have a right to view policy effects on a scale that reflects their interests. For example, a state government might wish to determine the effects of a state-financed transportation program to that particular state, whereas for a federally financed policy, this disaggregation might be inappropriate. It would be illogical for a state to use state tax dollars to finance a project that does not convey benefits to state residents. Similarly, a federal agency should generally consider benefits and costs from a national accounting perspective. However, a proper BCA employing a state accounting stance should provide decision-makers with estimates of *all* significant effects, including those to non-residents, alongside the summary of net benefits to state residents. Beyond ensuring an objective analysis, the inclusion or discussion of effects accruing to parties outside the given geographic boundary can prove highly useful in identifying potential feedbacks to the targeted population and fostering effective, comprehensive, and ethical policy decisions. The professional approach is to be explicit about omitted effects and policy impacts outside of the targeted population.

One policy area that frequently demonstrates the need to show benefits and costs accruing outside of the targeted accounting stance are criminal justice programs. Even though an analysis prepared for a county or state might focus on net benefits to that particular jurisdiction, presentation of crime policy options must acknowledge potential spillover and interaction effects between abutting and overlapping jurisdictions (Lott, Chapter 4 this volume). This is because a project might engender large net benefits to the targeted area through simply altering the spatial distribution of criminal behavior instead of reducing overall occurrence. Similar concerns typically arise in most policy sectors.

Thus, while a geographic or political accounting stance is appropriate for the disaggregation of benefits and costs, no constraint is an appropriate justification for omitting significant effects. Whether an effect cannot be estimated or whether it falls outside of the targeted accounting stance, the presentation of BCA should still inform decision-makers as to the implications and importance of these effects.

Market Extent Technical Standard 3: The law and the policy question under consideration can furnish a guide as to values that are offset by opposing values.[2] *This provides an objective justification for the exclusion (or inclusion) of illegally derived benefits.*

While some contend that the exclusion of illegally derived benefits injects subjectivity into what is ideally an objective exercise, the use of the law should rather be seen as furnishing information, though not perfect information, about social values that justifies the exclusion even in benefit–cost terms. That is, the law serves as a guide to provide rough estimates of aggregate sentiments and thus is not particularly subjective. The implication of an act being illegal furnishes information for BCA about broader sentiments, just as if an earlier "rough" BCA were already conducted (Zerbe, 2001, 2007). Thus, by recognizing the law we follow established principle.

Consider whether a BCA commissioned to evaluate policy responses to theft should include the value held by the thief towards the stolen goods. If the goods are worth more to the thief than to the victim, a decision based upon narrowly defined net benefits will recommend that the thief be allowed to retain the goods. However, if this is in fact the ruling, the end result will be an increase in theft and its attendant costs. Some of these costs are in terms of the violation of the moral sentiments of members of society that would consider such results unjust. Though these sentiments may be difficult to quantify directly, it is reasonable to infer from the present illegality of theft that the public's WTP to have stolen goods returned is greater than any excess value of the good to the thief compared to that of the victim.

If, however, the policy question is whether or not theft *should* be illegal, then the value to thieves should count (see Market Extent Technical Standard 4 below). Thus, the exclusion of legally proscribed values does not represent a subjective constraint. Rather, the justification for excluding illegally derived benefits is based upon the supposition that the existence of a law represents the results of a prior, de facto BCA.

Finally, while this discussion takes a broad, theoretical perspective to the economic standing of illegal benefits and costs, and discusses this largely in the context of criminal law, it is important to note that there is a much more specific component not discussed herein. BCA is commonly employed by and for government agencies in regulatory decision-making. There is a vast body of literature and legal casework regarding how analyses of government agency regulations, for instance, should account for (or exclude) some values that, while not necessarily illegal, run counter to a legislative aim or agency mandate. For example, consider whether the US Environmental Protection Agency should count the benefit of pollution to the polluting firm when conducting a BCA. For issues such as pollution control (as well as crime, transportation, or public health) the optimal economic outcome is never likely to be zero pollution (or zero crime, zero traffic, or zero illness). Thus, when analyzing programs it is often necessary to count bad utility so as to more accurately determine an optimal level of regulatory enforcement.

The legislative or regulatory context of the policy decision in such cases can require (or prohibit) including certain benefits or costs; this is determined by administrative law, in terms of: (1) whether the appropriate legislative body has spoken directly to the question at hand; and if not (2) whether the agency's interpretation of the statute is reasonable and not arbitrary (Sunstein, 2001). These issues are much more intricate and fluid, reflecting ongoing legal proceedings and legislative actions. Nonetheless, the approach recommended in this section can be applied according to administrative law as well. Sunstein's (2001) excellent discussion of default principles for regulatory BCA provides more detailed guidance as to how to proceed in a regulatory setting.

Market Extent Technical Standard 4: Where the policy question under consideration concerns a change in a point of law itself, or when the value of an illegal act is used to structure policy, effects accruing to those acting illegally should be counted.

Illegally derived benefits should be excluded in BCA, except in cases where the policy question at hand concerns a change in law, or when the illegal values serve to determine appropriate policy. A BCA for a marijuana legalization policy, for instance, should obviously relax the constraint of illegality to include benefits and costs resultant from marijuana usage within each policy alternative. This allows for the sentiments of all stakeholders to be given accurate weight. Likewise, in setting criminal penalties, the value of the illegal act is often crucial to effective policy-making. For instance, Becker's (1968) optimal penalties approach bases crime deterrence upon setting penalties such that the criminal internalizes the cost of the action; thus, when expected benefits are exceeded by these costs, the crime is deterred. In order to effectively structure penalties then, the analyst needs to incorporate benefits to the criminal resulting from the illegal action.

It is crucial to note that the change in law under consideration need not necessarily be explicit. The example is given of whether or not the time-saving value gained by a speeding motorist should be considered in a BCA analysis. If the issue is whether or not the speed limit should be changed, then the answer is unequivocally yes. If, however, the question is whether or not a fine is justified for speeders, it is reasonable to take as given that there is a social willingness to pay for fining speeders. For instance, analysis of a transportation project might find that road improvements would alleviate traffic such that cars desiring to speed would now generally be able to travel at five miles per hour greater than the posted speed limit. If local law enforcement officials will not ticket cars travelling five miles an hour over the speed limit on the road, and travel at such speed is facilitated by the new project, then implicitly part of the analysis at hand is a consideration of whether cars should be allowed to travel at this new, increased speed. Given this, the benefits and costs of this illegal act should be included in BCA, as the legality of the act is implicitly being analyzed.

Market Extent Technical Standard 5: Where legal rights are substantially controversial, they cannot be used to determine economic standing or reference points.

Using the law to inform the market extent of a BCA is not feasible in every application. For example, in estimating benefits and costs for a BCA of a potential change in abortion law, it would not be proper to consider using WTP values for those on one side of the issue and WTA for those on the other side, as the legal reference point must be regarded as fragile (Zerbe, 2001). The WTP should be used for both, as neither part has ownership, and the analyst would include sentiments on both sides of this issue. Even if current policy questions did not actually consider whether or not abortion should be legal, but merely altered the rate of occurrence (e.g., a public health project), one would have to include sentiments on both sides of this issue. It would not be legitimate to simply assume that current abortion law reflects the full weight of public sentiments. In such cases, two sets of results should be presented such that both sides are alternatively given full economic standing. Moreover, it should be acknowledged that the language of economic efficiency is not best suited, nor the only language to be used, for this type of constitutional discussion (ibid.).

Notes

1. The actual situation posed by Sen is a bit more complicated, involving several other actors and touching on several notions of utilitarian and welfare theory. However, the basic premise remains the same.
2. Economic standing is not the same as legal standing. A litigant must have legal standing in order to be able to bring a case to court. Generally speaking, the litigant must have suffered (or be in immediate danger of suffering) a particularized injury of some sort, that injury must have been caused by the conduct of the defendant, and it must be likely that a favorable court decision will redress the injury. Three requirements are commonly referred to as "injury-in-fact," "causation," and "redressability." Certain cases may involve additional requirements of standing established by statutes or by the courts. Whereas legal standing is primarily a procedural mechanism to regulate access to the judicial system, market extent in BCA refers to the extent of the effects of an action. The relationship between economic and legal standing often proves complicated. Legal standing can often provide guidance as to what (and whose) values should be included, but proper BCA should consider significant direct and indirect policy effects regardless of whether such effects are borne out upon those who would have legal standing to challenge the policy in court. Likewise, legality does not necessarily bound the inclusion of benefits or costs. Not all outcomes proscribed by law should be excluded in a BCA.

References

Becker, Gary S. (1968), "Crime and punishment: An economic approach," *The Journal of Political Economy*, **76** (2), 169–217.
Nozick, Robert (1974), *Anarchy, State, and Utopia*, New York: Basic Books.
Posner, Richard A. (1979), "Utilitarianism, economics, and legal theory," *The Journal of Legal Studies*, **8** (1), 103–40.
Sen, Amartya (1982), "Rights and agency," *Philosophy and Public Affairs*, **11** (1), 3–39.
Smith, V. Kerry (1993), "Welfare effects, omitted variables, and the extent of the market," *Land Economics*, **69** (2), 121–31.
Sunstein, Cass R. (2001), "Cost–benefit default principles," *Michigan Law Review*, **99** (7), 1651–723.
Trumbull, William M. (1990), "Who has standing in cost–benefit analysis?," *Journal of Policy Analysis and Management*, **9** (2), 201–18.
Whittington, Dale and Duncan MacRae (1986), "The issue of standing in cost–benefit analysis," *Journal of Policy Analysis and Management*, **5** (4), 665–82.
Whittington, Dale and Duncan MacRae (1990), "Judgments about who has standing in cost–benefit analysis," *Journal of Policy Analysis and Management*, **9** (4), 536–47.
Zerbe, Jr., Richard O. (1992), "Does benefit cost analysis stand alone? Rights and standing," *Journal of Policy Analysis and Management*, **10** (1), 96–105.

Zerbe, Jr., Richard O. (2001), *Economic Efficiency in Law and Economics*, Cheltenham, UK and Northampton, MA, USA: Edward Elgar.
Zerbe, Jr., Richard O. (2007), "The legal foundation of cost–benefit analysis," *Charleston Law Review*, **2** (1), 93–184.

9 STANDARDS FOR ADDRESSING RISK AND UNCERTAINTY

Risk and uncertainty are inevitable components of BCA predictions. The treatment of risk and uncertainty is fundamental to achieving a faithful assessment of policy options and ensuring that decision-makers can base policy decisions upon a best possible understanding of potential and/or expected outcomes and ramifications. Following a definition of risk and uncertainty as applied to BCA, this introduction summarizes the concept of risk and uncertainty to provide background for the principles and standards outlined in this section.

The precise definitions of risk and uncertainty have long been the subject of scholarly debate. In this document we assume that *risk* refers to a source of imprecision for which a probability of engendering a desired or undesired outcome can be assigned. Commonly this is summarized as an event with a known probability distribution. *Uncertainty* denotes an unknown or stochastic process for which precise quantitative description is unfeasible or unavailable. Uncertainty is often summarized as an event with an unknown probability distribution. Though we provide this distinction between risk and uncertainty, it is important to note that in the context of policy decision-making, the probabilities of adverse outcomes are treated similarly whether precisely quantified or poorly understood (Farrow and Viscusi, Chapter 5 this volume).

9.1 Risk

Fischhoff et al. (1984) caution that the precise meaning of "risk" remains embedded in controversy, as the choice (whether conscious or not) of a particular definition greatly affects policy choices, resource allocation, and the distribution of political power. As noted below, the definition of risk in BCA is an operative question that affects how benefit–cost outcomes are presented. For example, known probabilities might allow for direct incorporation within BCA, whereas uncertainty as to parameter precision and model accuracy might be better dealt with in a supplementary fashion alongside BCA output.

Though colloquially risk often implies potential for adverse outcomes and carries a negative connotation, risk is neither "good" nor "bad." Although known probabilities may be incorporated mechanistically into BCA, risk analysis and management depend upon the context of the decision-maker. Even well-quantified risks can complicate the use and interpretation of BCA. Almost three centuries ago Daniel Bernoulli demonstrated that few empirical decisions are made in a risk-neutral fashion according to the expected value criterion that multiplies the size of a payout by its probability of occurrence (Bernoulli, 1954). Risk neutrality implies one to be indifferent when faced with a choice between a policy that with absolute certainty would cause one death and another policy with a one in a million chance of causing one million deaths; in fact, people appear not to be indifferent.

Policy-makers tend to operate in a risk-averse setting, where more-certain outcomes are prioritized over outcomes with a greater potential gain but also a greater possibility of failure. Often, decision-makers can qualitatively evaluate the relative merits of expected values against potential harms side by side with BCA results; in such cases where regulation mandates strict adherence to formal BCA criteria, decision-making thresholds can be inserted directly into the model to allow for the analysis to faithfully represent political or societal risk treatment preferences.

One example of systematized risk aversion is the precautionary principle, whereby a proposed action or policy must demonstrate prior to its implementation that with reasonable certainty it will not engender irreversible harm (Stewart, 2002). For BCA it is key to note that risk aversion (as well as risk-seeking behavior) can be incorporated into analyses as is socially or politically desired. Analysts can employ thresholds to guide probabilistic decision-making within a BCA model so as to adhere to a desired treatment of risk rather than employ strict probability theory. If decision-makers desire precautionary management, thresholds can preclude an action holding a greater expected payoff but lacking the desired degree of certainty (Vining and Weimer, Chapter 1 this volume). In a simple example, for a policy scenario where weighted outcome values reveal that selecting "Option A" maximizes expected net benefits whenever "Option A" has at least a 40 percent chance of "success," policy-makers might still desire to restrict the model to only select "Option A" where there exists a 70 percent chance of success.

9.2 Uncertainty

Policy decision-making requires action despite uncertainty; even a decision not to act engenders its own consequences (IRGC, 2010). BCA is designed to be a decision-making aid for policy decisions in the face of uncertainty.

A crucial component of BCA then is its ability to improve understanding of risks and risk perception, and provide appropriate guidance on making risk management decisions (North, 1998).

Uncertainty may be separated into different components. Morgan and Henrion (1990) detail seven aspects through which uncertainty might be introduced into quantitative analysis: (1) random error and statistical variation; (2) systematic error and subjective judgment; (3) linguistic imprecision; (4) variability across time and space engendered by aggregation; (5) inherent randomness and unpredictability; (6) disagreement; and (7) approximations. Note that these categories also refer to non-stochastic processes, such as uncertainty as to whether a policy has a causal effect on a given outcome.

Even though a precise probability distribution is unavailable, uncertainty can often be addressed quantitatively. Appropriate BCA uses sensitivity analyses, probabilistic methods such as Monte Carlo simulation, and other means to reflect uncertainties in order to provide decision-makers with sufficient knowledge as to the relative significance of various sources of uncertainty and a fuller picture of possible policy outcomes. For instance, a sensitivity analysis might prove a BCA model to be robust to an approximation error of a certain variable, thus obviating concern (or further expense towards reducing uncertainty).

As discussed previously, risk and uncertainty are treated in much the same way in BCA. The primary importance to analysts of distinguishing between the two is that uncertainty can point to an opportunity to learn more about the level of probabilities (Farrow and Viscusi, Chapter 5 this volume). The following theoretical standards provide a conceptual foundation for addressing risk and uncertainty in BCA. Subsequent technical standards outline empirical steps to be taken when conducting BCA.

9.3 Theoretical Standards for Addressing Risk and Uncertainty

Risk and Uncertainty Theoretical Standard 1: The treatment of risk and uncertainty when conducting BCA is itself subject to at least an informal BCA test.

Further investment towards increased information or decreased uncertainty, in terms of both greater costs and further delay, should be in proportion to the expected benefit of the resultant improvement in decision-making ability (Wiener et al., 2009). In short, research expenditures should be commensurate with the value of the information gained. Of course, the analyst cannot know with certainty how investing resources to reduce uncertainty about a parameter will improve decision-making ability. However, the analyst can still strategically allocate resources in order to best estimate overall policy effects and improve decision-making. There are numerous ways to achieve proportionate allocation, for instance qualitatively determining that a certain aspect of a BCA is particularly important to the policy decision, or applying sensitivity analysis to different parameters in the model to identify significant relationships between parameter variability and overall model variability. In any case, careful thought must go into data gathering, and the rationale for a particular investment of resources should be carefully justified and clearly stated.

Finally, given this need for a treatment of uncertainty that is in proportion to the magnitude of policy implications, though discussing parameter uncertainty is essential, the existence of such uncertainty should not necessarily be a barrier to identifying a policy that maximizes the difference between the level of expected benefits and expected costs (Farrow and Viscusi, in Chapter 5). Greater refinement of an analysis might not affect the overall policy assessment or optimal policy choice (ibid.); in such cases, further expenditure towards data gathering is unwarranted.

Risk and Uncertainty Theoretical Standard 2: Analyses should account for multiple sources of risk and uncertainty.

Within a BCA model, there are two basic forms of uncertainty: (1) parameter uncertainty (e.g., sampling error); and (2) model uncertainty (e.g., scale-up effects) (Cook, Chapter 3 this volume). Both types should be addressed by furnishing decision-makers with a full range of decision approaches (Farrow and Viscusi, in Chapter 5). Similarly, the International Risk Governance Council (IRGC) identifies two broad categories of risk governance "deficits," where (1) requisite elements (such as sufficient and/or accurate data) are lacking or (2) actions are either untaken or unsuccessful. One instance of a deficit regarding assessing and understanding risks would be the provision of biased or selective information. A related deficit due to untaken action would be a failure to consider a suitable range of alternatives (IRGC, 2010).

The means and methods for addressing risk and uncertainty will be tailored for the requirements of a particular BCA. Farrow and Viscusi (in Chapter 5) recommend that analysts present the full range of relevant policy options. This provides a means by which to minimize the possibility of bias by omission. Cook (in Chapter 3) formalizes the way to account for the two central forms of uncertainty in addressing policy-makers by both: (1) communicating the distribution of benefits at the parameter level to show the implications of parameter uncertainty; and (2) communicating the distribution of model outcomes given varied inputs and parameters to demonstrate how scaling effects and parameter uncertainty amplify model uncertainty. Together these two forms of presentation provide the policy-maker with an appropriate conception of parameter and model uncertainty in the BCA model.

A crucial element of accounting for multiple sources of risk and uncertainty is to work in an iterative and recursive process (Wiener et al., 2009). Consultation with scientists, stakeholders, policy-makers, and oversight bodies should not merely be an ex ante occurrence but rather a continuous dialogue so as to promote high-quality information and furnish insight into both direct and ancillary policy effects (ibid.).

Risk and Uncertainty Theoretical Standard 3: Assumptions of rationality may need to be modified in the face of risk or uncertainty.

Research in both neoclassical economics and behavioral economics suggests that individuals often misunderstand or misinterpret probabilities. In addition, even if probabilities are well understood, individuals may overweight small changes in probabilities close to "0" or "1," and may be averse to ambiguity (Robinson and Hammitt, Chapter 10 this volume). These findings suggest that researchers will need to take care to ensure that probabilities are clearly communicated, and will need to consider how overweighting and ambiguity aversion affect related values. Given that BCA is the basic economic method of risk assessment and risk management (Farrow, 2004), proper analysis must then strive to pragmatically represent empirical economic decision-making.

North (1998) notes that understanding and managing risk involves both normative and behavioral aspects, as both risk and risk *perception* are critical to decision-making regarding uncertainty. Thus, risk assessment within BCA should be oriented towards subjective aspects of decision-making, emphasizing procedures and processes for dealing with risk (ibid.); BCA should then reflect current understanding of such behavioral responses to risk and uncertainty so as to best represent economic reality (Farrow and Viscusi, Chapter 5 this volume). Echoing this concept, a recent paper by the Committee of Past Presidents of the Society for Risk Analysis in response to the White House OMB's request for public comment on the current federal system of Regulatory Review stresses this need to greatly enhance the role of social and behavioral sciences in risk analysis (and thus BCA) so as to better understand how and why groups and individuals behave and act as they do in the face of risk and uncertainty (Wiener et al., 2009).

Risk and Uncertainty Theoretical Standard 4: BCA should not impose a particular form of risk-treating behavior, but should rely on empirical analysis.

The IRGC (2010) notes that sound, forward-looking policy requires a suitable mix of risk taking and risk avoidance. While the appropriate role of BCA is not to support a particular philosophy of risk management (e.g., precautionary principle), few empirical decisions are made on a risk-neutral basis. Zerbe (2007) argues that BCA should reflect the philosophy of risk appropriate for the policy problem, not the values of the analyst.

The treatment of risk may be dictated by agency mandate or legal constraint, or it may be dictated by the affected population. Some agencies are required to choose policy options that maximize net benefits, other agencies are required to select policy options that minimize harm or avoid certain risks. When preparing analysis in the context of such binding regulations, risk management standards are best included within the BCA model so that they are internalized within estimated net benefits. For instance, issues such as thresholds and irreversibility can be addressed a priori using a two-period (Gollier, 2001) or canonical (Dixit and Pindyck, 1994) model to optimize the timing of action (Farrow, 2004). Essentially, such a model delays action until benefits significantly exceed costs given a predefined amount of precaution (ibid.).

Decisions regarding risk management (e.g., a precautionary principle) can also be made post hoc through deliberation and public process. This helps ensure that the policy selected faithfully reflects public sentiment. In other settings, a baseline BCA might appropriately be conducted in risk-neutral fashion, and an ex post facto analysis and delineation of risk factors, probability thresholds, and various risk behaviors presented alongside model outcomes. Even basic sensitivity analyses demonstrating the relative outcomes engendered by various risk behaviors can help policy-makers manage risks more efficaciously, and varying the treatment of risk in complementary analyses helps identify current deficiencies in risk governance.

Risk and Uncertainty Theoretical Standard 5: The analyst should carefully account for the difference between predictions and estimates when transferring estimates and modeling outcomes.

BCA must recognize the statistical distinction between estimates and predictions. In most settings, parameter estimation focuses on the statistical relationship between the estimated parameter and the data set used for this estimation, evaluating to what degree the parameter accurately represents the given data. However, BCA usually entails using parameters derived in various studies (the "study sample") to predict policy outcomes (the "policy sample"); the issue for BCA then is not the representativeness of the parameter relative to its underlying data set, but rather the degree to which the study sample is appropriate for application to the policy sample (Vining and Weimer, Chapter 1 this volume).

Often, this transfer of WTP/WTA functions and parameter estimates from the study sample to a policy context proves problematic. Statistical literature recognizes that best estimates often do not facilitate accurate predictions (Efron and Morris, 1977). Predictions generated using said estimates tend to be overly optimistic given the stochastic nature of real-world events and the powerful force of regression to the mean, producing values that prove too large in absolute value terms (Vining and Weimer, in Chapter 1). Thus, analysis should account for regression to the mean (the statistical tendency that given an extreme sample from a data set, a second sample from that same set will tend to be closer in value to the mean value of the set) and optimism biases (that individuals tend to be overly optimistic about the potential outcomes of policies they generate or advocate [ibid.]), as research demonstrates that small, systematically selected, and carefully controlled programs typically demonstrate better outcomes relative to when the program is subsequently employed in empirical settings (Drake et al., 2009).

A related issue to optimism bias and regression to the mean is that of scale-up effects. Scale-up effects are of particular concern for social policy BCA, as analyses generally extrapolate findings derived on smaller, more manageable scales to make decisions regarding wide-scale policy implementation. Often there is little basis for knowing the direction or magnitude of the scaling factor for parameter estimates when such an action or policy is applied at large (Karoly, Chapter 2 this volume).

Risk and Uncertainty Theoretical Standard 6: Statistical significance levels for program and policy effect size are not relevant to BCA. Regardless of the associated level of significance, all estimated effects should be included in the BCA model with the appropriate standard error.

Statistical significance is not the same as economic significance (McCloskey and Ziliak, 1996). The decision to use a variable in a BCA model should be based upon economic theory instead of statistical significance. Given the importance of comprehensiveness in BCA of social policies, all effects, including those that might not achieve conventional levels of statistical significance in particular studies, should be included. The heightened uncertainty associated with using a statistically insignificant parameter will be internalized within the BCA model by the larger standard error value (relative to statistically significant parameters) accompanying the probability distribution of that parameter within a Monte Carlo simulation (Vining and Weimer, Chapter 1 this volume). The distribution of benefits to costs modeled by the Monte Carlo simulation or other simulation approach will reflect the increased degree of risk resultant from the use of statistically insignificant estimates. While this increases the degree of comprehensiveness, it also underscores the necessity of conducting a Monte Carlo simulation to account for the resultant increase in uncertainty (ibid.). For a fuller discussion of Monte Carlo simulations and the treatment of uncertainty related to estimated effects, see Vining and Weimer (ibid.).

9.4 Technical Standards for Addressing Risk and Uncertainty

Risk and Uncertainty Technical Standard 1: Clearly delineate the accuracy and precision of numerical values and identify sources of uncertainty.

To denote modeling assumptions and chapter numerical values, the analysis should convey information about the accuracy of the estimates. Explanation should be provided as to the resource limitations or inherent uncertainties currently unresolved (Farrow and Viscusi, Chapter 5 this volume).

The presence of uncertainty represents a potential for acquiring information that fosters more precise understanding (ibid.). Along with explicitly accounting for uncertainty, analyses should identify priorities for further characterization, denoting highly consequential areas of uncertainty whereby adherence to the principle of proportionate analysis mandates increased or better information (Wiener et al., 2009). These sources of uncertainty that are of great significance to model outcomes are a priority for further research expenditure.

Risk and Uncertainty Technical Standard 2: Explicitly define the concept of risk used in the analysis.

Fischhoff et al. (1984) write that the definition of risk is a political decision. This includes: (1) the degree of objectivity in defining a risk, for instance the attribution of deaths to predisposing causes such as poor nutrition instead of immediate causes such as disease; (2) a risk's dimensionality, in terms of the spate of consequences included in characterizing the risk; (3) the choice of summary statistic, such as deaths per ton of coal mined versus deaths per thousands of coal miners; and (4) risk bounding, which includes the attribution of partial consequences and the relevant time scale. All of these decisions play a significant role in determining the outcome(s) of BCA, as even a slight shift in the characterization of a risk might dramatically change model results and the decision context. For instance, Herbert et al. (1979) describe how a significant source of discrepancy and controversy in the debate over various energy technologies is predicated upon choices made regarding the inclusion (or lack thereof) of back-up energy sources. Thus, the analysis should carefully denote the operative definition of risk and provide justification for the choices made regarding characterization.

Risk and Uncertainty Technical Standard 3: Use sensitivity analyses to evaluate implications of estimates and modeling assumptions.

Conduct sensitivity analyses to examine implications of choices made regarding valuation and methodology, so as to reveal the impact of such decisions hold in the model. Such evaluation should include, but not be limited to different discount rates, the subject age to which policies are discounted, shadow price estimates, methods of future outcome projection, and scaling factors (Karoly, Chapter 2 this volume). Though risk traditionally connotes the potential for negative impact and/or costs, sensitivity analyses and other statistical approaches to the characterization of risk apply equally to questions of beneficial impact and positive values (Farrow, 2004).

Risk and Uncertainty Technical Standard 4: Utilize probabilistic techniques to calculate net benefits so as to account for multiple uncertainties.

BCA typically entails a number of uncertain precisions multiplied by uncertain shadow prices, requiring a probabilistic framework to accurately predict the value and precision of net benefits. Generally, the point estimate of net benefits should be the mean net benefits across all *simulations*, as opposed to the net benefit predicted from a calculation using the mean value of each *parameter*. Where the mean is unduly influenced by a small number of trials with large net benefits, it is appropriate to utilize a trimmed mean (Vining and Weimer, Chapter 1 this volume); when doing so, justification for ignoring extreme results must be made. Monte Carlo simulation is the most frequently employed, but not the only means by which to address these multiple sources of uncertainty, including imprecision in effect predictions, uncertainty regarding monetized shadow price estimates, and potential interaction effects (ibid.).[1] The results of a Monte Carlo simulation can also be presented to policy-makers using a histogram that shows the distribution of net benefits across all simulations, accompanied by appropriate summary statistics (e.g., mean, inter-quartile range). This supplements point estimates and provides greater analysis transparency.

Risk and Uncertainty Technical Standard 5: Analyze every value as a random variable, unless given evidence to the contrary.

Assume statistical randomness: if a numerical value is considered important and not analyzed as a random variable, one should explain why not (Farrow and Viscusi, Chapter 5 this volume). When there is only one source of data, and thus a single probability distribution, for a variable, this distribution can be incorporated directly in the simulation. However, when numerous studies are applicable, the analyst can pool these studies. One such approach is for each model iteration to first randomly select a particular study and then sample from that particular parameter distribution; the resulting meta-distribution accounts for uncertainty across studies (Farrow, 2004). Justification should be provided for studies and data sources used or not used in analysis (Farrow and Viscusi, in Chapter 5).

Risk and Uncertainty Technical Standard 6: Account for the legislatively mandated or desired stance towards risk at different agencies and levels of government.

Decisions regarding risk management (e.g., a precautionary principle) can be made post hoc through deliberation and public process. In cases where legislation mandates strict adherence to BCA outcomes, issues of uncertainty, thresholds, and irreversibility are to be addressed a priori using a two-period (Gollier, 2001) or canonical (Dixit and Pindyck, 1994) model to optimize the timing of action (Farrow, 2004). Essentially, such a model delays action until benefits significantly exceed costs given a predefined amount of precaution (ibid.).

Risk and Uncertainty Technical Standard 7: Address potential for regression to mean, publication bias, and optimism bias when necessary by adjusting estimates.

Though no definitive consensus exists as to the appropriate way to account for regression to the mean and optimism bias in predictions, often it is appropriate to downwardly adjust estimates to account for regression to the mean, optimism bias, and sample size issues in light of the incongruous nature of estimates and predictions (Vining and Weimer, Chapter 1 this volume). For example, the Washington State Institute for Public Policy often discounts effects engendered outside of an empirical setting by as much as 50 percent when evaluating educational projects (Drake et al., 2009). Selection bias can be either positive or negative however, thus in some cases an upward adjustment of effect estimates might be necessary.

Sample size is also a concern. Vining and Weimer in Chapter 1 discuss the danger of using too few (especially single) estimates of a parameter. Parameter estimates are a single value in a distribution of possibilities, and large numbers of estimates will regress to the mean value of the distribution. Thus, a mean value of a distribution is more likely to be accurate than a single observation from a distribution. The optimal method then is to incorporate as many parameter estimates as are available to identify a range of possible parameters through meta-analysis. Estimates gathered from meta-analyses, utilizing multiple studies, likely require less reduction given the benefit of increased sample size and differing methodologies (ibid.).

Finally, publication bias, the tendency for researchers and editors to submit and accept manuscripts for publication based upon the strength or direction of research findings, might influence meta-analyses of related studies. Even optimism bias, that people tend to be overly optimistic about policies they develop or advocate, can hinder accurate representation (Vining and Weimer, ibid.). To determine the appropriateness of adjusting an estimate, the analyst should carefully evaluate differences in the context from which the data stem and the empirical environment in which the program will be enacted; in turn, this should inform a clear, pointed justification of the analyst's actions to downgrade (or upgrade) an estimate of effects.

Risk and Uncertainty Technical Standard 8: Low-probability, high-consequence (i.e., catastrophic) risks should be treated with special attention according to contemporary protocol.

High-consequence/low-probability events demand special attention within BCA because of the magnitude of economic damages resulting from catastrophic events (Kunreuther and Michel-Kerjan, 2009). For an overview of current discussion and protocol for dealing with catastrophic events, see Kunreuther and Michel-Kerjan (ibid.). Analysis of such events should also be a priority of the iterative discussion process, with an eye towards priority setting and further research (Wiener et al., 2009).

Note

1. For a more detailed overview of conducting a Monte Carlo simulation for BCA, see Vining and Weimer in Chapter 1.

References

Bernoulli, Daniel (1954), "Exposition of a new theory on the measurement of risk," *Econometrica*, **22** (1), 23–36.

Dixit, Avinash and Robert Pindyck (1994), *Investment Under Uncertainty*, Princeton, NJ: Princeton University Press.

Drake, Elizabeth, Steve Aos, and Marna Miller (2009), "Evidence-based public policy options to reduce crime and criminal justice costs: Implications in Washington State," *Victims and Offenders*, **4** (2), 170–96.
Efron, Bradley and Carl Morris (1977), "Stein's paradox in statistics," *Scientific American*, **236** (5), 119–27.
Farrow, Scott (2004), "Using risk assessment, benefit–cost analysis, and real options to implement a precautionary principle," *Risk Analysis*, **24** (3), 727–35.
Fischhoff, Baruch, Stephen R. Watson, and Chris Hope (1984), "Defining risk," *Policy Sciences*, **17** (2), 123–39
Gollier, Christian (2001), *The Economics of Risk and Time*, Cambridge, MA: MIT Press
Herbert, John H., Christina Swanson, and Patrick Reddy (1979), "Risky business," *Environment*, **21** (6), 28–33.
IRGC (International Risk Governance Council) (2010), "Risk governance deficits: Analysis, illustration, and recommendations," Geneva: International Risk Governance Council, accessed 17 October 2012 at http://www.irgc.org/IMG/pdf/IRGC_RiskGovernanceDeficits_PolicyBrief2010.pdf.
Kunreuther, Howard C. and Erwann O. Michel-Kerjan (2009), "The development of new catastrophe risk markets," *Annual Review of Resource Economics*, **1** (1), 119–37.
McCloskey, Deirdre N. and Stephen T. Ziliak (1996), "The standard error of regressions," *Journal of Economic Literature*, **34** (1), 97–114.
Morgan, M. Granger and Max Henrion (1990), *Uncertainty: A Guide to Dealing with Uncertainty in Quantitative Risk and Policy Analysis*, Cambridge, UK: Cambridge University Press.
North, D. Warner (1998), "Comments on 'Three decades of risk research'," *Journal of Risk Research*, **1** (1), 73–6.
Stewart, Richard B. (2002), "Environmental regulatory decision making under uncertainty," *Research in Law and Economic*, **20**, 71–126.
Wiener, J.B., C.G. Whipple, P. Slovic, E.I. Anderson, R.C. Schwing, D.W. North, R.G. Tardiff, M.E. Paté-Cornell, R. Zimmerman, Y.Y. Haimes, G. Charnley, R. Kasperson, J. Ahearne, R. Cantor, B. Goldstein, B. Fischhoff, H.C. Frey, and A.C. Cullen, SRA (Society for Risk Analysis) (2009), Committee of Past Presidents, *Recommendations to OMB on Regulatory Review*, 16 March 2009.
Zerbe, Jr., Richard O. (2007), "The legal foundation of cost–benefit analysis," *Charleston Law Review*, **2** (1), 93–184.

10 STANDARDS FOR SELECTING AND IMPLEMENTING APPROPRIATE DISCOUNTING PROCEDURES

Perhaps no methodological question within benefit–cost analysis (BCA) has been so widely addressed as the discounting of future benefits and costs. The body of literature regarding this subject is vast. However, it is also unresolved. Little consensus can be found, either on issues such as what should be discounted, or the choice of a discount rate. Sources of discrepancy include: (1) the effects of risk; (2) displacement of private capital; (3) rate of time preference; (4) whether rates should be hyperbolic with respect to the time period in which effects are felt (an issue related to the use of time preferences); and (5) ethical issues such as whether the changing wealth of future generations should allow for rates that reflect preferences for income (a marginal utility of money that is different from those at the time the project is initiated) (Weitzman, 2001; Moore et al., 2004; Dasgupta, 2008). Part of the problem lies in the fact that proponents of different approaches to discounting are frequently unclear about what they are maximizing, or what function the discount rate is supposed to perform. This chapter assumes that the purpose of discounting is to select that rate that will lead to selection of the best projects in terms of rate of return.

The case for discounting arises from the concepts of time preference, uncertainty, and the opportunity cost of capital, all of which coalesce to underlie the simple premise that a dollar in hand today is held to be worth more than receiving that same dollar at any future point (US OMB, 1992, 2003).[1] Time preference refers to a demonstrated behavioral economic preference for immediate or near-term benefits over future accruement, which skews economic decision-making towards near-term benefits. In order to forgo a dollar of current consumption an individual must receive more than a dollar's worth of future consumption. Similarly, the opportunity cost of capital reflects the value that funds allocated towards a project would have generated in another one (i.e., lost earning potential). Whether because of taxes on capital income, myopia, or uncertainty, this productivity cost of capital is typically held to be higher than the time preference rate.

In determining the discount rate, concern does not lie with default risk, but with variance and covariance with other projects. The covariance risk can be estimated by models such as the capital asset pricing model (CAPM). Default risk is best handled by adjusting the value of benefits and costs and considering these values themselves.

Some argue for a zero discount rate (i.e., no discounting of future benefits and costs) on philosophical and/or economic grounds (see Goodin, 1982, p. 20 for an even-handed discussion of the limitations of discounting in policy analysis). These moral concerns seem better addressed by attaching values to projects with future benefits that reflect the WTP of the current generation to achieve a moral result, and not by cluttering the discount rate. In fact, discounting remains a widely recognized professional standard. Discounting is conducted in almost all empirical market transactions and used in finance. Thus, discounting should always be incorporated where appropriate in BCA.

10.1 Main Approaches

There are three main approaches to determining discounting rates: (1) the social opportunity cost of capital (SOC) (Sandmo and Dreze, 1971 [see also Harberger, 1972]; Sjasstad and Wisecarver, 1977; Harberger, 1987, 2010; Burgess, 2010a, 2010c); (2) the shadow price algorithm (SPA) (Marglin, 1963; Feldstein, 1972; Bradford, 1975; Lind, 1982), (3) the marginal cost of funds criterion (MCF) (Liu, 2003; Liu et al., 2004).[2]

All approaches recognize that the displacement of private capital is central to determining the rate. Under certain conditions the SOC and the MCF and the SPA approaches can be reconciled so that they become the same (Burgess, 2010a, 2010c). Liu's (2003) and Liu et al.'s (2004) MCF approach depends upon an exogenous rate of return to capital whereas the SOC approach is more general. Although in what follows brief attention is given to all of these, the SOC approach is found to be the most practicable. The SOC rate is justified by the straightforward principles of applied welfare economics—demand price (measures of marginal benefit), competitive supply price (marginal cost), and adding up. The basic exercise is the extraction of resources from the economy, which displaces investment and stimulates saving. The discount rate should be consistent with choosing a project that is more productive over another that is less productive. The rate then must cover the productivity that is forgone as a consequence of displaced investment, and the net-of-tax supply price of the newly induced savings. Any lower rate than the weighted average represented by the SOC will fail this test.[3] Though one can find a number of ways to motivate lower rates, one cannot escape the penalty of ignoring the correspondingly higher social productivity of investment funds.

The "debt" incurred through displacing investment and stimulating savings comes from the extraction of funds (resources) from the economy, not from the nature of their use. Thus, the shadow price of investible funds (SPIF) should properly apply to policemen's and teachers' salaries and soldiers' meals as well as to investments in public roads and dams. The SOC discount rate would apply to these sorts of government expenditures as well as traditional investments.

10.2 Theoretical Standards for Discounting

Discounting Theoretical Standard 1: All benefits and costs expected to accrue in the future should be discounted.

The manner in which BCA addresses intertemporal comparison is highly significant to project outcomes, as well as highly controversial philosophically. Though it is commonly accepted that *money* should be discounted, both due to time preference and the investment value of money, the discounting of life and health (as is done in many social policy BCAs) is disputed (Sunstein, 2007). Philosophers and legal scholars often question such discounting on ethical or legal grounds (e.g., Cowen and Parfit, 1992; Revesz, 1999; Ackerman and Heinzerling, 2002, 2004; Shapiro and Glicksman, 2003). This concern is summarized by the principle of intergenerational neutrality (Sunstein, 2007), which holds that members of any particular generation should not be favored over members of any other. However, this principle *does not* repudiate discounting life and health values. In fact, the justification for discounting adheres to the idea of intergeneration neutrality, as a failure to discount can often injure, instead of promote, the interests of future generations (ibid.).

Discounting can lead to an increase in investment, which in turn engenders long-term benefits to future generations, whereas a refusal to discount can delay action or protective program implementation (since a zero discount rate always favors program delay) and result in future generations being worse off (ibid.). Thus, the moral and philosophical implications of discounting should be addressed directly through consideration of the value of benefits and costs; given the goal of increased efficiency (as reflected by increased net benefits), all future effects should be appropriately discounted in BCA.

Discounting Theoretical Standard 2: A single, numerical discount rate should be applied consistently throughout the analysis. Where the current generation has moral values that apply to future generations these should be counted in terms of WTP at present and not incorporated into the discount rate.

The same discount rate should be applied to all benefits and costs estimated within an analysis (NOAA, 2010). Mitigating factors such as competing ethical or political stances, behavioral considerations, and policy goals should be incorporated into a profile of costs and benefits and not into the discount rate. Where the current generation has moral values that apply to future generations these should be counted in terms of WTP at present and not incorporated into the discount rate. The US Office of Management and Budget (US OMB, 1992) holds that, "[I]f one expects future generations to be better off, then giving them the advantage of a lower discount rate would in effect transfer resources from poorer people today to richer people tomorrow." Thus, the analyst should not adjust the discount rate for potential declining marginal utility of income over time. The method by which to avoid this problem is to count present intergenerational equity concerns in terms of the current populations' WTP for such a moral value instead of into the discount rate. An example is shown by Zerbe (2004). This provides an effective means to address equity concerns without having to adjust the discount rate used in the analysis. Thus, the equity rate calculation as recommended within this section is meant to entirely reflect discounting preferences of the present generation; further ethical considerations are then included as costs or benefit values within the analysis.

Discounting Theoretical Standard 3: No single rate will reflect the marginal preferences of all users.

One needs to separate the rate of return forgone from the displacement of private investment and the cost associated with the displaced consumption. On the displaced consumption side, it is true that people now deprived of a consumer loan may have a time preference of 20 percent. However, if it costs 15 percent for the financial institutions to intermediate this loan, then the economic opportunity cost of the consumption forgone is only 5 percent. This arises because the intermediation cost of the loan to the government is much less than the intermediation cost of a consumer loan.

Frederick et al. (2002) suggest that people have different discount rates for different activities and contexts. Thus, rates individuals might feel to be most appropriate for application to government social policy analyses might differ significantly from the rates they use in their own investment or consumption decisions. Robinson and Hammitt (Chapter 10 this volume) recommend that this behavior be factored into the discount rate used for the analysis so that derived estimates best reflect economic time preferences. If the aim is economic efficiency, however, time preference rates are not the main basis on which to base the discount rate. In addition, surveys of rates of time preference are so varied that no single rate seems possible (Frederick et al., 2002). More importantly there is no compelling rationale or motivation for using such rates even if available, since their use would result in a loss of efficiency. (As efficiency is used in this document it encompasses the WTP for moral outcomes.)

In so far as these rates are not shaped materially by the rate of return to capital, they can lead one to undertake a project that displaces one yielding better returns. This creates a potential Pareto improvement. Moreover, it is difficult to discover what these rates are. Finally the diversity of rates opens up a possible morass of arguments about what time preference rate is appropriate. The use of time preference rates is not, therefore, recommended as the government discount rate.

Weitzman (1998) fits a gamma distribution to the distribution of rates suggested by experts (a sample of economists). Economists as a general class are unlikely to be experts on the discount rate. Weitzman assumes an equal probability of each economist being correct (a uniform distribution); however, there is no reason to assume the sample of experts consists of the most knowledgeable people, or that their opinions should have equal weight. In using a sample of discount factors (the present value calculation for different people) one will necessarily find social rates to be hyperbolic and find very low rates for projects in the far future. The US OMB (1992) recommends against time-varying discount rates on the grounds that it results in time inconsistency and that it is not ethically attractive.[4]

Hyperbolic rates are inconsistent with the SOC recommended rate, and thus are not recommended. This is because capital markets are imperfect and tax rates differ among individuals and firms. More importantly, empirical work shows that there are substantial differences in rates. Weitzman (2001) asked 50 eminent economists for the discount rate appropriate for global warming mitigation policies, after explaining that all benefits and costs had been converted into consumption-equivalent real dollars for that year: the responses ranged from 0 percent to 15 percent. Much greater spreads have been found by Frederick et al. (2002). By controlling for confounding factors, Harrison (2010) finds rates that seem both more reasonable and less divergent.

10.3 Technical Standards for Discounting

Discounting Technical Standard 1: The discount rate should be based on the social opportunity cost (SOC). The SOC will take into account both the displacement of capital and forgone consumption, and the use of foreign funds in an open economy. Its use is simpler than other similarly derived rates.

This rate associated with the SOC is:

$$SDR = \sum \beta_i r_i + \sum \theta_j p_j + \alpha f \tag{11.1}$$

Where:

$$\sum \beta_i + \sum \theta_j + \alpha = 1 \tag{11.2}$$

And:

β_i = proportion of funds from increased savings of group i;
r_i = marginal rate of time preference, typically after-tax real rate of return, as perceived by group;
θ_j = proportion of funds from displaced investment in sector j;
p_j = marginal rate of capital productivity in sector j in home country;

α = proportion of funds from foreign funding;
f = marginal cost of foreign funding.

While the SOC is conceptually straightforward, it is empirically challenging to arrive at a reliable estimate; not only must rates of return on alternative sources of funds be estimated, so must the proportions of funding drawn from each source. A reasonable estimate of the opportunity cost of displaced investment is the pre-tax rate of return on capital in place. Accounting rates of return calculated using either national accounts or company accounts tend to be fairly stable over time. Jorgenson and others have estimated these rates of return for the US economy over many years (see Jorgenson and Yun, 1996). Poterba (1999) estimated an average pre-tax rate of return in the US non-financial corporate sector of 8.5 percent. Under certain conditions the average cost of foreign funding can be approximated as the rate of return that foreign investors earn on the capital invested in the country net of all taxes paid to the host government. If the supply price of foreign funding is upward sloping the average cost will understate the marginal cost. If the withholding tax corrects the divergence between average and marginal cost the marginal cost of foreign funding will be the rate of return to capital net of corporate and property taxes but gross of withholding taxes. Assuming a pre-tax rate of return of 8.5 percent and a combined corporate and property tax rate of 35 percent, the implied marginal cost of foreign funding is approximately 5.5 percent. The consumer rate of interest is usually calculated as a group's after-tax rate of return, but for some groups (e.g., negative savers) it is the real interest rate on credit cards and other debt. Since the aggregate household sector is a net saver, a reasonable estimate of the marginal cost of incremental saving (forgone consumption) is the pre-tax rate of return to capital net of all taxes on income from capital. Applying the corporate, property and personal tax rates to Poterba's 8.5 percent estimate of the pre-tax rate of return gives an after-tax rate of return of approximately 3.5 percent.

According to the SOC approach the marginal source of funding for all projects is the capital market. This ensures a level playing field for all projects and avoids situations where a project is judged to be worthwhile because it is proposed to fund it using an efficient tax. If a particular tax is being proposed to finance a particular project, the revenue from the tax could be used to pay down the debt instead of funding the project so the alternative use of funds for any project is to pay down the debt.

The weights that enter the SOC formula reflect the proportions of an incremental dollar of funding that is obtained from each source when funding is drawn from a well-functioning but distorted capital market. Harberger (1969) and Sandmo and Drèze (1971) show that these weights can be expressed in terms of the rate of return elasticities of supply and demand for each source and the proportions of existing funding drawn from each source. Estimates of the elasticity of demand for investment with respect to the cost of capital typically range from −1.0 to −0.7 (Department of Finance Canada, 2008), while the compensated elasticity of supply of indigenous saving with respect to the after-tax rate of return is in the range of 0.1 to 0.2 (Elemendorf, 1996).

The elasticity of supply of foreign funding with respect to the rate of return is more problematic. Some would argue that this elasticity is close to infinite given the high degree of capital market integration, but it is crucial to recognize that what is relevant is the responsiveness of the supply of real capital from abroad with respect to the real rate of return offered to attract this capital. Burgess (2010b) shows that the SOC formula can be rewritten in a way that does not depend (directly) upon an estimate of the elasticity of supply of external funding but instead upon an estimate of the "saving retention coefficient." The saving retention coefficient is the ratio of an increase in indigenous saving (induced by an exogenous shock to saving) that is invested within the country rather than being invested abroad. Beginning with the path-breaking paper by Feldstein and Horioka (1980), saving retention coefficients have been estimated by numerous researchers. The saving retention coefficient for OECD countries has been estimated to be in the range of 0.5 to 0.7 by Helliwell (1998). Since the USA is the largest OECD country, and larger countries have more market power, they will have larger saving retention coefficients. At the same time, national saving and investment rates have become increasingly decoupled in recent years. In light of these considerations a reasonable estimate of the saving retention coefficient for the USA is 0.6, with an upper bound of 0.67 and a lower bound of 0.5.

Burgess (2010b) shows that the SOC rate can be written as the following function of the relevant rates of return (opportunity cost of displaced private investment p, opportunity cost of postponed consumption r, and marginal cost of incremental foreign funding r^*), the (compensated) elasticity of supply of indigenous saving e, the elasticity of demand for investment n, the proportion of investment that is financed by indigenous saving S/I, and the saving retention coefficient SRC:

$$SOC = \{p - (e/n)(S/I)r + ((1/SRC) - 1)r^*\}/D \tag{11.3}$$

Where:

$$D = -(e/n)(S/I) + 1/SRC \tag{11.4}$$

Table 11.3 SOC rate for the United States

SRC	$e = 0.1, n = -1.0$	$e = 0.2, n = -1.0$	$e = 0.2, n = -0.7$
0.5	6.9%	6.7%	6.6%
0.6	7.1%	7.0%	6.7%
0.67	7.3%	7.1%	6.9%

Using the estimates for the rates of return p, r and r^* identified above, the elasticity values $e = 0.2$ and $n = -1.0$, an assumed ratio of indigenous saving to investment S/I equal to 0.9 (which implies that 10 percent of private investment is financed from abroad), and a saving retention coefficient SRC equal to 0.6, the implied estimate of the SOC rate is 7.0 percent. The proportions of an incremental dollar of funding that is obtained from displaced investment, postponed consumption, and incremental foreign funding are 0.54, 0.10, and 0.36 respectively.

It is possible that the benchmark estimates of the rates of return are biased upward or downward. The weights indicate the extent to which the SOC rate will change in response to a one percentage point change in the respective rate of return. For example, if the opportunity cost of displaced investment is underestimated by one percentage point the SOC rate will be underestimated by 0.54 percentage points.

Table 11.3 shows the sensitivity of the SOC rate to alternative values of the saving retention coefficient and alternative values of the elasticity parameters e and n. If plausible ranges for e are 0.1 to 0.2 and plausible ranges for n are -0.7 to -1.0 it is conceivable that the ratio could be as low as 0.1 and as high as 0.28. It is also possible that the saving retention coefficient could be as high as 0.67 or as low as 0.5. The results indicate that the implied SOC rate is in the range from 6.6 percent to 7.3 percent. Finally, the ratio of S/I could be as low as 0.8 but the implied SOC rate is only mildly affected by this change. It seems reasonable to conclude that an appropriate range of values for the SOC rate for the US economy is a lower bound 6 percent and an upper bound of 8 percent.

Thus, the recommended discount rate is between 6 percent and 8 percent. This is the range recommended for sensitivity or stimulation analysis.

A frequent point of criticism is that the use of SOC rates will materially reduce effects felt much beyond 50 years. However, there is nothing inherently wrong with this. Nor will this mean that really large effects that occur in the future will necessarily be ignored. Suppose that unless corrective mitigation is taken now the world's GDP will suddenly fall to zero in 100 years. The current world GDP is about \$62 trillion. This will grow to

$1192 trillion (constant dollars) in 100 years at a 3 percent annual rate. Assume that with the mitigation, GDP will continue to grow forever at 3 percent. The present value of the lost future GDP at year 100 will be $30 quadrillion, assuming infinite life for the world. When this is discounted at 7 percent, its present value today is $34 trillion. This is not a trivial sum to consider to place on the side of mitigating the future harm. (When the time period to destruction becomes 1000 years, however, the PV becomes negative. This is what happens when the discount rate becomes much greater than the growth rate of the economy.)

Discounting Technical Standard 2: The discount rate period should match the period of the cash flow stream being analyzed.

The selected discount rate should be applied according to the same time interval as the project cash flow stream. For example, if the cash flow is allocated monthly, a monthly discount rate should be used. In reality, receiving $100 once a year is not the same as receiving $50 twice a year. This can be accounted for by matching the period discount rate with the cash flow period. It can also be accounted for by using effective rate of yearly interest. The effective yearly interest rate is:

$$\left(1 + \frac{r}{h}\right)^h - 1 \tag{11.5}$$

where h is the number of cash flow periods in the year, and r is the nominally yearly rate.

Discounting Technical Standard 3: Health and mortality risks should be discounted.

This directly accords with Discounting Theoretical Standard 1. OMB Circular A-4 (US OMB, 2003) notes that although some have questioned whether health or lives should be discounted, resources that used to save lives today could instead be invested to save more lives in the future, thus justifying discounting. The Circular states, "For such reasons there is a professional consensus that future health, both benefits and costs, should be discounted at the same rate" (ibid.). Moreover, health and lives should be discounted at the same rate as other goods. The capital penalty is the same, health and lives are also investment goods and there is no compelling reason to use a different rate. There, however, may be special values that the current generation attaches to future health and safety of others and these values should be represented in the valuations given to risk reduction and increased health, but not incorporated into the discount rate.

Discounting Technical Standard 4: Adjustments for risk and uncertainty about the benefits and costs themselves should be applied to estimates of benefits and costs, and should not be factored into the discount rate. The sort of risk for which a risk premium should be attached to the discount rate is risk associated with covariance with other projects.

As discussed in Discounting Theoretical Standard 1, and section 9, Risk and Uncertainty, uncertainty associated with benefit and cost figures should be incorporated directly into the estimation of such values rather than factored into the discount rate used within the analysis. To the extent possible, the discount rate should be freed from uncertainty about the estimated benefit and cost figures. Uncertainty about these amounts should be addressed directly by gathering further data, finding certainty equivalents, or conducting sensitivity analysis and Monte Carlo simulations varying benefit and cost values. Using a probabilistic technique to explicitly adjust estimates of benefits and costs serves to improve the informational value of a BCA relative to using discounting to reflect uncertainty. It is preferable over factoring risk into the discount rate since it better compartmentalizes decisions regarding reasons to adjust benefits and costs.

Discounting Technical Standard 5: As an initial basis for developing a range of discount rates for social policy BCA, consult relevant published literature and standard government recommendations (such as that from the White House OMB).

Published academic literature and government analysis standards should form the initial basis for choosing a discount rate for use in BCA. For instance, the US OMB Circular A-94 (1992), which states that a real discount rate of 7 percent should be used as a base-case for regulatory analysis, provides a convincing initial standard. This is a reasonable recommendation. However, the Circular goes on to say, "[I]f we take the rate that the average saver uses to discount future consumption as our measure of the social rate of time preference, then the real rate of return on long-term government debt may provide a fair approximation. Over the last thirty years, this rate has averaged around 3% in real terms on a pre-tax basis" (US OMB, 1992).

Table 11.4, taken from Harrison (2010), summarizes discount rates as employed throughout the world for BCA:

Table 11.4 Current real discount rates in practice internationally

Country/Organization	Agency	Discount Rate (%)
Philippines		15[a]
India		12[a]
Pakistan		12[a]
International multilateral development banks	World Bank	
	Asian Development Bank	10–12[a]
	Inter-American Development Bank	12[a]
	European Bank for Reconstruction & Development	10[a]
	African Development Bank	10–12[a]
New Zealand	Treasury and Finance Ministry	8–9. From 1982 to 2008 it was 10[abf]
Canada	Treasury Board	8[c]. From 1976–2007 it was 10 (and test 8–12)[ab]
China (People's Republic)		8[a]
South Africa		8 (and test 3 and 12)[d]
United States	Office of Management and Budget	7 (and test 3). Used 10 until 1992[a]
European Union	European Commission	5. From 2001–06 was 6[a]
Italy	Central Guidance to Regional Authorities	5[a]
The Netherlands	Ministry of Finance	4 (risk-free rate)[e]
France	Commissariat Général du Plan	4. From 1985–2005 used 8[ab]
United Kingdom	HM Treasury	3.5 (declining to 1 for benefits and costs received more than 300 years in the future) from 2003. From 1969–78 used 10[a]
Norway		From 1978–98 used 7[ab]
Germany	Federal Finance Ministry	3. From 1999–2004 used 4[ab]
United States	Environmental Protection Agency	2–3 (and test 7)

Table 11.4 (continued)

Notes:

a. Zhuang et al. (2007, Table 4, pp. 17–18, 20).
b. Spackman (2006, Table A1, p. 31).
c. Treasury Board of Canada (1998, p. 45; 2007, p. 37).
d. South African Department of Environmental Affairs and Tourism (2004, p. 8), www.environmental.gov.za.
e. van Ewijk and Tang (2003, p. 1).
f. Use of 10% rate by New Zealand government is confirmed by Young (2002, p. 12); Abusah and de Bruyn (2007, p. 4).
g. New Zealand Treasury (2008) recommends a default rate of 8% (after adjusting the market risk premium of 7% for gearing).

Source: Original table found in Harrison (2010).

Notes

1. Inflation expectations also affect nominal rates but not significantly real rates.
2. Gramlich (1981) uses the growth rate of the economy to determine a government discount rate. This fails to take into account taxes and other distortions in the long run. The idea is to accumulate that quantity of capital that maximizes steady state consumption per effective worker. One reaches this state by the Golden Rule. This involves increasing the amount of capital when, and as long as, the increase in the marginal capital product is greater than the rate of depreciation of the increased capital, the rate of technological change and population growth. To reach the Golden Rule steady state the net (of depreciation) marginal product of capital should equal the growth of population and technical change per worker. The population growth rate multiplied by the rate of technical change will equal the growth rate of the economy. The long-run sustainable growth rate for a mature economy appears to be about 3 percent to 3.5 percent in real (inflation-adjusted) terms. The Golden Rule approach, however, is one of determining the optimal quantity of capital and should not be used to justify an interest rate that displaces more productive investments. That is, the Golden Rule is addressing the appropriate long-run productivity of capital and not the appropriate discount rate. The Golden Rule analysis suggests that the current capital stock, and the rate of capital accumulation, is lower than the Golden Rule rate. That is, the savings rate is too low.
3. This is why Marglin (1963) and those who followed him inserted the shadow price of investible funds (SPIF). Treating benefits as income, the simplest and most natural formula for SPIF is simply SOC divided by whatever lower rate is used. Thus if the SOC rate is 7.5 percent and desired discount rate is 5 percent, an SPIF of 1.5 should be used—that is, multiply all resource costs by 1.5, assuming that benefits return as income. If a discount rate of 2.5 percent is desired, Marglin et al. (1963) propose that an SPIF multiple of 3 must then be used in order to pay the "debt" incurred by displacing investment and stimulating savings in the first place. If the discount rate is chosen to be equal to SOC, the SPIF shadow price is equal to 1 and life is made simple once again. The shadow price approach requires that ordinary benefits as well as costs should be multiplied by an amount that depends also on the amount they return to public funds in the case of benefits or in the amount they take from public funds in the case of investment funds. This would require a separate estimation of these additions and displacements for every project. If the amount returned to public funds and the amount taken from public funds are equal, the multipliers would change the magnitude but not the sign of the NPV (Zerbe and Dively, 1994). These sorts of estimates are not, in general,

feasible and the use of the SOC again makes life simpler, and tends to give the correct answer.

4. However, time inconsistency and hyperbolic rates for individuals appear to arise from uncertainty and risk (Farmer and Geanakoplos, 2009). Once risk is accounted for, no time inconsistency exists and individual rates are constant, that is, exponential. Time inconsistency exists when individual choices are different at different times without a change in preferences or in information. Time consistency requires no difference. A more formal definition of time consistency is given by Farmer and Geanakoplos (ibid.) as, "The utility at one time s and the utility at another time s' are consistent with the discounting function. For successive time periods the utility Us from contemplating consumption stream X at time s should be equal to the utility of consuming at time s plus the utility of contemplating that same stream at time $s + 1$ discounted by one time period. Where there is certainty in the cash flows, hyperbolic discounting appears to be irrational and exponential discounting. The lack of hyperbolic discounting found by Anderson et al. (2008) appears due to the time certainty of their benefits, given the experimental setting. As time grows the uncertainty about future rates decreases and this, rather than irrationality or time inconsistency, explains the hyperbolic nature of discounting."

References

Abusah, Sam and Clinton de Bruyn (2007), "Getting Auckland on track: Public transport and New Zealand's economic transformation," Ministry of Economic Development Working Paper, August, accessed 17 October 2012 at http://www.knowledgeauckland.org.nz/home/publications/publications_home.cfm?oID=15399F48-EAA1-BFF0-4BA5-EC9076C0D9E4.

Ackerman, Frank and Lisa Heinzerling (2002), "Pricing the priceless: Cost–benefit analysis of environmental protection," *University of Pennsylvania Law Review*, **150** (5), 1553–84.

Ackerman, Frank and Lisa Heinzerling (2004), *Priceless: On Knowing the Price of Everything and the Value of Nothing*, New York: New Press.

Andersen, Steffen, Glenn W. Harrison, M.I. Lau, and E. Elisabet Rutstrom (2008), "Eliciting risk and time preferences," *Econometrica*, **76** (3), 583–618.

Bradford, David F. (1975), "Constraints on government investment opportunities and the choice of discount rate," *American Economic Review*, **65** (5), 887–99.

Burgess, David F. (2010a), "Towards a reconciliation of alternative views on the social discount rate," in D. Burgess and G. Jenkins (eds), *Discount Rates for the Evaluation of Public Private Partnership*, Montreal and Kingston: McGill-Queen's University Press, pp. 131–56.

Burgess, David F. (2010b), "Comment on 'The economic opportunity cost of capital for Canada: An empirical update,' by Glenn P. Jenkins and Chun-Yan Quo," in David Burgess and Glenn Jenkins (eds), *Discount Rates for the Evaluation of Public Private Partnerships*, Montreal and Kingston: McGill-Queen's University Press, pp. 289–97.

Burgess, David F. (2010c), "Reconciling alternative views about the appropriate social discount rate," working paper, Department of Economics, University of Western Ontario, 15 July 2010.

Cowen, Tyler and Derek Parfit (1992), "Against the social discount rate," in Peter Laslett and James Fishkin (eds), *Justice Between Age Groups and Generations*, New Haven, CT: Yale University Press.

Dasgupta, Partha (2008), "Discounting climate change," *Journal of Risk and Uncertainty*, **37** (2), 141–69.

Department of Finance Canada (2008), "Considerations in setting Canada's corporate income tax rate," *Tax Expenditures and Evaluations 2008*, Part 2 – Research Chapter.

Elemendorf, Douglas W. (1996), "The effect of interest rate changes on household saving and consumption: A survey," Federal Reserve Board, accessed 17 October 2012 at http://www.federalreserve.gov/pubs/feds/1996/ 199627/199627pap.pdf.

Farmer, J. Doyne and John Geanakoplos (2009), "Hyperbolic discounting is rational valuing the far future with uncertain discount rates," Cowles Foundation Discussion Paper No. 1719, New Haven, CT: Yale University, Cowles Foundation for Research in Economics.

Feldstein, Martin (1972), "The inadequacy of weighted discount rates," in Richard Layard (ed.), *Cost–Benefit Analysis*, Harmondsworth, UK: Penguin.

Feldstein, Martin and Charles Horioka (1980), "Domestic saving and international capital flows," *Economic Journal*, **90** (2), 314–29.

Frederick, Shane, George Loewenstein, and Ted O'Donoghue (2002), "Time discounting and time preference: A critical review," *Journal of Economic Literature*, **40** (2), 351–401.

Goodin, Robert E. (1982), "Discounting discounting," *Journal of Public Policy*, **2** (1), 53–71.

Gramlich, Edward M. (1981), *Benefit–Cost Analysis of Government Programs*, Englewood Cliffs, NJ: Prentice Hall.

Harberger, Arnold C. (1969), "On measuring the social opportunity cost of public funds," in *Proceedings of the Committee on Water Resources and Economic Development of the West: The Discount Rate in Public Investment Evaluation*, Western Agricultural Economic Research Council, Denver, CO.

Harberger, Arnold C. (1972), *Project Evaluation, Collected Papers of A.C. Harberger*, Chapter 4, Chicago, IL: University of Chicago Press.

Harberger, Arnold C. (1987), "Reflections on social project evaluation," in G.M. Meier, (ed.), *Pioneers in Development*, Oxford: Oxford University Press/World Bank.

Harberger, A.C. (2010), "On growth, investment, capital and the rate of return," in D.F. Burgess and G.P. Jenkins (eds), *Discount Rates for the Evaluation of Public Private Partnerships*, Montreal and Kingston: McGill-Queen's University Press. pp. 205–28.

Harrison, Mark (2010), "Valuing the future: The social discount rate in cost–benefit analysis," Visiting Researcher Paper, Australian Government Productivity Commission, Canberra, Australia.

Helliwell, John F. (1998), *How Much Do National Borders Matter?*, Washington, DC: Brookings Institution.

Jorgenson, Dale W. and Kun-Young Yun (1996), *Investment*, Cambridge, MA: MIT Press.

Lind, Robert C. (1982), "A primer on the major issues relating to the discount rate for evaluating national energy options," in Robert C. Lind (ed.), *Discounting for Time and Risk in Energy Policy*, Washington, DC: Resources for the Future.

Liu, Liqun (2003), "A marginal cost of funds approach to multi-period project evaluation: Implications for the social discount rate," *Journal of Public Economics*, **87** (7), 1707–18.

Liu, Liqun, Andrew Rettenmaier, and Thomas Saving (2004), "A generalized approach to multigenerational project evaluation," *Southern Economic Journal*, **71** (2), 377–96.

Marglin, Stephen A. (1963), "The opportunity cost of public investment," *Quarterly Journal of Economics*, **77** (2), 274–89.
Moore, Mark A., Anthony E. Boardman, Aidan R. Vining, David L. Weimer, and David H. Greenberg (2004), "Just give me a number! Practical values for the social discount rate," *Journal of Policy Analysis and Management*, **23** (4), 789–812.
New Zealand Treasury (2008), "Public sector discount rates for cost benefit analysis," *Guidance and Instructions: Cost Benefit Analysis*, accessed 17 October 2012 at http://www.treasury.govt.nz/publications/guidance/planning/costbenefitanalysis.
NOAA (US National Oceanic and Atmospheric Administration) (2010), "Restoration economics: Discounting and time preference," Charleston, SC: Coastal Services Center.
Poterba, James M. (1999), "The rate of return to corporate capital and factor shares: New estimates using revised national income accounts and capital stock data," NBER Working Paper No. 6263 (also published in Carnegie Rochester Series on Public Policy, 1998, **48**, 211–46).
Revesz, Richard L. (1999), "Environmental regulation, cost–benefit analysis, and the discounting of human lives," *Columbia Law Review*, **99** (4), 941–1017.
Sandmo, Agnar and Jacques H. Drèze (1971), "Discount rates for public investment in closed and open economies," *Economica*, **38** (152), 395–412.
Shapiro, Stuart A. and Robert L. Glicksman (2003), *Risk Regulation at Risk: Restoring a Pragmatic Approach*, Stanford, CA: Stanford University Press.
Sjaastad, Larry A. and Daniel L. Wisecarver (1977), "The social cost of public finance," *Journal of Political Economy*, **85** (3), 513–47.
Spackman, Michael (2006), "Social discount rates for the European Union: An overview," in M. Florio (ed.), *Cost–Benefit Analysis and Incentives in Evaluation. The Structural Funds of the European Union*, Cheltenham, UK and Northampton, MA, USA: Edward Elgar, pp. 253–79.
Sunstein, Cass R. (2007), *Worst-case Scenario*, Cambridge, MA: Harvard University Press.
Treasury Board of Canada (1998), *Benefit–Cost Analysis Guide*, July, 1998, Ottawa.
Treasury Board of Canada (2007), *Canadian Cost–Benefit Analysis Guide: Regulatory Proposals*, accessed 17 October 2012 at http://www.tbs-sct.gc.ca.
US OMB (US Office of Management and Budget) (1992), "Guidelines and discount rates for benefit–cost analysis of Federal programs," OMB Circular A-94, Washington, DC: US Government Printing Office.
US OMB (US Office of Management and Budget) (2003), "Regulatory analysis," Circular A-4, Washington, DC: US Government Printing Office.
van Ewijk, C. and Tang, P. (2003), "How to price the risk of public investment?," *De Economis*, **151** (3), 317–28.
Weitzman, Martin (1998), "Why the far-distant future should be discounted at its lowest possible rate," *Journal of Environmental Economics and Management*, **36** (3), 201.
Weitzman, Martin L. (2001), "Gamma discounting," *The American Economic Review*, **91** (1), 260–71.
Young, Louise (2002), "Determining the discount rate for government projects," New Zealand Treasury Working Paper, No. 02/21, accessed 17 October 2012 at http://www.treasury.govt.nz/publications/research-policy/wp/2002/02-21/twp02-21.pdf.

Zerbe, Jr., Richard O. (2004), "Should moral sentiments be incorporated into benefit–cost analysis? An example of long-term discounting," *Policy Sciences*, **37** (3/4), 305–18.
Zerbe, Jr., Richard O. and Dwight Dively (1994), *Benefit–Cost Analysis in Theory and Practice*, The HarperCollins Series in Economics, New York: HarperCollins College Publishers.
Zhuang, Jun, Vicki M. Bier, and Ashish Gupta (2007), "Subsidies in interdependent security with heterogeneous discount rates," *Engineering Economists*, **52** (1), 1–19.

11 STANDARDS FOR ADDRESSING EQUITY AND DISTRIBUTIONAL ISSUES

BCA inevitably faces concerns about how to appropriately deal with issues of equity. Early BCA economists feared that should BCA engage in the more subjective issues of distribution, it would be labeled as unscientific (Zerbe, 2007). Partially to avoid problematic interpersonal utility comparisons, the original Kaldor–Hicks (KH) model and the potential compensation test separate equity and efficiency by asserting that as long as beneficiaries could potentially compensate the "losers" from a program, the project was overall beneficial and thereby justified in benefit–cost terms (ibid.).

Many have been critical of the reliance on potential compensation, instead arguing that equity and distributional effects deserve consideration or valuation within the model (e.g., Zerbe, 2007, 2009). Economists have pointed out that the existence of significant charitable giving makes the notion of individuals acting solely to maximize their personal utility somewhat dubious (Sugden, 1984). For this reason, moral sentiments should not be ignored in BCA, and recent development in BCA has focused on expanding analyses to better include and address equity effects (Zerbe, 2007; Loomis, 2009). Empirically, politicians, decision-makers, and those affected by a policy care a great deal about the distributed effects of a potential decision; simply put, it matters who wins and who loses.

For instance, the environmental justice movement represents one aspect of this, where there is concern that decisions regarding the distribution of industrial activities, toxic pollution, and hazardous waste management unduly harm the poor and disadvantaged, subsequently further amplifying a cycle of poor health and low quality of life (US EPA, 2010). To address this issue of environmental justice Farrow (1998) proposes a modified criterion wherein a project is deemed to pass a benefit–cost test if the identified group either receives net benefits or is at least fully compensated for its losses (and similarly for environmental sustainability, if the compensation is larger than the net value of the resource, and the net value of the resource is reinvested). Krutilla (2005) proposes the KH tableau framework, which disaggregates the benefits and costs of an intervention among stakeholders and records all between-stakeholder financial transfers. Though this can prove highly complex, a fully implemented KH tableau can provide a comprehensive understanding of economic effects at the chosen level of stakeholder grouping.

Typically, BCAs present data on equity and distribution effects, for example potentially differential effects by race, socioeconomic level, or geographical distribution, however these elements have traditionally been an afterthought in BCA (Loomis, Chapter 9 this volume). Some government agencies require this analysis, and explicitly disfavor programs that have disproportionate effects on certain populations. However, generally analyses have not employed a full accounting framework for benefit distribution such as the KH tableau method.

Further, once a decision-making party decides to pay attention to a particular disaggregation, the methodology of weighting is at issue as well. For instance, WTP for a given benefit is often employed to reflect the relative utility of a good or service to different people or populations and thus guide weighting. If WTP is found to be strongly linked to income based upon empirical findings, however, it is preferable to measure WTP as a percentage of income to adequately consider equity with respect to low-income residents (Loomis, Chapter 9 this volume). The use of WTA values instead of WTP values also has the potential to increase equity, as values for WTA are affected by income or present wealth, but not bounded by these metrics. Moreover, weighting can prove highly problematic, and thus it is the formal recommendation of this chapter that distributional weights not be used. We discuss them herein nonetheless however, in acknowledgement of the fact that this issue is far from settled.

In the section that follows, we provide theoretical standards aimed at improving the ability of BCA to address equity and distributional concerns. The technical standards that follow then provide more specific action items for practitioners when conducting a BCA.

11.1 Theoretical Standards for Addressing Equity and Distributional Issues

Equity and Distribution Theoretical Standard 1: Explicitly include the distribution of net benefits in the discussion and presentation of BCA results.

This is consistent with principles of completeness and transparency. Ideally, BCA efforts should fully detail the equity effects of a proposed project, such that the analysis provides a basis for constructive debate. Comprehensive presentation of project equity effects serves to make the true decision-making trade-offs readily apparent. Equity effects should be presented clearly and discussed coherently so that the policy discussion centers on political questions and not scientific or methodological issues. Thus, BCA should strive to present equity effects in such a manner that frames the policy debate clearly in terms of the fundamental political, social, or ethical question rather than allowing the scientific mechanics of the analysis to be a point of controversy and thus obfuscate the true nature of the policy decision.

Finally, it is important to note that an "equity effect" does not simply refer to an unequal distribution of benefits and costs, and that personal losses do not necessarily represent a "fairness" issue. If equity considerations become too diffuse, policy decision-making degenerates into a battle for special interest favors (Graham, 2008). A pollution policy, for instance, that aims to make polluters pay a greater share of pollution mitigation costs might unequally distribute net benefits, but would certainly not be considered unequal in an analytical or philosophical sense. Careful distinction between an unequal distribution of net benefits and true equity effects is crucial, as otherwise the concept of equity and distribution merely serves as a political vehicle for interested parties.

This document does not provide a rigorous definition of what constitutes an "equity effect," as the particular issue of equality facing a BCA will differ given the policy realm and context. However, broadly conceived, a true "equity effect" is likely to entail a disproportionate allocation of costs upon a population lacking the means to exert their political interests upon the policy decision, for instance those living in poverty, lacking English proficiency, or possessing a disability. Graham (ibid.) posits equity concerns to pertain primarily to those who lack basic capabilities to pursue a good life, primary goods, or access to the central entitlements that define humanity in a modern, civilized society. Protecting or advancing the interests of such groups is a significant policy concern (and sometimes a legal mandate, as with government agencies forced to consider environmental justice), and thus it is important to provide information regarding net benefit distribution to underrepresented populations.

Equity and Distribution Theoretical Standard 2: Present differentiated policy effects either implicitly or explicitly, but do not explicitly weight disaggregated benefits and costs (if effects are weighted, the analyst should take extreme care so that weighting does not distort estimates such that it fosters sub-optimal policy decisions).

The issue of distributional weighting remains highly contentious, and future principles and standards updates will require revisiting this issue.

Harberger (1978), Loomis (Chapter 9 this volume), and others recommend *not* weighting differentiated benefits and costs (i.e., explicit weighting), since such weighting can undermine the utility-theoretic foundation of the estimated benefits and costs (Loomis, ibid.). Instead, implicit weighting, where unweighted values are presented in a disaggregated fashion (e.g., by income bracket, ethnicity, or other relevant factor), is usually most appropriate (Zerbe and Dively, 1994). If weights are used, weighting methodology must utilize an appropriate source. For instance, the federal income tax rate is progressive, and the respective rates per income bracket reflect a comparison of marginal utilities of income as approved by Congress and the President of the United States (Loomis, in Chapter 9). This representative authority lends justification for use of such figures.

Harberger (1978) cautions that limits must be put in place when considering distribution of benefits to individuals as a function of a proposed project. Weighting should not be used to produce a benefit estimate that exceeds the most cost-efficient way of achieving that same benefit. For example, a project that has an estimated real cost of $2 million and a real benefit of $1.6 million, but when weighted for an equity concern a net benefit figure that exceeds the $2 million project cost, is not justified, as it would be more efficient to simply transfer $1.6 million to the intended recipients. Essentially, distributional weighting should not cause an inefficient project to "pass" a BCA when the same effects could have been achieved via a less costly project.

Equity and Distribution Theoretical Standard 3: Beyond displaying the distributed effects of a policy, BCA should aim to provide decision-makers with information as to how the current distribution of net benefits could be altered if so desired.

Loomis (Chapter 9 this volume) notes the importance of providing feedback such that analysts and planners can modify a project to more equitably distribute benefits if that is a policy concern. For instance, a Lorenz curve reflecting the cumulative percentage of income as a function of cumulative percentage of population can be compared to a Lorenz curve demonstrating the cumulative distribution of project benefits against the cumulative population of beneficiaries to examine the distributional effects of a project relative to the existing distribution of income (Farrow and Viscusi, Chapter 5 this volume). Also, for very large-scale policies, before-project and after-project Lorenz curves of the focal population can be contrasted to demonstrate how a given policy alters the distribution of income (Loomis in Chapter 9). The Gini coefficient, a summary statistic for a Lorenz curve, is the ratio of the area between the line of complete equity (a straight-line Lorenz curve that would result from a one-to-one relationship between cumulative income and population) and the actual Lorenz curve of the given population, over the total area underneath the equality line. Comparing the project-specific Gini coefficient against the societal figure similarly addresses concerns as to whether a project improves or worsens the present income distribution (Loomis, ibid.). An empirical example of how a policy-maker might use such information would be to then alter the project funding mechanism within the BCA model, for instance an income tax instead of a sales tax, and again use the Gini coefficient to evaluate whether a project betters or worsens present income distribution (ibid.).

11.2 Technical Standards for Addressing Equity and Distributional Issues

Equity and Distribution Technical Standard 1: Disaggregate benefits and costs according to policy relevance and data availability.

At minimum, net benefits should be disaggregated by broad stakeholder type, in terms of government (i.e., taxpayers), participants, and the "rest of society" (Karoly, Chapter 2 this volume). The degree to which disaggregated net benefits should be estimated differs given project context. For instance, a comparison of educational policies might be concerned with increasing opportunities for currently underrepresented groups by income, ethnicity, and gender, whereas health policy might require disaggregation by age as well. Subject-specific guidance, for instance US Environmental Protection Agency (EPA) publications regarding environmental justice, can provide practitioners with tools and information such as appropriate disaggregations and indicators.

Data availability can also constrain disaggregation. Though poverty is to some extent endogenous, it represents a reasonable surrogate for more difficult to quantify disadvantages, and thus presenting net benefits to the affected population below the official US poverty line can help address equity concerns in data-limited situations (Graham, 2008). Where a stakeholder of concern is identified by a very specific combination of multiple characteristics (e.g., low-income, single parent, urban ESL [English as a second language] households), and data limitations render such disaggregation effectively impossible, the analyst might present side by side disaggregations of what information is available (e.g., by income, by geographic location, or by number of adults in household) to at the very least allow decision-makers to better infer benefit distribution.

There are multiple ways to appropriately disaggregate net benefits, some much more complex than others. For instance, if project costs are borne by taxes or user fees, it will be relatively straightforward to determine the distribution of costs. However, estimating benefits in such a case proves more difficult. One commonly employed method is to utilize accompanying population data from a contingent valuation survey to indicate how individual benefits might vary with respect to income, demographic, or other factor. Loomis in Chapter 9 suggests disaggregating total economic values by income brackets and examining the pattern of benefit distribution. Using multiple regression analysis, demographic characteristics can be coded as factors and subsequently tested against individual benefits for model "fit," in terms of whether there is a significant difference in response to price or consumer surplus by factor. Given that BCA is concerned with economic significance and not statistical significance, when using multiple regression it is also to determine percentage change in value or absolute change in net benefits (Loomis, ibid.).

Equity and Distribution Technical Standard 2: When comparing projects, use congruent benefit and cost disaggregations.

Often, projects are weighted according to the aims and/or needs of a particular locality or jurisdiction. This proves problematic when comparing projects across political boundaries, as different weighting frameworks produce benefit and cost estimates that are relevant only to that particular context; for instance, a city mayor might be concerned about the effects of a capital improvement project on underrepresented groups, whereas another official convening a different analysis might have desired weighting to address potential effects on the poor.

Loomis in Chapter 9 notes that utilizing federal tax figures allows for standardization of weighting for valid comparisons across states and other nested jurisdictions. Thus in the absence of another metric, these figures should be used for standardization when distributional weighting, against the recommendation of this chapter, is used. However, even if both studies weight using progressive tax rates as proxy for marginal utility of income, discrepancies in bounding can make comparisons problematic. Unless weight groupings are congruent across projects, disaggregated net benefit estimates do not necessarily provide a valid means of project comparison. Given such concerns, it is typically preferable simply to present unweighted net benefits, which already include to the degree possible the WTP for realization of moral sentiments, and let the decision-maker implicitly weight distributional concerns when comparing projects.

Equity and Distribution Technical Standard 3: Address potential relationship between distributional effects and policy valuation.

Though typically BCAs proceed on the assumption that distributional concerns are separable from efficiency concerns, and thus that project equity issues can be addressed subsequent to conducting the BCA, recent findings suggest that equity issues can in fact greatly affect policy valuation. Cai et al. (2010) demonstrate for climate policy that the distributional consequences of a given policy option can greatly affect an individual's WTP value. This calls into question the validity of the assumption that it is possible to produce a single WTP value without specifying the distribution of benefits and costs to those being surveyed. Without specification of policy effects, each individual is likely to impute what consequences seem most likely to them and these perceptions can differ across individuals in unobserved ways (ibid.). More research is required to make such findings operational for BCA, but it is important to note that distribution of net benefits likely plays a more significant role in policy valuation than has generally been assumed. Thus, when an analysis relies significantly on contingent valuation, the distribution of net benefits might need to be incorporated into the valuation process instead of addressed post analysis. This will be an area of future BCA refinement, however, and will require further address as these principles and standards are updated.

References

Cai, Beilei, Trudy Cameron, and Geoffrey Gerdes (2010), "Distributional preferences and the incidence of costs and benefits in climate change policy," *Environmental and Resource Economics*, **46** (4), 429–58.

Farrow, Scott (1998), "Environmental equity and sustainability: Rejecting the Kaldor–Hicks criteria," *Ecological Economics*, **27** (2), 183–8.

Graham, John (2008), "Saving lives through administrative law and economics," *University of Pennsylvania Law Review*, **157** (2), 101–245.

Harberger, Arnold C. (1978), "On the use of distributional weights in social cost–benefit analysis," *Journal of Political Economy*, **86** (2), S87–S120.

Krutilla, Kerry (2005), "Using the Kaldor–Hicks tableau format for cost–benefit analysis and policy evaluation," *Journal of Policy Analysis and Management*, **24** (4), 864–75.

Loomis, John (2009), "How two non-market valuation techniques can improve compliance with environmental justice requirements: Three case studies using hedonic property and contingent valuation methods to quantify the distribution of benefits by ethnicity and income," in *2009 Conference of Society for Environmental Law and Economics*, Vancouver, BC, Canada.

Sugden, Robert (1984), "Reciprocity: The supply of public goods through voluntary contributions," *The Economic Journal*, **94** (376), 772–87.

US EPA (US Environmental Protection Agency) (2010), "Environmental justice," accessed 17 October 2012 at http://www.epa.gov/environmentaljustice/.
Zerbe, Jr., Richard O. (2007), "The legal foundation of cost–benefit analysis," *Charleston Law Review*, **2** (1), 93–184.
Zerbe, Jr., Richard O. (2009), "Ethical benefit cost analysis as art and science: Ten rules for benefit–cost analysis," *University of Pennsylvania Journal of Law and Social Change*, **12** (1), 73–105.
Zerbe, Jr., Richard O. and Dwight Dively (1994), *Benefit–Cost Analysis in Theory and Practice*, New York: Harper Collins.

12 STANDARDS FOR ANALYSIS PRESENTATION

The presentation of benefit–cost analysis (BCA) findings is critical to the useful application of BCA in policy-making. In many cases, the consequences of a policy decision result directly from the quality of methods used to display and assess quantitative data (Tufte, 1997). BCA has been criticized in the past for combining a huge amount of data into a figure that gives a "thumbs up" or "thumbs down" to a project, with little transparency as to how the analysts arrived at that ratio. Opaque presentation hinders decision-making, and often serves to delegitimize BCA in the eyes of non-practitioners; if BCA is to be used most effectively in policy-making, there is a need for analysts to make models and outcomes available and accessible to the larger public (Caulkins, 2002).

Greater transparency as to how analysts arrived at specific values enables decision-makers to make better-informed use of BCAs and provides a basis for constructive debate about the true trade-offs of a policy decision. Clear presentation of assumptions about parameter values, modeling choices, discount rates, time horizons, and other choices made by the analyst allows policy-makers to verify that the researchers' choices are consistent with those of the policy-maker. Openness and clarity regarding the decisions made by the analyst indicates responsibility and increases accountability (Tufte, 1997). Moreover, providing model and process details, rather than simply a single estimate of net benefits, enables others to replicate or conduct comparative analyses. Efforts increasing BCA transparency will likely also foster a greater acceptability to the public of BCA employed in social policy decision-making.

The following theoretical standards outline broad concepts as to how BCA should be implemented and incorporated into policy decision-making, as well as how modeling results should be presented. More pointed standards then detail best practices for meeting such principles in conducting BCA.

12.1 Theoretical Standards for Analysis Presentation

Presentation Theoretical Standard 1: Presentations of benefit–cost analyses must be understandable, meaningful, and accountable to the audience.

Presentations of BCA results should avoid overwhelming the audience with technical details that obscure the data or make the results difficult to understand. However, overly simple presentations can belie the complex, uncertain nature of BCA estimates. Thus, BCA should be presented in a manner that is accessible and yet still reflects the true meaning and implications of analysis results. Depending on the audience and feasibility, a presentation of a BCA should include—or at least make available to those interested—each element discussed in the technical standards below.

Presentation Theoretical Standard 2: Analysis presentation should not overly emphasize the final estimate of net benefits. Each component of the analysis, from data gathering to modeling processes, potentially generates highly relevant policy information that deserves equal footing alongside model results in presentation.

Generating estimates of net benefits for different policy options is the fundamental output of BCA. Without context, however, net benefit estimates lack meaning and can result in ill-informed decision-making. Information and findings garnered throughout the analysis, such as model distributions, sensitivity analyses, and current data deficiencies, provide context and depth to model outputs that greatly enhance the overall usefulness of BCA for policy decision-making.

Communicating probabilistic results to policy-makers who tend to seek a final, numerical figure proves to be a significant challenge for BCA (Caulkins, 2002). Though there is an understandable tendency for policy-makers to simply look for a final net benefit summation, BCA practitioners should resist this pressure to "just provide a number." A single numerical BCA output can unhealthily dominate thinking and discussion, and moreover focusing on a single number belies the uncertainty associated with BCA model results. Morgan and Henrion (1990) and Krupnick et al. (2006) provide guidance as to presenting probabilistic information to decision-makers.

Similarly, unquantified effects must be purposefully presented so that they are not "lost" to the policy process. "Hard" data tends to drive out "soft" data, and so analysis presentation must ensure that unquantified effects are not ignored. The presentation of BCA should strive to provide the best information possible to policy-makers regarding the risks, implications, and assumptions underlying estimates so that they can be fully understood and utilized; this includes whatever quantitative or qualitative information is relevant to the decision.

12.2 Technical Standards for Analysis Presentation

Presentation Technical Standard 1: Provide a brief (~ten page) summary for decision-makers describing analysis process, results, and implications.

Though the actual analysis chapter might be longer, especially given technical appendixes, a project summary should also be composed that concisely details the analysis process, results, and implications. The summary should not over-simplify the analysis or over-generalize findings, but it should be worded in non-technical language that makes the chapter accessible to non-experts and policy-makers lacking economic expertise. This document should include, but not be limited to:

- a step-by-step discussion of how the analysis was conducted;
- visual or graphic displays of quantitative data such as Monte Carlo simulation results;
- explicit statements regarding model assumptions, baseline for comparison, and selection of parameter values, and other analyst-defined aspects;
- description of the subset of outcomes that are measured, and that are observed versus projected;
- qualitative analysis of elements not included in the model;
- tables or graphs of relevant figures, such as net benefit disaggregations;
- discussion of policy alternatives.

Presentation Technical Standard 2: Design models to allow replication and future revision. If possible, create models with accessible user interfaces so policy-makers can explore scenarios interactively.

Data and model information should be made available to facilitate replication, revision, and refinement of the analysis, whether provided in a technical appendix, supporting documents, or made available digitally. This is in keeping with best practices for scientific research overall, and greatly contributes to the legitimacy of BCA and development and growth in the field.

One method that can help demonstrate the implications of analysis decisions and communicate policy risks is to create interactive models that are accessible to policy-makers (Cook, Chapter 3 this volume). For instance, models may be designed so that policy-makers may change point estimates of parameters to observe the impact on the BCA outcome. This method can be used to improve communication of estimates with individuals less familiar with probabilistic statistical modeling techniques.

References

Caulkins, Jonathan P. (2002), "Using models that incorporate uncertainty," *Journal of Policy Analysis and Management*, **21** (3), 486–91.

Krupnick, Allen, Richard D. Morgenstern, Michael B. Batz, Per-Kristian C. Nelson, Dallas Burtraw, Jhih-Shyang Shih, and Michael R. Williams (2006), *Not a Sure Thing: Making Regulatory Choices Under Uncertainty*, Washington, DC: Resources for the Future Press.

Morgan, M. Granger and Max Henrion (1990), *Uncertainty: A Guide to Dealing with Uncertainty in Quantitative Risk and Policy Analysis*, Cambridge, UK: Cambridge University Press.

Tufte, Edward R. (1997), *Visual Explanations: Images and Quantities, Evidence and Narrative*, Cheshire, CT: Graphics Press.

APPENDIX

Table 11A.1 Glossary of terms and abbreviations

Term	Abbreviation	Definition
Benefit–cost analysis	BCA	Benefit–cost analysis (BCA) is an accounting framework that is used to evaluate the financial and the social consequences of decisions and to compare alternatives in financial terms. BCA attempts to furnish data about the gains and losses from a decision that are often missing from market data. Benefit–cost analysis and cost–benefit analysis are equivalent terms
Benefit–cost ratio	BCR	The ratio of benefits to costs (total present value of benefits divided by total present value of costs)
Benefits		Benefits are the positive effects of a policy or program, and are measured by the willingness to pay (WTP) for gains or the willingness to accept (WTA) for a loss restored. This is a proxy for the price people would pay for the goods were the market to provide them
Cost–benefit analysis	CBA	See benefit–cost analysis above. Benefit–cost analysis and cost–benefit analysis are equivalent terms
Cost-effectiveness analysis	CEA	Type of economic analysis that compares relative costs given a certain pre-decided outcome
Costs		Costs are the actual social costs and the value of negative effects of a policy or program. Costs are determined by the amount those bearing the costs would be willing to accept to bear the burden of the project or decision
Contingent valuation method	CVM	A survey-based method for valuing non-market resources. The survey typically asks people how much they would be willing to pay to maintain the existence of a certain feature (or willing to accept to be compensated for its loss) in a scenario given in the survey. Also called a "stated preference" model
Disability-adjusted life year	DALY	Disability-adjusted life year is a metric that combines mortality and morbidity by incorporating equivalent years of healthy life lost as a result of poor health and/or disability along with years lost due to premature death. It is derived using the formula DALY = Years of Life Lost + Years Lived with Disability

Discount rate		Typically represented as a percentage. The rate at which future values are reduced by time period to reflect present value. This is done according to personal time preference and/or market interest rates
Expected value		Savings or costs over time multiplied by the probability of those savings or costs being realized
Externality		A cost or benefit, not reflected by the transaction price, incurring/accruing to an individual not party to the actual market transaction. From a societal perspective, externalities cause too little or too much production/consumption, as prices do not reflect true costs/benefits of a good or service and producers/ consumers do not incur all costs or accrue all benefits
General equilibrium analysis	GE	An analysis in which many markets are taken into account, in contrast with partial equilibrium analysis
Least-cost alternative	LCA	The policy option that requires the lowest input of net present costs out of all alternatives. See cost-effectiveness analysis
Least-cost planning	LCP	Least-cost planning (LCP) is a sub-division of BCA. In LCP the benefits are taken as given in the form of some objective to be obtained. For example one might wish to reduce the high school dropout rate by 20%. LCP would seek to discover the least expensive method of achieving this goal. See cost-effectiveness analysis
Marginal cost of funds	MCF	
Multi-criteria decision analysis	MCDA	A disciplinary term describing various methodological tools designed to facilitate tractable decision-making in the face of numerous, conflicting analyses. Such methods aim to highlight and alleviate conflicts that cause different decision methods to produce conflicting answers
Net present value	NPV	The present value of benefits minus the present value of costs
Nominal interest rates		Market rates, which include expected inflation
Non-market values		Values for items not always counted in business accounting, e.g., the recreational value of a visit to a national park
Office of Information and Regulatory Affairs	OIRA	The Office of Information and Regulatory Affairs (OIRA) is located within the Office of Management and Budget. OIRA's functions include reducing paperwork burdens, reviewing federal regulations, and overseeing policies relating to privacy, information quality, and statistical programs

Table 11A.1 (continued)

Term	Abbreviation	Definition
Office of Management and Budget	OMB	The Office of Management and Budget (OMB) is a federal executive branch agency whose predominant mission is to assist the president in overseeing the preparation of the federal budget and to supervise its administration in Executive Branch agencies. As part of this, OMB evaluates the effectiveness of agency programs, policies, and procedures, assesses competing funding demands among agencies, and sets funding priorities. OMB also helps develop better performance measures
Partial equilibrium analysis	PE	An analysis that is limited in its inclusion of markets. Contrast with general equilibrium analysis
Present value	PV	The value, in today's dollars, of a future benefit or cost. Also can be described as the amount of money you would have to invest today at N% to yield X value a given number of years in the future
Quality-adjusted life year	QALY	Statistical metric designed to measure disease burden, in terms of quality and length of life added by a given policy intervention (or the converse). This can then be used to most efficiently allocate funds in terms of maximizing the marginal benefit of a policy intervention (in QALYs)
Real interest rate		Rate with inflationary expectations eliminated. Real rates show less variability than nominal rates
Risk		Technically defined as the likelihood (probability) of an occurrence (positive or negative) adjusted by the magnitude of said event
Risk-informed decision framework		Decision-making approach that incorporates probabilistic risk assessment techniques into regulatory decision-making
Shadow prices		Prices used to value non-market goods
Standing, economic		A person or group has economic standing in an analysis if the effects of the program or policy on that group are included in the analysis

Social opportunity cost of capita	SOC	
Standing, legal		Whether or not an individual or group is able to bring a lawsuit in court over a certain matter or against a specific defendant. In order to have standing, the plaintiffs must show (1) specific individualized injury (2) caused by the conduct of the defendant (3) of the type a favorable court decision can redress
Social rate of time preference	STP	
Travel cost method	TCM	A non-market valuation method, typically applied to recreational values, that derives a proxy value for a recreational site based upon actual market transactions (i.e., travel expenditures) incurred in order to access the site
Uncertainty		Typically, an uncertain outcome that is not/cannot be described probabilistically, where either the current state or future outcomes cannot be precisely described
Value of a statistical life	VSL	A misleading term referring to statistical value used to reflect the marginal cost of reducing deaths within a certain set of circumstances (e.g., worker deaths on a bridge building project). Essentially, VSL represents an equilibrium value between wealth and a reduction the probability of death. Where the cost of a statistical death reduction is lower than the VSL, such expenditure is then warranted. Values are adjusted to reflect demographics and characteristics of affected population, in terms of income level and life cycle
Willingness to accept payment	WTA	The price someone who has a good would accept to sell it. Also can be expressed as the minimum amount of money one would accept to forgo some good or to bear some harm
Willingness to pay	WTP	The price someone would pay to acquire a good or benefit. The willingness to pay is bounded by the ability to pay

Index

addiction 27, 51–4, 320
aggregation 249

baseline 322, 369, 385
behavioral 19, 175, 321–2, 335–7, 406
benefit transfer 183–4, 369, 390, 407–8
benefit–cost analysis (BCA) 101–4, 117–20, 128, 139, 264, 321, 379, 440
benefits 200–208, 299, 301–2, 320
  incremental 204
  intangible 92, 99–101
bias 411–12
  cognitive 46
budget constraint 187

capital 249
Carolina Abecedarian Program 67, 69–70, 72
catastrophe 412
Centers for Disease Control 114
childhood development 16, 38–9, 63–109
communication 373, 381, 405–6, 437–9
conscience goods 27
consumer surplus 51–4, 181, 186
contingent valuation 39, 49, 306–8, 392, 440
cost 160, 162, 166, 299–301, 320, 440
  incremental 204
cost of illness (COI) 118–19
cost–benefit 380; *see also* benefit–cost analysis
cost-effectiveness 115–17, 121, 128, 133–4, 138–9, 380, 440
  compared to BCA 111–12
crime 17, 91–2, 153–4
  costs 29–32, 160, 162
  deterrence 153–4, 161–6
  penalties versus reputational penalties 153, 156–7, 160–63
criticism (of BCA) 13–15, 267–9, 286–7, 374–5

demand curve 167
demographic factors 299
disability adjusted life year 116, 119, 134, 440
discount rate 81–2, 90, 93, 95–6, 164–5, 184–5, 188, 281–2, 335–6, 371, 416–18, 423–4
  exponential 334–5
  social 248, 251–5, 371, 418–22, 443
  time horizon 188, 256–8, 334, 422
discounting 18–19, 130–32, 247–59, 332–4, 335–7, 371–2, 413–15, 423, 441
distribution 5–7, 19, 47–9, 189, 294–313, 372, 429–33
  of income 157–8,–195, 204–5, 216–34

education 16–18, 36–8
efficiency 3, 5, 180, 272, 379
  allocative 117
  technical 117
elasticity 253–4
environment 168–9, 197, 202, 217, 295–6, 306
Environmental Protection Agency (EPA) 120–21, 128, 295
equity 7, 49–50, 132–3, 189, 270–71, 294–313, 319, 339–42, 372, 429–33
  intergenerational 258
ethics 18–19, 258, 264–85
evaluation 11
exact surplus 186
expected utility 173–4, 318–19
expected value 174, 182, 441
experiment 327, 336
expert 274–8
externalities 161, 167–8, 441

Flood Control Act 3–4
fraud 160–64

gambling 42
general equilibrium analysis 18, 127–9, 194–5, 202, 228–34, 297, 369, 387–8, 441
computable 209–13, 298
Gini coefficient 305
GMM estimation 225
Green Book (UK) 28, 46

handgun permits 166–7
health 17, 49, 258, 295–6, 328–9, 334, 372
hedonic property valuation method 199, 300, 308–13
history 2–13, 265, 373
human capital 32–4, 154

incarceration 31–2, 153–6, 164–6
income distribution 157–8, 225
income weights 302–3
insurance 187
internal rate of return 71, 102–3, 386
international guidance 12

Kaldor–Hicks 5–7, 117, 247

law and BCA 270, 278–81, 326, 370, 398–401, 411
law enforcement 17
location 214–34, 297
attributes 311–12
Lorenz curve 304–6

marginal utility of money 47–8
monetization 370, 393
Monte Carlo analysis 27, 43, 44, 46, 55, 130, 188, 404, 408, 410–11

net benefits 35, 369, 386–7, 437
net present value 247, 441
non-market goods 6, 19, 197, 199, 207–13, 235, 327, 369, 391–3

Office of Management and Budget 8–11, 28, 120, 128, 129–35, 373, 441
Circular A-4 9, 120, 334

opportunity cost 27, 34–6, 39–40, 248, 333
option price 186

pandemic 110–11, 114–15, 122–7
Pareto test 117, 247
partial equilibrium analysis 387–8
Perry Preschool 38, 67–9, 72, 74
pollution 188
precautionary principle 407
precision 409
present value, discounted net 71
presentation 373, 381, 437–9
principles and standards 8–12, 20, 172, 176–80, 368–9
probability 371
productivity gains 32–4, 36–7
prospect theory 319, 329, 385
public health 17, 172–3
preparedness 112, 120–21

quality adjusted life years 116, 119, 128, 133

rate of return 252–3
real 372
recreation 307–8
regulation 8–10
Regulatory Flexibility Act 295
resource cost method 73
risk 17, 172–5, 277–8, 302, 325, 329, 370–71, 402–3, 409, 423, 442
aversion 174
mortality risk 134–5

safety 17, 172–3
Scitovsky paradox 267–9, 326, 375
sensitivity analysis 40, 82, 90, 100–101, 184
shadow price 29, 76–81, 93, 118, 183, 386, 390, 442
social net benefits, *see* net benefits
social policy 2, 16, 324, 337
standing 197–8, 273–4, 370, 396–401, 442
stated preferences 119–20, 392
states and benefit–cost 12–13
statistical estimation 43–6, 182, 185, 188, 408

structural models 128, 208
substance abuse 40–43
Suits Index 305–6
surplus 181

taxes 196, 203–5, 249, 253, 308
  marginal excess burden 34–6
Tiebout models 214
transparency 436
travel cost 443

uncertainty 3, 43–55, 90, 93, 97–8, 129, 382, 402, 404, 443
utility 6

value
  of information 404–5
  of a statistical life 166, 328, 390, 443
  of statistical life year 119–20
volunteer time 27, 39–40

water 3, 11
welfare 319–20
willingness to accept 181, 201–2, 266–7, 271–2, 325–8, 369, 384–5, 389, 392, 408, 430, 443
willingness to pay 27–8, 118, 134–5, 181, 200–202, 207–8, 229–33, 266–7, 271–2, 325–8, 369, 384–5, 389, 392, 408, 430, 443